MI(E)RCE
NORÐWEALAS
EASTENGLE
EASTSEAXE
CENT
SUÐSEAXE
WESTSEAXE
ANDREDESWEALD
HAMTUNSCIR
WILSÆTAN
ÆSCESDUN
SUMURSÆTE
DEF(E)NAS
CORNWALAS
WIHT
FRONCLOND
NORÞSÆ
Maserfeld
Hreopedun
Snotengaham
(Peterborough)
Peodford
(Ely)
Grantebrycg
Sturmere
Gipeswic
Buttingtun
Cwatbrycg
Saefern
Wiogoraceaster
(Evesham)
Gleawceaster
(Eynsham)
(Oxford)
Beorhhamstede
Mældun
Meresig
Cirenceaster
(Abingdon)
Dorceceaster
(Wallingford)
Lyge
Beamfleot
Sceoburg
Lunden
Colun
Temes
Cippanhamm
Englafeld
Readingas
Fullanhamm
Hrofesceaster
Middeltun
Meratun
Basengas
Fearnhamm
Cantuareburg
Sandwic
Weþmor
Eþandun
Iglea
Stan
Glæstingaburg
Alor
Wiltun
Wintanceaster
Pryfet
Apuldor
Æþelingaeig
Pedrede
Scireburne
Limene
(Cerne Abbas)
Cisseceaster
Hæstingap
Pefnesea
Bunne
Escanceaster
Ascanmynster
Winburne
Werham
(Corfe)
Swanawic

 Bright, James Wilso
Bright's Old Engl rammar
& reader.

OLD ENGLISH GRAMMAR & READER

The Sacrifice of Isaac.
London, British Museum, MS *Cotton Claudius B. iv*, fol. 38[r].
(See Reader selection 15)

THIRD EDITION

SECOND CORRECTED PRINTING

BRIGHT'S OLD ENGLISH GRAMMAR & READER

Edited by

FREDERIC G. CASSIDY

and

RICHARD N. RINGLER

HOLT, RINEHART AND WINSTON, INC.
New York Chicago San Francisco Atlanta
Dallas Montreal Toronto London Sydney

Library of Congress Catalog Card Number: **76–179921**
ISBN: 0–03–084713–3
Printed in the United States of America
56 038 98765432

preface

The present edition of *Bright's Anglo-Saxon Reader* represents a thorough revision and updating of what has been for many years a favorite text for beginning studies in Old English. The revisers have sought to preserve the virtues of the original as far as possible while seeking to make it more teachable in present terms and furnishing a much more useful selection of texts, freshly edited.

A number of recent Old English textbooks have proposed to "get the student as fast as possible into the reading of the literature." This is our aim as well, but we do not believe the literature can be accurately translated or sensitively read without a basic grasp of Old English grammar, the origins of the language, and its position in relation to Modern English. These things cannot be taken for granted. To read acceptably and listen critically one must gain a reasonable understanding of the sounds of Old English and how they are arrived at. Finally, scholarly and critical writings on Old English literature require at least that the student begin to appreciate the language in its context as an early Germanic tongue under cultural and linguistic pressure of outside forces, chiefly Latin, Celtic and Scandinavian.

Something must be said of the ways in which this edition differs from its predecessors.

The Grammar no longer confronts the student as a pathless wilderness of philological data, but is articulated in a series of graded lessons liberally sprinkled with exercises and easy readings.

Hulbert's "Sketch of Anglo-Saxon Literature" has been omitted; it would have served no purpose to update it in the light of two recently published and easily accessible books, Stanley B. Greenfield's *A Critical History of Old English Literature* (New York 1965), with its superb bibliographical aids, and C. L. Wrenn's *A Study of Old English Literature* (London 1967), with its exhaustive and stimulating scholarship. On roughly the same principle, bibliographical references in the headnotes to the readings have been kept to a minimum: the student can now find the major bibliography quickly and easily not only in Greenfield but in Fred C. Robinson's indispensable introduction to scholarly and critical materials, *Old English Literature: A Select Bibliography* (Toronto 1970).

Of the prose selections, *The Conversion of King Eadwine* and *The Reigns of Æðelred and Ælfred* have been considerably expanded. *1066* and *Sermo Lupi ad Anglos* are included for the first time. In order to accommodate these additions (and to provide space for the amplification of other parts of the book, notably the Grammar and the explanatory notes) a number of seldom-taught prose texts—all but one of them translations from Latin—have been omitted.

The number of lines of poetry has been increased by almost half and an effort has been made to include complete poems, or, failing that, uninterrupted stretches of extract from longer poems. *Judith* has been added in order to supply one fairly substantial poetic text beyond *The Battle of Maldon*. The two metrical Charms have been omitted. Bright's very useful treatment of versification has been retained in a slightly modified form and prefaced with an introduction to various other aspects of Old English poetry.

The prose selections are arranged chronologically according to the date of their composition (to the degree that this can be ascertained) with two exceptions. Bede is assigned priority of place on the basis of the date of the Latin, not the OE text, and the four Chronicle excerpts have been grouped together for obvious reasons, though they span a period of three hundred years. This arrangement offers no clue to the order of increasing difficulty of these prose texts. The following grouping of selection numbers is the suggested order of increasing difficulty: 10, 12; 3, 4, 6, 8; 11; 7, 9, 13; 1, 2; 14.

For the order of the poetry selections in this book, and a suggested order of increasing difficulty, see p. 264 n. 3.

Eight of the texts in this book are translations, paraphrases or expansions of Latin originals. In four cases we have printed the relevant Latin text in the middle of the page: in *The Conversion of King Eadwine* and *The Miracle of Cædmon*, it not only illuminates the procedures of the Anglo-Saxon translator, but often explains them (and is thus of direct help in translating his OE into MnE); in *The Sacrifice of Isaac* and *Neorxnawang*, on the other hand, consultation of the Latin original is a *sine qua non* for studying the poets' techniques of paraphrase and expansion. In the case of the other four OE texts, we confine ourselves to occasional Latin citation in the explanatory notes: the authors of *Homily on the Assumption of Saint John*, *Homily on the Death of Saint Oswald*, and *Judith* expand or alter their Latin originals so freely that there seemed no point in reproducing them, while in the case of *The Acts of Matthew and Andrew in the City of the Cannibals*, the immediate source is lost.

When Latin is quoted in the introductory or explanatory notes, a Modern English translation is ordinarily provided, unless the quotation is only a word or two in length.[1] Modern English translations are *not* provided, however, for Old

[1]This procedure is not followed in the explanatory notes to Selections 10 and 11, however, where the philological apparatus is fuller than usual and the Latin is generally adduced to illuminate minute syntactic or textual problems in the OE.

English passages appearing in the same places: the vocabulary of these passages has been included in the Glossary, and teacher and student are urged to treat them as additional exercises in translation.

For a statement of our editorial and lexicographical principles and procedures, see the introductions to the Textual Notes and the Glossary.

We have included a number of reproductions of pages from OE MSS. Our selection has been governed by two criteria: the page must be one which is not easily available in facsimile or it must contain the text of some important moment in one of the selections. In most instances we have been able to satisfy both criteria at once. We hope that the student, by comparing these MS pages with our edited texts, will obtain some foundation in reading OE MSS. To further this purpose, we have printed a detailed analysis of p. 14 of MS Junius 11 on p. 297, facing the reproduction. Furthermore the whole of Selection 11 has been edited in a way that will suggest to the student what an OE MS looks like and that will facilitate his comparison of the edited text with the collotype facsimile (*EEMSF*, XIII).

There remains now, *eoletes æt ende*, the pleasant duty of thanks. We are grateful to the Clarendon Press for permission to print extracts from *Venerabilis Baedae Opera Historica*, ed. Charles Plummer, 2 vols. (Oxford 1896), and from Sir Frank M. Stenton's *Anglo-Saxon England*, 3rd ed. (Oxford 1971); to the Trustees of the British Museum, London, for permission to reproduce the frontispiece and the photographs facing pp. 172, 175, 192, 246, 257 and 373; to the Keeper of Western MSS. of the Bodleian Library, Oxford, for permission to reproduce those facing pp. 129, 297 and 365; and to the President and Fellows of Corpus Christi College, Oxford, for permission to reproduce that facing p. 118. We add our thanks to the staffs of these institutions, as well as to that of University Library, Cambridge, and to R. I. Page, Librarian of Corpus Christi College, Cambridge, for amenities shown to the junior editor in the summer of 1969. We thank Professors J. B. Bessinger, Jr., R. F. Leslie, Fred C. Robinson and Robert D. Stevick for the care with which they reviewed our manuscript on behalf of the publisher: they caught a host of inaccuracies and made numerous helpful suggestions, most of which we took to heart, a few of which we chose to ignore—no doubt at our peril. Finally we must thank several generations of students who have suffered through early versions of both the Grammar and the Reader in dittoed, mimeographed and xeroxed forms.

It would be foolish to suppose that a work of this sort should not be riddled with errors. The editors would be grateful for having their attention called to stupidities and misprints alike, and would welcome suggestions as to how future editions of this book can be made more serviceable.

Frederic G. Cassidy
Richard N. Ringler

Madison, Wisconsin
September 1971

contents

GRAMMAR

READER

Note to the Second Printing

In this reprinting a substantial number of errors have been corrected and a few changes have been made in the explanatory notes to the texts. We wish to thank colleagues who took the trouble to notify us of errors or to disagree with our opinions. We hope that they will apprise us of any further errors remaining in this printing.

Through inadvertence on our part, the Preface omits to mention two debts of gratitude: to our *editrix* Priscilla Van Haverbeke of Holt, Rinehart and Winston, without whose energetic attentions this book would be much less satisfactory; and to Lindsay Holichek, who helped us in the time-consuming task of proofreading the Glossary.

F. G. C.
R. N. R.

Madison, Wisconsin
January 1974

ABBREVIATIONS

acc. accusative.
A.D. Anno Domini.
adj(s). adjective(s).
ad loc. ad locum, i.e. to the place (cited).
adv. adverb; adverbial.
Ang. Anglian.
Anm. Anmerkung, i.e. note.
A-SE Sir Frank Stenton, *Anglo-Saxon England*, 3rd ed. (Oxford 1971).
ASPR *The Anglo-Saxon Poetic Records: A Collective Edition*, ed. George Philip Krapp and Elliott Van Kirk Dobbie, 6 vols. (New York 1931–53).
B Dorothy Bethurum, ed., *The Homilies of Wulfstan* (Oxford 1957).
Brit. British.
BT Bosworth-Toller, i.e. *An Anglo-Saxon Dictionary, Based on the Manuscript Collections of the Late Joseph Bosworth. . .*, ed. and enlarged by T. Northcote Toller. . . . (Oxford 1898).
BTS Bosworth-Toller Supplement, i.e. T. Northcote Toller, Supplement to *An Anglo-Saxon Dictionary, Based on the Manuscript Collections of the Late Joseph Bosworth* (Oxford 1921).
c circa, i.e. about, approximately.
Campbell A. Campbell, *Old English Grammar*, reprinted . . . from corrected sheets of the first [1959] edition (Oxford 1962).
cf. confer, i.e. compare.
cogn. cognate with.
col. column.
comp. comparative.
CVC Cleasby-Vigfusson-Craigie, i.e. *An Icelandic-English Dictionary*, initiated by Richard Cleasby, subsequently revised, enlarged and completed by Gudbrand Vigfusson, M.A., 2nd ed. with a Supplement by Sir William A. Craigie. . . . (Oxford 1957).
d. died.
del. delete.
dat. dative.
d.o. direct object.
ed. edited by.

ed. cit. editione citata, i.e. in the edition cited.
eds. editors.
EEMSF *Early English Manuscripts in Facsimile.*
EETS Early English Text Society.
e.g. exempli gratia, i.e. for example.
EGmc East Germanic.
EGS English and Germanic Studies.
EHD *English Historical Documents, I: c540–1042*, ed. Dorothy Whitelock (London 1955).
Ericson Eston Everett Ericson, *The Use of Swa in Old English, Hesperia* XII (Göttingen 1932).
esp. especially.
etc. et cetera.
EWS Early West Saxon.
f. and [the page or line] following.
Farr James Marion Farr, *Intensives and Reflexives in Anglo-Saxon and Early Middle English* (Baltimore 1905).
fem. feminine.
ff. and [the pages or lines] following.
fol(s). folio(s).
gen. genitive.
Ger. German.
GK Grein-Köhler, i.e. C. W. M. Grein, *Sprachschatz der Angelsächischen Dichter. . .*, neu herausgegeben von J. J. Köhler (Heidelberg 1912).
Gmc. Germanic.
Gr. Greek.
IE Indo-European.
i.e. id est, i.e. that is, to wit.
Íf *Íslenzk fornrit.*
ind. indirect.
indef. indefinite.
indic. indicative.
inf. infinitive.
inst. instrumental.
IPA International Phonetic Association.
JEGP *Journal of English and Germanic Philology.*
K Kentish.
Ker N. R. Ker, *Catalogue of Manuscripts Containing Anglo-Saxon* (Oxford 1957).
l. line.
Lat. Latin.
lit. literally.
ll. lines.
LWS Late West Saxon.
MÆ *Medium Ævum.*
masc. masculine.
ME Middle English.
MLN *Modern Language Notes.*

MLR *Modern Language Review.*
MnDan Modern Danish.
MnE Modern English.
MnGer Modern German.
MnNor Modern Norwegian.
Mossé Fernand Mossé, *Manuel de l'Anglais du Moyen Âge*, I (Vieil-Anglais), Paris 1950.
MS *Medieval Studies.*
MS(S) manuscript(s).
MW Magoun-Walker, i.e. F. P. Magoun, Jr. and J. A. Walker, *An Old-English Anthology: Translations of Old-English Prose and Verse* (Dubuque 1950).
n. note.
neut. neuter.
NGmc North Germanic.
NM *Neuphilologische Mitteilungen.*
nom. nominative.
OE Old English.
OF Old Frisian.
OHG Old High German.
ON Old Norse.
op. cit. opere citato, i.e. in the work cited.
OS Old Saxon.
p. page.
PBA *Proceedings of the British Academy.*
pl. plural.
PL *Patrologia Latina.*
Plummer[1] *Two of the Saxon Chronicles Parallel*, ed. Charles Plummer, 2 vols. (Oxford 1892–9); reprinted 1952 with additional material by Dorothy Whitelock.
Plummer[2] *Venerabilis Baedae Opera Historica.* ed. Carolus Plummer. 2 vols. (Oxford 1896).
PMLA *Publications of the Modern Language Association.*
Pope[1] John Collins Pope, *The Rhythm of Beowulf*, revised edition (New Haven 1966).
Pope[2] *Seven Old English Poems*, ed. John C. Pope (Indianapolis 1966).
Pope[3] *Homilies of Ælfric: A Supplementary Collection*, ed. John C. Pope, EETS, 259–60 (1967–8).
pp. pages.
PrehOE Prehistoric OE.
pret. preterit.
PrGmc Primitive Germanic.
pron. pronoun.
PrON Primitive Old Norse.
q.v. quod vide, i.e. which see.
QW Quirk-Wrenn, i.e. Randolph Quirk and C. L. Wrenn, *An Old English Grammar*, 2nd ed. (London 1958).
r recto, i.e. on the front (of an MS leaf).

refl. reflexive.
rel. relative.
RES *Review of English Studies.*
SB Sievers-Brunner, i.e. Karl Brunner, *Altenglische Grammatik nach der Angelsächsischen Grammatik von Eduard Sievers*, 3rd. ed. (Tübingen 1965).
sc. scilicet, i.e. to wit (used before a word that is to be supplied or understood).
sg. singular.
Sisam Kenneth Sisam, *Studies in the History of Old English Literature* (Oxford 1953).
Skt Sanskrit.
SN *Studia Neophilologica.*
SP *Studies in Philology.*
Sprockel C. Sprockel, *The Language of the Parker Chronicle*, I (The Hague 1965).
SS. Saints.
St. Saint.
subj. subjunctive.
s.v. sub verbo, i.e. under the word (in question).
Sweet^{14} *Sweet's Anglo-Saxon Reader in Prose and Verse*, 14th ed., rev. C. T. Onions (Oxford 1959).
Sweet^{15} *Sweet's Anglo-Saxon Reader in Prose and Verse*, 15th ed., rev. Dorothy Whitelock (Oxford 1967).
US United States.
v verso, i.e. on the back (of an MS leaf).
Voges F. Voges, "Der Reflexive Dativ im Englischen," *Anglia*, VI (1883), 317–374.
W *Sermo Lupi ad Anglos*, ed. Dorothy Whitelock, 3rd ed. (London 1963).
WGmc West Germanic.
WS West Saxon.
Wrenn C. L. Wrenn, *A Study of Old English Literature* (London 1967).
Wülfing J. Ernst Wülfing, *Die Syntax in den Werken Alfreds des Grossen*, 2 vols. (Bonn 1894–1901).
ZfdA *Zeitschrift für deutsches Altertum.*

Chapter 1

The Place of Old English

1.1. Scholars of the English language divide it for historical treatment into three stages:

Old English (OE), or Anglo-Saxon[1]	c500—c1100
Middle English (ME)	c1100—c1500
Modern English (MnE)	c1500—the present

Though these dates are set up partly for convenience, they nevertheless reflect a linguistic reality: by each of the boundary times, 1100 and 1500, the accumulation of gradual changes has become so considerable that in each case the language is clearly seen to have entered a new phase.

1.2. In its earliest phase one cannot even properly speak of the language as "English"; it was a collection of dialects brought over to Britain from the continent by Germanic invaders (the familiar Angles, Saxons, and Jutes[2]). These dialects were members of the Germanic (Gmc) branch of Indo-European (IE), the "family" to which most present European languages belong. The history of Old English cannot be fully understood unless its Gmc and IE connections are recognized. The accompanying Diagram 1 shows how the chief members of the IE family are related to one another:

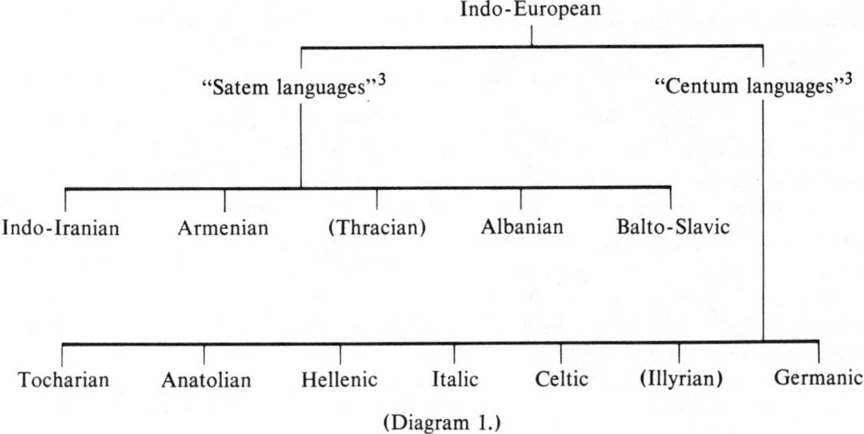

(Diagram 1.)

1.3. Since the Gmc branch is at the center of our present interest, it needs to be seen in fuller detail than the others (Diagram 2):

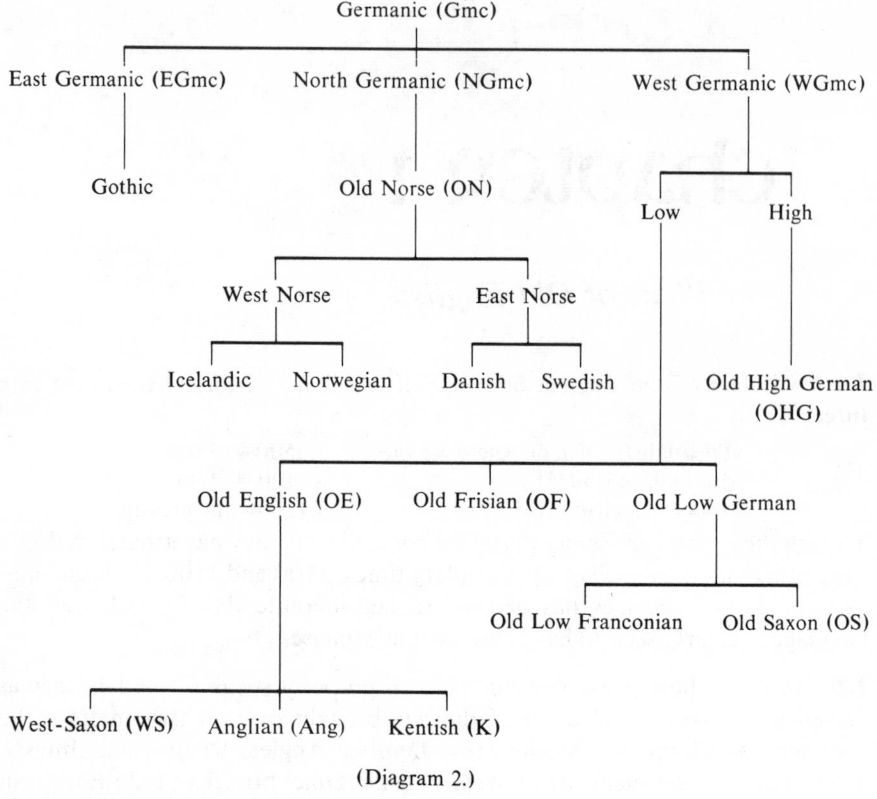

(Diagram 2.)

Language Relationships

1.4. A word in any language which can be shown to have descended from the same source as one in another language is said to be *cognate*[4] with it. For example, the English word *bear*, carry, is descended from OE *beran*, which is cognate (within the Gmc branch) with OS and OHG *beran*, ON *bera*, and Gothic *bairan*, all having the same meaning. Scholars have hypothesized a common Primitive Germanic (PrGmc) source form or base **ber-*[5] from which all of these could have developed regularly. These Gmc forms are in turn cognate with forms from other IE branches: Latin *fer-* (Italic branch), Greek *φερ-* (Hellenic branch), Sanskrit *bhar-* (Indo-Iranian branch). And in turn an IE base **bher-* is hypothesized from which all the historically attested forms in the various branches could have developed regularly.

1.5. Generally speaking, the farther apart two languages are in time and/or space, the less alike their cognate forms will look. The preceding diagrams suggest a much nearer relationship between OE and ON than between either of these languages and Latin, and a comparison of cognate forms in the three languages bears out this conclusion:

Lat. *pecus*, ON *fé*, OE *feoh* (MnE *fee*)
Lat. *quod*, ON *hvat*, OE *hwæt* (MnE *what*)

It is not often that a series of cognates from distantly related languages shows consistently similar forms, but consider the case of the humble mouse: OE *mūs*, Old Irish *mús*, Lat. *mūs*, Gr. *μυς*, Skt *mūṡ*, all going back to an IE base **mūs*-.

1.6. What we know of these complex interrelationships is the product of Comparative Indo-European Philology, a study which has occupied many of the greatest language scholars since the late eighteenth century. The plentiful remains preserved in OE were of considerable value in working out the details of the Gmc branch, hence also the larger scheme of IE. Old English, then, should be seen in its historical context, not only as the earliest phase of the present English language, but also as a member of the Gmc branch, and in relation to the other IE languages. (No systematic account of IE or of Gmc will be given in this book, however.)

1.7. Because of the paucity of documents surviving in the other OE dialects, all introductory study of the language is based on West Saxon (WS), the language of King Ælfred the Great (reigned 871–899) and of the writers who followed him until the Norman Conquest.[6] Hence the texts in this book are WS, as is also the outline of grammar. Even a cursory inspection of the texts will show, however, that the usage and spelling of Ælfred's time differed considerably from those of the time of Ælfric (c955–c1012), about a century later. It is therefore necessary to distinguish between Early West Saxon (EWS), which is presented in the grammar and exemplified in texts 1, 2, 7 and 8, and Late West Saxon (LWS), which is exemplified in texts 11, 12, 13, and 14.

1.8. Though many changes have come into the language as OE has developed through ME to MnE, there has always been a high degree of continuity. The impression of strangeness which one receives at the first sight of an OE text is therefore somewhat misleading. It results largely from the presence of three unfamiliar symbols (þ, ð, and æ) and a number of unfamiliar clusters of otherwise familiar symbols (hw-, -cg, -sc, etc.). Most of these represent sounds still present in MnE though now spelled differently. For example, OE *pæð* is the familiar MnE *path* and sounded the same in OE as it does for most speakers today. As soon as these OE spellings become familiar the text will no longer have the look of a foreign language. One will begin to discover, in fact, that a great many OE words or word bases can be recognized by their MnE descendants.

Vocabulary

1.9. Vocabulary-counts of present day English have shown that, of the 1000 words most frequently used, about 83 percent are of OE origin. The proportion decreases rapidly in the less frequent thousands but remains throughout at about 30 percent despite the large number of non-English words that have been borrowed down through the centuries.[7]

1.10. Similar word-counts of the OE poetic vocabulary[8] test this continuity in the other direction: of the 1000 most frequently used words, fully 55 percent have survived in recognizable form into MnE, and of the 100 most frequent, 76 percent have survived.

1.11. Analyzing only this last group, the one hundred or so most frequently used words in OE poetry, we find the following:

NOUNS:	Surviving into MnE with little or no change in form or meaning (about 40 percent)	*god*, God *mann*, man *heofon*, heaven *eorðe*, earth *weorold*, world *līf*, life *lufu*, love *word*, word *weorc*, work *dæg*, day *hand*, hand *cynn*, kin *riht*, right *þanc*, thank *engel*, angel
	With greater change in form or meaning (about 30 percent)	*cyning*, king *mōd*, (mood), courage *folc*, (folk), people *mynd*, (mind), memory *dōm*, (doom), judgment *fēond*, (fiend), enemy *fæsten*, (fastness), fortification *gāst*, (ghost), spirit *sōþ*, (sooth), truth *burg*, (borough), walled town
	With no Standard English descendant (about 30 percent)	*dryhten*, lord *hyge*, mind, thought *rīce*, dominion (cogn. Ger. *Reich*) *þēod*, people, nation *wuldor*, glory *æðeling*, nobleman, prince *scop*, poet, singer *līc*, body, corpse *feorh*, life *wer*, man (cogn. Lat. *vir*)

Thus about 70 percent survive in recognizable form, though 30 percent of these have changed their meanings more or less. The rest have either died out entirely or are preserved only locally in dialect forms.

PRONOUNS:	Surviving with little change (about 80 percent)	*ic*, I *þū*, thou *hē*, he *hit*, it *þæt*, that *hwā*, who *hwæt*, what *þis*, this *self*, self, same *hwelc*, which
	Essentially different forms (about 20 percent)	*hēo*, she *sē*, *sēo*, the *þēs*, *þēos*, this
VERBS:	Surviving with little change of the base form or of meaning (about 35 percent)	*sittan*, sit *sēcan*, seek *healdan*, hold *beran*, bear *giefan*, give *cuman*, come *sēon*, see *bēon*, *wæs*, be, was *dōn*, *dyde*, do, did
	Surviving with considerable change (about 46 percent)	*wieldan*, (wield), control *habban*, *hæfde*, have, had *mæg*, *meahte*, may, might *willan*, *wolde*, will, would *sculan*, *sceolde*, shall, should *mōtan*, *mōste*, be able, must *āgan*, own *secgan*, say *faran*, (fare), journey, travel *cunnan*, *cūðe*, (can, couth), know *cweðan*, *cwæð*, (quoth), say, said *scieppan*, (shape), create
	Not surviving in Mn Standard English (about 18 percent)	*hātan*, *hātte*, (ME hight), be called *weorðan*, (ME worth), become *beorgan*, protect *witan*, (wit), know *munan*, remember
ADJECTIVES:	Surviving with little	*gōd*, good

	change (about 57 percent)	*wīd*, wide *fæst*, fast *hālig*, holy *rīce*, rich *ān*, *nān*, one, none *hēah*, *hīerra*, *hīehst*, high, -er, -est *micel*, *māra*, *mǣst*, much, more, most
	Surviving with considerable change (about 14 percent)	*swelc*, such *lēof*, (lieve), beloved
	Not surviving in Mn Standard English (about 29 percent)	*ēce*, eternal *swīð*, strong *æðele*, noble (cogn. Ger. *edel*) *eft*, later
ADVERBS:	Surviving with little change (about 53 percent)	*tō*, too *eall*, all *swā*, so, as *þǣr*, there *þanne*, then *nū*, now *ǣr*, ere, before *wīde*, widely
	Surviving with considerable change (about 27 percent)	*ēac*, (eke), also *swelce*, (so-like), likewise *ā*, *nā*, aye; never, not at all *gelīc*, like
	Not surviving in MnE (about 20 percent)	*ne*, not, neither *þā*, then, when *swīðe*, very, extremely
PREPOSITIONS:	Surviving with little change (about 82 percent)	*in*, in, on *on*, in, on *tō*, to, toward *for*, for *ofer*, over *under*, under *æfter*, after *æt*, at *þurh*, through
	Surviving with changed meaning (about 9 percent)	*wið*, (with), against, opposite
	Not surviving in MnE (about 9 percent)	*mid*, with, accompanying (cogn. Ger. *mit*)

CONJUNC-TIONS:	Surviving with little change (about 75 percent)	*and*, *ond*, and *gif*, if *þēah*, though
	Not surviving	*ac*, but

1.12. In sum, it should be evident that there is a considerable degree of continuity in the core of the English vocabulary between OE times and the present. The enormous increase in the number of words has been due to addition rather than to wholesale replacement. In any present-day use of English the ancient native element is virtually inescapable and stays normally at the center. Almost all our MnE function-words (prepositions, conjunctions, articles) are from OE, as also the pronouns, numerals, and auxiliary verbs. Thus even if a writer today were to avoid the native nouns, verbs, adjectives, and adverbs, using borrowed ones instead, the structural framework of most sentences would remain Anglo-Saxon. The first sentence of this paragraph (a random example which was not written to be used as such) would look like this if only the native words were retained and the others deleted:

In ______, it should be ______ that there is a ______ of ______ in the ______ of the English ______ between OE times and the ______.

More than 77 percent of the words in this sentence are native. The others are from Latin, directly or through French.

FOOTNOTES

[1]"Anglo-Saxon" is properly used of the people, their history, their literature, and frequently of their language. "Old English" specifically refers to the language, or to the literature written in it.

[2]So named by the Venerable Bede. Precisely who the "Jutes" were is not known; they can hardly have been from present Jutland. Scholarly opinion now inclines to identify them with the Frisians.

[3]IE languages have been broadly divided into *centum* [kɛntum] and *satem* [satɛm] (the Latin and the Avestan words for "one hundred"), indicating that a *k* sound found in languages of the first group was palatalized to an *s* or similar sound in languages of the second. This does not however reflect any basic split within the IE family. (For items in parentheses the evidence is not conclusive.)

[4]Lat *co-gnatus*, "of common origin," sprung from the same stock. To be properly called *cognate*, two words must share a common ancestor. If one is the source of the other the relationship is different. For example, MnE *garage* is a *loanword* (borrowing) from MnFrench.

[5]Hypothetical or reconstructed forms are regularly preceded by an asterisk (*) to distinguish them from historically recorded or attested forms.

[6]West-Saxon was spoken in southwestern England (south of the Thames and west of Kent). Other dialects were Kentish (in Kent and adjoining parts of Sussex and Surrey) and the Anglian dialects, which included Northumbrian (northward from the Humber to Scotland) and Mercian (between the Thames and the Humber—the large midland area). King Ælfred's capital was at Winchester (the "Casterbridge" of Thomas Hardy's novels).

[7]A. H. Roberts, *A Statistical Analysis of American English*, The Hague (Mouton) 1965, p. 37.

[8]J. F. Madden and F. P. Magoun, Jr., *A Grouped Frequency Word-List of Anglo-Saxon Poetry*, Dept. Of English, Harvard University, 1960.

chapter 2

Speech Sounds

2.1. In order to understand how OE was pronounced and how certain OE sounds changed before, during, and after the OE period, it is necessary to know the basic principles of phonetics, the science of speech sounds. How the sounds of speech are produced, what kinds there are, how they affect each other, how and why they change—these are the questions that need to be answered. The following brief account will touch only on features relevant to OE.

Speech Production

2.2. The sounds of speech are produced by air expelled from the lungs and modified variously by organs in the throat, the mouth passage, and the nose passage. The air leaves the lungs through the *trachea* or *windpipe* but produces no sounds before entering the *larynx* ("Adam's apple," the cartilaginous "box" at the top of the trachea). In the larynx the air meets two membranes (*vocal cords*, *bands*, or *folds*) which are attached along its inner sides from front to back. When stretched, these membranes draw together, closing the air passage or leaving only a slit between; when relaxed, they leave a wide opening. (This passage between the vocal cords is called the *glottis*.) The air coming from the lungs, when impeded by the vocal cords, causes them to vibrate, producing the sound called *voice*. But when the cords are relaxed and the glottis is open, the air is unimpeded and produces no vibration, hence no sound. All speech sounds are either *voiced* to some degree or *voiceless*. In the latter, the sound we hear is produced somewhere above the vocal cords (in the throat, mouth, or nasal passage).

Consonants and Vowels

2.3. When the air from the lungs enters the mouth passage (*oral cavity*) it may produce sounds of two main types: if it is shut off at some point and then suddenly released, an explosive or *stop* sound is produced—for example, [**k**]. However, if it encounters such a narrow aperture that, in forcing its way through, the friction becomes audible a *spirant* (or *fricative*) sound is produced—for example, [s]. Sounds made in either of these ways, or by impeding the breath in other ways, are *consonants*. Consonants accompanied by vocal cord vibration are *voiced*; others are *voiceless*.

2.4. When air from the lungs, after producing vibration in the larynx, encounters no stoppage or constriction in the throat or mouth but passes freely through, vowels are produced. The difference in the *quality* of vowels (for example the audible difference between [o] and [u]) is due to modifications made in the shape of the oral cavity, tongue position, and action of the lips as the breath passes through. (Pronounce the vowels of *toe* and *too*, noting the differences in each of these three factors.) Vowels, as their name implies, are voiced.

Classifying Consonants

2.5. Consonants are classified by three factors taken together:

1. presence or absence of voice,
2. the organ or organs chiefly involved in producing them,
3. their type—stop, spirant, etc.

Organs involved in producing the consonants, in addition to the larynx, are:

velum or soft palate: *velar* sounds
hard palate or roof of the mouth: *palatal* sounds
alveolar ridge or gum ridge: *alveolar* sounds
teeth: *dental* sounds
lips: *labial* sounds.

Usually the *tongue* articulates with one or more of these organs, either pressing against it or coming close enough to form a narrow aperture with it. The areas of the tongue which do this are the *tip*, the *blade* (behind the tip), and the *back*.

2.6. In addition to stops and spirants, already described, the class of consonants includes:

affricates, in which a stop changes immediately into a spirant in the same position,
nasals, in which the mouth passage is closed off and the breath comes out through the nasal passage instead,
sonorants, in which the voice resonance is partially impeded in the mouth but not enough to produce spirancy, and
glides or *semivowels*, which begin with a narrower aperture than that of the vowel articulated in the same position, and continue immediately to the position of whatever vowel follows. (Thus the position from which a glide starts is its stable feature; the position at which it ends depends on what follows it.)

2.7. The accompanying Diagram 3 shows the consonants of OE and MnE. The sounds of these consonants are given in the symbols of the International Phonetic Association (IPA).[1] A MnE keyword, with its relevant part printed in boldface type, is also supplied to indicate the value of the IPA symbol. The consonants are arranged from left to right on the diagram according to their relative position of articulation from the front to the back of the mouth. Most of the sounds indicated occur in both OE and MnE; however, EWS did not have [g] and [ʒ] and MnE does not have [ɣ] and [x].

Diagram 3

	Bilabial	*Labio-dental*	*Inter-dental*	*Alveolar*	*Post-alveolar*	*Palatal/Velar*
Voiced Stop	[b] **b**ine			[d] **d**ine		[g] **g**rind
Vcless Stop	[p] **p**ine			[t] **t**ine		[k] **k**ind
Voiced Spir		[v] **v**ine	[ð] **th**y	[z] **z**ing	[ʒ] a**z**ure	[ɣ] N Ger ma**g**en
Vcless Spir		[f] **f**ine	[θ] **th**igh	[s] **s**ing	[ʃ] a**sh**es	[x] Ger ma**ch**en
Voiced Affr				[dʒ] **g**in		
Vcless Affr				[tʃ] **ch**in		
Nasal	[m] **m**ine			[n] **n**ine		[ŋ] lo**ng**
Sonorant				[l] **l**ine		
Sonorant				[r] **r**ye		
Glide					[j] **y**et	[w] **w**ine

Another voiceless spirant is [h] as in *him*, *hoot*, but its position of articulation varies with its environment. The sonorants differ as to the action of the tongue: in [l] it is free laterally; in [r] it is retroflexed (turned back) or trilled. Further details about these sounds will be taken up in Chapter 4.

2.8. Any of the consonants may be designated or identified by naming its three characterizing features as they appear on the diagram. Thus, [p] is a *voiceless bilabial stop*; [n] is a (*voiced*) *alveolar nasal*, and so on. (When a feature is the same for a whole class of sounds it need not be mentioned—e.g., *voice* for nasals, sonorants, and glides.)

Exercise 1. Following the examples given for [p] and [n], write descriptions for the other consonants of Diagram 3.

FOOTNOTES

[1]Enclosing a symbol in square brackets indicates that it is being used phonetically, i.e., consistently and exclusively to represent a given sound. The phonetic alphabet of the IPA is premised on this one-to-one correspondence. Thus, in a phonetic transcription using the IPA alphabet, the symbol [f] will be used to represent the final consonant of all four words *laugh*, *luff*, *lymph*, *aloof*, where our English spelling has four separate ways of representing the same sound.

chapter 3

Speech Sounds. Vowels

3.1. In the OE manuscripts (MSS), long vowels and diphthongs are sometimes marked with an acute accent (ʹ); edited modern texts, the present one included, usually indicate etymologically long vowels with a macron (¯), leaving the short unmarked. Thus *gōd*, good, but *God*, God; *wītan*, to keep, but *witan*, to know; and so on. Scholars know which to mark or leave unmarked after comparisons made with cognate forms in other Gmc languages and from observing how these vowels later developed in ME and MnE. Another valuable source of evidence is OE poetry, where vowel length is often indicated by the meter (see pp. 274–288).

Classifying Vowels

3.2. Vowels may differ from one another in *quantity* (i.e. length), *quality*, or both. They are classified as regards quality chiefly by three factors taken together: the degree of openness of the oral cavity, the position of the tongue, and the shape of the lips. In fuller detail:

1) The cavity may be slightly open, half open, or wide open: the vowels produced are accordingly *high*, *mid*, or *low* (compare MnE *beat*, *bait*, *bat*).
2) The tongue may be pushed forward, left at the center, or humped backward within the mouth: vowels are accordingly *front*, *central*, or *back* (compare MnE *beat*, *but*, *boot*).
3) The lips may be more or less pouted or they may be left inactive: vowels are accordingly *round* or *unround* (compare MnE *boot*, *beat*).

The accompanying diagram 4 shows the vowels of OE.

Diagram 4

	Front	*Central*	*Back*
High	[i:] beat [y:] Ger kühn [ɪ] bit [y] Ger küss		[u:] boot [ʊ] put
Mid	[e:] bait [ɛ] bet	[ə] but	[o:] boat [ɔ] Brit pot
Low	[æ:] S-SW US buy [æ] bat	[a] Scot man	[ɑ:] baah [ɑ] US pot

The rounded vowels are: [y:, y, u:, ʊ, o:, ɔ]. The sound [æ:] has no MnE standard keyword but is widely used in Southern and Southwestern U.S. The sound [ə] is found in EWS only as the second element of diphthongs. The vowels [y:, y] lost rounding and did not survive into MnE.

Note that within each of the two pairs [æ:] and [æ] and [y:] and [y] the difference is *quantitative*, whereas within the other pairs there is a *qualitative* difference as well.

3.3. Any of these vowels may be designated (described) by its three characterizing features and by whether it is long or short. (In IPA the diacritic [:] following a symbol indicates that it is long.) For example, [ɑ:] is a *low back unround long* vowel; [y] is a *high front round short* vowel.
Exercise 1. Following the examples given for [ɑ:] and [y], write designations for the other vowels of Diagram 4.

3.4. A *diphthong* (Gr *di-*, two + *phthongos*, sound) is made by starting in the position of one vowel and moving smoothly and rapidly to the position of another, the shift taking place within a single syllable. MnE has diphthongs in such words as *bout* [ɑ + ʊ], *bite* [ɑ + ɪ], boy [ɔ + ɪ]; the vowels in such a word as *chaos* do not form a diphthong, however. (The OE diphthongs are described in 4.15.)

Sound Change

3.5. To know the elements of phonetics makes it possible to understand all the regular sound-changes of OE, such as diphthongization, assimilation, palatalization, and others described in later chapters. The sounds of every language are constantly subject to change for several reasons. Though any normal human being can hear and produce a very large number of different sound-features, no language utilizes more than a fraction of those possible. The feature through which one sound is *distinct* from others similar to it will be accompanied by *non-distinctive* features which native speakers and hearers learn to ignore or to discount. For example, we recognize nasality as distinctive in the consonant phoneme[1] /n/ because on its presence or absence depends the difference of meaning between *pie* and *pine*, or between *sea* and *scene*. But if nasality is added to vowels, as it is in some individuals' speech, it does not affect the meaning of what is said; we ignore it and notice only those features necessary to the distinctiveness of the linguistic signal. (For example, [mæ̃n] said nasally means the same as [mæn] without nasality.) Over the course of time, with many speakings and hearings, a formerly non-distinctive feature may become more prominent, or one that was sporadic or contingent may become established. The former interrelation of sounds has been altered: there has been a sound-change.

3.6. Such changes are usually the result of the influence which sounds exert upon one another within the sequences of which words are built. It is well known that the [æ] in *at* is shorter than the [æ] in *add*—why? Because the vibration of the vocal cords in the first word must stop for voiceless *t*, whereas in the second vibrations of [æ] do not stop but continue into *d*, which is a voiced sound. The greater length of the [æ] in *add* is due simply to its environment. (As far as meaning is concerned, this difference of length is quite non-significant.)

3.7. Speech is a continuum. As sounds are spoken, they normally flow into each other with small adjustments that make articulation easier. By itself, [p] (a voiceless bilabial stop) would require an explosion to be heard, yet in context it is not always exploded. In the compound word *hop-pole* we do not have two explosions: the *p* of *hop* makes the bilabial closure and holds it for a moment; then the *p* of *pole* makes the explosion. Thus, in fact, two *p*'s have been reduced to one lengthened [p:] which requires less complex articulation.

3.8. One of the commonest sound-changes is *assimilation*, in which one sound or sound-feature becomes *more like* or *similar to* another near it. The past tense of *have* in OE is *hæfde* (*f* representing the sound [v]). By ME this has changed to *hadde*, the [v] becoming [d] by assimilation to the following [d].[2] (As with *hop-pole* the double letter represents length, not two explosions.) During most of the ME period *hadde* remains disyllabic, but by early MnE it has become *had* and is now even further reduced to *'d* in such condensed forms as he*'d* promised, they*'d* arrived. Such progressive simplification occurs gradually enough not to destroy the functioning of the linguistic signal. Many features of OE show the effects of assimilation; one special type, *umlaut* or *mutation*, has left interesting traces in MnE. (See Ch 11.)

3.9. Very important sound-changes result also from the feature called *stress*, which is simply the differential physical force exerted in producing syllables. This feature typifies the Gmc branch of IE; it has been in operation throughout the history of English and continues in force today. Every English word of two or more syllables places considerably more stress on one syllable than on the other or others. At least three distinctive degrees of stress exist in OE: primary, secondary, and weak. In the word *gūð-cyning*, war-king, they are found respectively in the first, second, and third syllables: ´ ` ˟.

3.10. Strong stress tends to preserve sounds: weak stress lays them open to change. A striking example of stress working in cooperation with other phonetic factors to simplify the linguistic signal is furnished by the history of our MnE word *lord*. It goes back to Prehistoric OE **hlāf-ward*, loaf-guardian, i.e. the master of a household in his capacity as distributor of food. As separate monosyllables, *hlāf* and *ward* (in WS *weard*) normally took primary stress. Joined together as a compound word, the second element had to have less stress than the first, thus ´ `. With a further reduction of stress to ´ ˟, further change ensued: between the voiced sounds represented by *ā* and *w*, the sound represented by *f* became voiced: phonetically, [f] to [v]. This is a type of assimilation. Further, the rounded semivowel represented by *w* was simplified altogether out of existence but left a ghostly reminder of itself in the rounding of the second vowel from *a* to *o*. Thus by the time of our historical OE records, **hlāf-ward* had become *hlāford*, and its etymology was doubtless obscure to most OE speakers. In ME we find the word as *loverd*: now the voiceless *hl-* of OE[3] has been voiced (perhaps through assimilation to the following vowel) as [l]; the unstressed vowel has lost rounding, hence *o* is now spelled *e*, which probably represents [ə].[4] Finally, internal *v*, occurring in an unstable position between vowels, disappears; the vowel of the primary-stressed syllable is preserved, the vowel of the weak-stressed syllable is lost, and a monosyllable is the result: *lord*. Through a similar if less sweeping series of changes, PrehOE **hlāf-dige*, bread-kneader, became MnE *lady*.

3.11. One of the most sweeping effects of the stress-differential in changing a language may be observed toward the end of the OE period. Strong stress remains on the base syllable of words; prefixes and suffixes accordingly become weaker by contrast and tend to be at first reduced, then entirely lost. Inflectional syllables, coming at the ends of words, are especially subject to this erosion; indeed, it is their widespread disappearance more than anything else which marks the boundary between OE and ME.

3.12. Sound changes are not of equal importance. Those which affect an entire category of sounds, or which even produce a realignment in the structure or system of the language, are obviously the more profound. Others may affect only a few words or may operate for a limited time then be overcome by countervailing forces. The final outcome of any sound-change is also greatly subject to such nonlinguistic factors as the prestige of one dialect over others (hence its spread at their expense) or serious dislocations in society because of war, plague, economic collapse, foreign influence. The language reflects the society: traditionalism fosters linguistic conservatism; social change fosters change in the language. Since it is probably true that English society has undergone more cultural change than any other in Western Europe, it is not surprising that the English language should have been less conservative than any other. Old English, richly varying in its dialects and everywhere reflecting the many changes and influences it underwent during the six hundred years in which it was the vernacular language of England, may be seen as a microcosm of the whole English language—though emphasis will be placed, in this Grammar, on the relatively circumscribed and stable stage of EWS.

FOOTNOTES

[1]A phoneme is a minimal unit of distinctive sound-feature which contrasts structurally with all other phonemes in the same language or form of speech. Differences in meaning are signaled by this distinctiveness of the phoneme. Phonemic symbols are regularly put between virgules: /n/, etc. See further Appendix II.

[2]In fuller detail: [v] was already voiced, like [d]; its assimilation consisted in its partial spirant closure becoming full stop closure and its position of articulation moving from labio-dental to dental.

[3]See further below, Ch 4, footnote 11.

[4]The change of OE *ā* > ME *o* in the first syllable reflects the *isolative change* (i.e., one occurring without reference to an immediate phonetic environment) by which every OE *ā* became ME *o* (phonetically [ɑ:] > [ɔ:])—compare OE *bāt*, ME *bote* (MnE *boat*). Most of the changes hitherto exemplified in the development of **hlāf-ward* have been *combinative changes* (i.e. those conditioned by an immediate phonetic environment).

Chapter 4

OE Spelling and Pronunciation

4.1. The growth of literacy and literary culture among the Anglo-Saxons was a consequence of their conversion to Christianity. The Latin alphabet, introduced by missionaries, displaced the Germanic *fuþark* (runic alphabet), which in any event had only been used for brief inscriptions of a magical, monumental, or practical nature and never for the transcription of extended texts. It was in the *scriptoria* of the early monasteries that writing was done on a large scale for the first time in Anglo-Saxon England. The monks were concerned first and foremost with the creation and transmission of Latin texts, which they had been taught to write by Irish monks. When they started writing their own vernacular language they naturally maintained the same correspondence between sound and symbol to which they were accustomed in writing Latin. As a consequence, OE spelling before Ælfred's reign, and to some extent after it, approached a phonetic rendering of the actual speech of various districts and periods.[1] It is thanks to this situation, where regional or individual variations in pronunciation are directly reflected in writing, that scholars have been able to establish the dialect characteristics and the historical development of OE sounds.

4.2. A number of sounds existed in OE, however, for which the Roman alphabet did not provide since they were not present in the pronunciation of Latin. The missing letters were supplied in a number of ways. From the runic alphabet þ ("thorn") was borrowed and used to represent both interdental spirants: voiced [ð] as in *thy* and voiceless [θ] as in *thigh*. Another letter was later invented for the same sounds by "crossing" a *d*: ð ("eth"). These two letters, *þ* and ð, are virtual alternatives in OE writing.[2]

4.3. The other character borrowed from the runic alphabet is Ƿ ("wen" or "wynn"), used for the sound [w]. Most modern texts (including this one) substitute *w* for it to avoid confusion with *p*, which it closely resembles.

4.4. The Latin diphthong *ae*, written as a ligature, *æ*, is used for the simple vowel articulated somewhere between [a] and [ϵ], as in MnE *bat*. The runic name for this symbol is "ash", OE *æsc*.

4.5. Every letter written was intended to be pronounced—there were no "silent" letters.[3] Doubling of a letter indicates prolongation in its pronunciation.[4]

Consonants

4.6. OE b, d, l, m, p, t, w, and x ([ks]) are pronounced as in MnE.
Examples: **bedd**, bed; **dol**, dull, stupid; **lamb**, lamb; **meolc**, milk; **pinn**, pin; **tacan**, take; **waru**, ware; **fyxe**, vixen.

4.7. It is thought (with some differences of scholarly opinion) that r was trilled, rather than simply retroflex as in MnE.
Examples: **rāp**, rope; **byrig**, city; **fær**, journey.

4.8. Three consonant symbols, f, s, and þ/ð, have dual values: they represent *voiced* sounds when they occur singly (not doubled) between voiced sounds (except when the first is a part of a prefix: e.g., the f in **gefoh** remains [f]). Everywhere else they represent *voiceless* sounds.
Examples:

Letter		*Sound*	*Words*
f	voiced	[v]	**ofer**, over; **efne**, even; **hærfest**, autumn.
	voiceless	[f]	**feld**, field; **æfter**, after; **hōf**, hoof; **Offa**, Offa.
s	voiced	[z]	**wīse**, wise; **hæslen**, of hazel.
	voiceless	[s]	**saet**, sat; **hūs**, house; **ēast**, east; **acsian**, to ask; **cyssan**, to kiss.
þ/ð	voiced	[ð][5]	**ōþer**, other; **hoðma**, darkness; **weorðan**, to become.
	voiceless	[θ]	**þis**, this; **bæð**, bath; **oðþe**, or.

These alternant forms are examples of assimilation (3.9.): the factor of *voice* is present or absent according to the environment in which the consonant occurs.

4.9. Two letters, *g* and *c*, have dual values according to their environment: the original sounds were velar [γ, k], but in PrehOE those occurring with front vowels (dental to palatal region) were fronted; those occurring with back vowels (velar region) remained back. (These alternants, like the preceding, exemplify assimilation: this time the *position of articulation* changed to agree with that of environing sounds.)

Letter		*Sound*	*Words*
g	velar	[ɣ]	**gān**, to go; **lagu**, law; **slōg**, struck.
	palatalized	[j]	**gīet**, yet; **fæger**, fair; **dæg**, day.
c	velar	[k]	**caru**, care; **tacan**, to take; **hōc**, hook.
	palatalized	[tʃ][6]	**ceaf**, chaff; **ēce**, eternal; **dīc**, ditch.

Specifically, *g* is fronted to [j] when it comes:

1. before long or short *i*, *e*, (*ī̆*, *ē̆*)[7] and the diphthongs which begin with them: **gif,** if; **gēar,** year;
2. between front vowels (*ī̆*, *ē̆*, *ǣ̆*): **siges,** of victory; **leger,** couch, lair;
3. at the end of a syllable, following a front vowel: **hīeg,** hay; **lægdon,** (they) laid;
4. when it had been followed in PrehOE by *i* or *j*:[8] **cīegan,** to name, call; **byrg,** of (the) town.

Otherwise *g* remains velar[9] (except in the combination *cg*—see **4.12.**).
Specifically, *c* is fronted when it comes:

1. before *ī*, *ē*, and the diphthongs beginning with *ī*, *ē*: **ciele,** chill; **cīdan,** to chide;[10]
2. between *ī* and a front vowel: **rīces,** of the kingdom;
3. at the end of a syllable, following *ī*: **pic,** pitch;
4. when it had been followed in PrehOE by *ī̆* or *j*:[8] **tǣcan,** show, teach.

In all other situations, *c* (or *k* when that is used) remains a back sound—i.e., is pronounced [k].

4.10. The letter *n* also has two values: it represents ordinary [n] except before *c* (or *k*) and *g*, in which cases it is pronounced [ŋ]. In such combinations the nasal and the following consonant are *both* pronounced: [ŋk, ŋɣ].

4.11. The letter *h* has two values: in initial position it is like MnE [h], a light voiceless spirant or simple aspirate; internally and finally, however, it has much stronger spirancy: [x]. This latter value is preserved today in Scots **nicht,** night, **loch,** lake (and may be heard in German **ich,** I, **buch,** book), but it does not survive in MnE.[11]

4.12. The cluster *sc*, originally pronounced [sk], became changed in WS when *c* was palatalized. It may be pronounced [ʃ].[12] Similarly, the cluster *cg* (representing palatalized *gg*) is pronounced [dʒ] as in MnE bridge (< OE **brycg**).

Vowels

4.13. The short vowels of OE, written *i*, *e*, *æ*, *u*, *o*, *a*, were probably pronounced much the same as the corresponding sounds today: [ɪ, ϵ, æ, ʊ, ɔ, ɑ] in *bit*, *bet*, *bat*, *put*, Brit. *pot*,[13] Scots or Ger. *man*.[14] The long vowels should be lengthened in pronunciation:[15] [i:, e:, æ:, u:, o:, ɑ:] as in *beet*, *bait*, *buy*,[16] *boot*, *boat*, *baah*.[17] OE *ȳ*, *y* were lost in ME; they are like *ī*, *i* but said with the lips closely rounded (cf. Ger. *kühn*, keen, *küss*, kiss).

4.14. The following is a practice list for pronouncing OE vowels:

Letter	*Sound*	*Words*
ȳ	[y:]	**ȳð,** wave; **brȳce**, useful; **þȳ**, by that
y	[y]	**yrre,** anger; **byre,** youth; **ymbe**, about
ī	[i:]	**īs,** ice; **bītan,** to bite; **hī,** they
i	[ɪ]	**ic,** I; **biten,** bitten; **hit,** it
ē	[e:]	**ēðel**, native land; **þēs**, this; **mē**, me
e	[ɛ]	**eft,** again; **tellan,** to count; **here,** army
ǣ	[æ:]	**ǣr,** before; **mǣre,** famous; **sǣ,** sea
æ	[æ]	**æt,** at; **hæft,** captive; **sæd,** heavy, sad
ū	[u:]	**ūt**, out; **fūl**, foul; **þū**, thou
u	[ʊ]	**uppe,** up; **hund,** dog; **caru,** care
ō	[o:]	**ōfer,** shore; **hrōf,** roof; **tō,** to
o	[ɔ]	**of,** of; **from,** from; **ealo,** ale
ā	[ɑ:]	**āð,** oath; **hāma,** cricket; **wā,** woe
a	[a]	**ac,** but; **camp,** battle; **cuma,** visitor.

Diphthongs

4.15. OE diphthongs include some sound combinations which do not survive in standard MnE. Like the vowels, they were paired, long and short. (Note the presence of [ə], which was not an independent phoneme in OE.)

Letters	*Sounds*	*Words*
ēa	[æ:ə]	**ēage**, eye; **gēar**, year; **fēa,** few
ea	[æə]	**eald**, old; **fealu**, fallow, yellow
ēo/īo	[e:ɔ, i:ɔ][18]	**ēoh,** yew tree; **nēod,** desire; **bēo,** be
eo/io	[ɛɔ, ɪɔ]	**eom,** am; **seolc,** silk; **teoru,** tar
īe	[i:ə]	**īeðe,** easy; **hīene,** frail; **hīe,** she
ie	[ɪə]	**hiera,** their; **ieldo,** old age.

Note: Both long and short diphthongs are stressed on the first element.

Accentuation

4.16. OE words are accented or stressed according to two rules:

1) Simple words, and words with inflectional or derivational suffixes, are stressed on the first syllable. Especially in poetry, some of these suffixes may receive a secondary stress.

Examples: dágas, grḗne, ḗage, ḗagena, swéotole, hélpan; swḗtèst. ðúrstìg, bódùng, léornùnga, dýrlìng, mícelnès, wýnsùm, glǽdlìce, bérènde, wúndrìan, wúndròde.

2. Compound words include substantive compounds and verbal compounds. Substantive compounds (except those beginning with **ge-**, **be-**, and **for-**, which are weak-stressed) take primary stress on the first component and secondary stress on the second.

Examples: góld-smìð, mónn-cỳnn, swī́ð-mṑd, sélf-wìlles, ónd-swàru, bī́-gòng, fóre-wèard, mís-dǣ̀d, tṓ-wèard, ýmb-hwỳrft; but note: ge-bód, be-góng, for-wýrd.

Verbal compounds are stressed on the base or root syllable, hence the prefix is weak-stressed.

Examples: a-rī́san, be-hā́tan, for-lǣ́tan, ge-bíddan, mis-fáran, ofer-cúman, tō-wéorpan, wið-stóndan, ymb-síttan.

FOOTNOTES

[1]In the ninth century, however, largely through Ælfred's influence, OE spelling tended to become more consistent, and after his time—even more after Ælfric's—the language had a more or less standard spelling. Toward the end of the OE period, nevertheless, irregularities in spelling show that pronunciation is changing.

[2]During the ME period ð disappeared; þ continued into the sixteenth century.

[3]Silent letters merely testify to the fact that pronunciation changes more quickly than spelling. Even after sounds have ceased to be pronounced, traditional spelling may continue to use the letters which formerly represented them.

[4]In MnE consonants are long only in compound words such as hea*dd*ress, ca*tt*ail, shee*p*-*p*en. Other doubled letters are pronounced short, like single letters.

[5]Note that though the letter ð is *written* in manuscripts for both voiced and voiceless sounds, as a phonetic symbol it is used only for the voiced sound.

[6]In becoming palatalized, k probably passed through the sequence [k > kj > tj > tʃ].

[7]Exception: When e was the result of *i-umlaut* (see Ch 11), the preceding g was not palatalized.

[8]The **i** or **j** which caused umlaut (and before which **g** or **c** was fronted) was changed or disappeared before the time of historic OE. (See Chap 11.)

[9]Spirant [ɣ] tended to close and become the stop [g].

[10]Before front vowels resulting from *i-umlaut*, however, c remained unpalatalized [k]. Examples: **cemban** < ***kambjan**, to comb; **cyning** < ***kuning**, king. See footnote 7 above.

[11]Initially in the clusters hl-, hn-, hr-, hw-, the consonants that follow h are devoiced by assimilation to it: [hl̥-, hn̥-, hr̥-, hw̥-]. Similarly, the other clusters fn-, fl-, fr-, þr- were probably pronounced [fn̥-, fl̥-, fr̥-, θr̥-].

[12]In becoming palatalized, sk probably passed through the sequence [sk > skj > sxj > sj > ʃ].

[13]As said in British "Received Pronunciation" (RP): a short, rounded, mid-back vowel.

[14]A short, unrounded, low-central vowel.

[15]The "long" vowels of OE have commonly become diphthongs today, especially [e:, o:], which usually are [eɪ, oʊ] as in *day* and *low*; but also [i:, u:], which are often [ij, uw] as in *me, you* (though several other variants are in use).

[16]The OE sound [æ:] or [ɛ:] survives only locally, not in Standard English. See diagram 4 (Chap 3).

[17]In MnE dialects, especially those where postvocalic r is lost: in English "RP", eastern New England, and the south Atlantic coast.

[18]In EWS manuscripts the etymological distinctions between ē̆o and ī̆o were not preserved: in effect, they were written alternatively: ēo or īo and eo or io, though ē̆o forms appear more frequently than ī̆o forms. The sound [ɔ] probably varied with [ə] allophonically in ē̆o/ī̆o.

chapter 5

Phonological Changes

5.1. In learning OE it is necessary to take careful note of the sound-changes which occurred in it and which give it its characteristic differences from other Low Germanic languages. These sound-changes also underlie, of course, the sounds which developed in ME and MnE. They will be outlined in chronological order in this and following chapters, beginning here with the three earliest. The vowel changes dealt with concern only those in syllables having primary or secondary, not weak stress.

Gemination

5.2. A type of consonant lengthening, traditionally called *gemination*, occurred in the WGmc stage (see Diagram 2), hence it affected not only OE but all the other WGmc dialects as well.
Rule: A single consonant (except **r**), when preceded in Gmc[1] by a short vowel and followed by **j**, was lengthened in WGmc.[2]
Examples: Thus Gmc ***cunja-** became WGmc ***cunnja-** (and ultimately OE **cynn**).[3] Similarly, Gmc ***saljan** > WGmc ***salljan** (> OE **sellan**).[4] But **r** was not lengthened, hence Gmc ***harja-** remained unchanged in WGmc (and ultimately became **here** in OE). Gmc **f** and **g** were regularly geminated in WGmc; the forms descended from them are written in OE as **bb** and **cg** respectively.[5]
Exercise 1. Write out the WGmc forms which would have resulted from gemination of the following Gmc forms: ***cwaljan**, ***sōcjan**, ***hafjan**, ***lagjan**, ***farjan**, ***dōmjan**, ***satjan**, ***sandjan**. (Note that it did not change *all* these forms.)

The Change of a to o

5.3. This change occurred in Prehistoric OE (PrehOE) but not in all dialects.
Rule: Before a nasal, the vowel [a] became [ɔ], **a** being respelled as **o** in most instances in EWS. (By the time of LWS, however, the **a** spellings had become predominant, even where the [ɔ] pronunciation survived.[6])

Examples: EWS **ond, lomb, monig, long**—(MnE and, lamb, many, long) LWS **and, lamb, manig, lang.**
Note: When **on** (< PrehOE ***an**) occurs before a voiceless spirant (**h, f, þ, s**). the nasal disappears and, in compensation, the vowel is lengthened to **ō**. Under the same conditions **in** and **un** become **ī** and **ū**. Thus EWS **sōft** (< ***sonft** < ***sanft**), soft; **ōðor** (< ***onðor** < ***anðar**), other; **gōs** (< ***gons** < ***gans**), goose; **fīf** (< ***finf**) five; **ðūhte** (< ***ðunhte**) thought. Compare Mn German **sanft, ander, gans, fünf, dünkte**, where cognate **n** was not lost.

The Change of a to æ

5.4. ***Rule:*** In PrehOE, **a** (except when followed by a nasal as above) was generally fronted and raised to (or nearly to) the position of **æ** unless the phonetic environment was such as to counteract this fronting tendency.
Examples: 1. In monosyllables, **dæg**, day, **bæc**, back, **sæd**, sad, heavy; 2. In polysyllables when PrehOE **e** or **i** (front vowels) come in the syllable following the base: **dæges**, day's, **togædere**, together. But **a** is unchanged when followed by **w** or by **a, o,** or **u** (back sounds) in the next syllable: **clawe**, of a claw, **dagas**, days, **nacod**, naked, **racu**, explanation. (The **a** in past participles such as **slagen** is not exceptional but results from the fact that **-en** < earlier **-an**. Thus there was a back environment counteracting the fronting tendency.)
Note. One effect of this sound-change was to make the base irregular in paradigms, as in the examples just given: NomSg **dæg**, GenSg **dæges**, but NomPl **dagas**; similarly, NomSg **sacu**, DatSg **sæcce**, etc. (Further changes undergone by this **æ** are detailed in Ch. 8.)
***Exercise* 2.** Write out the EWS forms which result from the change of **a** > **æ** in the following PrehOE forms: ***acer**, ***sadol**, ***craftig**, ***water**, ***aðele**, ***lawer-bēam.**

FOOTNOTES

[1]"Gmc" refers to the stage of development after PrGmc changes have taken place but before the branching into NGmc, EGmc, and WGmc.

[2]Later, when the dialects came to be written, lengthening was indicated by doubling the consonant—hence the term "gemination," from Lat *geminatio*, a doubling.

[3]In PrehOE the **j** changed the quality of some of the vowels preceding it, and ultimately it disappeared. (See Ch. 11, *i-umlaut*.)

[4]Compare, in other WGmc dialects, OFris **sella**, OS **sellian**, OHG **sellen**—but EGmc (i.e. Gothic) **saljan**, NGmc (i.e. ON) **selja**, both ungeminated.

[5]Gmc **f** represents a voiced bilabial spirant [ƀ]; **g** represents [ɣ]. Examples: Gmc ***liƀjan** by gemination > WGmc ***libbjan** (> OE **libban**); Gmc ***bugjan** > WGmc ***bugg-jan** (> OE **bycgan**).

[6]Phonetically, this change means that, under influence of the nasal, the low vowel [a] was raised and rounded in the WS area, though not in Kent or East Anglia. The change in the sound must have been distinct enough so that the EWS spelling was changed to reflect it. The growing importance of the London area may be responsible for the LWS return to the **a** spelling. The [ɔ] sound has survived till today in the W Midland dialect area: see Harold Orton, *Survey of English Dialects*.

chapter 6

Personal Pronouns

6.1. The personal pronoun in OE, like that of MnE, has singular and plural forms. It also preserves the IE *dual* forms. The dual is especially effective for showing close association between two people—as two men fighting side by side, or husband and wife, or lovers. (See, for example, Selection 22/21a–3a.) The dual forms, however, disappeared early in the ME period.

6.2. Like MnE, OE has forms for the three persons, with masculine, feminine, and neuter genders in the third person. As against the three case forms of MnE, however, OE has four, since it distinguishes dative from accusative. (In ME these fell together under the dative form to produce the MnE "object case.")

First Person	*Sg.*	*Dual*	*Pl.*
Nom	**ic**, I	**wit**, we two	**wē**, we
Gen	**mīn**	**uncer**	**ūser, ūre**[1]
Dat	**mē**	**unc**	**ūs**
Acc	**mec, mē**	**uncit, unc**	**ūsic, ūs**

Second Person			
N	**ðū**, thou	**git**, you two	**gē**, you
G	**ðīn**	**incer**	**ēower**
D	**ðē**	**inc**	**ēow**
A	**ðec, ðē**	**incit, inc**	**ēowic, ēow**

Third Person	*Masc.*	*Neut.*	*Fem.*	*All Gend.*
N	**hē**, he	**hit**, it	**hēo, hīe**, she	**hēo, hīe**, they
G	**his**	**his**	**hire**	**hira**
D	**him**	**him**	**hire**	**him, heom**
A	**hine**	**hit**	**hēo, hīe**	**hēo, hīe**

6.3. The Genitive forms of the first and second persons, all numbers, are also used as strong adjectives. (See Chap. 10.8.)

Reflexive Use

6.4. OE has no special reflexive pronoun forms; the personal pronoun forms are used to perform this grammatical function. For example: **Ic sceal mec hȳdan.** Standard MnE requires a form with *-self* in such situations, but the simple form is still found in archaic and folk speech: *I'll hide me.*

Exercise 1. Read the following sentences aloud. Translate them (no use of the glossary should be necessary). Identify person, number, case, and gender of each personal pronoun.

1) Hē is his brōðor.
2) Þǣr wæs hire bōc.
3) Ic þancie him.
4) Wē sungon monige songas.
5) Fīf menn sōhton uncit.
6) Hīe wǣron blīðe.
7) Gief hit mē.
8) Hit is hire horn.
9) Hēo ne lufiað ēowic.
10) "Ælfred" is ðīn nama.

Note: The Genitive is translated with *-'s*, *-s'*, or *of*; the Dative is usually translated with *to* or *for*.

Interrogative Pronouns

6.5. Though the interrogative has no distinctive feminine, it has five different case forms: N, G, D, A, and I (Instrumental[2]).

	Masc.	*Neut.*
Sg N	**hwā**, who	**hwæt**, what
G	**hwæs**	**hwæs**
D	**hwǣm, hwām**	**hwǣm, hwām**
A	**hwone**	**hwæt**
I	**hwī, hwon**	**hwī, hwon**

Note: From the Instrumental also comes the adverb **hū**, how. Two other interrogatives, **hwæðer**, which (of two), and **hwilc, hwelc**, which, are declined like strong adjectives. (See Chap 10.)

Exercise 2. Read the following sentences aloud. Translate them. Identify the number and case of the interrogative pronouns.

1) Hwæs is ðæt cild?
2) Hwā cumað hēr?
3) Hwæt sægde hē?
4) Hwī singeð ðes monn?
5) Hwæðer wæs þīn brōðor?

FOOTNOTES

[1]These and other multiple forms are alternates, sometimes one, sometimes the other being found in the MSS.

[2]The Instrumental case, used to show *means by which* or *thing with which* something is done, is translated with the prepositions *with* or *by*. *Examples*: **Ic hine cwealde ðȳ spere**, I killed him with the spear. **Hwī stearf hē**? Why (by what cause) did he die?

chapter 7

Anomalous Verbs

7.1. Several common OE verbs are so irregular ("anomalous") that they stand apart. These verbs are: 1. **bēon (wesan)**, to be; 2. **willan**, to will, to wish; 3. **dōn**, to do, to cause; 4. **gān**, to go.

7.2. The verb *to be* is a composite of parts supplied from three separate stems: **bēon, is,** and **wesan.**

			Present		*Preterit (Past)*
			INDICATIVE		
Sing.	1	ic	eom	bēo	wæs
	2	þū	eart	bist	wǣre
	3	hē / hit / hēo	is	bið	wæs
Plur.	1	wē			
	2	gē	sind, sint, sindon	bēoð	wǣron
	3	hīe			
			SUBJUNCTIVE		
Sing.	1–3		sīe, sī, sēo	bēo	wǣre
Plur.	1–3		sīen, sīn	bēon	wǣren
			IMPERATIVE		
Sing.	2		bēo, wes		
Plur.	2		bēoð, wesað		
			INFINITIVE	INFLECTED INFINITIVE[1]	
			bēon, wesan	tō bēonne	
			PARTICIPLE		
			bēonde, wesende		

7.3. OE verbs lack an inflected Future tense; they use the Present tense forms to express future time as well as present. (This is still true of the MnE present tense.) The verb *to be* is unique in OE in having alternate forms, **bēon** and

wesan. Forms of **bēon** are generally limited to the future, those of **wesan** to the present. (See for example the sentence in Selection 9, the Blickling Homily, p. 201, ll. 98–99.)

Negative Forms

7.4. Negative forms are produced by *contraction* when the negative particle **ne**, prefixed to the form, becomes combined with it. The **n-** becomes the initial consonant of the contracted form (displacing initial **w** if there is one) and the stressed vowel is preserved. Thus **ne** + **eom** > **neom**; **ne** + **wæs** > **næs**. Similarly formed are **nis, nǣre, nǣron**.

Exercise 1. Read the following sentences aloud. Translate them. Identify the person, number, tense, and mood of the finite forms; identify also the infinitive and participle forms.

1. Bēoð gē stille.
2. Hīe ne sindon englas.
3. Wes ðū beald!
4. Wē nǣron on Engla londe.
5. Sōna biþ hēo mid ēow.
6. Hwǣr wǣre ðū?
7. Þæt wæs mīn wīf.
8. Wīs is hālig tō bēonne.
9. Neom ic ðīn brōðor?
10. Ic wille þæt gē sīen hēr.

7.5. Willan

	Present	*Preterit*
	INDICATIVE	
Sing. 1	wille, wile	wolde
2	wilt	woldest
3	wille, wile	wolde
Plur. 1–3	willað	woldon
	SUBJUNCTIVE	
Sing. 1–3	wille, wile	wolde
Plur. 1–3	willen	wolden
	IMPERATIVE	
Plur. 2	nyllað, nellað (only in the negative)	
	INFINITIVE	
	willan	
	PARTICIPLE	
	willende	

Note: Negatives (produced by contraction as with the forms of **bēon**) are: **nyllan, nolde, noldon**, etc.

7.6. dōn

	Present	Preterit
	INDICATIVE	
Sing. 1	dō	dyde
2	dēst	dydest
3	dēð	dyde
Plur. 1–3	dōð	dydon
	SUBJUNCTIVE	
Sing. 1–3	dō	dyde
Plur. 1–3	dōn	dyden
	IMPERATIVE	
Sing. 2	dō	
Plur. 2	dōð	
	INFINITIVE	
	dōn	(Inflected) tō dōnne
	PARTICIPLE	
	dōnde	dōn

7.7. gān

	Present	Preterit
	INDICATIVE	
Sing. 1	gā	ēode
2	gǣst	ēodest
3	gǣð	ēode
Plur. 1–3	gāð	ēodon
	SUBJUNCTIVE	
Sing. 1–3	gā	ēode
Plur. 1–3	gān	ēoden
	IMPERATIVE	
Sing. 2	gā	
Plur. 2	gāð	
	INFINITIVE	
	gān	(Inflected) tō gānne
	PARTICIPLE	
	gānde	gān

Exercise 2. Read the following sentences aloud. Translate them. Identify the person, number, tense, and mood of the finite forms. Identify also the infinitive and participle forms.

1. Dōð þæt weorc.
2. Wilt ðū mē helpan?
3. Hē gæð hwǣrswā [wherever] hēo bēo.
4. Hīe woldon hēr cuman.
5. Ic dyde þæt hīe eoden.

FOOTNOTE

[1]The "Inflected Infinitive" is, specifically, its Dative case. (Some grammars call this the "OE Gerund" though the term does not properly apply.) It is regularly preceded by the preposition tō, forming with it a phrase often best translated into MnE by the Infinitive. It is frequently used to express purpose.

Chapter 8

Phonological Changes (contin.)

Breaking: Short Vowels

8.1. Rule: In PrehOE the vowels **æ** (which had developed < **a**—see 5.4 above), **e**, and **i**, when they occur before **r** + consonant, **l** + consonant, or **h**, are "broken" into short diphthongs, becoming respectively **ea**, **eo**, **io**.[1]

Examples: 1. **æ** > **ea**—***hærd** > **heard**, hard; ***hælf** > **healf**, half; ***fællan** > **feallan**, to fall; ***æhta** > **eahta**, eight.

2. **e** > **eo**—***werðan** > **weorðan**, become; ***herte** > **heorte**, heart. Before **l** this breaking occurs only if the following consonant is **c** ([k]) or **h**: ***melcan** > **meolcan**, to milk; ***selh** > **seolh**, seal; but **helpan**, to help, **swelgan**, to swallow, **sweltan**, to die, remain unbroken. Before **h** breaking is regular: ***fehtan** > **feohtan**, to fight, etc.

3. **i** > **io**—***Piht** > ***Pioht** (later **Peoht**), Pict; ***hirdi-** > ***hiordi-**,[2] herdsman; ***tihhian** > **tiohhian**, to arrange.

Breaking: Long Vowels

8.2. Rule: Long vowels break before **h**. (Examples with **i** are the most numerous.)

Examples: ***līht** > **līoht** (frequently **lēoht**), light; ***betwīh** > **betwīoh** (frequently **betwēoh**), betwixt; ***nǣh** > **nēah**, nigh.

Exercise 1. Write out the EWS forms which would result from the breaking (when possible) of the following PrehOE forms: ***bergan**, ***belgan**, ***tīhð**, ***wærþ**, ***rehhe**, ***hæll**, ***welc**, ***weltan**, ***cwern**.

Diphthongization after Initial Palatal g, c, sc,

8.3. Rule: When the palatals **g**, **c**, and **sc** occur initially in a stressed morpheme, certain vowels following them are diphthongized: **æ** > **ea**, **ǣ** > **ēa**, and **e** > **ie**.[3]

Examples: **æ** > **ea**— **gæf** > **geaf**, gave; ***cæf** > **ceaf**, chaff; Lat. **castra** > ***cæster** > **ceaster**, town; ***scæl** > **sceal**, shall.

ǣ > **ēa**— ***gǣfon** > **gēafon**, gave; Lat. **cāseus** > ***cǣsi** > ***cēasi** > **cīese** (by **i**-Umlaut, see Chap. 11), cheese; ***scǣp** > **scēap**, sheep.

e > **ie**—***gefan** > **giefan**, give; ***getan** > **gietan**, get; ***sceran** > **scieran**, to shear.

Exercise 2. Write out the EWS forms which would result from the diphthongization after initial palatals of the following PrehOE forms: ***scær**, ***sceld**, ***gæt**, ***scǣron**, ***gestran**, ***gǣton**, ***scæft**, ***geman**, ***cæp**, ***cælf**.

Final Double Consonants

8.4. Double consonants at the end of a word are usually simplified.
Examples: **monn**, **mon**, man; **menn**, **men**, men; **eall**, **eal**, all; **cynn**, **cyn**, kin; **bedd**, **bed**, bed; **sibb**, **sib**, peace.

But **cg**, though it historically represents a doubled consonant (see 4.12, 5.2 above), had changed phonetically ([ɣɣ > dʒ]) and was not simplified.

FOOTNOTES

[1]In broad phonetic terms: [æ > ǽə, ϵ > ϵ́ə, ɪ > ɪ́ə]. In each case an unstressed glide-vowel has crept in as the tongue moved from a front vowel position to that of a consonant somewhat farther back—in the first examples, [r, l, x].

[2]Later > **hierde**. See Chap. 11.

[3]Phonetically: [æ > æə, æ: > æ:ə, ϵ > ɪə]. Here the diphthong is due to movement of the tongue from palatal position, which is high, to that of the mid and low front vowels. This produces a glide-sound *after* **æ** and **ǣ**, making them phonetically [ǽə] *and* [ǽ:ə], spelled *ea* and *ēa* But the glide-sound developed *before* **e**, and later the stress was moved back and placed on it; thus: [ϵ > ɪϵ́ > ɪ́ϵ > ɪ́ə], spelled *ie*.

CHAPTER 9

Demonstrative Pronouns

9.1. The Demonstrative Pronouns of OE are sē, *that*, and its forms, and þēs, *this*, and its forms. The first is by far the more important since it serves also as the Definite Article. In demonstrative use these pronouns are stressed, hence the two forms þæt and þis come down to MnE virtually unchanged (though other case forms are lost). In definite article use, however, being but weakly stressed, sē and its forms were worn down phonetically in ME to produce MnE *the*, now used without distinction of number, gender, or case.

9.2. The OE paradigm formally distinguishes 2 numbers, 3 genders, and 5 cases:

	Masc.	*Neut.*	*Fem.*
S.N.	sē	ðæt	sēo
G.	ðæs	ðæs	ðǣre
D.	ðǣm, ðām	ðǣm, ðām	ðǣre
A.	ðone	ðæt	ðā
I.	ðȳ, ðē, ðon	ðȳ, ðē, ðon	
		ALL GENDERS	
P.N.A.		ðā	
G.		ðāra, ðǣra	
D.I.		ðǣm, ðām	

9.3. The second demonstrative, þēs, with an equally elaborate paradigm, was similarly reduced in ME. The resultant MnE forms are *this* and *these*.

	Masc.	*Neut.*	*Fem.*
S.N.	ðēs	ðis	ðēos
G.	ðis(s)es	ðis(s)es	ðisse, ðeosse
D.	ðis(s)um	ðis(s)um	ðisse, ðeosse
A.	ðisne	ðis	ðās
I.	ðȳs, ðīs	ðȳs, ðīs	
		ALL GENDERS	
P.N.A.		ðās	
G.		ðissa, ðeossa	
D.I.		ðis(s)um, ðeos(s)um	

Note: When sē and þēs are used as modifiers, they take weak stress, hence the vowels are usually shortened: **se, þes**. (In the oblique cases the vowels remain long.)

Exercise. Read the following sentences aloud. Translate them. Identify the number, gender, and case of each demonstrative (or definite article):

1. Þes monn is mīn fæder.
2. Ic rīde tō þǣre healle.
3. Þis līf is sceort.
4. Ealle þā stānas sind hēr.
5. Lufiað gē þās cildru?
6. Hē blissiað þȳs songe.
7. Hīe cwealdon þone fēond þȳ spere.
8. Hēo is sēo mōdor þisses lȳtlinges.
9. Ðæs hūses weallas sindon gōde.
10. Se hūsbond þǣre cwēne is se cyning.

The Relative Pronoun.

9.4. OE has no paradigm of inflected relative pronouns. This function is expressed in three ways: (1) most frequently, by use of the relative particle **þe**, which serves for all cases and numbers; (2) often by forms of the demonstrative sē (or sometimes a personal pronoun) + the particle **þe**; (3) sometimes by use of sē and its forms alone.

Example: **Hē ceas þone monn {þe / þone þe / þone} ic lufie,** He chose the man *whom* I love.

Note: Other words which sometimes serve as relatives are **swilc**, such, and **swā**, as.

Translation: *A Dialog*

Lārēow:[1] Gōdne dæg, leorneras.[2]

Leorneras: Gōdne dæg, lārēow.

Lār.: Tōdæg sculon wē specan Westseaxna þēode.[3] Bēoð gē gearwe?[4]

Leorn.: Gēa, lēof,[5] wē sindon gearwe.

Lār.: Ðū, leorningcniht,[6] and þū, leorningmægden[7]—secgað[8] mē nū—hwæt is Westseaxna þēod?

L-mægden: Ðæt is sēo þēod ūserra ealdfædera.[9]

Lār.: Ðæt is sōð.[10] Ūre ealdfæderas spǣcon Westseaxna þēode þūsend gēara ǣr ðissum.[11]

L-cniht: Ðūsend gēara ǣr þissum! Ðæt is fela[12] gēara. Lēof, sæge mē, for ic nylle dol[13] bēon—

Lār.: Hwæt wilt þū cnāwan?[14]

L-cniht: Ūre ealdfæderas sindon dēade þūsend gēara?

Lār.: Gēa, þæt is sōþ. Heora līc[15] sindon dēad.

L-cniht: Hīe ne specað nū—þonne is heora þēod dēad ealswā[16] swā hīe. Hwæt is ūs nīed[17] Westseaxna ðēode tō leornienne?

VOCABULARY

1. **lārēow,** teacher
2. **leorneras,** students
3. **þēod,** language
4. **gearwe,** ready, (Shaks. yare)
5. **lēof,** (dear) sir
6. **leorningcniht,** young man student
7. **leorningmægden,** young woman student
8. **secgað,** say, tell
9. **ealdfæderas,** ancestors'
10. **sōþ,** true
11. **ǣr ðissum,** ago (lit. before this)
12. **fela,** many
13. **dol,** foolish
14. **cnāwan,** to know
15. **līc,** body, corpse; also plural
16. **ealswā,** also
17. **nīed,** necessity

chapter 10

Adjectives; Analogy; Possessive Pronouns

10.1. In common with the Gmc languages generally, OE has a twofold classification of adjectives: the Strong or Indefinite declension (in this chapter), and the Weak or Definite declension (in Chap. 12). The Strong declension is used except when conditions calling for use of the Weak declension are present (see 12.1, 2).

10.2. Adjectives (and nouns) are classified by their stem vowels. This system of classification rests on the forms they had during the Gmc stage, when they were composed of *base* + *stem* + *inflectional suffix*: Those which had the same stem vowel are now classified together. Because it is convenient for comparative grammar this system is used even when (as frequently happens in OE) this distinctive stem has been lost through phonological change. Thus Gmc ***stainaz**, stone, composed of **stain** + **a** + **z** is classified as an "a-stem"; and so also is its descendant OE **stān**, even though in this word both stem and inflectional suffix have been lost.

Strong Declension of Adjectives

a- (o-) Stems. Monosyllabic bases, short and long.

		MASC.	NEUT.	FEM.
S.	N.	til *good*	til	til u, -o
	G.	~ es	~ es	~ re
	D.	~ um	~ um	~ re
	A.	~ ne	~	~ e
	I.	~ e	~ e	~ re
P.	N.A.	~ e	~ u, -o	~ a
	G.	~ ra	~ ra	~ ra
	D.I.	~ um	~ um	~ um

(*cont.*)

(*cont.*)		MASC.	NEUT.	FEM.
S.	N.	gōd *good*	gōd	gōd
	G.	~ es	~ es	~ re
	D.	~ um	~ um	~ re
	A.	~ ne	~	~ e
	I.	~ e	~ e	~ re
P.N.A.		~ e	~	~ a, -e
	G.	~ ra	~ ra	~ ra
	D.I.	~ um	~ um	~ um

Note 1: Some variations of form within the paradigm were the following: Bases having PrehOE a were of course subject to the change of **a** > **æ** (5.4); hence such a paradigm contains **æ** forms, e.g. **hræd, hrædes, hræde**, etc., as well as **a** forms, e.g. **hrada, hradu**, etc.
Note 2: In bases ending in **-h** [x], the **h** changes according to its phonetic environment. Thus it may disappear: **hēah,** *high*, fem. **hēa**, masc. gen. **hēas**. It may be assimilated to the following consonant: fem. gen. **hēahre, hēarre,** *higher*. It may be voiced > **g** [ɣ]: **wōh,** *wrong*, gen. **wōges**. Or it may be vocalized, replaced by w [**w**]: **rūh,** *rough*, gen. **rūwes**.

10.3. *ja- (jō-) and wa- (wō-) Stems. Disyllabic bases.*

		MASC.	NEUT.	FEM.
S.	N.	grēne *green*	grēne	grēnu, -o
	G.	~ es	~ es	~ re
	D.	~ um	~ um	~ re
	A.	~ ne	~ e	~ e
	I.	~ e	~ e	~ re
P.N.A.		~ e	~ u, -o	~ a, -e
	G.	~ ra	~ ra	~ ra
	D.I.	~ um	~ um	~ um
S.	N.	gearu, -o	gearu, -o	gearu, -o *ready*
	G.	~ wes	~ wes	~ (o)re
	D.	~ wum	~ wum	~ (o)re
	A.	~ one	~ u, -o	~ we
	I.	~ we	~ we	~ (o)re
P.N.A.		~ we	~ u, -we	~ wa, -e
	G.	~ (o)ra	~ (o)ra	~ (o)ra
	D.I.	~ wum	~ wum	~ wum

Note 3: The wa-stems often exhibit a parasitic vowel before **w**: **gear(o)wes, gear(e)wes, gear(u)we**, etc. Phonetically these spellings no doubt represent the

same sound: a weak, centralized vowel, [ə] or the like, induced by the transition from [r] to [w].

Effects of Analogy

10.4. In any language, the more frequent structural patterns or those having a larger number of members constantly exert pressure upon the less frequent to conform by analogy, and thus to reduce irregularity. Examples are numerous. From ME to MnE, the regular pattern for forming the plural of nouns is gradually substituted for irregular ones: ME *goot*, *geet* > MnE *goat*, *goats*. (Children generally say *foot*, *foots* following this pattern until they learn the correct, though less common, pattern *foot*, *feet*.)

10.5. The most conspicuous example of this kind of analogical force in English is the slow changeover of strong (irregular) verbs to weak (regular) verbs which began in the OE period and is still in progress. *Burn, chew, glide, grip, help, lock, reek, seethe, shove, sigh, slip, smoke, suck, yawn* are only a few of the verbs, strong in OE, which are now weak. Thus the OE principal parts *helpan*, *healp*, *hulpon*, *holpen* have yielded to MnE *help*, *helped*, *helped*. (The U.S. dialectal *holp*, sometimes spelled "hope": *He holp/hope me when I was sick*, is a relic of the older strong verb form.) Though phonological change frequently introduces inconsistencies into paradigms (see Note 1 above on the forms of *hræd*), analogy tends to level them out again, making the base the same for all members of the paradigm. Similarly with *dæg*-, *dagas*, etc. (see 5.4. Note) the *dag*- forms disappeared, the *dæg*- forms survived, though now spelled with *a* (MnE *day*, *days*).

10.6. Another phonological change (see Appendix I, Verner's Law) split some verb bases in another way, as *frēosan* (freeze), *frēas*, *fruron*, *froren*, with *s* in the first two, *r* in the other principal parts. But later, by analogy, the *r* forms were changed to *s* [z], restoring consistency: MnE *freeze*, *froze*, *frozen*.

10.7. As regards OE adjective classes (our immediate concern), analogy was responsible for reducing their number to three, when there had been five distinct classes in Gmc: the Gmc **i**-stems became **ja**-stems in OE, and the Gmc **u**-stems became either **ā**- or **ja**-stems.

Possessive Pronouns

10.8. The Possessive Pronouns, when used adjectivally, are declined like **gōd** (except **ūre**, which is declined like **grēne**): **mīn**, mine; **ðīn**, thine; **sīn**, his, hers, its; **ūre**, ours; **ēower**, yours; **uncer**, of us two; **incer**, of you two.

Translation: A Dialog (concluded)

Lār.: Ēalā,[1] geong mann, sege mē nū: ðæt ðæt is nīwe,[2] is hit eall gōd?
L-cniht: Nā, hlāford, nis hit eall gōd.
Lār.: And sōð is swā same:[3] ðæt ðæt is eald, nis hit eall yfel.[4]

L-cniht: Ðēahhwæþere[5] ne magon wē hīeran ūre ealdfæderas.

Lār.: Leorningmægden, hwæt sægst þū þærtō?

L-mægden: Ic sege þæt ðēah þe[6] wē ne mægen hīeran ūssera ealdfædera stefna,[7] þēahhwæðere magon wē rǣdan heora word, þā þe ðā bōceras[8] gewriten habbað.

Lār.: Gēa sōðlīce, leorneras ealle. On ūssera ealdfædera dagum lifdon mihtige cyningas, bealde rincas.[9] Hīe begēaton[10] ðis land and hit gesetton.[11] Fela gēara ðǣræfter wǣron hīe gefulwode[12] and gehwurfon[13] Crīstnan. Ðā wunnon[14] hīe wið ðā hǣðnan.[15] Manige bōceras brōhton wīsdōm in on land. Swēte songas sungon þā scopas[16] on healle. Nū sindon wē hīera ierfan.[17] Gif wē nyllað dolu bēon, uton[18] leornian ðā Westseaxna ðēode.

VOCABULARY

1. **ēalā**, lo! look here!
2. **nīwe**, new
3. **swā same**, likewise
4. **yfel**, evil, bad
5. **ðēahhwæðere**, nevertheless
6. **þēah þe**, although
7. **stefna**, voices
8. **bōceras**, writers
9. **rincas**, warriors
10. **begēaton**, took, won
11. **gesetton**, settled
12. **gefulwode**, baptized
13. **gehwurfon**, turned
14. **wunnon**, fought
15. **hǣðnan**, heathens
16. **scopas**, poets, singers
17. **ierfan**, heirs, inheritors
18. **uton**, let us

chapter 11

Phonological Changes (contin.)

i-Umlaut

11.1. The most regular and widespread form of assimilation to occur in OE is that called **i-umlaut**[1] (or **i-mutation**). It affects most of the stressed radical or base vowels, and, as the name implies, the change is due to a high-front vowel or semivowel [i:, i, j] in the following syllable, which, by anticipation, draws the base vowel upward and/or forward toward the high-front position. (It occurred during PrehOE but after Breaking.)

11.2. Rule: A stressed base vowel is moved toward high-front position (palatalized) by ī, i, or j occurring in the following syllable. Thus:

a (or o) before nasal	>	e
æ (< PrehOE a)	>	e
ū	>	ȳ
u	>	y
ō	>	ē
o	>	e
ā (< Gmc ai)	>	ǣ
ēa, ēo, īo	>	īe, later ī (in LWS often sp. ȳ)
ea, eo, io	>	ie, later i (in LWS often sp. y)

Diagram 5

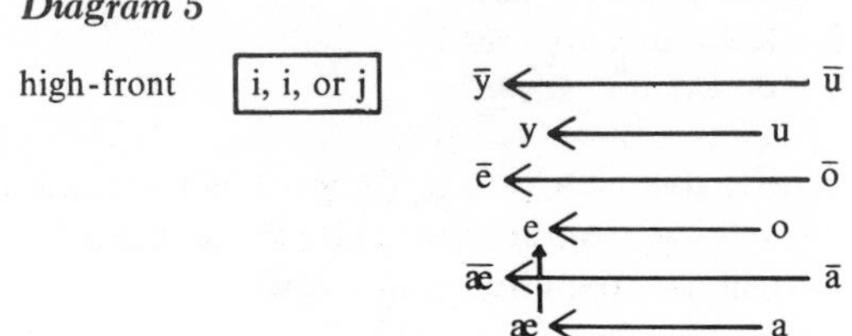

Note 1: The vowels ī, i, being already high-front, are not affected by **i**-umlaut. The change of **e** > **i** had already occurred in PrimGmc; its effects may be seen in the early stage of all Gmc languages.

Note 2: The ī, **i**, once they have caused umlaut, are later for the most part either changed to **e**, or lost (see examples following); the **j**, retained only after **r**, is there spelled **i**. After a long syllable, final **i** was lost. (A syllable is long if it contains a long vowel or diphthong—one marked with a macron: ¯, or if it contains a short vowel or diphthong followed by more than one consonant. All other syllables are short. See further p. 276, n. 23.)

Examples:

æ > e : ***hærjan** > **herian**, to raid; ***mæti** > **mete**, meat
a/o > e : ***monni** > **menn**, dat.sg., to a man; **wandian** > **wendan**, to turn
ā > ǣ : ***dāli** > **dǣl**, share; ***hāljan** > **hǣlan**, to heal
ō > ē : ***dōmian** > **dēman**, to deem; ***tōði** > **tēð**, teeth
o > e : ***morgin** > **mergen**, morrow; ***dohtri** > **dehter**, to a daughter
ū > ȳ : ***cūðian** > **cȳðan**, to inform; ***mūsi** > **mȳs**, mice.
u > y : ***cuning** > **cyning**, king; ***buggjan** > **bycgan**, to buy
ea,īo, etc. > īe, ie: ***ealdira** > **ieldra**; ***frīondi** > **frīend**.

Exercise. Write out the EWS forms which would result from **i**-umlaut of the following PrehOE forms (including the changes mentioned in Note 2).

1. * flāsci	6. * hæti	11. * lārjan
2. * slægi	7. * brūdi	12. * bandjan
3. * huldi	8. * hwearfjan	13. * bōci
4. * līohtjan	9. * sættjan	14. * frammjan
5. * sandjan	10. * wurmi	15. * hæfig

u-o-a-Umlaut

11.3. Rule: The stressed base vowels **æ, e, i,** if followed by a single consonant, are diphthongized by **u, o,** or **a** (back vowels) coming in the following syllable. (This process operated uniformly in the Mercian and Kentish dialects, irregularly in WS.)

Examples:

***æfora** > **eafora**, heir; ***ælu** > **ealu**, ale
***werold** > **weorold**, world; ***gelu** > **geolu**, yellow
***wita** > **wiota**, wise man; ***clipode** > **cliopode** (> **cleopode**), cried out.
But: WS **hafoc**—Merc. **heafoc**, hawk
WS **medu**—Kent. **meodu**, mead
WS **sinu**—Kent. **sionu**, sinew.

Note 3: Phonetically, this change exactly parallels Breaking (8.1): the same vowels change into the same diphthongs. This time, however, the back sound which led to the intrusion of the glide was a vowel.

Translation: Luke VIII, 4–8

Sōþlīce þā micel menigu cōm and of þām ceastrum tō him efeston. Hē sǣde heom ān bīspell.

Sum mann his sǣd sēow. Đā hē þæt sēow, sum fēoll wið þone weg and wearð fortreden. And heofenes fuglas hit frǣton.

And sum fēoll ofer þone stān and hit forscranc for þām þe hit wǣtan næfde.

And sum fēoll on þā þornas and þā þornas hit forþrysmodon.

And sum fēoll on gōde eorðan and worhte hundfealde wæstm.

Đā clipode hē and cwæð, "Gehīere sē ðe ēaran hæbbe."

VOCABULARY

bīspell, parable
ceaster, city
clipian, to call, speak
ēare, ear
efestan, to hasten
fēoll, PastT of **feallan,** to fall
forscrincan, to shrink up
fortredan, to tread down
for þām (þe), because
forþrysmian, to choke
fugol, bird
fretan, to devour
gehīeran, to hear, listen
hæbbe, Subjunc. of **habban,** to have
hundfeald, hundredfold
menigu, multitude
micel, great, large
of, from
sēow, PastT of **sāwan,** to sow
þā, then, when
wæstm, increase, harvest
wǣta, moisture
wearð, PastT of **weorðan,** to become
wið, against, beside
worhte, PastT of **wyrcan,** to work, make, produce

FOOTNOTE

[1]German *Umlaut* = a sound which goes around (from one position of articulation to another).

chapter 12

Weak Adjectives; Participles; Comparison

Weak Declension of Adjectives

12.1. The "weak" adjectives are so called because they have fewer distinctive inflectional endings than the Strong adjectives. The strong and weak types fell together in ME; in MnE, adjectives have lost all inflection except that for comparison.

12.2. The Weak declension is used in four situations especially:

1. When the adjective is preceded by a demonstrative (sometimes a possessive) pronoun;
2. In direct address;
3. Often in poetry where prose would normally use the strong forms;
4. In the comparative degree and often in the superlative.

The Weak declension is also used for ordinal numbers except **ǣrest, fyrmest, fyrst,** *first,* which are declined both strong and weak; and **ōðer**, *second*, which is declined strong only.

12.3.

	Masc.	*Neut.*	*Fem.*
S.N.	gōda, *good*	gōde	gōde
G.	~ an	~ an	~ an
D.I.	~ an	~ an	~ an
A.	~ an	~ e	~ an
		ALL GENDERS	
P.N.A.		gōdan	
G.		~ ena, -ra	
D.I.		~ um	

Note 1: The GenPl sometimes occurs in **-ana, -an** (conforming to the other cases); or in **-na,** and **-a** (conforming to noun endings). In later texts the case inflection **-an** sometimes appears as **-on;** and **-um** often becomes **-un; -on.**

Note 2: Adjectives ending in **-h** are contracted, with loss of the **h: hēah**, high: **hēa, hēan**, etc.; **ðweorh**, athwart: **ðwēora, -e**, etc.; **woh**, wrong: **wōna**, etc. (See 10.2. *Note 2*, **hēah**, etc.)

12.4. The Demonstrative **ilca**, *the same*, is generally declined like a Weak adjective. **Self (seolf, sylf)**, *self*, may be declined like either a Strong or a Weak adjective.

Declension of Participles

12.5. Participles may be inflected like either the Strong or the Weak adjective. The Present Participle, when strong, is declined like a **ja-** (**jō-**) stem (**grēne**, 10.3.). The Past Participles are declined like **a-** (**ō-**) stems (**til, gōd**, 10.2.).

Comparison of Adjectives

12.6. Rule: The *majority* of OE adjectives form the comparative with **-ra** (< * **-ora**) and the superlative with **-ost**.

Examples:

ceald, *cold*	cealdra	cealdost
earm, *poor*	earmra	earmost
heard, *hard*	heardra	heardost
hlūd, *loud*	hlūdra	hlūdost

12.7. A *limited number* of OE adjectives, however, form the comparative with **-ra** (< * **-ira**) and the superlative with **-est** (< ***-ist**); in these the **i** causes umlaut of the base vowel.

Examples:

eald, *old*	ieldra	ieldest
ēaðe, *easy*	īeðra	īeðest
geong, *young*	giengra	giengest
grēat, *great*	grīetra	grīetest
hēah, *high*	hīehra (hīerra)	hīeh(e)st
long, *long*	lengra	lengest
sceort, *short*	sciertra	sciertest

Note 3: The ending **-ost** (which is often represented by **-ust, -ast**) is occasionally transferred to umlauted forms; and **-est** is often found with the unumlauted forms, especially when these are inflected: **heardesta, rīcestan**, etc. (In other words, both umlauted and unumlauted forms exerted analogical attraction on each other.)

12.8. *Some few* comparatives and superlatives have no positive degree form but are based on corresponding adverbs or prepositions.

Examples:

(nēah, *near*)	nēarra	nīehst
(ǣr, *earlier*)	ǣrra	ǣrest
(fore, *before*)	furðra	fyr(e)st

12.9. A trace of superlatives in **-m** survives in **forma**, *the first*, and **hindema**, *the hindmost*. But to this **-m** the regular ending **-est** has been added; the result is a (double) superlative ending **-mest**. These adjectives, also, are usually based upon adverbs or prepositions and usually have the comparative in **-erra**.

Examples:

(sīð, *late*)	sīðra	sīðemest, sīðest
(læt, *late*)	lætra	latemest, lætest
(inne, *within*)	inn(er)ra	innemest
(ūte, *without*)	ūt(er)ra, ȳttra	ȳtemest, ūtemest
(ufan, *above*)	uferra, yfer(r)a	yfemest, ufemest
(niðan, *below*)	niðerra	niðemest
(æfter, *after*)	æfterra	æftemest
(norð, *northward*)	norðra, nyrðra	norðmest

Note 4: The MnE forms *utmost*, *foremost*, *northmost*, etc. have changed **e** > **o** under the influence of the word *most*, which is also used for periphrastic comparison.

12.10. In the following list comparison is irregular: the base of the comparative and superlative forms differs from that of the positive. (In other words, the paradigm is composed by suppletion.)

gōd, *good*	bet(e)ra, bettra	bet(e)st
yfel, *evil*	wiersa	wierrest, wierst
micel, *great*	māra, mǣra	mǣst
lȳtel (lȳt), *little*	lǣssa	lǣs(e)st

Note 5: With **gōd** is to be associated (in meaning) the adverb **sēl**, *better*, comparative adj. **sēlla, sēlra**, superlative adj. **sēlost, sēlest**; and the adverb and substantive **mā (mǣ)**, *more*, belongs to **māra**.

Translation: *Luke IX, 12–13*

Ðā gewāt se dæg forð. And hīe twelfe him genēahlǣhton and sǣdon him, "Lǣt þās menigu þæt hīe faren on þās castelu and on þās tūnas þe hēr ābūtan sind, and him mete finden, for þām þe wē sind hēr on wēstere stōwe."

Ðā cwæð hē tō him, "Sellaþ gē him etan." Ðā cwǣdon hīe, "We nabbaþ būtan fīf hlāfas and twēgen fiscas, būton wē gān and ūs mete bycgen and eallum þissum werode." Ðǣr wǣron nēah fīf þūsenda wera.

VOCABULARY

ābūtan, about
būton, except, only; unless
bycgan, to buy
castel, town
cwǣdon, Past T of **cweðan**, to say
faran, to go, to travel
fisc, fish
genēahlǣcan, to approach
gewāt, PastT of **gewītan**, to depart, to go
hlāf, loaf of bread
lǣtan, to permit, to cause to
mete, food
nēah, nigh, near(ly)
stōw, place
sellan, to sell, to give
tūn, village
twēgen, two
wer, man
werod, multitude
wēste, uninhabited, waste

Chapter 13

Nouns: the a-Declension

13.1. The a-declension (including also **ja-** and **wa-**stems) comprises masculine and neuter (no feminine) nouns with both *monosyllabic* and *disyllabic* bases. The greater number of masculine and neuter nouns in OE belong to this declension.

13.2. Masculine a-stems, monosyllabic:

S.N.A.	stān, *stone*	dæg, *day*	mearh, *horse*	fugol, *bird*
G.	~ es	~ es	mēares	fugles
D.I.	~ e	~ e	~ e	~ e
P.N.A.	~ as	dagas	~ as	~ as
G.	~ a	~ a	~ a	~ a
D.I.	~ um	~ um	~ um	~ um

Note 1: Of the examples above, **stān** represents the norm; **dæg**[1] illustrates the change of **a** > **æ** (See 5.4.); **mearh** illustrates loss of **h** (See 16.4.); the base of **fugol** is monosyllabic **fugl-**, and the **o** of the Nom. is epenthetic—i.e., it comes in to facilitate pronunciation.[2]

13.3. Masculine a-stems, disyllabic:

S.N.A.	ēðel, *property*	fǣtels, *tub*	heofon, *heaven*
G.	ēðles	~ es	~ es
D.I.	~ e	~ e	~ e
P.N.A.	~ as	~ as	~ as
G.	~ a	~ a	~ a
D.I.	~ um	~ um	~ um

Note 2: Of these examples, **ēðel** illustrates syncope[3] of **e** in the oblique cases; the **e** of **fǣtels** is not syncopated, however, because the syllable it is in is long; **o** is sometimes syncopated in **heofon** and similar words, usually not.

13.4. Neuter a-stems, monosyllabic:

S N.A.	scip, *ship*	word, *word*	fæt, *vessel*	feoh, *cattle*	tungol, *star*
G.	~ es	~ es	~ es	fēos	tungles
D.I.	~ e	~ e	~ e	fēo	~ e
P.N.A.	~ u	~	fatu		tungol
G.	~ a	~ a	~ a		tungla
D.I.	~ um	~ um	~ um		~ um

Note 3: Of these examples, **scip** and **word** represent the norm, differing from one another only in the P.N.A., where the **-u** is retained after a short syllable (**scip**) but disappears after a long syllable (**word**). For stem changes compare **fæt** with **dæg**, **feoh** with **mearh**, and **tungol** with **fugol** (Note 1 above).

13.5. Neuter a-stems, disyllabic:

S.N.A.	hēafod, *head*	fulwiht, *baptism*	werod, *troop, multitude*
G.	hēafdes	~ es	~ es
D.I.	~ e	~ e	~ e
P.N.A.	~ u	fulwiht	werod
G.	~ a	~ a	~ a
D.I.	~ um	~ um	~ um

Note 4: For stem changes compare **hēafod** with **ēðel**, and **fulwiht** with **fǣtels** (Note 2 above).

13.6. The **ja-** and **wa-**stems follow the patterns above, respectively as Masc. or Neut., monosyllabic or disyllabic.

Examples:

Masc,	monosyllabic,	ja-stems:	**hierde,** shepherd; **here,** army
	disyllabic,	′ :	**ǣfen,** evening; **fiscere,** fisher
	monosyllabic,	wa-stems:	**þēow**, servant
	disyllabic,	′ :	**bearu,** grove
Neut,	monosyllabic,	ja-stems:	**wīte,** punishment, **cynn,** kin
	disyllabic,	′ :	**wēsten,** waste, desert; **fæsten,** fortress
	monosyllabic,	wa-stems:	**cnēo,** knee
	disyllabic,	′ :	**searu,** device

Exercise For each of the PrehOE S.N. forms listed in the first column, supply the EWS form called for in the second column. (See also Ch. 16.4)

1.	***farh**, pig (Masc)	S.D.
2.	***hwal**, whale (Masc)	S.A.
3.	***selh** (< PrGmc ***selhaz**), seal (Masc)	P.N.
4.	***coss**, kiss (Masc)	P.D.
5.	***pleh**, danger (Neut)	S.D.

Note that not only inflectional endings but some stem changes are involved.

Translation: *Luke IX, 14–17*

Ðā cwæð hē tō his leorningcnihtum, "Dōþ þæt hīe sitten þurh gebēorscipas fīftegum." And hīe swā dydon and hīe ealle sǣton.

Ðā nam hē þā fīf hlāfas and þā twēgen fiscas, and on þone heofon beseah, and blētsode hīe, and bræc, and dǣlde his leorningcnihtum þæt hīe āsetton hīe beforan þām menigum.

Ðā ǣton hīe ealle and wurdon gefyllode. And man nam þā gebrotu þe þǣr belifon twelf cȳpan fulle.

VOCABULARY

ǣton, PastT of **etan,** to eat
āsetton, PastT of **āsettan,** to set, place
belīfan, to remain over
beseah, PastT of **besēon,** to look
blētsian, to bless
bræc, PastT of **brecan,** to break
cȳpa, basket
dǣlan, to divide
fiftig, (a set of) fifty
gebēorscipe, feast, seated group
gebrot, scrap
leorningcniht, disciple
sǣton, PastT of **sittan,** to sit (down)
sitten, Subjunc of **sittan,** to sit (down).

FOOTNOTES

[1]**Mǣg**, kinsman, usually P.N.A. **māgas**, exhibits a similar variation in a long base vowel (ǣ/ā). In a noun like **geat**, gate, P.N.A. **gatu**, there is a further change: [a > æ > ea], the last due to the initial palatal g (See 8.3.).

[2]Epenthetic vowels develop before **l**, **r**, **m**, and **n**. *Examples:* **nægel**, nail (cf ON **nagl**); **æcer**, field (ON **akr**); **māþum**, treasure (Goth **maiþms**); **hræfen**, raven (ON **hrafn**). Note that the epenthetic vowel harmonizes with (i.e., is a front or back vowel according to) the vowel of the base syllable. (Such vowels are found in MnE dialect pronunciations such as [ɛləm] for *elm*, [hɛnərɪ] for *Henry*, [fɪləm] for *film*, etc.)

[3]Syncope is the loss of a vowel with weakest stress. It occurs at all stages of the language (cf MnE *int'resting*; Brit *jewellery*, US *jewelry*, both ['dʒuwɪlrɪ]; Brit. *speciality*, without syncope, US *specialty* with *i* syncopated) but it is not wholly uniform in its operation at any time.

Chapter 14

Nouns: the o-Declension

14.1. All nouns of the ō-Declension (which includes the **jō-** and **wō-**stems) are feminine.

ō-Stems

Monosyllabic, short: **giefu**, *gift*; long: **lār**, *lore, learning.*

Disyllabic, short: **firen**, *sin*; long: **frōfor**, *consolation*; **costung**, *temptation.*

S. N.	giefu, -o	lār	firen	frōfor	costung
A.	~ e	~ e	~ e	frōfre	~ a, -e
G.D.I.	~ e	~ e	~ e	~ e	~ a, -e
P.N.A.	~ a, -e	~ a, -e	~ a, -e	~ a, -e	~ a, -e
G.	~ a, -ena	~ a, -ena	~ a	~ a	~ a
D.I.	~ um	~ um	~ um	~ um	~ um

Note 1: As before, the S.N. inflectional ending **-u** is retained only in words with short radical syllable (like **giefu**). The P.G. inflection **-ena** is taken over from the **n**-Declension (See below 14.7), probably because it is more distinctive than **-a**. As before, the middle vowel is syncopated after a long radical syllable (**frōfre**). Nouns in **-ung** (**costung**) commonly have the inflectional ending **-a** in the Sing. oblique cases.

14.2. *jō*-Stems

Long: **wylf**, *she-wolf*; **byrðen**, *burden*; **hālignes**, *holiness.*

Note 2: These are declined like **firen**, above. In **byrðen**, **n** may be doubled in oblique cases; in **hālignes** and similar words, s is regularly doubled in oblique cases: **byrðenne**, **hālignessum**, etc.

14.3. *wō*-**Stems**

Short: **beadu**, battle.

Long: **stōw**, place; **mǣd**, mead, meadow.

S. N.	beadu	stōw	mǣd
A.	beadwe	~ e	~ (w)e, (mǣd)
G.D.I.	~ e	~ e	~ (w)e

P.N.A.	~ a, -e	~ a, -e	~ (w)a, -e
G.	~ a	~ a	~ (w)a
D.I.	~ um	~ um	~ (w)um

Note 3: An epenthetic vowel **u**, **o**, or **e** (probably [ə]) may be developed before **w**: **bead(u)we, bead(o)we, near(o)we, geat(e)we**, etc.

The *i*-Declension

14.4. The **i**-declension includes nouns of all genders, but it has been much affected analogically by the **a**-declension, whose inflectional endings it has adopted.

14.5. Masculine and Neuter *i*-Stems

Masculine: **hryre**, *fall*; **frēondscipe**, *friendship*; plural only, **Dene**, *the Danes*, **Engle**, *the Angles*.

Neuter: **sife**, sieve.

S.N.A.	hryre	frēondscipe			sife
G.	~ es	~ es			~ es
D.I.	~ e	~ e			~ e
P.N.A.	~ as		Dene	Engle	~ u
G.	~ a		~ (ige)a	~ a	~ a
D.I.	~ um		~ um	~ um	~ um

Note 4: The original **i** of the stem has produced umlaut of the radical vowel; when the radical syllable is short, this **i** > **e** in the Sing. N.A., e.g. in WGmc ***hruri** > EWS **hryre**. Except in proper nouns (**Dene, Engle**, etc.) the historical Masc. Plur. N.A. ending **-e** has been almost wholly displaced by **-as** of the **a**-declension.

14.6. Feminine *i*-Stems

Long: **dǣd**, *deed*; **scyld**, *guilt*.

S. N.	dǣd	scyld
A.	~ (e)	~
G.D.I.	~ e	~ e
P.N.A.	~ e	~ e, (-a)
G.	~ a	~ a
D.I.	~ um	~ um

Note 5: The endings Sing. A. **-e**, Plur. N.A. **-a** are often brought over from the **ō**-declension. Original **i**-stems with short radical syllable have "gone over" or conformed to the **ō**-declension.

The Weak Declension (n-Declension)

14.7. Masculine: **noma**, *name*; **gefēa**, *joy*.
Neuter: **ēage**, *eye*.
Feminine: **tunge**, *tongue*.

	noma	ēage	tunge	gefēa
S. N.	noma	ēage	tunge	gefēa
A.	~ an	~ e	~ an	~ an
G.D.I.	~ an	~ an	~ an	~ an
P.N.A.	~ an	~ an	~ an	~ an
G.	~ ena	~ ena	~ ena	~ ana
D.I.	~ um	~ um	~ um	~ a(u)m

Note 6: The ending of Plur. G. **-ena** (which may also occur as **-ana, -ona, -una**) is sometimes reduced to **-na**, or even to **-a** (in conformity with other declensions); **-an** often becomes **-on. Gefēa** exemplifies a small class of stems ending in a vowel which absorbed the vowels of the inflectional endings. Other words of this class are: **frēa**, *lord*; **ðrēa**, *threat*; **flā**, *arrow*. Beside **ēage**, the only other full Neuter **n**-stem is **ēare**, *ear*.

Translation: *Luke VI, 39–42*

Ðā sægde hē heom sum bigspell: Segst þū, mæg se blinda þone blindan lædan? Hū ne feallaþ hīe bēgen on þone pytt?

Nis se leorningcniht ofer þone lārēow. Ælc bið fulfremed gif hē is swilce his lārēow.

Hwī gesihst þū þā egle on þīnes brōðor ēagan and ne gesihst þone bēam on þīnum ēagan? And hū meaht þū secgan þīnum brēðer, "Brōðor, læt þæt ic ātēo þā egle of þīnum ēage," and þū seolf ne gesiehst þone bēam on þīnum āgenum ēagan? Ēalā līcettere! Tēoh ǣrest þone bēam of þīnum ēage, and þonne þū gesihst þæt þū ātēo þā egle of þīnes brōðor ēage.

VOCABULARY

ǣlc, each
ǣrest, first
āgen, own
ātēon, to draw out
bēam, beam
bēgen, both
blinda, blind man
brēðer, Sing.D. of **brōðor**
brōðor, Sing.N.G., brother
ēalā, int., alas
egl, mote
fullfremman, to fulfill
hū, how
lǣdan, to lead
lǣtan, to let, permit
līcettere, hypocrite
mæg, PresT of **magan**, to be able
meaht, PresT of **magan**
pytt, pit
secgst, PresT of **secgan**, to say
swilce, like
tēoh, imperative of **tēon**, to pull

Chapter 15

Nouns: Minor Declensions

15.1. The "minor" noun declensions, those which have fewer members, are in general much affected by analogical attraction of "major" declensions having more members. The former tend to adopt some of the inflectional endings of the latter, or even to "go over" completely to them, taking on the entire paradigm of inflections. Sometimes this even involves a shift of gender.

The *u*-Declension

15.2. Masculine: **sunu**, son. Feminine: **hond**, hand.

S.N.A.	sunu, -a	hond
G.	~ a	~ a
D.I.	~ a, -u	~ a
P.N.A.	~ a, -u	~ a
G.	~ a	~ a
D.I.	~ um	~ um

This declension has been reduced to comparatively few members. The commonest are: Masc. **wudu**, *wood*; **sidu**, *custom*; **medu**, *mead*; **feld**, *field*; **ford**, *ford*; **winter**, *winter*; **sumor**, *summer*; **weald**, *forest*. Fem. **duru**, *door*. Neut. **fela**, *much*.

Feminine Abstract Nouns in -u, -o

15.3. Examples: **wlencu**, *pride*; **strengðu**, *strength*.

S.N.	wlencu, -o	strengðu, -o
A.G.D.I.	~ e; -u, -o	~ e; -u, -o
P.N.A.	~ (e)a; -u, -o	~ e, -a; -u, -o
G.	~ (e)a	~ a
D.I.	~ um	~ um

Note 1: The **-u** of the S.N. has been obtained from the **o**-declension and extended to other cases so as to produce often an uninflected singular. There is always more or less conformity to the **o**-declension, especially by nouns in ***-iðu.**

The *r*-Declension

15.4. Nouns of relationship: **fæder, mōdor, brōðor, dohtor.** With these belong the collective plurals **gebroðor**, *brethren*, and **gesweostor**, *sisters*.

	MASCULINE		FEMININE	
S.N.A.	fæder	brōðor	mōdor	sweostor, -er
G.	~ , -(e)res	~	~	~
D.I.	~	brēðer	mēder	~
P.N.A.	fæd(e)ras	brōðor, -ru	mōdru, -a	sweostor, -ru, -ra
G.	~ a	~ ra	~ a	~ ra
D.I.	~ um	~ rum	~ um	~ rum

Note 2: The datives **mēder** and **brēðer**, and sometimes **dehter** (from **dohtor**) are examples of **i**-umlaut: **mēder** < ***mōdri; brēðer** < ***brōðri; dehter** < ***dohtri**. (These forms are sometimes transferred from D. to G. case.)

The *nd*-Declension

15.5. Examples: **frēond**, friend (loving one); **hettend**, *enemy* (hating one).

S.N.A.	frēond	hettend
G.	~ es	~ es
D.I.	~ frīend, frēonde	~ e
P.N.A.	frīend, frēond, frēondas	~ , -as, -e
G.	frēonda	~ ra
D.I.	~ um	~ um

This declension comprises Masculine nouns of agency derived from present participles. Like **frēond** is declined **fēond,** *foe*; like **hettend** are declined **āgend,** *owner*; **dēmend,** *judge*; **ēhtend,** *persecutor*; **fultum(i)end,** *helper*; **Hǣlend,** *Savior*; **wealdend,** *ruler*; **wīgend,** *warrior*; etc.

Note 3: Some inflectional endings of this class show analogical conformity to other classes: S.G. **-es**, D. **-e**, P.N. **-as** follow the **a**-declension; P.N. **-e**, G. **-ra** are derived from the regular strong adjective declension of present participles.

The *er*-Declension

15.6. Neuter: **lomb,** *lamb*; **cealf,** *calf*; **ǣg,** *egg*.

S.N.A.	lomb	cealf	ǣg
G.	~ es	~ es	~ es
D.I.	~ e	~ e	~ e

P.N.A.	lombru (lomb)	cealfru	ǣgru
G.	~ ra (lomba)	~ ra	~ ra
D.I.	~ rum (lombum)	~ rum	~ rum

Note 4: The plurals in **r** just given in the paradigms, to which may be added the occasional P. **cildru,** *children,* conserve notable traces of the primitive stem-formation. These may also be recognized in **dōgor,** *day;* **sigor,** *victory;* **hrȳðer,** *cattle,* which, however, have gone over to the a-declension, often with a change of gender.

The Radical Consonant Declension[1]

15.7. Masculine: **monn,** *man;* **fōt,** *foot;* **tōð,** *tooth.* Feminine: **bōc,** *book;* **burg,** *borough, fortified town.*

S.N.A.	monn	fōt	tōð	bōc	burg
G.	~ es	~ es	~ es	bēc, bōce	byr(i)g
D.I.	menn	fēt	tēð	~	~
P.N.A.	~	~	~	~	~
G.	monna	fōta	tōða	bōca	burga
D.I.	~ um	~ um	~ um	~ um	~ um

Note 5: Some occasional analogical forms are: S.A. **monnan;** P.N.A. **fōtas, tōðas.** Other nouns of this declension are: Neut. **scrūd,** *garment, shroud;* Fem. **brōc,** *breeches;* **gāt,** *goat;* **gōs,** *goose;* **lūs,** *louse;* **mūs,** *mouse;* **cū,** *cow.* Most of these come down into MnE as the "Umlaut Plurals."

Translation: *The Creation*

Ealle gesceafta, heofonas and englas, sunnan and mōnan, steorran and eorðan, ealle nȳtenu and fugolas, sǣ and ealle fiscas, and ealle gesceafta God gesceōp and geworhte on six dagum; and on ðām seofoðan dæge hē geendode his weorc, and geswāc þā and gehālgode ðone seofoðan dæg, for þām þe hē on ðām dæge his weorc geendode. And hē behēold ðā ealle his weorc þe hē geworhte, and hī wǣron ealle swīðe gōde.

Ealle ðing hē geworhte būton ǣlcum antimbre. Hē cwæð, "Geweorðe lēoht"; and ðǣrrihte wæs lēoht geworden. Hē cwæð eft, "Geweorðe heofon"; and ðǣrrihte wæs heofon geworht, swā swā hē mid his wīsdōme and mid his willan hit gedihte.

Hē cwæð eft, and hēt ðā eorðan þæt hēo sceolde forðlǣdan cwicu nȳtenu; and hē ðā gesceōp of ðǣre eorðan eall nȳtencynn, and dēorcynn, ealle ðā þe on fēower fōtum gāð; ealswā eft of wætere hē gesceōp fiscas and fuglas, and sealde ðām fiscum sund, and ðām fuglum fliht; ac hē ne sealde nānum nȳtene ne nānum fisce nāne sāwle; ac heora blōd is heora līf, and swā hraðe swā hī bēoð dēade, swā bēoð hī mid ealle geendode.

VOCABULARY

ǣlc, any
antimber, building material, matter
cwicu, live, quick
ealswā, also
forðlǣdan, to bring forth
gedihtan, to dispose, arrange
gehālgian, to hallow, bless
gesceaft, created thing
gesceop, PastT of **gescieppan,** to create
geswāc, PastT of **geswīcan,** to cease.
geweorðan, to come about
hraðe, quickly
nȳten, animal
sāwol, soul
sund, power of swimming
swā, so, as
swīðe, very
ðǣrrihte, immediately

FOOTNOTE

[1]This name indicates that the inflection, in this class of nouns, is added directly to the consonant of the root or base, rather than to a stem.

Chapter 16

Later Sound Changes

16.1. The sounds spelled **g** and **h** underwent considerable change according to their phonetic environments. As we have already seen (Ch. 4), by the time of EWS each represents two different sounds: In a back-vowel environment, **g** retains its original velar quality [ɣ]; in a front-vowel environment, it is palatalized to [j]. Similarly, in velar environments **h** remains as a voiceless spirant [x] (corresponding to voiced [ɣ]), but in initial position in words it is weakened to [h].

Other changes undergone by **g** and **h** in the WS period and later are the following:

Loss of Medial *g*

16.2. Palatal g followed by **d** or **n** often disappears and, in compensation, the vowel which preceded it is lengthened.

Examples: **bregdan, brēdan**, to brandish; PastT, S **brægd, brǣd**
secgan, to say, PastT S **sægde, sǣde**; PastPple **gesægd, gesǣd**
frignan, frīnan, to inquire
mægden, mǣden, maiden
ðegn, ðēn, servant.

Note 1: By analogy to such forms velar **g** occasionally disappears even after back vowels. *Examples*: **brugdon, brūdon; brogden, brōde.**

Devoicing of *g*

16.3. Final (and occasionally medial) **g**, especially after a long back vowel, or **l**, or **r**, frequently became **h** [ɣ > x].

Examples: **bēag, bēah**, ring — **burg, burh**, borough
flōg, flōh, flayed — **dolg, dolh**, wound.

Loss of Medial *h*

16.4. Medial **h** (but not **hh**) preceded by **r** or **l** and followed by an inflectional vowel disappears, and, in compensation, the stem-vowel is lengthened.

Examples: **mearh**, G **mēares**, horse; **seolh**, G **sēoles**, seal.

Loss of Intervocalic *h*

16.5. Intervocalic **h** disappears, and the vowel which followed it is absorbed into the vowel or diphthong which preceded it, by compensation lengthening it (if it was not long already). The resulting forms are said to be *contracted*, and verbs in which this process occurs are called *Contract Verbs* (see 19.3.).
Examples: **feoh**, G **fēos** (< ***feohes**), property; **hēah**, G **hēas** (< ***hēahes**), high; **slēan** (< ***sleahan** < ***slahan**), to strike; **fōn** (< ***fōhan** < ***fonhan**) to seize.

Note 2: **h** disappears similarly sometimes before inflectional syllables beginning with **n** or **r**, before the comparative ending in **r**, and in compounds: **hēah**, MascA **hēane**; FemD **hēare**; Comp **hīera** (**hīerra**); **hēalic**, high.

Influence of *w*

16.6. The diphthongs **eo**, **io** (produced by Breaking or by **u-o-a-Umlaut** of **e**, **i**) are sometimes labialized[1] by a preceding **w** and become **u** or **o**.
Examples: **weorðan** (< ***werðan**), to become, appears also as **wurðan**
weorðian, wurðian, to honor
weorold, worold, woruld, world
wita, wiota, weota, wuta, wise man
sweord, swurd, sword.

Exercise. Write the EWS forms which would result if the changes described above were to occur to the following:

Loss of medial **g: wægn** > , wagon; **ðegnian** > , to serve.
Devoicing of **g: earg** > , cowardly; **sorg** > , sorrow.
Loss of medial **h: feorh** > SingG , life; **pohha** > , bag.
Loss of Intervocalic **h: eoh** > SingG , horse; **pleohlic** > , perilous.

Translation: ***Jonah***

God spræc tō ānum wītegan, sē was Jōnas gehāten, "Far tō ðǣre byrig Niniuen, and boda ðǣr ðā word þe ic þē secge." Ðā wearð se wītega āfyrht, and wolde forflēon Godes gesihðe, ac hē ne mihte. Fērde þā tō sǣ, and stāh on scip. Ðā ðā þā scipmen cōmon ūt on sǣ, þā sende him God tō micelne wind and hrēohnisse, swā þæt hīe wǣron orwēne heora līfes. Hīe þā wurpon heora wara oferbord, and se wītega læg and slēp. Hīe wurpon þā tān betweox him, ond bǣdon þæt God sceolde gesweotolian hwanon him þæt ungelimp becōme. Ðā cōm ðæs wītegan tā upp. Hīe āxodon hine, hwæt hē wǣre, oððe hū hē faran wolde. Hē cwæð, þæt hē wǣre Godes ðēow, sē ðe gesceōp sǣ and land, and þæt hē flēon wolde of Godes gesihðe. Hīe cwǣdon: "Hū dō wē ymbe ðē?" Hē andwyrde: "Weorpað mē oferbord; ðonne geswīcð þēos gedreccednis." Hīe ðā swā dydon, and sēo hrēohnis wearð gestilled, and hīe offrodon Gode heora lāc, and tugon forð.

(Concluded in next chapter)

VOCABULARY

āfyrht, afraid
boda, Imp of **bodian**, to proclaim
far, Imp of **faran**, to travel
forflēon, to flee from
gedreccednis, distress
gesihðe, sight, vision
gesweotolian, to reveal
geswīcan, to cease
hrēohnis, rough weather
hū, what, how
hwanon, whence
lāc, sacrifice
Niniuen, Niniveh
offrian, to offer
orwēne, despairing
spræc, PastT of **sprecan**, speak
stāh, PastT of **stīgan**, to mount
tā, tān, twig, lot
tugon, PastT of **tēon**, draw, move
ðā, then, when
ungelimp, misfortune
waru, ware(s), cargo
weorpan, to cast, throw
ymbe, about, concerning

FOOTNOTE

[1]Rounded. In this case the lip-rounding of [w] induces a closer rounding in the following vowel or diphthong.

chapter 17

Verb Classes

17.1. OE verbs fall into two large classes and two smaller ones:

1. *Strong* verbs form their Principal Parts by varying the base vowel or diphthong (by Ablaut or Gradation—see Chs. 19–22).
2. *Weak* verbs form the Past Tense and Past Participle by addition of a morpheme containing /d/ or /t/ (see this chapter).
3. *Anomalous* verbs (see Ch. 7).
4. *Preterit-Present* verbs (see Ch. 23).

17.2. The *Principal Parts* of any verb are those basic forms upon which the entire conjugation may be constructed. They are not the same for all verbs; differences will be noted as each class is introduced.

The Principal Parts of a Weak Verb are:

1. The *Infinitive*: from this all Present Tense forms may be derived.
2. The *Past Tense Singular*: from this all Past Tense forms may be derived.
3. The *Past Participle*: this is used with auxiliaries to form phrasal verb constructions.[1]

Classification of Weak Verbs

17.3. Weak Verbs are of three classes: (I) the **ja**-class, (II) the **ō**-class, (III) the **ai**-class.

Most Weak verbs are derivative—that is, they are formed from nouns, adjectives, or other verbs. For example:

From nouns: **dōm,** judgment, + **-jan** > ***dōmian** > **dēman,** to judge
tāc(e)n, token, + **-ōjan** > ***tācnōjan** > **tācnian**, to betoken.

From adjs.: **cūð**, known, + **-jan** > ***cūðian** > **cȳðan**, to make known
hāl, whole, + **-jan** > ***hālian** > **hǣlan**, to heal.

From verbs: ***sat** (Past Sing. of **sittan**, to sit) + **-jan** > ***sattian** > ***sættian** > **settan,** to set
dranc (Past Sing. of **drincan**, to drink) + **-jan** > ***drancian** > **drencan,** to drench.

Note: Weak verbs formed as in the last examples are transitive (and causative); the Strong verbs on whose Preterits (Past Tenses) they are formed are intransitive. Thus, for example, in MnE:

Strong, intrans.	*sit*;	Weak, trans. (causative)	*set*, cause to sit
~ ~	*lie*;	~ ~ ~	*lay*, cause to lie.

Conjugation of Class I Weak Verbs

17.4. ***Examples:*** **fremman**, to perform; **herian**, to praise; **dēman**, to judge.

		PRESENT: **Indicative**	
Sing. 1.	fremme	herie	dēme
2.	fremest	herest	dēm(e)st
3.	fremeð	hereð	dēm(e)ð
Plur. 1–3.	fremmað	heriað	dēmað
		Subjunctive	
Sing. 1–3.	fremme	herie	dēme
Plur. 1–3.	fremmen	herien	dēmen
		Imperative	
Sing. 2.	freme	here	dēm
Plur. 2.	fremmað	heriað	dēmað
Infinitive	fremman	herian	dēman
Infl. Infin.	tō fremmanne	tō herianne	tō dēmanne
Pres. Pple.	fremmende	heriende	dēmende
		PRETERIT: **Indicative**	
Sing. 1.	fremede	herede	dēmde
2.	~ est	~ est	~ est
3.	~ e	~ e	~ e
Plur. 1–3.	~ on	~ on	~ on
		Subjunctive	
Sing. 1–3.	fremede	herede	dēmde
Plur. 1–3.	~ en	~ en	~ en
Past Pple.	fremed	hered	dēmed

Exercise. Review the sound changes of Chaps. 5.2. (Gemination); 11.1, 2 i-Umlaut); 13.3, Note 2, and Footnote 3 (Syncope). Then answer the following questions:

1. Why do some forms of **fremman** have **-mm-** while others have **-m-**?
2. Why does not the same variation hold for **herian** and **dēman**?
3. Why does the parenthetic **-e-** in **dēm(e)st** sometimes disappear?
4. Of these three verbs only **herian** has **-i-** in the Present forms. Whence comes this **-i-**, and why is it lacking in the other two verbs?

Verbs Without the Middle Vowel

17.5. Certain verbs form the Preterit and Past Participle without the middle vowel **e**(<**i**). These verbs therefore have two special features: 1) the absence of **i**-Umlaut in the Preterit and Past Participle; 2) the change (which took place in Gmc) of original **c** before **d**, or **g** before **d**, > **ht**.

Examples: **cweccan**, to shake, < ***cwæcjan**, Pret. **cweahte** < ***cwæhte.**
sēcan, to seek, < ***sōcian**, Pret. **sōhte.**
ðyncan, to seem, Pret. **ðūhte** < ***ðunhte.**

Some verbs of this group are:

sellan, give, sell	**sealde**	**seald**
rǣcan, reach	**rǣhte**	**rǣht**
ðencan, think	**ðōhte**	**ðōht**
bycgan, buy	**bohte**	**boht**

Translation: *Jonah (concluded)*

God þā gegearcode ānne hwæl, and hē forswealh þone wītegan, and ābær hine tō ðām lande þe hē tō sceolde, and hine ðǣr ūt āspāw. Ðā cōm eft Godes word tō ðām wītegan, and cwæð: "Ārīs nū, and gā tō ðǣre micelan byrig Niniuen, and boda swā swā ic ðē ǣr sǣde." Hē fērde, and bodode, þæt him wæs Godes grama onsīgende, gif hī tō Gode būgan noldon. Ðā ārās se cyning of his cynesetle, and āwearp his dēorwyrðe rēaf, and dide hǣran tō his līce, and ascan uppan his hēafod, and bēad ðæt ǣlc man swā dōn sceolde; and ǣgðer ge men ge þā sūcendan cild and ēac ðā nȳtenu ne onbyrigdon nānes ðinges binnan ðrim dagum. Ðā ðurh þā gecyrrednisse, þæt hī yfeles geswicon, and ðurh þæt strange fæsten, him gemiltsode God, and nolde hī fordōn, swā swā hē ǣr þā twā burhwara Sodomam and Gomorram, for heora leahtrum, mid heofonlicum fȳre forbærnde.

VOCABULARY

āberan, to bear, carry
asce, ash, dust
āspīwan, to spew up
binnan (be + innan), within
būgan, to bow
burhwaru, city
cynesetl, throne
dōn . . . tō, to put on
fæsten, fasting
gecyrrednis, conversion
gegearcian, to prepare
gemiltsian, to have mercy upon
geswīcan, to cease from
grama, wrath
hǣre, hair shirt, sackcloth
hwæl, whale, great fish
leahtor, sin, vice
onbyr(i)gan, to taste
onsīgan, to come upon
rēaf, garment
sūcan, to suck, suckle

FOOTNOTE

[1]In MnE, Principal Parts 2) and 3) have fallen together into one, always the same: OE **dēman**, **dēmde**, **dēmed**; MnE *deem*, *deemed*.

Chapter 18

Weak Verbs Classes II, III

Weak Verbs, Class II

18.1. The verbs of Class II, as noted above, are ō-stems. To this ō was added the infinitive ending **-jan**, producing ***-ōjan**, which by **i-Umlaut** > ***-ējan**, then by contraction > **-īan**, and finally > **-ian.**

Conjugation

	PRESENT:	**Indicative**
Sing. 1.	bodie, *proclaim*	smēage, *consider*
2.	~ ast	smēast
3.	~ að	~ ð
Plur. 1–3.	~ iað	smēag(e)að
	Subjunctive	
Sing. 1–3.	~ ie	smēage
Plur. 1–3.	~ ien	~ en
	Imperative	
Sing. 2.	~ a	smēa
Plur. 2.	~ iað	smēag(e)að
Infinitive	~ ian	~ (e)an
Infl. Infin.	~ ianne	~ (e)anne
Pres. Pple.	~ iende	~ ende
	PRETERIT:	**Indicative**
Sing. 1.	bodode	smēade
2.	~ est	~ est
3.	~ e	~ e
Plur. 1–3.	~ on	~ on
	Subjunctive	
Sing. 1–3.	~ e	~ e
Plur. 1–3.	~ en	~ en
Past Pple.	bodod	smēad

Most weak verbs of Class II are conjugated like **bodian**. Only a few are conjugated like **smēag(e)an: fēog(e)an**, to hate, **frēog(e)an**, to love, **scōg(e)an**, to shoe, **twēog(e)an**, to doubt, **ðrēag(e)an**, to rebuke.

Weak Verbs, Class III

18.2. Verbs of Class III, as noted above, are **ai**-stems. Only a few examples survive, and even these are defective. Their tendency in PrehOE was to "go over" to the pattern of Class II verbs.

Conjugation

		PRESENT: **Indicative**		
Sing.	1.	hæbbe, *have*	libbe, lifge, *live*	secge, *say*
	2.	hafast, hæfst	lifast	sægst, segst
	3.	hafað, hæfð	lifað	sægeð, segð
Plur.	1–3.	habbað	libbað	secgað
			Subjunctive	
Sing.	1–3.	hæbbe	libbe	secge
Plur.	1–3.	~ en	~ en	~ en
			Imperative	
Sing.	2.	hafa	liofa	saga, sege
Plur.	2.	habbað	libbað, lifiað	secg(e)að
Infinitive		habban	libban, lifian	secg(e)an
Infl. Infin.		tō habbanne	tō libbanne, lifienne	tō secg(e)anne
Pres. Pple.		hæbbende	libbende, lifigende	secgende
		PRETERIT: **Indicative**		
Sing.	1.	hæfde	lifde	sægde, sǣde
	2.	~ est	~ est	~ est, sǣdest
	3.	~ e	~ e	~ e, sǣde
Plur.	1–3.	~ on	~ on	~ on, sǣdon
			Subjunctive	
Sing.	1–3.	hæfde	lifde	sægde, sǣde
Plur.	1–3.	~ en	~ en	~ en, ~ en
Past Pple.		hæfd	lifd	sægd, sǣd

Translation: *St. Cuthbert*

A.D. 687. On þone ilcan dæg [March 20] biþ Sancte Cūðberhtes gelēornes þæs hālgan biscopes; sē wæs on þisse Brytene on þǣre mǣgðe ðe is nemned Transhumbrensium, þæt is Norðanhymbra ðēod. Þone wer oft englas sōhton, and him tō brōhton heofonlīce gereorde; and hē hæfde þā mihte þæt hē mihte gesēon manna sāwla, þā clǣnan and þā ōðre, þonne hēo of þǣm līchaman lēordon, and ealle untrumnesse hē mihte hǣlan mid his gebedum.

Þæt wæs his wundra sum, þæt hē wæs æt gereordum on sumre æðelre abbudissan mynster. Þā hē ārās on dæge of undernræste, þā sǣde hē ðæt hine þyrste, and hēt him beran wæter tō þæt hē mihte onbergan. Þā blētsode hē þæt wæter and his onbergde, and sealde his mæssepreōste; and hē hit sealde heora þegne; heora þegn wæs þæs ilcan mynstres mæssepreōst. Þā ondranc sē þæs wæteres, and sealde hit þǣm brēðer þe him ætstōd, þæs mynstres profoste, and sē gedranc ēac ðæs wætres, and hī gefēldon bēgen þæt þæt wæs þæt betste wīn; and þā hī þā tīd hæfdon ymb þæt tō sprecanne, þā ondette heora ǣgþer ōðrum þæt hī nǣfre ǣr sēlre wīn ne druncon.

VOCABULARY

abbudissa, abbess
ætstandan, to stand beside
blētsian, to bless
clǣne, pure
gebed, prayer
gefēlan, to feel, perceive
gelēornes, departure, death
gereord, food; plur. feast
ilca, same
lēoran, to depart from, leave
mǣgð, people, country
mæssepreōst, masspriest
miht, power
mynster, monastery
onbergan, to drink
ondettan, to confess, avow
profost, provost, prior
sēlre, better
þegn, servant
þēod, people
þyrstan, to thirst
tīd, occasion
undernræst, morning rest
untrumnes, sickness
wundor, wonder, miracle.

POINTS OF SYNTAX

Line 2 – Why the **-an** ending on **hālgan**?
– What is the relationship between **biscopes** and **Cūðberhtes**?
3–4 – Note the word-order of the two clauses, different from that of MnE.
7 – What is the syntax of **sum**?
8 – Note the use of **þyrste** without expressed subject.
– The verb **hātan** is regularly followed, as here, by an infinitive with unexpressed subject. (In MnE the subject of such an infinitive is expressed and has the object case form.)
9 – Note that **tō** is a postposed preposition. What is its object?
10 – Some OE verbs take an object in a case other than the accusative. In what case is the object of **onbergde**?
– Note that **sealde** (first occurrence) has no direct object.
– Note that **sealde** (second occurrence) has a direct object.
11 – In what case is the object of **ondranc**?
14 – What form is **tō sprecanne**?
– Note the construction **nǣfre . . . ne**. (In ME it was literary. What is its present status?)

chapter 19

Strong Verbs, Classes 1 and 2

19.1. As was stated above, the Strong Verbs are characterized by ablaut or gradation of the radical vowel. (The system is familiar to speakers of MnE in such verbs as *sing*, *sang*, *sung*, or *ride*, *rode*, *ridden*.) Though ablaut is a feature of IE, only in the Gmc branch was it used organically in a verbal system, functioning so in all the Gmc Languages. In accordance with the bases and ablauts used, the OE strong verbs are divided into seven classes. In all of these the Principal Parts are the Infinitive, Preterit 3 Singular, Preterit Plural, and Past participle.

Class 1

19.2. The PrGmc series of ablaut vowels was **ī, ai, i, i**. From these developed respectively in OE the vowels of the four Principal Parts of this class: **ī, ā, i, i**. Most verbs of this class were regular—see (a) below—but sound changes already described, and others, produced sub-classes by the time of historical EWS—see (b), (c):

	Infinitive	*Pret. 3 Sing.*	*Pret. Plur.*	*Past Pple.*
(a)	bīdan, *bide*	bād	bidon	biden
	bītan, *bite*	bāt	biton	biten
	glīdan, *glide*	glād	glidon	gliden
	rīsan, *rise*	rās	rison	risen
	wrītan, *write*	wrāt	writon	writen
(b)	snīðan, *cut*	snāð	snidon	sniden
(c)	ðēon, *thrive*	ðāh	ðigon	ðigen

Note 1: In (b) and (c) it will be noticed that the final consonant of the base differs in the first two principal parts and the second two principal parts, **ð** alternating with **d**, and **h** with **g**. This is due to Grammatical Change or "Verner's Law" (see Appendix I).

Note 2: The form **ðēon** does not have the expected ablaut vowel **i**, nor is the **h** corresponding to **g** preserved (though it is in **ðāh**). This is due to Breaking (**8.1.**), Loss of Intervocalic **h** (**16.5.**), and change of **īo** to **ēo**: PrehOE ***ðīhan** > ***ðīohan** > **ðīon** > **ðēon.**

Contract Verbs

19.3. **Đēon** and other verbs like it are called Contract Verbs because they lost intervocalic **h** (see 16.5) and were contracted, with accompanying vowel changes. Other examples are: **lēon,** to lend, **sēon,** to strain, sift, **tēon,** to censure, **wrēon,** to cover. Their accidental similarity to contract verbs of Class 2 has led to the formation of many analogical forms of the latter conjugation. Thus **tēon** has the following forms, those in parentheses made by analogy to Class 2 forms:

tēon   tāh (tēah)   tigon (tugon)   tigen (togen).

(**Tēon** also has some forms analogical to Class 3 verbs.)

Class 2

19.4. The PrGmc series of ablaut vowels was **eu, au, u, u**. From these developed respectively the vowels of the four Principal Parts of this class: **ēo, ēa, u, o**. A few verbs have **ū** in the Present instead of **ēo**. Sound changes within the PrehOE period have produced four sub-classes in EWS, as follows:

(a)	bēodan, *command*	bēad	budon	boden
	clēofan, *cleave*	clēaf	clufon	clofen
	crēopan, *creep*	crēap	crupon	cropen
	drēogan, *endure*	drēag	drugon	drogen
(b)	brūcan, *enjoy*	brēac	brucon	brocen
	būgan, *bow*	bēag	bugon	bogen
	dūfan, *dive*	dēaf	dufon	dofen
(c)	cēosan, *choose*	cēas	curon	coren
	frēosan, *freeze*	frēas	fruron	froren
	sēoðan, *seethe*	sēað	sudon	soden
(d)	flēon, *flee*	flēah	flugon	flogen
	tēon, *draw*	tēah	tugon	togen

Note 3: The **ū** of (b) is not satisfactorily explained. It may be due to analogy of some kind.
Note 4: (c) and (d) offer further examples of Grammatical Change, or Verner's Law (Appendix I).

Translation: *Doomsday*

Uton nū geþencan hū micel egesa gelimpeð eallum gesceaftum on þās andweardan tīd þonne se dōm nēalǣceþ. And sēo openung þæs dæges is swīðe egesful eallum gesceaftum. On þǣm dæge gewīteð heofon and eorðe and sǣ and ealle þā þing þe on þǣm sindon. Swā ēac for þǣre ilcan wyrde gewīteþ sunne and mōna, and eal tungla lēoht āspringeð; and sēo rōd ūres Drihtnes bið ārǣred on þæt gewrixle þāra tungla, sēo nū on middangearde āwergde gāstas flīemeð. And on þǣm dæge heofon biþ befealden swā swā bōc; and on þǣm dæge eorðe biþ forbærned tō ascan; and on þǣm dæge sǣ ādrūgað; and on þǣm dæge eall heofona mægen biþ onwended and onhrēred . . .

Ðȳ fīftan dæge æt underne se heofon tōberst from þǣm ēastdǣle oþ þone westdǣle, and þonne eall engla cynn lōciaþ þurh þā ontȳnnesse on manna cynn. Ðonne gesēoþ ealle menn þæt hit wile bēon æt þisse worlde ende: flēoþ þonne tō muntum and hīe hȳdað for þāra engla onsīene, and þonne cweþaþ tō þǣre eorðan and biddaþ þæt hēo hīe forswelge and gehȳde, and wyscað þæt hīe nǣfre nǣron ācennede from fæder ne from mēder.

VOCABULARY

ācennan, to bring forth
ādrūgan, to dry up
andweard, present
ārǣran, to raise up
asce, ash(es)
āspringan, to fail
āwergan, to curse
befealdan, to fold up
biddan, to beseech
ēastdǣl, east side
egesa, awe, fear
egesful, fearful
flēon, to flee
flīeman, to put to flight
for, because of
forbærnan, to burn up
forswelgan, to swallow up
gāst, spirit
gelimpan, to happen
gesceaft, creature
geþencan, to consider
gewītan, to pass away
gewrixl, exchange
hȳdan, to hide
mægen, host
middangeard, the earth
munt, mountain
nēalǣcan, to draw near
onhrēran, to arouse
onsīen, countenance
ontȳnnes, opening
onwendan, to overturn
openung, manifestation
rōd, cross
tōberstan, to burst open
tungol, star
undern, morning (9am–12)
westdǣl, west side
wyrd, event
wyscan, to wish

POINTS OF SYNTAX

Does **eal** (line 5) modify **tungla** or **lēoht**?
What is the subject of **āspringeð** (line 5)?
What use is made of **sēo** (line 6)? (Contrast its use in line 5.)
What tense is **biþ** (lines 7, 7, 9)?
What are the case and gender of **þisse worlde** (line 12)?
What is the case of **mēder** (line 15)?

Chapter 20

Strong Verbs, Classes 3 and 4

Class 3

20.1. The PrGmc series of ablaut vowels was **e, a, u, u.** From these developed, because of the functioning of various sound changes in PrehOE, four distinct sub-classes, as follows:

(a) Verbs having nasal + consonant after the radical vowel:

bindan, *bind*	band (bond)	bundon	bunden
drincan, *drink*	dranc (dronc)	druncon	druncen
singan, *sing*	sang (song)	sungon	sungen
swimman, *swim*	swamm (swomm)	swummon	swummen

Note 1: In the infinitive, PrGmc **e** has been raised to **i** under the influence of the following nasal. In the Pret. Sing. we meet variants due to change of **a** > **o** before nasals (5.3.).

(b) Verbs having the conditions for Breaking (8.1.) in the Infinitive:

beorgan, *protect*	bearg	burgon	borgen
ceorfan, *carve*	cearf	curfon	corfen
feohtan, *fight*	feaht	fuhton	fohten
fēolan, *reach*	fealh	fulgon	fulgen

Note 2: Breaking occurs also in the Pret. Sing. following the change of PrGmc **a** > **æ** (5.4.). **Fēolan** is contracted from ***feolhan** after loss of the **h** (16.5; 19.3.); it also exemplifies Verner's Law in the latter two principal parts (Appendix I). The vowel **o** of the fourth principal part is the regular one for Class 3 verbs, in which PrGmc **u** became **o** unless followed by a nasal (as in (a) above).

(c) Verbs having an initial palatal in the Infinitive, hence diphthongization of the radical vowel (8.3.):

gieldan, *yield*	geald	guldon	golden
giellan, *yell*	geall	gullon	gollen
gielpan, *boast*	gealp	gulpon	golpen

Note 3: This variation occurs only in these three verbs. Note that the second principal part had already been affected by Breaking.

(d) Verbs having only Change of a > **æ** in the second principal part:

stregdan, *strew*	strægd	strugdon	strogden
ðerscan, *thresh*	ðærsc	ðurscon	ðorscen

Note 4: A number of verbs historically of this class developed analogical weak forms alongside the regular strong ones. (Since OE times, and still continuing in MnE, there has been a slow movement of Strong Verbs going over by analogy to the Weak Verb pattern.)

20.2. Exercise 1. Following the models and rules given above, write out the principal parts of the following Class 3 verbs: **smeortan**, *smart*; **bregdan**, *brandish*; **grindan**, *grind*; **berstan**, *burst*; **meltan**, *melt*.

Class 4

20.3. The PrGmc series of ablaut vowels was **e, a, ǣ, o**; in EWS these became regularly **e, æ, ǣ, o**:

beran, *bear*	bær	bǣron	boren
helan, *conceal*	hæl	hǣlon	holen
scieran, *shear*	scear	scēaron	scoren
niman, *take*	nam (nom)	nāmon	numen

Note 5: **Scieran** and **niman** are affected by sound changes of the same kinds as those affecting Class 3 verbs.

Translation: *The Description of Britain*

Britannia þæt īgland hit is norþēastlang; and hit is eahta hund mīla lang, and twā hund mīla brād. Ðonne is be sūþan him on ōðre healfe þæs sǣs earmes Gallia Belgica; and on westhealfe on ōðre healfe þæs sǣs earmes is Ibernia þæt īgland. Ibernia, þæt wē Scotland hātaþ, hit is on ǣlce healfe ymbfangen mid gārsecge; and for þon þe sēo sunne þǣr gǣð nēar on setl þonne on ōðrum landum, þǣr sindon liðran wederu þonne on Britannia. Ðonne be westannorðan Ibernia is þæt ȳtemeste land þæt man hǣt Thīla, and hit is fēawum mannum cūð for þǣre oferfyrre.

Hēr sindon on Brytene þām īglande fīf geþēodu, Englisc, Brytwylsc, Scyttisc, Pihtisc, and Bōclǣden. Ǣrest wǣron būend þisses landes Bryttas; þā cōmon of Armenia, and gesǣton sūðanwearde Brytene ǣrest. Ðā gelamp hit þæt Pihtas cōmon sūðan of Sciþia mid langum scipum nā manigum, and þā cōmon ǣrest on Norþ-Ibernian ūp, and þǣr bǣdon Scottas þæt hī þǣr mōsten wunian; ac hī noldon him līefan, for þon þe hī cwǣdon þæt hī ne mihton ealle ætgædere gewunian þǣr. And þā cwǣdon Scottas: "Wē magon ēow hwæðere rǣd gelǣran. Wē witon ōðer īgland hēr be ēastan þǣr gē magon eardian, gif gē willað. And gif hwā ēow wiðstent, wē ēow fultumiað, þæt gē hit magon gegangan." Ðā fērdon þā Pihtas, and gefērdon þis land norþanweard. Sūðanweard hit hæfdon Bryttas, swā swā wē ǣr cwǣdon; and þā Pihtas him ābǣdon wīf æt Scottum, on gerād þæt hī gecuron heora cynecynn ā on þā wīfhealfe; þæt hī heoldon swā lange siþþan. And þā gelamp ymbe gēara ryne þæt Scotta sum dǣl gewāt of Ibernian on Brytene, and þæs landes sumne dǣl geēodon, and wæs heora heretoga Rēoda gehaten; from þām hī sind genemnode Dālrēodi.

VOCABULARY

ā, always
ābiddan, request
ætgædere, together
be sūðan, south of
be westannorþan, northwest of
būend, inhabitant
cynecynn, royal family
eardian, to dwell
earm, arm
fultumian, to assist
gārsecg, ocean
gecuron, Pret Subjunc of **gecēosan**, choose
gefēran, to conquer
gegangan, to overcome
gelǣran, teach
gelimpan, to occur
gerād, Plur., conditions
geþēod, language
gewītan, to depart, go out
healf, side
heretoga, leader
hwæðere, however
līefan, to permit
līðe, mild
norþēastlang, extending to the northeast
oferfyrre, excessive distance
rǣd, advice
ryne, course
setl, seat, setting
Thīla, Thule (Iceland)
westhealf, westerly direction
wīfhealf, female side
wiþstandan, to resist
wunian, to dwell
ymbfōn, to surround
ӯtemest, outermost

POINTS OF SYNTAX

To what noun does **him** (line 2) refer?
Judging by the form of the noun **būend** (l. 9), from what verb form is it derived?
What mood is **mōsten** (l. 12), and why?
What mood is **wiþstent** (l. 16), and why?

chapter 21

Strong Verbs, Classes 5, 6, and 7

Class 5

21.1. The PrGmc series of ablaut vowels was **e, a, ǣ, e**; in EWS these usually became **e, æ, ǣ, e** (as in the first examples below), but sound changes in PrehOE produced variants. Class 5 verbs are also characterized by having the ablaut vowels followed by a *single* consonant (in contrast to Class 4 verbs) other than **l**, **r**, or a nasal.

Examples:

(**a**)	metan, *measure*	mæt	mǣton	meten
	lesan, *collect*	læs	lǣson	lesen
	sprecan, *speak*	spræc	sprǣcon	sprecen

Note 1: Two verbs, **etan**, eat, and **fretan**, devour, are exceptional in having the vowel of the Pret. Sing. long: **ǣt, frǣt.**

(**b**)	giefan, *give*	geaf	gēafon	giefen
	gietan, *get*	geat	gēaton	gieten

Note 2: Changes here are due to the initial palatals (8.3.).

(**c**)	gefēon, *rejoice*	gefeah	gefǣgon	gefegen
	sēon, *see*	seah	sǣgon, sǣwon	segen, sewen

Note 3: These are forms contracted from ***gefehan** and ***sehan** respectively. Also present are the effects of Verner's Law.

(**d**)	biddan, *bid*	bæd	bǣdon	beden
	licgan, *lie*	læg	lǣgon	legen

Note 4: The infinitives, formed with **-jan**, underwent Gemination (5.2.) and the radical vowel **e** underwent **i**-Umlaut (lines 11.1, 2.).

21.2. Exercise 1. Form the Principal Parts of the following Class 5 Strong

Verbs: **tredan**, tread; **sittan**, sit; **drepan**, strike; **plēon**, risk; **wegan**, carry; **cweðan**, say (with effect of Verner's Law).

Class 6

21.3. The PrGmc series of ablaut vowels was **a, ō, ō, a**; these remained unchanged in EWS, except when PrehOE sound changes produced variants.
Examples:

(a)	faran, *go, travel*	fōr	fōron	faren
	bacan, *bake*	bōc	bōcon	bacen
	hladan, *load*	hlōd	hlōdon	hladen

Note 5: Such forms as **stondan**, stand, and **sponan**, entice, show the change of **a** > **o** (5.3.).

(b)	flēan, *flay*	flōh	flōgon	flagen
	lēan, *blame*	lōh	lōgon	lagen

Note 6: These are forms contracted from ***flahan** and ***lahan** respectively. (E.g.: ***flahan** > ***flæhan** > ***fleahan** > **flēan**.)

(c)	hebban, *heave*	hōf	hōfon	hafen
	scieppan, *create*	scōp	scōpon	scapen

Note 7: These are variously affected by Gemination, Diphthongization by Initial Palatal, and Verner's Law.

21.4. Exercise 2 Form the Principal Parts of the following Class 6 Strong Verbs: **sacan**, contend; **sc(e)acan**, shake; **dragan**, draw; **slēan**, strike; **steppan**, step.

Class 7

21.5. This is a mixed class including several kinds of stems, a variety of ablauts, and some reduplicative forms. These last were formed by prefixing to the stem a syllable composed of the first consonant of the stem + **e**. (Reduplicated forms are found also in Gothic, Latin, and Greek.) Thus, OE **heht** is derived from the base of **hātan**, *call*, by prefixing **he-** to **hāt**: ***hehā́t**. When stress moves back to the first syllable, this is reduced to **héht**; (ā, now unsupported by stress, is lost).

Class 7 verbs have two sub-classes, those with **ē** and those with **ēo** in the **Preterit, both Sing.** and **Plur.** The Infinitive and the Past Participle have the same vowel.
Examples:

(a)	blondan, *blend*	blēnd	blēndon	blonden
	hātan, *call*	hēt	hēton	hāten
	rǣdan, *counsel*	rēd	rēdon	rǣden
	fōn, *seize*	fēng	fēngon	fongen

Note 8: **Fōn** is a contracted form from ***fahan.**

(b)	fealdan, *fold*	fēold	fēoldon	fealden
	bēatan, *beat*	bēot	bēoton	bēaten
	grōwan, *grow*	grēow	grēowon	grōwen
	crāwan, *crow*	crēow	crēowon	crāwen

Translation: ***Bede—St. Gregory and the English Slaves.***[1]

Grēgōrius se hālga pāpa is rihtlīce Engliscre þēode apostol, for þām þe hē, þurh his rǣd and sande, ūs fram dēofles biggengum ætbrǣd, and tō Godes gelēafan gebīgde. Manega hālige bēc cȳðaþ his drohtnunge and his hālige līf, and ēac "Historia Anglorum," þā þe Ælfred cyning of Lēdene on Englisc āwende. Sēo bōc sprecþ genōh sweotollīce be þissum hālgan were. Nū willað wē sum þing sceortlīce ēow be him gereccan, for þām þe sēo foresǣde bōc nis ēow eallum cūð, þeah þe hēo on Englisc āwend sīe.

Đes ēadiga pāpa Grēgōrius wæs of æðelborenre mǣgðe ācenned; Rōmānisce witan wǣron his māgas; his fæder hātte Gordiānus, and Fēlix, se ēawfæsta pāpa, wæs his fifta fæder. Hē wæs fram cildhāde on bēclicum lārum getȳd, and hē on þǣre lāre swā gesǣliglīce þēah, þæt on ealre Rōmāna byrig næs nān his gelīca geþōht.

Hit gelamp æt sumum sǣle, swā swā gīet foroft dēþ, þæt Englisce cēapmenn brōhton heora ware tō Rōmāna byrig, and Grēgōrius ēode be þære strǣt tō þām Engliscum mannum, heora þing scēawigende. Đā geseah hē betweox þām warum cēapcnihtas gesette; þā wǣron hwītes līchaman and fægeres andwlitan menn, and æðellīce gefeaxode.

(Concluded in next chapter.)

VOCABULARY

ætbregdan, to deliver
æþelboren, noble
æþellīce, nobly, excellently
āwendan, to translate
andwlita, countenance
bēclic, literary
biggeng, worship
cēapcniht, young slave
cēapman, merchant
drohtnung, conduct
ēawfæst, pious
fifta fæder, great-great-great-grandfather
foroft, very often
gebīgan, to convert
gefeaxod, haired
gereccan, to relate
gesǣliglīce, happily
getȳd, educated
hālig, holy
līchama, body
mǣgþ, family, kindred
pāpa, pope
sǣl, occasion
sand, mission
scēawian, to look at, examine
sweotollīce, clearly
þēon, to thrive, flourish
þing, goods
wita, counsellor

FOOTNOTE

[1]See pp. 105–107 for an account of the Venerable Bede and his work.

Chapter 22

Conjugation of Strong Verbs

22.1. Representative verbs are: **singan**, to sing (Class 3); **beran**, to bear (Class 4); **healdan**, to hold (Class 7).

	PRESENT:	**Indicative**	
Sing. 1.	singe	bere	healde
2.	~ est[1]	bir(e)st	~ est, hieltst
3.	~ eð	~ (e) ð	~ eð, hielt
Plur. 1–3.	~ að	berað	~ að
		Subjunctive	
Sing. 1–3.	singe	bere	healde
Plur. 1–3.	~ en	~ en	~ en
		Imperative	
Sing. 2.	sing	ber	heald
Plur. 2.	~ að	~ að	~ að
Infinitive	singan	beran	healdan
Infl. Inf.	tō singanne	tō beranne	tō healdanne
Pres. Pple.	singende	berende	healdende
	PRETERIT:	**Indicative**	
Sing. 1.	song	bær	hēold
2.	sunge	bǣre	~ e
3.	song	bær	~
Plur. 1–3.	sungon	bǣron	~ on
		Subjunctive	
Sing. 1–3.	sunge	bǣre	hēolde
Plur. 1–3.	~ en	~ en	~ en
Past Pple.	sungen	boren	healden

22.2. *Contracted Presents*: **sēon**, to see; **fōn**, to seize.
Presents in **-jan: biddan**, to bid; **licgan**, to lie.

		PRESENT:	**Indicative**	
Sing. 1.	sēo[2]	fō	bidde	licge
2.	siehst	fēhst	bid(e)st, bitst	lig(e)st
3.	siehð	fēhð	bideð, bit(t)	lig(e)ð, līð
Plur. 1–3.	sēoð	fōð	biddað	licgað
			Subjunctive	
Sing. 1–3.	sēo	fō	bidde	licge
Plur. 1–3.	sēon	fōn	~ en	~ en
			Imperative	
Sing. 2.	sēoh	fōh	bide	lige
Plur. 2.	sēoð	fōð	biddað	licgað
Infinitive	sēon	fōn	biddan	licgan
Infl. Inf.	tō sēonne	tō fōnne	tō biddanne	tō licganne
Pres. Pple.	sēonde	fōnde	biddende	licgende
		PRETERIT:	**Indicative**	
Sing. 1.	seah	fēng	bæd	læg
2.	sāwe		bǣde	lǣge
3.	seah		bæd	læg
Plur. 1–3.	sāwon		bǣdon	lǣgon
			Subjunctive	
Sing. 1–3.	sāwe	fēnge	bǣde	lǣge
Plur. 1–3.	~ en	~ en	~ en	~ en
Past Pple.	sewen	fongen	beden	legen

Gemination, *i*-Umlaut, Syncope and Assimilation.

22.3. The Present Indicative 2 and 3 Sing. forms have 3 special features:

a. Since, in Presents in **-jan**, these two forms (and the Imperative 2 Sing.) lacked a **-j-**, the radical consonant was not geminated (5.2.). All other forms had the **-j-** and were geminated. Thus **ic bidde**, but **ðū bidest, hē bideð**, etc.

b. In the same forms (2 and 3 Sing.) the radical vowel is umlauted when umlaut is possible, since both **-j-** and **-i-** cause umlaut. Likewise, **e** becomes **i**. Thus, **ic sēo**, but **ðū siehst, hē siehð**, etc.

c. In WS (though not in the other dialects) the personal endings of these forms were regularly syncopated—that is, the vowel, coming under weak stress, was lost. The consonants thus brought together were then phonetically assimilated (3.8.): the voiced forms became voiceless to correspond to the voiceless endings. (Some further simplifications also followed.) Thus:

	Voiced		*Voiceless*		*Assimilated to*	*Second Person*
biddan:	d	+	st	>	tst	bid(e)st>bitst
snīðan:	ð	+	st	>	tst	snīð(e)st>snītst
stīgan:	g	+	st	>	hst	stīg(e)st>stīhst
						Third Person
biddan:	d	+	ð	>	t(t)	bid(e)ð>bit(t)
snīðan:	ð	+	ð	>	ð	snīð(e)ð>snīð
stīgan:	g	+	ð	>	hð	stīg(e)ð>stīhð

Voiceless forms coming together could not be further assimilated—e.g. **bītan, ðū bītst; brūcan, ðū brȳcst.** But some other reductions or simplifications occurred—e.g., **cēosan, hē ciest.**

Inflectional Simplifications

22.4. 1. When **wē**, we, and **gē**, ye, come immediately after the verb, its ending is often reduced to **-e**. Thus:

wē/gē cweðað, but cweðe wē/gē
wē/gē magon, but mage wē/gē
wē/gē nimen, but nime wē/gē

2. The older ending of Pret. Indic. Plur., **-un**, was already weakening in EWS. Though it still appears frequently, **-on** (**-an**) takes its place even more frequently, and by LWS this has become the regular form. In MSS of about 1000, scribes begin to show uncertainty about the spelling, often writing **-an**, **-un**, or **-en**. (This kind of uncertainty indicates that they can no longer rely on pronunciation to guide spelling: pronunciation has changed, the vowel sound having become [ə].) The Subjunctive is similarly affected: EWS Pres. and Pret. Plur. **-en** appears in LWS as **-on**, **-an**, or **-un**. (Neutralization of the vowels to [ə] in these unstressed inflectional endings was one factor in the breakdown of inflection which characterizes ME.)

Translation: *St. Gregory and the English Slaves (concluded)*

Grēgōrius þā behēold þǣre cnapena wlite, and befrān of hwilcere þēode hī gebrōhte wǣron. Ða sǣde him mon þæt hī of Englalande wǣron, ond þæt þǣre þēode mennisc swā wlitig wǣron. Eft þā Grēgōrius befrān hwæðer þæs landes folc Crīsten wǣre þe hǣðen. Him man sǣde þæt hī hǣðene wǣron. Grēgōrius þā of innweardre heortan langsume siccetunge tēah, and cwæð: "Wālāwā þæt swā fægeres hīwes menn sindon þām sweartan dēofle underþēodde!"

Eft hē āxode hū þǣre þēode nama wǣre, þe hī of cōmon. Him wæs geandwyrd þæt hī Angle genemnode wǣron. Ðā cwæð hē: "Rihtlīce hī sind Angle gehātene, for þām þe hī engla wlite habbað, and swilcum gedafenað þæt hī on heofonum engla gefēran bēon." Gȳt þā Grēgōrius befrān hū þǣre scīre nama wǣre, þe þā cnapan of ālǣdde wǣron. Him man sǣde þæt þā scīrmen wǣron Dēre gehātene.

Grēgōrius andwyrde: "Wel hī sind Dēre gehātene, for þām þe hī sind fram graman generede, and tō Crīstes mildheortnesse gecȳgde." Gȳt þā hē befrān: "Hū is þǣre lēode cyning gehāten?" Him wæs geandswarod þæt se cyning Ælle gehāten wǣre. Hwæt þā Grēgōrius gamenode mid his wordum tō þām naman and cwæþ: "Hit gedafenað þæt Alleluia sīe gesungen on þām lande, tō lofe þæs ælmihtigan Scieppendes."

VOCABULARY

ālǣdan, to bring
befrinan, to inquire
Dēre, from Deira, Deiran
fram graman, Lat. *dē irā,* from wrath
gamenian, to play
geandwyrdan, to answer
gecȳgan, to summon
gedafenian, to be fitting
gefēra, companion
generian, to deliver, save
hīw, hue, color
lof, praise
mennisc, people
mildheortnes, mercy, pity
scīr, shire, district
Scieppend, Creator
siccetung, sigh
sweart, black
þe, or (line 4)
ðēod, nation
underþēodan, to subject
wālāwā, wellaway! alas!
wlite, beauty
wlitig, beautiful

POINTS OF SYNTAX

Note the frequent variations of word order in the passage. Inversion of subject and verb is normal after introductory adverbs, e.g. **Ðā sǣde him mon** (line 2). See 26.28., Word Order.

What type of constructions (Voice) are **Him wæs geandwyrd** (line 7) and **wæs geandswarod** (line 14)? (This text, translated from Latin, reflects Latin syntax.) Other examples of this type of construction are found throughout the selection.

Note the Mood of **wǣre** (line 10).

Is **lofe** (line 16) a noun or a verb?

FOOTNOTES

[1]The formation of **-est** is interesting. Historically this was **-es** (< ***is**); it is sometimes found in EWS texts. However, the pronoun **ðū** frequently followed it and became added to it, producing ***-esðū**; this in turn was reduced to EWS **-esð**, an occasional form, and further to **-est**, the regular form.

[2]The long diphthong is due to contraction: **sēo** < ***seohe**. It was this short **eo** which was umlauted to **ie** in the 2 and 3 Sing. forms.

Chapter 23

Preterit-Present Verbs

23.1. Certain verbs in the Germanic languages are called Preterit-Presents because, in them, *strong* verb preterits are shifted to present tense use, and new preterits are formed with *weak* verb inflectional endings. In effect, this produces a new set of Principal Parts (see Diagram 6 below): (a) the old Infinitive is lost; (b) the old Pret. Sing. furnishes the base of the new Pres. Sing.; (c) the old Pret. Plur. furnishes the base of the new Pres. Plur., the new Infinitive, and all other Present forms; (d) the new Pret. is formed with weak verb endings on the base of the old Past Pple. (The old Past Pple. remains, but it is not a Principal Part.)

23.2. The paradigms of Preterit-Present verbs are seldom complete but **dugan,** to avail, will serve as an example of the group.

Diagram 6

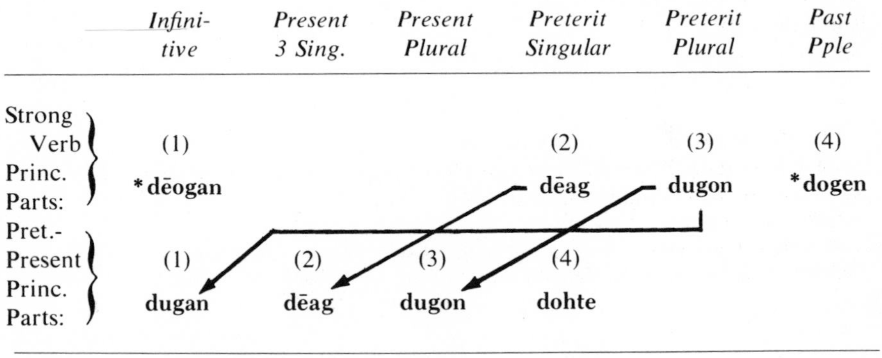

	Infinitive	*Present 3 Sing.*	*Present Plural*	*Preterit Singular*	*Preterit Plural*	*Past Pple*
Strong Verb Princ. Parts:	(1) ***dēogan**			(2) **dēag**	(3) **dugon**	(4) ***dogen**
Pret.-Present Princ. Parts:	(1) **dugan**	(2) **dēag**	(3) **dugon**	(4) **dohte**		

The new form **dohte** is composed of the participial base **dog-** + weak preterit **-te,** with **g** [ʒ] devoiced by assimilation to **t:** [ht].

INDICATIVE

Pres. Sing. 1.	dēag, dēah		*Pret.* Sing. 1.	dohte
2.	—		2.	dohtest
3.	dēag, dēah		3.	dohte
Plur. 1–3.	dugon		Plur. 1–3.	dohton

SUBJUNCTIVE

Pres. Sing. 1–3.	duge, dyge	*Pret.*	—
Infinitive: dugan	Pres. Pple. dugende	*Past Pple.*	—

23.3. Preterit-Present verbs are derived from the first six classes of strong verbs, as follows:

Class	*Infinitive*	*Present 3 Sing.*	*Present Plural*	*Preterit 3 Sing.*
1	witan, *know*	wāt	witon	wisse, wiste
	āgan, *possess*	āh	āgon	āhte
2	dugan, *avail*	dēag	dugon	dohte
3	cunnan, *know*	cann, conn	cunnon	cūðe
	durran, *dare*	dearr	durron	dorste
	ðurfan, *need*	ðearf	ðurfon	ðorfte
	unnan, *grant*	ann, onn	unnon	ūðe
4	munan, *remember*	man, mon	munon	munde
	sculan, *be obligated*	sceal	sculon	scolde
5	magan, *be able*	mæg	magon	meahte
	nugan, *suffice*	neah	nugon	nohte
6	mōtan, *be permitted*	mōt	mōton	mōste

Note 1: These verbs are special in retaining some features of the more primitive conjugation of ablaut verbs: (a) the Present Indicative 2 Sing. is in **-t** or **-st** without change of the radical syllable; (b) there is partial survival of the umlauted subjunctive, e.g., in **dyge** beside **duge, ðyrfe** beside **ðurfe**. On the other hand, analogy to the regular conjugation has produced such forms as Plur. **(ge)munað**; Imperative 2 Plur. **witað**.

Exercise 1: The normal ablaut series of Class 2 Strong Verbs was **ēo, ēa, u, o** (19.4); as just shown in Diagram 6, ***dēogan** would have been the Infinitive form if **dugan** had not replaced it. Answer:

1. If **faran** (Class 6) had become a Preterit-Present verb, what would have been its Principal Parts? (Label your forms.)
2. If **witan** (Pret-Pres. 1) had not become a PP verb, what would have been its Principal Parts?

Translation: *St. Hilda*

A.D. 680. On þone seofontēoðan dæg þæs mōnðes [November] biþ þǣre hālgan abbudessan gewītennes on Brytene þǣre nama wæs Sancta Hilda. Hēo wæs sēo ǣreste timbrend þæs mynstres þe is nemned Strēonesheallh. Hire fæder nama wæs Hererīc, and hire mōdor nama wæs Bregoswīþ; and þǣre mēder wæs on slǣpe ætīewed, þā hēo mid þām bearne wæs, þæt hire man stunge ān sigle on þone bōsm, and sēo ongunne scīnan ofer ealle Brytene. Ðæt tācnode þone blysan þǣre fǣmnan hālignesse. And Sancta Hilda wæs þrēo and þrītig gēara under hāligryfte, and hēo þā gewāt tō Crīste. And hire Godes þēowena sum geseah hū englas hire gāst tō heofonum lǣddon, and hēo glitenode on þǣra engla midle swā scīnende sunne oððe nīgslīcod hrægl. And sēo ylce Godes þēowen gehȳrde, on þā ylcan tīd þā hēo gewāt, wundorlicre bellan swēg on þǣre lyfte, and hēo geseah ēac þæt englas hōfon up ongēan hire gāst swīðe micle and wundorlice Crīstes rōde, and sēo sceān swā heofones tungol, and mid swylcere blisse Sancta Hildan gāst wæs gelǣded on heofones cyneþrym, þǣr hēo nū ā būtan ende gesyhþ ūrne Drihten, þæs willan hēo ǣr fremode þā hwīle hēo on līfe wunode on hire līchaman.

VOCABULARY

abbudessa, abbess
ætīewan, to show, reveal
belle, bell
blysa, radiance
bōsm, bosom
cyneþrym, royal glory
fǣmne, woman
gewītennes, passing away
glitenian, to glitter
Godes þēowa, nun
hāligryft, veil
hōfon, Pret Pl of **hebban,** to raise
hrægl, garment
lǣdan, to conduct, take
mynster, monastery, nunnery
nīgslīcod, newly smoothed
onginnan, to begin
on lyft, aloft, in the sky
sigle, necklace
stingan, to thrust
Strēonesheallh, Whitby
swēg, sound
tungol, star, the sun
timbrend, builder
þēowen, handmaiden
ylce, same

Chapter 24

Adverbs; Indefinite Pronouns

Adverbs of Place

24.1. Following are some of the more important adverbs of place. They fall with fair consistency into three related groups:

Simple Position	*Motion Toward*	*Motion From*
hwǣr (LWS hwār), where	**hwider**, whither, whereto	**hwonan**, whence, wherefrom
ðǣr (LWS ðār), there	**ðider, ðidres**, thither	**ðonan**, thence
hēr, here	**hider, hidres**, hither	**heonan**, hence
inne, inside	**in(n)**, into, on, at, to	**innan**, from within
ūte, outside	**ūt**, out, outwardly	**ūtan**, from outside
uppe, up, above	**ūp, upp**, upward, up	**uppan**, on, upon
ufan, above		**ufan**, from above
neoðan, beneath	**niðor**, downward, down	**neoðan**, from below
foran, before	**forð**, forward, onward	**foran**, before, in front
hindan, behind	**hinder**, hindward	**hindan**, from behind
	east, east(ward)	**ēastan**, from the east
	west, west(ward)	**westan**, from the west
	norð, north(ward)	**norðan**, from the north
	sūð, south(ward)	**sūðan**, from the south
feorran, far, distant	**feor(r)**, afar, far away	**feorran**, from afar
nēah, (nēh), near, nigh	**nēar**, near by	**nēan**, from near by

Adverbs Formed from Adjectives and Nouns

24.2. Many adverbs are derived from adjectives and nouns. The largest class is derived from adjectives by addition of the ending **-e** (which originally was the instrumental locative singular case-ending of nouns). Adjectives already having **-e** remained unchanged. Examples:

Adj.	*Adv.*	*Adj.*	*Adv.*
georn, eager	**georne**	**blīðe**, joyful	**blīðe**
hlūd, loud	**hlūde**	**clǣne**, clean	**clǣne**
hlūtor, clear	**hlūtre**		
long, long	**longe**		
dēop, deep	**dēope**		
dēoplic, deep	**dēoplīce**		

Note 1: Adverbs in **-līce** (the source of MnE **-ly**) already in OE were more numerous than adjectives in **-lic.**
Note 2: The adverbs **sōfte**, **swōte** are without the umlaut of the corresponding adjectives **sēfte**, soft, **swēte**, sweet. (In ME this distinction was confused: note Chaucer's *shoures sote* and *swete breeth* within five lines of each other. By MnE it was leveled out.)

24.3. Other Adverbial endings are **-a** and **-unga** (**-enga**, **-inga**). Examples:

gēara, of yore (Gen. Pl. of **gēar**, year)
sōna, soon, at once
tela (**teola**, **teala**), properly
tūwa (**twūwa**, **twīwa**), twice
ðrīwa, thrice
ǣninga (**āninga**, **ānunga**), entirely
eallunga (**eallinga**), altogether
grundlunga (**grundlinga**), completely
somnunga (**semninga**), suddenly
wēninga, perhaps

24.4. Oblique cases of nouns and adjectives are used adverbially. From these, and from prepositional phrases, have sprung more or less permanent adverbial forms. Examples:

Genitive Advs.	*Accusative Advs.*	*Dat.-Instr. Advs.*
dæges, by day	(**ge**)**fyrn**, formerly	**hwēne**, somewhat
nihtes, by night	**full**, fully	**hām**, **hāme**, home
ealles, altogether	**genōg**, enough	**sāre**, sorely
elles, otherwise	**hwon**, somewhat	**hwīlum**, sometimes
micles, very	**lȳtel**, **lȳt**, little	**stundmǣlum**, time after time
nēades, needs	**ungemet**, immeasurably	**lȳtlum**, little
simbles, **singāles**, always	**ūpweard**, upward	**miclum**, very
willes, willingly		
self-willes, voluntarily		
ūpweardes, upwards		
tōgegnes, against		
ungewisses, unconsciously		
nēde, f, necessarily		
hū gēares, at what time of year		

Note 3: Colloquial MnE preserves some of these: "He works *nights* and sleeps *days*." Others are archaic: *needs*; or poetic: *whilom*; or somewhat old fashioned: "He won't come *else*", "You know full *well*". Others are in daily use: *home*, *upward(s)*, *little*. But many others have disappeared.

Comparison of Adverbs

24.5. Adverbs (chiefly those derived from adjectives) adopt the comparative and superlative endings **-or, -ost (-ust, -ast)**: **georne**, eagerly; **geornor, geornost**.

Certain monosyllabic comparatives are without the comparative ending. These were originally in **-iz** and therefore have umlaut:

ǣr, earlier (< *__āriz__ < * __airiz__, Goth *airiz*).
bet, better (< *__batiz__, Goth *batis*).
fierr, farther
īeð (ēað), easier
lǣs, less
leng, longer
mǣ (mā), more
nӯr (nēar), nearer
sēft, softer
sēl, better
sīð, later
tylg, more willingly

Indefinite Pronouns

24.6. The Indefinite Pronouns form three general groups:

1. The true Indefinites:

ǣlc, each
ān, a, an
ǣnig, any
sum, a certain (one)
swilc, such
ōðer, a second, other
nǣnig, none

The Nom. Sing. **mon**, man, is used as an indefinite, one. (Cf. the cognate Ger. *man*.)

2. Interrogatives, often used as indefinites:

hwā, anyone, someone, etc.
hwæðer, whichever
hwilc, whichever, whosoever

Interrogatives in combination with **swā**:

swā hwā swā, who(so)ever
swā hwæðer swā, which(so)ever (of two)

Interrogatives in composition:

āhwā, any one
āhwæt, anything
ǣghwā, æthwā, gehwā, each, every
āhwæðer, āðer, ōðer, either
ǣghwæðer, ǣgðer, either
nāhwæðer, neither
ǣghwilc, gehwilc, each
sumhwylc, someone
hwæthwega, something
hwilchwega, any one
æthwega, somewhat

3. Other substantival Indefinites:

āwiht (āwuht, āuht, āht, ōwiht, ōwuht, ōht), aught, anything
nāwiht (nāuht, nāht, nōht, etc.), **nānwuht,** naught, nothing

Translation: *The Mandrake*

Ðēos wyrt þe man Mandragoram nemneð is micel and mǣre on gesihþe, and hēo is fremful. Ðā ðū scealt þissum gemete niman; þonne þū tō hire cymst, þonne ongietst þū hī, be þām þe hēo on nihte scīneð ealswā lēohtfæt. Ðonne ðū hire hēafod ǣrest gesēo, þonne bewrīt þū hī wel hraðe mid īserne, þȳlæs hēo þē ætflēo. Hire mægen is swā micel and swā mǣre, þæt hēo unclǣnne mann, þonne hē tō hire cymeð, wel hraðe forflēon wile. For þȳ þū hī bewrīt, swā wē ǣr cwǣdon, mid īserne.

And swā þū scealt onbūtan hī delfan, swā þū hire mid þǣm īserne nā æthrīne; ac þū geornlīce scealt mid elpendbǣnenan stæfe ðā eorðan delfan, and þonne þū hire handa and hire fēt gesēo, þonne gewrīð þū hī. Nim þonne þone ōðerne ende, and gewrīð tō ānes hundes swēoran, swā þæt se hund hungrig sīe: wurp him siþþan mete tōforan, swā þæt hē hine ārǣcan ne mæge, būton hē mid him þā wyrte ūpābregde. Be þisse wyrte is sægd þæt hēo swā micele mihte hæbbe, þæt swā hwilc þing swā hī ūpātēohþ, þæt hit sōna scule þām selfan gemete bēon beswicen; for þȳ sōna swā þū gesēo þæt hēo ūpābrogden sīe, and þū hire geweald hæbbe, genim hī sōna on hand, swā andwealc hī, and gewring þæt wōs of hire lēafum on āne glæsene ampellan, and þonne ðē nēod becume þæt þū hwilcum menn þǣrmid helpan scule, þonne help þū him ðissum gemete.

VOCABULARY

ætflēon, to escape
æthrīnan, to touch
ampelle, flask, vial
andwealcan, to twist
ārǣcan, to reach
beswīcan, to deceive
bewrītan, to mark around
delfan, to dig
ealswā, like
elpendbǣnen, of ivory
forflēon, to escape
fremful, profitable
gemet, manner
gesihð, appearance
geweald, power, control
gewrīðan, to bind, tie
glæsen, of glass
hraðe, quickly
īsern, iron
lēoht-fæt, lamp
mægen, power, strength
mǣre, noble
onbūtan, around, about
ongīetan, to recognize
swā þæt, so that, provided that
swēora, neck
toforan, in front of
þȳlæs, lest
ūpābregdan, to pull up
ūpātēon, to pull up
wōs, juice
wurp, Imperative of **weorpan**
wyrt, plant

Chapter 25

Numerals

25.1.

	Cardinal	*Ordinal*
1	ān	forma, formesta, fyrmest, fyrest, fyrst; ǣrest
2	twēgen, tū, twā	ōðer; æfterra
3	ðrīe, ðrīo, ðrēo	ðridda
4	fīower, fēower	fēowerða, fēorða
5	fīf	fīfta
6	siex, six	siexta
7	siofon, seofon	seofoða, -eða
8	eahta	eahtoða, -eða
9	nigon	nigoða, -eða
10	tīen, tȳn	tēoða
11	endlefan, -leofan, -lufan	endlefta, ellefta
12	twelf	twelfta
13	ðrēotīene, -tēne, -tȳne	ðrēotēoða
14	fēowertīene	fēowertēoða
15	fīftīene	fīftēoða
16	siextīene	siextēoða
17	seofontīene	seofontēoða
18	eahtatīene	eahtatēoða
19	nigontīene	nigontēoða
20	twēntig	twēntigoða, -tigða, -tiga
21	ān ond twēntig	ān ond twēntigoða
30	ðrītig	ðrītigoða
40	fēowertig	fēowertigoða
50	fīftig	fīftigoða
60	siextig	siextigoða
70	(hund)seofontig	(hund)seofontigoða

(Cont.)

(Cont.)	Cardinal	Ordinal
80	(hund)eahtatig	(hund)eahtatigoða
90	(hund)nigontig	(hund)nigontigoða
100	(hund)tēontig, hund, hundred	(hund)tēontigoða
110	hundendlefantig, hundǣlleftig	(hund)endleftigoða
120	hundtwelftig	(hund)twelftigoða
200	twā hund, tū hund	
1000	ðūsend	

Declension of Numerals

25.2. 1. The cardinal **ān** is generally declined like a strong adjective, with Masc. Acc. Sing. **ǣnne, ānne,** and Instr. Sing. **ǣne, āne**. When it means *alone* it is often declined weak. (Cf. Indefinite Pronouns, 24.6.)

2. The cardinals **twēgen** and **ðrīe** have the following forms:

	Masc.	Neut.	Fem.
N.A.	**twēgen**	**tū, twā**	**twā**
G.		**twēga, twēgra**	
D.		**twǣm, twām**	
N.A.	**ðrīe, ðrī**	**ðrīo, ðrēo**	**ðrīo, ðrēo**
G.		**ðrīora, ðrēora**	
D.		**ðrīm**	

3. Like **twēgen** is declined **bēgen**, *both*; Neut. **bū**; Fem. **bā**; Gen. **bēgra, bēga**; Dat. **bǣm, bām.**

Note: Gender is not strictly held to in the above forms; **twā** is sometimes used for **twēgen, bā** and **bū** for **bēgen**, etc. When nouns of different genders are referred to, the Neut. form of the numeral is generally employed.

4. The cardinal numbers from 4 to 19 are not inflected, except when used absolutely (i.e. without a noun); they then take the case endings N.A. **-e**, G. **-a**, D. **-um**.

5. The cardinal numbers in **-tig** are often not inflected; when inflected, the case endings are G. **-a, -ra**, D. **-um**, and sometimes Sing. G. **-es**.

6. **hund**, usually uninflected, has the Sing. D. **hunde**, and the Plur. N.A. **hunde**, D. **hundum**. When inflected, **hundred** has the following case endings: Sing. G. **-es**, D. **-e**; Plur. N.A. **-u, -o**, G. **-a**, D. **-um**. The same occur with **ðūsend**, and also Plur. G. **-ra**.

7. All ordinals are declined like weak adjectives, except **ǣrest, fyrmest, fyrest, fyrst**, which may be strong or weak, and **ōðer**, which is only strong.

Review of Sound Changes

25.3. The major sound changes which affected OE and produced its most regular forms were:

1. The PrGmc umlaut of **e** > **i** (11.2. Note 1) and of **eu** > **iu** (ultimately > OE **īo**).
2. The PrGmc change of **eu** > **eo** (ultimately > OE **ēo**).
3. The PrGmc change of **e** > **i** before a nasal + other consonant (20.1. Note 1).
4. The WGmc Change of Gemination (5.2.).
5. The PrehOE change of **a** > **o** before nasals (5.3.).
6. The PrehOE change of **a** > **æ** (5.4.).
7. The PrehOE change of Breaking (8.1.).
8. The PrehOE change of Diphthongization after Initial Palatal (8.3.).
9. The PrehOE change of **i**-Umlaut (11.1-2.).
10. The PrehOE change of **u-o-a**-Umlaut (11.3.).
11. Loss of final **-i** or **-u** after long syllables (11.2. Note 2; 13.4. Note 3).
12. Syncope of unstressed **e, i, o**; loss of medial **j**. (Chap 4, footnote 8; 11.2. Note 2.)
13. Changes of unstressed **i** > **e** (11.2. Note 2).
14. Loss of Intervocalic **h** (16.5.).

These are given in chronological order; one should be able to follow the PrGmc or other source form down to the EWS form by noting the change or changes to which it was susceptible. Each change may be designated by its number in the list. *Examples:*

PrGmc ***framjan(an)** > ***frammjan** (4) > ***fremmjan** (9) > EWS **fremman** (12).
PrGmc ***sehið** > ***sihið** (1) > ***siohið** (7) > ***siehið** (9) > EWS **siehð** (12).
PrehOE ***dōmide** > ***dēmide** (9) > EWS **dēmde** (12).

(The parenthetic (**an**) on PrGmc infinitives—as ***framjan(an)** above—disappeared probably by the Gmc period.)

Exercise. Show each of the forms through which the following would have passed in developing from PrGmc or PrehOE into EWS. Indicate each change with the number of the sound-change which produced it. (*Note*: No forms were open to *all* the changes; most underwent only two or three. Be sure to take into account the conditions under which changes did or did not occur.)

PrGmc forms:	* **drencan(an)**	* **beriþ**	* **lagjan(an)**
	* **helpis**	* **hlunjan(an)**	* **saljan(an)**
	* **sagjan(an)**	* **dōmjan(an)**	* **creupan(an)**
PrehOE forms:	* **fliohiþ**	* **stragd**	* **ānfald**
	* **druhti**	* **tamið**	* **hefon**
	* **hand**	* **scarp**	* **wandjan**
	* **galp**	* **caru**	* **aldira**
	* **guldjan**	* **lūsi**	* **gefan**
	* **teohan**	* **elhes**	* **swehor**
	* **fehes**	* **wrehan**	* **gǣt**

Chapter 26

Syntax

26.1. Syntax is the set of rules by which the meaning-bearing units of any language work together. These units (morphemes and combinations of morphemes constituting 'words') when syntactically structured, produce organized, more fully meaningful expressions. *Hills*, *the*, *over* consists of three meaningful words (the first having two morphemes) which in this sequence are meaningless together. In the phrase *over the hills*, however, where rules of syntax organize them, they form a meaningful group. Larger groups still (clauses, sentences) are similarly structured under syntactic rules to produce meaningful discourse.

26.2. A language may be said to have a syntactic category (such as Number, Mode, Case) only to the extent that it is formally distinct, the form clearly indicating the function. Inflection, word order, use of specific function words, are such formal devices in MnE. In the course of time both forms and functions may change: OE had some that MnE lacks, and MnE has some that OE lacked. The following brief account will touch on those syntactic features of OE which differ markedly from the corresponding features of MnE. It should be noted that, as in phonology, OE morphology and syntax exhibit considerable variation throughout the period. No rules are absolute, though some are firmer than others.

Pronouns

26.3. Like MnE, OE has Personal, Interrogative, Demonstrative, Possessive, and Indefinite pronouns. It has no Reflexive or Relative pronouns as such though these functions are expressed (see 6.4, 9.4).

26.4. Personal Pronoun. Like MnE, OE distinguishes the usual three persons (for speaker, person addressed, other person or thing) with gender distinction also in the singular of the third person.

26.5. Number distinction is more complex: OE has forms not only for singular and plural but for *dual* (see 6.1, 2). The second person singular forms

(MnE *thou, thine, thy, thee* now largely disused) are fully active in OE (6.2); the OE plural forms are thus distinctive of number, as MnE *you, your, yours* are not.

26.6. Though MnE pronouns to some extent preserve distinct *Case* forms, the category of case as such is functionally inactive: the distinct forms must follow the rules of *word order* (see below) which has superseded case as the functionally active feature in MnE syntax. In OE the case system is still functional, however.

26.7. OE formally and functionally distinguishes a maximum of *five* cases in the Interrogative and Demonstrative pronoun and the Strong adjective (6.5; 9.2, 3; 10.2, 3), a maximum of *four* cases in the Personal pronoun and the Weak adjective (6.2, 12.3), and a maximum of *three* cases in the Noun (13.2 ff.). In the plural there are never more than three distinct case forms. These cases are:

Nominative (to express the subject relation),
Genitive (to express possessive and similar relations; also, with certain verbs, the object relation: (see 26.24),
Dative (to express the indirect object and similar relations; also, with certain verbs, the sole object: (see 26.24),
Accusative (to express the direct object relation),
Instrumental (to express means; see Ch 6, footnote 2).

26.8. Interrogative Pronoun. The OE Interrogative pronoun has distinctive forms only for Masculine and Neuter, and only for the Singular. The Masculine, however, has all five distinct case forms (6.5). (The MnE relative pronouns *who, whom, what, which* developed out of the OE interrogatives.)

26.9. Demonstrative Pronoun. OE has demonstrative pronouns for both far and near (MnE *that, this*), with three genders distinguished in the singular, none in the plural. Masculine has the full range of five distinctive case forms, Neuter only four, Feminine three with the Instrumental lacking (see 9.2, 3). Both Demonstrative pronouns could be used adjectivally to modify nouns (as in MnE).

26.10. Forms of the first OE Demonstrative, when weakly stressed, also function as the Definite Article (**sē, sēo, þæt**). (Much reduced, they are the source of the MnE Definite Article *the*. The stressed forms survived in MnE *that*, which is still distinguished from Relative *that* by strong stress.)

26.11. Possessive Pronoun. The first and second person forms, in all numbers, are identical in form with the Genitive of the Personal pronoun. The third person forms, however, are different (see 6.2, 10.8). Both may function adjectivally.

26.12. Gender in OE is *grammatical* (not *natural* as in MnE). Normally, each noun is of a specific gender, though some shift gender (especially between

Masculine and Neuter) and some survive in rare or nonce examples of uncertain gender. Gender has no necessary correspondence with the nature of the thing named: **stān,** stone, is Masculine, **word,** word, is Neuter, **duru,** door, is Feminine, though all refer to inanimate things (hence are Neuter in MnE). The same is true of nouns naming some animate things: **wīf,** woman, **mægden,** maiden, **cild,** child, are Neuter. The same for abstracts: **fæstness,** firmness, is Feminine, **mægdenhād,** maidenhood, is Masculine. On the other hand, the nouns of family relationship generally correspond to nature: **fæder, brōþor** are Masculine, **mōdor, sweostor** are Feminine.

26.13. Pronouns agree in Gender and Number with the nouns they stand for. Thus **wīf** requires **hit, duru** requires **hēo, stān** requires **hē,** etc. The sense of natural gender, distinguishing animate from inanimate referents, begins to assert itself in later texts: **wīf** may then take **hēo,** and so on. (The system of grammatical gender breaks down in the ME period and is replaced by natural gender, which continues into MnE.)

26.14. Indefinite Pronoun. (See 24.6.)

Adjectives

26.15. OE has two classes of adjectives, called *strong* and *weak* (see 10.1, 12.1) according to the two systems of inflectional morphemes they employ, the 'strong' system having more distinctive case forms in the singular (5 Masc., 4 Neut., 3 Fem.) than has the 'weak' (2 in each gender—see 10.2, 12.3). With few exceptions, any adjective may be declined strong or weak, according to its situation (12.2). (The weak adjective developed in the Gmc branch of IE and is one of its distinctive features.)

26.16. Though the terms 'strong' and 'weak' are also used about nouns and verbs they are merely metaphorical: no grammatical agreement is involved. Strong or weak nouns may be modified by strong or weak adjectives, and strong or weak verbs may take strong or weak nouns as subjects, objects, etc.

26.17. Adjectives regularly agree in Number, Gender, and Case with the nouns or pronouns they modify. When they are verb complements, however, usage varies and they may agree with the noun or pronoun modified or be invariable in form. (In MnE the adjective has lost all morphological distinctions for number, gender, and case, hence has no concord relationships. Except for inflection for degree of comparison it is invariant in form.)

26.18. Numerals are declined like adjectives (see 25.2).

26.19. Participles are inflected like both strong and weak adjectives (12.5).

Nouns

26.20. OE nouns have fewer distinctive inflectional morphemes than do pronouns or adjectives: no more than 3 in the strong or vowel-stem declensions (13;

14.1–6; 15.1–6) and 2 in the singular of the weak or consonant-stem declension (14.7). The cases without distinctive forms (e.g. Dative and Instrumental syncretized under a single form) often depend on concord (agreement) with adjectives or pronouns to show their case, number, or gender. Lacking this, the word order may indicate syntactic structure. Sometimes, however, non-distinctiveness of forms produces ambiguity.

26.21. Apposition, much used in OE poetry, requires concord of number, gender, and case between appositives: **Godes candel beorht, ēces Drihtnes**, etc.

Verbs

26.22. OE has four classes of verbs: Strong, Weak, Anomalous, and Preterit-Present (see 17.1 ff). OE verbs have distinctive forms for:

Three Modes:	*Indicative*—for statements without contingency; *Subjunctive*—for statements involving contingency, possibility, unrealized situations, etc.; *Imperative*—for orders and requests.
Four non-finite forms:	*Infinitive*, the *Inflected Infinitive* (see Ch 7, footnote 1), *Present Participle*, and *Past Participle*.
Two Tenses:	*Present*, and *Preterit* (or *Past*). There is no *Future* tense as such (see 7.3); futurity is indicated instead with the Present Tense form and with time words.
Three Persons:	But this is true only in the singular of the Present and Preterit Indicative; in the plural a single form serves for all persons.

26.23. In common with other Gmc languages, OE has no inflected Passive Voice forms (apart from a few relics surviving from IE). During the OE period we find phrases of passive sense developing, chiefly in translation of Latin passives. By the end of the period these are well established. (From them the MnE analytic Passive is descended.)

26.24. In OE the case of the Object depends upon the verb, each verb regularly requiring its object or objects to be in a specific case or cases. Following is a partial list of verbs with the cases of their objects:

Verbs taking a single object in the **Accusative** (the great majority): **āgan, brengan, cemban**, etc., etc.

Verbs taking a single object in the **Dative** (a fair number): **andswarian, bēodan, beorgan, bodian, bregdan, dēman, fylgan, gebiddan, gelȳfan, helpan, līcian, miltsian, onfōn, þegnian, þyncan, wealdan**, etc.

Verbs taking a single object in the **Genitive** (a fair number): **bedǣlan, benǣman, beburfan, bīdan, blissian, brūcan, fægnian, gelȳfan, gewyrcan, gyrnan, helpan, onfōn, reccan, swīcan, twēon, þurfan, wēnan, wealdan, wilnian, wundrian**, etc.

Verbs taking two *Accusative* objects (a few): **āscian, gelǣran**, etc.

Verbs taking two objects, in **Dative** and **Accusative** (a fair number): **cweþan, etan, feccan, findan, giefan, lecgan, sellan, sendan,** etc.

Verbs taking two objects, in **Genitive** and **Accusative** (a few): **æmtigan, biddan, gelystan, lettan, sceamian,** etc.

Verbs taking two objects, in Dative and Genitive (a few): **forwyrnan, gestȳran, geunnan, gewanian, ofþyncan, onlēon, tilian, tīþian, þancian, wyrnan,** etc.

Adverbs

26.25. See Ch. 24, 1–5.

26.26. Many adverbs are formed from oblique cases of nouns and adjectives (24.4); the inflectional morphemes they bear belong to the nouns or adjectives, however, not to the adverbs as such. The only adverbial inflection is for degree of comparison (24.5).

Prepositions

26.27. Certain prepositions take their object in a specific case, as follows:

Usually with a *Dative* object: **æfter, ǣr, æt, be, būton, ēac, fram, mid, nēah, of, ongemang, oninnan, onufan, wiþūtan.**

Usually with an *Accusative* object: **geond, ongēan, oþ, siþþan, wiþ, ymbūtan.**

With a *Genitive* object: **andlang, andlanges.**

With a *Dative* or an *Accusative* object: **betwux, binnan, fore, in, on, under, ymbe.**

There are many exceptions, however.

Prepositional forms without objects, often coming finally in the phrase or clause, are adverbial in function: **þā ēode hē tō**, then he walked *thereto*.

Word-Order

26.28. The sequence of words in discourse follows certain patterns, one of which is structurally basic: this is the customary order, used unless there is some reason to vary it. Variations upon this basic order[1] may serve a syntactic function (for example, to shift from the declarative to the interrogative or from active to passive), or a stylistic function, as when their difference from the basic order gives prominence or calls attention to one or another element of the sentence.

26.29. The word-order of MnE is often called "fixed": it is far less flexible than that of OE. Nevertheless, the "freedom" usually attributed to OE word-order has been exaggerated. It has recently been shown[2] that, in ninth-century OE:

> Subject (S) and Object (O) are distinguished by inflection in only 41 percent of instances; they are *not* distinguished by inflection in 59 percent of instances. Of the 59 percent not distinguished by inflection, the word-order is Subject before

Object (S-O) in 94 percent of instances; of the 41 percent distinguished by inflection, the word-order is still S-O in 93 percent of instances.

It is evident that already in ninth-century OE the basic word-order is S-O. Further, it probably has syntactic force, functioning to distinguish Subject from Object. (As inflection progressively breaks down during the ME period, word-order is left to bear this burden almost alone. The establishment of the S-O order may even have contributed to the breakdown of inflection.)

26.30. Reversal of the basic S-O word order has syntactic force in questions: **Hwæt sindon gē searohæbbendra? Hwær cwōm mearg? Canst þū ænig þing?** (This word-order survives in MnE only with the verbs *be* and *have*: *Is he here? Has he come?* Other questions require the interrogative auxiliary *do*, unless they depend entirely on intonation.)

26.31. In Gmc languages generally, the normal position of the verb (V) is at the end of the clause. In OE this order is by no means uncommon; for example, S-O-V: **hē hit self ne geseah; hē mē āðas swōr; bearwas blōstmum nimað.** It is far more frequent with pronoun objects. But even in early OE the S-V-O order (or Subject-Verb-Complement, S-V-C) is used nearly half the time, and by the early ME period S-V-O is the norm (as it is in MnE): **hīe brōhton sume þǣm cyninge; hē syxa sum ofslōge syxtig on twām dagum; hundas bedrifon hine tō mē; Ætla wēold Hūnum.**

26.32. Basic S-V word-order is reversed after a clause-initial adverb: **Þā fōr hē norðryhte; Þǣr læg secg mænig; Forð ðā ēode Wīstān; Swā cwæð snottor on mōde; Ne hȳrde ic cȳmlīcor cēol gegyrwan.**

26.33. Any element other than the S placed first in a clause is given emphasis. ***Examples:***

With O first: **Fela spella him sǣdon þā Beormas; Mē þīn mōdsefa līcað; Ðæt fram hām gefrægn Higelāces þegn.**
With C first: **Dēad is Æschere; Bēowulf is mīn nama; Frōd wæs se fyrdrinc.**
With V first: **Cōm þā tō lande lidmanna helm; Gyrede hine Bēowulf; Gelpan ne þorfte beorn blandenfeax.**

These emphatic variants are much used in OE poetry, homilies, and other literature.

26.34. The word-order of **æt, in, on, beforan, tō, ūt,** etc., must be carefully observed: *before* a nominal they are almost certainly prepositions; *after* the nominal they are likely to be adverbial, especially if a verb follows. Even here, however, there is uncertainty, since they may be a part of the verb even though not an integral part of it. Compare **dælan, tō dælan, tōdælan; beran, æt beran, ætberan.** In the *Chronicle*, **him māra fultum tō cōm,** without **tō**, would still mean "more aid came to him"; the **tō** in this position is probably to be taken as adverbial and translated "in addition (to what he had already)"—the source of MnE *too*. (See 26.27.)

FOOTNOTES

[1]Paul Bacquet, *La Structure de la Phrase Verbale à l'Epoque Alfrédienne*, Pub. Faculté des Lettres de l'Université de Strasbourg, Paris (Belles Lettres) 1962. Our term "basic order" translates Bacquet's "l'ordre de base", p. 13 *et passim*. Bacquet also proposes "l'ordre sélectif" in which an element's position is varied to throw it into relief, and "l'ordre de liaison" in which an element is moved forward in the sentence to give it prominence.

[2]Robert L. Saitz, *Functional Word Order in Old English Subject-Object Patterns*, Unpub diss., Madison, Wis., 1955. See especially Chap IV.

appendix I

Grimm's Law and Verner's Law

The "laws" of language, like those in any other scientific field, are statements of observed regularity in the way the language behaves. If the law has been stated on the basis of adequate observation and understanding of the data, it should be valid for features similar to the ones already observed. When these do not behave as expected, we conclude that the law is inadequately stated; it must then be revised to take care of the irregularities as well as possible.

Two such laws are basic to Germanic studies: that of Jacob Grimm,[1] also called the "first Germanic consonant shift," and that of Karl Verner, which accounted for certain "exceptions" to Grimm's law. The effects of these laws may be readily observed in OE and still to some degree in MnE.

Grimm's Law

The "branch" languages of the IE family tree grew away from each other as a result of slow changes over many centuries. Most basic of these for Germanic, the one which set that branch apart from all others, was a regular "shifting" of the stop consonants such that in the non-Gmc languages the original sounds were generally retained, whereas in the Gmc branch they were changed. The result, in somewhat simplified form, was as follows:

1. The voiceless stops [p, t, k] became the corresponding voiceless spirants [f, θ, x].
2. The voiced stops [b, d, g] became the corresponding voiceless stops [p, t, k].
3. The voiced aspirated stops [bh, dh, gh] became the voiced stops [b, d, g].

Examples:

	Non-Gmc Languages		Gmc Languages
p	Gr *pella*, Lat *pellis*	> f	Goth *-fill*, Icel *fell*, OE *fell*, hide, skin
t	Skt *tat*, Gr *tó*, Lith *tas*	> θ	Goth *thata*, Icel *þat*, OE *þæt*, that
k	Lat *cornu*, Gael, Ir, W *corn*	> x	Goth *haurn*, Ger *horn*, OE *horn*, horn
b	Gr *baíte*, goatskin coat	> p	Goth *páida*, OS *pēda*, OE *pād*, coat, cloak
d	Skt *ad*, Gr *édein*, Lat *edere*	> t	Goth *itan*, Icel *eta*, OE *etan*, to eat
g	Gr *genos*, Lat *genus*	> k	Icel *kyn*, OS *kunni*, OE *cynn*, kin, tribe
bh	Skt *bhratar*, Gael *brathair*, Lat *frater*	> b	Goth *brōthar*, Icel *bróðir*, OE *brōðor*, brother
dh	Gr *thumos*, spirit, Lat *fumus*, smoke, Russ *dukh*, breath	> d	Ger *dunst*, fine dust, vapor, OE *dūst*, dust
gh	IE **ghostis*, Lat *hostis*, Russ *goste*	> g	Goth *gasts*, OE *gæst*, *giest*, guest

This shift occurred with a high degree of regularity when the sounds came in initial position in words. When they came internally irregularities sometimes appeared. The reason for this was discovered by Verner.

Verner's Law

Alongside the first consonant shift the Gmc branch developed a second distinctive characteristic. In IE, word stress was variable and might come on any syllable according to the word. In Gmc it was also variable to begin with but later became fixed on the base syllable. Verner saw a connection, as others had not, between this fixing of the Gmc stress and the irregularity of the consonants in internal positions. He hypothesized that the consonant shift had begun in early PrimGmc and that [p, t, k] had already changed to [f, θ, x] before the stress became fixed on the base. Then in later Prim Gmc [f, θ, x] coming initially or just after a stressed vowel remained without further change, but in any other position they became voiced: [ƀ, ð, ɣ]. The spirant [s] also took part in this development, becoming voiced: [z]. When, later on, stress moved to the base syllable, the phonetic reason for this voicing was no longer evident, hence the appearance of irregularity. In the later WGmc stage these four voiced sounds [ƀ, ð, ɣ, z] underwent further change, appearing in OE as *f*, *d*, *g*, and *r*.

As evidences of Verner's law we find in OE such verb Infinitives as *frēosan*, freeze, *cēosan*, choose, alongside their PretPl *fruron*, *curon*, with *r* in the latter two for *s* [z] in the first two. In MnE similarly we find *was* and *were*, *lose* and *(for)lorn*. The sequence of these changes was:

Early PrimGmc		*Later PrimGmc*	*Stress moved to Base*	*WGmc*	*OE*	*MnE*
Infin	* kéusanan	* kéusan		* kéosan	cēosan	choose
PretPl	*kusón	* kuzón	kúzon	* kúron	curon	chose

During ME the analogical influence of the Infinitive and Pret3Sg generalized [z] throughout the verb at the expense of [r]; MnE therefore has *chose*, *chosen* rather than * *chore*, * *choren*.

A few further examples will show other effects. If the first Gmc consonant shift had had no exceptions and IE [k, t] had always produced Gmc [x, θ], the cognate of Lat *centum* would have been **hunthred* rather than *hundred*. Why do we have *d* rather than *th*? The stress in early PrimGmc must have been on the syllable after *t*, as it is in Skt *çatám* and Gr *'ekatón*, hence IE [t] > early PrimGmc [θ] > late PrimGmc [ð], before the Gmc stress was shifted back to the base; and so into OE and MnE as *d*. In the light of this and other evidence PrimGmc **xumðóm* is reconstructed as the ancestor of all the later Gmc words for 'hundred.'

Again, as noted, PrimGmc [s] > [z] was followed in WGmc by change of [z] > [r], the result being visible in OE *curon*, *(for)loren*, etc. In the NorthGmc sub-branch, however, [z] remained—did not become [r]; hence we find the cognates OE *rǣran*, to rear, alongside ON *reisa*, to raise. *Rǣran* has come down directly through the WGmc sub-branch into OE and MnE, whereas our MnE *raise* is from the ON word, borrowed into ME, and making a doublet with *rear*.

FOOTNOTE

[1]Grimm made the first full attempt to articulate it, though Rasmus Rask had seen the basis of it earlier. It has been considerably revised by later scholars.

appendix II

The Phonemes of OE

It is a matter of general observation that when attention is paid not to the *meaning* of a linguistic unit (sentence, phrase, word) but to its *sounds* when spoken, these turn out to be noticeably different from individual to individual and even within the usage of any one individual: the "same" thing is not said identically twice over. Though small, these differences are undeniable.

For the exact study of sounds, as under laboratory conditions, attention must be paid to every least detail. In everyday speech, however, speakers simply ignore such small differences, or remain quite unaware of them. We do not often notice the sounds of language until communication threatens to break down (as with inadequate enunciation, a speech defect, or a foreigner's distortions), or unless the sounds themselves are a subject of esthetic interest (as in literary use). In normal communication we respond only to the larger, distinctive units of sound which, for our language, are structurally significant: those which make each word identifiable, hence decodable.

Any speech sound, as sound, is called a *phone*. Phones having phonetic similarity (for example, various types of *b*-sounds, exploded, unexploded, aspirated, devoiced, etc.) and to which a hearer responds in the same way, ignoring their differences, are called *allophones* (i.e., "other-sounds") and constitute together a class called a *phoneme*. Put the other way round, a phoneme is a class of phones to any of which, in a given language, the hearer responds in the same way.

It follows that what is actually said and heard is a phone, an audible physical sound, but the speaker produces it and the listener hears it as an allophone, since he refers it to the abstract class of a single phoneme. Every language uses a number of phonemes, each of which is necessarily distinctive from all others in the language—otherwise, combinations of phonemes into larger units (words, phrases, sentences) would not have consistent symbolic value—would not carry meaning.

When sounds are *heard*, the phonic details can be observed. Writing systems, by which the past stages of languages are preserved, do not record these details. Ideographic systems record no sounds at all. Alphabetic systems, especially when a language is written down for the first time, record the sound-classes (phonemes) which the writers recognize as distinctive in that language. There would be no occasion for them to use letters without sounds, nor would the system be adequate if some distinctive sound had no letter to represent it. The ideal alphabet therefore has one letter for each phoneme, no more and no less.

As has been pointed out above (4.1–3), when the Latin alphabet was first used to write OE, some letters proved superfluous and were not used; others had to be supplied for sounds which Latin lacked. All the phonemes were accounted for, but not the phones. This is normal: the ordinary writing system does not give phonetic information below the level of the phoneme. Hence, when scholars reconstruct past stages of a language on the basis of alphabetic records, it should be understood that they are often dealing not with facts but with presumptions—the best hypothesis they can make on the basis of the way living language behaves under similar conditions. (An example of this may be seen above, Ch 4, footnote 12.)

Once a spelling system is established, however—even a perfect one with one letter for each phoneme—it becomes to some extent a thing apart. In the course of time phonemes may be merged (that is, fall together so that now there is one where there were two before), but the established spelling tradition may continue as it was. For example, WS /y/ appears to have lost its distinctive rounding and to have fallen together with /i/, but both letters continue in spelling and are often interchanged. (In fact, it is the interchange which tells us they are no longer distinct.)

On the other hand, a phoneme may split, but the spelling system may fail to introduce a new letter or letter combination to make the distinction. (When, in ME, /ŋ/ split off from /n/, no letter was introduced for it; so in MnE it is sometimes written *ng*, as in *sing*, sometimes *n* as in *sink*.) Styles in writing may also lead to inconsistencies: OE had both þ and ð—though it needed only one letter since there was only one phoneme to be spelled. Then in ME this phoneme split into our present /θ/ and /ð/ as in *thin* and *then*, but both the OE characters later became disused and MnE has only *th* for two phonemes. Alphabets do not automatically or necessarily keep in line with the sounds of the language.

The phonemes and chief allophones of WS were:

Consonant Phonemes	*Probable Allophones*	*Examples*
/p/	[p]	pinn : b̄inn
/b/	[b]	~
/t/	[t]	tiht : diht
/d/	[d]	~
/k/	[k]	calan : galan
/g/	[g]	~
/č/	[kj, tj, tʃ]	ece : ecge
/ǰ/	[gj, dj, dʒ]	~

(Cont.)

(Cont.)	Consonant Phonemes	Probable Allophones	Examples
	/f/	[f]	fyllan : syllan
		[v]	ōfer : ōðer
	/þ/	[θ]	þæt : sæt
		[ð]	ōðer : ōfer
	/s/	[s]	syllan : fyllan
		[z]	oser : ofer
	/h/	[c, x]	byht, lōh : byge, lōc
		[h]	hōs : gōs
	/ʒ/	[ɣ]	saga : saca
	/m/	[m]	mān : nān
	/n/	[n, n̥]	næs, fnæs : wæs
		[ŋ]	ðanc, (ge) ðang : ðan
	/l/	[l, l̥]	lēow, hlēow : rēow
	/r/	[r, r̥]	rīm, hrīm : līm
	/w/	[w, w̥]	won, hwon : mon
	/y/	[j]	git : wit

Long consonants (written doubled) contrasted in EWS with single consonants, especially in internal position. Examples are, ǣne : ǣnne, hetan : hettan.[1]

There is less agreement about the status of the vowels and diphthongs, some of which changed within the period of OE. For example, EWS /ȳ, y/ were in contrast with /ī, i/; but in LWS the rounding appears to have been lost, the vowels merged, and ī, i or ȳ, y became alternative spellings for the two phonemes /ī, i/. The diphthongs [ie, ea, eo] that resulted from Breaking (see above 8.1–2) and other causes are in complementary distribution with [i, æ, e], hence are allophones of /i, æ, e/.[2]

Those of which we can be sure for EWS are:

Phonemes	Allophones	Examples
/ī/	[i:]	pīc : pic
/i/	[ɪ, ɪɛ, ɪə]	~
/ē/	[e:]	rēcan : recan
/e/	[ɛ, ɛɔ, ɛə]	~
/ǣ/	[æ: , ɛ:]	hǣlan : hēlan
/ā/	[a:]	hāt : hæt
/a/	[a, æ]	~
/ō/	[o:]	sōc : soc
/o/	[ɔ]	~
/ū/	[u:]	fūl : ful
/u/	[ʊ]	~
/ȳ/	[y:]	bȳgeð : bygeð
/y/	[y]	~
/īe/	[i:ɛ, i:ə]	hīe : hēa
/ēa/	[æ:ə, ɛ:ə]	tēah : tēoh
/ēo/	[e:ɔ, e:ə]	tēoh : tīehð

FOOTNOTES

[1]See further, H. Kurath, The Loss of Long Consonants . . . in Middle English, *Language* 32 (1956) 435–445.

[2]See further, A. J. Van Essen, Some Remarks on Old English Phonology, *Linguistics* 32 (1967) 83–86; Sherman M. Kuhn, On the Syllabic Phonemes of Old English, *Language* 37 (1961) 522–538; and On the Consonantal Phonemes of Old English, in *Philological Essays . . . in Honour of Herbert Dean Meritt*, ed. James L. Rosier, The Hague (Mouton) 1970, 16–49.

READER

the old english translation of bede's historia ecclesiastica gentis anglorum

(Ecclesiastical History of the English People)

Much of our knowledge of the life and career of the Venerable Bede comes from the autobiographical postscript which he appended to his masterpiece, the *Historia Ecclesiastica*. Here he identifies himself as

> Bēda Crīstes þīow, ond mæssepreōst þæs minstres þāra ēadigra apostola Pētrus ond Paulus þæt is æt Wīramūþon ond on Gyrwum.[1] Wæs ic ācenned on sundurlonde þæs ylcan mynstres. Mid þȳ ic wæs seofanwintre, þā wæs ic mid gīmene mīnra māga seald tō fēdanne ond tō lǣrenne þām ārwyrþan abbude Benedicte, ond Cēolferþe æfter þon. Ond siðþan ealle tīd mīnes līfes on þæs ilcan mynstres eardunge ic wæs dōnde;[2] ond ealle geornesse ic sealde tō leornien*ne*[3] ond tō smēagenne hālige gewritu. Ond betwih gehild regollices þēodscipes ond þā dæghwāmlican gīmene tō singanne on cyrcan, mē symble swēte ond wynsum wæs ðæt ic oþþe leornode oþþe lǣrde oððe write.[4]

---

[1]**ond on Gyrwum** = "and Jarrow." The *on* is part of the place name: elsewhere in the OE Bede the place is referred to as *ðǣre stōwe ðe is gecȳged on Gearwum*. Cf. *æt Hæþum*, 8/75 and n.

[2]**ealle tīd . . . ic wæs dōnde** "I passed the whole time."

[3]MS *leorniende*.

[4]Baeda famulus Christi, et presbyter monasterii beatorum apostolorum Petri et Pauli, quod est ad Uiuraemuda, et in Gyruum. Qui natus in territorio eiusdem monasterii, cum essem annorum septem, cura propinquorum datus sum educandus reuerentissimo abbati Benedicto, ac deinde Ceolfrido; cunctumque ex eo tempus uitae in eiusdem monasterii habitatione peragens, omnem meditandis scripturis operam dedi; atque inter obseruantiam disciplinae regularis, et cotidianam cantandi in ecclesia curam, semper aut discere, aut docere, aut scribere dulce habui.

He goes on to say that he was ordained a deacon at nineteen and a priest at thirty, then cites for posterity an enormous bibliography of the books he had written up to the time when he completed the *Historia Ecclesiastica* in 731. A touching and inspiring eyewitness account of his death, on May 25th four years later, is found in the brief *Epistola Cuthberti de Obitu Bedae*, written by one of his students.[5] Here we are told of the poem he composed on his deathbed and of his healthy-minded acceptance both of his past life and of his approaching death:

> Tempus est, si sic Factori meo uidetur, ut ad eum modo absolutus ex carne ueniam, qui me, quando non eram, ex nihilo formauit. Multum tempus uixi, beneque mihi pius Iudex uitam meam praeuidit.[6]

In later years a number of legends grew up to explain how Bede acquired the cognomen Venerable. One of the most entertaining is cited here in the lively version of Thomas Fuller:

> He is generally surnamed *Venerable*, but why, Authours differ therein. Some say, a Dunce-Monk, being to make his Epitaph, was *non-pluss'd* to make that *Dactyle*, which is onely of the *Quorum* in the Hexameter, and therefore at Night left the Verse thus gaping,
>
> *Hic sunt in fossa* Bedæ__________*ossa*.[7]
>
> till he had consulted with his Pillow, to fill up the *Hiatus*. But returning in the morning, an Angel (we have often heard of their Singing, see now of their Poetry) had filled up the *Chasma* with *Venerabilis*.[8]

Bede's immense learning and his expert, unaffected Latin would have been impossible without the splendid libraries with which Benedict Biscop had enriched Wearmouth and Jarrow, the sister monasteries of his foundation. Here was the mine from which Bede extracted his many books on subjects as diverse as metrics, astronomy, hagiography, meteorology and medicine. In the *Historia Ecclesiastica*, which is the most important of these works and the crowning glory of a lifetime of prolific literary activity, he displays a scientific and judicious attitude toward his sources which has earned for him the title of "the first modern historian." An important innovation is his use, for the first time in

---

[5]It is cited by Charles Plummer, *Venerabilis Baedae Opera Historica*, 2 vols. (Oxford 1896), I, clx–clxiv (and an English translation is given, I, lxxii–lxxviii). Plummer's edition of the Latin text of the *Historia Ecclesiastica*, which was for many years the best available and is accompanied by an excellent introduction and notes, has recently been superseded (at least in part) by *Bede's Ecclesiastical History of the English People*, ed. Bertram Colgrave and R. A. B. Mynors (Oxford 1969).

[6]"It is time for me, if it be His will, to return to my Maker, Who formed me, when as yet I was not, out of nothing. I have lived long, and my merciful Judge has well disposed my life" (Plummer's translation).

[7]Here in this grave are the bones of______ Bede.

[8]*The Church-History of Britain* (London 1655), p. 98 f.

any historical work—and following the suggestion of the sixth-century Scythian monk Dionysius Exiguus—of the year of Christ's incarnation as the basis of his chronological system. Like Richard Hooker, Bede was concerned "that posteritie may know we haue not loosely through silence permitted things to passe away as in a dreame," and it is due to his efforts that we know as much as we do about the history of early Anglo-Saxon England.

The popularity of Bede's history is attested by the large number of surviving MSS of the Latin text—well over 150.[9] It was early regarded as a masterpiece, and as such it was a natural choice for inclusion in King Ælfred's program of translating the "great books" of medieval Latinity into the vernacular (see p. 178). The OE version was composed in the later ninth century, probably not by the king himself, and perhaps in Mercia. It gives ample evidence of the awkwardness which frequently characterizes early efforts to write literary prose. The translator often follows his Latin original so literally that the resulting OE is highly unidiomatic, and his work is chiefly useful as showing how much cultivation OE prose, with its naturally paratactic syntax, would require before it would be capable of imitating the graceful hypotaxis of Bede's Latin. On the other hand, it is sometimes capable of a great beauty and simplicity of its own. The translator is at his best in passages of direct, straightforward narration. For a lucid introduction to the OE translation and the problems which surround it, see *PBA*, XLVIII (1962), 57–90. The most useful edition is that of Thomas Miller, *The Old English Version of Bede's Ecclesiastical History of the English People*, EETS, Original Series, 95–6 (1890–91), 110–11 (1898).

Listed below are the five MSS of the OE Bede which have survived in relatively complete form. Each is preceded by the traditional abbreviation, called a *siglum* (pl. *sigla*), which is used for purposes of quick identification and reference. Note that in four cases the siglum is derived from some distinguishing element in the description of the MS; B is derived from Benet, the old name of Corpus Christi College, Cambridge.

T = MS Tanner 10, Bodleian Library, Oxford (Ker 351); first half of the tenth century.

B = MS 41, Corpus Christi College, Cambridge (Ker 32); first half of the eleventh century.

C = MS Cotton Otho B. xi, British Museum, London (Ker 180); a Winchester MS, for the most part mid tenth century. This MS was largely destroyed in the Cottonian fire of 1731, but not before a copy (now British Museum Additional MS 43703) had been made by Laurence Nowell; this copy is known as N, and we are largely dependent upon it today for the readings of C.

O = MS 279 (II), Corpus Christi College, Oxford (Ker 354); early eleventh century.

---

[9]The Latin version printed here in the middle of the pages is based upon the Moore MS (Cambridge University Library Kk. 5. 16 [Ker 25]), which dates from about 737, only two years after Bede's death. It has been normalized to a form "which may be taken to represent fairly the Latin orthography of the eighth century" (Plummer, I, lxxxv).

Ca = MS Kk. 3. 18, University Library, Cambridge (Ker 23); a Worcester MS, second half of the eleventh century.

The relationship between the texts of these five MSS is indicated (in highly simplified fashion) by the following family tree, which is called technically a *stemma* (pl. *stemmata*):

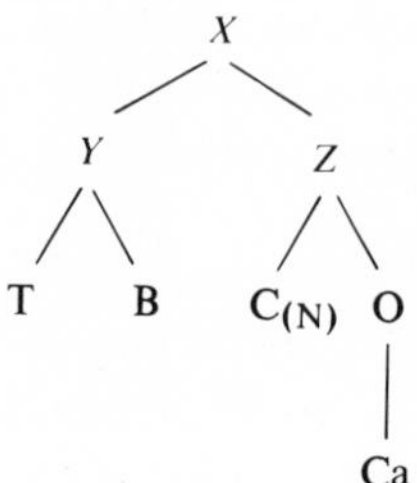

X, the translator's holograph (i.e. his original version in his own handwriting), is referred to as the archetype. It no longer exists. *Y* and *Z* are the exemplars of two subsequent branches of the text, i.e. they were the first MSS in which occurred the major textual differences now serving to distinguish T and B on the one hand from C (together with the copy N), O and Ca on the other. *Y* and *Z* are no longer extant; their existence is inferred from a study of the differences between the surviving MSS. The lines between sigla do not necessarily imply direct descent: several recopyings may have intervened between *Y* and T, for instance.

The basis of our text is T, with a large section of the first selection (where a leaf is missing from T) taken from O, and the excerpt at the beginning of this headnote taken from C.

1 / the conversion of king Eadwine of Northumbria

(Book II, Chapters IX–XI)

The Christianization of Anglo-Saxon England began in 597 with Augustine's arrival in Kent and his subsequent conversion of Æðelberht, the Kentish king. Some years later Æðelberht's daughter Æðelbeorg married Eadwine, the pagan king of Northumbria, on condition that she and her attendants be allowed to practice their Christianity at his court undisturbed. The newly consecrated bishop Paulinus accompanied her north as her chaplain in A.D. 625 and, once arrived in Northumbria, set to work zealously converting the kingdom. He discovered that in practice this would mean converting the king.

It was not long before an episode occurred which, though for a moment it threatened disaster to Paulinus' hopes, was ultimately to turn the king's mind firmly in the direction of Christianity:

Ðā wæs þȳ æfteran gēare, cwōm sum monn in Norðanhymbra mǣgðe; wæs his noma Ēomǣr. Wæs hē sended from Westseaxna cyninge, sē wæs hāten Cwichelm, þæt hē scolde Ēadwine þone cyning somed ge rīce ge līfe beneoman. Hæfde hē ond wæg mid him twīecge handseax geǣttred, þæt gif[1] sēo wund tō lȳt genihtsumode tō þæs cyninges dēaðe, þæt þæt āttor gefultmade.[2] Cwōm hē tō þām cyninge þȳ ǣrestan Eastordæge bii Deorwentan þǣre ēa, þǣr wæs þā cyninges aldorbold; þā ēode hē inn, swā swā hē his hlāfordes ǣrendo secgan scolde. Ond mid þȳ hē þā geswippre mūþe līccetende ǣrend wreahte ond lēase fleosewade, þā āstōd hē semninga ond, getogene þȳ wǣpne[3] under his scēate, rǣsde on þone cyning. Þā þæt þā Lilla geseah, se cyninges þegn him se holdesta,[4] næfde hē scyld æt honda, þæt hē þone cyning mid scyldan meahte;[5] sette þā his

---

[1]**gif** MS *gis*.

[2]**þæt þæt . . . gefultmade** "The poison might help." The first (conjunctive) *þæt* is redundant.

[3]**getogene þȳ wǣpne** Inst. absolute, translating the Lat. ablative absolute *euaginata . . . sica*.

[4]**se[1] . . . holdesta** "The thane of (the) king (who was) the most loyal to him."

[5]**mid scyldan meahte** I.e. *meahte scyldan mid*.

līchoman betweoh beforan þām stynge. Ond þurhstong[6] þone cyninges þegn ond þone cyning gewundade. Þā wæs sōna ǣghwonan mid wǣpnum ymbhēped. Hwæt þā gēna ōðerne cyninges þegn in þǣm ungerecce, sē wæs Forðhere hāten, mid þȳ mānfullan wǣpne ācwealde.[7]

The wounded Eadwine told Paulinus that if God would let him live and would grant him victory over Cwichelm, hē would adopt the Christian faith. In the military campaign which he now mounted against the West Saxons, Eadwine was entirely successful. But upon returning to Northumbria, although he had by now given up the worship of idols, he was reluctant to embrace the faith precipitantly. He insisted that Paulinus give him a complete course of instruction in Christianity. Meanwhile he discussed what action he should take with his counsellors:

ge ēac hē seolfa, mid þȳ þe hē wæs in gecynde se glēawesta mon, oft longe āna sæt swīgende mūðe, ac mid inneweardre heortan monig[8] mid hine sprecende; smēade, hwæt him sēlest tō dōnne wǣre ond hwylce ǣfæstnis him tō healdenne wǣre.[9]

[IX.]

Dǣre tīde ēac swylce þæs apostolican seðles biscop, Bonefātius pāpa, sende Ēadwini grētinge ond gewrit mid þȳ hē hine trymede tō onfōnne Crīstes lēafan. Swylce ēac wæs sum godgesprǣce ond heofonlic onwrigenis, þe him gēo sēo godcunde ārfæstnis onwrāh, þā hē wrecca wæs mid Rǣdwald, Ēastengla cyning, sēo

---

XII.

Haec quidem memoratus papa Bonifatius de salute regis Aeduini ac gentis ipsius litteris agebat. Sed et oraculum caeleste, quod illi quondam exulanti apud Redualdum

---

[6]**þurhstong** I.e. *(he) þurhstong*; similarly *wæs* (*hē*) and (*hē*) *ācwealde* in what follows. Eomær is the subject. The pronouns are omitted in slavish imitation of the Latin.

[7]Anno autem sequente uenit in prouinciam quidam sicarius uocabulo Eumer, missus a rege Occidentalium Saxonum nomine Cuichelmo, sperans se regem Aeduinum regno simul et uita priuaturum; qui habebat sicam bicipitem toxicatam; ut si ferri uulnum minus ad mortem regis sufficeret, peste iuuaretur ueneni. Peruenit autem ad regem primo die paschae iuxta amnem Deruuentionem, ubi tunc erat uilla regalis, intrauitque quasi nuntium domini sui referens; et cum simulatam legationem ore astuto uolueret, exsurrexit repente, et, euaginata sub ueste sica, impetum fecit in regem. Quod cum uideret Lilla minister regi amicissimus, non habens scutum ad manum, quo regem a nece defenderet, mox interposuit corpus suum ante ictum pungentis; sed tanta ui hostis ferrum infixit, ut per corpus militis occisi etiam regem uulneraret. Qui cum mox undique gladiis inpeteretur, in ipso tumultu etiam alium de militibus, cui nomen erat Fordheri, sica nefanda peremit.

[8]**monig** "Many (a thing);" cf. Lat. *multa*.

[9]Sed et ipse, cum esset uir natura sagacissimus, saepe diu solus residens ore quidem tacito, sed in intimis cordis multa secum conloquens, quid sibi esset faciendum, quae religio seruanda tractabat.

swīðe gefultumede his ondgit tō onfōnne ond tō ongeotonne monunge þǣre hālwendan lāre. Mid þȳ hē ðā, se biscop Paulīnus, geseah þæt hē unēaðelīce meahte ðā hēannesse þæs cynelican mōdes tō ēaðmōdnesse gecerran, *þæt* hē onfōn wolde his ǣcre hǣlo ond þǣm gerȳne þǣre līffæstan rōde Crīstes, ond hē somed fore his hǣlo (þæs cyninges), ond þǣre þēode þe hē fore wæs, ge mid worde trymenesse mid monnum wonn, *ge ēac mid ðā godcundan ārfæstnesse mid worde his gebeda won* þæt hē foreþingode, þā æt nȳhstan geleornade hē in gāste ond him onwrigen wæs hwelc onwrigenis gīu heofonlic ætēawde þǣm cyninge, þā hē wrecca wæs. Ne ylde hē hit þā leng, ac ēode sōna tō þām cyninge ond hine monade þæt hē his gehāt gefylde þæt hē in þǣre *on*wrignesse geheht, þe him ætēawed wæs, gif hē þǣre tiide

---

regem Anglorum pietas diuina reuelare dignata est, non minimum ad suscipienda uel intellegenda doctrinae monita salutaris sensum iuuit illius. Cum ergo uideret Paulinus difficulter posse sublimitatem animi regalis ad humilitatem uiae salutaris, et suscipiendum mysterium uiuificae crucis inclinari, ac pro salute illius simul et gentis, cui praeerat, et uerbo exhortationis apud homines, et apud diuinam pietatem uerbo deprecationis ageret; tandem, ut uerisimile uidetur, didicit in spiritu, quod uel quale esset oraculum regi quondam caelitus ostensum. Nec exinde distulit, quin continuo regem ammoneret explere uotum, quod in oraculo sibi exhibito se facturum promise-

---

1 f. **Đǣre . . . lēafan** Bede devotes two chapters to the text of the letters which Boniface wrote to Eadwine and Æðelbeorg; the OE translator omits them entirely. This is his usual practice, and accounts for the fact that the chapter-numbers of the Lat. and OE versions frequently do not correspond.

1 **Đǣre tīde** Temporal dat.

Bonefātius Boniface V (consecrated A.D. 619).

4 **sēo** "Which," with the gender of the closest member (*onwrigenis*) of its compound antecedent.

7 **þæt** "So that." MS N has *ond þæt*, a reading which reproduces the syntactic structure of the Latin more closely by making the *þæt*-clause parallel to the phrase *tō ēaðmōdnesse*.

8 **ond hē** I.e. *ond mid þȳ hē þā*, introducing the second of the two coordinated "when" clauses which are correlative to the "then" clause beginning with *þā* in l. 11. Correlation of *mid þȳ* "when" and *þā* "then" occurs frequently in this text; cf. ll. 16 ff.

9 **þæs cyninges** This explanatory phrase is necessitated by the separation of *his* and its antecedent (*hē*—i.e. Eadwine—in l. 7), and the intervention between them of *hē* (i.e. Paulinus) in l. 8.

9 f. **mid . . . mid . . . mid . . . mid** "By means of . . . with . . . with . . . by means of," somewhat awkwardly reproducing a chiasmus in the Lat.

trymnesse, gebeda Descriptive gen.; similarly *þisses gemetes* in l. 16.

11 **þæt hē foreþingode** The purpose clause is tacked on to supply the sense of intercession lacking in the word *gebeda*; cf. Lat. *uerbo deprecationis ageret*. *Foreþingode* may well be a scribal error, since intransitive use of this verb is highly suspicious and B N O Ca agree in reading *fore hīe þingade* (O).

12 **onwrigenis gīu heofonlic** I.e. *heofonlic onwrigenis gīu*; the actual word order imitates the Lat.

13 **hit** I.e. action based upon this new information.

14 **þæt . . . gif** The translator has failed to reproduce the sense of Lat. *se facturum*. His meaning would have been clearer had he written: *þæt hē, in þǣre onwrigenesse þe him ætēawed wæs, geheht þæt hē gefyllan wolde gif* etc.

tiide Cf. 2/61 n.

ærmþa biswicade ond tō hēannisse cynerīces becwōme.

Wæs þis godgesprǣce ond þēos onwrigenis þisses gemetes: Mid þȳ hine ēhte Æðelfrið, sē ðe ǣr him cyning wæs, ond þurh missenlice stōwe hē monigra gēara tīde flȳma wæs, ðā gesōhte hē æt nȳhstan ond cwōm tō Rǣdwolde, Ēastengla cyninge, ond hine bæd þæt hē his līf gescylde wið swā micles ēhteres sǣtingum ond him feorhyrde wǣre. Ond hē lustlīce hine onfēng ond him geheht þæt hē swā dōn wolde swā hē hine bæd. Æfter þon, þā Æþelfrið se cyning hine þǣr geāhsode, þæt hē mid Rǣdwold þone cyning wæs, þā sende hē sōna ǣrendwrecan tō him ond micel feoh wið þon ðe hē hine ofslōge oðþe him tō cwale āgēfe; ne hwæðre ōwiht on þon fromade. Sende hē eft æfteran sīðe ǣrendwrecan; synde þriddan sīða ond māran gife micle ond feoh þonne hē him ǣr sende wið his cwale, ond hēt ēac him onbēodan þæt hē hine wolde mid fyrde tō gefeohte gesēcan gif hē his word ond his gife forhogode. Þā wæs his mōd ǣghwæðer ge mid þǣm bēotungum gebrēged ge mid þǣm geofum gewemmed, þæt hē geþafode þæs cyninges bēne ond gehēt þæt hē Ēadwine ofslōge oðþe fēondum tō cwale gēfe. Þā wæs sum cyninges þegn, his

---

rat, si temporis illius erumnis exemtus ad regni fastigia perueniret.

Erat autem oraculum huiusmodi. Cum persequente illum Aedilfrido, qui ante eum regnauit, per diuersa occultus loca uel regna multo annorum tempore profugus uagaretur, tandem uenit ad Redualdum obsecrans, ut uitam suam a tanti persecutoris insidiis tutando seruaret; qui libenter eum excipiens, promisit se, quae petebatur, esse facturum. At postquam Aedilfrid in hac eum prouincia apparuisse, et apud regem illius familiariter cum sociis habitare cognouit, misit nuntios, qui Redualdo pecuniam multam pro nece eius offerrent; neque aliquid profecit. Misit secundo, misit tertio, et copiosiora argenti dona offerens, et bellum insuper illi, si contemneretur, indicens. Qui uel minis fractus, uel corruptus muneribus, cessit deprecanti, et siue occidere se Aeduinum, seu legatariis tradere promisit. Quod ubi fidissimus quidam amicus illius

---

17 **Æðelfrið** King of Bernicia, 593–616. His father Æðelric had gained control of the neighboring kingdom of Deira in 588 upon the death of its ruler Ælle. Ælle's three-year-old son Eadwine was thereby driven into an exile of almost thirty years. During this time—which was spent in Wales, Mercia and East Anglia—he had to be continually on guard against the machinations of Æðelfrið, who naturally wanted no heir of Ælle's to contest his title to the throne of Deira. The flashback which begins with this sentence is full of the melancholia of exile, a theme dear to the Anglo-Saxon heart.

18 **tīde** Acc. of duration (cf. Lat. dat. *tempore*).

Rǣdwolde Rædwald died c624; the events narrated here as taking place at his court probably occurred in 616.

20 **him**[1] "To him (Eadwine)."

22 **him** Rædwald. The student will not have difficulty figuring out the referents of the following pronouns if he keeps the situation and relative interests of the three protagonists firmly in mind.

23 **him** Ind. object of *āgēfe* and referring to Æðelfrið (or his messengers).

tō "For purposes of"; similarly in ll. 26, 29.

24 **on þon** "By that." Æðelfrið is the (unexpressed) subject of *fromade*.

sīða Acc. sg. MSS B N O Ca have *sīðe*.

24 f. **. . . cwale** I.e. *ond (sende), wið his cwale, micle māran gife ond feoh þonne hē him ǣr sende.*

29 **his** Eadwine's.

frēond se getrēowesta, þe ðās þing gehȳrde ond onget. Þā ēode hē tō his inne, þǣr hē inne rēstan wolde—wæs foreweard niht—ond hine ācēgde ūt ond him sægde ond cȳðde hū him mon emb dōn wolde. Cwæð him þā gȳt tō: "Gif ðū wilt, in þās seolfan tīd ic þē ālǣdo of þisse mǣgðe ond in þā stōwe ālǣde þǣr þē nǣfre Rǣdwald ne Æðelfrið gemētan magon." Cwæð hē tō him: "On þonce mē synd þīn word ond þīn lufo, ond hwæðre ne mæg ic þæt dōn þæt þū mē lǣrest, þæt ic ǣrest þā wǣre forlǣte, þe ic tō swā miclum cyninge nōm, mid þȳ hē mē nōht yfeles dyde ne lāðes ætēawde. Ac gif ic dēað þrōwian sceal, lēofre mē is þæt hē mec tō dēaðe sylle þonne unæðelra mon. Oððe lā, hwider mæg ic nū leng flēon? Monigra gēara tīda ofer ealle Breotone ic flȳma wæs, þæt ic mē his hete bearh ond warenode." Þā ēode sē his frēond onweg from him ond hē Ēadwini āna þǣr ūte gewunade: sæt swīðe unrōt on stāne beforan þǣre healle ond ongon mid monegum hǣtum his geþōhta swenced bēon, ond ne wiste hwider hē ēode oððe hwæt him sēlest tō dōnne wǣre.

Mid þȳ hē þā longe swīgendum nearonissum his mōdes ond mid þȳ blindan fȳre soden wæs, þā geseah hē semninga on midre niht sumne mon wið his gongan uncūþes ondwlitan ond uncūðes gegyrlan. Þā hē ðā tō him cwōm, þā wæs hē forht

---

animaduertit, intrauit cubiculum, quo dormire disponebat, erat enim prima hora noctis, et euocatum foras, quid erga eum agere rex promisisset, edocuit, et insuper adiecit: "Si ergo uis, hac ipsa hora educam te de hac prouincia, et ea in loca introducam, ubi numquam te uel Reduald, uel Aedilfrid inuenire ualeant." Qui ait: "Gratias quidem ago beneuolentiae tuae; non tamen hoc facere possum, quod suggeris, ut pactum, quod cum tanto rege inii, ipse primus irritum faciam, cum ille mihi nil mali fecerit, nil adhuc inimicitiarum intulerit. Quin potius, si moriturus sum, ille me magis quam ignobilior quisque morti tradat. Quo enim nunc fugiam, qui per omnes Brittaniae prouincias tot annorum temporumque curriculis uagabundus hostium uitabam insidias?" Abeunte igitur amico, remansit Aeduini solus foris, residensque mestus ante palatium, multis coepit cogitationum aestibus affici, quid ageret, quoue pedem uerteret, nescius.

Cumque diu tacitis mentis angoribus, et caeco carperetur igni, uidit subito intempesta nocte silentio adpropinquantem sibi hominem uultus habitusque incogniti; quem uidens, ut ignotum et inopinatum, non parum expauit. At ille accedens salutauit

---

31 **inne** The other MSS have *hine*, which is undoubtedly right. T's *inne* is no doubt influenced by *inne* three words before.

32 **emb, tō** Postpositions (governing *him*[1,2] respectively).

mon Note this impersonal rendering of Lat. *rex*.

35 **ǣrest** I.e. before Rǣdwald.

37 **lēofre mē is** "(It) is preferable to me."

39 **þæt** Introducing a result clause: "(in such a way) that."

his hete "Against his hate."

41 **mid monegum hǣtum his geþōhta** "With many a feverish thought" (Miller). The oddity of the passage, translated literally, results from slavish imitation of the Lat.

43 f. **swīgendum . . . fȳre** Note the author's freedom to express instrumentality either with or without a preposition.

The images here are traditional poetic images for anxiety and are often found associated in OE poetry with the anxiety of exile; cf. esp. 20/7a, 10b–11a. On the other hand the striking phrase *mid þȳ blindan fȳre soden wæs* (Lat. *caeco carperetur igni*) is Vergilian: cf. *Aeneid* IV.2.

44 **wið his** I.e. *tōweard him*.

45 **uncūþes . . . gegyrlan** Descriptive gen., complement of *mon*.

geworden. Þā ēode hē tō him, grētte hine, ond frægn for hwon hē in þǣre tīde þe ōðre men slēpon ond reston āna swā unrōt on stāne wæccende sǣte. Đā frægn hē hine hwæt þæs tō him lumpe, hwæðer hē wacode þe slēpe ond hwæðer hē þe ūte þe inne wǣre. Đā ondswarade hē ond him tō cwæð: "Ne tala þū mē þæt ic ne cunne þone intingan þīnre unrōtnisse ond þīnre wæcene ond *ānlē*pnesse þīnes seðles. Ac ic cūðlīce wāt ge hwæt þū eart ge for hwon þū gnornast ond hwylc tōweard yfel þū þē in n*ēa*hnesse forhtast. Ac gesaga mē hwylce mēde þū wille syllan þām men—gif hwylc sȳ—þætte þec from þissum nearonessum ālȳse ond Rǣdwalde on mōd beswāpe þæt hē nōht lāðes ne gedō, ne þec þīnum fēondum tō cwale āgife?" Þā ondswarede ond cwæð þæt hē ealle ðā gōd þe hē meahte for mēde þislicre fremsumnesse syllan wolde. Þā *æ*tēcte hē þā gȳt his gesprec ond cwæð: "Ond nū gif hē ðē ēac, ādwǣsctum þīnum fēondum, in sōðe tōweard cynerīce gehāteð, swā ðæt nales þæt ān ealle þīne yldran ac ēac ealle cyningas, þā ðe in Breotone wǣron ǣr, þū in meahte ond in rīce feor oferstīgest?" Þā wæs hē Ēadwine baldra geworden in þǣre frignesse ond sōna gehēt, sē ðe him swā micle fremsumnesse forgēfe, þæt hē him þæs wolde wyrðelice þoncunce dōn. Cwæð hē þriddan sīðe tō him, sē þe him wið spræc: "Ono gif se mon, sē ðe þyslice gife ond swā micle sōðlīce þē tōwearde

---

eum, et interrogauit, quare illa hora, ceteris quiescentibus, et alto sopore pressis, solus ipse mestus in lapide peruigil sederet. At ille uicissim sciscitabatur, quid ad eum pertineret, utrum ipse intus an foris noctem transigeret. Qui respondens ait: "Ne me aestimes tuae mestitiae et insomniorum, et forinsecae et solitariae sessionis causam nescire; scio enim certissime qui es, et quare meres, et quae uentura tibi in proximo mala formidas. Sed dicito mihi, quid mercedis dare uelis ei, siqui sit, qui his te meroribus absoluat, et Redualdo suadeat, ut nec ipse tibi aliquid mali faciat, nec tuis te hostibus perimendum tradat." Qui cum se omnia, quae posset, huic tali pro mercede beneficii daturum esse responderet, adiecit ille: "Quod si etiam regem te futurum exstinctis hostibus in ueritate promittat, ita ut non solum omnes tuos progenitores, sed et omnes, qui ante te reges in gente Anglorum fuerant, potestate transcendas?" At Aeduini constantior interrogando factus, non dubitauit promittere, quin ei, qui tanta sibi beneficia donaret, dignis ipse gratiarum actionibus responderet. Tum ille tertio: "Si autem," inquit, "is, qui tibi tanta taliaque dona ueraciter aduentura praedixerit,

---

46 **þe** "In which" (see l. 155 n.).

48 **hwæt þæs** "How much of that," lit. "what of that," *þæs* being partitive gen. (cf. 8/26 n.).

50 **seðles** The other MSS read *ūtsetles* here.

53 f. **ond . . . þæt** "And sweep into Rædwald's mind (the idea) that" etc.; *Rǣdwalde* is possessive dat. and the *þæt*-clause is the d.o. of *beswāpe*.

55 **ondswarede** Sc. *hē*.

55 f. **for . . . fremsumnesse** "As (the) reward of such a favor."

57 **ādwǣsctum þīnum fēondum** Dat. absolute, reproducing an ablative absolute in the Lat. (*exstinctis hostibus*). The construction is not native to OE.

58 **nales þæt ān** "Not only."

60 **sē . . . forgēfe** A dependent clause which modifies *him*[1] in l. 61 and which would normally be placed after the clause containing this antecedent (cf. the arrangement *him . . . sē* in l. 66 f.); it is displaced, here, because of the translator's desire to reproduce the idea-order of the Lat.

61 **þæs** "In return for that"; neuter, since the antecedent is not so much *fremsumnes* as the idea of giving *fremsumnes*.

62 ff. **sē . . . þonne** Word order and phrasing: *sē ðe forecwið | þyslice ond swā*

forecwið, ond ēac swylce geþeahte þīnre hǣlo ond betran līfes ond nyttran þē ætēawan mæg, þonne ǣnig þīnra māga oðþe yldrena ǣfre gehȳrde—cwist þū hwæðer þū his þā hālwendan monunge onfōn wille ond him hēarsum bēon?" Þā ne ˌelde hē Ēadwini ōwiht, ac sōna gehēt þæt hē wolde in eallum þingum him hēarsum bēon ond his lāre lustlīce onfōn, sē þe hine from swā monegum ermþum ond tēonum generede ond tō hēanisse cynerīces forðgelǣdde. Þā hē ðā þisse ondsware onfēng, sē þe mid hine spræc, þā instæpe sette hē mid þā swīðron hond him on ðæt hēafod ond þus cwæð: "Þonne þis tācen þislic þē tō cyme, þonne gemyne þū þās tīde uncres gespreces ond ne yld þū þæt þū þā þing gefylle þe ðū mē nū gehēte." Þā hē ðā þās word spræc, þā ne wiste hē semninga hwǣr hē cwōm; wolde þæt hē in þon ongēte þæt þæt mon ne wæs, sē ðe him ætēawde, ac þætte þæt gāst wæs.

Ond mid þȳ hē ðā, se geonga æþeling, āna þǣr þā gȳt sæt ond wæs swīðe gefēonde bī þǣre frōfre þe him gehāten wæs, ac hwæðre sorgende mōde geornlīce þōhte hwæt sē wǣre oðþe hwonan hē cwōme, sē ðās þing tō him sprecende wæs, þā cōm eft tō him se foresprecena his frēond ond mid blīðe ondwleotan hine hālette ond grētte ond þus cwæð: "Ārīs, gong in, gerest þīnne līchoman ond þīn mōd būton sorgum, for ðon þæs cyninges heorte is oncerred: ne wile hē ðē ōwiht lāðes gedōn,

---

etiam consilium tibi tuae salutis ac uitae melius atque utilius, quam aliquis de tuis parentibus aut cognatis umquam audiuit, ostendere potuerit, num ei obtemperare, et monita eius salutaria suscipere consentis?" Nec distulit Æduini, quin continuo polliceretur in omnibus se secuturum doctrinam illius, qui se tot ac tantis calamitatibus ereptum, ad regni apicem proueheret. Quo accepto responso, confestim is, qui loquebatur cum eo, inposuit dexteram suam capiti eius dicens: "Cum hoc ergo tibi signum aduenerit, memento huius temporis ac loquellae nostrae, et ea, quae nunc promittis, adimplere ne differas." Et his dictis, ut ferunt, repente disparuit, ut intellegeret non hominem esse, qui sibi apparuisset, sed spiritum.

Et cum regius iuuenis solus adhuc ibidem sederet, gauisus quidem de conlata sibi consolatione, sed multum sollicitus, ac mente sedula cogitans, quis esset ille, uel unde ueniret, qui haec sibi loqueretur, uenit ad eum praefatus amicus illius, laetoque uultu salutans eum: "Surge," inquit, "intra, et sopitis ac relictis curarum anxietatibus, quieti membra simul et animum conpone, quia mutatum est cor regis, nec tibi aliquid mali

---

micle gife | sōðlīce tōwearde þē, | ond ēac swylce mæg ætēawan þē | geþeahte þīnre hǣlo ond betran ond nyttran līfes | þonne etc.

63 **geþeahte þīnre hǣlo** An unidiomatic reproduction of the Lat. objective gen. (*consilium tuae salutis*). Translate: "a plan for achieving your salvation."

69 **mid²** Cf. l. 102.

him Possessive dat.

70 **þislic** "In this manner, thus." When used predicatively the adj. *þyslic*, though agreeing with its noun in case and number, often seems to function syntactically almost as an adv., equivalent in meaning to *þus*.

72 **he²** Eadwine.

hwǣr hē cwōm "Where he [Eadwine's visitant] disappeared to"; cf. 19/92.

wolde Sc. *hē* (the visitant).

74 **wæs . . . gefēonde** This verbal periphrasis was often employed mechanically by Anglo-Saxons—and without any intention of emphasizing duration—to translate Lat. present participles and deponent verbs. Further examples in this selection are l. 76 *sprecende wæs* (*loqueretur*), l. 101 *wæs . . . ingongende* (*ingrediens*), l. 118 f. *wæs frignende* (*sciscitabatur*), l. 167 *wæs . . . gefēonde* (*gauisus*).

ac hē mā wile his trēowa ond his gehāt wið þē gehealdan ond þē feorhhyrde bēon." Sægde him þā: "Æfter þon þæt se cyning his geþōht, bī ðǣm þe ic ðē ǣr sǣde, þǣre cwēne in dēagolnesse onwrēah, ðā onwende hēo hine from þǣre yflan inngehygde his mōdes, lǣrde hine ond monade þætte þæt nǣnige þinga gedafenode swā æðelum cyninge ond swā geþungennum þæt hē sceolde his frēond þone betstan, in neede gesetum, in gold bebycgan ond his trēowe for fēagītsunge ond -lufan forlēosan, sēo wǣre dēorwyrð*re* eallum māðmum." Hwæ*t* sculon wē þæs nū mā secgan? Dyde se cyning swā hit ǣr cweden wæs, nales þæt ān þæt hē ðone wreccan tō cwale ne gesealde, ac ēac swylce him gefultumade þæt hē tō rīce becwōm. For þon sōna siðþan þā ǣrendwrecan hām cerdon þe his cwale ǣrendodon, þā gebēon Rǣdwald his fyrd ond micel weorod gesomnade tō gewinnenne wið Æþelfriðe. Þā fōr hē him tōgegnes ungelīce weorode, for þon hē ne wolde him fyrst ālȳfan þæt hē mōste his weorod eal gesomnian. Ðā gefōron hēo tōsomne ond gefuhton on gemǣre Mercna þēode æt ēastdǣle þǣre ēa þe is Īdle nemned, ond þǣr mon Æðelfrið þone cyning slōg. Swylce ēac in ðǣm ilcan gefeohte mon slōh Rǣdwoldes sunu, sē wæs hāten Regenhere. Ond swā Ēadwine æfter þām godgesprēce, þe hē ǣr onfēng, nales þæt ān þæt hē him þā sǣtunge gewearonode þæs unholdan cyninges, ac ēac swylce æfter his slege him in þæs rīces wuldor æfterfylgde.

---

facere, sed fidem potius pollicitam seruare disponit; postquam enim cogitationem suam, de qua tibi ante dixi, reginae in secreto reuelauit, reuocauit eum illa ab intentione, ammonens, quia nulla ratione conueniat tanto regi amicum suum optimum in necessitate positum auro uendere, immo fidem suam, quae omnibus ornamentis pretiosior est, amore pecuniae perdere." Quid plura? Fecit rex, ut dictum est; nec solum exulem nuntiis hostilibus non tradidit, sed etiam eum, ut in regnum perueniret, adiuuit. Nam mox redeuntibus domum nuntiis, exercitum ad debellandum Aedilfridum colligit copiosum, eumque sibi occurrentem cum exercitu multum inpari (non enim dederat illi spatium, quo totum suum congregaret atque adunaret exercitum), occidit in finibus gentis Merciorum ad orientalem plagam amnis, qui uocatur Idlæ; in quo certamine et filius Redualdi, uocabulo Rægenheri, occisus est. Ac sic Aeduini iuxta oraculum, quod acceperat, non tantum regis sibi infesti insidias uitauit, uerum etiam eidem peremto in regni gloriam successit.

---

80 **mā** "Rather" (Lat. *potius*).

81 **bī ðǣm þe** Ca has the same reading (*big þām ðe*). B, O and apparently N (whose text is corrupt here) agree in omitting the *þe*, which obviously makes better sense. Cf. Lat. *de qua*.

83 **nǣnige þinga** "By no means" (lit. "by none of things").

84 f. **in neede gesetum** "Situated (as he was) in (desperate) need." Either this is a dat. absolute (where there is no corresponding ablative absolute in the Lat.), or else *gesetum* = *gesetne*, with inadvertent reproduction of the Lat. acc. sg. masc. ending of *positum*. On the spelling *neede* cf. 2/61 n.

85 **in gold** "For gold."

86 **eallum māðmum** B has *þonne ealle mādmas*, an equivalent way of saying the same thing.

þæs Gen. of respect.

90 **hē** Æðelfrið. In the next line, *he*[1] is Rædwald.

91 **ungelīce weorode** Instrumental of accompaniment ("comitative instrumental"). *Ungelīce* translates Lat. *multum inpari* "greatly unequal."

93 **Īdle** A tributary of the Trent. This battle was fought in 616.

95 **æfter** "In accordance with."

Mid þȳ hē þā, Paulīnus se biscop, Godes word bodade ond lǣrde, ond se cyning elde þā gȳt tō gelȳfanne ond þurh sume tīde—swā swā wē ǣr cwǣdon—gelimplicum āna sæt ond geornlīce mid him seolfum smēade ond þōhte hwæt him sēlest tō dōnne wǣre, þā wæs sume dæge se Godes wer ingongende tō him, þǣr hē āna sæt, ond sette his þā swīðran hond him on þæt hēafod ond hine āhsode hwæðer hē þæt tācen ongytan meahte. Þā oncnēow hē hit sōna sweotole ond wæs swīðe forht geworden ond him tō fōtum fēoll, ond hine se Godes monn ūp hōf ond him cūðlīce tō spræc ond þus cwæð: "Ono hwæt, þū nū hafast þurh Godes gife þīnra fēonda hond beswicade, þā ðū ðē ondrēde, ond þū þurh his sylene ond gife þǣm rīce onfēnge þe ðū wilnadest. Ac gemyne nū þæt þū þæt þridde gelǣstest þæt þū gehēte, þæt þū onfō his gelēafan ond his bebodu healde, sē ðe þē from wīlwendlecum earfeðum generede ond ēac in āre wīlwendlices rīces āhōf. Ond gif ðū forð his willan hēarsum bēon wilt, þone hē þurh mē bodað ond lǣreð, hē þonne þē ēac from tintregum genereð ēcra yfela, ond þec dǣlneomende gedēð mid him þæs ēcan rīces in heofonum."||

[X.]

Þā se cyning þā þās word gehȳrde, þā andswarode hē him and cwæð þæt hē ǣghwæþer ge wolde ge sceolde þām gelēafan onfōn þe hē lǣrde; cwæð hwæþere, þæt hē wolde *mid* his frēondum and mid his wytum gesprec and geþeaht habban,

---

Cum ergo praedicante uerbum Dei Paulino rex credere differret, et per aliquod tempus, ut diximus, horis conpetentibus solitarius sederet, quid agendum sibi esset, quae religio sequenda, sedulus secum ipse scrutari consuesset, ingrediens ad eum quadam die uir Dei, inposuit dexteram capiti eius et, an hoc signum agnosceret, requisiuit. Qui cum tremens ad pedes eius procidere uellet, leuauit eum, et quasi familiari uoce affatus. "Ecce," inquit, "hostium manus, quos timuisti, Domino donante euasisti; ecce regnum, quod desiderasti, ipso largiente percepisti. Memento, ut tertium, quod promisisti, facere ne differas, suscipiendo fidem eius, et praecepta seruando, qui te et a temporalibus aduersis eripiens, temporalis regni honore sublimauit; et si deinceps uoluntati eius, quam per me tibi praedicat, obsecundare uolueris, etiam a perpetuis malorum tormentis te liberans, aeterni secum regni in caelis faciet esse participem."

XIII.

Quibus auditis, rex suscipere quidem se fidem, quam docebat, et uelle et debere respondebat. Uerum adhuc cum amicis principibus et consiliariis suis sese de hoc

---

98 **Mid þȳ . . . þā** Correlative with *þā* in l. 101.

99 **þurh sume tīde** "For a certain period."

99 f. **gelimplicum** Sc. *tīdum*, "at convenient times" (Lat. *horis conpetentibus*); cf. 2/20.

101 **wǣre** After this word the other MSS have *and hwylc ǣfæstnes him tō healdanne wǣre* (O), corresponding to Lat. *quae religio sequenda*. N reads *æfternes* instead of *ǣfæstnes*.

wæs . . . ingongende Cf. l. 74 *wæs . . . gefēonde* and n.

sume dæge Temporal instrumental.

106 **þā** The antecedent is *þīnra fēonda*.

113–149 **Þā . . . wīg-** A leaf is lost from T here; the text follows O.

116 **þæt¹, þæt³** Translate: "so that . . . then."

þæt gif hī mid hine þæt geþafian woldan, þæt hī ealle ætsomne on līfes willan Crīste gehālgade wǣran. Þā dyde se cyning swā swā hē cwæð, and se bisceop þæt geþafade. Þā hæfde hē gesprec and geþeaht mid his witum, and syndriglīce wæs fram him eallum frignende hwylc him þūhte and gesawen wǣre þēos nīwe lār and þǣre godcundnesse bīgong þe þǣr lǣred wæs.

Him þā andswarode his ealdorbisceop, Cēfi wæs hāten: "Geseoh þū, cyning, hwelc þēos lār sīe þe ūs nū bodad is. Ic ðē sōðlīce andette þæt ic cūðlīce geleornad hæbbe, þæt eallinga nāwiht mægenes ne nyttnesse hafað sīo ǣfæstnes þe wē oð ðis hæfdon and beēodon. For ðon nǣnig þīnra þegna nēodlīcor ne gelustfullīcor hine underþēodde tō ūra goda bīgange þonne ic; and nōht þon lǣs monige syndon, þā þe māran gefe and fremsumnesse æt þē onfēngon þonne ic and on eallum þingum māran gesynto hæfdon. Hwæt ic wāt, gif ūre godo ǣnige mihte hæfdon, þonne woldan hīe mē mā fultumian, for þon ic him geornlīcor þēodde and hȳrde. For þon mē þynceð wīslic, gif þū gesēo þā þing beteran and strangran þe ūs nīwan bodad syndon, þæt wē þām onfōn."

Þæs wordum ōþer cyninges wita and ealdormann geþafunge sealde, and tō þǣre sprǣce fēng and þus cwæð: "Þyslic mē is gesewen, þū cyning, þis andwearde līf manna on eorðan, tō wiðmetenesse þǣre tīde þe ūs uncūð is, swālic swā þū æt

---

conlaturum esse dicebat, ut, si et illi eadem cum illo sentire uellent, omnes pariter in fonte uitae Christo consecrarentur. Et adnuente Paulino, fecit, ut dixerat. Habito enim cum sapientibus consilio, sciscitabatur singillatim ab omnibus, qualis sibi doctrina haec eatenus inaudita, et nouus diuinitatis, qui praedicabatur, cultus uideretur.

Cui primus pontificum ipsius Coifi continuo respondit: "Tu uide, rex, quale sit hoc, quod nobis modo praedicatur; ego autem tibi uerissime, quod certum didici, profiteor, quia nihil omnino uirtutis habet, nihil utilitatis religio illa, quam hucusque tenuimus. Nullus enim tuorum studiosius quam ego culturae deorum nostrorum se subdidit; et nihilominus multi sunt, qui ampliora a te beneficia quam ego, et maiores accipiunt dignitates, magisque prosperantur in omnibus, quae agenda uel adquirenda disponunt. Si autem dii aliquid ualerent, me potius iuuare uellent, qui illis inpensius seruire curaui. Unde restat, ut si ea, quae nunc nobis noua praedicantur, meliora esse et fortiora, habita examinatione perspexeris, absque ullo cunctamine suscipere illa festinemus."

Cuius suasioni uerbisque prudentibus alius optimatum regis tribuens assensum, continuo subdidit: "Talis," inquiens, "mihi uidetur, rex, uita hominum praesens in terris, ad conparationem eius, quod nobis incertum est, temporis, quale cum te resi-

---

116 **woldan** Subjunctive; similarly *wǣran* in the next line.

117 **Crīste** In apposition to **willan.**

119 **þūhte and gesawen wǣre** *Gesawen wǣre* (a Latinism; again in l. 132) is synonymous with *þūhte*, and both are used to translate *uideretur*. The tradition of translating a Latin word by a pair of English synonyms lasted well into the Renaissance. Other doublets in this text: l. 124 *hæfdon and beēodon* (for Lat. *tenuimus*); *nēodlīcor ne gelustfullīcor* (for Lat. *studiosius*).

121 **Cēfi wæs hāten** "(Who) was called Cefi": zero correlation.

122 **þæt** "That which" (Lat. *quod*).

131 **Þæs wordum** "To his words."

132 f. **Þyslic . . . swālic swā** In Bede's Latin, life is *talis . . . quale cum . . . unus passerum domum . . . peruolauerit*, "such a thing as when a sparrow traverses a hall." In the OE it is *þyslic . . . swālic swā þū . . . sitte*, "such a thing, as if you should be sitting" etc.

The difficulty of attempting to reproduce in OE the correlation *talis . . .*

THE FLIGHT OF A SPARROW. Oxford, Corpus Christi College, MS *279 (II)*, fol. 18r.
(See p. 107 and cf. 1/127–144)

swǣsendum sitte mid þīnum ealdormannum and þegnum on wintertīde, and sīe fȳr onǣlæd and þīn heall gewyrmed, and hit rīne and snīwe and styrme ūte; cume ān spearwa and hrædlīce þæt hūs þurhflēo, cume þurh ōþre duru in, þurh ōþre ūt gewīte. Hwæt, hē on þā tīd þe hē inne bið ne bið hrine*n* mid ðȳ storme þæs wintres, ac þæt bið ān ēagan bryhtm and þæt lǣsste fæc, ac hē sōna of wintra on þone winter eft cymeð. Swā þonne þis monna līf tō medmiclum fæce ætȳweð; hwæt þǣr foregange oððe hwæt þǣr eftfylge, wē ne cunnun. For þon gif þēos nīwe lār ōwiht cūðlicre and gerisenlicre brenge, þæs weorþe is þæt wē þǣre fylgen." Þeossum wordum gelīcum ōðre aldormen and þæs cyninges geþeahteras sprǣcan.

Þā gēn tōætȳhte Cǣfi and cwæð þæt hē wolde Paulīnus þone bisceop geornlīcor gehȳran be þām Gode sprecende, þām þe hē bodade. Þā hēt se cyning swā dōn. Þā hē þā his word gehȳrde, þā clypode hē and þus cwæð: "Geare ic þæt ongeat, þæt

---

dente ad caenam cum ducibus ac ministris tuis tempore brumali, accenso quidem foco in medio, et calido effecto caenaculo, furentibus autem foris per omnia turbinibus hiemalium pluuiarum uel niuium, adueniens unus passerum domum citissime peruolauerit; qui cum per unum ostium ingrediens, mox per aliud exierit. Ipso quidem tempore, quo intus est, hiemis tempestate non tangitur, sed tamen paruissimo spatio serenitatis ad momentum excurso, mox de hieme in hiemem regrediens, tuis oculis elabitur. Ita haec uita hominum ad modicum apparet; quid autem sequatur, quidue praecesserit, prorsus ignoramus. Unde si haec noua doctrina certius aliquid attulit, merito esse sequenda uidetur." His similia et ceteri maiores natu ac regis consiliarii diuinitus admoniti prosequebantur.

Adiecit autem Coifi, quia uellet ipsum Paulinum diligentius audire de Deo, quem praedicabat, uerbum facientem. Quod cum iubente rege faceret, exclamauit auditis eius sermonibus dicens: "Iam olim intellexeram nihil esse, quod colebamus; quia

---

quale cum seems to have given scribes and editors trouble. Our MS (O) reads *swa lic swa*, with *a*[1] subsequently erased. (Did the eraser intend his *sw lic swa* to represent *swilc swā*? This assumption must underlie Miller's emendation *swylc swā*.) B has simply *swylc* here, N *swa ic swa*, Ca *swa gelíc swa*. Mossé emends to *swylce*.

137 **þe** "In which" (cf. l. 155 n.).

hrinen "Touched": thus B, correctly reproducing Lat. *tangitur*. N and Ca have *rīned* "rained upon." The scribe of our MS (O) originally wrote the latter, then inserted an *h* before the *r*, but neglected to correct *d* to *n* (or else assumed a weak past participle *hrīned* of *hrīnan*). The erroneous reading *rīned* was no doubt originally caused by the occurrence of this verb a few lines earlier (l. 135).

138 **ac**[2] "For."

139 **tō medmiclum fæce ætȳweð** "Appears for a small space of time" (cf. Lat. *ad modicum apparet*).

141 **þæs . . . fylgen** "(Then it) is worthy of this, that we should adopt it."

141 f. **þeossum wordum gelīcum** "In words similar to these" (Lat. *his similia*).

144 **sprecende** I.e. *sprecendne*; present participles often remain uninflected, especially when remote from their nouns (here *þone bisceop*).

þām þe More regular would be *þone þe* (or simply *þe*). The relative pronoun is not inflected here as demanded by the syntax of the clause to which it belongs, but has assumed the case of its antecedent.

ðæt nōwiht wæs þæt wē beēodan, for þon swā micle swā ic geornlīcor on þām bīgange þæt sylfe sōð sōhte, swā ic hit lǣs mētte. Nū þonne ic openlīce ondette þæt on þysse lāre þæt sylfe sōð scīneð þæt ūs mæg þā gyfe syllan ēcre ēadignesse and ēces līfes hǣlo. For þon ic þonne nū lǣre, cyning, þæt þæt templ and þā wīg||bedo, þā ð*e* wē būton wæstmum ǣnigre nytnisse hālgodon, þæt wē þā hraþe forlēosen ond fȳre forbærne." Ono hwæt, hē þā wæs, se cyning, openlīce ondette þām biscope ond him eallum þæt hē wolde fæstlīce þām dēofolgildum wiðsacan ond Crīstes gelēafan onfōn. Mid þȳ þe hē ðā, se cyning, from þǣm foresprecenan biscope sōhte ond āhsode heora hālignesse þe hēo ǣr biēodon, hwā ðā wīgbed ond þā hergas þāra dēofolgilda—mid heora heowum þe hēo ymbsette wǣron—hēo ǣrest āīdligan

---

uidelicet, quanto studiosius in eo cultu ueritatem quaerebam, tanto minus inueniebam. Nunc autem aperte profiteor, quia in hac praedicatione ueritas claret illa, quae nobis uitae, salutis, et beatitudinis aeternae dona ualet tribuere. Unde suggero, rex, ut templa et altaria, quae sine fructu utilitatis sacrauimus, ocius anathemati et igni contradamus." Quid plura? praebuit palam adsensum euangelizanti beato Paulino rex, et, abrenuntiata idolatria, fidem se Christi suscipere confessus est. Cumque a praefato pontifice sacrorum suorum quaereret, quis aras et fana idolorum cum septis, quibus erant circumdata, primus profanare deberet; ille respondit: "Ego. Quis enim ea, quae

---

146 f. **swā micle swā ic geornlīcor . . . swā ic . . . lǣs** Notice this rendering of the Lat. construction *quanto . . . tanto* with comparative adverbs: "the more eagerly I . . . , the less I . . ."

149 **hǣlo** Considering both the Lat. and the word order of *þā gyfe* and *syllan*, *hǣlo* is probably gen. sg. (parallel to *ēadignesse*), rather than acc. sg. (parallel to *gyfe*).

150 **þæt** This word repeats, somewhat redundantly, the first (conjunctive) *þæt* in l. 149; the following *þā* (acc. pl. neut.) recapitulates the d.o. (*þæt templ and þā wīgbedo*) after the intervening clause.

150 f. **forlēosen ond fȳre forbærne** *Fȳre* is inst. dat. For the archaic form of the pl. subj. without final *-n* (and its use in sequence with the normal form) see *JEGP*, XXIX (1930), 100–13. O has *forlēose and fȳre forbærne*, with a final *-n* added to both verbs above the line, whether by the original scribe or by another hand is not clear.

151 **wæs . . . ondette** "Acknowledged," lit. "was an acknowledger." So too N: *wæs . . . ondetta*. O and Ca read *andette* but omit *wæs* (apparently taking *andette* as 3 sg. pret. indic.). B has *wæs . . . andettende*.

153 f. Word order: *sōhte ond āhsode from þǣm foresprecenan biscope* [i.e. Cefi] *heora hālignesse þe hēo* [nom. pl. masc.] *ǣr biēodon* etc.

155 **þe** "With which" (Lat. *quibus*). The indeclinable relative particle *þe* cannot be preceded by a preposition; hence, in subordinate clauses which it introduces, the preposition is either deferred until just before the verb (Wülfing ʃ299), or, if it is identical with the preposition of the main clause, omitted entirely (ʃ300). The translator has followed the second procedure here, though if he had thought more carefully and realized the enormous notional difference between comitative *mid* and instrumental *mid*, he would probably have followed the second and written: *þe hēo mid ymbsette wǣron*.

On the architecture of pagan temples see E. O. G. Turville-Petre, *Myth and Religion of the North* (London 1964), p. 236 sq.

hēo² Acc. pl. neut. The translator imagines that the sense will be clearer if, after all the intervening material, he inserts a pronoun recapitulating his d.o. (*ðā wīgbed ond þā hergas*).

ond tōweorpan scolde, þā ondsworede hē: "Efne *ic*. Hwā mæg þā nū ēað, þe ic longe mid dysignesse beēode, tō biseɲe ōðerra monna gerisenlecor tōweorpan þonne ic seolfa, þurh þā snytro þe ic from þǣm sōðan Gode onfēng?" Ond hē ðā sōna from him āwearp þā īdlan dysignesse þe hē ǣr beēode, ond þone cyning bæd þæt hē him wǣpen sealde ond stōdhors þæt hē meahte on cuman ond dēofolgyld tōweorpan, for ðon þām biscope heora hālignesse ne wæs ālȳfed þæt hē mōste wǣpen wegan ne elcor būton on mȳran rīdan. Þā sealde se cyning him sweord þæt hē hine mid gyrde—ond nōm his spere on hond ond hlēop on þæs cyninges stēdan ond tō þǣm dēofolgeldum fērde. Þā ðæt folc hine þā geseah swā gescyrpedne, þā wēndon hēo þæt hē teola ne wiste, ac þæt hē wēdde. Sōna þæs þe hē nēalēhte tō þǣm herige, þā scēat hē mid þȳ spere, þæt hit sticode fæste on þǣm herige, ond wæs swīðe gefēonde þǣre ongytenisse þæs sōðan Godes bīgonges. Ond hē ðā heht his gefēran tōweorpan ealne þone herig ond þā getimbro ond forbærn*an*. Is sēo stōw gȳt ætēawed gū ðēara dēofulgilda nōht feor ēast from Eoforwīcceastre begeondan Deorwentan þǣre ēa, ond gēn tō dæge is nemned Gōdmundingahām, þǣr se biscop, þurh þæs sōðan Godes inbryrdnesse, tōwearp ond fordyde þā wīgbed þe hē seolfa ǣr gehālgode.

---

per stultitiam colui, nunc ad exemplum omnium aptius quam ipse per sapientiam mihi a Deo uero donatam destruam?" Statimque, abiecta superstitione uanitatis, rogauit sibi regem arma dare et equum emissarium, quem ascendens ad idola destruenda ueniret. Non enim licuerat pontificem sacrorum uel arma ferre, uel praeter in equa equitare. Accinctus ergo gladio accepit lanceam in manu, et ascendens emissarium regis, pergebat ad idola. Quod aspiciens uulgus, aestimabat eum insanire. Nec distulit ille, mox ut adpropiabat ad fanum, profanare illud, iniecta in eo lancea, quam tenebat; multumque gauisus de agnitione ueri Dei cultus, iussit sociis destruere ac succendere fanum cum omnibus septis suis. Ostenditur autem locus ille quondam idolorum non longe ab Eburaco ad orientem, ultra amnem Doruuentionem, et uocatur hodie Godmunddingaham, ubi pontifex ipse, inspirante Deo uero, polluit ac destruxit eas, quas ipse sacrauerat, aras.

---

156 **þā[2] . . . þe** "Those (pagan objects) which."

ēað It is possible to take this word as a comparative adv. ("more easily"), but this makes the sentence somewhat clumsy; furthermore the idea is wanting in the Latin. Bright plausibly suggested that we have here a phantom word which was originally caused by the inadvertent insertion into the OE text of Lat. *ea*.

157 **ōðerra monna** Cf. l. 63 n. More idiomatic here would be *ōðrum monnum*.

165 **hēo** Pl., since *folc* is collective.

165 sq. **Sōna þæs þe** "As soon as." The procedure followed by Cefi here suggests that he may have been a priest of Woden; see H. R. Ellis Davidson, *Gods and Myths of Northern Europe* (Harmondsworth 1964), p. 50 f.

168 f. **sēo stōw . . . gū ðēara dēofulgilda** "The place (which was) formerly (the site) of those devil-shrines"; cf. Lat. *locus ille quondam idolorum*.

170 **Gōdmundingahām** Goodmanham, about 20 mi. ESE of York.

[XI.]

Ðā onfēng Ēadwine cyning—mid eallum þǣm æðelingum his þēode ond mid micle folce—Crīstes gelēafan ond fulwihte bæðe þȳ endlyftan gēare his rīces: wæs hē gefulwad from Paulīni þǣm biscope his lārēowe in Eoforwīcceastre, þȳ hālgestan Ēastordæge, in Sancte Pētres cirican þæs apostoles, þā hē þǣr hræde geweorce of trēo cirican getimbrode siðþan hē gecrīstnad wæs; swylce ēac his lārēowe ond biscope Paulīni biscopseðl forgeaf. Ond sōna þæs þe hē gefulwad wæs, hē ongon mid þæs biscopes lāre māran cirican ond hȳrran, stǣnenne, timbran ond wyrcan ymb þā cirican ūtan þe hē ǣr worhte. Ac ǣr þon hēo—sēo hēannis þæs wealles—gefylled wǣre ond geendad, þæt hē se cyning mid ārlēasre cwale ofslegen wæs ond þæt ilce geweorc his æfterfylgende Ōswalde forlēt to geendianne.

XIV.

Igitur accepit rex Aeduini cum cunctis gentis suae nobilibus ac plebe perplurima fidem et lauacrum sanctae regenerationis anno regni sui XI, qui est annus dominicae incarnationis DCXXVII, ab aduentu uero Anglorum in Brittaniam annus circiter CLXXX^mus^. Baptizatus est autem Eburaci die sancto paschae pridie Iduum Aprilium in ecclesia Petri apostoli, quam ibidem ipse de ligno, cum cathecizaretur, atque ad percipiendum baptisma inbueretur, citato opere construxit. In qua etiam ciuitate ipsi doctori atque antistiti suo Paulino sedem episcopatus donauit. Mox autem ut baptisma consecutus est, curauit, docente eodem Paulino, maiorem ipso in loco et augustiorem de lapide fabricare basilicam, in cuius medio ipsum, quod prius fecerat, oratorium includeretur. Praeparatis ergo fundamentis in gyro prioris oratorii per quadrum coepit aedificare basilicam. Sed priusquam altitudo parietis esset consummata, rex ipse impia nece occisus, opus idem successori suo Osualdo perficiendum reliquit. Paulinus

---

176 **Ēastordæge** April 12th, 627.
þā "Which" (rel. pron., acc. sg. fem.; cf. Lat. *quam*), needlessly recapitulated by *cirican* (in the next line), which is in apposition to it.

176 f. **hræde geweorce** Inst. denoting manner (cf. Lat. *citato opere*).

177 **siðþan hē gecrīstnad wæs** "After he had been *gecrīstnad*." According to BTS (s.v. *gecrīstnian*), the rite of *crīstnung* "was introductory, and preceded, sometimes by years, that of baptism. The person who had undergone [it] became a Catechumen," *i.e.* one who is receiving preliminary instruction in the faith. (In place of this clause the Lat. has "when he was being catechized and instructed for receiving baptism.")

179 **stǣnenne** For this spelling (as a variant of *stǣnene*) see SB ʃ231.4 Anm. 3.

181 **þæt** "(It happened) that" (see BT s.v. *þæt* conj. V.(1)).

182 **ofslegen wæs** October 12th, 632: *Ono hwæt hē Ēadwine, æfter þon þe hē seofontēone winter Ongolþēode ond Bretta in cynedōme wuldorlīce fore wæs —of þǣm wintrum hē syx winter Crīstes rīce compade,—þā wonn wið hine Ceadwealla, Bretta cyning, ond him Penda on fultome wæs, se fromesta esne of Mercna cyningcynne. . . . Þā wæs geðēoded hefig gefeoht ond micel on Hǣðfelda, ond þǣr mon Ēadwine þone cyning slōh þȳ fēorðan dæge Iduum Octobrium: hæfde hē þā seofon ond fēowertig wintra. Ond eall his weorod oððe ofslegen wæs oððe geflȳmed. (At uero Aeduini cum X et VII annis genti Anglorum simul et Brettonum gloriosissime praeesset, e quibus sex etiam ipse, ut diximus, Christi regno militauit, rebellauit aduersus eum Caedualla rex Brettonum, auxilium praebente illi Penda uiro strenuissimo de*

Of þǣre tīde Paulīnus se biscop syx gēr ful, þæt is oð endan þæs cyninges rīces, þæt hē mid his fultome in þǣre mǣgðe Godes word bodode ond lǣrde. Ond men gelȳfdon ond gefulwade wǣron, swā monige swā fortēode wǣron tō ēcum līfe.

---

autem ex eo tempore sex annis continuis, id est ad finem usque imperii regis illius, uerbum Dei, adnuente ac fauente ipso, in ea prouincia praedicabat; credebantque et baptizabantur quotquot erant praeordinati ad uitam aeternam.

---

regio genere Merciorum; . . . et conserto graui proelio in campo, qui uocatur Haethfelth, occisus est Æduini die IIII Iduum Octobrium, anno dominicae incarnationis DCXXXIII, cum esset annorum XL et VII; eiusque totus uel interemtus uel dispersus est exercitus.)

Ōswalde For an account of him and his career, based upon Bede's account, see Selection 12.

183 **Of þǣre tīde** I.e. the conversion.

endan The other MSS have the regular strong form *ende*.

184 **þæt hē** Anacoluthic (i.e. syntactically inconsistent) and to be ignored in translating.

2 / the story of cædmon

(Book IV, Chapter XXIV)

We know the names of only two major Anglo-Saxon poets whose work in the vernacular has survived; all the rest are anonymous. We know a great deal about Cynewulf's poetry, nothing about Cynewulf himself. Cædmon's biography—for which we are entirely dependent on the following account by Bede—is relatively full, but only nine lines of verse can be attributed to him with any confidence.

Cædmon—a cowherd at a Yorkshire monastery—was a man shamed and tormented by his inability to sing secular songs at social gatherings. Then one night, at the bidding of a mysterious visitant, he suddenly found himself able to "sing the Creation." The result of this miraculous gift of song was nine lines of poetry so famous that they survive in seventeen MSS dating from the early eighth to the late fifteenth centuries.

It is hard to sort out fact and fancy in Bede's account, since Cædmon's miracle is simply one version of the widespread and well-attested folk-motif of poetic powers acquired during sleep. It is possible that the attraction of this legendary material to the historical figure of Cædmon, and the slight repatterning of his biography which it presupposed, have obscured what may have been his real contribution: the inspired discovery of how to adapt the ancient, heroic formulas of Germanic oral poetry to the expression of Christian themes and ideas (see p. 270 ff.).

Excellent commentary on this chapter of Bede, and a handy MnE translation of the Latin text, will be found in Wrenn, pp. 92–7.

In ðeosse abbudissan mynstre wæs sum brōðor syndriglīce mid godcundre gife gemǣred ond geweorðad, for þon hē gewunade gerisenlice lēoð wyrcan, þā ðe tō ǣfæstnisse ond tō ārfæstnisse belumpen, swā ðætte, swā hwæt swā hē of godcundum stafum þurh bōceras geleornode, þæt hē æfter medmiclum fæce in scopgereorde mid þā mǣstan swētnisse ond inbryrdnisse geglængde, ond in Engliscgereorde wel geworht forþbrōhte. Ond for his lēoþsongum monigra monna mōd oft tō worulde forhogdnisse ond tō geþēodnisse þæs heofonlican līfes onbærnde wǣron. Ond ēac swelce monige ōðre æfter him in Ongelþēode ongunnon ǣfæste lēoð wyrcan, ac nǣnig hwæðre him þæt gelīce dōn meahte: for þon hē nales from monnum ne þurh mon gelǣred wæs þæt hē þone lēoðcræft leornade, ac hē wæs godcundlīce gefultumed ond þurh Godes gife þone songcræft onfēng. Ond hē for ðon nǣfre nōht lēasunge ne īdles lēoþes wyrcan meahte, ac efne þā ān þā ðe tō ǣfæstnesse belumpon ond his þā ǣfestan tungan gedeofanade singan.

In huius monasterio abbatissae fuit frater quidam diuina gratia specialiter insignis, quia carmina religioni et pietati apta facere solebat; ita ut, quicquid ex diuinis litteris per interpretes disceret, hoc ipse post pusillum uerbis poeticis maxima suauitate et conpunctione conpositis, in sua, id est Anglorum, lingua proferret. Cuius carminibus multorum saepe animi ad contemtum saeculi, et appetitum sunt uitae caelestis accensi. Et quidem et alii post illum in gente Anglorum religiosa poemata facere temtabant; sed nullus eum aequiparare potuit. Namque ipse non ab hominibus, neque per hominem institutus, canendi artem didicit, sed diuinitus adiutus gratis canendi donum accepit. Unde nil umquam friuoli et superuacui poematis facere potuit, sed ea tantummodo, quae ad religionem pertinent, religiosam eius linguam decebant.

---

1 **ðeosse abbudissan mynstre** The double Benedictine monastery at Streoneshealh (Whitby), in the North Riding of Yorkshire. Its founder and abbess between c657 and 680, the years during which the miracle occurred, was Hild, a grandniece of King Eadwine of Northumbria and the greatest of all English abbesses (cf. the reading selection on p. 80).

2 **gemǣred ond geweorðad** A doublet translating Lat. *insignis*; cf. 1/119 n. Further examples of the technique occur in l. 27 f. (*þā fers ond þā word* rendering Lat. *uersus*) and often subsequently.

3 **belumpen** Probably not subjunctive, but rather a spelling variant of *belumpon*; cf. 12/235a. B O Ca read *belumpon* here (though in O the *-on* is a correction in a later hand of something else, probably *-en*); N reads *belumpun*.

4 **þæt** Correlative with *swā hwæt swā* in l. 3 and d.o. of *geglængde* l. 5 and *forþbrōhte* l. 6.

9 **him . . . meahte** I.e. *meahte dōn þæt gelīce him*.

9 f. **nales . . . mon** Cf. Galatians 1:1: *non ab hominibus neque per hominem, sed per Iesum Christum et Deum Patrem* ("not of men, neither by man, but by Jesus Christ, and God the Father").

12 **lēasunge ne īdles lēoþes** Partitive gen. (complement of *nōht*).

efne þā ān þā ðe "Only those (things) which" (lit. "just those only, those which").

13 **his þā ǣfestan tungan** "That religious tongue of his." The use of both a possessive pronoun and a definite article is not felt to be redundant as in MnE; cf. l. 59. Note that the phrase *þā ǣfestan tungan* is acc. (the case governed by Lat. *decere*) rather than dat. (which is normal in OE with the verb *gedafenian*).

gedeofanade B N have *gedafenade*, O Ca *gedafenode*. T's spelling is unusual but not unexampled (see BTS s.v.).

Wæs hē, se mon, in weoruldhāde geseted oð þā tīde þe hē wæs gelȳfdre ylde, ond næfre nǣnig lēoð geleornade. Ond hē for þon oft in gebēorscipe, þonne þǣr wæs blisse intinga gedēmed þæt hēo ealle scalde þurh endebyrdnesse be hearpan singan, þonne hē geseah þā hearpan him nēalēcan, þonne ārās hē for ˌ scome from þǣm symble ond hām ēode tō his hūse. Þā hē þæt þā sumre tīde dyde, þæt hē forlēt þæt hūs þæs gebēorscipes ond ūt wæs gongende tō nēata scipene, þāra heord him wæs þǣre neahte beboden, þā hē ðā þǣr in gelimplice tīde his leomu on reste gesette ond onslēpte, þā stōd him sum mon æt þurh swefn ond hine hālette ond grētte ond hine be his noman nemnde: "Cedmon, sing mē hwæthwugu." Þā ondswarede hē ond cwæð: "Ne con ic nōht singan; ond ic for þon of þeossum gebēorscipe ūt ēode ond hider gewāt, for þon ic nāht singan ne cūðe." Eft hē

Siquidem in habitu saeculari usque ad tempora prouectioris aetatis constitutus, nil carminum aliquando didicerat. Unde nonnumquam in conuiuio, cum esset laetitiae causa decretum, ut omnes per ordinem cantare deberent, ille, ubi adpropinquare sibi citharam cernebat, surgebat a media caena, et egressus ad suam domum repedabat. Quod dum tempore quodam faceret, et relicta domu conuiuii egressus esset ad stabula iumentorum, quorum ei custodia nocte illa erat delegata, ibique hora conpetenti membra dedisset sopori, adstitit ei quidam per somnium, eumque salutans, ac suo appellans nomine: "Caedmon," inquit, "canta mihi aliquid." At ille respondens: "Nescio," inquit, "cantare; nam et ideo de conuiuio egressus huc secessi, quia cantare non

---

14 **gelȳfdre ylde** Descriptive gen.

15 **ond** After this word B N O Ca have *hē*.

geleornade Pret. with past perfect force; similarly *gehȳrde* in l. 28.

15 ff. *þonne* in l. 15 and *þonne*[1] in l. 17 introduce two asyndetic "when" clauses, correlative to the "then" clause which begins with *þonne*[2] in l. 17. Precisely the same pattern is repeated in the next sentence: *þā* . . . *þā* (l. 18) = "when," *þā* . . . *ðā* (l. 20) = "when," and *þā* (l. 21) = "then."

þonne þǣr wæs blisse intinga gedēmed þæt etc. Taking the OE in isolation, we might regard the *þæt*-clause as an explanation of *blisse intinga*: "when a cause of merriment was settled upon, (i.e.) that" etc. But reference to the corresponding Latin—*cum esset laetitiae causa decretum, ut* etc., "when it was decided, for the sake of merriment, that" etc.—shows that the OE translator has misconstrued Bede's *laetitiae causā* "for the sake of merriment" as *laetitiae causă* "a cause of merriment," and this explains the form of the OE text.

16 **scalde** MS *sealde*. B has *sceoldon*, C and Ca *sceoldan*. O has *sceolde*, with a final *-n* added above the line, whether by the original scribe or by another hand is not clear. All of this suggests that T's erroneous *sealde* is the result of a West-Saxon scribe's dismayed response to *scalde* in his exemplar: this *scalde* would have been the archaic 3 pl. pret. subj. without final *-n* (see 1/150 f. n.) in a common Anglian spelling (SB ʃ59 Anm. 1).

17 **for** MS *for for*, an example of the scribal error known as dittography ("double writing").

18 **sumre tīde** Temporal dat.; similarly *þǣre neahte* in l. 20.

19 **wæs gongende** Cf. 1/74 n.

21 **æt** Postposition governing *him*.

22 **Cedmon** The name—which the MSS give in a number of variant spellings —is Celtic in origin.

23 f. **for þon . . . for þon** Correlative: "for that reason . . . that."

CÆDMON'S HYMN. Oxford, Bodleian Library, MS *Tanner 10*, fol. 100r. (See p. 107 and cf. 2/22–50)

cwæð, sē ðe wið hine sprecende wæs: "Hwæðre þū meaht singan." Þā cwæð hē: "Hwæt sceal ic singan?" Cwæð hē: "Sing mē frumsceaft." Þā hē ðā þās andsware onfēng, þā ongon hē sōna singan in herenesse Godes Scyppendes þā fers ond þā word þe hē nǣfre gehȳrde, þǣre endebyrdnesse þis is:

"Nū sculon herigean   heofonrīces Weard,
Meotodes meahte   ond his mōdgeþanc,
weorc Wuldorfæder,   swā hē wundra gehwæs,
ēce Drihten,   ōr onstealde.
Hē ǣrest sceōp   eorðan bearnum
heofon tō hrōfe,   hālig Scyppend;
þā middangeard   monncynnes Weard,

---

poteram." Rursum ille, qui cum eo loquebatur, "Attamen," ait, "cantare habes." "Quid," inquit, "debeo cantare?" Et ille, "Canta," inquit, "principium creaturarum." Quo accepto responso, statim ipse coepit cantare in laudem Dei conditoris uersus, quos numquam audierat, quorum iste est sensus:

"Nunc laudare debemus auctorem regni caelestis, potentiam Creatoris et consilium illius, facta Patris gloriae. Quomodo ille, cum sit aeternus Deus, omnium miraculorum auctor extitit, qui primo filiis hominum caelum pro culmine tecti, dehinc terram custos humani generis omnipotens creauit."

---

25 **meaht** "Can, are able." T's *þū meaht singan* corresponds to *cantare habes* in Latin MSS of the Cotton Tiberius C. ii type, whereas B's *þū mē miht singan* and N O Ca's *þū meaht mē singan* correspond to *mihi cantare habes* in Latin MSS of the Moore type; see the headnote to the textual notes, p. 376. For further discussion see Mossé's n. ad loc. and *NM*, LXX (1969), 369–80.

28 **þǣre endebyrdnesse** Dat. or gen. sg. is inexplicable here. One expects *þāra* (cf. Lat. *quorum*) *endebyrdnes*—which is in fact the reading of O.

Note that whereas the OE translator promises to give the *endebyrdnes* of Cædmon's poem—i.e. the poem itself—Bede in his Latin translation of it can offer no more than the *sensus*.

29 sq. **Nū sculon** etc. For excellent critical comment and bibliography on this poem see Wrenn, pp. 92–103.

The version of the hymn in our text is naturally in West Saxon, as are a dozen more of the surviving copies. Cædmon presumably composed it in Anglian (Northumbrian), and four Anglian versions have come down to us. The earliest of these (and the earliest of all surviving copies) appears at the top of the last page of the Moore MS of the *Historia Ecclesiastica* (see p. 107, n. 9). It was written in 737, some seventy-five years after Cædmon composed the hymn:

Nū scylun hergan   hefaenrīcaes Uard,
Metudæs maecti   end his mōdgidanc,
uerc Uuldurfadur,   suē hē uundra gihuaes,
ēci Dryctin,   ōr āstelidæ.
Hē ǣrist scōp   aelda barnum
heben til hrōfe,   hāleg Scepen;
thā middungeard   moncynnæs Uard,

ēce Drihten, æfter tēode,
fīrum foldan, Frēa ælmihtig."

Þā ārās hē from þǣm slǣpe ond eal þā þe hē slǣpende song fæste in gemynde hæfde, ond þǣm wordum sōna monig word in þæt ilce gemet Gode wyrðes songes tōgeþēodde.

Þā cōm hē on morgenne tō þǣm tūngerēfan þe his ealdormon wæs; sægde him hwylce gife hē onfēng, ond hē hine sōna tō þǣre abbudissan gelǣdde ond hire þā cȳðde ond sægde. Þā heht hēo gesomnian ealle þā gelǣredestan men ond þā leorneras ond him ondweardum hēt secgan þæt swefn ond þæt lēoð singan, þæt

---

Hic est sensus, non autem ordo ipse uerborum, quae dormiens ille canebat; neque enim possunt carmina, quamuis optime conposita, ex alia in aliam linguam ad uerbum sine detrimento sui decoris ac dignitatis transferri. Exsurgens autem a somno, cuncta, quae dormiens cantauerat, memoriter retinuit, et eis mox plura in eundem modum uerba Deo digni carminis adiunxit.

Ueniensque mane ad uilicum, qui sibi praeerat, quid doni percepisset, indicauit, atque ad abbatissam perductus, iussus est, multis doctioribus uiris praesentibus, indicare somnium, et dicere carmen, ut uniuersorum iudicio, quid uel unde esset, quod

---

ēci Dryctin, æfter tīadæ,
fīrum foldu, Frēa allmectig.
Primo cantauit Caedmon istud carmen ("Cædmon first sang this song").

A study of all the MSS of the hymn shows that the text of this poem was preserved with great fidelity and that the disagreement of our two texts in l. 33—where one has *eorðan* and the other *aelda* (= WS *ylda*), the latter agreeing with Bede's *filiis hominum*—cuts across dialectical lines and probably arose at a fairly early stage in the transmission of the text. On this question, and on the reasons for believing that *aelda* represents Cædmon's original choice, see *ASPR* VI, c.

37 After giving his Latin version of the hymn, Bede offers the following perspicacious remarks on the difficulties of translating poetry: "This is the sense, not however the precise sequence of words which he sang while sleeping; for poems, no matter how well written they are, cannot be translated literally from one language to another without detriment to their beauty and dignity." These remarks were naturally omitted by the OE translator.

38 **eal þā þe** "All those (things) which."

39 **þǣm wordum** Governed by *tōgeþēodde* in the next line.

in þæt ilce gemet The phrase is calculated on Lat. *in eundum modum*; normal OE practice would require that *in* govern dat. in a situation of rest: *in þǣm ilcan gemete*.

Gode wyrðes songes "Of song worthy of God" (calculated upon Lat. *Deo digni carminis*, even to the highly un-OE dat. rection of *wyrðe*). The entire OE phrase is a complement of *word*, not *gemet* (as comparison with the Lat. makes clear).

42 **þā** Probably acc. pl. neut., "those (things)," but possibly acc. sg. fem. (with *gife* as its antecedent). B C O Ca read *þæt*. There is nothing corresponding in the Lat.

44 **him ondweardum** The corresponding Lat. (*multis doctioribus uiris praesentibus*) could be either an ablative absolute or an ind. object.

ealra heora dōme gecoren wǣre, hwæt oððe hwonon þæt cumen wǣre. Þā wæs him eallum gesegen—swā swā hit wæs—þæt hit wǣre from Drihtne sylfum heofonlic gifu forgifen. Þā rehton hēo him ond sægdon sum hālig spell ond godcundre lāre word; bebudon him þā, gif hē meahte, þæt hē in swinsunge lēoþsonges þæt gehwyrfde. Þā hē ðā hæfde þā wīsan onfongne, þā ēode hē hām tō his hūse ond cwōm eft on morgenne ond, þȳ betstan lēoðe geglenged, him āsong ond āgeaf þæt him beboden wæs.

Ðā ongan sēo abbudisse clyppan ond lufigean þā Godes gife in þǣm men, ond hēo hine þā monade ond lǣrde þæt hē woruldhād ānforlēte ond munuchād onfēnge, ond hē þæt wel þafode. Ond hēo hine in þæt mynster onfēng mid his gōdum ond hine geþēodde tō gesomnunge þāra Godes þēowa, ond heht hine lǣran þæt getæl þæs hālgan stǣres ond spelles. Ond hē eal þā hē in gehȳrnesse geleornian meahte mid hine gemyndgade ond, swā swā clǣne nēten eodorcende, in þæt swēteste lēoð gehwerfde. Ond his song ond his lēoð wǣron swā wynsumu tō gehȳranne þætte seolfan þā his lārēowas æt his mūðe wreoton ond leornodon. Song hē ǣrest be

---

referebat, probaretur. Uisumque est omnibus caelestem ei a Domino concessam esse gratiam. Exponebantque illi quendam sacrae historiae siue doctrinae sermonem, praecipientes eum, si posset, hunc in modulationem carminis transferre. At ille suscepto negotio abiit, et mane rediens, optimo carmine, quod iubebatur, conpositum reddidit.

Unde mox abbatissa amplexata gratiam Dei in uiro, saecularem illum habitum relinquere, et monachicum suscipere propositum docuit, susceptumque in monasterium cum omnibus suis fratrum cohorti adsociauit, iussitque illum seriem sacrae historiae doceri. At ipse cuncta, quae audiendo discere poterat, rememorando secum, et quasi mundum animal ruminando, in carmen dulcissimum conuertebat, suauiusque resonando doctores suos uicissim auditores sui faciebat. Canebat autem de creatione

---

45 **gecoren wǣre** "(It) might be decided"—an unidiomatic meaning suggested by Lat. *probaretur*.

hwæt . . . wǣre A telescoping of two constructions, *hwæt þæt wǣre* and *hwonon þæt cumen wǣre*.

45 f. **wæs him eallum gesegen** "(It) was seen by them all"; another Latinism (*Uisum . . . est omnibus*).

46 **hit**[2] Probably an error for *him* (the reading of the other MSS, confirmed by the Latin); as it stands it must be taken as the subject, with *heofonlic gifu* in apposition to it.

49 **onfongne** A syncopated form of *onfongene*, acc. sg. fem. *Habban* + d.o. + a past participle inflected to agree with the latter is idiomatic OE (cf. 23/64b).

50 **geglenged** The *þæt* which follows stands for the demonstrative plus the relative (i.e. *þæt þæt*); *geglenged* is to be construed with the former.

53 **ānforlēte** B C O have *forlēte*, Ca *forlǣte*.

54 **mid his gōdum** A misunderstanding of Lat. *cum omnibus suis* "with all her (people)."

56 **eal þā** I.e. *eal þā þe* (cf. l. 38).

57 **mid hine** "In himself." *Mid* + acc. is an Anglian feature.

swā swā clǣne nēten eodorcende This image, which is frequent in Bede, is based upon Leviticus 11:3 and Deuteronomy 14:8. The standard commentaries on these passages interpreted the dividing of the hoof and the chewing of the cud to signify discretion and continual meditation on the law of God.

59 **seolfan þā his lārēowas** "Those very same teachers of his." The other MSS have *þā seolfan* (variously spelled), which is the more normal word order (see Farr p. 18).

middangeardes gesceape ond bī fruman moncynnes ond eal þæt stǣr Genesis (þæt is sēo ǣreste Moyses booc), ond eft bī ūtgonge Israhēla folces of Ǣgypta londe ond bī ingonge þæs gehātlandes ond bī ōðrum monegum spellum þæs hālgan gewrites canōnes bōca, ond bī Crīstes menniscnesse ond bī his þrōwunge ond bī his ūpāstīgnesse in heofonas, ond bī þæs Hālgan Gāstes cyme ond þāra apostola lāre. Ond eft bī þǣm dæge þæs tōweardan dōmes ond bī fyrhtu þæs tintreglican wiites ond bī swētnesse þæs heofonlecan rīces hē monig lēoð geworhte. Ond swelce ēac ōðer monig be þǣm godcundan fremsumnessum ond dōmum hē geworhte. In eallum þǣm hē geornlīce gēmde þæt hē men ātuge from synna lufan ond māndǣda, ond tō lufan ond tō geornfulnesse āwehte gōdra dǣda. For þon hē wæs, se mon, swīþe ǣfæst, ond regollecum þēodscipum ēaðmōdlīce underþēoded. Ond wið þǣm þā ðe in ōðre wīsan dōn woldon, hē wæs mid welme micelre ellenwōdnisse onbærned. Ond hē for ðon fægre ænde his līf betȳnde ond geendade.

For þon þā ðǣre tīde nēalǣcte his gewitenesse ond forðfōre, þā wæs hē fēowertȳnum dagum ǣr þæt hē wæs līchomlicre untrymnesse þrycced ond hefgad, hwæðre tō þon gemetlīce þæt hē ealle þā tīd meahte ge sprecan ge gongan. Wæs þǣr in nēaweste untrumra monna hūs, in þǣm heora þēaw wæs þæt hēo þā untrumran ond þā ðe æt forðfōre wǣron inlǣdon sceoldon ond him þǣr ætsomne

---

mundi, et origine humani generis, et tota genesis historia, de egressu Israel ex Aegypto, et ingressu in terram repromissionis, de aliis plurimis sacrae scripturae historiis, de incarnatione dominica, passione, resurrectione, et ascensione in caelum, de Spiritus Sancti aduentu, et apostolorum doctrina. Item de terrore futuri iudicii, et horrore poenae gehennalis, ac dulcedine regni caelestis multa carmina faciebat; sed et alia perplura de beneficiis et iudiciis diuinis, in quibus cunctis homines ab amore scelerum abstrahere, ad dilectionem uero et solertiam bonae actionis excitare curabat. Erat enim uir multum religiosus, et regularibus disciplinis humiliter subditus; aduersum uero illos, qui aliter facere uolebant, zelo magni feruoris accensus; unde et pulchro uitam suam fine conclusit.

Nam propinquante hora sui decessus, XIIII diebus praeueniente corporea infirmitate pressus est, adeo tamen moderate, ut et loqui toto eo tempore posset, et ingredi. Erat autem in proximo casa, in qua infirmiores et qui prope morituri esse uidebantur,

---

61 **booc** Graphic doubling is occasionally used by scribes to indicate vowel length; cf. *wiites* in l. 66.

62 f. **þæs**[2] **. . . bōca** "Of the books of the canon of Holy Writ."

63 f. **menniscnesse, þrōwunge, ūpāstīgnesse** Cf. Lat. *incarnatione*, *passione*, *ascensione* and observe that whereas OE made use of native elements to translate the Latin, MnE uses the Latin words themselves. (Note also that a word translating *resurrectione*, which occurs between *passione* and *ascensione* in the Lat., fails to appear in any of the OE MSS, and must reflect an error in their common ultimate source.)

65 **dæge** The other MSS all have *ege*, which correctly renders Lat. *terrore*. T's *dæge* makes excellent sense (which no doubt explains how the error arose), though of course it ruins Bede's carefully contrived series of abstract nouns (*terrore . . . horrore . . . dulcedine*).

72 **fægre ænde** Inst. dat.; similarly *līchomlicre untrymnesse* in l. 74.

74 **þæt hē wæs** Redundant (and not corresponding to anything in the Lat.).

76 f. **in þǣm . . . sceoldon** I.e. (*Þæt*) *wæs heora þēaw*, *þæt hēo sceoldon* ["were accustomed to," cf. Lat. *solebant*] *inlǣdon* [infinitive] *in þǣm* [sc. *hūse*] *þā untrumran* [d.o., adj. used substantivally] *and þā ðe æt forðfōre wǣron*. *Untrumran* is a comparative adj. used absolutely—"(the) more ill (ones)," i.e. "those who were seriously sick"—in direct imitation of Lat. *infirmiores*.

þegnian. Þā bæd hē his þegn, on ǣfenne þǣre neahte þe hē of worulde gongende wæs, þæt hē in þǣm hūse him stōwe gegearwode, þæt hē gerestan meahte. Þā wundrode se þegn for hwon hē ðæs bǣde, for þon him þūhte þæt his forðfōr swā nēah *ne* wǣre; dyde hwæðre swā swā hē cwæð ond bibēad. Ond mid þȳ hē ðā þǣr on reste ēode ond hē gefēonde mōde sumu þing mid him sprecende ætgædre ond glēowiende wæs þe þǣr ǣr inne wǣron, þā wæs ofer middeneaht þæt hē frægn hwæðer hēo ǣnig hūsl inne hæfdon. Þā ondswarodon hēo ond cwǣdon: "Hwylc þearf is ðē hūsles? Ne þīnre forþfōre swā nēah is, nū þū þus rōtlīce ond þus glædlīce tō ūs sprecende eart." Cwæð hē eft: "Berað mē hūsl tō." Þā hē hit þā on honda hæfde, þā frægn hē hwæþer hēo ealle smolt mōd ond būton eallum incan blīðe tō him hæfdon. Þā ondswaredon hȳ ealle ond cwǣdon þæt hēo nǣnigne incan tō him wiston, ac hēo ealle him swīðe blīðemōde wǣron; ond hēo wrixendlīce hine bǣdon þæt hē him eallum blīðe wǣre. Þā ondswarade hē ond cwæð: "Mīne brōðor, mīne þā lēofan, ic eom swīðe blīðemōd tō ēow ond tō eallum Godes monnum." Ond swā wæs hine getrymmende mid þȳ heofonlecan wegneste ond him ōðres līfes ingong gegearwode. Þā gȳt hē frægn hū nēah þǣre tīde wǣre þætte þā brōðor ārīsan scolden ond Godes lof rǣran ond heora ūhtsong singan. Þā ondswaredon hēo: "Nis hit feor tō þon." Cwæð hē: "Teala! Wuton wē wel þǣre

---

induci solebant. Rogauit ergo ministrum suum uespere incumbente, nocte qua de saeculo erat exiturus, ut in ea sibi locum quiescendi praepararet; qui miratus, cur hoc rogaret, qui nequaquam adhuc moriturus esse uidebatur, fecit tamen, quod dixerat. Cumque ibidem positi uicissim aliqua gaudente animo, una cum eis, qui ibidem ante inerant, loquerentur ac iocarentur, et iam mediae noctis tempus esset transcensum, interrogauit, si eucharistiam intus haberent. Respondebant: "Quid opus est eucharistia? neque enim mori adhuc habes, qui tam hilariter nobiscum uelut sospes loqueris." Rursus ille: "Et tamen," ait, "afferte mihi eucharistiam." Qua accepta in manu, interrogauit, si omnes placidum erga se animum, et sine querela controuersiae ac rancoris haberent. Respondebant omnes placidissimam se mentem ad illum, et ab omni ira remotam habere, eumque uicissim rogabant placidam erga ipsos mentem habere. Qui confestim respondit: "Placidam ego mentem, filioli, erga omnes Dei famulos gero." Sicque se caelesti muniens uiatico, uitae alterius ingressui parauit; et interrogauit, quam prope esset hora, qua fratres ad dicendas Deo laudes nocturnas excitari deberent. Respondebant: "Non longe est." At ille: "Bene, ergo exspectemus

---

80 f. **þæt his . . . wǣre** "That his departure was not so near." Though *forðfōr* (nom. sg.) makes excellent sense, it is no doubt a corruption: B N O Ca all read *forðfōre* (dat. sg.) here, and cf. the usage—in T itself—in ll. 85 and 93.

81 **mid þȳ** Correlative with *þā* in l. 83.

84 "It would seem that the . . . Sacrament was kept in the infirmary of the monastery, so as to be ready in case of any of the inmates becoming suddenly worse" (Plummer[2]).

86 **Berað mē hūsl tō** Between *mē* and *hūsl*, N O Ca have *hwæþere* (*hwæþere þæt* B), thus expressing the sense of Lat. *tamen.*

88 **blīðe** Sc. *mōd.*

89 **him²** "Towards him."

91 **mīne** This word occurs only in T.

92 **wæs hine getrymmende** Sc. *hē*. For *wæs . . . getrymmende* (= *getrymmede*) see 1/74 n.; similarly *wæs forlǣtende* (= *forlēt*) in l. 100.

tīde bīdan," ond þā him gebæd ond hine gesegnode mid Crīstes rōdetācne ond his hēafod *on*hylde tō þām bolstre ond medmicel fæc onslēpte, ond swā mid stilnesse his līf geendade. Ond swā wæs geworden þætte swā swā hlūttre mōde ond bilwitre ond smyltre wilsumnesse Drihtne þēode, þæt hē ēac swylce swā smylte dēaðe middangeard wæs forlǣtende ond tō his gesihðe becwōm. Ond sēo tunge þe swā monig hālwende word in þæs Scyppendes lof gesette, hē ðā swelce ēac þā ȳtmæstan word in his herenisse, hine seolfne segniende ond his gāst in his honda bebēodende, betȳnde. Ēac swelce þæt is gesegen þæt hē wǣre gewis his seolfes forðfōre, of þǣm wē nū secgan hȳrdon.

---

horam illam." Et signans se signo sanctae crucis reclinauit caput ad ceruical, modicumque obdormiens ita cum silentio uitam finiuit. Sicque factum est, ut, quomodo simplici ac pura mente tranquillaque deuotione Domino seruierat, ita etiam tranquilla morte mundum reliquens ad eius uisionem ueniret, illaque lingua, quae tot salutaria uerba in laudem Conditoris conposuerat, ultima quoque uerba in laudem ipsius, signando sese, et spiritum suum in manus eius commendando clauderet; qui etiam praescius sui obitus extitisse ex his, quae narrauimus, uidetur.

---

96 **him** Refl. with *gebæd*.

98 **līf** D.o. (as in l. 72).

98 f. **þætte swā swā . . . þæt hē ēac swylce** Correlative (and redundant): "that as (he) . . . so also he" (cf. Lat. *quomodo . . . ita etiam*).

After *swa*[3] in l. 98, N O Ca have *hē* (and this is supported by the reading of B).

100 **Ond sēo tunge** The translator should have written *ond mid þǣre tungan* in order to correctly render the Lat. ablative phrase *illāque linguā*. Apparently he mistook the latter for the subject, reading it as *illăque linguă* in the nominative. The result is an anacoluthon when he reaches the real subject *hē* in l. 101.

103 f. **of . . . hȳrdon** "From those (things) we just heard tell."

the anglo-saxon chronicle

Annalistic writing among the Anglo-Saxons probably had its origin in the Easter Tables. These were long lists of consecutive years, kept by the clergy and used for computing the date of Easter. For purposes of identifying the individual years with something more palpable than a date, it became customary to jot the major, identifying event of a given year in the wide right margin of the table. A gradual development in the length and scope of these entries led at last to the keeping of true annals. The end result of this process of evolution is the group of annals which are known collectively as the Anglo-Saxon Chronicle, and which constitute the most important single source for the history of Anglo-Saxon England between the time of Bede and the Norman Conquest.[1]

Six manuscripts of the Chronicle have survived, in relatively complete form, to modern times. Up through 891 all these manuscripts derive ultimately from a set of annals compiled, in or shortly after that date, somewhere in southwest England. Soon afterwards there seems to have been a great copying and circulation of MSS, perhaps at the instigation of King Ælfred the Great, certainly with his benediction. The various copies were now continued independently in different locations. Occasionally they were sent bulletins from some central source, but they also begin to incorporate material of local interest and to go their independent ways in other matters, too; consequently their texts begin to diverge radically from one another. "Down to the year 915 a large amount of material is common to most of these manuscripts, but the question of their mutual relations has already become a serious critical problem, and it increases in complexity as the annals are followed downwards towards the Norman Conquest" (*A–SE* 688). The six major MSS are available in a parallel-text edition by Benjamin Thorpe, *The Anglo-Saxon Chronicle*, in *Rerum Britannicarum Medii Ævi Scriptores* (generally referred to as the "Rolls Series"), 2 vols. (London 1861).

[1]See further *The Anglo-Saxon Chronicle*, tr. G. N. Garmonsway, revised ed. (London 1954), pp. xix–xxv.

For our purposes, five of these MSS deserve notice and are described briefly below. Our first three excerpts from the Chronicle are based upon A, which is the earliest surviving MS. But early as it is, it is at least two removes from the author's original, and some of the later MSS occasionally preserve better readings, or contain interesting variants which are mentioned in the notes. Our fourth excerpt is edited from C and D. The five MSS are:

A = Cambridge, Corpus Christi College 173 (Ker 39); often referred to as the Parker MS or Parker Chronicle.[2] This is the oldest MS. Its early entries, up through almost the end of 891, were written by a single scribe whose hand can be dated to about 900. After that it was continued by a series of scribes; the third (who entered the annals for 925–55) was writing at Winchester, and it is possible that this MS was written there from the beginning. Its record of events is full and detailed up to 920, after which time "it shares in the general decay in historical writing and is the scantiest of our texts" (*EHD*, p. 110). Sometime in the eleventh century it was moved to Christ Church, Canterbury, and its last entry was made there in 1070.

This MS and MS E were made the basis of the standard edition of the Anglo-Saxon Chronicle by Charles Plummer, *Two of the Saxon Chronicles Parallel*, 2 vols. (Oxford 1892–99; reprinted 1952 with additional material by Dorothy Whitelock). There is an excellent translation of Plummer's text, which keeps the same pagination, by G. N. Garmonsway: *The Anglo-Saxon Chronicle* (London 1954). The section of MS A from which our second excerpt is drawn has been separately edited by A. H. Smith, *The Parker Chronicle (832–900)* (London 1935). A facsimile edition of A, *The Parker Chronicle and Laws*, edited by Robin Flower and Hugh Smith, was published by EETS in 1941 (Original Series, 208); students are encouraged to consult it while studying the texts of the first three selections.

B = British Museum, Cotton Tiberius A. vi (Ker 188).

C = British Museum, Cotton Tiberius B. i (Ker 191); often referred to as the Abingdon Chronicle.

These two MSS are very closely related. The older theory was that up to the year 977, which is where B ends, they are copies of a common original, which was located at Abingdon at the time; but more recent investigations suggest that from 491 to 652 C is a direct copy of B, and that after 652 C made use of B in conjunction with another source.

B was written at Abingdon, quite possibly between 977 and 979; later it was moved to Canterbury, where it was located shortly after the Norman Conquest. It has not been independently edited.

C was written at Abingdon and remained there. It breaks off in the middle of the annal for 1066. It prefaces its version of the Chronicle with two poems, the second of which is printed below (p. 373 ff.). It has been independently edited by Harry August Rositzke, *The C-Text of the Old English Chronicles* (Bochum-Langendreer 1940).

D= British Museum, Cotton Tiberius B. iv (Ker 192); often referred to as the Worcester or Evesham Chronicle.

---

[2]It was bequeathed to Corpus Christi by Matthew Parker, Archbishop of Canterbury from 1559 to 1575.

E= Oxford, Bodleian Library, Laud Misc. 636 (Ker 346); often referred to as the Peterborough Chronicle.

These two MSS must be discussed together, since between them they represent what is known as the northern recension of the Chronicle, and go back to a common archetype which was probably compiled at York. Both show a greater interest in northern affairs than do the other three versions. The relationship between them is very complicated. D was written at either York or Worcester and ends in 1079; E was written at Peterborough and continues until 1154, much later than any of the other four MSS. D has been independently edited by E. Classen and F. E. Harmer, *An Anglo-Saxon Chronicle* (Manchester 1926). E is edited in Plummer's great edition (see above under A), and a facsimile, edited by Dorothy Whitelock, has been issued as the fourth volume (1954) of *EEMSF*.

Furthermore, early versions of the Chronicle which have since been lost were drawn upon, while still extant, by Latin writers of the period, who sometimes also add valuable information of their own which can be used to supplement the Chronicle account. For our purposes two of these writers are of importance: (1) Ælfred's biographer, Bishop Asser of Sherborne (d. 909), whose *De Rebus Gestis Ælfredi* (c893) makes extensive use of the Chronicle (in a version not greatly dissimilar to A) between 851 and 887, and (2) Ælfric's patron Æðelweard,[3] who wrote a Latin Chronicle (*Chronicon Æthelweardi*) in the late 980's, making frequent use of a recension of the Chronicle that may be dated to the time of Ælfred's son and successor Eadweard, and adding many original details of its own, especially about events in Æðelweard's own area, the south-west of England. Frequent reference will be made to the versions of both these writers in the notes to the first two selections. The best editions are: *Asser's Life of King Alfred*, ed. William Henry Stevenson (Oxford 1904; reprinted 1959), and *The Chronicle of Æthelweard*, ed. A. Campbell (London 1962).

[3]Æðelweard was a descendant of King Ælfred's brother Æðelred; he was ealdormann of the western provinces (*Occidentalium prouinciarum dux*) in the reign of Æðelred the Unready and died in or shortly after 998.

3 / Cynewulf and Cyneheard

This entry in the Chronicle recounts two clusters of related incidents—separated from one another by almost thirty years—in a dynastic struggle between two branches of the West-Saxon royal house. It stands out from all the entries which precede it, and many of those which follow, in its detail and spirit, and in its careful analysis of motivation. Not only its central themes (the duty of vengeance; loyalty to one's lord vs. loyalty to one's kin), but several of its motifs (*sjálfdæmi*, *útganga*; see the notes to ll. 23 and 27), its objective tone, and certain features of its style (the colloquialism, the sudden switch from indirect to direct discourse in l. 29, the rather unclear use of pronouns throughout) are reminiscent of the Icelandic family sagas, and scholars have speculated that it—like the sagas—may have been developed and transmitted orally for some time before being written down in its present form.

Plummer[1] has this to say about the closing sentences of the account: "The poverty of the English language in demonstrative pronouns as compared with the Latin *hic*, *ille*, *is*, *iste*, *ipse* appears very strongly in this passage, and makes it very difficult to follow." Modern readers who find themselves non-plussed by the confusing welter of pronouns may perhaps derive some comfort from the fact that Æðelweard—himself a native speaker of the language—blundered badly when he translated the passage into Latin. Probably, however, most Anglo-Saxon readers or hearers of the story would have had little difficulty following the course of events. They would have known that a man's loyalty to his lord is everything: that he must sacrifice his life for him if need be, and avenge his death at any cost—even at the cost of ignoring the other cardinal loyalty of the Germanic world, loyalty to one's kin. The two protagonists of this story are related by blood; so are many of their supporters. Events put these supporters in the position of having to choose between (1) loyalty to their lord and life itself, (2) loyalty to their lord and loyalty to their kinsmen. All the characters in this little tale are faithful to the heroic code and make the "correct" choice. Hence the story is not only exemplary, but also perfectly clear: the logic of loyalty makes the behavior of the actors and the sequence of events patterned and predictable. If one keeps this in mind, the referents of the pronouns are rarely ambiguous.

no dcclv

Hēr Cynewulf benam Sigebryht his rīces ond Westseaxna wiotan for unryhtum dǣdum, būton Hamtūnscīre. Ond hē hæfde þā oþ hē ofslōg þone aldormon þe him lengest wunode, ond hiene þā Cynewulf on Andred ādrǣfde ond hē þǣr wunade oþ þæt hiene ān swān ofstang æt Pryfetes flōdan; ond hē wræc þone aldormon Cumbran.

Ond sē Cynewulf oft miclum gefeohtum feaht uuiþ Bretwālum. Ond ymb xxxi wintra þæs þe hē rīce hæfde, hē wolde ādrǣfan ānne æþeling sē was Cyneheard hāten; ond sē Cyneheard wæs þæs Sigebryhtes brōþur. Ond þā geāscode hē þone

---

1 **Hēr** Referring to the date-entry (755) which introduces the annal. Due to an error, it predates events by two years: the deposition of Sigebryht actually occurred in 757.
Cynewulf For a brief account of this important West-Saxon king see *A-SE* 209.
benam Inflected sg. with the nearest member of the compound subject *Cynewulf . . . ond Westseaxna wiotan*. Note the double rection of *beniman*: to deprive someone (acc. sg.) of something (gen. sg.).
Sigebryht Cynewulf's predecessor. MSS D and E add the significant fact that he was Cynewulf's *mǣg*.

2 **þā** Acc. sg. fem.; the antecedent is *-scīre*.
þone aldormon Cumbra (cf. l. 4 f.), probably *ealdorman* of Hampshire.
him "With him" (comitative dat.).

3 **on Andred ādrǣfde** Æðelweard has: *expulit in inuia loci qui apellatur Andred*, "drove into the pathless tracts of the area which is called Andred." The *Andredesweald* was an extensive tract of forest stretching from Kent to Hampshire; in 4/133 f. it is said to be 120 miles long and 30 miles broad. Many swine were pastured there.
ond he þǣr wunade Æðelweard renders this: *sicque migrando mansit de denso in condenso*, "and thus he lived wandering from thicket to thicket."

4 **Pryfetes flōdan** Modern Privet(t), Hampshire. The word *flōde* here may mean a spring whose flow is irregular.
hē The *swān*, who was presumably a dependent of Cumbra's. The date of Sigebryht's slaying is not known.

6 **sē Cynewulf** "This Cynewulf"; cf. l. 8. (On this use of *sē* as a deictic demonstrative see QW ʃ117 f.).
miclum gefeohtum Instrumental.

6 f. **xxxi wintra** An error. The events which the annalist is about to relate occurred in 786, 29 (and not 31) years after Cynewulf's accession.

7 **þæs þe** "After."

7 f. **hē wolde . . . brōþur** According to l. 34, both Cynewulf and Cyneheard claimed direct male descent from Cerdic (the invader of Wessex and founder of the West-Saxon kingdom), and nothing would be more likely to bring these two kinsmen into conflict in an age when "supremacy in Wessex was . . . open to any representative of any line which could claim descent from Cerdic" (*A-SE* 72).

cyning lȳtle werode on wīfcȳþþe on Merantūne ond hine þǣr berād ond þone būr ūtan beēode ǣr hine þā men onfunden þe mid þām kyninge wǣrun. Ond þā ongeat se cyning þæt, ond hē on þā duru ēode ond þā unhēanlīce hine werede oþ hē on þone æþeling lōcude, ond þā ūt rǣsde on hine ond hine miclum gewundode; ond hīe alle on þone cyning wǣrun feohtende oþ þæt hīe hine ofslægenne hæfdon.

Ond þā on þæs wīfes gebǣrum onfundon þæs cyninges þegnas þā unstilnesse, ond þā þider urnon swā hwelc swā þonne gearo wearþ, ond radost. Ond hiera se æþeling gehwelcum feoh ond feorh gebēad, ond hiera nǣnig hit geþicgean nolde: ac hīe simle feohtende wǣran oþ hīe alle lǣgon būtan ānum Bryttiscum gīsle, ond sē swīþe gewundad wæs.

Þā on morgenne gehīerdun þæt þæs cyninges þegnas þe him beæftan wǣrun, þæt se cyning ofslægen wæs. Þā ridon hīe þider, and his aldormon Ōsrīc ond Wīferþ his þegn ond þā men þe hē beæftan him lǣfde ǣr, ond þone æþeling on þǣre byrig mētton þǣr se cyning ofslægen læg. Ond þā gatu him tō belocen hæfdon, ond

---

9 **lȳtle werode** Inst. of accompaniment ("comitative" inst.).
on wīfcȳþþe *Cum quadam meretrice* ("with a certain prostitute") according to Æðelweard.
Merantūne Not certainly identified; perhaps Merton, Surrey. At the time of the events recorded here we may imagine it to consist of a palisade or (earthwork) wall with a gate. Inside this fortification are a large *heall* (in which Cynewulf's retainers are bedded down) and a number of outbuildings or *būras* (cooksheds, storerooms, womens' quarters). The king is *on wīfcȳþþe* in one of these.
hine Cynewulf.
būr So A D E; B C have *burh*.

10 **hine** Cyneheard.

11 f. **oþ hē** etc. Recognition of his antagonist provokes the king into leaving his tactically advantageous position inside the doorway.

12 f. **hīe alle** etc. *Nec obliti socii minas arma eleuant*, says Æðelweard, "[Cyneheard's] retainers, not forgetting their boasts, ply their weapons": cf. 24/198–201, 212–5, and esp. 289–93.

13 **wǣrun feohtende** "Kept on fighting"; cf. ll. 17, 30.

15 **ond radost** MS E omits the conjunction, reading *swā hwilc swā ðonne gearo wearð hraðost*, "whoever got ready (i.e. armed himself) most quickly"; similarly MS D. MSS B and C omit both words.
hiera Complement of *gehwelcum*, which is the ind. object.

16 **feoh ond feorh gebēad** I.e. if they would surrender.
ond[2] . . . nolde Æðelweard adds the heroic motif: *Post dominum desiderant orcum*, "they desire death after their lord" (and cf. 24/317b–19).

17 **ānum Bryttiscum gīsle** Why he should be found in Cynewulf's retinue may be inferred from l. 6. It was not unusual for hostages to behave as if they were "honorary" members of the *comitatus* of the king who held them in pledge: cf. 24/265 sq., or the example of Walter of Aquitaine who, sent as a hostage to the court of Attila the Hun, rose to become the leader of his armies.

19 f. **þæt . . . þæt** *þæt*[1] is d.o. of *gehīerdun*; *þæt*[2] is correlative with it and introduces an explanatory clause.

19 **him beæftan** Perhaps in Winchester, the West-Saxon royal seat. *Him beæftan* = *beæftan him*; the author of this annal is fond of placing prepositions after the nouns they govern (postposition).

22 f. **Ond . . . ēodon** In the first half of this sentence, a pronoun *hīe* (referring to Cyneheard and his men) must be supplied as the subject; it occurs in MSS B C D E. In the second half of the sentence, *þā* is probably the subject and refers to

þā þǣrtō ēodon. Ond þā gebēad hē him hiera āgenne dōm fēos ond londes, gif hīe him þæs rīces ūþon, ond him cȳþdon þæt hiera mǣgas him mid wǣron, þā þe him from noldon. Ond þā cuǣdon hīe þæt him nǣnig mǣg lēofra nǣre þonne hiera hlāford, ond hīe nǣfre his banan folgian noldon, ond þā budon hīe hiera mǣgum þæt hīe gesunde from ēodon. Ond hīe cuǣdon þæt tæt ilce hiera gefērum geboden wǣre þe ǣr mid þām cyninge wǣrun; þā cuǣdon hīe þæt hīe hīe þæs ne onmunden

---

the royal forces (or if *þā* is an adv., then another *hīe* must be supplied). Compare the text of this sentence in MS B: *And hīe þā þā geatu him tō belocen hæfdan, and hīe ðǣrtō ēodan.*

22 **him tō** Either "upon themselves" or "against them" (the royal forces), probably the latter: Æðelweard took it this way (*firmantur ex aduerso fores*) and cf. the use of the equivalent idiom *intō him* in the Chronicle entries for 901 (A) and 1083 (E).

23 **hē** Cyneheard.

him The royal forces.

hiera āgenne dōm Cf. the phrase *hyra sylfra dōm* (24/38b) and the ON legal term *sjálfdœmi* "self-assessment (of the damages owed to one)." Giving your opponent *sjálfdœmi*—letting him write his own ticket—was something generally done only when your back was to the wall. Cyneheard had eighty-four men with him (see l. 30 f. n.); the royal forces must have greatly outnumbered his.

24 **ūþon** Probably subjunctive (cf. QW ∫133d); indic. and subj. pl. are not distinguished by spelling in MS A, and one can reasonably ask whether there is still a distinction in usage (see C. Sprockel, *The Language of the Parker Chronicle*, I (The Hague 1965), p. 217 Note).

cȳþdon Note the change of subject, from Cyneheard (sg.) to Cyneheard and his men (pl.). MSS B D E have a sg. form here, MS C has the pl., like A.

hiera The members of the royal forces.

him[3,4] Both pronouns can be interpreted either as dat. sg. (referring to Cyneheard alone) or dat. pl. (referring also to his men).

25 **noldon** Supply the infinitive of a verb of motion.

hīe The royal forces. The next two *hīe*'s in this sentence also refer to them; the fourth *hīe* to their kinsmen inside the gate.

him . . . lēofra "Dearer to them."

27 **þæt**[1] **. . . ēodon** In the feuds described in the Icelandic family sagas—where farmsteads were often surrounded by night and set afire and everyone inside them either burned alive or else cut down at the exit while trying to escape—it was customary for the attackers to offer *útganga*—the chance to walk out unharmed—to such of their kinsmen as were within, and also to the women, children and servants. The offer was often rejected.

hīe gesunde from ēodon MSS B C D have a *him* (E *heom*) between the first two words: this could be either reflexive with the verb, or else the object of *from* (in which case it refers to Cyneheard and his men).

ēodon Subjunctive; but see l. 24 *ūþon* n.

hīe[2] The kinsmen inside. The other *hīe*'s in this sentence also refer to them.

þæt tæt I.e. *þæt þæt*; cf. the frequent spelling *þætte* for *þæt þe*.

tæt ilce "That same (thing)," i.e. *feorh*. Cf. l. 16.

hiera The kinsmen outside.

28 **hīe**[3] This reflexive *hīe* is a later addition to MS A (and does not appear in B C D E). MS B strengthens the subject here with an added *hīe sylfe*, which helps emphasize the determination of the relatives inside to live up to the example set by the men who died with the king.

"þon mā þe ēowre gefēran þe mid þām cyninge ofslægene wǣrun." Ond hīe þā ymb þā gatu feohtende wǣron oþ þæt hīe þǣrinne fulgon ond þone æþeling ofslōgon ond þā men þe him mid wǣrun, alle būtan ānum: sē wæs þæs aldormonnes godsunu ond hē his feorh generede, ond þēah hē wæs oft gewundad.

Ond sē Cynewulf rīcsode xxxi wintra ond his līc līþ æt Wintanceastre, ond þæs æþelinges æt Ascanmynster; ond hiera ryhtfæderencyn gǣþ tō Cerdice.

---

29 **"þon . . . wǣrun"** The sudden switch to direct discourse, signalized by *ēowre* (MSS A and C), is conceivably a holdover from an earlier (oral? poetic?) form of this story in which the introduction to the battle at the gate took the form of a direct report of alternating speeches; cf. the technique in 24/25–61. (The other MSS regularize the usage here, reading *heora* instead of *ēowre*.)

30 **hīe** The royal forces. The previous *hīe* could also refer to them, or else to both sides.

30 f. **þone æþeling . . . wǣrun** The Chronicle entry for 784 (an error for 786, see 1.1 *Hēr* n.) begins: *Hēr Cyneheard ofslōg Cynewulf cyning, ond hē þǣr wearþ ofslægen ond lxxxiiii monna mid him.*

31 **þæs aldormonnes** Cf. 1. 20.

33 **xxxi wintra** The same mistake as in l. 6 f.

34 **Cerdice** For an account of him see *A-SE* 19–27.

4 / the reigns of æðelred and ælfred

It was under Cynewulf's successor Beorhtric (786–802) that Wessex—and Anglo-Saxon England—received their first ominous hint of future disaster. *On his dagum*, says the Chronicle, *cuōmon ǣrest iii scipu.*[1] *Ond þā se gerēfa þǣrtō rād, ond hīe*[2] *wolde drīfan tō þæs cyninges tūne, þȳ hē nyste hwæt hīe wǣron: ond hiene mon ofslōg. Þæt wǣron þā ǣrestan scipu Deniscra monna þe Angelcynnes lond gesōhton.* These "Danish men" were of course the Vikings, and the band which killed Beaduheard the reeve[3]—perhaps sometime in the late 780s—was the advance guard of the terrible Viking armies which were to ravage England and Europe during the anxious centuries which followed.

The next recorded Viking descent upon England is not only more precisely dated but was far more spectacular. It did not strike out of a clear blue sky but was heralded by suitable portents:

Anno dccxciii Hēr wǣron rēðe forebēcna cumene ofer Norþanhymbra land, and þæt folc earmlīce brēgdon: þæt wǣron ormēte līgræscas, and wǣron geseowene fȳrene dracan on þām lyfte flēogende. Þām tācnum sōna fyligde mycel hunger. And lītel æfter þām þæs ilcan gēares, on vi Idus Ianuarii,[4] earmlīce hēðenra manna hergung ādīligode Godes cyrican in Lindisfarena ee þurh rēaflāc and mansleht.[5]

---

[1]MS E adds here *Norðmanna of Hereðalande* (=ON *Hǫrðaland* < **Haruþaland*), on the Hardangerfjord in Norway.

[2]**hīe** Acc. pl. (referring to the crews of the ships).

[3]Æðelweard's *Chronicle* has preserved his name for us.

[4]The 6th (or 7th) of the Ides of *June*, according to other sources—which are almost certainly right, since a Viking fleet was not likely to be on the prowl in midwinter.

[5]The text here is from E; this annal is not found in A.

These earliest desultory raids were probably made by Norwegian Vikings. Greater organization and persistence were shown by the Danish Vikings of the next century, who initiated a series of large-scale inroads against the Franks in 834 and the Anglo-Saxons in 835. More than twelve Danish assaults against various parts of England are recorded during the next thirty years, and twice during this period large Danish forces remained in England over winter.

With the accession of Æðelred to the throne of Wessex in the autumn of 865, another critical change occurred in the nature of the Viking attacks on England: a *micel here* arrived in East Anglia, "prepared to spend many consecutive years in the deliberate exploitation of all the opportunities for profit which England offered" (*A–SE* 246). Our excerpt from the Chronicle resumes at this point.

Historical and military notes have been kept to a bare minimum on the assumption that the student will consult *A–SE* 239–69 in conjunction with this excerpt. Students who wish to follow these campaigns on a map may be referred to the front endpaper of this book.

Anno dccclxui

Hēr fēng Æþered Æþelbryhtes brōþur tō Wesseaxna rīce. Ond þȳ ilcan gēare cuōm micel here on Angelcynnes lond ond wintersetl nāmon on Ēastenglum, ond

---

1 **Hēr** etc. It is now generally agreed that in this part of the Chronicle—up to the year 890—the year begins not on January 1st but on September 24th, the so-called "Caesarean indiction" (see Plummer[1], II, cxxxix–cxlii*d*). According to our modern reckoning the accession of Æðelred and the movement of the Viking army into winter quarters occurred in the autumn of 865; in the Chronicle, however, events taking place after September 23rd are dated in the new year which began then. "It follows that the movements of the Danish army, which usually took place in the autumn, are consistently dated a year too late" (*A-SE* 246 n. 3). Students should bear this crucial difference in chronology in mind throughout their reading of these annals. See further G. N. Garmonsway, *The Anglo-Saxon Chronicle* (London 1954), pp. xxvi–xxx.

Æþered < **Æþelred,** with assimilation and simplification: *lr* > *rr* > *r* (Campbell §484, 457 n. 3).

Æþelbryht Æðelred's older brother and predecessor. He, Æðelred and Ælfred the Great were all sons of Æðelwulf (reigned 839–858).

2 **micel here** MS E has *mycel hǣðen here* (with which MSS B C D agree). The word *here* is related to *herian* "to plunder" and always denotes the Vikings in these annals, whereas the English forces are called the *fierd* (a noun related to the verb *faran*). The derived verb *fierdian* means "to campaign with the *fierd*."

The *micel here* was led by the sons of the famous ninth-century Viking Ragnarr Loðbrók. The commander-in-chief, at least in the beginning, was Inwær (ON Ívarr, but preserved in MS A in an archaic form without loss of *n*), who according to tradition was responsible for the death of the East Anglian king Eadmund (see ll. 22 f.). Associated with him in command was his brother Healfdene (ON Hálfdanr), who is mentioned three times in these annals (see ll. 34, 81f., 94). A third brother, Ubba (ON Ubbi), also seems to have been associated with the expedition and is identified by the twelfth-century writer

þǣr gehorsude wurdon; ond hīe him friþ *wiþ* nāmon.

no dccclxuii

Hēr fōr se here of Ēastenglum ofer Humbremūþan tō Eoforwīcceastre on Norþhymbre. Ond þǣr wæs micel ungeþuærnes þǣre þēode betweox him selfum, ond hīe hæfdun hiera cyning āworpenne Ōsbryht, ond ungecyndne cyning underfēngon Ællan. Ond hīe late on gēare tō þām gecirdon þæt hīe wiþ þone here winnende wǣrun, ond hīe þēah micle fierd gegadrodon ond þone here sōhton æt Eoforwīcceastre ond on þā ceastre brǣcon ond hīe sume inne wurdon. Ond þǣr was ungemetlic wæl geslægen Norþanhymbra, sume binnan, sume būtan, ond þā cyningas bēgen ofslægene, ond sīo lāf wiþ þone here friþ nam.

Ond þȳ ilcan gēare gefōr Ealchstān bisceop, ond hē hæfde þæt bisceoprīce 1 wintra æt Scīreburnan, ond his līc līþ þǣr on tūne.

no dccclxuiii

Hēr fōr se ilca here innan Mierce tō Snotengahām ond þǣr wintersetl nāmon. Ond Burgræd Miercna cyning ond his wiotan bǣdon Æþered Westseaxna cyning ond Ælfred his brōþur þæt hīe him gefultumadon þæt hīe wiþ þone here gefuhton. Ond þā fērdon hīe mid Wesseaxna fierde innan Mierce oþ Snotengahām ond þone here þǣr mētton on þām geweorce. Ond þǣr nān hefelic gefeoht ne wearþ, ond Mierce friþ nāmon wiþ þone here.

no dccclxix

Hēr fōr se here eft tō Eoforwīcceastre ond þǣr sæt i gēar.

Gaimar as the Viking chieftain slain in Devon in the winter of 867–68 (see ll. 94 ff.).

nāmon Inflected pl. because *here* is collective. This usage is frequent in the following annals.

on Ēastenglum "In East Anglia." Historically a noun like this denotes the people themselves, hence is pl.; but by this time it has come to be used of the territory which they inhabited. Cf. *Norþhymbre* in l. 5 f., *Mierce* in l. 14, *Westseaxe* in l. 26, and often thereafter. See further 12/128a n.

3 **hīe** I.e. the *Ēastengle.*

him . . . nāmon I.e. *nāmon friþ wiþ him.* Such a peace, here as elsewhere in these annals, was purchased for a large sum of tribute.

4 **tō Eoforwīcceastre** According to other sources, York was taken on November 1st. Many generations were to pass before it was recovered from the Vikings.

4 f. **on Norþhymbre** This adv. phrase is to be construed with *fōr* (not with *Eoforwīcceastre*), as is shown by the acc. rection of *on.*

6 **Ōsbryht** In apposition with *cyning.*

7 **hīe**[1] Perhaps the two rival kings (united by their common peril), or perhaps the Northumbrians in general.

7 f. **tō þām . . . wǣrun** "Addressed themselves to fighting with the *here*" (lit. "set about it, that they were fighting" etc.); cf. BTS *gecirran* B.III.(a).

8 **þēah** I.e. even though it was *late on gēare* for initiating a military campaign: it was March, according to other sources.

9 **hīe . . . wurdon** "Some of them got inside." *Sume* is in apposition to *hīe.*

11 **ofslægene** Sc. *wǣron.*

16 **gefultumadon, gefuhton** Subjunctives (but see 3/24 *ūþon* n.).

18 **geweorce** MS E adds *and hine inne besetton*; the other MSS also mention this siege.

Anno dccclxx

Hēr rād se here ofer Mierce innan Ēastengle ond wintersetl nāmon æt Þēodforda. Ond þȳ wintre Ēadmund cyning him wiþ feaht, ond þā Deniscan sige nāmon ond þone cyning ofslōgon ond þæt lond all geēodon.

Ond þȳ gēare gefōr Cēolnōþ ærcebisceop, ond Æþered Wīltūnscīre biscop wearþ gecoren tō ærcebiscpe tō Cantuareberi.

Anno dccclxxi

Hēr cuōm se here tō Rēadingum on Westseaxe, ond þæs ymb iii niht ridon ii eorlas ūp. Þā gemētte hīe Æþelwulf aldorman on Englafelda ond him þǣr wiþ gefeaht ond sige nam. Þæs ymb iiii niht Æþered cyning ond Ælfred his brōþur þǣr micle fierd tō Rēadingum gelǣddon ond wiþ þone here gefuhton, ond þǣr wæs micel wæl geslægen on gehwæþre hond, ond Æþelwulf aldormon wearþ ofslægen, ond þā Deniscan āhton wælstōwe gewald.

Ond þæs ymb iiii niht gefeaht Æþered cyning ond Ælfred his brōþur wiþ alne þone here on Æscesdūne, ond hīe wǣrun on twǣm gefylcum: on ōþrum wæs Bāchsecg ond Halfdene, þā hǣþnan cyningas, ond on ōþrum wǣron þā eorlas. Ond þā gefeaht se cyning Æþered wiþ þāra cyninga getruman, ond þǣr wearþ se cyning Bāgsecg ofslægen; ond Ælfred his brōþur wiþ þāra eorla getruman, ond þǣr wearþ Sidroc eorl ofslægen se alda, ond Sidroc eorl se gioncga, ond Ōsbearn eorl, ond Frǣna eorl, ond Hareld eorl; ond þā hergas bēgen geflīemde, ond fela þūsenda ofslægenra, ond on feohtende wǣron oþ niht.

---

22 **þȳ wintre** I.e. of 869–70.

23 **þone cyning ofslōgon** "The contemporary West Saxon author of the *Chronicle* records his death without any sign of interest, but within a quarter of a century he had come to be honoured as a saint in East Anglia" (*A-SE* 248), and soon thereafter throughout all England.

Æðelweard adds that the leader of the Vikings, Inwær, died this same year.

24 f. **ond² . . . Cantuareberi** This statement was inserted in the text of MS A after its removal to Christ Church, Canterbury (see p. 136).

26 **on Westseaxe** Cf. l. 2 *on Ēastenglum* n.

þæs . . . niht "Three days later" (lit. "at three nights after that").

27 **eorlas** "The OE adaptation of ON *jarl*, equivalent as a designation of rank to OE *aldormon*" (Smith).

ūp "Up-country" (from Reading), on a reconnaissance or raiding expedition.

Æþelwulf aldorman Of Berkshire.

29 **to Rēadingum** Amplifying *þǣr*.

31 **āhton wælstōwe gewald** "Had control of the place of slaughter," i.e. ended up in possession of the battlefield. This traditional phrase is often used in the Chronicle (and elsewhere) to identify the victors in a battle.

33 **on Æscesdūne** The Berkshire Downs. Asser adds several details to the Chronicle account, among them "that Alfred had to begin the battle alone, since his brother was hearing Mass and refused to leave until it was over; that the Danes had the higher ground, and that the battle raged round a thorn-tree which he had himself seen" (*EHD*, p. 177 n. 11).

34 **Bāchsecg ond Halfdene** For the ON forms of these names, and of those which follow, see Smith, note ad loc. Only Halfdene can be identified with certainty: cf. 1.2 n.

38 f. **ond³ . . . niht** "And both those divisions (were) routed, and (there were) many thousands of slain, and (they) were engaged in fighting until nightfall."

Ond þæs ymb xiiii niht gefeaht Æþered cyning ond Ælfred his brōður wiþ þone here æt Basengum, ond þǣr þā Deniscan sige nāmon.

Ond þæs ymb ii mōnaþ gefeaht Æþered cyning ond Ælfred his brōþur wiþ þone here æt Meretūne, ond hīe wǣrun on tuǣm gefylcium; ond hīe būtū geflīemdon ond longe on dæg sige āhton. Ond þǣr wearþ micel wælsliht on gehwæþere hond, ond þā Deniscan āhton wælstōwe gewald. Ond þǣr wearþ Hēahmund bisceop ofslægen ond fela gōdra monna. Ond æfter þissum gefeohte cuōm micel sumorlida.

Ond þæs ofer Ēastron gefōr Æþered cyning. Ond hē rīcsode u gēar, ond his līc līþ æt Winburnan.

Þā fēng Ælfred Æþelwulfing his brōþur tō Wesseaxna rīce. Ond þæs ymb ānne mōnaþ gefeaht Ælfred cyning wiþ alne þone here lȳtle werede æt Wīltūne, ond hine longe on dæg geflīemde, ond þā Deniscan āhton wælstōwe gewald.

Ond þæs gēares wurdon uiiii folcgefeoht gefohten wiþ þone here on þȳ cynerīce be sūþan Temese, ond būtan þām þe him Ælfred þæs cyninges brōþur ond ānlīpig aldormon ond cyninges þegnas oft rāde on ridon þe mon nā ne rīmde. Ond þæs gēares wǣrun ofslægene uiiii eorlas ond ān cyning. Ond þȳ gēare nāmon Westseaxe friþ wiþ þone here.

no dccclxxii

Hēr fōr se here tō Lundenbyrig from Rēadingum ond þǣr wintersetl nam, ond

---

43 **æt Meretūne** This is too common a name for the place to be identified with certainty.

hīe[1] Presumably the Danes, as in l. 33.

hīe[2] The Anglo-Saxons; *būtu* is the d.o.

44 **ond . . . āhton** "And had the advantage late into the day" (when some sort of reversal seems to have occurred).

45 f. **Hēahmund bisceop** Of Sherborne.

47 **sumorlida** MSS B C D E add: *tō Rēadingum* (which was still the base of operations of the *micel here*).

48 **Ēastron** April 15th.

49 **æt Winburnan** MSS B D E read (more precisely) *æt Winburnan mynster* (E).

50 **Þā** The scribe of MS A signalizes the importance of this statement by beginning a new paragraph—his only example of intra-annal paragraphing—and using a very large capital *Þ*. Further emphasis is given by a large cross in the margin.

51 **lȳtle werede** Cf. 3/9 n. Æðelweard claims that the English force was small "due to the absence of the king, who was taking care of his brother's funeral at the time."

52 **hine** I.e. *þone here*.

ond[2] **. . . gewald** According to Asser they feigned a rout and then turned on their pursuers.

53 **þæs gēares** "During that year."

54 **ond**[1] This awkward conjunction does not appear in MSS B C D E and is probably a scribal error.

him Either a reflexive (referring collectively to the English) or the object of *on* (and referring to the Vikings). In the latter case *rāde* must be taken either as the object of *ridon* or else as an inst. sg. attached to it as an adverbial complement.

55 **ānlīpig aldormon** "(One or another) individual *ealdorman*." MSS B C D E omit the adj. and give the noun in the pl.

þā nāmon Mierce friþ wiþ þone here.

Anno dccclxxiii

Hēr fōr se here on Norþhymbre. Ond hē nam wintersetl on Lindessē æt Turecesīege, ond þā nāmon Mierce friþ wiþ þone here.

Anno dccclxxiiii

Hēr fōr se here from Lindessē tō Hreopedūne ond þǣr wintersetl nam, ond þone cyning Burgræd ofer sǣ ādrǣfdon ymb xxii wintra þæs þe hē rīce hæfde, ond þæt lond all geēodon. Ond hē fōr tō Rōme ond þǣr gesæt, and his līc līþ on Sancta Marian ciricean on Angelcynnes scōle.

Ond þȳ ilcan gēare hīe sealdon ānum unwīsum cyninges þegne Miercna rīce tō haldanne, ond hē him āþas swōr ond gīslas salde þæt hē him gearo wǣre swā hwelce dæge swā hīe hit habban wolden ond hē gearo wǣre—mid him selfum ond on allum þām þe him lǣstan woldon—tō þæs heres þearfe.

Anno dccclxxu

Hēr fōr se here from Hreopedūne. Ond Healfdene fōr mid sumum þām here on Norþhymbre ond nam wintersetl be Tīnan þǣre ēi, ond se here þæt lond geēode ond oft hergade on Peohtas ond on Stræcledwālas. Ond fōr Godrum ond Ōscytel ond Anwynd, þā iii cyningas, of Hreopedūne tō Grantebrycge mid micle here ond sǣton þǣr ān gēar.

Ond þȳ sumera fōr Ælfred cyning ūt on sǣ mid sciphere ond gefeaht wiþ uii sciphlæstas ond hiera ān gefēng ond þā ōþru geflīemde.

Anno dccclxxui

Hēr hiene bestæl se here intō Werhām Wesseaxna fierde. Ond wiþ þone here se

---

60 **Hēr . . . Norþhymbre** It is thought that the purpose of this expedition was to investigate a revolt against the puppet-king whom they had established in Northumbria.

65 **scōle** "Literally 'school,' but not in any modern sense of the word. It was first applied to the contingent supplied to the Roman militia by Englishmen in Rome, but by this time had clearly also acquired a local sense. It was on the Vatican Hill and was inhabited by ecclesiastics, pilgrims and others whose business took them to Rome" (*EHD*, p. 170 n. 7).

66 **ānum . . . þegne** His name, Ceolwulf, is given by the other MSS (and Æðelweard).

66 f. **tō haldanne** I.e. as a puppet king.

67 **hē**[2] MSS B C D E read *hit* (i.e. *Miercna rīce*), and this makes the meaning more immediately obvious.

him gearo wǣre "Would be at their disposal."

67 f. **swā hwelce dæge swā** "On whatever day."

68 **ond** Sc. *þæt*.

69 **on** = *mid* (which is the reading of MSS B C D E). For the sense of *on* here see BT s.v. A.III.(4–6), (10).

72 **oft** Corrected in MS A from *eft*.

77 **hiene . . . fierde** "The *here* [the one at *Grantebrycg*] slipped past the *fierd* of the West Saxons into *Werhām*." Literally *hine bestæl . . . fierde* is "bestole it-

cyning friþ nam, ond him þā āþas swōron on þām hālgan bēage, þe hīe ǣr nānre þēode noldon, þæt hīe hrædlīce of his rīce fōren. Ond hīe þā under þām hīe nihtes bestǣlon þǣre fierde—se gehorsoda here—intō Escanceaster.

Ond þȳ gēare Healfdene Norþanhymbra lond gedǣlde ond ergende wǣron ond hiera tilgende.

no dccclxxuii

Hēr cuōm se here intō Escanceastre from Werhām. Ond se sciphere sigelede west ymbūtan, ond þā mētte hīe micel ȳst on sǣ ond þǣr forwearþ cxx scipa æt Swānawīc. Ond se cyning Ælfred æfter þām gehorsudan here mid fierde rād oþ Exanceaster, ond hīe hindan ofrīdan ne meahte ǣr hīe on þām fæstene wǣron, þǣr him mon tō ne meahte. Ond hīe him þǣr foregīslas saldon, swā fela swā hē habban

---

self . . . with reference to the *fierd*" (or "away from the *fierd*," depending upon whether one takes *fierde* as gen. sg. [like most eds.] or dat. sg. [like BTS *bestelan* II.(1a)]).

Ond The other MSS add *siððan* (C E) or *syþþan* (B D).

78 **nam** Æðelweard adds: "giving them money at the same time." The other MSS (supported by Asser and Æðelweard) add: *and him þā gīslas sealdon þe on þām here weorþuste wǣron tō þām cyninge* (E), "and (they) gave him those hostages who in that army were most important next to the king," i.e. next to Godrum, who seems to have acted as leader among the three Viking kings. This passage reflects the original Chronicle text and has been somehow omitted from A.

ond . . . swōron Sc. *hīe* (the Vikings) as the subject.

þām hālgan bēage ON *stallahringr*, an armlet of silver or gold, weighing more than 1 lb. avoir. Ordinarily it was kept on the altar in a heathen temple: the priest wore it on his arm during sacrifices and oaths were sworn upon it after it had been reddened in sacrificial blood. Such oaths were unusually serious and binding—though this fact does not seem to have restrained the present group of Vikings.

78 f. **þe hīe . . . noldon** "(A thing) which they would not (do) before for any people."

79 **under þām** "Meanwhile; in the meantime."

79 f. **hīe³ . . . bestǣlon þǣre fierde** See l. 77 n. for the construction.

80 **se gehorsoda here** In apposition to the subject, *hīe*² in l. 79.

81 **Ond . . . gedǣlde** This is "the first of the three great partitions of territory which established Danish armies in more than a third of eastern England" (*A-SE* 252).

ergende wǣron Sc. *hīe*.

82 **hiera tilgende** "Providing for themselves," i.e. by farming instead of raiding.

83 **Hēr . . . Werhām** Recapitulating information from the preceding annal.

83 f. **west ymbūtan** "Westward along the coast," en route to reinforce the *here* at Exeter. The point of origin of this fleet is not known.

85 f. **Exanceaster** Acc.; cf. gen. sg. *Exanceastres* in l. 167. Forms like this are not uncommon when *ceaster* is used as the second element of a place-name; as a simplex, however, it is regularly declined as a fem. **o**-stem (like *frōfor*, p. 49).

87 **foregīslas** Either hostages "given as security for the performance of a promise" (BTS s.v.) or else " 'preliminary hostages' . . . given while the final terms (which might include permanent hostages) were being discussed" (Sweet[15], p. 237).

wolde, ond micle āþas swōron, ond þā gōdne friþ hēoldon. Ond þā on hærfeste gefōr se here on Miercna lond ond hit gedǣldon sum ond sum Cēolwulfe saldon.

Anno dccclxxuiii

Hēr hiene bestæl se here on midne winter ofer tuel*f*tan niht tō Cippanhamme ond geridon Wesseaxna lond ond gesǣton, *ond* micel þæs folces ofer sǣ ādrǣfdon, ond þæs ōþres þone mǣstan dǣl hīe geridon ond him tō gecirdon, būton þām cyninge Ælfrede: ond hē lӯtle werede uniēþelīce æfter wudum fōr ond on mōrfæstenum.

Ond þæs ilcan wintra wæs Inwæres brōþur ond Healfdenes on Westseaxum on Defenascīre mid xxiii scipum; ond hiene mon þǣr ofslōg ond dccc monna mid him ond xl monna his heres.

Ond þæs on Ēastron worhte Ælfred cyning lӯtle werede geweorc æt Æþelingaēigge, ond of þām geweorce was winnende wiþ þone here ond Sumursǣtna se dǣl sē þǣr nīehst wæs. Þā on þǣre seofoðan wiecan ofer Ēastron hē gerād tō Ecgbryhtesstāne be ēastan Sēalwyda, ond him tō cōm*on* þǣr ongēn Sumorsǣte

---

88 **þā**[1] "This time."

on hærfeste Since *hærfest* began on August 7th, this movement must have occurred between then and September 23rd (see 1.1 n.).

89 **on Miercna lond** Æðelweard implies that they made Gloucester their headquarters.

hit . . . sum[1] "Some of it"—in fact the eastern half of the kingdom.

Cēolwulfe See l. 66 f. and n.

90 **Hēr . . . tō Cippanhamme** "This treacherous move by the Danes at an unusual season took Wessex by surprise" (Smith). The *here* was led by Godrum and consisted of those warriors who had chosen not to settle in Mercia.

tuelftan niht The feast of the Epiphany, January 6th.

91 **ond micel þæs folces** The text of MS A (*micel þæs folces ond*) is emended on the basis of the other MSS.

92 **þæs ōþres** "Of the rest."

him tō gecirdon I.e. *gecirdon tō him* (the Danes).

93 **wudum, mōrfæstenum** Asser locates these in Somerset.

94 **Inwæres brōþur** Probably Ubba (see l. 2 n.). Asser gives much additional information about this encounter.

95 **ond**[1] **. . . ofslōg** Æðelweard identifies the English leader as Odda, *ealdorman* of Devon.

96 **ond xl monna his heres** Thus all MSS (except B C, who give the number as 60). It is hard to explain why these 40 (or 60) men should be singled out from the other 800; some scholars assume an error and read *hīredes* for *heres*, or else *hēafodmonna* for *monna*.

MSS B C D E all add: *and þār wæs se gūðfana genumen þe hī "Ræfen" hēton* (E). According to a twelfth-century source this banner had been woven by Ragnarr Loðbrók's daughters and could predict the issue of battles: before a victory there appeared *in medio signi quasi corvus vivus volitans* ("as it were a live raven flying in the center of the banner"), but before a defeat the banner hung limp.

97 **on Ēastron** March 23rd.

98 f. **Sumursǣtna se dǣl** This phrase is part of the subject.

100 **Ecgbryhtesstān** Unidentified.

cōmon The scribe of MS A wrote the sg. *cō* (= *cōm*); a later hand corrected it to pl.—the reading of the other MSS—by adding *-mon* above the line.

alle ond Wīlsǣtan ond Hamtūnscīr—se dǣl sē hiere behinon sǣ was—ond his gefægene wǣrun. Ond hē fōr ymb āne niht of þām wīcum tō Īglēa, ond þæs ymb āne tō Ēþandūne, ond þǣr gefeaht wiþ alne þone here ond hiene geflīemde ond him æfter rād oþ þæt geweorc ond þǣr sæt xiiii niht. Ond þā salde se here him foregīslas ond micle āþas þæt hīe of his rīce uuoldon, ond him ēac gehēton þæt hiera kyning fulwihte onfōn wolde: ond hīe þæt gelǣston swā.

Ond þæs ymb iii wiecan cōm se cyning tō him Godrum, þrītiga sum þāra monna þe in þām here weorþuste wǣron, æt Alre; ond þæt is wiþ Æþelinggaēige. Ond his se cyning þǣr onfēng æt fulwihte, ond his crismlīsing was æt Wēþmōr. Ond hē was xii niht mid þām cyninge; ond hē hine miclum ond his gefēran mid fēo weorðude.

no dccclxxix

Hēr fōr se here tō Cirenceastre of Cippanhamme ond sæt þǣr ān gēar. Ond þȳ gēare gegadrode *ān* hlōþ wīcenga ond gesæt æt Fullanhamme be Temese. Ond þȳ ilcan gēare āþīestrode sīo sunne āne tīd dæges.

no dccclxxx

Hēr fōr se here of Cirenceastre on Ēastengle ond gesæt þæt lond ond gedǣlde. Ond þȳ ilcan gēare fōr se here ofer sǣ, þe ǣr on Fullanhomme sæt, on Fronclond tō Gend, ond sæt þǣr ān gēar.

---

101 **se dǣl . . . was** "That portion of it which was on this side of the sea." Depending on one's identification of *sǣ*, this clause could refer to (1) the part of Hampshire west of Southampton Water, (2) its mainland territory north of the Solent (thus excluding the Isle of Wight), or (3) the portion of its populace which had not fled across the English Channel (cf. l. 91). Asser endorses the latter interpretation: *omnes accolae Hamtunensis qui non ultra mare pro metu paganorum nauigauerunt* ("all the inhabitants of Hampshire who had not sailed beyond the sea out of fear of the heathens").

102 **Iglēa** Iley (Oak) near Warminster, Wiltshire; its precise location is unknown.

104 **þæt geweorc** Probably at *Cippanhamm*.

107 **Godrum** In apposition to *se cyning*.

þrītiga sum Literally "one of thirty," i.e. with twenty-nine others; but by Ælfred's time the idiom has come to be carelessly used, and here it probably means "with thirty others."

109 **crismlīsing** "It was a very ancient custom for the newly baptized to be clad in white garments . . . to symbolise their purification. In these garments and with lighted tapers they appeared daily for a week with their sponsors in the church, finally laying them aside on the octave of the baptism-day. . . . With [this ceremony] was associated the 'chrisom-loosing,' the undoing of the 'chrismale' or linen fillet . . . which was bound round the head of the newly baptized to keep the chrism or unction on the head during the week [after baptism]" (Plummer[2], II, 280).

110 **hē[2]** Ælfred.

112 **fōr . . . Cirenceastre** Autumn, 878. The eclipse mentioned at the end of the annal occurred on October 29th, 878.

113 **ān** MS A reads *on*; all the others agree in reading *ān*.

After fourteen years of wreaking havoc in England, the *micel here* of 865 had finally disbanded. Its men had made large-scale permanent settlements in Northumbria (876), Mercia (877) and finally East Anglia (880). The decision of the new force (which rowed up the Thames and encamped at Fulham in the autumn of 878) to go to Ghent gave England a much-needed breathing-spell: for the next thirteen years the activities of this new Viking army were to be largely confined to the continent, though the Chronicle follows events there with close and anxious attention.

Not that the years from 879 to 892 were wholly without incident in England: in 882 *fōr Ælfred cyning mid scipum ūt on sǣ ond gefeaht wiþ fēower sciphlæstas Deniscra monna.* Late in 884 the *here*—which was then at Amiens—split in two; one group came to England and besieged Rochester. When this siege was relieved by Ælfred and the *fierd*, part of the Viking force returned immediately to the continent, while the other part left the next summer (885) after some raiding in which they were abetted by the Danes who were now settled in East Anglia. In retaliation, Ælfred launched a naval expedition against the latter, and the next year (886) he wrested London from them. This was a very important feat, the first consequence of which was that *him all Angelcyn tō cirde þæt būton Deniscra monna hæftnīede was.* Another important result of this struggle was a treaty between Ælfred and Godrum which defines the boundary between Wessex and the Danelaw (OE *Dena lagu*, ON **Danalǫg*, "the area in which the laws of the Danes are in force.").

The absence from England for thirteen years of a large invading army gave Ælfred much-needed time to reorganize the national defense system by establishing a series of permanent garrisons. The system was only brought to completion in the reign of his son Edward, in whose time "no village in Sussex, Surrey and Wessex east of the Tamar was distant more than twenty miles from a fortress which formed a unit in a planned scheme of national defence" (*A-SE* 264). It is clear that Ælfred was determined that this time he would be ready for the *here*, if and when it should decide to return to England.

Our excerpt resumes—in the middle of the annal for 891—with a miracle and a portent.

Þrīe Scottas cōmon tō Ælfrede cyninge on ānum bāte būtan ǣlcum gerēþrum of Hibernia, þonon hī hī bestǣlon for þon þe hī woldon for Godes lufan on elþīodignesse bēon, hī ne rōhton hwǣr. Se bāt wæs geworht of þriddan healfre

118 sq. **Scottas** Irishmen. The Old Irish *immrama* ("voyages") and saints' lives are rich in accounts of similar pilgrims, who are motivated by the same desire for exile and make the same absolute commitment to the will and guidance of God by putting out to sea without *gerēþru* ("oars, including rudder") and taking along inadequate provisions. The curraghs [ˈkərəks] or coracles in which they voyaged were amazingly sturdy vessels made of a basket-like wicker framework covered with hides sown together. They could be either rowed or sailed, and came in all sizes.

120 f. **of þriddan healfre hȳde** "Out of two and a half hides," lit. "out of (two full hides and) a third half hide."

hȳde þe hī on fōron, ond hī nāmon mid him þæt hī hæfdun tō seofonnihtum mete. Ond þā cōmon hīe ymb uii niht tō londe on Cornwālum ond fōron þā sōna tō Ælfrede cyninge. Þus hīe wǣron genemnde: Dubslane ond Maccbethu ond Maelinmun. Ond Swifneh, se betsta lārēow þe on Scottum wæs, gefōr.

no dcccxcii

Ond þȳ ilcan gēare ofer Ēastron, ymbe gangdagas oþþe ǣr, ætēowde se steorra þe mon on bōclǣden hǣt cometa; *sume* men cweþaþ on Englisc þæt hit sīe feaxede steorra, for þǣm þǣr stent lang lēoma of, hwīlum on āne healfe, hwīlum on ǣlce healfe.

no dcccxcii

Hēr on þysum gēare fōr se micla here, þe wē gefyrn ymbe sprǣcon, eft of þǣm

---

121 **ond . . . mete** "And they took along with them what they had (or should have [subjunctive]) as a week's food." Cf. Æðelweard: *alimentum sibi ebdomadarium subplent* ("they provided a week's food for themselves").

123 f. **Dubslane** etc. "Delaney and Macbeth." *Maelinmun* (MnIr *Maol Ionmhain*) means "the well-loved disciple."

124 **Swifneh** Suibhne ("Sweeney") mac Maelumha, anchorite and scribe of Clonmacnoise. News of his death—which Irish sources confirm as having occurred in this year—may have been brought to England by the three pilgrims.

Anno dcccxcii The first scribe of MS A laid aside his pen with this date entry for 892, leaving four blank lines at the bottom of the page (fol. 16^{r}). The second scribe, when he began writing at the top of the next page, did not start in at once on the new annal for 892, but added additional material to 891 (hence his phrase *þȳ ilcan gēare*). Unfortunately he forgot to cancel his predecessor's now inappropriate date entry, instead repeating it himself when he actually *did* reach 892 (after l. 128). A later scribe, finding what were apparently two annals for 892, altered the date of the latter to 893—and went on adding a year to every date entry all the way to 929. Our text ignores these erroneous corrections.

125 **Ēastron** April 4th.

gangdagas See p. 196.

126 **sume** MS A has *same* ("similarly"), which is not contextually inappropriate, since Lat. *cometa* is a loan from Gr. κομήτης [ἀστηρ], "long-haired [star]." However, MSS B C D all agree in reading *sume* here, and it would have been very easy for the scribe of A to have mistaken a *u* in his exemplar for an open *a*; furthermore *same* is not found apart from the combination *swā same* (*swā*). Cf. 6/5 f.

127 f. **on ǣlce healfe** "On every side." For the acc. rection of *on* in this situation of rest, see BT s.v. B.I.(3).

129 **Hēr** R. H. Hodgkin claims that for the annals 892–6 indictional dating (see 1.1 n.) is dropped, and the annalistic year begins at Christmas. Dorothy Whitelock, however, while acknowledging that these annals "do not keep to a year from September to September," attributes it to the fact that in them, written as they apparently are "all in a piece, in a distinctive style, the writer is more concerned to mark the end of a campaigning year than of a calendar year." Since the annual campaigns "went on until the army took up winter quarters, his annals go on after 23 September. Even if, however, we accept Hodgkin's view that he begins his year at Christmas, we should attribute this change to an individual writer, for after he ceases we find at 900 the September beginning still in use" (Plummer[1], II, cxli f.).

ēastrīce westweard tō Bunnan, ond þǣr wurdon gescipode, swā þæt hīe āsettan him on ānne sīþ ofer mid horsum mid ealle, ond þā cōmon ūp on Limenemūþan mid ccl hunde scipa. Se mūþa is on ēastweardre Cent, æt þæs micla*n* wuda ēastende þe wē Andred hātað: se wudu is ēastlang ond westlang hundtwelftiges mīla lang oþþe lengra, ond þrītiges mīla brād. Sēo ēa þe wē ǣr ymbe sprǣcon līð ūt of þǣm wealda. On þā ēa hī tugon ūp hiora scipu oþ þone weald, iiii mīla fram þǣm mūþan ūteweardum, ond þǣr ābrǣcon ān geweorc inne on þǣm fenne: sǣton fēawa cirlisce men on, ond wæs sāmworht.

Þā sōna æfter þǣm cōm Hǣstēn mid lxxx scipa ūp on Temesemūðan ond worhte him geweorc æt Middeltūne, ond se ōþer here æt Apuldre.

Anno dcccxciii

On þȳs gēare—þæt wæs ymb twelf mōnað þæs þe hīe on þǣm ēastrīce geweorc geworht hæfdon—Norþhymbre ond Ēastengle hæfdon Ælfrede cyninge āþas geseald, ond Ēastengle foregīsla ui. Ond þēh, ofer þā trēowa, swā oft swā þā ōþre hergas mid ealle herige ūt fōron, þonne fōron hīe, oþþe mid oþþe on heora healfe.

---

129 f. **eft of þǣm ēastrīce** There they had been defeated the year before by Arnulf, king of the East Franks, in a battle on the River Dyle (at Louvain); a famine coming on the heels of this defeat was responsible for their return to England late in 892.

131 **mid horsum mid ealle** "With all their horses." The adv. phrase *mid ealle* means literally "altogether, completely"; cf. ON *með ǫllu*.

on Limenemūþan "Into the estuary of the Lympne," a river which has changed its course and dwindled considerably since 892. It flowed past Appledore and into the sea at Lympne.

132 **ccl hunde** The *hunde* (ostensibly an irregular dat. pl.) is redundant. (It may well result from corruption; cf. the reading of MSS E F: *þridde healf hund*).

miclan MS *miclam* (itself apparently corrected from *miclum*). The error arose through the scribe's careless assumption that this adj. was part of a dat. phrase governed by *æt*, rather than part of the gen. phrase complementary to *ēastende*.

133 **Andred** See 3/3 n.

hundtwelftiges Gen. of measure, complement of *lang*.

135 **tugon** "Rowed."

136 **fenne** So too MS E. MSS B C D agree in reading *fæsten(n)e* here, which could also be right.

137 **ond wæs sāmworht** I.e. the *geweorc*.

138 **Hǣstēn** A Viking leader active on the continent since 866 (ON *Hásteinn*).

139 **Apuldre** E adds *Hic obiit Wulfhere Norðanhymbrorum archeipiscopus* ("Here died Wulfhere, archbishop of the Northumbrians"), whereupon there begins a long series of blank annals in E, which does not resume until the year of Ælfred's death (see 11. 286 ff. n.).

140 **geweorc** The *micla here* had encamped at Louvain over the winter of 891–2, after its defeat at the Dyle: cf. l. 129 f. n.

141 **Norþhymbre ond Ēastengle** I.e. the Danes who had been settled there since 876 and 880 respectively, and whose neutrality Ælfred hoped to insure by collecting oaths and hostages from them.

142 **foregīsla** Cf. l. 87 n.

142 f. **þā ōþre hergas** From Appledore and Milton.

143 **mid ealle herige** "In full force."

heora healfe Either "their own behalf" or "their (the two armies') behalf."

Ond þā gegaderade Ælfred cyning his fierd ond fōr þæt hē gewīcode betwuh þǣm twām hergum, þǣr þǣr hē nīehst rȳmet hæfde for wudufæstenne ond for wæterfæstenne, swā þæt hē mehte ǣgþerne gerǣcan gif hīe ǣnigne feld sēcan wolden. Þā fōron hīe siþþan æfter þǣm wealda hlōþum ond flocrādum, bī swā hwaþerre efes swā hit þonne fierdlēas wæs: ond hī ˌ mon ēac mid ōþrum floccum sōhte mǣstra daga ǣlce, oþþe on niht, ge of þǣre fierde ge ēac of þǣm burgum. (Hæfde se cyning his fierd on tū tōnumen, swā þæt hīe wǣron simle healfe æt hām, healfe ūte, būtan þǣm monnum þe þā burga healdan scolden.) Ne cōm se here oftor eall ūte of þǣm setum þonne tuwwa: ōþre sīþe þā hīe ǣrest tō londe cōmon, ǣr sīo fierd gesamnod wǣre; ōþre sīþe þā hīe of þǣm setum faran woldon.

Þā hīe gefēngon micle herehȳð ond þā woldon ferian norþweardes ofer Temese, in on Ēastseaxe ongēan þā scipu, þā forrād sīo fierd hīe foran ond him wið gefeaht æt Fearnhamme, ond þone here geflīemde ond þā herehȳþa āhreddon; ond hīe flugon ofer Temese būton ǣlcum forda, þā ūp be Colne on ānne iggað. Þā besæt sīo fierd hīe þǣr ūtan þā hwīle þe hīe þǣr lengest mete hæfdon. Ac hī hæfdon þā heora stemn gesetenne ond hiora mete genotudne: ond wæs se cyng þā þiderweardes

---

144 **Ond** MS A reads *on heora healfe an* followed by a *punctus* (see p. 225). It is just barely possible that this *an* = *ān* (adv.) "only," in which case the entire phrase would mean "solely on their (own) behalf." MS B has *on* here; C and D have the symbol for *ond*.

145 **þǣr[1] . . . hæfde** "Where he could get closest" (lit. "where he had room most close by").

145 f. **for[1] . . . wæterfæstenne** There are three possible interpretations: (1) "with regard to (both) the stronghold in the wood and the stronghold by the water" (i.e. Appledore and Milton respectively, which are some twenty-five miles apart); (2) "(and yet) with a view to (assuring himself and his troops) the protection offered by wood and water"; (3) "considering the (natural) barrier presented by forest and water."

146 **ǣgþerne** Sc. *here*.

146 f. **gif . . . wolden** "In case they should come out into the open" (lit. "in case they wished to make for any open country"). Or *feld* here could mean "a pitched battle."

147 **hīe** The Danes.

148 **hit** Redundant; cf. 24/195b.

149 **oþþe on niht** MSS C D precede this phrase with *oþþe on dæg* (C); B agrees with A.

150 f. **(Hæfde . . . scolden)** Referring to an important innovation of Ælfred's whereby only half the men who were available for military service were called up at one time, the other half staying home until their turn (*stemn*) came. The system provided for a continuously existing army. See ll. 158 ff.

151 **se here** At Appledore.

154 **Þā** "When" (correlative with *þā* "then" in l. 155). The second *þā* in this line is a pronoun (acc. sg. fem., *herehȳð* being the antecedent).
gefēngon "(Had) seized."

155 **ongēan þā scipu** "To meet the ships," which had presumably been despatched from the Lympne estuary after the debarkation of the *here*. (But compare the sequence of events according to Æðelweard, in the note to ll. 161 ff. below.)
sīo fierd Æðelweard says that this division was led by Ælfred's son Eadweard.

157 **ānne iggað** Thorney Island (Hertfordshire).

158 **hīe[2]** The English.

159 **stemn** MSS B C D have *stem(n)inge*, which has the same meaning.

on fære mid þǣre scīre þe mid him fierdedon.

Þā hē þā wæs þiderweardes, ond sīo ōþeru fierd wæs hāmweardes, ond ðā Deniscan sǣton þǣr behindan (for þǣm hiora cyning wæs gewundod on þǣm gefeohte þæt hī hine ne mehton ferian), þā gegaderedon þā þe in Norþhymbrum būgeað ond on Ēastenglum sum hund scipa ond fōron sūð ymbūtan, ond sum fēowertig scipa norþ ymbūtan ond ymbsǣton ān geweorc on Defnascīre be þǣre Norþsǣ; ond þā þe sūð ymbūtan fōron ymbsǣton Exancester. Þā se cyng þæt hīerde, þā wende hē hine west wið Exanceastres mid ealre þǣre fierde būton swīþe gewaldenum dǣle ēasteweardes þæs folces: þā fōron forð oþ þe hīe cōmon tō Lundenbyrg, ond þā mid þǣm burgwarum ond þǣm fultume þe him westan cōm fōron ēast tō Bēamflēote. Wæs Hǣstēn þā þǣr cumen mid his herge þe ǣr æt Middeltūne sæt, ond ēac se micla here wæs þā þǣrtō cumen þe ǣr on Limenemūþan sæt æt Apuldre. Hæfde Hǣstēn ǣr geworht þæt geweorc æt Bēamflēote, ond wæs þā ūt āfaren on hergaþ, ond wæs se micla here æt hām. Þā fōron hīe tō ond geflīemdon þone here ond þæt geweorc ābrǣcon ond genāmon eal þæt þǣr binnan wæs—ge on fēo ge on wīfum ge ēac on bearnum—ond brōhton eall intō Lundenbyrig, ond þā scipu eall oððe tōbrǣcon oþþe forbærndon oþþe tō Lundenbyrig brōhton oþþe tō Hrōfesceastre. Ond Hǣstēnes wīf ond his suna twēgen mon brōhte tō þǣm cyninge, ond hē hī him eft āgeaf, for þǣm þe hiora wæs ōþer his godsunu, ōþer Æðeredes ealdormonnes: hæfdon hī hiora onfangen ǣr Hǣstēn tō Bēamflēote cōme, ond hē him hæfde geseald gīslas ond āðas, ond se cyng him ēac wel feoh sealde (ond ēac

---

161 ff. **ðā Deniscan . . . ferian** The next time the Chronicle mentions the *micla here*, it has joined Hæsten in his new quarters at Benfleet (l. 171). Æðelweard fills in the gap as follows: when Eadweard (see l. 155 n.) was still besieging the Danes on Thorney, Æðelred, *ealdorman* of Mercia, "set out from the city of London, and gave the prince help. The barbarians asked for peace, and for conditions set out by treaty. Hostages were given." The Danes agreed to leave Æðelred's province. "They set out then for East Anglia, . . . and their ships sped round from the harbour of the Lympne to [meet] them at Mersea" (Campbell).

164 f. **sum feowertig scipa** Sc. *fōron* or *ond fōron*. This entire clause *ond . . . ymbūtan*[2] is missing in B C D.

165 **þǣre Norþsǣ** The Bristol Channel. "It is still so called by Plymouth fishermen" (Sweet[15]).

168 **ēasteweardes þæs folces** Probably "of the eastern part of the army," i.e. those whose homes were in the east; cf. a phrase like *on easteweardum þissum middangearde* in the OE Orosius (see Sweet's edition 136/6 f. and 26 f.). It is less likely that *ēasteweardes* is an adv. here and that the phrase means "of the army (which continued) eastwards."

þā "They."

172 **ǣr** I.e. before the arrival there of the *micla here*.

173 **tō** "Thither."

175 **eall**[2] An adj. (acc. pl. neut.) in apposition to *scipu*.

178 **hiora wæs ōþer** I.e. *ōþer hiora wæs*.

Æðeredes Cf. ll. 161 ff. n.

179 **hī** Ælfred and Æðered.

hiora onfangen Sc. *æt fulwihte*, cf. l. 109.

179 f. **hæfdon . . . sealde** Ælfred must have started negotiating with Hæsten soon after the latter's arrival at Milton: "Within a few weeks he was able to impose a treaty upon Hæsten, as a result of which he and his men left Kent for Essex, and his two sons were baptized" (*A-SE* 266).

swā þā hē þone cniht āgef ond þæt wīf). Ac sōna swā hīe tō Bēamflēote cōmon ond þæt geweorc geworct wæs, swā hergode hē his rīce, þone ilcan ende þe Æþered his cumpæder healdan sceolde. Ond eft ōþre sīþe hē wæs on hergað gelend on þæt ilce rīce, þā þā mon his geweorc ābræc.

Þā se cyning hine þā west wende mid þǣre fierde wið Exancestres, swā ic ǣr sǣde, ond se here þā burg beseten hæfde, þā hē þǣrtō gefaren wæs, þā ēodon hīe tō hiora scipum.

Þā hē þā wið þone here þǣr wæst ābisgod wæs, ond þā hergas wǣron þā gegaderode bēgen tō Scēobyrig on Ēastseaxum ond þǣr geweorc worhtun, fōron bēgen ætgædere ūp be Temese, ond him cōm micel ēaca tō, ǣgþer ge of Ēastenglum ge of Norþhymbrum; fōron þā ūp be Temese oþ þæt hīe gedydon æt Sæferne, þā ūp be Sæferne. Þā gegaderode Æþered ealdormon ond Æþelm ealdorman ond Æþelnōþ ealdorman ond þā cinges þegnas þe þā æt hām æt þǣm geweorcum wǣron, of ǣlcre byrig be ēastan Pedredan ge be westan Sēalwuda ge be ēastan, ge ēac be norþan Temese ond be westan Sæfern, ge ēac sum dǣl þæs Norðwēalcynnes. Þā hīe þā ealle gegaderode wǣron, þā offōron hīe þone here hindan æt Buttingtūne on Sæferne staþe, ond hine þǣr ūtan besǣton on ǣlce healfe on ānum fæstenne.

Þā hīe ðā fela wucena sǣton on twā healfe þǣr*e* ē, ond se cyng wæs west on Defnum wiþ þone sciphere, þā wǣron hīe mid metelīeste gewǣgde ond hæfdon micelne dǣl þāra horsa freten, ond þā ōþre wǣron hungre ācwolen. Þā ēodon hīe ūt tō ðǣm monnum þe on ēasthealfe þǣre ē wīcodon ond him wiþ gefuhton, ond þā Crīstnan hæfdon sige. Ond þǣr wearð Ordhēh cyninges þegn ofslægen, ond ēac monige ōþre cyninges þegn*as*; *ond þāra Deniscra þǣr wearð swīðe mycel ge*slegen, ond se dǣl þe þǣr āweg cōm wurdon on flēame generede.

---

182 **geworct wæs** The *t* of *geworct* was written in later, above the line. The reading of B C D here is *geworht hæfdon* (D).
hē After this word, a later hand has added *on* above the line; the correction (which is not supported by C D) is entirely a matter of style. B has *swā hergode hē on his rīces þone ende þe* etc.

182 f. **his**[1,2] Referring respectively to Ælfred and Hæsten.

185 f. **Þā** in l. 185 and *þā*[1] in 186 introduce two non-coordinate (asyndetic) "when" clauses, both correlative to the "then" clause beginning with *þā*[2] in 186.

188 **wæst** This spelling in A probably results from anticipation of the following *wæs*; cf. l. 198 n.
þā hergas The *micla here* and the force commanded by Hæsten.

189 **fōron** Introducing the main clause, with zero correlation. B C D add *þā*.

192 **gegaderode** "Came together," inflected sg. to agree with the first member of the complex subject.

192 f. **Æþelm . . . ealdorman** Of Wiltshire and Somerset respectively.

193 f. **of ǣlcre byrig** An adv. phrase modifying *gegaderode*.

197 **on ǣlce healfe** Cf. 1 . 127 f. n.
on ānum fæstenne "There are still traces of an island between two branches of the Severn at . . . Buttington," which is near Welshpool (*A-SE* 267 n. 2).

198 **hīe** The English.
wæs west The scribe at first conflated these two words, writing *wæst*. Then he noticed his error and added the missing letters (*wes*) above the line. Cf. l. 188.

199 **hīe** The Danes.

200 **þā ōþre** Sc. *hors*.

203 **þegnas . . . geslegen** Thus B and (substantially) C D. The reading of A here is: *þegn* (with *-as* added above the line by a later corrector) *ofslægen*. The

Þā hīe on Ēastseaxe cōmon tō hiora geweorce ond tō hiora scipum, þā gegaderade sīo lāf eft of Ēastenglum ond of Norðhymbrum micelne here onforan winter, ond befæston hira wīf ond hira scipu ond hira feoh on Ēastenglum ond fōron ānstreces dæges ond nihtes þæt hīe gedydon on ānre wēstre ceastre on Wīrhēalum, sēo is Lēgaceaster gehāten. Þā ne mehte sēo fird hīe nā hindan offaran ǣr hīe wǣron inne on þǣm geweorce; besǣton þēah þæt geweorc ūtan sume twēgen dagas, ond genāmon cēapes eall þæt þǣr būton wæs, ond þā men ofslōgon þe hīe foran forrīdan mehton būtan geweorce, ond þæt corn eall forbærndon, ond mid hira horsum fretton, on ǣlcre efenēhðe. Ond þæt wæs ymb twelf mōnað þæs þe hīe ǣr hider ofer sǣ cōmon.

Anno dcccxciv

Ond þā sōna æfter þǣm, on ðȳs gēre, fōr se here of Wīrhēale in on Norðwēalas, for þǣm hīe ðǣr sittan ne mehton: þæt wæs for ðȳ þe hīe wǣron benumene ǣgðer ge þæs cēapes ge þæs cornes ðe hīe gehergod hæfdon. Þā hīe ðā eft ūt of Norðwēalum wendon mid þǣre herehȳðe þe hīe ðǣr genumen hæfdon, þā fōron hīe ofer Norðhymbra lond ond Ēastengla, swā swā sēo fird hīe gerǣcan ne mehte, oþ þæt hīe cōmon on Ēastseaxna lond ēasteweard on ān īgland þæt is ūte on þǣre sǣ, þæt is Meresīg hāten.

Ond þā se here eft hāmweard wende þe Exanceaster beseten hæfde, þā hergodon hīe ūp on Sūðseaxum nēah Cisseceastre; ond þā burgware hīe geflīemdon ond hira monig hund ofslōgon ond hira scipu sumu genāmon.

Ðā þȳ ilcan gēre onforan winter þā Deniscan þe on Meresīge sǣton tugon hira scipu ūp on Temese, ond þā ūp on Lȳgan. Þæt wæs ymb twā gēr þæs þe hīe hider ofer sǣ cōmon.

---

scribe probably reproduced the phrase *þegn ofslægen* from 1. 202 by dittography; then his eye jumped from the *-slægen* which he had just written to *-slegen* in 203, and he continued on from there—omitting the clause *ond . . . geslegen* in its entirety.

swīðe mycel "A very great (part)." D adds *wæl* (unnecessarily).

209 **Lēgaceaster** Chester, no doubt a *wēste ceaster* since the great battle fought there, sometime in the years 613–16, by Æðelfrið of Northumbria against the Britons (see Bede, *Historia Ecclesiastica*, II. ii; *A-SE* 77 f.). *Lēgaceaster* < *Legionis* (or *-um*) *Castra*, "Fortress of the Legion(s)": in Roman times it had been the headquarters of the twentieth legion.

213 **fretton** "Grazed up, grazed to ruin"; cf. *ettan* "to graze" (8/49). These two verbs are causatives from *fretan* and *etan* respectively.

on ǣlcre efenēhðe "Within a (certain) radius," lit. "in every (place of) equal nearness." *Efenēhðe* is dat. sg. of **efennīehðu*, with which cf. the adj. *efennēah*.

217 **hīe**[1] The English.

219 **ond Ēastengla** MS B has *ond swā on Ēastengle*, with which C D agree substantially.

swā swā Probably introducing a purpose clause in the subjunctive (see BT *swā* VI.(Ia)), and hence equivalent to *swā þæt*.

223 **þā burgware** Subject.

224 **sumu** In apposition to *scipu*.

225 **onforan winter** MSS B and C have *on forewe(a)rdne winter*, and D (substantially) agrees.

no dcccxcv

On þȳ ilcan gēre worhte se foresprecena here geweorc be Lȳgan, xx mīla bufan Lundenbyrig. Þā þæs on sumera fōron micel dǣl þāra burgwara, ond ēac swā ōþres folces, þæt hīe gedydon æt þāra Deniscana geweorce, ond þǣr wurdon geflīemde ond sume fēower cyninges þegnas ofslægene. Þā þæs on hærfeste þā wīcode se cyng on nēaweste þǣre byrig þā hwīle þe hīe hira corn gerypon, þæt þā Deniscan him ne mehton þæs rīpes forwiernan. Þā sume dæge rād se cyng ūp bī þǣre ēæ ond gehāwade hwǣr mon mehte þā ēa forwyrcan, þæt hīe ne mehton þā scipu ūt brengan. Ond hīe ðā swā dydon: worhton ðā tū geweorc on twā healfe þǣre ēas. Þā hīe ðā þæt geweorc furþum ongunnen hæfdon, ond þǣrtō gewīcod hæfdon, þā onget se here þæt hīe ne mehton þā scipu ūt brengan; þā forlēton hīe hīe ond ēodon ofer land þæt hīe gedydon æt Cwatbrycge be Sæfern, ond þǣr gewerc worhton. Þā rād sēo fird west æfter þǣm herige, ond þā men of Lundenbyrig gefetedon þā scipu, ond þā ealle þe hīe ālǣdan ne mehton tōbrǣcon, ond þā þe þǣr stælwyrðe wǣron binnan Lundenbyrig gebrōhton. Ond þā Deniscan hæfdon hira wīf befæst innan Eastengle ǣr hīe ūt of þǣm geweorce fōron. Þā sǣton hīe þone winter æt Cwatbrycge. Þæt wæs ymb þrēo gēr þæs þe hīe on Limenemūðan cōmon hider ofer sǣ.

no dcccxcvi

Ðā þæs on sumera on ðysum gēre tōfōr se here, sum on Ēastengle, sum on Norðhymbre; ond þā þe feohlēase wǣron him þǣr scipu begēton ond sūð ofer sǣ fōron tō Sigene.

Næfde se here, Godes þonces, Angelcyn ealles forswīðe gebrocod, ac hīe wǣron micle swīþor gebrocede on þǣm þrim gēarum mid cēapes cwilde ond monna, ealles swīþost mid þǣm þæt manige þāra sēlestena cynges þēna þe þǣr on londe wǣron forðfērdon on þǣm þrim gēarum: þāra wæs sum Swīðulf biscop on Hrōfesceastre, ond Cēolmund ealdormon on Cent, ond Beorhtulf ealdormon on Ēastseaxum, ond Wulfred ealdormon on Hamtūnscīre, ond Ealhheard biscop æt Dorceceastre, ond Ēadulf cynges þegn on Sūðseaxum, ond Beornulf wīcge*rēf*a on Winteceastre, ond Ecgulf cynges horsþegn, ond manige ēac him, þēh ic ðā geðungnestan nemde.

Þȳ ilcan gēare drehton þā hergas on Ēastenglum ond on Norðhymbrum Westseaxna lond swīðe be þǣm sūðstæðe mid stælhergum, ealra swīþust mid ðǣm æscum þe hīe fela gēara ǣr timbredon. Þā hēt Ælfred cyng timbran lang scipu ongēn ðā æscas; þā wǣron fulnēah tū swā lang swā þā ōðru. Sume hæfdon lx āra, sume mā;

---

228 f. **On . . . Lundenbyrig** "The first sentence of this annal would have been better placed at the end of the previous one" (*EHD*, p. 188 n. 4). The sentence is introduced by *On* in A B, by *Ond* in C D.

231 **þā** Omitted B C D, as is *ðā*[2] in l. 235.

235 **þǣre ēas** Compare 8/19 and see Campbell ∫625. The other MSS read *ēa* here.

240 **ealle** Nom. pl. neut. (for the final *-e* see l. 258 n.), in apposition to *þā* ("those"). **mehton** B C D add *hī*.

245 **þā . . . wǣron** And therefore unable to purchase land for themselves?

247 **Godes þonces** "Through God's grace" (*Dei gratia*); *þonces* is adv. gen.

248 **ealles** B C D have *ealra*.

253 **wīcgerēfa** So B C D. A's reading *wīcgefēra* has inadvertently substituted the familiar noun *gefēra* for *gerēfa*.

255 **on** "(Originating) in."

258 **þā**[1] Pronoun (so too *þā*[1] in l. 259).

lang An *-e* has been added above the line, perhaps by another hand: note that

þā wǣron ǣgðer ge swiftran ge unwealtran ge ēac hīeran þonne þā ōðru. Nǣron nāwðer ne on Frēsisc gescæpene ne on Denisc, būte swā him selfum ðūhte þæt hīe nytwyrðoste bēon meahten.

Þā æt sumum cirre þæs ilcan gēares cōmon þǣr sex scipu tō Wiht, ond þǣr micel yfel gedydon, ǣgðer ge on Defenum ge welhwǣr be ðǣm sǣriman. Þā hēt se cyng faran mid nigonum tō þāra nīwena scipa, ond forfōron him þone mūðan foran on ūtermere. Þā fōron hīe mid þrim scipum ūt ongēn hīe, ond þrēo stōdon æt ufeweardum þǣm mūðan on drȳgum: wǣron þā men uppe on londe of āgāne. Þā gefēngon hīe þāra þrēora scipa tū æt ðǣm mūðan ūteweardum, ond þā men ofslōgon; ond þæt ān oðwand. On þǣm wǣron ēac þā men ofslægene būton fīfum; þā cōmon for ðȳ onweg ðe ðāra ōþerra scipu āsǣton. Þā wurdon ēac swīðe unēðelīce āseten: þrēo āsǣton on ðā healfe þæs dēopes ðe ðā Deniscan scipu āseten wǣron, ond þā ōðru eall on ōþre healfe, þæt hira ne mehte nān tō ōðrum. Ac ðā þæt wæter wæs āhebbad fela furlanga from þǣm scipum, þā ēodon ðā Deniscan from þǣm þrim scipum tō þǣm ōðrum þrim þe on hira healfe beebbade wǣron, ond þā þǣr gefuhton. Þǣr wearð ofslægen Lucumon cynges gerēfa, ond Wulfheard Frīesa, ond Æbbe Frīesa, ond Æðelhere Frīesa, ond Æðelferð cynges genēat, ond ealra monna, Frēsiscra ond Engliscra, lxii, ond þāra Deniscena cxx. Þā cōm þǣm Deniscum scipum þēh ǣr flōd tō, ǣr þā Crīstnan mehten hira ūt āscūfan, ond hīe for ðȳ ūt oðrēowon. Þā wǣron hīe tō þǣm gesārgode þæt hīe ne mehton Sūðseaxna lond ūtan berōwan, ac hira þǣr tū sǣ on lond wearp; ond þā men mon lǣdde tō Winteceastre tō þǣm cynge, ond hē hīe ðǣr āhōn hēt. Ond þā men cōmon on

---

lang stands uncorrected in the previous line. B C D read *lange* in both instances. These (unhistorical) final *e*'s have been extended from the masc. pl. (see Sprockel p. 191).

259 **hīeran** For *hīerran*, with simplification of *-rr-* (see Sprockel §6.10.3.(1)).
Nǣron B C D add *hī(e)*.

260 **on Frēsisc** "On the Frisian (model)." The Frisians, like the Vikings, were famous shipbuilders and merchants, and Ælfred's new fleet was to some extent commanded by Frisians (cf. ll. 274 ff.).

264 **tō** Adv. with *faran* (cf. l. 173).
forfōron Sc. *hīe* (the English) as the subject.
him "For them, against them (the Danes)."
þone mūðan It is not possible to identify with certainty the estuary or harbor along the south coast of England where this engagement occurred. For a survey of the various suggestions and a detailed (but often highly speculative) play-by-play account of the battle, see *MLR*, XXXVII (1942), 409–14.

264 f. **foran on ūtermere** "At the seaward end."

269 **þā . . . āsǣton** "They got away because the ships of the others (i.e. the English) were aground." They may well have drifted into shoal water while their oarsmen were busy fighting, and then been stranded there by the outgoing tide (cf. ll. 271–74).
Þā Pronoun.

270 **āseten**[2] One expects *on āseten*.

271 **ōðru** Omitted B C D.

272 **āhebbad** I.e. *āebbad* (the reading of C D), with "incorrect addition of the symbol *h*" (Campbell §61); B has *geebbad*.

273 **ond** After this word a later hand has added *hīe* above the line; B C D also read *hī(e)* here.

277 **hira** Sc. *scipu*.

279 **hira** Sc. *scipa*.

Ēastengle þe on þǣm ānum scipe wǣron, swīðe forwundode. Þȳ ilcan sumera forwearð nō lǣs þonne xx scipa mid monnum mid ealle be þǣm sūðriman.

Þȳ ilcan gēre forðfērde Wulfrīc cynges horsðegn, sē wæs ēac Wealhgefēra.

no dcccxcvii

Hēr on þysum gēre gefōr Æðelm, Wīltūnscīre ealdormon, nigon nihtum ǣr middum sumere; ond hēr forðfērde Hēahstān, sē wæs on Lundenne biscop.

no dcccxcviii

no dcccxcix

no dcccc

Hēr gefōr Ælfred Aþulfing, syx nihtum ǣr ealra hāligra mæssan. Sē wæs cyning ofer eall Ongelcyn, būtan ðǣm dǣle þe under Dena onwalde wæs, ond hē hēold þæt rīce ōþrum healfum lǣs þe xxx wintra. Ond þā fēng Ēadweard his sunu tō rīce.

---

282 **mid ealle** See l. 131 n.

283 **Wealhgefēra** Since B C D agree in reading *-gerēfa*, the scribe of A may well have made the same mistake here as he made in l. 253, q.v. *Wealhgefēra* (A) has been interpreted as the commander of a troop of men (the *Walhfæreld*) assigned to patrol the Welsh marches; *Wealhgerēfa* (B C D) as the reeve in charge of the king's Welsh serfs. But these are both guesses.

285 **Hēahstān** B C D *Ealhstān* (erroneously).

286 ff. **Hēr . . . wintra** The reading of E (and substantially D) is: *Hēr gefōr Ælfred cyning vii Kalendarum Novembris, and hē hēold þet rīce xxviii wintra and healf gēar*. Ælfred's death occurred on October 26th, 899; the fact that it is entered under 900 shows that indictional dating is in use here (see 1.1 n., 129 n.).

288 **ōþrum healfum** B C add *gēare*. *Ōþer healf (gēar)* = "one and one half (years)."

5 / The Battle of Brunanburh

In 937 a West-Saxon and Mercian army led by King Æðelstan of Wessex and his brother Eadmund defeated a coalition of Scandinavians and Scots under the command of Ólafr Guðfriðarson, King of Dublin, and Constantinus III, King of Scotland. This English triumph, one episode in a long struggle between Æðelstan and the Norse kings of Dublin for control of Northumbria, can be seen in retrospect as a climactic step in the series of events, beginning in the reign of Ælfred, Æðelstan's grandfather, that assured the ultimate unity of England. Even in its own day it was felt to be an engagement of the first importance: legend quickly accumulated around it and it came to be referred to simply as *bellum magnum* ("the great battle"). There is a very stirring (and highly fabulous) account of it in the Icelandic *Egils saga Skallagrímssonar*; Egill had himself been present, fighting on Æðelstan's side. Ironically the site of the battle, *ymbe Brūnanburh* ("around Brown's fort"), near *Dinges mere* ("the Sea of Storm"), has never been satisfactorily identified. It was probably somewhere along the west coast of England between Chester and Dumfries.

The song that was composed to celebrate this battle moves on two traditional poles, the contrasting emotions of unrestrained panegyric for the victors and ironic scorn for the defeated. Although it sets out to lavish praise upon the royal house of Wessex, it goes further, conceiving of the battle as a victory of the whole English nation. The absence of references to the *comitatus* relationship is symptomatic of this new national consciousness, as is also the highly effective conclusion, where the battle is placed in a large context of racial history and aspiration. Though the poem is very conventional in subject matter and versification, it is clearly the work of a man who handles the traditional tools of poetic composition with great authority, vitalizing convention by his own emotional force and fitting traditional halflines and themes into a coherent and eloquent whole.

The poem survives today in four MSS of the Anglo-Saxon Chronicle, A B C and D (see above, p. 136). The version contained in A seems nearest to the poet's original, therefore it is adopted by modern editors as the basis of their texts. This version was entered on vellum at Winchester, soon after 955, by the third scribe of A (who was responsible for the annals for 925–965). It exhibits a large number of peculiar forms and is rich in examples of uncertainty as to the spelling of weakly stressed inflectional syllables: for example the 3 pl. pret. indic. of verbs ends in both *-an* and *-un* (in addition to more usual *-on*), and the dat. pl. of nouns and adjs. ends in *-an* or *-un* (as well as historical *-um*).

The best modern edition is Alistair Campbell's *The Battle of Brunanburh* (London 1938), which contains an excellent and exhaustive treatment of all aspects of the poem. There is a famous translation by Tennyson and an interesting critique by Milton: "the *Saxon* Annalist [,] wont to be sober and succinct. . , now labouring under the weight of his Argument, and over-charg'd, runs on a sudden into such extravagant fansies and metaphors, as bare him quite beside the scope of being understood."[1]

[1] *The History of Britain*, in *The Works of John Milton*, X (New York 1932), 233.

Anno dccccxxxvii

Hēr Æþelstān cyning, eorla dryhten,
beorna bēahgifa, ond his brōþor ēac,
Ēadmund æþeling, ealdorlangne tīr
geslōgon æt sæcce sweorda ecgum
ymbe Brūnanburh. Bordweal clufan,
hēowan heaþolinde hamora lāfan
afaran Ēadweardes, swā him geæþele wæs
from cnēomægum, þæt hī æt campe oft
wiþ lāþra gehwæne land ealgodon,
hord ond hāmas. Hettend crungun,
Sceotta lēoda ond scipflotan,

1a **Hēr** "In this year." The word refers to the date entry and is not likely to have been part of the original composition. In fact it somewhat misleadingly suggests that the poem was composed to celebrate a date rather than a deed.

3a **Ēadmund æþeling** He was sixteen years old at the time of the battle. Succeeding Æðelstan in 939, he ruled until 946.

4b **sweorda ecgum** "With the edges of swords": *ecgum* is dat. pl., instrumental in function.

5a **Brūnanburh** Before *n*[1] another *n* has been added above the line by another hand.

5b **bordweal** D.o.; the subject is *afaran* in 7a.

6b **hamora lāfan** "With leavings of hammers": a kenning (see p. 268) for swords, which are "left" (i.e. produced) by the hammers of weapon-smiths.

7b–8a The clause *swā . . . cnēomægum* plays two syntactic roles, first subordinate clause to the main clause which precedes it, then main clause to the subordinate clause which follows it. This construction (known as apo koinou) pivots on *swā*, which functions as an adverbial conjunction ("as") vis-à vis the preceding clause (cf. *Genesis A* 2772 f.), and as a simple adverb ("thus") vis-à-vis the following clause.

fǣge fēollan: feld dænede
secga *s*wāte siðþan sunne ūp
on morgentīd, mǣre tungol,
glād ofer grundas, Godes condel beorht,
ēces Drihtnes, oð sīo æþele gesceaft
sāh tō setle. Þǣr læg secg mænig
gārum āgēted, guma norþerna
ofer scild scoten, swilce Scittisc ēac,
wērig, wīges sæd. Wesseaxe forð
ondlongne dæg ēorodcistum
on lāst legdun lāþum þēodum,
hēowan herefl̄ēman hindan þearle
mēcum mylenscearpan. Myrce ne wyrndon
hęardes hondplegan hæleþa nānum
þǣ*ra þe* mid Anlāfe ofer ǣra gebland
on lides bōsme land gesōhtun,
fǣge tō gefeohte. Fīfe lǣgun
on þām campstede cyninges giunge,

12b **dænede** In the MS a second *n* was added afterwards above the line, it is uncertain whether by the original scribe or by another hand. MSS B C read *dennade*, D *dennode*.

There is much disagreement among scholars as to the word intended by the poet; most feel that it was either *ðānode* (from *ðānian* "to become wet") or *dunnode* (from *dunnian* "to grow dark)".

13a **secga swāte** "With the blood of men." Emended from B C D; the reading of A is *secgas hwate*.

13b **ūp** Construe with *glād* in 15a.

18b **guma norþerna** Sc. *mænig* from the line before. In 19b supply both *mænig* and *guma*.

20b **Wesseaxe** An assimilated form of *Westseaxe*; cf. mod. Wessex.
forð "Continuously."

21b **ēorodcistum** "In troops" (adv. dat.).

22 **on lāst . . . þēodum** Since the phrase *lāstas lecgan* "to make tracks" occurs frequently in OE verse, and since *lecgan* is not elsewhere intransitive, Campbell in his edition (p. 105) suggests that this line represents a telescoping of *on lāst legdun lāstas lāþum þēodum*, "made tracks on the trail of the hostile peoples."

26a **Anlāf** ON *Óláfr* (< PrON **AnulaifaR*).

26b **ǣra gebland** "Seas' commotion" (with *ǣr* an unusual spelling variant of *ēar* "sea"). However MSS B C D all agree that the compound *ēargebland* is to be read here, and they may well be right—especially since the halfline *ofer·ēargebland* occurs twice elsewhere in the poetry.

28a **fǣge tō gefeohte** Either sc. *cōmon* (the idea of which is implicit in *gesōhtun* in the preceding line), or translate *tō* here as "in, at" (cf. 24/12a, also BT s.v. I.(5)(g)).

29b **cyninges** Nom. pl. (B C D read *-as*). While it is possible that A's reading is a mere slip, it could also be a precocious example of *-es* as a legitimate spelling variant of historical *-as* (and symptomatic of late vowel-reduction in weakly-stressed syllables); cf. *Wēales* (acc. pl.) in 72b, and note the comparable reduced spellings *en* in 35a (where B C D and MS Cotton Otho B. xi [Ker

sweordum āswefede,   swilce seofene ēac
eorlas Anlāfes,   unrīm heriges,
flotan ond Sceotta.   Þǣr geflēmed wearð
Norðmanna bregu,   nēde gebēded
tō lides stefne   lītle weorode;
crēad cnear en flot,   cyning ūt gewāt
on fealene flōd,   feorh generede.
Swilce þǣr ēac se frōda   mid flēame cōm
on his cȳþþe norð,   Costontīnus,
hār hildering,   hrēman ne þorfte
mǣcan gemānan: hē wæs his mǣga sceard,
frēonda gefylled   on folcstede,
beslagen æt sæcce,   ond his sunu forlēt
on wælstōwe   wundun fergrunden,
giungne æt gūðe.   Gelpan ne þorfte
beorn blandenfeax   bilgeslehtes,
eald inwidda,   ne Anlāf þȳ mā;

180] have *on*), *fealene* in 36a (where B C have *fealone*), and *fergrunden* in 43b (where B C D all have *forgrunden*).

32a **flotan** Thus all four MSS. In order to make the word parallel to *Sceotta*, many editors emend it to *flotena*; but it is possible to leave it as it stands and interpret it as a LWS gen. pl.; see 17/146b n. (and also SB ∫276 Anm. 5). Yet another approach is to take *flotan* as gen. sg. of the collective noun *flota* "fleet" (BTS s.v. (2) and (2a))—though this is less satisfactory stylistically.

33a **Norðmanna bregu** Anlaf.

34a **tō lides stefne** Ships of the period were drawn up on shore and boarded by gangways attached to their prows.

34b **lītle weorode** See 3/9 n.

35a **crēad** Probably intransitive (with *cnear* the subject), though possibly transitive (with *cnear* the d.o. and *cyning* the subject).

cnear en MS *cnea ren*. B C D read *cnear on*. The badly damaged MS Cotton Otho B. xi, which was a copy of A, also read *cnear on* here (see Campbell's edition, p. 141), thus indicating that its scribe understood his exemplar perfectly, in spite of the misleading word-division and the odd spelling. This suggests that a different word-division is all that is necessary in modern editions of A, and not (with most eds.) emendation of *en* to *on*: note that in the very next line the scribe of A again gives us *en* for historical *on* in an unstressed syllable. See further 1. 29b n.

38b **Costontīnus** B C D have *Constantīnus*. A's form is a Vulgar Latin spelling of the name (with loss of *n* before *s*; cf. Campbell, *Grammar*, ∫541.(1).

39b–40a **hrēman . . . gemānan** "Had no reason to boast about the shared swords," i.e. those which the armies had shared (in a highly pregnant sense) on the battlefield. *Mǣcan gemānan* is an odd but defensible spelling of *mēcum gemǣnum*. B C read *mēc(e)a gemānan* "(the) sharing of swords."

40b–42a **hē wæs . . . sæcce** Though Constantine himself had not been literally wounded in the battle, metaphorically he had been "gashed with respect to kinsmen, felled on the battlefield with respect to friends, smitten in combat." *Mǣga* and *frēonda* are genitives of respect. (The passage is usually taken literally, which involves giving both *sceard* and *gefylled* the unattested sense "deprived of.")

43b **fergrunden** See 29b n., and cf. also 16/301b and Campbell (*Grammar*) ∫73 n. 4.

mid heora herelāfum hlehhan ne þorftun
þæt hēo beaduweorca beteran wurdun
on campstede, cu*m*bo*l*gehnā*st*es,
gārmittinge, gumena gemōtes,
wǣpengewrixles, þæs hī on wælfelda
wiþ Ēadweardes afaran plegodan.
Gewitan him þā Normen nægledcnearrum,
drēorig daraða lāf, on Dinges mere,
ofer dēop wæter Difelin sēcan,
eft Īra land, ǣwiscmōde;
swilce þā gebrōþer bēgen ætsamne,
cyning ond æþeling, cȳþþe sōhton,
Wesseaxena land, wīges hrēmige.
Lētan him behindan hrǣ bryttian
saluwigpādan, þone sweartan hræfn,
hyrnednebban, ond þane hasewanpādan,
earn æftan hwīt, ǣses brūcan,
grǣdigne gūðhafoc, ond þæt grǣge dēor,
wulf on wealde. Ne wearð wæl māre
on þīs ēiglande ǣf*re* gīeta

---

48 **beaduweorca beteran wurdun** Probably: "were superior with regard to battle-works," though the use of *weorðan* instead of *wesan* suggests an alternate translation: "came to be (any) better off, with regard to battle-works." *Beaduweorca* is gen. of respect, as is the itemizing series of singular nouns which follow in apposition to it (49b–51a).

49b **cumbolgehnāstes** Thus B C D. A has the meaningless reading *culbodgehnades*, over the first element of which a perceptive contemporary reader wrote: *vel cumbel* (i.e. "or *cumbel-*").

51b **þæs** This word may be taken either as an adverbial conjunction ("because," "after," "by virtue of the fact that"), or a relative pronoun ("which") attracted to the case of its antecedent *wǣpengewrixles*.

53a **him þā** *Him* is refl. and *þā* is an adv. (cf. *Beowulf* 301a, 1125a).

Normen B C D read *Norðmen(n)*, and a *þ* has been added above the line in A, probably not by the original scribe. By a century later the form without ð was common: see 6/41, 55.

54b **Dinges mere** Unidentified.

56a **eft Īra land** Emendation from B C D. MS A has *and eft hira land*, with the sign for *and* added above the line, seemingly in a different hand.

59b **hrēmige** MS *hramige*, with *a* marked for deletion and *e* added above the line (seemingly by the original scribe).

60a–65a **Lētan . . . wealde** This trio of scavengers is a traditional motif in OE battle poetry; cf. 23/205b–12a.

60b **hrǣ** A final *w* has been added to this word above the line by another hand.

61a **saluwigpādan** Usually interpreted as acc. sg., anticipating *hræfn*. Pope[2] however suggests that it is acc. pl. and refers to all three animals.

63a **earn æftan hwīt** Metrical considerations precluded the poet's use of acc. *hwītne*, which is demanded by strict syntax.

The Gray Sea Eagle (*Haliaeetus albicilla*) is not a true eagle at all, but a carrion bird related to the kite. Its most distinctive feature is its white tail.

64a **gūðhafoc** Probably a kenning for the eagle.

folces gefylled   beforan þissum
sweordes ecgum,   þæs þe ūs secgað bēc,
ealde ūðwitan,   siþþan ēastan hider
Engle ond Seaxe   ūp becōman,
ofer brād brimu   Brytene sōhtan,
wlance wīgsmiþas   Wēales ofercōman,
eorlas ārhwate,   eard begēatan.

67a **folces gefylled** Construe *gefylled* with *wearð*, and *folces* as gen. complement of *wæl*. Cf. 4/9 f.

67b **þissum** Dat. sg., and not to be construed with *ecgum* in the next line (on which see 4b n.).

68b **þæs þe** "According to what" (lit. "as regards that which"); *þæs* is gen. of respect. Cf. 14/145.

72b **Wēales** Acc. pl., cf. 29b n.

6 / 1066

As the year 1065 drew to a close and it became clear that King Edward the Confessor was dying, the burning question throughout Europe was: who would follow him as master of England? Edward himself, who had no direct heir, seems to have wished to be succeeded by Duke William of Normandy, whose father—Duke Robert—had sheltered Edward during his long exile at the Norman court (when Canute the Great was on the throne of England). Norman sources in fact assert that in 1051–52, on the occasion of a state visit by William, Edward had actually recognized him as heir-designate.

But the years which followed had seen the rise to a position of all but unchallenged authority in England of Harold, Earl of Wessex. As recently as 1062–63 Harold had won a reputation as the greatest warrior and strategist in England by a series of brilliant campaigns against the redoubtable Welsh warrior-king Gruffydd ap Llywelyn, and for the next two years he was at the height of his power. He had no reason to doubt that the crown itself might be within his grasp. Then in 1064 he unfortunately compromised his position: despatched by King Edward to Normandy, perhaps on a mission to confirm Edward's grant of the succession to William, he accepted a gift of arms from the latter—thus becoming his man—and apparently even swore a solemn oath to assist William to the English throne. Harold may have felt that he could later repudiate this oath by claiming that it had been sworn under psychological duress. However that may be, it was his betrayal of this oath that William would later use as his moral pretext for invading England.

The third candidate for the English crown was King Haraldr Sigurðarson of Norway: Harald Hardrada, warrior and poet, the last heroic figure of the Viking age and one of the most brilliant. Driven from his native Norway at the age of 15, he had come to maturity as a Viking mercenary in the service of the Eastern Roman emperors at Constantinople, where he was personally credited with blinding the emperor Michael Calaphates in 1042. Returning to Scandinavia, he came to the throne of Norway in 1047. For the next twenty years he ruled Norway with an iron hand and waged a never-ending war against King Sveinn of Denmark, earning the reputation of a great warrior, ruthless and ambitious. He based his claim to the throne of England on a treaty made in 1038–39 between his predecessor King Magnúss the Good and Harðacnut, the son of Canute. The threat of a Norwegian invasion, with Harald at its head, had hung over England for many years.

Over Christmas of 1065 Edward the Confessor lay dying at Westminster while his council met in London. Acutely aware of the dangers threatening England, they had no alternative but to choose as his successor the strongest and most capable man in the country. In the end even King Edward saw the virtue—or at least the necessity—of this choice and concurred in it, sometime before his death on January 5th, 1066. He was buried the day after, and on the same day—with a haste appropriate to the anxiety of the times—Harold was consecrated in his place. William at once sent messengers of protest to England and when these were ignored he began to make preparations for an invasion, first enlisting the support of Pope Alexander II, then assembling his warriors and building an armada to carry them across the channel.

For the events of the year 1066 there are many sources, English, Scandinavian and Norman. Two of these—the one reflecting a Scandinavian, the other a Norman point of view—are of great interest in and for themselves. The first is Snorri Sturluson's biography of Harald of Norway, written in ON some 170 years after the king's death (and now available in a fine translation by Magnus Magnusson and Hermann Pálsson: *King Harald's Saga* [Harmondsworth 1966]). The climax of this saga—as of its hero's career—is of course the Battle of Stamfordbridge. On the other hand the Battle of Hastings, and the events leading up to it, are portrayed from the Norman point of view on the magnificent Bayeux Tapestry (which is best approached through *The Bayeux Tapestry: A Comprehensive Survey*, 2nd [revised and enlarged] ed. [London 1965], where it is reproduced in full and expertly introduced).

The Chronicle account which is printed below has the extraordinary interest of reflecting the point of view of the vanquished. Our text follows C (see p. 136), which is the fullest version and strictly contemporary, until this MS breaks off mutilated in the middle of its account of the Battle of Stamfordbridge; after that we follow D, which is a somewhat later conflate (after 1070) of two texts similar to C and E. The difference in tone between C and D is striking: whereas C manages to remain fairly detached while describing the events of 1066, D is the work of an outraged patriot: he tries to be objective, but his emotional involvement in the last campaign of *Harold ūre cyng* is very obvious—and very moving.

Though it is hoped that the notes will make the sequence of events relatively clear, the student is urged to study *A–SE* 581–600 for full background and interpretation.

Millesimo lxvi

*O*n þisum gēare cōm Harold kyng of Eoforwīc tō Westmynstre tō þām Ēastran þe wǣron æfter þām middanwintr*e* þe se kyng forðfērde, and *wǣron* þā Ēastran on þone dæig xvi Kalendarum Mai.

Þā wearð geond eall Engla land swylc tācen on heofenum gesewen swylce nān mann ǣr ne geseh. Sume menn cwǣdon þæt hyt cometa se steorra wǣre, þone sume menn hātað þone fexedan steorra*n*, and hē ætēowde ǣrest on þone ǣfen Letania Maiora, þæt ys viii Kalendarum Mai, and swā sceān ealle þā uii-niht.

And sōna þāræfter cōm Tostig eorl fram begeondan sǣ intō Wiht mid swā myclum liðe swā hē begytan mihte, and him man geald þār ǣigðer ge feoh ge metsunge; and fōr þā þano*n* and hearmas dyde ǣgwār be þām sǣriman þār hē tō mihte, oð þæt hē becōm tō Sandwīc. Ðā cȳdde man Harolde kynge, þe on Lundene wæs, þæt Tostig his brōðor wæs cumen tō Sandwīc. Þā gegadorade hē swā mycele scipfyrde and ēac landfyrde swā nān cingc ǣr hēr on lande ne gegaderade, for

---

1 **On þisum gēare** After 1065 both C and D begin their annalistic year at a date in the spring, either Easter or the Annunciation. This is why they relegate Edward's death (January 5th) and Harold's accession (January 6th) to the close of the annal for 1065, and also why the present annal reports events well into 1067. See further Plummer[1] [1952 reprint], II, cxlii*b* f.

of Eoforwīc Harold's visit to York early in the spring was prompted by the reluctance of the Northumbrians to recognize him as king; this they did only after he had convinced them of the need for unity on the eve of the forthcoming crisis.

3 **dæig** Cf. *ǣigðer* in l. 9. For these spellings see Campbell §269, SB §126.2.

xvi Kalendarum Mai April 16th. The phrase is in apposition to *þone dæig.*

5 **geseh** I.e. *geseah.* MS C is very rich in forms showing this LWS "smoothing" (see Campbell §312).

Sume . . . wǣre It was in fact Halley's Comet.

se In the MS this word is partially obscured by a vellum repair.

6 f. **Letania Maiora** The Feast of the Greater Litany, April 25th. The date *viii Kalendarum Mai* (April 24th) is that of the *ǣfen.*

8 **Tostig eorl** Harold's brother, and a favorite of the late King Edward. Tostig had been earl of Northumbria from 1055 until late September of 1065, when he was deposed by a revolt. He and Edward wished to oppose this rebellion with force, but Harold, who was anxious to avoid civil war, opened negotiations with the rebels which resulted in the confirmation of Morkere as earl of Northumbria and the banishment of Tostig. He left England on November 1st and stayed over the winter at Bruges, in the protection of Baldwin, Count of Flanders (who was a kinsman of his wife). Henceforth Tostig regarded his brother Harold as a bitter personal enemy, and this fact goes a long way toward explaining his alliance with Harald of Norway in 1066.

10 **fōr** Sc. *hē.*

ǣgwār I.e. *ǣghwār* (as in l. 25), with omission of the symbol *h* (see Campbell §61).

11 **mihte** Sc. *cuman.*

12–15 **Þā gegadorade . . . āeode** Harold apparently regarded Tostig as William's harbinger, which suggests that over the winter Tostig had been in touch with Normandy as well as Norway.

12 **gegadorade** The *ge-* was added above the line, apparently by the original scribe; D has *gegædrade.*

ðām þe him wæs tō sōðan gesǣd þæt Willelm eorll fram Normandīge, Ēadwardes cingces mǣg, wolde hider cuman and þis land gegān—eall swā hit syððan āēode.

Þā Tostig þæt geāxode, þæt Harold cing wæs tōward Sandwīc, þā fōr hē of Sandwīc and nam of þām būtsekarlon sume mid him—sume þances, sume unþances—and gewende þā norð intō   , and þǣr hergode on Lindesēge and þǣr manega gōde men ofslōh. Þā Ēadwine eorl and Morkere eorl þæt undergēaton, þā cōman hī þyder and hine of þǣm lande ādrifon. And hē fōr ðā tō Scotlande, and Scotta cynning hine griðede and him tō metsunge fylste, and þǣr ealne sumor wunode.

Đā cōm Harold ciningc tō Sandwīc and þǣr his liðes ābād, for þām þe hit wæs lang ǣr hit man gegaderian mihte. And þā his lið gegaderad wæs, þā fōr hē intō Wiht and þǣr læg ealne þone sumor and þone hærfest; and man hæfde landfyrde ǣghwār be sǣ, þēh hit æt þām ende nāht ne forstōde.

Þā hit wæs tō Natiuitas Sanctæ Mariæ, þā wæs manna metsung āgān, and hig nān man þār nā leng gehealdan ne mihte. Đā lȳfde man mannum hām, and se cyngc rād ūp, and man drāf þā scypu tō Lunde*ne*, and manega forwurdon ǣr hī þyder cōmon.

Þā ðā scipu hām cōman, þā cōm Harold cyning of Norwegan norð intō Tīnan

---

14 f. **Willelm . . . mǣg** Mention of William's and Edward's relationship may imply some recognition of the former's claim. The reading of D here is blunt and chauvinistic: *Wyllelm bastard.*

16–21 **Þā . . . wunode** The briefer version of these events in D and E furnishes some useful complementary information: *And þā wīle* [cf. SB ∫217 Anm. 1 and 2] *cōm Tostig eorl intō Humbran mid sixtigum scipum, and Ēadwine eorl cōm mid lanferde and ādrāf hine ūt; and þā būtsacarlas hine forsōcan. And hē fōr tō Scotlande mid xii snaccum* (D).

17 **of . . . sume**[1] I.e. some of Harold's sailors (and also, apparently, some of his ships). *Būtsekarlas* were men in the king's pay who were equally adept at fighting on land and sea. *Būtse-* is a loan from ON *búza*, "a kind of merchant ship."

18 **intō** The scribe of C left a blank space after this word. On the basis of D and E's report of this campaign (see ll. 16–21 n.) the missing word ought to be *Humbran* (and this has in fact been inserted into C by a much later hand).

manega The scribe appears to have first written *manege* and then to have extended *e*[2] into an *a* (but without erasing the loop of the *e*). The respelling conforms to his practice with this word in l. 28.

19 **Ēadwine eorl and Morkere eorl** Of Mercia and Northumbria respectively.

20 f. **Scotta cynning** Malcolm Canmore (the Malcolm of Shakespeare's *Macbeth*). Tostig and he had become good friends during the former's ten year tenure as earl of Northumbria.

21 **cynning** is probably spelled with a double *n* on the analogy of etymologically related *cynn*.

and[2] Sc. *hē* (Tostig).

26 **Natiuitas . . . Mariæ** The Feast of the Nativity of St. Mary, September 8th.

hig Both the land and sea levies.

27 **hām** Sc. *tō farenne.*

28 **rād ūp** "Rode inland," i.e. travelled overland to London.

30–34 **Þa . . . ward** Instead of this, and immediately following the passage cited in ll. 16–21 n., D and E have: *And hine gemētte þǣr Harold cyng of Norwegon mid þrēo hund scypum, and Tostig him tō bēah and his man wearð. And hī fōron þā bēgen intō Humbran oð þæt hī cōmon tō Eoforwīc* (D).

30 **Tīnan** MS *tinian* with *i*[2] erased.

on unwaran mid swȳðe miclum sciphere and nā lȳtlan—þæt mihte bēon oððe mā—and Tostig eorl him cōm tō mid eallum þām þe hē begiten hæfde, eall swā hȳ ǣ*r* gesprecen hæfdon; and fōran þā bēgen mid eallum ðām liðe andlang Ūsa*n* ūp tō Eoferwīc ward.

Ðā cȳdde man Harolde cynge be sūðan, þā h*ē* of scipe cumen wæs, þæt Harold cyng on Norwegan and Tostig eorl wǣron ūp cumene nēh Eoferwīc. Þā fōr hē norðweard dæges and nihtes swā hraðe swā hē his fyrde gegaderian mihte. Þā, ǣr þām þe se cynning Harold þyder cuman mihte, þā gegaderode Ēadwine eorl and Morkere eorll of heora eorldōme swā mycel werod swā hī begitan mihton and wið þone here gefuhton and mycel wæl geslōgon, and þǣr wæs þæs Engliscan folces mycel ofslagen and ādrenct and on flēam bedrifen, and Normen āhton wælstōwe gewald. And þis gefeoht wæs on Vigilia Mathei Apostoli, and wæs Wōdnesdæg. And þā æfter þām gefeohte fōr Harold cyningc of Norwegan and Tostig eorl intō Eoferwīc mid swā miclum folce swā heom þā geþūhte, and hi*m* mon gīslade of þǣre burh and ēac tō metsunge fylste; and swā þanon tō scipe fōran, and tō fullan friðe gesprǣcon þæt hig ealle mid him sūð faran woldon and þis land gegān.

Ðā āmang þissan cōm Harold Engla cyningc mid ealre his fyrde on ðone Sunnandæg tō Tāda, and þǣr his lið fylcade, and fōr þā on Mōnandæg þurhūt Eoferwīc. And Harold cyningc of Norwegan and Tostig eorl and heora gefylce wǣron āfaren of scipe begeondan Eoferwīc tō Stānfordbrycge, for þām þe him wǣron behāten tō gewissan þæt him man þǣr of ealre þǣre scīre ongēan hȳ gīslas bringan wolde. Ðā

---

31 **bēon** After this word the scribe of C left another blank space, probably intending to come back later and fill in the number of ships (which is given by D and E as 300; see the note before last). A much later hand has inserted *mið ðrēo hund scypum* into the blank space in C.

33 f. **andlang ... ward** "Up along the Ouse toward York." We learn from the twelfth-century chronicler Florence of Worcester that they disembarked at Riccall, which is on the Ouse some ten miles south of York.

39 **eorldōme** Logically this should be pl.; the sg. is probably influenced by *gegaderode*.

40 **gefuhton** Near the village of Fulford, two miles south of York.

41 **Normen** A mark resembling an *i* appears above the line between *e* and *n*; if it is a letter at all, it is certainly not by the original scribe.

42 **Vigilia ... Apostoli** The eve of St. Matthew the Apostle, September 20th.

45 **and² ... fōran** I.e. Harald and Tostig returned to their fleet at Riccall.

45 f. **and³ ... woldon** "And they agreed, (as a condition) for an abiding peace, that they all (i.e. the men of York) would march south with him" etc.

47 f. **on ðone Sunnandæg** September 24th.

48 **Tāda** Tadcaster, nine miles southwest of York: the form is either an abbreviation or else an affectionate nickname.

49 ff. **And ... wolde** Before marching south against the heart of England, the Norwegian king "took the obvious precaution of calling for hostages from the Yorkshire thegns who had survived the battle of Fulford [and] decided to await them in the presence of his army at a site seven miles east of York, where roads from all parts of eastern Yorkshire converged on the crossing of the Derwent known as Stamfordbridge" (*A-SE* 589).

50 f. **for þām þe ... wolde** The syntax is peculiar here and the text may be corrupt. Strictly speaking, *wǣron* in l. 50 ought to be *wæs*, and *ongēan hȳ* in l. 51 is redundant after the preceding *him*.

THE BATTLES OF FULFORD AND STAMFORDBRIDGE. London, British Museum, MS *Cotton Tiberius B. i*, fol. 162 . (See p. 136 and cf. 6/32–55)

7 rume tac forbærnde. 7 swa mislice forfarene þ hæs wæs lyt 80
to lafe. 7 engle ahton wælstowe geweald. Se kyng þa geaf grið
olafe þæs norna cynges suna 7 heora bisceope 7 þan eorle of orcan
ege. 7 eallon þan þe on þam scypum to lafe wæron. 7 hi foron þa
upp to uran kyninge 7 sworon aðas þ hi æfre woldon frið
7 freondscype into þisan lande haldan. 7 se cyng hi let ham
faran mid .xxiiii. scypum. Þas twa folcgefeoht wæron ge
fremmede binnan fif nihtan. Ða com Willelm eorl of
normandige into Pefnesea on sancte Michaeles mæsse æfen.
7 sona þæs hi fere wæron worhton castel æt hæstinga port.
Þis wearð þa Harolde cynge gecydd. 7 he gaderade þa mycel
ne here 7 com him togenes æt þære haran apuldran.
7 Willelm him com ongean on unwær ær þis folc gefylced
wære. Ac se kyng þeah him swiðe heardlice wið feaht
mid þam mannum þe him gelæstan woldon. 7 þær wearð
micel wæl geslægen on ægðre healfe. Ðær wearð ofslægen
harold kyng. 7 leofwine eorl his broðor. 7 Gyrð eorl his
broðor. 7 fela godra manna. 7 þa frencyscan ahton wæl
stowe geweald eallswa heom god uðe for folces synnon.
Aldred arceb 7 seo burhwaru on lundene woldon habban
þa Eadgar cild to kynge eallswa him wel gecynde wæs
7 Eadwine 7 Morkere him beheton þ hi mid him feohtan
woldon. ac swa hit æfre forðlicor beon sceolde swa
wearð hit fram dæge to dæge lætre 7 wyrse. eallswa hit

THE BATTLE OF HASTINGS. London, British Museum, MS *Cotton Tiberius B. iv*, fol. 80[r]. (See p. 136 and cf. 6/57–76)

cōm Harold Engla cyning heom ongēan on unwaran, begeondan þǣre brycge, and hī þǣr tōgædere fēngon and swȳðe heardlīce lange on dæg feohtende wǣron. And þǣr wæs Harold cyning of Norwegan and Tostig eorl ofslagen and ungerīm folces mid heom, ǣgðer ge Normana ge Englisca. And þā Normen|| þe þǣr tō lāfe wǣron wurdon on flēame, and þā Engliscan hī hindan hetelīce slōgon oð þæt hig sume tō scype cōman; sume ādruncen, and sume ēac forbærnde, and swā mislīce forfarene þæt þǣr wæs lȳt tō lāfe. And Engle āhton wælstōwe geweald.

Se kyng þā geaf gryð Ōlāfe, þæs Norna cynges suna, and heora biscope, and þān eorle of Orcanēge, and eallon þān þe on þām scypum tō lāfe wǣron. And hī fōron þā upp tō ūran kyninge and swōron āðas þæt hī ǣfre woldon fryð and frēondscype intō þisan lande haldan, and se cyng hī lēt hām faran mid xxiiii scypum.

Þās twā folcgefeoht wǣron gefremmede binnan fīf nihtan.

Ðā cōm Wyllelm eorl of Normandīge intō Pefnesēa on Sancte Michaeles mæsseǣfen. And sōna þæs hī fēre wǣron, worhton castel æt Hǣstingaport. Þis wearð þā Harolde cynge gecȳdd, and hē gaderade þā mycelne here and cōm him tōgēnes æt þǣre hāran apuldran. And Wyllelm him cōm ongēan on unwær, ǣr þis folc gefylced wǣre; ac se kyng þēah him swīðe heardlīce wið feaht mid þām mannum þe him gelǣstan woldon, and þǣr wearð micel wæl geslægen on ǣgðre healfe. Ðǣr wearð ofslægen Harold kyng and Lēofwine eorl his brōðor and Gyrð eorl his

---

52 **Harold Engla cyning** The reading of D is significantly different: *Harold ūre cyng*.

55 **Normana ge Englisca** I.e. *Normanna ge Engliscra*. The first form shows reduction of *nn* > *n* owing to weakened stress (see Campbell §457); the second shows the adj. *Englisc* inflected as if it were a noun (probably because it follows *Normana* and is parallel to it).

And þā Normen With these words the text of C breaks off at the bottom of a folio. It was originally followed by an added page on which a twelfth-century scribe continued the text briefly by telling the famous story of a lone Norwegian's attempt to hold the bridge against the advancing English army.

57 **sume[1] . . . forbærnde** Sc. *wǣron* or *wurdon*. (Cf. D's annal for 1079: *fela þǣr wurdon ofslægen, and ēac gefangene*—a passage showing similar inconsistency in the inflection of syntactically parallel participles.)

60 **þān . . . Orcanēge** Páll Þorfinnsson. According to Florence of Worcester he had been left to guard the ships.

64 f. **Sancte . . . mæsseǣfen** Michaelmas Eve, September 28th. William had set sail from the mouth of the Somme the evening before, entering Pevensey Bay at 9:00 the next morning.

65 **æt Hǣstingaport** Some twelve miles east of Pevensey along the coast.

65 ff. **Þis wearð** etc. "Harold was at York when he learned of William's landing. Within thirteen days at most he had . . . covered the 190 miles between York and London, expanded the force at his command into the dimensions of an army, and brought it by a march of 50 miles to a point within a short ride of Hastings" (*A-SE* 592).

67 **æt . . . apuldran** The phrase "indicates that the site of the battle was then a wilderness, where an ancient tree formed the only landmark" (*The Bayeux Tapestry*, p. 20).

þis Above the *þ* in the MS is written *h*, possibly (but not certainly) a correction by the original scribe.

68 f. **mid þām . . . woldon** According to Florence of Worcester, many of Harold's men left the battle because the position taken up by the English was too cramped to hold them.

brōðor and fela gōdra manna. And þā Frencyscan āhton wælstōwe geweald, eall swā heom God ūðe for folces synnon.

Aldred arcebiscop and sēo burhwaru on Lundene woldon habban þā Ēadgār cild tō kynge, eall swā him wel gecynde wæs, and Ēadwine and Morkere him behēton þæt hī mid him feohtan woldon. Ac swā hit æfre forðlīcor bēon sceolde, swā wearð hit fram dæge tō dæge lætre and wyrre, eall swā hit æt þām ende eall geferde.

Þis gefeoht wæs gedōn on þone dæg Calesti pāpe. And Wyllelm eorl fōr eft ongēan tō Hǣstingan and geanbidode þǣr hwæðer man him tō būgan wolde. Ac þā hē ongeat þæt man him tō cuman nolde, hē fōr upp mid eallon his here þe him tō lāfe wæs and him syððan fram ofer sǣ cōm, and hergade ealne þone ende þe hē oferfērde, oð þæt hē cōm tō Beorhhāmstede. And þǣr him cōm ongēan Ealdred arcebiscop and Ēadgār cild and Ēadwine eorl and Morkere eorl and ealle þā betstan men of Lundene and bugon þā for nēode, þā mǣst wæs tō hearme gedōn—and þæt wæs micel unrǣd þæt man ǣror swā ne dyde, þā hit God bētan nolde for ūrum synnum—and gȳsledan and swōron him āðas. And hē heom behēt þæt hē wolde heom hold hlāford bēon; and þēah onmang þisan hī hergedan eall þæt hī oferfōron.

Ðā on midwintres dæg hine hālgode tō kynge Ealdred arcebiscop on Westmynstre. And hē sealde him on hand mid Crīstes bēc and ēac swōr—ǣr þān þe hē wolde þā corōna him on hēafode settan—þæt hē wolde þisne þēodscype swā wel haldan swā ǣnig kyngc ætforan him betst dyde, gif hī him holde bēon woldon. Swā þēah leide gyld on mannum swīðe stīð, and fōr þā on þām lengtene ofer sǣ tō Normandīge and nam mid him Stīgand arcebiscop and Ægelnāð abbod on Glæstingabiri

---

73 **Aldred arcebiscop** Of York.

73 f. **Ēadgār cild** "The princeling Eadgar," a great grandson of Æðelred the Unready and the last male of the line of Cerdic. He can have been no more than a boy in 1066, since he is known to have lived until 1125.

74 **eall swā . . . wæs** "As was indeed due him by birth."

75 f. **Ac . . . geferde** "But the more constantly forward it should have been, the more dilatory and worse it turned out to be from day to day, just as it all came to pass in the end."

76 **wyrre** An assimilated form of *wyrse*, perhaps influenced by the ON cognate *verri*. The later annals in D show extensive Scandinavian influence on vocabulary and forms, strongly suggesting that this MS was compiled at York.

77 **on . . . pāpe** "On the day of Pope Calixtus": Saturday, October 14th.

80 **him . . . cōm** For the construction without *tō*, see 16/255b and BTS *cuman* V.

80 f. **ealne . . . oferfērde** After finding that it would be inadvisable to storm London, which was the center of loyalist resistance, William began a campaign to isolate and reduce it by ravaging the surrounding countryside. His route took him westward through Surrey, northern Hampshire and Berkshire, where he crossed the Thames at Wallingford.

83 **þā mǣst . . . gedōn** "After most damage had been done."

84 **þā** "In view of the fact that."

86 **and . . . oferfōron** William felt that "until London was in his hands a display of force was still necessary, and he allowed his army to ravage the whole country along the twenty-five miles of road between Berkhamstead and the city" (*A-SC* 597).

88 **And hē . . . bēc** "And he (i.e. William) promised him on Christ's book (i.e. the Gospels)."

hē[2] Ealdred.

91 **on þām lengtene** See 1.1 n.

92 **Stīgand arcebiscop** Of Canterbury.

and Ēadgār cild and Ēadwine eorl and Morkere eorl and Wælþēof eorl and manege ōðre gōde men of Engla lande, and Ōda biscop and Wyllelm eorl belifen hēr æfter and worhton castelas wīde geond þā þēode and earm folc swencte; and ā syððan hit yflade swīðe. Wurðe se ende þonne God wylle.

Glæstingabiri The MS has the abbreviation *Glbr*, which has been expanded to *Glæstingabiri* above the line, probably by another hand.

93 **Wælþēof eorl** His earldom comprised the shires of Huntingdon, Northampton, Bedford and Cambridge.

94 **Ōda biscop** Of Bayeux; William's half-brother and the commissioner of the famous tapestry.

Wyllelm eorl William fitz Osbern, the Conqueror's seneschal; he had recently been made earl of Hereford.

belifen Possibly a past participle (in which case sc. *wǣron*), possibly 3 pl. pret. indic. (= *belifon*).

95 **þā** In the MS an *s* has been added to this word, possibly (but not certainly) a correction by the original scribe.

swencte Perhaps a late, reduced spelling for *swencton*. But it is also possible that the annalist's mind has reverted to William, and that he is the subject here. Cf. the beginning of the obituary poem about him in E's annal for 1086: *Castelas hē lēt wyrcean and earme men swīðe swencean.*

95 f. **and . . . swīðe** The perspective here suggests that D's annal was composed some time after 1066.

96 **Wurðe** Optative subjunctive. In the MS the word *gōd* has been added above the line after this word, possibly (but not certainly) by the original scribe.

7 / King Ælfred on the advancement of learning

In addition to being one of our most valuable sources for the study of the Early West Saxon language, the present document is of great importance for both Anglo-Saxon history and Old English literature. It is in the form of a royal letter, composed by King Ælfred the Great and sent to each of the bishops of his realm. Writing probably in 894, the king looks back nostalgically to the great flowering of Latin culture in England during the age of Bede and Alcuin, then describes its decay in the ninth century. He regards the Viking wars, which had destroyed so many cultural centers and their manuscripts, as God's judgment on a people who had failed in their duty to maintain this cultural heritage. He acknowledges that there has been some recovery in recent years, but it has not been sufficient. Hence he wishes to initiate an educational program which will have two major aspects: first, the sons of all freemen will be taught to read; second, some of the classical works of medieval Christendom will be translated into the vernacular, so that their substance will continue to be available, whatever the state of Latin learning in England.

Ælfred's letter was designed to serve as the preface to the first volume in this projected series, the king's own translation of the *Liber Regulae Pastoralis* or *Pastoral Rule* of Gregory the Great (c540–604), the greatest of early medieval popes and a figure particularly dear to the Anglo-Saxons because he had been instrumental in their conversion. Gregory had written this work in 591 on the occasion of his accession to the papacy; in it he conducted a careful examination of his own conscience by means of outlining his ideal conception of a "shepherd of souls." In attempting to describe the ideal prelate, he was often concerned with the shepherd's responsibility for the education of his flock. This fact made the book an excellent and indeed obvious choice on Ælfred's part, since he knew that it was his bishops who must support, implement and advance his educational program.

Our text of Ælfred's letter is based upon the copy of the translation of Gregory's book that was sent to Bishop Wærferð of Worcester; it is now MS Hatton 20 in the Bodleian Library at Oxford (Ker 324). This MS, known as H, was one of the first copies made by Ælfred's scribes. It remained at Worcester probably until 1643, when it passed into the possession of Christopher, first Baron Hatton; it was sold to the Bodleian in 1671. A facsimile edition (ed. N. R. Ker) is available as the sixth volume of *EEMSF*, and the student is strongly urged to examine it. He will notice that a number of later writers have been busy on the four pages which contain Ælfred's letter. The most important of these is an early eleventh-century reviser who has been tentatively identified as the homilist Wulfstan (see p. 255), Bishop of Worcester and Archbishop of York. He has made a number of corrections and modifications of the text, repunctuating extensively and in general trying to bring spelling usage into line with that of his own period: ī̆ are often altered to ȳ̆, *swǣ* to *swā*, *þætte* to *þæt*. In all cases we have restored the original text, though some of the reviser's more interesting substantive changes are registered in the notes.[1] Our text tries to reproduce the text of H in the form in which it left Ælfred's scriptorium at Winchester, sometime in the last decade of the ninth century.

Three other copies of Ælfred's letter survive. The most important is in British Museum Cotton Tiberius B. xi (Ker 195), known as C, which is probably nearest of all to Ælfred's first draft. This MS was written (sometime between 890 and 897) by the same scribe who wrote the copy of Ælfred's letter in H. It suffered fire damage twice (once in 1731 and again in 1864) and now consists of eight charred fragments.[2] Fortunately while still intact it had been transcribed by Franciscus Junius (see p. 289), and his copy (now Bodleian MS Junius 53) was printed, together with the text of H (on facing pages), by Henry Sweet in *King Alfred's West-Saxon Version of Gregory's Pastoral Care* (EETS, Original Series, 45 [1871], 50 [1872]). In C the space for the name of the recipient of the letter was left blank, hence it has been conjectured that this was a copy made to be kept at Winchester. This view is borne out by the very interesting memorandum which, according to Junius and Humfrey Wanley, once stood at the beginning of the MS: *Plegmunde arcebiscepe is āgifen his bōc, ond Swīðulfe biscepe, ond Wērferðe biscepe.* This note gives us a priceless, momentary glimpse into the shipping department of Ælfred's publishing firm!

A third MS, Cambridge, Corpus Christi College 12 (Ker 30), known as D, is from the late tenth century and may be a copy of C. Even later, and closely related to H instead of to C, is U, Cambridge University Library Ii. 2. 4 (Ker

[1] Later yet an early thirteenth-century Worcester scribe who is known as "the tremulous hand" entered a number of Latin glosses; and further Latin glosses were added in the sixteenth century by Archbishop Parker's Latin secretary, John Joscelyn.

[2] And an entire leaf (now in Kassel, Germany) which had become detached from the codex at an earlier date. Facsimiles of the fragments and the leaf are printed at the end of *EEMSF*, VI, where there is also a transliteration of the fragments made from photographs taken under ultra-violet light.

19), which was written at Exeter in the mid-eleventh century and derives from the copy sent originally to Bishop Wulfsige of Sherborne. The versions of Ælfred's letter in D and U were edited by F. P. Magoun, Jr., in *Mediaeval Studies*, XI (1949), 113–22.

✠ ÐĒOS BŌC SCEAL TŌ WIOGORACEASTRE

Ælfred kyning hāteð grētan Wǣrferð biscep his wordum luflīce ond frēondlīce; ond ðē cȳðan hāte ðæt mē cōm swīðe oft on gemynd hwelce wiotan iū wǣron giond Angelcynn, ǣgðer ge godcundra hāda ge woruldcundra; ond hū gesǣliglica tīda ðā wǣron giond Angelcynn; ond hū ðā kyningas ðe ðone onwald hæfdon ðæs folces Gode ond his ǣrendwrecum hīersumedon; ond hīe ǣgðer ge hiora sibbe ge hiora siodo ge hiora onweald innanbordes gehīoldon, ond ēac ūt hiora ēðel rȳmdon; ond hū him ðā spēow ǣgðer ge mid wīge ge mid wīsdōme; ond ēac ðā godcundan hādas, hū giorne hīe wǣron ǣgðer ge ymb lāre ge ymb liornunga ge ymb ealle ðā ðīowotdōmas ðe hīe Gode scoldon; ond hū man ūtanbordes wīsdōm ond lāre hieder on lond sōhte, ond hū wē hīe nū sceoldon ūte begietan, gif wē hīe habban sceoldon. Swǣ clǣne hīo wæs oðfeallenu on Angelcynne ðæt swīðe fēawa wǣron behionan Humbre ðe hiora ðēninga cūðen understondan on Englisc, oððe furðum ān ǣrendgewrit of Lǣdene on Englisc āreccean; ond ic wēne ðætte nōht monige begiondan Humbre nǣren. Swǣ fēawa hiora wǣron ðæt ic furðum ānne ānlēpne ne mæg geðencean be sūðan Temese, ðā ðā ic tō rīce fēng. Gode ælmihtegum sīe ðonc ðætte wē nū ǣnigne onstal habbað lārēowa. Ond for ðon ic ðē bebīode ðæt ðū dō swǣ ic gelīefe ðæt ðū wille, ðæt ðū ðē ðissa woruldðinga tō ðǣm geǣmetige swǣ ðū oftost mæge, ðæt ðū ðone wīsdōm ðe ðē

Title **ÐĒOS . . . WIOGORACEASTRE** This direction was added to H after the entire codex had been assembled, perhaps even after it had been bound.

1 **hāteð** Sc. *mon*, which is generally omitted in acc. + inf. constructions involving verbs of commanding and hearing.

Wǣrferð biscep Of Worcester, from 873 to 915. He made his own contribution to Ælfred's educational program by translating Gregory's *Dialogues* at the king's request.

2 **ond ðē cȳðan hāte** A shift from the third person of formal epistolary salutation to first person is very common at the beginning of OE letters and writs (cf. 12/1 f. and BTS *grētan* VI.(5))—though the omission of the pronoun *ic* here is atypical.

cōm The subject is the clause *hwelce . . . Angelcynn*.

5 **ðæs folces** The eleventh-century reviser adds *on ðām dagum*.

ond² After this word MSS C D U all have *hū*, which the scribe of H probably omitted through carelessness.

9 **ge** C D U have *ond* instead.

Gode Sc. *dōn* (which has been added above the line by the eleventh-century reviser. It occurs in C D, but not in U).

11 **hīo** I.e. *lār*.

17 **Ond** This does not occur in C D U.

17 f. **ðæt ðū ðē ðissa woruldðinga . . . mæge, ðæt** The syntax of this passage is ca-

God sealde ðǣr ðǣr ðū hiene befæstan mæge, befæste. Geðenc hwelc wītu ūs ðā becōmon for ðisse worulde, ðā ðā wē hit nōhwæðer ne selfe ne lufodon ne ēac ōðrum monnum ne lēfdon! Đone naman ǣnne wē lufodon ðætte wē Crīstne wǣren, ond swīðe fēawe ðā ðēawas.

Đā ic ðā ðis eall gemunde, ðā gemunde ic ēac hū ic geseah—ǣr ðǣm ðe hit eall forhergod wǣre ond forbærned—hū ðā ciricean giond eall Angelcynn stōdon māðma ond bōca gefylda, ond ēac micel mengeo Godes ðīowa, ond ðā swīðe lȳtle fiorme ðāra bōca wiston, for ðǣm ðe hīe hiora nānwuht ongiotan ne meahton, for ðǣm ðe hīe nǣron on hiora āgen geðīode āwritene. Swelce hīe cwǣden: "Ūre ieldran, ðā ðe ðās stōwa ǣr hīoldon, hīe lufodon wīsdōm, ond ðurh ðone hīe begēaton welan ond ūs lǣfdon. Hēr mon mæg gīet gesīon hiora swæð, ac wē him ne cunnon æfter spyrigean. Ond for ðǣm wē habbað nū ǣgðer forlǣten ge ðone welan ge ðone wīsdōm, for ðǣm ðe wē noldon tō ðǣm spore mid ūre mōde onlūtan."

---

pable of two interpretations: (1) "that you detach yourself from these worldly affairs as often as you can, to the end that" etc., taking *tō ðǣm* as correlative with the following *ðæt*; (2) "that you take time out from these worldly affairs for those (other things) as often as you can, so that" etc., with *tō ðǣm* referring in a general way to *lār* and *leornung*, and *ðæt* introducing a purpose clause.

Dorothy Whitelock points out (Sweet[15]) that this passage recalls the acts of the Council of Clofesho (747), in which priests are urged *a saecularibus negotiis causisque, in quantum praevaleant, vacare* ("to free themselves from worldly affairs and concerns as much as they can").

18 f. **ðū ðone wīsdōm . . . befæste** "You may apply that wisdom which God has given you wherever you may be able to apply it." Here Ælfred has in mind the parable of the talents, Matthew 25:14–30.

19 **hiene** I.e. *wīsdōm* (but note the shift to natural gender with *hit* in l. 20).

20 **for** "As regards; with respect to."

20 f. **ne selfe . . . lēfdon** Ælfred is perhaps recalling his translation of Gregory's paraphrase of Matthew 23:13 (about the scribes and pharisees): *nāðer ne hīe selfe on ryhtne weg gān noldon ne ōðrum geðafigean.*

21 **lufodon** C and D read *hæfdon* here. This is likely to be what Ælfred originally wrote, since he clearly has in mind Augustine's much-imitated *Non se autem glorietur Christianum, qui nomen habet et facta non habet.* ("Let him not boast himself a Christian who has the name but does not have the deeds"). (H's reading also appears in U [*lufdon*] and probably goes back to a common ancestor of these two MSS in which this word was repeated accidentally from l. 20.)

22 **wǣren** C D U have the indicative *wǣron*, which is undoubtedly more original. **swīðe . . . ðēawas** *Fēawe* is acc. pl., with *ðā ðēawas* standing in apposition to it: "very few (of) the practices." (The other possible interpretation—"very few [of us loved] the practices"—is much less satisfactory rhetorically.)

23 sq. Note that according to this passage the decay of learning in England *preceded*, and was not a consequence of, the Viking wars.

25 **ond[2]** Sc. *ðǣr wæs.*

25 f. **ond[3] . . . wiston** "And they received very little sustenance from those books."

26 **for ðǣm ðe** Before these words the eleventh-century reviser inserts: *and þæt wæs.*

27 **Swelce hīe cwǣden** "(It was) as if they said."

30 **Ond** This does not occur in C D U.

30 f. **for ðǣm . . . for ðǣm ðe** Correlative: "therefore . . . because."

Ðā ic ðā ðis eall gemunde, ðā wundrade ic swīðe swīðe ðāra gōdena wiotona ðe giū wǣron giond Angelcynn ond ðā bēc eallæ be fullan geliornod hæfdon, ðæt hīe hiora ðā nǣnne dǣl noldon on hiora āgen geðīode wendan. Ac ic ðā sōna eft mē selfum andwyrde ond cwæð: "Hīe ne wēndon ðætte ǣfre menn sceolden swǣ reccelēase weorðan ond sīo lār swǣ oðfeallan. For ðǣre wilnunga hīe hit forlēton, ond woldon ðæt hēr ðȳ māra wīsdōm on londe wǣre ðȳ wē mā geðēoda cūðon."

Ðā gemunde ic hū sīo ǣ wæs ǣrest on Ebriscgeðīode funden, ond eft, ðā hīe Crēacas geliornodon, ðā wendon hīe hīe on hiora āgen geðīode ealle, ond ēac ealle ōðre bēc. Ond eft Lǣdenware swǣ same, siððan hīe hīe geliornodon, hīe hīe wendon ealla ðurh wīse wealhstodas on hiora āgen geðīode. Ond ēac ealla ōðra Crīstna ðīoda sumne dǣl hiora on hiora āgen geðīode wendon. For ðȳ mē ðyncð betre, gif īow swǣ ðyncð, ðæt wē ēac suma bēc, ðā ðe nīedbeðearfosta sīen eallum monnum tō wiotonne, ðæt wē ðā on ðæt geðīode wenden ðe wē ealle gecnāwan mægen, ond gedōn, swǣ wē swīðe ēaðe magon mid Godes fultume, gif wē ðā stilnesse habbað, ðætte eall sīo giogūð ðe nū is on Angelcynne frīora monna, ðāra ðe ðā spēda hæbben ðæt hīe ðǣm befēolan mægen, sīen tō liornunga oðfæste, ðā hwīle ðe hīe tō nānre ōðerre note ne mægen, oð ðone first ðe hīe wel cunnen Englisc gewrit ārǣdan. Lǣre mon siððan furður on Lǣdengeðīode ðā ðe mon furðor lǣran wille ond tō hīeran hāde dōn wille.

---

33 **wundrade** This verb has two parallel objects, *ðāra gōdena wiotona* and the *þæt*-clause beginning in 1.35.

wiotona C D U have *witena*; on H's form with *-ona* see SB ∫276 Anm. 3.

34 **eallæ be fullan** The word order in C D U is *be fullan ealla* (C).

36 **sceolden** C D U have *sceoldon*.

37 **sīo lār** Sc. *sceolde*.

For ðǣre wilnunga I.e. that learning should *not* fall off (this desire being implicit in the previous statement). On the other hand, Klaeber (*Anglia*, XLVII [1923], 59 n. 3) may be right in regarding *ond* etc. as an explanatory clause introduced paratactically (where hypotaxis would be more normal: cf. *for þǣre gewilnunge þe hē wolde* in Ælfred's translation of Orosius, 112/2 in Sweet's edition).

38 **ðȳ . . . ðȳ** Correlative: "to the degree . . . that," i.e. "in proportion as."

40 **sīo ǣ** Presumably Ælfred uses this term to mean the Heptateuch, i.e. the first seven books of the Old Testament.

ðā Thus also U; C D have *ðā ðā* (D).

hīe The antecedent is *ǣ*.

42 **ealle ōðre bēc** I.e. of the Old Testament. The eleventh-century reviser struck out *ealle* and wrote *mænige* above it.

hīe² The antecedent is *bēc*.

43 **ealla²** Struck out by the eleventh-century reviser.

45 **īow** Note that Ælfred now addresses *all* the bishops.

46 **ðæt wē ðā** The first two words are redundant, recapitulating the previous *ðæt wē* after the intervening clause. The *ðā*, too, could be part of the redundancy (acc. pl. fem., recapitulating *suma bēc*), or it could be the adv. "then."

48 **frīora monna** Partitive gen. dependent on *eall sīo giogūð*.

50 **tō . . . mægen** The phrase *magan tō* means "to be good for; to have the strength for."

52 **hīeran hāde** I.e. the clergy. For the spelling *hīeran* with one *r* see 4/259 n.

Đā ic ðā gemunde hū sīo lār Lǣdengeðīodes ǣr ðissum āfeallen wæs giond Angelcynn, ond ðēah monige cūðon Englisc gewrit ārǣdan, ðā ongan ic, ongemang ōðrum mislicum ond manigfealdum bisgum ðisses kynerīces, ðā bōc wendan on Englisc ðe is genemned on Lǣden "Pastoralis" ond on Englisc "Hierdebōc," hwīlum word be worde, hwīlum andgit of andgiete, swǣ swǣ ic hīe geliornode æt Plegmunde mīnum ærcebiscepe ond æt Assere mīnum biscepe ond æt Grimbolde mīnum mæssepriōste ond æt Iōhanne mīnum mæsseprēoste. Siððan ic hīe ðā geliornod hæfde, swǣ swǣ ic hīe forstōd ond swǣ ic hīe andgitfullīcost āreccean meahte, ic hīe on Englisc āwende, ond tō ǣlcum biscepstōle on mīnum rīce wille āne onsendan, ond on ǣlcre bið ān æstel sē bið on fīftegum mancessa. Ond ic bebīode on Godes naman ðæt nān mon ðone æstel from ðǣre bēc ne dō, ne ðā bōc from ðǣm mynstre: uncūð hū longe ðǣr swǣ gelǣrede biscepas sīen swǣ swǣ nū, Gode ðonc, welhwǣr siendon. For ðȳ ic wolde ðætte hīe ealneg æt ðǣre stōwe wǣren, būton se biscep hīe mid him habban wille, oððe hīo hwǣr tō lǣne sīe, oððe hwā ōðre bī wrīte.

---

53 **āfeallen** C D *oðfeallen.*

56 **"Pastoralis"** The usual medieval title of Gregory's work was *Liber Pastoralis* or *Pastorale.*

57 **hwīlum[1] . . . andgiete** This very popular tag derives ultimately from St. Jerome's preface to the Vulgate translation of Job: *vel verbum e verbo, vel sensum e sensu.*

58 f. **Plegmunde . . . Iōhanne** None of Ælfred's mentors was a native West Saxon. Plegmund (Archbishop of Canterbury from 890 to 914) was Mercian; Asser (who became Ælfred's biographer, see p. 137) was Welsh; Grimbold was from Flanders and John was a continental Saxon. See further on these men *A-SE* 271 f.

60 **forstōd** The eleventh-century reviser altered this to *betst understandon cūðe.* **swǣ[3]** Omitted D U.

62 **æstel . . . mancessa** On the etymology and meaning of the word *æstel* and the value of a *mancus* see *Mediaeval Studies*, X (1948), 104 ff. and Sweet[15] p. 225. **bið on** "Will be in (the value of)," i.e. "will be worth."

64 **uncūð** "(It is) unknown."

65 **hīe** Pl., referring to both *bōc* and *æstel.*

67 **oððe . . . wrīte** "Or someone should be writing another (copy) from (it)."

8 / the voyages of ohthere and wulfstan

Another landmark in Ælfred's translation program was the Old English version of Orosius, though it is not certain whether this is the king's own work or was simply done at his direction.

The priest Paulus Orosius, born c385 at Braga in northern Portugal, wrote the seven books of his *Historiae adversum Paganos* in the years 417–18. His work, which had been undertaken at the suggestion of St. Augustine and was intended to supplement the latter's *De Civitate Dei*, furnishes a synopsis of world history from Adam to the year 417. Orosius' polemical purpose was to absolve Christianity of responsibility for the trouble and violence of his times by showing that before the coming of Christianity things had been even worse. The book came to be highly regarded during the Middle Ages as a sort of universal chronicle; Ælfred valued it above all for its Christian interpretation of history, and also no doubt because he regarded it as complementary to Bede's *Historia Ecclesiastica*, supplying the background against which the latter work should be read.

For purposes of general orientation, Orosius introduced his *Historiae* with a geographical survey. He notes the traditional division of the world into three parts, Asia, Europe and Africa, which he then proceeds to describe in that order. The OE translation follows him meekly enough across Asia, but when Orosius reaches Europe, Ælfred (or his staff) ignores the original altogether and makes a famous double insertion: (1) an enumeration, on fresh evidence, of the tribes and boundaries of Europe from the Danube north to Scandinavia; (2) the well-known *periplus Ohtheri*, an eyewitness description of Scandinavia and the Baltic, narrated to Ælfred by two experienced navigators of those northern waters. It is the latter passage that we print here. Interestingly enough, it is the first piece of OE ever to be mentioned in print (by Robert Recorde in 1557).

The first of the two voyagers was a Norwegian named Ohthere who lived high up on the west coast of Norway and told Ælfred about two voyages which he had made, one north around Norway (past Murmansk and into the White Sea), the other south to Denmark; Wulfstan, whose nationality is uncertain, told of a voyage from Denmark east to the area near Danzig. Wulfstan reports the marvels he has seen with wide-eyed wonder; Ohthere gives a more pragmatic account of life in northern Norway. Nothing illuminates Ohthere's background and circumstances better than the first twenty-two chapters of the Old Norse *Egils saga Skallagrímssonar*,[1] which, though it was written much later (in the early thirteenth century), seems to preserve accurate memories of the time and milieu in which Ohthere lived. The first part of this saga tells the unforgettable story of the brilliant and ill-fated Þórólfr Kveld-Úlfsson, who had an estate at Sandnes in southern Hálogaland, a mere 300 miles down the coast from Ohthere. They may well have known each other—or so one would like to think.

Students who are studying these voyages will almost certainly want to refer to the series of maps printed as the back endpaper of this book.

The Ælfredian translation of Orosius' *Historiae adversum Paganos* survives, in complete or nearly complete form, in two closely related MSS. The older of these, British Museum Additional MS 47967 (Ker 133), also known as the Tollemache or Lauderdale Orosius, dates from the first quarter of the tenth century and may very well be from Winchester: according to Ker, it is "written in one hand contemporary with and from the same scriptorium as the hand (or hands) of the annals for 892–924 in the Parker chronicle." It was acquired by the British Museum in 1953 and a facsimile (ed. Alistair Campbell) is now available as the third volume of *EEMSF*. This MS was made the basis of his text by Henry Sweet, *King Alfred's Orosius*, EETS, Original Series, 79 (1883). Historically, linguistically and paleographically this MS is of great importance and we print our text from it as long as we can. Unfortunately at some point prior to the late seventeenth century, someone abstracted from the MS the gathering which contains the final three quarters of Ohthere's and Wulfstan's narratives. Consequently the text of the latter portion of this excerpt must be based on the other MS, British Museum Cotton Tiberius B. i (Ker 191), written perhaps a century later.[2] It is likely that its text of Orosius—which is complete—and the text in the Tollemache MS descend from a common exemplar, though some scholars have held the later MS to be a direct copy of the earlier. There is no facsimile of this MS; its text of Orosius was made the basis of his edition by Joseph Bosworth, *King Alfred's Anglo-Saxon Version of the Compendious History of the World by Orosius* (London 1859).

[1] Available in a fine translation by Gwyn Jones, *Egil's Saga* (Syracuse 1960).

[2] The Cotton MS also contains two poems (the *Menologium* and *Maxims II*, which is edited below, p. 373 ff.) and the C-Version of the Anglo-Saxon Chronicle (see pp. 136, 169).

Ōhthere sǣde his hlāforde, Ælfrede cyninge, þæt hē ealra Norðmonna norþmest būde. Hē cwæð þæt hē būde on þǣm lande norþweardum wiþ þā Westsǣ. Hē sǣde þēah þæt land sīe swīþe lang norþ þonan; ac hit is eal wēste, būton on fēawum stōwum styccemǣlum wīciað Finnas, on huntoðe on wintra ond on sumera on fiscaþe be þǣre sǣ.

Hē sǣde þæt hē æt sumum cirre wolde fandian hū longe þæt land norþryhte lǣge, oþþe hwæðer ǣnig mon be norðan þǣm wēstenne būde. Þā fōr hē norþryhte be þǣm lande: lēt him ealne weg þæt wēste land on ðæt stēorbord ond þā wīdsǣ on ðæt bæcbord þrīe dagas. Þā wæs hē swā feor norþ swā þā hwælhuntan

---

1 **Ōhthere** He is known only from the present account. His name in ON would have been *Óttarr*, of which *Ōhthere* is the OE adaptation.

his hlāforde The phrase suggests that he was in Ælfred's service, whether for a winter or a decade no one can tell. In fact we can only speculate whether Ohthere, impelled by that same combination of business acumen and wanderlust that had taken him to the White Sea, had visited Ælfred only briefly and then returned to Norway with a cargo of English wheat, honey, wine and cloth (see *Egils saga*, Chapter 17); or whether he was one of the great Norwegian magnates who fled permanently abroad in the wake of King Harald Fairhair's consolidation of the Norwegian kingdom in the years prior to c885 (see G. Turville-Petre, *The Heroic Age of Scandinavia* [London 1951], pp. 109–19). Ælfred's court would not be an unusual place for such a person to come: in fact, in the autumn of c888, Þórólfr Kveld-Úlfsson's father advised him to leave Norway (because of King Harald's hatred towards him) and enter the service of the King of England (*Egils saga*, Chapter 18).

2 **on þǣm lande norþweardum** "In the north of the country." In 1.82 he adds that he lived in *Hālgoland* (ON *Hálogaland*, MnNor *Helgeland*). Scholars generally locate Ohthere's home in the region around Malangen (a large fjord southwest of present-day Tromsö).

3 **Westsǣ** I.e. the sea off the west coast of Norway: the nomenclature reflects Ohthere's Scandinavian viewpoint.

þæt The Cotton MS has *þæt þæt*.

sīe Subjunctive in indirect discourse. Translate: "extends; stretches."

norþ Actually "northeast." Malone has argued (*Speculum*, V [1930], 139–67) that the cardinal points in these two voyages show a 45° clockwise displacement; Ekblom (*SN*, XIV [1941–42], 115–44) argued for a 60° displacement. But Binns (see l. 7 f. n.) argues that the apparent displacement is simply a result of Ohthere's vagueness and that his "compass directions are to be taken much more with reference to an assumed trend of the coastline than to any quarter of the heavens" (p. 51).

4 **Finnas** The Lapps of northern Norway (who are still called *finner* in MnNor).

6 **fandian** "See; acquire (personal) experience of." Ohthere was not the first Norwegian to explore these northern waters: grave finds from the north Norwegian area suggest that, as early as the Migration Period, his homeland in Norway and northern Russia were linked by trade routes around the North Cape, and that by his day commercial traffic along them must have been brisk.

7 f. **Þā fōr hē norþryhte** For details of the voyage—which he thinks began in mid-April—see A. L. Binns, "Ohtheriana VI: Ohthere's Northern Voyage," *EGS*, VII (1961), 43–52.

8 f. **stēorbord . . . bæcbord** Since the rudder was fastened to the right side of the stern, this came to be called the "steering side," and the side opposite (to which the helmsman turned his back) the *bæcbord*.

firrest faraþ. Þā fōr hē þā gīet norþryhte swā feor swā hē meahte on þǣm ōþrum þrim dagum gesiglan. Þā bēag þæt land þǣr ēastryhte, oþþe sēo sǣ in on ðæt lond, hē nysse hwæðer, būton hē wisse ðæt hē ðær bād westanwindes ond hwōn norþan, ond siglde ðā ēast be lande swā swā hē meahte on fēower dagum gesiglan. Þā sceolde hē ðǣr bīdan ryhtnorþanwindes, for ðǣm þæt land bēag þǣr sūþryhte, oþþe sēo sǣ in on ðæt land, hē nysse hwæþer. Þā siglde hē þonan sūðryhte be lande swā swā hē mehte on fīf dagum gesiglan. Ðā læg þǣr ān micel ēa ūp in on þæt land. Þā cirdon hīe ūp in on ðā ēa, for þǣm hīe ne dorston forþ bī þǣre ēa siglan for unfriþe, for þǣm ðæt land wæs eall gebūn on ōþre healfe þǣre ēas. Ne mētte hē ǣr nān gebūn land siþþan hē from his āgnum hām fōr, ac him wæs ealne weg wēste land on þæt stēorbord, būtan fiscerum ond fugelerum ond huntum, ond þæt wǣron eall Finnas; ond him wæs ā wīdsǣ on ðæt bæcbord. Þā Beormas hæfdon swīþe wel gebūd hira land; ac hīe ne dorston þǣron cuman. Ac þāra Terfinna land wæs eal wēste, būton ðǣr huntan gewīcodon, oþþe fisceras, oþþe fugeleras. Fela spella him sǣdon þā Beormas, ǣgþer ge of hiera āgnum lande ge of þǣm landum þe ymb hīe ūtan wǣron; ac hē nyste hwæt þæs sōþes wæs, for þǣm hē hit self ne geseah. Þā Finnas, him þūhte, ond þā Beormas sprǣcon nēah ān geþēode.

---

11 f. **Þā bēag . . . hwæðer** He had reached Nordkinn (the frequent spelling -kyn comes from Dutch maps), the northernmost tip of the Scandinavian mainland. He seems to have been uncertain whether the coastline took a permanent tack to the (south)east, or whether he had simply reached the mouth of a large bay.

12 f. **ond[1] ðā** The Cotton MS has respectively *oððe, þanon*.

13 **swā swā** Elliptical; cf. *swā feor swā* in l. 10.

14 **ðǣr** A number of prominent capes along the northeast coast of the Poluostrov Kol'skiy (Kola Peninsula)—e.g. Svyatoy Nos, Orlov, Korabelnyy—have been suggested as the point off which Ohthere waited for his change of wind.

16 f. **ān micel ēa** One of the rivers flowing southward through the Poluostrov Kol'skiy into Kandalakshskaya Guba (Kandalaks Bay); probably the Varzuga.

18 **for unfriþe** I.e. lest their sudden and unannounced arrival should result in their being taken for Viking marauders. During the next two centuries the White Sea was a scene of enthusiastic Viking activity; see for example *Egils saga*, Chapter 37.

19 **þǣre ēas** The Cotton MS has *ēa*. For the form *ēas* see 4/235 n.

20 **hām** An endingless locative (cf. Campbell ʃ572). The Cotton MS has *hāme*.

21 **eall** Sg., agreeing with *þæt*. The Cotton MS has *ealle* pl., agreeing with *wǣron . . . Finnas*.

22 **Beormas** ON *Bjarmar*. Probably Karelians, who in Ohthere's day seem to have been widely distributed around the White Sea. He had apparently run into a settlement of theirs on the north shore of Kandalakshskaya Guba. (Here and in l. 27 the first limb of the *m* in *Beormas* has been partially erased, and in l. 24 its third limb, all of this no doubt by a later reader who did not recognize the ethnic name and thought that the common noun *beornas* "men" had been intended.)

gebūd The Cotton MS has *gebūn*, the strong form of the participle.

23 **Terfinna land** The *Terfinnas* were Lapps living in the southeast of the Poluostrov Kol'skiy (the coast still known as the Terskiy Bereg in their memory).

26 **hwæt þæs sōþes wæs** "How much of that was true," lit. "what of the truth (that) was," *þæs sōþes* being partitive gen. (see Wülfing ʃ311ß).

27 **nēah ān geþēode** Both the Lapps and the Karelians spoke Finno-Ugrian languages.

Swīþost hē fōr ðider, tōēcan þæs landes scēawunge, for þǣm horshwælum, for ðǣm hīe habbað swīþe æþele bān on hiora tōþum—þā tēð hīe brōhton sume þǣm cyninge—ond hiora hȳd || bið swīðe gōd tō sciprāpum. Sē hwæl bið micle lǣssa þonne ōðre hwalas: ne bið hē lengra ðonne syfan elna lang. Ac on his āgnum lande is se betsta hwælhuntað: þā bēoð eahta and fēowertiges elna lange, and þā mǣstan fiftiges elna lange; þāra hē sǣde þæt hē syxa sum ofslōge syxtig on twām dagum.

Hē wæs swȳðe spēdig man on þǣm ǣhtum þe heora spēda on bēoð, þæt is on wildrum. Hē hæfde þā gȳt, ðā hē þone cyningc sōhte, tamra dēora unbebohtra syx hund. Þā dēor hī hātað "hrānas." Þāra wǣron syx stælhrānas: ðā bēoð swȳðe dȳre mid Finnum, for ðǣm hȳ fōð þā wildan hrānas mid. Hē wæs mid þǣm fyrstum mannum on þǣm lande; næfde hē þēah mā ðonne twentig hrȳðera and twentig scēapa and twentig swȳna, and þæt lȳtle þæt hē erede, hē erede mid horsan. Ac hyra ār is mǣst on þǣm gafole þe ðā Finnas him gyldað. Þæt gafol bið on dēora fellum, and on fugela feðerum, and hwales bāne, and on þǣm sciprāpum þe bēoð of hwæles hȳde geworht and of sēoles. Ǣghwilc gylt be hys gebyrdum: se byrdesta sceall gyldan fīftȳne mearðes fell and fīf hrānes, and ān beran fel, and tȳn ambra feðra, and berenne kyrtel oððe yterenne, and twēgen

---

28 **horshwælum** Thus the Cotton MS. The Tollemache MS has *horschwælum*: in his unfamiliarity with the word, which appears only here (and is perhaps a loan from ON *hrosshvalr*), the scribe seems to have substituted the OE adj. *horsc* "active, daring" as the first element of the compound.

29 f. **þā tēð . . . cyninge** While it is possible to interpret *þā tēð* as the d.o. of *brōhton*, and *sume* as in apposition to it (cf. 4/224), it is more likely that we have a colloquial anacoluthon here, with *þā tēð* introduced as the subject and then an immediate switch of subject to *hīe*: "those teeth, they brought some to the king." Cf. 9/7 ff. *þā . . . forsyhþ*.

30 **hȳd** After this word begins the gap in the Tollemache MS (see p. 185); from here on our text follows the Cotton MS.
Sē hwæl *Sē* is deictic: "this (particular kind of) whale."

32 **fēowertiges** Gen. of measure (numerals in *-tig* are sometimes declined as neuter nouns).

33 **syxa sum** Cf. 4/107 n.

36 f. **þā gȳt . . . unbebohtra** The phrase *þā gȳt* can be taken as suggesting that Ohthere had attempted (and failed) to realize the value of his reindeer herd on the eve of a permanent departure from Norway: cf. *Egils saga*, Chapter 25, where Kveld-Úlfr emigrates and no one dares buy his land because they know that King Harald dislikes him and will almost certainly confiscate it after his departure (which he in fact does in Chapter 30).

37 **hī** Altered to *hȳ* by a later hand (as are a number of subsequent *hī*'s).
hrānas The word *hrān* occurs nowhere else in OE and may have been coined by Ælfred (or his scribes) to be the phonological equivalent of Ohthere's ON *hreinn*. *Hreinn* is related to OE/MnE *horn* and to OE *hrȳðer* (l. 39) and has the etymological meaning of "the horned animal." (Note that MnE *rein* [*deer*] descends from the ON, not the OE form.)

40 f. **mid horsan** Oxen were used for this purpose in England. Note the late dat. pl. in *-an*.

41 **is mǣst on** "Consists for the most part in."
þǣm gafole . . . gyldað This is the notorious *finnskattr* or "Lapp-tax," which can be read about in *Egils saga*, Chapter 10 sq. Since Ohthere and his neighbors seem to be collecting this tax for themselves, and not on behalf of King Harald—who made it into a royal monopoly as soon as he had gained control of the area—the account seems to reflect the state of affairs prior to c885.

sciprāpas: ǣgþer sȳ syxtig elna lang, ōþer sȳ of hwæles hȳde geworht, ōþer of sīoles.

Hē sǣde ðæt Norðmanna land wǣre swȳþe lang and swȳðe smæl. Eal þæt his man āþer oððe ettan oððe erian mæg, þæt līð wið ðā sǣ; and þæt is þēah on sumum stōwum swȳðe clūdig; and licgað wilde mōras wið ēastan and wið uppon, emnlange þǣm bȳnum lande. On þǣm mōrum eardiað Finnas. And þæt bȳne land is ēasteweard brādost, and symle swā norðor swā smælre. Ēastewerd hit mæg bīon syxtig mīla brād oþþe hwēne brǣdre, and middeweard þrītig oððe brādre; and norðeweard hē cwæð (þǣr hit smalost wǣre) þæt hit mihte bēon þrēora mīla brād tō þǣm mōre: and se mōr syðþan on sumum stōwum swā brād swā man mæg on twām wucum oferfēran, and on sumum stōwum swā brād swā man mæg on syx dagum oferfēran. Đonne is tōemnes þǣm lande sūðeweardum, on ōðre healfe þæs mōres, Swēoland, oþ þæt land norðeweard; and tōemnes þǣm lande norðeweardum, Cwēna land. Þā Cwēnas hergiað hwīlum on ðā Norðmen ofer ðone mōr, hwīlum þā Norðmen on hȳ. And þǣr sint swīðe micle meras fersce geond þā mōras; and berað þā Cwēnas hyra scypu ofer land on ðā meras and þanon hergiað on ðā Norðmen: hȳ habbað swȳðe lȳtle scypa and swȳðe lēohte.

Ōhthere sǣde þæt sīo scīr hātte Hālgoland þe hē on būde. Hē cwæð þæt nān man ne būde be norðan him. Þonne is ān port on sūðeweardum þǣm lande, þone man hǣt Scīringesheal. Þyder hē cwæð þæt man ne mihte geseglian on ānum mōnðe, gyf man on niht wīcode and ǣlce dæge hæfde ambyrne wind; and

---

46 **ǣgþer sȳ** "Let each be," i.e. "both must be;" *sȳ* is optative subjunctive.

49 **man** "Servant" (or even "slave"; cf. Haddan and Stubbs, III, 235: *Gif man his mæn an wiofode freols gefe* etc.).

52 **ēasteweard** "In the east." Ohthere was thinking of the west shore of the Oslofjord (ON *Vík*). From the point of view of residents of western Norway, this area was the eastern extension of the Norwegian coastline conceived as an uninterrupted stretch; hence to go there by sea or land from anywhere in the country was to travel *austr í Vík*, "east to Oslofjord." (Note however that in l. 65, when Ohthere thinks of this area in relation to his own home, he calls it more accurately *sūðeweard*.)

57 ff. **Đonne . . . Cwēna land** I.e. *Swēoland* is across the mountains from and parallel to the southern half of Norway, *Cwēna land* across from and parallel to the northern half. The Swedes at this time controlled the southeast quarter of present-day Sweden, roughly the provinces from Uppland south to Blekinge. The northeast quarter belonged to the *Cwēnas*, a north Finnish people known in their own language as *Kainulaiset*. The southwest quarter (Bohuslän south to Skåne) belonged to the Danes.

59–63 **Þā Cwēnas . . . lēohte** The *finnskattr* was probably the chief bone of contention (cf. *Egils saga*, Chapters 10, 14). For an interpretation of the geography of this passage see Alan S. C. Ross, "Ohthere's 'Cwenas and Lakes'," *The Geographical Journal*, CXX (1954), 337–46.

66 **Scīringesheal** ON *Skíringssalr*. Probably not the name of the port, but the district (corresponding to modern *Tjölling herred*) in which it was located. Today the site—near Larvik on the west side of the Oslofjord—is occupied by a group of farms which still go by the name of Kaupang, "market town." In the ninth century the place was an important local marketing center, and archaeological investigations (since 1950) have suggested a strong connection with

ealle ðā hwīle hē sceal seglian be lande. And on þæt stēorbord him bið ǣrest Īraland, and þonne ðā īgland þe synd betux Īralande and þissum lande. Þonne is þis land oð hē cymð tō Scīrincgesheale, and ealne weg on þæt bæcbord Norðweg. Wið sūðan þone Scīringesheal fylð swȳðe mycel sǣ ūp in on ðæt land. Sēo is brādre þonne ǣnig man ofer sēon mæge, and is Gōtland on ōðre healfe ongēan and siððа Sillende. Sēo sǣ līð mænig hund mīla ūp in on þæt land.

And of Scīringesheale hē cwæð ðæt hē seglode on fīf dagan tō þǣm porte þe mon hǣt æt Hǣþum: sē stent betuh Winedum and Seaxum and Angle, and hȳrð in on Dene. Ðā hē þiderweard seglode fram Scīringesheale, þā wæs him on þæt bæcbord Denamearc and on þæt stēorbord wīdsǣ þrȳ dagas; and þā

---

the British Isles. (See Charlotte Blindheim, "The Market Place in Skiringssal: Early Opinions and Recent Studies," *Acta Archaeologica* [Copenhagen], XXXI [1960], 83–100.)

66 **ne** The scribe first wrote an *m*, then altered it to *ne*. The most likely explanation is that he had started to write *mihte*, and had finished its first letter, when he noticed that he had omitted a *ne* which stood in his exemplar.

68 ff. **And on . . . Scīrincgesheale** The many interpretations of this vexed passage are reviewed by William C. Stokoe, Jr. (*Speculum*, XXXII [1957], 299–306), who argues that Captain Ohthere was not thinking of the relationship between these land masses in precise geographical terms, but rather of the sea-routes which one would take to reach them from the north Norwegian coast. Stokoe's map (p. 303) makes the whole matter instantly clear and lends great weight to his argument.

69 **ðā īgland** The Shetlands and Orkneys.

þissum lande England.

71 **swȳðe mycel sǣ** The Skagerrak and Kattegat are thought of as an arm of the ocean.

72 **ǣnig . . . mæge** "Any man can see across" (cf. BT s.v. *ofer* III). Mossé prints the compound *oferseōn* and would translate the clause: "it is larger than any (other which) one can see" (§181 Rem. I)—but this is most unlikely (see BT s.v. *þanne* D.III).

Gōtland ON *Jótland*, "Jutland." One expects an OE form like *Geōtland* (with diacritic *e* indicating the palatal pronunciation of *g* before a back vowel).

73 **siððа** Usually emended to *siððan*. But the reduced spelling occurs elsewhere (e.g. *Beowulf* 2996b and in the mid-tenth century MS Cotton Otho A. vi of Boethius [*Metres* 24, 30a]); see further Campbell §217.

Sillende Roughly the East Jutland coast from Fredericia south to the Schlei.

75 **æt Hǣþum** Hedeby (ON Runic *Haiþabu*, MnDan *Haddeby*), at the head of the Schlei near modern Schleswig. In Ohthere's time it was a large, fortified international trading center which controlled commercial traffic across the neck of the Jutland peninsula. (See Herbert Jankuhn's exhaustive *Haithabu: Ein Handelsplatz der Wikingerzeit*, 4th ed. [Neumünster 1963].)

The use of *æt* before OE place names was not unusual; cf. MnE place names like Attercliffe (< OE *æt þǣm clife*) or Attington (< OE *æt þǣm dūnum*).

Winedum etc. Literally "the Wends," but used by Ælfred for the Slavic peoples generally; in the present passage it refers to the Slavic inhabitants of the South Baltic coast. The *Seaxan* lived in Holstein; *Angel* is Angeln, the region east of Flensburg and north of the R. Schlei.

77 **Denamearc** After leaving Skíringssalr, Ohthere has the Skagerrak and Kattegat (*wīdsǣ*) to starboard for three days as he coasts south along the shore of present-day Sweden, which (according to him) belonged to Denmark at the

twēgen dagas, ǣr hē tō Hǣþum cōme, him wæs on þæt stēorbord Gōtland and Sillende and īglanda fela. On þǣm landum eardodon Engle, ǣr hī hider on land cōman. And hym wæs ðā twēgen dagas on ðæt bæcbord þā īgland þe in *on* Denemearce hȳrað.

Wulfstān sǣde þæt hē gefōre of Hǣðum, þæt hē wǣre on Trūsō on syfan dagum and nihtum, þæt þæt scip wæs ealne weg yrnende under segle. Weonoðland him wæs on stēorbord, and on bæcbord him wæs Langaland and Lǣland and Falster and Scōnēg, and þās land eall hȳrað tō Denemearcan. "And þonne Burgenda land wæs ūs on bæcbord, and þā habbað him sylf cyning. Þonne æfter Burgenda lande wǣron ūs þās land þā synd hātene ǣrest Blēcinga ēg and Mēore and Ēowland and Gotland on bæcbord, and þās land hȳrað tō Swēon. And

---

time of his voyage. The northern half of this coast was conquered by Harald Fairhair in the early 880's, so Ohthere's voyage to Hedeby must have preceded that date (if he is speaking precisely, which is by no means certain).

77 f. **and þā twēgen dagas** "And then for two days." The rest of Ohthere's itinerary is clear if we presume that he sails through the Samsø Bælt and Store Bælt, coasts the east side of Langeland and then steers west to Hedeby. Samsø, Fyn, Langeland etc. are the islands he sees to starboard (l. 79); Sjælland, Falster, Lolland etc. the islands he sees to port (l. 80 f.). For a slightly different suggestion (and a useful map) see *SN*, XII (1939–40), 177–90.

80 **on**[2] Not in MS. A later reader felt the lack and added *tō* above the line, and in fact *hīeran in tō* + dat. is the normal OE idiom. Modern editors prefer *hīeran in on* + acc., however, since this has just occurred in l. 76.

82 **Wulfstān** His nationality is not known. It has been suggested (*JEGP*, XXIV [1925], 396 f.) that he was an Anglo-Saxon and that his speech (assuming that it was accurately transcribed) shows a number of Anglian features.

Trūsō A great trading center in the southeast Baltic, probably a colony of the island of Gotland.

84 f. **Langaland . . . Scōnēg** The first three are the Danish islands of Langeland, Lolland and Falster; the fourth is Skåne, the southwestern portion of modern Sweden (corresponding to the counties of Malmöhus and Kristianstad).

85 **And** etc. The pronoun *ūs* in this and the following two sentences suggests that here (and perhaps for the remainder of the account) we are hearing Wulfstan's own voice, recorded but not edited by Ælfred's scribes. The likelihood that we have here an undoctored transcript of actual speech may explain some of the colloquial constructions and anacolutha which occur later in the account.

86 **Burgenda land** Bornholm (< ON *Borgundarhólmr*, "the high-lying island"): the original home of the Burgundians, and the source of their name.

þā . . . cyning "They have their own king," lit. "they (them)selves have them(selves) a king," *him* being refl. with *habban* and *sylf* intensifying the subject *þā*. Already in OE the frequent juxtaposition of *him* and *sylf* in sentences of this type was causing misunderstanding of their true syntactic relationship, a misunderstanding which led ultimately to MnE *himself* (see Wülfing ʃ239b).

sylf Nom. pl. masc. agreeing with *þā*; such uninflected forms of *sylf* are not uncommon in either MS of the Ælfredian Orosius (for further examples see Sweet's edition 42/23, 112/20, 144/32 and 236/24). See also BT s.v. *self* IV.

87 **þā** Relative pronoun.

87 f. **Blēcinga ēg . . . Gotland** Respectively Blekinge (today the southeastern county of Sweden), Möre (today the southern part of the county of Kalmar) and the islands of Öland and Gotland.

Weonodland wæs ūs ealne weg on stēorbord oð Wīslemūðan. Sēo Wīsle is swȳðe mycel ēa, and hīo tōlīð Wītland and Weonodland; and þæt Wītland belimpeð tō Estum. And sēo Wīsle līð ūt of Weonodlande and līð in Estmere, and se Estmere is hūru fīftēne mīla brād. Þonne cymeð Ilfing ēastan in Estmere of ðǣm mere ðe Trūsō standeð in staðe. And cumað ūt samod in Estmere, Ilfing ēastan of Ęstlande and Wīsle sūðan of Winodlande, and þonne benimð Wīsle Ilfing hire naman, and ligeð of þǣm mere west and norð on sǣ; for ðȳ hit man hǣt Wīslemūða.

"Þæt Ęstland is swȳðe mycel, and þǣr bið swȳðe manig burh, and on ǣlcere byrig bið cyningc. And þǣr bið swȳðe mycel hunig, and fiscað; and se cyning and þā rīcostan men drincað mȳran meolc, and þā unspēdigan and þā þēowan drincað medo. Þǣr bið swȳðe mycel gewinn betwēonan him. And ne bið ðǣr nǣnig ealo gebrowen mid Estum, ac þǣr bið medo genōh.

"And þǣr is mid Estum ðēaw, þonne þǣr bið man dēad, þæt hē līð inne unforbærned mid his māgum and frēondum mōnað, ge hwīlum twēgen, and þā kyningas and þā ōðre hēahðungene men swā micle lencg swā hī māran spēda habbað: hwīlum healf gēar þæt hī bēoð unforbærned and licgað bufan eorðan on hyra hūsum. And ealle þā hwīle þe þæt līc bið·inne, þǣr sceal bēon gedrync and plega, oð ðone dæg þe hī hine forbærnað. Þonne þȳ ylcan dæg hī hine tō þǣm āde beran wyllað, þonne tōdǣlað hī his feoh, þæt þǣr tō lāfe bið æfter þǣm gedrynce and þǣm plegan, on fīf oððe syx, hwȳlum on mā, swā swā þæs fēos andefn bið. Ālecgað hit ðonne forhwaga on ānre mīle þone mǣstan dǣl

---

88 **Swēon** For this LWS form of the dat. pl. (instead of *Swēom*) see Campbell §572 n. 4.

91 **Estum** The *Este* (Tacitus' *Æstii*) were an Old Prussian tribe who lived east of the Wisła (Vistula) and spoke a Baltic language.

Estmere The Zalew Wislany, an enormous lagoon off the Gulf of Danzig. The eastern mouth of the Wisła (now called the Nogat) flows into it, as does the Elbing (Wulfstan's *Ilfing*).

92 **ēastan** This and the following directions seem to show the clockwise displacement (see l. 3 *norþ* n.).

93 **ðǣm mere** The Drausen See, now a large marshy lake some eight miles up the Elbing (*Drausen* preserves the name *Trūsō*).

ðe "Of which" (see Wülfing §279C.I.b).

cumað Sc. *hīe*.

96 **Wīslemūða** The predicate complement of the d.o. of *hātan* may be inflected either nom. or acc. (see BTS s.v. III).

99 **mȳran meolc** I.e. koumiss.

107 **dæg²** In the MS another hand has added an *e* to this word, but unnecessarily: the endingless locative is well attested (cf. l. 20 *hām* n. and Campbell §572).

After *dæg* sc. *þe*, the omission of which is perhaps a result of the highly colloquial character of this selection.

109 **on fīf oððe syx** As is shown by what follows, the portions are not of equal size but range from large to small down a graduated scale.

110 **Ālecgað** Sc. *hīe*.

forhwaga Altered to *forhwæga* by a later hand (as is the reoccurrence of this word in l. 115).

on Here probably: "at (a distance of)," though in the next line it means "within."

⁊ sconeg. ⁊ þas land eall hyrað to denemearcan.
⁊ þonne burgenda land wæs us onbæcbord. ⁊ þa
habbað him sylf cyning. þonne æfter burgenda
lande. wæron us þas land. þa synd hatene ærest
blecingaeg. ⁊ meore. ⁊ eowland. ⁊ gotland onbæc
bord. ⁊ þas land hyrað to sweon. ⁊ weonodland wæs
us ealne weg onsteorbord. oð wisle muðan; seo
wisle is swyðe mycel ea. ⁊ hio tolið witland. ⁊ weo
nodland. ⁊ þæt witland belimpeð to estum. ⁊ seo
wisle lið ut of weonod lande. ⁊ lið in estmere. ⁊ se
estmere is huru fiftene mila brad. þonne cymeð
ilfing eastan. in estmere. of ðæm mere. ðe truso
standeð in staðe. ⁊ cumað ut samod in estmere. ilfing
eastan of eastlande. ⁊ wisle suðan of winodlande.
⁊ þon benimð wisle ilfing hire naman. ⁊ ligeð of
þæm mere west. ⁊ norð on sæ. forðy hit man hæt
wisle muða; þæt eastland is swyðe mycel. ⁊ þær bið
swyðe manig burh. ⁊ on ælcere byrig bið cyninge.
⁊ þær bið swyðe mycel hunig. ⁊ fiscnað. ⁊ se cyning. ⁊ þa
ricostan men drincað myran meolc. ⁊ þa unspe
digan. ⁊ þa þeowan. drincað medo. þær bið swyðe my
cel gewinn betweonan him. ⁊ ne bið ðær nænig ealo
gebrowen mid estum. ac þær bið medo genoh. ⁊ þær
is mid estum ðeaw. þonne þær bið man dead. þæt he
lið inne unforbærned. mid his magum. ⁊ freondum.

THE VISTULA AND THE LAND OF THE ESTS. London, British Museum, MS *Cotton Tiberius B. i*, fol. 14r. (See p. 185 and cf. 8/85–103)

fram þǣm tūne, þonne ōðerne, ðonne þæne þriddan, oþ þe hyt eall ālēd bið on þǣre ānre mīle: and sceall bēon se lǣsta dǣl nȳhst þǣm tūne ðe se dēada man on līð. Đonne sceolon bēon gesamnode ealle ðā menn ðe swyftoste hors habbað on þǣm lande, forhwaga on fīf mīlum oððe on syx mīlum fram þǣm fēo. Þonne ærnað hȳ ealle tōweard þǣm fēo. Đonne cymeð se man sē þæt swifte hors hafað tō þǣm ǣrestan dǣle and tō þǣm mæstan, and swā ǣlc æfter ōðrum, oþ hit bið eall genumen: and sē nimð þone lǣstan dǣl sē nȳhst þǣm tūne þæt feoh geærneð. And þonne rīdeð ǣlc hys weges mid ðan fēo and hyt mōtan habban eall; and for ðȳ þǣr bēoð þā swiftan hors ungefōge dȳre. And þonne hys gestrēon bēoð þus eall āspended, þonne byrð man hine ūt and forbærneð mid his wǣpnum and hrægle; and swīðost ealle hys spēda hȳ forspendað mid þan langan legere þæs dēadan mannes inne, and þæs þe hȳ be þǣm wegum ālecgað, þe ðā fremdan tō ærnað and nimað. And þæt is mid Estum þēaw þæt þǣr sceal ǣlces geðēodes man bēon forbærned; and gyf þār man ān bān findeð unforbærned, hī hit sceolan miclum gebētan. And þǣr is mid Estum ān mǣgð þæt hī magon cyle gewyrcan, and þȳ þǣr licgað þā dēadan men swā lange and ne fūliað, þæt hȳ wyrcað þone cyle hine on. And þēah man āsette twēgen fǣtels full ealað oððe wæteres,

---

þone . . . dǣl In apposition to *hit*. There is a slight anacoluthon here, since the referent of *hit* is all the *feoh*, not just the largest portion of it.

114 **fram þǣm fēo** I.e. beyond the largest portion (and thus six or seven miles from the village).

115 **swifte** This is generally emended to the superlative *swiftoste*, and perhaps rightly. But there is at least a chance that it ought to be retained as being the king of intensified positive which is indicated by stress in spoken MnE and by italics in print: "the man who has the *fast* horse," i.e. the really fast one.

116 **tō þǣm¹ . . . mæstan** I.e. *tō þǣm ǣrestan and mæstan dǣle.*

118 **weges** Adv. gen.

mōtan "(They) may."

121 **and . . . forspendað** "And for the most part (lit. mostly) they spend up all his riches" etc.

122 **and þæs þe** Probably: "and through (the dispersion of) that (wealth) which" etc., with *þæs* a gen. of respect used in an instrumental sense.

123 **ǣlces geðēodes** Literally "of every tongue," distinctiveness of dialect (or language) being a criterion of tribe (or nationality).

125 **þæt hī magon** "Who can." The pronoun *hī* reiterates collective *mǣgð*, spelling it out in the pl.

cyle gewyrcan Precisely how this was done is not known. It has often been suggested that some kind of ice-chamber or ice-pit was used (see *MLR*, XLIII [1948], 73 f.), but this cannot be the whole answer, since ice by itself will freeze neither water nor ale (see 128 ff.). Perhaps the Este used freezing mixtures (i.e. mixtures of various chemical salts with either water or ice), which produce cooling far below 32° F. Or perhaps they used radiation cooling to produce a film of ice on pails of water or ale (though this would hardly explain their ability to refrigerate corpses inside houses). (See W. R. Woolrich, *The Men Who Created Cold: A History of Refrigeration* [New York 1967], pp. 30–37; 205–12 [Bibliography].)

126 **þȳ . . . þæt** Correlative: "for this reason . . . that."

127 **hine** Usually emended to *him* because of the pl. *men* in the preceding line. But sudden reversion to the generic sg. would hardly be surprising in this colloquial excerpt, and one certainly expects *on* to govern an acc. in this construction (cf. BT *on* B. III).

hȳ gedōð þæt ōþer bið oferfroren, sam hit sȳ sumor sam winter."

---

twēgen fǣtels full Usually *fǣtels* is masc., but it occurs at least one other time as a neut. (BT s.v., first citation). The use of *twēgen* (which is normally masc. in WS) instead of *twā* is perhaps an Anglian (Northumbrian) feature (SB ∫324 Anm. 1; Campbell ∫683).

128 **ōþer** "One of the two."

9 / the end of the world is at hand: Blickling homily X
(For Rogation Wednesday)

The imminence of Doomsday was a theme which fascinated the author of the Blickling Homilies and he returned to it again and again. It is natural to associate his interest with the anxiety, widespread in Europe in the late tenth century, that the turn of the millenium and the end of the world would arrive together. Orthodox thought combatted this attitude on the grounds that it was presumptuous for men to try to forecast Doomsday, and our author echoes this orthodoxy in Homily XI, where he tells us that the hour of its coming is so secret that there is *nǣnig tō þæs hālig mon on þissum middangearde, ne furþum nǣnig on heofenum, þe þæt ǣfre wiste, hwonne hē—ūre Drihten—þisse worlde ende gesettan wolde on dōmes dæg.* Still, he seems perennially conscious of the fact that he lives not only in the sixth and last age of the world,[1] but very much toward the latter end of it. It is *se mǣsta dǣl āgangen, efne nigon hund wintra and lxxi on þȳs gēare.* His apprehension has served to date him—if, as seems possible, this date is his own, and not that of a scribe recopying the text at some point in its history.[2]

The eighteen sermons of the Blickling Homiliary are intended as a cycle to cover the major saints' and festival days of the ecclesiastical year. Homily X is for Rogation Wednesday, the last of the three Rogation Days—OE *gangdagas*—which precede Ascension Day (i.e. Holy Thursday, forty days after Easter, when Christ's ascension is commemorated).

The portion of the MS which contains the homiliary has been dated to about the year 1000 (Ker 382). The student will find it very instructive to compare the text printed below with the collotype facsimile of the MS now conveniently

[1]See 20/89 f. n.

[2]But some scholars wish to see ninth-century originals behind the Blickling Homilies. The evidence of vocabulary suggests that the homilies were originally composed somewhere in Mercia.

available in the tenth volume of *EEMSF* (ed. Rudolph Willard), where Homily X occupies fols. 65^{r}–70^{r}. He will notice the frequent alternation of the hands of the two scribes who wrote out the MS. Furthermore he will notice that the margins are crowded with entries in a much later handwriting; these are "a whole series of lists of the city officials of Lincoln over a period of four hundred years. . . . For this eleventh century book of homilies found itself in the reign of Edward I turned into a city memorandum book, and its margins continued to serve that purpose until the reign of James I" (ibid. p. 7). In 1724 the Lincoln corporation gave away its memorandum book, "writ in ancient character and of no further use to the city" (p. 15), and it passed into private hands. For almost the next two centuries it was located in the library of Blickling Hall, Norfolk—hence its traditional name. While there it was consulted by Richard Morris for his edition of the text, which is still standard.[3] In 1932 it was sent to New York and sold in auction for $55,000; it was resold in 1938 for $38,000. Since then it has been part of the John H. Scheide Library and is currently located in Princeton, New Jersey. Consequently, the Blickling Homilies are of particular interest to Americans since they are found in the most important—and one of the very few—Anglo-Saxon MSS presently located in the United States.

Another copy of roughly the second half of this homily is found in MS Cambridge, Corpus Christi College 198 (Ker 48), fols. 314^{r}–16^{r}, tacked onto the end of a sermon on penitence. This partial text dates from the early eleventh century and differs from the Blickling text in a number of details. It has not been printed. We have used it to support our restorations of the Blickling text in the two places where the latter is now almost illegible; furthermore we have reported all its substantive variants (i.e. everything except spelling differences) in the textual notes and called attention to the more important of them in the explanatory notes.

[3] *The Blickling Homilies of the Tenth Century*, EETS, Original Series, 58, 63, 73 (1874–80).

Men ðā lēofostan, hwæt, nū ānra manna gehwylcne ic myngie and lǣre, ge weras ge wīf, ge geonge ge ealde, ge snottre ge unwīse, ge þā welegan ge þā þearfan, þæt ānra gehwylc hine sylfne scēawige and ongyte and, swā hwæt swā hē on mycclum gyltum oþþe on medmycclum gefremede, þæt hē þonne hrædlīce gecyrre tō þām sēlran and tō þon sōþan lǣcedōme. Þonne magon wē ūs God ælmihtigne mildne habban, for þon þe Drihten wile þæt ealle men sȳn hāle and

1 Originally Homily X bore a title in the MS, but this was later erased. "One would have expected the original title to have been something like *to þam þriddan gangdæge* (cf. Vercelli Homily XIII: *spel to þriddan gangdæge*)" (Willard p. 39).

4 **gefremede** "May have committed."

gesunde and tō þon sōþan andgite gecyrran. Swā Dāuid cwæþ, þā ēaðmōdan heortan and þā forhtgendan and þā bifigendan and þā cwacigendan and þā ondrǣdendan heora Scyppend, ne forhogaþ þā nǣfre God ne ne forsyhþ. Ah heora bēna hē gehȳreð, þonne hīe tō him cleopiað and him āre biddaþ.

Magon wē þonne nū gesēon and oncnāwan and swīþe gearelīce ongeotan þæt þisses middangeardes ende swīþe nēah is, and manige frēcnessa ætēowde, and manna wōhdǣda and wōnessa swīþe gemonigfealdode. And wē fram dæge tō ōþrum geāxiað ungecyndelico wītu and ungecyn*d*elice dēaþas geond þēodland tō mannum cumene. And wē oft ongytaþ þæt ārīseþ þēod wiþ þēode and ungelimplico gefeoht on wōlicum dǣdum. And wē gehȳraþ oft secggan gelōme worldrīcra manna dēaþ þe heora līf mannum lēof wǣre, and þūhte fæger and wlitig heora līf and wynsumlic. Swā wē ēac geāxiað mislice ādla on manegum stōwum middangeardes and hungras wexende. And manig yfel wē geāxiaþ hēr on līfe gelōmlīcian and wæstmian, and nǣnig gōd āwunigende and ealle worldlicu þing swīþe synlicu. And cōlaþ tō swīþe sēo lufu þe wē tō ūrum Hǣlende habban sceoldan, and þā gōdan weorc wē ānforlǣtaþ þe wē for ūre sāule hǣle begān sceoldan. Þās tācno þyslico syndon þe ic nū hwīle big sægde be þisse worlde earfoþnessum and frǣcnessum. Swā Crīst sylfa his geongrum sægde þæt þās þing ealle geweorþan sceoldan ǣr þisse worlde ende.

Uton wē nū efstan ealle mægene gōdra weorca and geornfulle bēon Godes miltsa, nū wē ongeotan magon þæt þis nēalǣcþ worlde forwyrde. For þon ic myngige and manige manna gehwylcne þæt hē his āgene dǣda georne smēage, þæt hē hēr on worlde for Gode rihtlīce lifge and on gesyhþe þæs hēhstan Cyninges.

Sȳn wē rūmmōde þearfendum mannum, and earmum ælmesgeorne. Swā ūs God sylfa bebēad þæt wē sōþe sibbe hēoldan and geþwǣrnesse ūs betwēonon habban. And þā men þe bearn habban, lǣran hīe þām rihtne þēodscipe and him tǣcean līfes

---

7 **gecyrran** 3 pl. pres. subj. Late forms with *-an* or *-on* instead of *-en* are common in this text.

Swā ll. 18, 24, 30, 35. Characteristic of the low-keyed colloquial style of the Blickling Homilies—and especially frequent as a device to introduce quotations (as in three of these examples)—is the use of *swā* "as a mere transitional link between clauses or at the head of a sentence. In such examples, the modal signification is so low that the *swa* approximates 'and' " (Ericson p. 19).

7 ff. **þā ēaðmōdan heortan** etc. Cf. Psalm 54:1–5, 17 f. (Vulgate). Note the highly rhetorical word order of the OE sentence, with deliberate anacoluthon (cf. 8/29 f. *þā tēð . . . cyninge*).

10 **him āre biddaþ** "Ask for mercy (gen. or acc.) for themselves"; cf. BTS *biddan* IV.(1)(a) or (e). Were the pronoun intended to refer to God (as assumed by both Morris and MW), the homilist would have written *hine* (IIa.(1)) or *æt him* (IIIa.(1) or even (2)).

15 f. **ungelimplico gefeoht** Sc. *ārīsaþ*.

17 **þe heora līf** "Whose life."

22 f. **Þās tācno þyslico syndon** "Such are the signs."

26 **ealle mægene** Inst.

27 **þæt þis nēalǣcþ worlde forwyrde** "That it (lit. this) is getting on toward the destruction of the world."

28 **þæt**[2] Introducing a purpose clause.

32 **lǣran . . . þēodscipe** "Let them teach them proper conduct." Cf. *Fæderas ic lǣrde þæt hīe heora bearnum þone þēodscipe lǣrdon Drihtnes egsan* (Blickling

weg and rihtne gang tō heofonum: and gif hīe on ǣnigum dǣle wōlīce libban heora līf, sȳn hīe þonne sōna from heora wōnessum onwende, and fram heora unrihtum oncyrron, þæt wē þurh þæt ealle Gode līcian. Swā hit eallum gelēaffullum folcum beboden standeþ, næs nā þām ānum þe Gode sylfum underþēodde syndon mid myclum hādum—biscopas and cyningas and mæssepreōstas and hēahdīaconas—ac ēac sōþlīce hit is beboden subdīaconum and munecum, and is eallum mannum nēdþearf and nytlic, þæt hīe heora fulwiht *and* hādas wel gehealdan.

Ne bēo nǣnig man hēr on worldrīce on his geþōhte tō mōdig, ne on his līchoman tō strang, ne nīþa tō georn, ne bealwes tō beald, ne bregda tō full;—ne inwit tō lēof, ne wrōhtas tō webgenne, ne searo tō rēnigenne.

Ne þearf þæs nān man wēnan þæt his līchama mōte oþþe mæge þā synbyrþenna on eorþscrafe gebētan: ah hē þǣr on moldan gemolsnaþ and þǣr wyrde bīdeþ, hwonne se ælmihtiga God wille þisse worlde ende gewyricean. And þonne hē his byrnsweord getȳhþ and þās world ealle þurhslyhþ and þā līchoman þurhscēoteð and þysne middangeard tōclēofeð and þā dēadan ūp āstandaþ, biþ þonne se flǣschoma āscȳred swā glæs, ne mæg ðæs unrihtes bēon āwiht bedīgled. For ðon wē habbaþ nēdþearfe þæt wē tō lange ne fylgeon inwitweorcum. Ac wē sceolan ūs geearnian þā siblecan wǣra Godes and manna and þone rihtan gelēafan fæste staðelian on ūrum heortum, þæt hē ðǣr wunian mæge and mōte, and þǣr grōwan and blōwan. And wē sceolan andettan þā sōþan gelēaffulnesse on ūrne Drihten Hǣlende Crīst and on his ðone ācendan Suna and on ðone Hālgan Gāst, sē is efnēce Fæder and Sunu. And wē sceolan gehyhtan on Godes þā gehālgodan cyricean and on ðā rihtgelēfedan. And wē sceolan gelȳfan synna forlǣtnessa and līchoman

Homily XV).

33 **hīe** I.e. the children.

37 **biscopas** etc. Note the use of the nominative in this parenthesis, though technically dat. is required.

39 **þæt . . . gehealdan** "That they honor their baptism and their stations (in society)." The MS has *fulwiht* | *hadas* with a line division falling between the two words: a situation very conducive to accidental omission of the symbol for *and*. A compound *fulwihthād* is nowhere else attested and does not make sense. The emendation is supported by an extract such as this: "*Mīn fulwiht and mīn*[*n*] *e hād . . . ic swīðe unmeodomlīce gehealdan hæbbe*" (cited BTS s.v. *hād* Va).

41 f. **ne inwit tō lēof** etc. The construction changes abruptly with this phrase: "nor (let) guile (be) too dear (to him), nor contriving slanders," etc.

43 **þæs** Object of *wēnan* and correlative with *þæt*.

44 f. **þǣr wyrde bīdeþ, hwonne** "There awaits the fateful event when" etc. *Wyrd* here refers to Doomsday and *hwonne* introduces an explanatory clause in apposition to it (see BTS s.v. *hwanne* II.(3a)).

45 **þonne** "When" (correlative with *þonne* in l. 47).

48 **ðæs unrihtes** Partitive gen. (complement of *āwiht*).

50 **þā siblecan wǣra** "The covenants of the peace" (lit. "peaceful covenants"). **þone rihtan gelēafan** I.e. the Creed, parts of which the homilist now proceeds to paraphrase.

52 f. **on ūrne . . . Suna** The original reading—bungled by a scribe at some point—was probably something like *on God Fæder and on ūrne Drihten Hǣlende Crīst, his ðone ācendan Suna.*

53 f. **efnēce Fæder and Sunu** "Co-eternal with (the) Father and Son." This dat. of comparison is the rule with *efn-* compounds.

ǣristes on dōm*e*s dæg. And wē sceolan gelēfan on þæt ēce līf and on þæt heofonlice rīce þæt is gehāten eallum þe nū syndan gōdes wyrhtan. Þis is se rihta gelēafa þe ǣghwylcum men gebyreð þæt hē wel gehealde and gelǣste, for ðon þe nān wyrhta ne mæg gōd weorc wyrcean for Gode būton lufon and gelēafan. And ūs is mycel nēdþearf þæt wē ūs sylfe geðencean and gemunan, and þonne geornost þonne wē gehȳron Godes bēc ūs beforan reccean and rǣdan and godspell secggean and hīs wuldorþrymmas mannum cȳþan.

Vton wē þonne georne teolian þæt wē æfter þon ðē beteran sȳn and þē sēlran for ðǣre lāre ðe wē oft gehȳrdon.

Ēalā men ðā lēofostan, hwæt, wē sceolan geðencean þæt wē ne lufian tō swȳþe þæt þæt wē forlǣton sceolan, ne þæt hūru ne forlǣtan tō swīþe þæt wē ēcelīce habban sceolan.

Gesēo wē nū forgeorne þæt nǣnig man on worlde tō ðæs mycelne welan nafað, ne tō ðon mōdelico gestrēon hēr on worlde, þæt sē on medmycclum fyrste tō ende ne cume and þæt eall forlǣteð þæt him ǣr hēr on worlde wynsumlic wæs and lēofost tō āgenne and tō hæbbenne. And se man nǣfre tō ðon lēof ne bið his nēhmāgum and his worldfrēondum, ne heora nān hine tō þæs swīþe ne lufað, þæt hē sōna syþþan ne sȳ onscungend, seoþþan se līchoma and se gāst gedǣlde bēoþ, and þincð his nēawist lāþlico and unfæger.

Nis þæt nān wundor. Hwæt biþ hit lā elles būton flǣsc, seoððan se ēcea dǣl of biþ, þæt is sēo sāwl? Hwæt biþ lā elles sēo lāf būton wyrma mete?

Hwǣr bēoþ þonne his welan and his wista? Hwǣr bēoð þonne his wlencea and his anmēdlan? Hwǣr bēoþ þonne his īdlan gescyrplan? Hwǣr bēoþ ðonne þā glengeas and þā mycclan gegyrelan þe hē þone līchoman ǣr mid frætwode? Hwǣr cumaþ þonne his willan and his fyrenlustas ðe hē hēr on worlde beēode? Hwæt, hē þonne sceal mid his sāule ānre Gode ælmihtigum riht āgyldan ealles þæs þe hē hēr on worlde tō wommum gefremede.

Magon wē nū gehēran s*ec*ggean be *sumum welegum men* and worldrīcum. Āhte hē on þysse worlde mycelne welan and swīðe mōdelico gestrēon and manigfealde,

---

59 **lufon** Note the spelling *-on* for *-an*; similarly in the inf. *forlǣton* in l. 66. **ūs** With this word begins the parallel version of this text in MS Corpus Christi College (Cambridge) 198 (hereafter referred to as C).

61 **gehȳron** Presumably subjunctive. C has *gehȳrað*.

63 **æfter þon** Context does not allow us to decide whether the phrase is temporal ("afterwards") or exemplary ("accordingly").

68 **Gesēo** For 1–2 pl. forms without final -ð, used when the pronoun follows immediately, see Campbell ∫730.
tō ðæs "So"; similarly *tō ðon* ("such") in the next line.

70 **þæt eall** D.o.

72 ff. **ne heora . . . unfæger** C has the following quite different version: *ne hē fram nǣnigum men tō þām swīþe gelufad bið, syþþan se līchama and se gāst gedǣlede bēoð, þæt hē sōna syþþan ne sȳ onscunigendlic and his nēawest lāðlic and unfæger*. This would appear to be a better reflection of the ultimate original since its syntax is less tortuous and it does not contain the questionable and otherwise unattested form *onscungend*.

72 **hē** The antecedent is *nān*.

73 **and þincð** I.e. *and þæt him ne þincð*.

79 f. **Hwǣr cumaþ** "What has become of" (cf. 19/92a and n.).

81 **Gode . . . þæs** The idiom is *agyldan* + dat. + *riht* + gen., "to render someone what is due for something."

and on wynsumnesse lifde.

Þā gelamp him þæt his līf wearð geendod and fǣrlic ende on becōm þisses lǣnan līfæs. Þā wæs his nēhmāga sum and his worldfrēonda þæt hine swȳþor lufode þonne ǣnig ōþer man. Hē þā for þǣre langunga and for þǣre geōmrunga þæs ōþres dēaþes leng on þām lande gewunian ne mihte. Ac hē unrōtmōd of his cȳþþe gewāt and of his earde and on þǣm lande feala wintra wunode, and him nǣfre sēo langung ne getēorode, ac hine swīþe gehyrde and þrēade. Þā ongan hine eft langian on his cȳþþe, for þon þæt hē wolde gesēon eft and scēawian þā byrgenne, hwylc sē wǣre þe hē oft ǣr mid wlite and mid wæstmum fægerne mid man*num* geseah. Him þā tō cleopodan þæs dēadan bān and þus cwǣdon: "For hwon cōme þū hider ūs tō scēawigenne? Nū þū miht hēr gesēon moldan dǣl and wyrmes lāfe, þǣr þū ǣr gesāwe godweb mid golde gefāgod. Scēawa þǣr nū dūst and drȳge bān, þǣr þǣr þū ǣr gesāwe æfter flǣsclicre gecynde fægre leomu on tō sēonne.

"Ēalā þū frēond and mīn mǣg, gemyne þis and ongyt þē sylfne, þæt þū eart nū þæt ic wæs īo—and þū byst æfter fæce þæt ic nū eom. Gemyne þis, and oncnāw þæt mīne welan þe ic īo hæfde syndon ealle gewitene and gedrorene, and mīne herewīc syndon gebrosnode and gemolsnode. Ac onwend þē tō þē sylfum and þīne heortan tō rǣde gecyr, and geearna þæt þīne bēna sȳn Gode ælmihtigum andfenge." Hē þā swā geōmor and swā gnorngende gewāt from þǣre dūstscēawunga, and hine þā onwende from ealre þisse worlde begangum. And hē ongan Godes lof leornian and þæt lǣran and þæt gāstlice mægen lufian, and þurh þæt geearnode him þā gife Hāliges Gāstes, and ēac þæs ōþres sāule of wītum generede and of tintregum ālēsde.

Magon wē þonne, men þā lēofestan, ūs þis tō gemyndum habban and þās bysene on ūrum heortum staþelian, þæt wē ne sceolan lufian worlde glengas tō swīþe, ne þysne middangeard, for þon þe þēos world is eall forwordenlic and gedrorenlic and gebrosnodlic and feallendlic, and þēos world is eall gewiten.

Uton wē þonne geornlīce geþencean and oncnāwan be þyses middangeardes fruman. Þā hē ǣrest gesceapen wæs, þā wæs hē ealre fægernesse full and hē wæs

---

84–107 For a discussion of this passage and its origins see *JEGP*, LVI (1957), 434–9.

86 **on becōm** Sc. *him.*

90 **on þǣm lande** I.e. the land of his voluntary exile. But C's reading *of þām lande* "away from that country" (i.e. his native country) is no doubt more original.

92 **hwylc sē wǣre** "(Wanted to see) what he was," i.e. what his present condition was.

93 **mid[1] . . . geseah** "Saw among men, lovely of countenance and form." But note that instead of *fægerne*, C has the adv. *fægere.*

94 **þæs dēadan** "Of the dead (man)."

96 f. **þǣr þǣr þū . . . tō sēonne** "Where you formerly beheld limbs (which were) —after the nature of flesh—fair to look upon."

99 **þæt[1,2]** I.e. *þæt þæt.*

111 **þēos . . . gewiten** C has instead *eall þēos woruld is gewitenlic.*

113 sq. **Þā hē ǣrest gesceapen wæs** etc. The rest of this paragraph is a close imitation of a passage in Gregory's *Homilia XXVIII in Evangelia* ʃ3 (see *NM*, LXVI [1965], 327–30). Gregory's sermon, originally preached on the day of the martyrs SS. Nereus and Achilleus, concludes with an elaborate comparison between the prosperity of the times in which the martyrs lived (early second century) and the misery of Gregory's own age. The point of the comparison is that whereas Nereus and Achilleus freely gave up a world that

blōwende on him sylfum on swȳþe manigfealdre wynsumnesse. And on þā tīd wæs mannum lēof ofor eorþan, and hālwende and hēal smyltnes wæs ofor eorþan, and sibba genihtsumnes and tūddres æþelnes. And þes middangeard wæs on þā tīd tō þon fæger and tō þon wy*n*sumlic þæt hē tēah men tō him—þurh his wlite and þurh his fægernesse and wynsumnesse—fram þon ælmihtegan Gode. And þā hē þus fæger wæs and þus wynsum, þā wisnode hē on Crīstes hāligra heortum, and *nū hē is wanigenne and scinddende*, nū *is hē* on ūrum heortum blōwende, swā hit gedafen *ne* is. Nū is ǣghwonon hrēam and wōp. Nū is hēaf ǣghwonon and sibbe tōlēsnes. Nū is ǣghwonon yfel and slege. And ǣghwonon þes middangeard flȳhþ from ūs mid mycelre biternesse—and wē him flēondum fylgeaþ and hine feallendne lufiaþ. Hwæt, wē on þām gecnāwan magon þæt þēos world is scyndende and heononweard.

Uton wē þonne þæs geþencean, þā hwīle þe wē magon and mōton, þæt wē ūs georne tō Gode þȳdon.

Uton ūrum Drihtne hȳran georne and him þancas secggan ealra his geofena and ealra his miltsa and ealra his ēaðmōdnessa and fremsumnessa þe hē wiþ ūs ǣfre gecȳþde, þǣm heofonlican Cininge þe leofað and rīxaþ on worlda world aa būton ende on ēcnesse. Amen.

---

was still desirable, men of Gregory's day perversely refuse to give up a world that is hateful.

The OE homilist, in line with his controlling eschatological purpose, transformed Gregory's comparison into a comparison between the newly-created world of the First Age and the disintegrating world of the latter part of the Sixth Age. In this new context, Gregory's references to the two martyrs were no longer appropriate; but the homilist apparently included them anyway. This generated an inconsistency which seems to have puzzled the scribes: the text of B is at one point quite incoherent; the text of C manages to make sense, but only as the result of a savage process of cutting on the part of a scribe (see the textual notes).

114 f. **wæs mannum lēof** "(It) was pleasant for men."

118–21 **And þā hē . . . gedafen ne is** The corresponding text in C is: *And þā hē þus fæger wæs and þus wynsum gesceapen wæs, and þā wæs hē ealra gōdnyssa ful. And nū hē is wanigenne and scinddende.*

119 **Crīstes hāligra** I.e. Nereus and Achilleus; see l. 113 sq. n.

119 f. **nū hē is . . . blōwende** Our restoration is based upon the text of C (for which see ll. 118–21 n.) and upon the corresponding Latin of Gregory: *tamen cum in seipso floreret, jam in eorum cordibus mundus aruerat. Ecce jam mundus in seipso aruit, et adhuc in cordibus nostris floret (PL*, LXXVI, col. 1212), "when it was still flourishing in itself, the world had withered in their hearts. Lo, now the world itself has withered, but it still flourishes in our hearts."

121 **ne** Not in MS; this emendation seems demanded by the sense.

125 **þæs . . . þæt** Correlative.

129 **þæm heofonlican Cininge** As it stands, this phrase must be taken as standing rather oddly in apposition with *him* in l. 127. C's reading is undoubtedly more original: *Ðām heofonlican Cyninge sȳ lof, sē lyfað* etc.

10 / the acts of matthew and andrew in the city of the cannibals

When Jesus appeared to his disciples after the Resurrection he instructed them to go "unto the uttermost part of the earth" (Acts 1:8) in order to "teach all nations" (Matthew 28:19). In general the New Testament is silent on the subject of these missions of the apostles and to remedy this situation there arose in the second century A.D. the legend of the *Sortes Apostolorum*, according to which the apostles, before separating and setting out on their journies, cast lots to decide where each of them was to go. Soon the careers of the major apostles—their deeds, travels, miracles and martyrdoms—had been fully developed in a series of large-scale apocryphal biographies. In general these narratives belong to popular legendary literature "though they sometimes contain an historical core. In a certain sense they may be considered parallels to the novels of antiquity."[1] They were often heretical in origin and sometimes contain a good deal of heretical doctrine.

It now seems probable that the present selection, the Acts of Matthew and Andrew in the City of the Cannibals, was composed in Greek by an anonymous Egyptian monk not long before the year 400 A.D. Hence it did not form part of the original Acts of Andrew, which are possibly Gnostic in origin and may date from as early as the second half of the second century. Rather it was an entirely independent work and represented "a new kind of apostolic romance, free of the doctrinal tendencies traceable in the original Acts of Peter, Paul, John, and Andrew [and] more imbued with orthodox Christian thinking."[2] It seems to

[1]Berthold Altaner, *Patrology*, tr. Hilda C. Graef (Freiburg 1960), p. 72. On the apocryphal Acts in general see Richard Adelbert Lipsius, *Die apokryphen Apostelgeschichten und Apostellegenden*, 2 vols. (Braunschweig 1883–84).

[2]Francis Dvornik, *The Idea of Apostolicity in Byzantium and the Legend of the Apostle Andrew* (Cambridge, Mass. 1958), p. 203. See also pp. 181–222.

have been from the very beginning one of the most popular of all the apocryphal stories of the apostles and survives today in Syriac, Ethiopic, Coptic, Greek, Latin and OE versions.

OE in fact can boast of having two quite different versions. One of them is the 1722-line heroic poem commonly known as *Andreas*; it survives in a unique copy in the Vercelli Book.[3] The other is the text printed here. This is a close (often slavishly close) translation into OE prose of a Latin version which is no longer extant.[4] This lost Latin version was itself a very faithful rendering of its Greek original.[5] This means, in effect, that the Greek version is by and large the closest we can now come to the translator's lost Latin source, and consequently we must rely on comparison with the Greek text to clear up some of the difficulties in the OE.

These most recent statements require two qualifications. A short Latin fragment (Val), corresponding to ll. 103–24 in our text, is preserved in an eleventh-century palimpsest.[6] This fragment belongs to the same recension as the lost Latin version and is consequently very close to the OE; we have printed its relevant portions in the middle of the appropriate pages. There is also a complete Latin prose version (Cas) in a twelfth-century MS.[7] Though it unfortunately belongs to a different and much expanded recension, it is often useful for elucidating some of the perplexities (both syntactic and contextual) of the OE translation.[8]

[3]See below, p. 310. The most recent edition is by Kenneth R. Brooks, *Andreas and the Fates of the Apostles* (Oxford 1961), but see also *Andreas and the Fates of the Apostles*, ed. George Philip Krapp (Boston 1906). For a discussion of the relation of this poem to the other extant versions, see Claes Schaar, *Critical Studies in the Cynewulf Group, Lund Studies in English*, XVII (Lund and Copenhagen 1949), pp. 15–23.

[4]Save for twenty-three words which have survived embedded in one of the two MSS of the OE translation; see l. 50 n.

[5]Πράξεις Ἀνδρέου καὶ Ματθεία εἰς τὴν πόλιν τῶν ἀνθρωποφάγων, printed from nine MSS by M. Bonnet, *Acta Apostolorum Apocrypha*, II, ι (Leipzig 1898). There is a close English translation in *The Ante-Nicene Christian Library*, ed. Alexander Roberts and James Donaldson, 24 vols., XVI (Edinburgh 1870), pp. 348–68, reprinted in *The Ante-Nicene Fathers*, 10 vols., VIII (New York 1903), pp. 517–25. This is the translation we have quoted in our notes. The English versions by Montague Rhodes James (in *The Apocryphal New Testament* [Oxford 1927], pp. 453–58) and Peter M. Peterson (in *Andrew, Brother of Simon Peter: His History and his Legends* [Leiden 1963]) are highly abridged and useless for purposes of comparison.

[6]Codex Vallicellensis; first printed by Bonnet, pp. 85–8.

[7]Codex Casanatensis 1104; most authoritatively available in Franz Blatt, *Die lateinischen Bearbeitungen der Acta Andreae et Matthiae apud anthropophagos, Zeitschrift für die Neutestamentliche Wissenschaften*, Beiheft 12 (Giessen 1930).

[8]Two other Latin versions are known, both representing independent recensions. One is found in MS 1576 of the University of Bologna; it is not yet available in its entirety, the text of the first two pages only having been printed by Holthausen in *Anglia*, LXII (1938), 190–92; it seems to offer a severely abridged version of the story and is probably much the shortest of all the extant Latin versions. The other is the (complete) rhythmic version in Codex Vaticanus lat. 1274, first printed by Blatt; it stands at a very far remove from the lost Latin original of the OE prose.

This OE translation survives in two copies, a complete text in the early eleventh-century MS Cambridge, Corpus Christi College 198 (Ker 48), and a fragment—just over ⅓ of the text—in the slightly earlier Blickling MS (Ker 382; and see p. 196 f. above). A comparison of these two texts suggests that C contains a very lightly abridged form of the text in B.[9] In a number of places, moreover, the readings of B are clearly superior to those of C[10] and this supports the inference which we might draw from the fact of abridgement and from the relative dates of the two MSS, i.e. that B is closer than C to the translator's holograph and is therefore of greater textual authority. On the other hand, though C can be shown to be descended from a MS which was very closely related to B,[11] it cannot be derived from B itself.[12]

We have chosen to print the complete text of C, without interpolating that of B, for two reasons: (1) we thus get a linguistically and orthographically coherent text; (2) whereas the C-text is not available in a reliable modern edition, the B-text is readily obtainable in collotype facsimile (see p. 196 f.). The textual notes report all of B's substantive variants and a few of the more interesting spelling variants; the explanatory notes report a few of the more interesting Latin glosses from C.

---

[9]Mostly this abridgement takes the form of the sporadic omission of a word or a group of two or three words not absolutely necessary to the sense (e.g. ll. 22, 23, 38, 40 *bis*, 45 *bis*, 70, 73 *bis*, etc.); on one occasion, however, the abridgement is more radical (l. 50). An exception to the abridging tendency is the insertion of numerous pronouns which are not strictly necessary (e.g. ll. 23, 58, 81, 96 etc.).

[10]E.g. ll. 50, 62, 82, 99, 105, 113, 118 f., 125.

[11]See especially l. 37 f. n.

[12]C has the spelling *Marmadonia* consistently for B's *Mermedonia*. Furthermore C has a number of superior readings, and though a few of these could perhaps be explained as rather obvious corrections by the scribe of C of rather obvious errors in B (e.g. ll. 84, 115 f.), others cannot (e.g. ll. 26, 102, 118, 127). Finally there is at least one case (l. 75) in which C seems to preserve an oddity of the translator's usage (see n. ad loc.) which has been normalized in B.

SANCTE ANDREAE

[1] Hēr segð þæt æfter þām þe Drihten Hǣlend Crīst tō heofonum āstāh þæt þā apostol(as) wǣron ætsomne, and hīe sendon hlot him betwēonum, hwider

---

1 **þæt . . . þæt** The intervention of the adv. clause *æfter . . . āstāh* causes the (to our way of thinking) unnecessary repetition of the conj. *þæt*; cf. the way in which the intervention of the descriptive clause *þe . . . wǣron* in l. 4 occasions the repetition not only of conjunctive *þæt* but of the subject of the sentence as well.

2 **hīe sendon hlot** "They cast lots" (lit. "sent a lot"). In the MS the phrase is glossed *illi miserunt sortem*; the OE phrase is a loan-translation of this Vulgate idiom.

hyra gehwylc faran scolde tō lǣranne. Segþ þæt se ēadiga Māthēus gehlēat tō Marmadonia þǣre ceastre. Segð þonne þæt þā men þe on þǣre ceastre wǣron þæt hī(e) hlāf ne ǣton ne wæter ne druncon, ac ǣton manna līchaman and heora blōd druncon. And ǣghwylc man þe on þǣre ceastre cōm ælþēodisc, segð þæt hīe hine sōna genāmon and his ēagan ūt āstungan, and hīe him sealdon āttor drincan þæt mid myclen lybcræfte wæs geblanden: and mid þȳ þe hīe þone drenc druncon, hraþe heora heorta wæs tōlēsed and heora mōd onwended.

[2] Se ēadiga Māthēus þā in ēode on þā ceastre, and hraðe hīe hine genāmon and his ēagan ūt āstungan. And hīe him sealdon āttor drinccan and hine sendon on carcerne. And hīe hine hēton þæt āttor etan and hē hit etan nolde, for þon þe his heorte næs tōlēsed ne his mōd onwended; ac hē wæs simle tō Drihtne biddende mid myclum wōpe and cwæþ tō him: "Mīn Drihten Hǣlend Crīst, for þon wē ealle forlēton ūre cnēorisse and wǣron þē fylgende and þū eart ūre ealra fultum, þā þe on þē gelȳfað, beheald nū and geseoh hū þās men þīnum þēowe dōð. And ic þē bidde, Drihten, þæt þū mē forgife mīnra ēagna lēoht þæt ic gesēo þā þe mē onginnað dōn on þisse ceastre þā weorstan tintrego; and ne forlǣt mē, mīn Drihten Hǣlend(e) Crīst, ne mē ne sele on þone bitterestan dēaþ."

[3] Mid þȳ þe hē þis gebed se ēadiga Mātheūs gecweden hæfde, mycel lēoht and beorht onlēohte þæt carcern and Drihtnes stefn wæs on þǣm lēohte cweþende: "Māthēus mīn se lēofa, beheald on mē." Māthēus þā lōciende, hē geseah Drihten Crīst, and eft Drihtnes stefn wæs cweþende: "Māthēus, wes þū gestran-

---

4 **Marmadonia** A town in Scythia, probably to be identified with ancient Myrmekion, which is located by the Greek geographer Strabo about 2¼ miles from modern Kerch (in the eastern Crimea).

7 **āstungan** I.e. 3 pl. pret. indic., with typical late confusion of back vowels in unstressed syllables (cf. Campbell §377). *Myclen* for *myclum* in l. 8 (for the *-m* > *-n* change see ibid. §378), *heorta* for *heorte* in l. 9, *derað* for *dereð* in l. 162, etc. represent the even later confusion in unstressed syllables of front and back vowels (ibid. §379). There are many further examples of these confusions in both MSS of this text.

11 **sendon** With this word the text of the Blickling MS begins.

12 **And hīe . . . nolde** That something is amiss here is indicated not only by the curious use of *etan* rather than *drincan*, but also by the two facts that (1) we may presume Matthew already to have drunk the poison in l. 11, and (2) if we accept the text as it stands, the OE prose becomes the only known version of the story in which Matthew *refuses* to take the poison. The corresponding passage in the Greek reads: "and [they] put beside him grass to eat, and he ate it not," and this is clearly the original reading. It is useless to conjecture when the corruption in the OE arose—whether in the course of transmission of the lost Latin intermediary or in the process of translating it into OE—though we may perhaps hazard a guess that the error was occasioned by the similarity between the Latin words *fenum* ("hay") and *venenum* ("poison").

14 f. **for þon** "Seeing that; since." The phrase is glossed *ex quo* in the MS. The Greek has "for whose sake," Cas *quoniam*.

15 **wē . . . fylgende** See Matthew 19:27.

17 **dōð** "Are treating."

18 **þā þe . . . dōn** "Those who are trying to inflict upon me."

22 **wæs** B adds *geworden tō him*; cf. Cas *facta . . . ad eum.*

23 **beheald on mē** Greek "receive thy sight."

god and ne ne ondrǣd þū þē, for þon ne forlǣte ic þē ǣfre, ac ic þē gefrēolsige of ealra frēcennesse, and nalæs þæt ān, ac simle ealle þīne brēþere and ealle þā þe on mē gelȳfað on eallum tīdum oþ ēcnesse. Ac onbīd hēr xxvii nihta, and æfter þan ic sende tō þē Andrēas þīnne brōþor and hē þē ūt ālǣdeþ of þissum carcerne and ealle þā þe mid þē syndon." Mid þȳ þe þis gecweden wæs, Drihten him eft tō cwæþ: "Sib sī mid þē."

Māthēus þā þurhwuniende mid gebedum and Drihtnes lof singende on þām carcerne. And þā unrihtan men in ēodon in þæt carcern þæt hīe þā men ūt lǣdan woldon and him tō mete dōn. Se ēadiga Māthēus þā betȳnde his ēagan þȳ lǣs þā cwelleras gesāwan þæt his ēagan geopenede wǣron, and he cwǣdon him betwȳnum: "III dagas nū tō lāfe syndon þæt wē hine willað ācwellan and ūs tō mete gedōn."

[4] Se ēadiga Māthēus, sē gefelde xx daga ðā Drihten Hǣlend(e) Crīst cwæþ tō Andrēae his apostolæ, mid þī þe hē wæs in Āchāia þām lande and þǣr lǣrde his discipulī. Hē cwæþ: "Gang on Marmadonia ceastre and ālǣd þanon Māthēus, for þon iii dagas tō (h)lāfe syndon þæt hīe hine willað ācwellan and him tō mete gedon."

Se hāliga Andrēas him andswarode and hē cwæþ: "Mīn Drihten Hǣlend(e)

---

25 **ne ne** Probably dittography for *ne*.
gefrēolsige Glossed *liberabo* in MS.

26 **ealra** I.e. *ealre* (see l. 7 n.).
and . . . ān Gr. has "and not only thee."
brēþere An odd but probably not impossible form of the acc. pl. (cf. Campbell §629–31). B has *brōþor*.

31 **mid gebedum** B adds *wæs* and omits the following *and*. Here and elsewhere in our text (ll. 212, 223) the omission of forms of *wesan* with participles is probably only apparent. What we in fact seem to have is the reproduction in OE of a peculiarity of the Latin original, i.e. its use of participles instead of finite verbs in a number of situations where strict syntax demands the latter. This usage is very frequent in Cas (see Blatt, ed. cit., p. 32, n. to l. 14; also his Index s.v. *Partizipia*) and even occurs once in Val (*Tunc respiciens Sanctus Andreas in caelum et dixit* etc.).

32 f. **þæt² . . . woldon** While it is possible that *þæt* introduces a causal clause and is to be translated "inasmuch as, because" (cf. BT s.v. IV and 17/34b below), *for þon (þe)* is the translator's normal usage in this function, and both Gr. and Cas (*qualiter*) suggest that there ought to be a purpose clause here. It is therefore possible that we should translate: "so that they might lead out the men," interpreting *lǣdan woldon* as a (clumsy) analytical subjunctive (see QW §134), used in place of inflected subjunctive *gelǣdden*.

34 **he** A peculiar (but not unattested) spelling of *hīe*; it occurs again in l. 298. See Campbell §703.

35 **þæt** "(Until the time) that"; cf. BT s.v. VI.

37 f. **Se . . . Andrēae** "The blessed Matthew, he (had) completed twenty days when (our) Lord (and) Savior Christ spoke to Andrew." In l. 37, B has *þā* instead of *sē*, and this makes for better correlation and a smoother reading. The dating error—twenty days instead of twenty-seven—occurs in both B and C and indicates their close relationship.

38 **Āchāia** A region of Scythia on the east coast of the Black Sea.

40 **tō (h)lāfe** I.e. *tō lāfe*; cf. ll. 142, 289. In all three instances the original scribe wrote *tō hlāfe*, with "incorrect addition of the symbol *h*" (Campbell §61). Later the *h* was erased in all three places, completely here and in l. 142, imperfectly in l. 289.

Crīst, hū mæg ic hit on þrim dagum gefaran? Ac mā wēn is þæt þū onsende þīnne engel, sē hit mæg hrædlīcor gefaran, for þon, mīn Drihten, þū wāst þæt ic eam flæsclic man, and ic hit ne mæg hrædlīce gefaran for þon se sīðfæt is þider tō lang and ic þone weg ne can."

Drihten him tō cwæþ: "Andrēas, gehēr mē, for þon þe ic þē geworhte and ic þīnne sīð gestaþelode and getrymede. Gang nū tō þæs sǣ*s* waroðe mid þīnum discipulum, and þū þǣr gemētest scip on þām waroðe: āstīg on þæt mid þīnum discipulum."

[5] Se hāliga Andrēas þā ārās on mergen and hē ēode tō þǣre sǣ mid his discipulum and hē geseah scip on þām waroðe and iii weras on þām sittende. And hē wæs gefēonde mid micle gefēan and him tō cwæþ: "Brōðor, hwider willað gē faran mid þīs medmiclum scipe?"

Drihten Hǣlend wæs on þām scipe swā (se) stēorrēðra, and his twēgen englas mid him, þā wǣron gehwyrfede on manna onsȳne. Drihten Crīst him tō cwæþ: "On Marmadonia ceastre."

Se hāliga Andrēas him andswarode and hē cwæþ: "Brōþor, onfōh ūs mid ēow on þæt scip and gelǣdað ūs on þā ceastre."

Drihten him tō cwæþ: "Ealle men flēoð of þǣre ceastre. Tō hwǣm willað gē þider fēran?"

Se hāliga Andrēas him andswarode. Hē cwæþ: "Nēdmycel ǣrende wē þider habbað and ūs is þearf þæt wē hit gefyllon."

Drihten Hǣlend him tō cwæþ, "Āstīgað on þis scip tō ūs [6] and sellað ūs ēowerne færsceat."

Se hāliga Andrēas him andswarode: "Gehȳrað gē, brōþor, nabbað wē færsceat. Ac wē syndon discipulī Drihtnes Hǣlendes Crīstes, þā hē gecēas, and þis bebod hē ūs sealde and hē cwæþ: 'Þonne gē faren godspel tō lǣrenne, þonne nabbe gē mid ēow hlāf ne feoh ne twīfeald hrægl.' Gif þu þonne wille mildheort-

---

43 **hit . . . gefaran** "Accomplish it (i.e. the journey)."
Ac . . . onsende "But more probably you should send" (cf. BT *wēn* IIIa).

50 **discipulum** B adds (corresponding to Gr.): *And mid þȳ þe hē þis cwæð, Drihten Hǣlend ðā gīt wæs sprecende and cwæð: "Sib mid þē and mid eallum þīnum discipulum." And hē āstāg on heofenas. Tunc Sanctus Andreas surgens mane abiit ad mare cum discipulis suis et uidit nauiculam in litore et intra naue sedentes tres uiros.* Presumably the second half of this addition is "an intentional learned insertion made by the translator" from his Latin original (Krapp p. xxii, n.1).

56 **þā** "Who" (glossed *qui* in the MS).

58 f. **onfōh . . . gelǣdað** Note the switch from imperative sg. to pl.

62 **Nēdmycel ǣrende** "An urgent mission." Although this makes excellent sense, B's *medmycel ǣrende* "a trifling errand" is proved to be the original reading by a comparison with Gr. ("some small business") and Cas (*parvulum negotium*). The error in C undoubtedly arose through a scribe's misreading his exemplar's *med-* as *nīed-* (a very easy mistake to make).

66 **gē, brōþor** Usually printed *gebrōþor* ("brethren"). We have followed the interpretation of the Anglo-Saxon reader who wrote the Latin gloss *vos* above *gē* in the MS.

68 f. **Þonne . . . hrægl** Cf. Matthew 10:9 f., Mark 6:8 f., Luke 9:3.

69 **nabbe** Imperative pl.
twīfeald hrægl Glossed *ij tunicas* (Cas *duas tunicas*).

nesse mid ūs dōn, saga ūs þæt hrætlīce; gif þū þonne nelle, gecȳð ūs þone weg."

Drihten Hǣlend him tō cwæþ: "Gif þis gebod ēow wǣre geseald fram ēowrum Drihtene, āstīgað hider mid gefēan on mīn scip." Se hālga Andrēas āstāh on þæt scip [7] and hē gesæt beforan þām stēorrēþran (þæt wæs Drihten Hǣlend Crīst).

Drihten Hǣlend him tō cwæþ: "Ic gesēo for þon þe þās brōðor synt geswencede of þisse sǣwe hrēohnesse. Ācsa hīe hwæþer hī woldon tō lande āstīgan and þīn þǣr onbīdan oþ þæt þū gefylle þīne þēnunge, tō þǣre þū eart sended; and þū eft hwyrfest tō him."

Se hālga Andrēas him tō cwæþ: "Mīne bearn, wille gē tō lande faran and mīn þǣr onbīdan?"

His discipulī (him) andswarodon and hīe cwǣdon: "Gif wē gewītað fram þē, þonne bēo wē fram eallum þām gōdum þe þū ūs gearwodest. Ac wē bēoð mid þē swā hwǣr swā þu færest."

[8] Drihten Hǣlend him tō cwæþ, tō þām hālgan Andrēa: "Gif þū sȳ sōðlīce his discipul sē is cweden Crīst, spec tō þīnum discipulum be þām mægenum þe þīn lǣrēow dyde, þæt sīe gebletsod hiere heorte and hīe ofergieton þisse sǣwe ege."

Se hāliga Andrēas cwæþ tō his discipulum: "Sumre tīde, mid þī þe wē wǣron mid ūrum Drihtne, wē āstigon mid him on scip. Hē ætȳwde ūs swā hē slǣpende wǣre tō costianne and dyde swīþe hrēoge þā sǣ: fram þām winde wæs geworden swā þæt þā selfan ȳþa wǣron āhafene ofer þæt scip. Wē ūs þā swīðe andrǣdon and cīgdon tō him, Drihtne Hǣlendum Crīste, and hē þā ārās and bebēad þām

---

69 f. **mildheortnesse . . . dōn** "Show us compassion."

70 **hrætlīce** I.e. *hrædlīce*. For the form see Campbell ∫450.

75 **for þon þe** "That" (Cas *quia*). Here and elsewhere the translator has rendered Latin *quia* and *quoniam*, in cases where they were used to introduce declarative object clauses (as frequently in post-classical Latin, e.g. the Vulgate and the fathers), by what would have been their correct OE equivalent had they been used to introduce causal or explanatory clauses. See Blatt's Index s.v. *Objektsatz* 2 and 3.

76 **sǣwe** Gen. sg. (cf. Campbell ∫610.(2)).

82 **bēo wē . . . gearwodest** Gr. has "may we become strangers to the good things which the Lord hath provided for us"; Cas *exteri efficiamur de omnia quod nos docuisti*. B adds *fremde* after *bēo wē*, and the Greek and Latin show that this reading is superior to that of C.

86 **lǣrēow** I.e. *lārēow*; the spelling is no doubt on the analogy of *lǣran* etc.
hiere I.e. *heora*. In addition to these two spellings we also find *hiora*, *hyra*, *hira*, *hieora* and *hera* in this text.

88 sq. **Sumre tīde** etc. See Mark 4:35–40, Matthew 8:23–7.

89 ff. **Hē ætȳwde . . . ȳþa** Translate: "He appeared to us as if he were sleeping in order to make trial of (us), and (he) made the sea very rough: it came about through the (agency of the) wind in such a way that the very waves" etc. But the text of both OE MSS seems seriously disturbed here (for *hrēoge þā sǣ*, B has *hrēonesse ðǣre sǣwe*). Gr. has: "He lay down to sleep in the boat, trying us; for he was not fast asleep. And a great wind having arisen, and the sea being stormy, so that the waves were uplifted, and came under the sail of the boat, and when we were in great fear, the Lord stood up" etc.

90 **hrēoge** Glossed *crudelem* in the MS.

winde þæt hē gestilde, and wæs geworden mycel smyltnes on þǣre sǣ; hīe ondrēdon, ealle þā þe his weorc gesāwon. Nū þonne, mīne bearn, ne ondrǣdaþ gē ēow, for þon þe ūre God ūs ne forlǣteð." [9–15]

[16] And þus cweþende se hālga Andrēas, hē sette his hēafod ofer ǣnne his discipul and slēp. Drihten Hǣlend þā wiste for þon þe se hālga Andrēas þā slēp. Hē cwæþ tō his englum: "Genimað Andrēas and his discipulī and āsettað hīe beforan Marmadonia ceastre, and mid þī þe gē hīe þǣr āsetton, h*weorf*að eft tō mē." And þā englas dydon swā heom beboden wæs, and hē āstāh on heofonas.

[17] Þā se mergen geworden wæs, þā se hāliga Andrēas licgende wæs beforan Marmadonia ceastre and his discipulos þǣr slǣpende wǣron mid him. And hē hīe āweahte and cwæþ: "Ārīsað, mīne bearn, and ongitað Godes mildheortnesse sīo is nū mid ūs geworden; wē witon þæt ūre Drihten mid ūs wæs on þām scipe and wē hine ne ongēaton. Hē hine geēadmēdde swā stēorrēþra and hē hine ætēowde swā man ūs tō costienne."

[18] Se hālga Andrēas þā lōcode tō heofonum and hē cwæþ: "Mīn Drihten Hǣlend Crīst, ic wāt þæt þū ne eart feor fram þīnum þēowum. And ic þē behēold on þām scype and ic wæs tō þē sprecende swā tō men. Nū þonne, Drihten, ic þē bidde þæt þū mē þē onȳwe on þisse stōwe."

. . . . doniae et respexit ad discipulos suos et uidit eos dormiente*s*. Et excitans eos dixit eis: "Surgite, filii mei, et uidete et cognoscite misericordiam Dei que facta est nobis, et scitote quia Dominus Iesus Christus nobiscum erat in nauem et non cognouimus eum. . . . nobis quas*i* homo ad tentandum nos."

. . . . Tunc respiciens Sanctus Andreas in caelum et dixit: "Domine meus Iesu Christe, ego enim scio quia non es ˌ longe a seruis tuis. Unde obsecro te indulgeas michi in unc locum."

---

93 **and wæs . . . sǣ** Cas *et facta est tranquillitas magna in mare.*
hīe B adds *hine* (but see BTS *ondrǣdan* IV.(2) for evidence of usage with neither d.o. nor refl. dat.).

96 f. **ǣnne his discipul** "One of his disciples." B has *discipula*, the more normal construction with partitive gen.

97 **for þon þe** "That" (see l. 75 n.).

102 **Þā . . . þā** "When . . . then."

103 **Marmadonia** The text of the Latin fragment Val (see p. 204) begins at this point and ends at a point corresponding to *wæter* in l. 124. We have printed the relevant parts in the middle of the page. (Most of Bonnet's corrections are adopted and his text is repunctuated to agree with our version of the OE.)
discipulos B has the same reading. The OE translator has carried over the Lat. acc. pl. ending from his original, though it is no longer syntactically appropriate (Cas agrees with Val in reading *discipulos* here).

105 **wē witon** B has *witon wē*, an optative subjunctive construction which makes better sense and answers better to the imperative in Gr., Val and Cas.

107 **swā man . . . costienne** After this in Gr., Val and Cas there is a passage in which Andrew's disciples tell how, while sleeping, they were carried to heaven by eagles and shown a vision of Christ sitting in glory. We have not printed this part of the text of Val, since there is nothing corresponding to it in the OE.

108–11 **Mīn . . . stōwe** In this passage the OE text is fuller and more coherent than Val (as comparison with Gr. shows).

Þā þis gecweden wæs, þā Drihten him ætȳwde his onsȳne on fægeres cildes hīwe and him tō cwæþ: "Andrēas, geseoh mid þīnum discipulum."

Se hālga Andrēas þā hine gebæd and cwæþ: "Forgif mē, mīn Drihten, þæt ic tō þē sprecende wæs swā tō men. And wēn is þæt ic gefirnode, for þon ic þē ne ongeat."

Drihten him þā tō cwæþ: "Andrēas, nǣnigwuht þū gefirnodest, ac for þon ic swā dyde, for þon þū swā cwǣde þæt þū hit ne meahtes on iii dagum þider gefēran. For þon ic þē swā ætēow*de*, for þon ic eom mihtig swā eall tō dōn*ne* and ānra gehwilcum tō ætēowenne swā swā mē līcað. Nū þonne ārīs, and gā on þā ceastre tō Māthēum þīnum brēþer, and lǣt þonne hine of þǣre ceastre and ealle þā þe mid him syndon. Ana ic þē gecȳþe, Andrēas, for þon þe manega tintrega hīe þē on bringað, and þīnne līchaman geond þisse ceastre lonan hīe tōstencaþ swā þæt þīn blōd flōwð ofer eorðan swā wæter. Tō dēaþe hīe þē willaþ gel*ǣ*dan, ac hī ne magon; *ac manega earfoðnessa hīe þē magon* on gebringan. Ac þonne hwæþere ārefna þū þā ealle, Andrēas, and ne dō þū æfter heora ungelēafulnesse. Gemune hū manega earfoðnesse fram Iūdēum ic wæs þrōwiende, þā hīe mē swungon and hīe mē spǣtton on mīne onsȳne; ac eall ic hit āræfnede

---

Hæc dicentem Sanctum Andream, uenit ad eum Dominus Iesus Christus in effigia pulcerrimi pueri et dixit ei: "Gaudeas cum tuis discipulis."

Et cum uidisset Sanctu*s* Andrea*s*, procidens in terra adorauit eum dicens: "Indulge michi, Domine Iesu Christe, quia ut hominem te extimaui in mari et ita tibi locutus sum. Quid enim pec*c*avi, Domine, ut non te michi manifestasti in mare?"

Et Dominus Iesus ait illi: "Andreas, nichil michi peccasti, set ideo hoc tibi feci ˌ quia dissisti: 'Non possum proficere in triduo in anc ciuitate.' Propterea hoc tibi hostendi qui*a* potens sum et omnia possum facere et unicuique ap*pare*re sicut michi placet. Et nunc surge, ingredere in ciuitatem ad Matheum fratrem tuum, et erue eum de carcere et omnes qui cum eo sunt peregrini. Ecce enim dico tibi quia multa tormenta tibi habent inferre isti nequissimi, *e*t carnes tuas in plateas ciuitatis et uicos exp*a*rg*u*nt. Ita sanguis tu*u*s fluet in terra sicut aqua, ita ut. . . ."

---

113 **geseoh** B has *gefeoh*, which obviously corresponds better to *gaudeas* in Val (and Cas).

115 f. **And wēn is . . . ongeat** In Val Andrew asks: "In what way have I sinned, Lord, that you did not manifest yourself to me on the sea?" This makes much better sense in the context.

118 **þider** B *hider*.

121 **ceastre**[2] So also B; but Gr., Val and Cas read "prison."

122 **for þon þe** "That" (Val *quia*); see l. 75 n.

124 f. **swā wæter . . . gebringan** The text of C is considerably disturbed here, apparently as the result of false pointing by a scribe at some point in its prehistory. Where MS B (unedited) reads *swa swa wæter · to deaðe hie* etc., C reads *swá wæt̄ to deaþe · ⁊ hie* etc. The confusion thus generated no doubt explains the omission from C of *ac*[2] . . . *magon* in l. 125.

It is interesting to note that in C another hand has written *sēaþe* as an alternative to *dēaþe*—an ingenious (but insufficiently radical) attempt, on the part of an Anglo-Saxon reader of this MS, to make some sense out of the passage.

128 **hīe**[1] **. . . onsȳne** Cf. Matthew 27:30.

þæt ic ēow ætēowe hwylce gemete gē sculon āræfnan. Gehīere mē, Andrēas, and āræfna þās tintrego, for þon manige synt on þisse ceastre þā sculon gelēofan on mīnne naman." Mid þī hē þis cwæð, Drihten Hǣlend Crīst, hē āstāh on heofonas.

[19] Se hāliga Andrēas þā in ēode on þā ceastre mid his discipulum, and nǣnig man hine ne mihte gesēon. Mid þī þe hīe cōmon tō þæs carcernes duru, hīe þǣr gemētton seofon hyrdas standan. Se hāliga Andrēas þā gebæd on his heortan and raðe hīo wǣron dēade. Se hālga Andrēas þā ēode tō þæs carcernes duru and hē worhte Crīstes rōdetācen, and raþe þā dura wǣron ontȳnede. And hē in ēode on þæt carcern mid his discipulum and hē geseah þone ēadigan Māthēus ǣnne sitton singende.

Se ēadiga Māthēus þā and se hāliga Andrēas hīe wǣron cyssende him betwēonon. Se hālga Andrēas him tō cwæþ: "Hwæt is þæt, brōþor! Hū eart þū hēr gemēt? Nū þrȳ dagas tō (h)lāfe syndon þæt hīe þē willaþ ācwellan and him tō mete gedōn."

Se hālga Māthēus him andswarode and hē cwæþ: "Brōþor Andrēas, ac ne gehȳrdest þū Drihten cweþende for þon þe 'ic ēow sende swā swā scēap on middum wulfum?' Þanon wæs geworden, mid þȳ þe hīe mē sendon on þis carcern, ic bæd ūrne Drihten þæt hē hine ætēowde, and hraþe hē mē hine ætēowde and hē mē tō cwæþ: 'Onbīd hēr xxvii daga and æfter þon ic sende tō þē Andrēas þīnne brōðor, and hē þē ūt ālǣt of þissum carcerne and ealle þā mid þē syndon.' Swā mē Drihten tō cwæþ, ic gesīe. Brōðor, hwæt sculon wē nū dōn?" [20]

[21] Se hālga Andrēas þā and se hālga Māthēus gebǣdon tō Drihtne. And æfter þon gebede se hāliga Andrēas sette his hand ofer þāra wera ēagan þā þǣr on lande wǣron, and gesihþe hīe onfēngon. And eft hē sette his hand ofer hiora heortan, and heora andg*ie*t him eft tō hwirfde. Se hāliga Andrēas him tō cwæþ: "Gangað on þās niþeran dǣlas þisse ceastre and gē þǣr gemētað mycel fīctrēow: sittað under him and etað of his wæstmum oð þæt ic ēow tō cyme."

---

129 **hwylce gemete** "In what manner."
āræfnan With this word the text of B breaks off.
Gehīere Imperative sg. (for this LWS form see Campbell ∫752, last paragraph).

139 **sitton** Infinitive.

140 **hīe** This pronoun recapitulates the compound subject.

140 f. **wǣron . . . betwēonon** Cas *osculati sunt se invicem*.

141 f. **Hwæt . . . gemēt** Gr. "Brother, how hast thou been found here?" Cas *quid est hoc frater quod video*.

142 **tō (h)lāfe** See l. 40 n.
þæt "(Until the time) that" (see BT s.v. *þæt* conj VI).

144 **ac** Used here (with no sense of antithesis) to introduce an interrogative clause; cf. *Beowulf* 1990b.

145 **for þon þe** "That" (see l. 75 n.).

145 f. **ic . . . wulfum** See Matthew 10:16.

146 **Þanon** "After that."

149 **ealle þā** "All who"; cf. l. 267.

150 **gesīe** Sc. *þē*? (see *ZfdA*, XXX [1886], 180). The form *gesīe* is non-WS (see Campbell ∫237.(3)).

153 **þā** "Who."

154 **on lande** Gr. "in the prison."

Hī cwǣdon tō þām hālgan Andrēa: "Cum nū mid ūs, for þon þe þū eart ūre wealdend, þȳ lǣs wēn is þæt hī ūs eft genimon and on þā wyrstan tintregu hīe ūs on gebringan."

Se hāliga Andrēas him tō cwæþ: "Farað þider, for þon þe ēow nǣnig wiht ne derað ne ne swenceþ." And hraðe hīe þā ealle fērdon, swā him se hālga Andrēas bebēad. And þǣr wǣron on þǣm carcerne twā hund and eahta and fēowertig wera and nigon and fēowertig wīfa, ðā se hāliga Andrēas þanon onsende. And þone ēadigan Māthēum hē gedyde gangan tō þām ēastdǣle mid his discipulum. And se hāliga Andrēas [. . .] and āsetton on þā dūne þǣr se ēadiga Pētrus se apostol wæs, and hē þǣr wunode mid him.

[22] Se hāliga Andrēas þā ūt ēode of þǣm carcerne and hē ongan gangan ūt þurh midde þā ceastre. And hē cōm tō sumre stōwe and hē þǣr geseah swer standan, and ofer þone swer ǣrne onlīcnesse. And hē gesæt be þām swere anbīdende hwæt him gelimpan scolde.

Đā unrihte men þā ēodon þæt hīe þā men ūt gelǣd*an woldon* and hi*m* tō mete gedōn, and hīe gemētton þæs carcernes duru opene and þā seofon hyrdas dēade licgan. Mid þȳ þe hīe þæt gesāwon, hīe eft hwirfdon tō hiora ealdormannum and hīe cwǣdon: "Þīn carcern open wē gemētton, and in gangende *n*ǣnige wē þǣr gemētton."

Mid þī þe hīe gehȳrdon þāra sācerda ealdormen and hīe cwǣdon him betwēonon: "Hwæt wile þis wesan? Wēn is þæt hwilc wundor in ēode on þæt carcern and þā hyrdas ācwælde and somnunga *ālȳsde þā þe* þǣr betȳnede wǣron." [23]

[24] Æfter þiossum him ætēowde dēofol on cnihtes onlīcnysse and him tō

---

158 f. **Cum . . . wealdend** Gr. "Go along with us, O our master."

159 **þȳ lǣs wēn is þæt** "Lest perchance" (Cas *ne forte*).

165 ff. **And þone . . . mid him** The corresponding Gr. clarifies the meaning of the OE and supplies the missing material: "and he made Matthias go along with his disciples out of the eastern gate of the city. And Andrew commanded a cloud, and the cloud took up Matthias and the disciples of Andrew; and the cloud set them down on the mountain where Peter was teaching, and they remained beside him." (The OE translator's Latin original no doubt read *nubes* [pl.], as does Cas, and this explains the number of *āsetton* in l. 166.)

170 **be** Gr. "behind."

172 **gelǣdan woldon** The MS has simply *gelǣddon*, and if we keep it we must emend *gedōn* to *gedydon*. But comparison with l. 32 f. suggests that the reading here was originally the same, and that a scribe—puzzled by the admittedly puzzling construction—altered *gelǣdan woldon* to *gelǣddon* (= *gelǣdden*), assuming that *þæt* was being used to introduce a purpose clause and rejecting the analytical in favor of the inflected subjunctive.

175 **Þīn** More accurate would be *Ēower*. The sg. is perhaps under the influence of a vocative sg. here in the translator's Latin source (cf. Cas *dixeruntque ad eos, Domine, carcerem apertum invenimus*).

177 **Mid þī . . . cwǣdon** "When they (had) heard (this), (those) leaders of the priests, they said" etc. The redundant *and* is probably yet another reflection of the bad Latin of the original (see Blatt, Index s.v. *que* III).

178 **Hwæt . . . wesan?** Cas *Quid sibi vult esse hec quod accidit.*

181 **on cnihtes onlīcnysse** Gr. "in the likeness of an old man" (Cas *in similitudinem hominis canuti*).

cwæþ: "Gehȳrað mē, and sēcað hēr sumne ælþēodigne man þæs nama is Andrēas and ācwellað hine. Hē þæt is sē þā gebundenan of þissum carcerne ūt ālǣdde and hē is nū on þisse ceastre. Gē hine nū witon: efstað, mīne bearn, and ācwellað hine."

Se hāliga Andrēas þa cwæþ tō þām dēofle: "Ana þū heardeste strǣl tō ǣghwilcre unrihtnesse, þū þe simle fihtest wið manna cyn: mīn Drihten Hǣlend(e) Crīst þē gehnǣde in helle."

Þæt dēofol, þā hē þis gehȳrde, hē him tō cwæþ: "Þīne stefne ic gehīere, ac ic ne wāt hwǣr þū eart."

Se hāliga Andrēas him tō cwæþ: "For þon þe þū eart blind, þū ne gesihst ǣnigne of Godes þām hālgum."

Þæt dēofol þā cwæþ tō þām folce: "Behealdað ēow and gesēoð hine, for þon þe hē þæt is sē þe wið mē spræc."

Ðā burhlēode þā urnon and hī betȳndon þǣre ceastre gatu and hīe sōhton þæne hālgan Andrēas þæt hīe hine genāmon. Drihten Hǣlend hine þā ætēowde þām hāligan Andrēa and him tō cwæþ: "Andrēas ārīs and gecȳð him, þæt hīe ongieton mīn mægen on þē wesan."

[25] Se hāliga Andrēas þā ārās on þæs folces gesihþe and hē cwæþ: "Ic eom sē Andrēas þe gē sēcaþ."

Þæt folc þā arn and hī hine genāmon and cwǣdon: "For þon þū ūs þus dydest, wē hit þē forgyldað." And hīe þōhton hū hīe hine ācwellan meahton.

Þā wæs se dēofol in gangende and cwæþ tō þām folce: "Gif ēow swā līcige, uton sendon rāp on his swyran and hine tēon þurh þisse ceastre lanan, and þis uton wē dōn oþ þæt hē swelte. And mid þī þe hē dēad sīe, uton wē dǣlan his līchaman ūrum burhlēodum."

And þā eall þæt folc þæt gehīerde, hit him līcode, and hraðe hīe sendon rāp on his swēoran and hīe hine tugon geond þǣre ceastre lanan. Mid þī þe se ēadiga Andrēas wæs togen, his līchama wæs gemengeð mid þǣre eorðan swā þæt blōd flēow ofer eorðan swā wæter.

Ðā ǣfen geworden wæs, hī hine sendon on þæt carcern and hīe gebunden his handa behindan and hīe hine forlēton, and eall his līchama gelȳsed.

[26] Swilce ōþre dæge þæt ilce hīe dydon. Se hāliga Andrēas þā wēop and hē

---

184 **Gē . . . witon** "Now you know who he is" (lit. "him"). The Gr. however has "you have not seen him" (or "you do not know him").

186 f. **Ana . . . unrihtnesse** Thus too the OE poem: *ðū dēofles strǣl*. The Gr. has "O Belial most fiendish." It has been plausibly suggested that *strǣl* renders *sagitta* or *telum* in the lost Latin original, and that this Latin reading resulted from confusion of Gr. Βελία "Belial" with βέλος "dart."

196 **þæne** I.e. *þone* (see Campbell §380).

197 **gecȳð him** Gr. "show thyself to them."

203 **Þā wæs . . . folce** A somewhat garbled version of Gr. "Then one of them, the devil having entered into him, said to the multitudes" etc.

204 **sendon** I.e. *sendan.*

swyran Cf. *swēoran* in l. 208, *swuran* in l. 277, and see Campbell §241.(2) n. 5.

209 **gemengeð** I.e. *gemenged* (an example of the confusion of *d* and *þ*/ð which is common in late MSS).

211 **gebunden** I.e. *gebundon.*

212 **gelȳsed** Sc. *wæs* (but cf. l. 31 n.).

cwæþ: "Mīn Drihten Hǣlend Crīst, cum and geseoh þæt hīe mē dōð, þīnum þēowe: and eall ic hit ārǣfnie for þīnum gebode þe þū mē sealdest. And þū cwǣde: 'Ne dō æfter hiora ungelēafulnesse.' Beheald, Drihten, and geseoh hū hīe mē dōð."

Mid þī hē þus cwæþ, þæt dēofol cwæþ tō þām folce: "Swingað hine on his muð, þæt hē þus ne sprece."

Đā geworden wæs þæt hīe hine eft betȳndon on þām carcerne. Đæt dēofol þā genam mid him ōþre seofon dēoflo, þā þe hāliga Andrēas þanon āflīemde, and in gangende on þæt carcern hīe gestōdon on gesihþe þæs ēadigan Andrēas and hine bismriende mid myclere bismre and hīe cwǣdon: "Hwæt is þæt þū hēr gemētest? Hwilc gefrēolseð þē nū of ūrum gewealde? Hwǣr is þīn gilp and þīn hiht?"

[27] Þæt dēofol þā cwæþ tō þām ōðrum dēoflum: "Mīne bearn, ācwellað hine, for þon hē ūs gescende and ūre weorc."

Þā dēofla þā blǣstan hīe ofer þone hālgan Andrēas, and hīe gesāwon Crīstes rōdetācen on his onsīene: hī ne dorston hine genēalǣcan ac hraðe hīe onweg flugon. Þæt dēofol him tō cwæþ: "Mīne bearn, for hwon ne ācwealdon gē hine?"

Hīe him andswarodon and hīe cwǣdon: "Wē ne mihton, for þon þe Crīstes rōdetānc on his onsīene wē gesāwon and wē ūs ondrǣdon. We witon *hine*, for þon þe ˌ ǣr *hē* on þæs earfoðnesse cōm he ūre wæs wealdend. Gif þū mæge, ācwel hine. Wē þē on þissum ne hērsumiað, þȳ lǣs wēn sīe þæt hine God gefrēolsige and ūs sende on wyrsan tintrego."

Se hāliga Andrēas him tō cwæþ: "Þēah þe gē mē ācwellan, ne dō ic ēowerne willan, ac ic dō willan mīnes Drihtnes Hǣlendes Crīstes." And þus hī gehērdon and onweg flugon.

[28] On mergen þā geworden wæs, eft hīe tugon þone hālgan Andrēas. And hē cīgde mid mycle wōpe tō Drihtne and cwæþ: "Mīn Drihten Hǣlend(e) Crīst, mē genihtsumiað þās tintrega, for þon ic eom getēorod. Mīn Drihten Hǣlend(e) Crīst, āne tīd on rōde þū þrōwodest, and þū cwǣde: 'Fæder, for hwon forlēte þū mē?' Nū iii dagas syndon syððan ic wæs getogen þurh þisse ceastre lanum. Þū wāst, Drihten, þā menniscan tȳddernysse. Hāt onfōn mīnne gāst. Hwǣr syndon þīne word, Drihten, on þām þū ūs gestrangodest and þū cwǣde: 'Gif gē mē gehȳrað and gē mē bēoð fylgende, ne ān locc of ēowrum hēafde forwyrð.' Beheald, Drihten, and geseoh, for þī *mīn* līchama ˌ and loccas mīnes hēafdes mid þisse eorðan synd gemengde. Ane, iii dagas syndon syððan ic wæs getogen tō

---

214 **þæt** I.e. *þæt þæt*.
221 **þā þe . . . āflīemde** Gr. "whom the blessed one had cast out of the countries round about."
223 **bismriende** I.e. *bismrodon* (cf. l. 31 n.).
myclere I.e. *mycelre*; cf. 11/114 *lytlere* n.
228 **blǣstan** I.e. *blǣston* (Cas *intenderunt*).
232 **rōdetānc** For this spelling see Campbell ∫400 n. 4.
232 f. **Wē witon . . . wealdend** The MS has *Wē witon for þon þe hē ǣr* etc. We base our emendations on the corresponding Gr. ("for we knew him before he came into the distress of his humiliation").
242 **āne tīd** Gr. "three hours" (with which compare Andrew's three days).
242 f. **Fæder . . . mē?** Cf. Matthew 27:46.
246 **ne . . . forwyrð** Cf. Luke 21:18.

þǣm wyrstan tintregum, and þū mē ne ætēowdest. Mīn Drihten Hǣlend Crīst, gestranga mīne heortan!"

Ðus gebiddende þām hālgan Andrēa, Driht(e)nes stefn wæs geworden on Ebrēisc cweþende: "Mīn Andrēas, heofon and eorðe mæg gewītan, mīn word nǣfre ne gewītaþ. Beheald æfter þē and gescoh þīnne līchaman and loccas þīnes hēafdes, hwæt hīe syndon gewordene."

Se hāliga Andrēas þā lōciende, hē geseah geblōwen trēow wæstm berende and hē cwæþ: "Nū ic wāt, Drihten, for þon þæt þū ne forlēte mē."

On ǣfenne þā geworden, hīe hine betȳndon on þām carcerne and hīo cwǣdon him betwȳnum for þon þe "þisse nihte hē swelt."

[29] Him ætēowde Drihten Hǣlend Crīst on þǣm carcerne, and hē āþenede his hand and genam, and hē cwæþ: "Andrēas, ārīs."

Mid þī þe hē þæt gehȳrde, hraþe hē þā ārās gesund and hē hine gebæd and hē cwæþ: "Þancas ic þē dō, mīn Drihten Hǣlend Crīst." Se hāliga Andrēas þā lōciende, hē geseah on middum þǣm carcerne swer standan, and ofer þone swer stǣnenne anlīcnesse. And hē āþenede his handa and hiere tō cwæþ: "Ondrǣd þē Drihten and his rōdetānc, beforan þǣm forhtigað heofon and eorþe. Nū þonne, anlīcnes, dō þæt ic bidde on naman mīnes Drihtnes Hǣlendes Crīstes: sænd mycel wæter þurh þīnne mūþ swā þæt sīen gewemmede ealle þā on þisse ceastre syndon."

Mid þī hē þus cwæþ, se ēadiga Andrēas, hraþe sīo st*ǣne*ne onlīcnes sendde mycel wæter þurh hiora mūþ swā sealt, and hi*t* ǣt man*n*a līchaman.

[30] And hit ācwealde heora bearn and hyra nȳtenu, and hīe ealle woldon flēon of þǣre ceastre. Se hāliga Andrēas þā cwæþ: "Mīn Drihten Hǣlend Crīst, ne forlǣt mē, ac send mē þīnne engel of heofonum on fȳrenum wolcne, þæt þā embgange ealle þās ceastre þæt ne magen genesan for þǣm fȳre." And þus

---

251 **Ðus . . . Andrēa** "St. Andrew praying in this fashion," etc.; a dat. absolute, no doubt representing an ablative absolute in the Latin original.

251 f. **Driht(e)nes . . . cweþende** Cas *facta est vox Domini sermo Ebraico dicens ad eum.*

252 f. **heofon . . . gewītaþ** See Mark 13:31, *Cælum et terra transibunt, verba autem mea non transibunt.*

255 **hē geseah . . . berende** Cas *apparuerunt caro et capilli sui sicut arbores florentes et fructum afferentes.*

256 **for þon þæt** Cf. l. 75 n. The form here seems to represent a conflation of *for þon þe* and *þæt.*

257 **On . . . geworden** Cas *Vespere autem facto.*

257 f. **and hīo . . . swelt** Cas *dicentes, quia iam caro eius et capilli destructi sunt, forsitan in hac nocte morietur.*

260 **genam** "Lay hold of (him)," see BTS s.v. *geniman* II.

264 **stǣnenne** Gr. "alabaster." For the spelling *stǣnenne* see 1/179 and n.

267 **swā** MS *swā swā*, with *swā*[1] erased. The use of *swā swā* to introduce a purpose clause is possible (BT *swā* VI.(1a)), but probably not if *þæt* follows (cf. Ericson p. 73).

270 **hiora** Compare the spelling *heora* in l. 287, and cf. l. 86 *hiere* n.

273 f. The OE text is disturbed here. Translate: "so that (he? it?) may surround all this town, so that (the inhabitants) cannot escape because of the fire." Gr. "but send Michael Thy archangel in a cloud of fire, and be a wall round the city, that no one may be able to escape out of the fire"; Cas *continuo mittas angelum tuum cum nubis igneis in circuitu civitatis istius, nec valeant quiscumque hominum vel iumentum exiliret.*

cweþende, fȳren wolc āstāh of heofonum and hit ymbsealde ealle þā ceastre. Mid þȳ þæt ongeat se ēadiga Andrēas, hē bletsode Drihten.

Þæt wæter wēox oþ mannes swuran and swīþe hit ǣt hyra līchaman, and hīe ealle cīgdon and cwǣdon: "Wā ūs, for þon þe þās ealle ūp cōman for þissum ælþēodigum þe wē on þissum carcerne betȳned hæbbað. Hwæt bēo wē dōnde?"

Sume hīe cwædon: "Gif ēow swālīce þūhte, utan gangan on þissum carcerne and hine ūt forlǣtan, þȳ lǣs wēn sīe þæt wē yfele forweorþon; and uton wē ealle cīgean and cweþan for þon þe wē gelēofað on Drihten þyses ælþēodigan mannes: þonne āfyrseþ hē þās earfoðnesse fram ūs."

Mid þī se ēadiga Andrēas ongeat þæt hīe tō Drihtene wǣron gehwyrfede, hē cwæþ tō þǣre stǣnenan anlīcnesse: "Āra nū þurh mægen ūres Drihtenes, and mā wæter of þīnum mūþe þū ne send." And þā gecweden, þæt wæter oflan, and mā of heora mūþe hit ne ēode.

Se hāliga Andrēas þā ūt ēode of þām carcerne, and þæt selfe wæter þegnunge gearwode beforan his fōtum. And þā þǣr tō hlāfe wǣron, hīe cōmon tō þæs carcernes duru and hīe cwǣdon: "Gemiltsa ūs, God, and ne dō ūs swā swā wē dydon on þisne ælþēodigan."

[31] Se hāliga Andrēas þā gebæd on þæs folces gesihþe, and sēo eorþe hīe ontȳnde and hīo forswealh þæt wæter mid þām mannum. Þā weras þā þæt gesāwon hīe him swīþe ondrǣdon and hīe cwǣdon: "Wā ūs, for þon þe þes dēað fram Gode is. And hē ūs wile ācwellan for þissum earfoðnessum þe wē þissum mannan dydon. Sōðlīce fram Gode hē is send, and hē is Godes þēowa."

Se hālga Andrēas him tō cwæþ: "Mīne bearn, ne ondrǣdaþ gē ēow, for þon þe þās þe on þīs wætere syndon, eft he libbað. Ac þis is for þon þus geworden, þæt gē gelēofon on mīnum Drihtne Hǣlendum Crīste."

---

274 f. **And þus cweþende** Note the dangling participle.

275 **wolc** An odd but not unexampled spelling of *wolc(e)n*; see BT s.v. passim.

278 **Wā ūs** "Woe is us."

279 **Hwæt . . . dōnde** "What should we do?" (no doubt a clumsy imitation of a Latin gerundive).

283 **hē** I.e. God.

285 f. **and mā . . . send** Cas *ne amplius mittas aquas per os tuum*, so *mā* in the OE is probably an adverb.

286 **And þā gecweden** "And these (things having been) said" etc., no doubt imitating an absolute construction in the Latin.

287 **mā** Adv.

288 f. **and . . . fōtum** Gr. "and the water ran this way and that from the feet of the blessed Andrew."

289 **þā** "Those who."

tō hlāfe See l. 40 n.

292 **hīe** Reflexive.

293 **þām mannum** Fourteen Marmadonian executioners and an unnatural old man who had wanted to have his own life at the expense of his children's.

293 f. **Þā weras . . . gesāwon** Probably "When men then saw that," possibly "The men who saw that."

298 **syndon** Sc. *dēad* (Cas *mortui*).

he I.e. *hīe*; cf. l. 34 n.

298 f. **Ac þis . . . Crīste** Cas *nam hec omnia que factum est, propter vos factum est, ut cognoscatis . . . Dominum Iesum Christum.*

[32] Se hāliga Andrēas þā gebæd tō Drihtne and cwæþ: "Mīn Drihten Hǣlend(e) Crīst, send þīnne þone Hālgan Gāst þæt āwecce ealle þā þe on þisse wætere syndon, þæt hīe gelīefon on þīnne naman." Drihten þā hēt ealle ārīsan þe on þām wætere wǣron.

And æfter þissum se hāliga Andrēas hēt cyrican getimbrian on þǣre stōwe þǣr se swer stōd, and hē him sealde bedodu Drihtnes Hǣlendes ˌ Crīstes. "And lufiað hine for þon mycel is his mægen." And ǣnne of heora aldormannum tō bisceope hē him gesette, and hē hī gefullode and cwæþ: "Nū þonne ic eom gearo þæt ic gange tō mīnum discipulum."

Hīe ealle hine bǣdon and hīe cwǣdon: "Medmycel fæc nū gȳt wuna mid ūs, þæt þū ūs gedēfra*n* gedō, for þon þe wē nīwe syndon tō þissum gelēafan gedōn."

Se hālga Andrēas hīe þā nolde gehīeran, ac hē hīe grētte and hīe swā forlēt. Him fylgede mycel manigo þæs folces wēpende and hrȳmende. And þā āscān lēoht ofer hieora hēafod.

[33] Mid þī se hālga Andrēas þanon wæs farende, him ætīwde Drihten Hǣlend(e) Crīst on þām wege on ansīne fægeres cildes and him tō cwæþ: "Andrēas, for hwan gǣst þū swā, būton wæstme þīnes gewinnes? And þū forlēte þā þe þē bǣdon and þū nǣre miltsiend ofer heora cild, þā þē wǣron fyliende and wēpende, þāra cirm and wōp mē āstāh on heofonas. Nū þonne hwyrf(e) eft on þā ceastre and bēo þǣr seofon dagas, oþ þæt þū gestrangie hera mōd on mīnne gelēafan. Gang þonne tō þǣre ceastre mid þīnum discipulum, and gē on mīnne gelēafan gelēofon." Mid þī hē þis cwæþ, Drihten Hǣlend (e) Crīst, hē āstāh on heofonas.

Se ēadiga Andrēas þā wæs eft hwyrfende on Marmadonia ceastre and hē cwæþ: "Ic þē bletsige, mīn Drihten Hǣlend Crīst, þū þe gehwyrfest ealle sāula, for þon þū mē ne forlēte ūt gangan mid mīnre hātheortan of þisse ceastre."

Hīo wǣron gefēonde mycle gefēan. And hē þǣr wunode mid him seofon da-

---

301 **þæt** Sc. *þū* (and cf. the similar omissions in l. 274). Cas *mitte spiritum sanctum tuum de celis, et allevas omnes animas* etc.

306 f. **And . . . gesette** Cas *ordinavit eis episcopum unum de principibus eorum.*

310 **gedēfran** Glossed *tranquillos* in the MS (but cf. Cas *quousque nos firmetur in dominicam integram fidem*).

313 **Him fylgede . . . hrȳmende** Gr. "And the children followed after, weeping and praying, with the men."

313 f. **And þā . . . hēafod** Gr. "and they cast ashes upon their heads." We can no doubt attribute the OE version to a scribe who mistook *ascan* ("ashes") in his exemplar for *āscān* ("shone") and adjusted the context to agree with him.

319 **hwyrf(e)** For the form see l. 129 *Gehīere* n.

321 f. **Gang þonne . . . gelēofon** Gr. "and then thou shalt go away into the country of the barbarians, thou and thy disciples. And after going into this city [i.e. Marmadonia], thou shalt proclaim my Gospel, and bring up the men who are in the abyss [cf. l. 293 n.]. And thou shalt do what I command thee."

321 **tō þǣre ceastre** Cas agrees with this senseless reading (*in istum civitatem*). In Gr. the phrase "the country of the barbarians" appears instead and serves to link this story to its sequel, the Acts of Peter and Andrew.

325 **þū þe . . . sāula** Gr. "who wishest to save every soul."

327 **Hīo . . . gefēan** Gr. "And when he had come into the city, they, seeing him, rejoiced with exceeding great joy."

gas, lǣrende and strangende hira heortan on gelēafan ūres Drihtnes Hǣlendes Crīstes. Mid þī þe þā wǣron gefyllede seofon dagas, swā swā him Drihten bebēad, hē fērde of (Mar)madonia ceastre, efstende tō his discipulum. And eall þæt folc hine lǣdde mid gefēan and hīe cwǣdon: "Ān is Drihten God, sē is Hǣlend(e) Crīst and se Hālga Gāst, þām is wuldor and geweald on þǣre Hālgan Þrȳnnysse þurh ealra worulda woruld sōðlīce ā būtan ende." (A)men.

ÆLFRIC

The works of Ælfric "the Grammarian" (c955–c1012), the most important literary figure of the late OE period, represent the high point of the religious and educational renaissance of the latter tenth century which is often referred to as the Benedictine Reform. Spearheaded by St. Dunstan (d. 988), this reform revitalized Anglo-Saxon monasticism and affected all areas of artistic activity. For the first time in Anglo-Saxon England we find a prose distinguished for sensitivity, sophistication, and plurality of imaginative effect.

Ælfric was trained at Winchester under St. Æðelwold (d. 984), one of the leaders of this renaissance. Ordained a priest at the usual age of thirty, he was for a time monk and mass-priest at Cerne Abbas in Dorset, where a Benedictine monastery was founded in 987. After a further period in Winchester, he became in 1005 the first abbot of Eynsham in Oxfordshire, another new Benedictine foundation. There he remained for the rest of his life.

Ælfric is not remarkable as an original thinker. What best characterizes him is his great learning, his firm sense of tradition, his productivity in the service of a clearly conceived and articulated educational program, his versatility in many forms, and his attention to style: in the latter area his accomplishment was truly remarkable. He wrote extensively in both Latin and English. His vernacular production as a whole represents a systematic attempt to make available in his native tongue what he considered to be the basic truths of orthodox Christian doctrine.

Most of his surviving sermons—the most characteristic and important body of his work—are found included in three great series, the two sets of *Catholic Homilies* and the *Lives of the Saints*. In addition he revised and adapted Bede's *De Temporibus Anni* into the vernacular; wrote a grammar of Latin, the first such grammar ever to be written in a European vernacular; wrote the famous *Colloquy*, a Latin dialogue between teacher and pupils, designed for pedagogical purposes (and accompanied in one MS by an interlinear OE gloss). He wrote paraphrases of portions of the Old Testament, drafted pastoral letters on behalf of Anglo-Saxon bishops, etc. For an Old English writer his corpus is enormous—and probably most of it has survived to our day.

Ælfric is deservedly famous as a stylist, a master of prose raised to the level of conscious art and developed in the direction of a clarity, economy and flexibility which make it the suitable vehicle for a number of different types of subject. He availed himself of all the resources of the *dulce* in order that he might most effectively transmit and inculcate the *utile*.

An excellent introduction to Ælfric's mind and work is to be found in Peter Clemoes' essay "Ælfric," in *Continuations and Beginnings: Studies in Old English Literature*, ed. Eric Gerald Stanley (London 1966), pp. 176–209.

11 / homily on the assumption of saint john the apostle
(For December 27th)

The present selection is the fourth homily in the First Series of *Sermones Catholici*, generally referred to as the *Catholic Homilies*. This First Series, Ælfric's earliest work, was written c989. It consists of homilies for forty Sundays and festivals, including certain saints' days, arranged in the order of the church year. The Second Series (c992) follows the same pattern and consists of forty-five homilies. Ælfric originally wrote these two sets of homilies in order to furnish himself with material for preaching at Cerne Abbas, and later revised them for more general distribution. He reissued them several times, each time introducing further changes into the text, a development which can be traced in the extant MSS.

The bulk of the present homily is an adaptation of parts of the apocryphal Acts of John.[1] The original Greek version of this work was written about the middle of the second century, allegedly by a certain Leucius Charinus, who compiled it by "taking the Canonical Acts as his model, but infusing into his work more romantic elements."[2] Ælfric was dependent on the Latin recension attributed to Mellitus of Laodicea.[3] In general it may be said that Ælfric handles his source very freely, sometimes following it faithfully over long sections, sometimes conflating passages or adding additional information, often omitting speeches and irrelevant detail. The student who wishes to compare Ælfric's treatment with the Latin will find a convenient version of the "interpolated

---

[1]On the apocryphal Acts in general, see p. 203.

[2]Montague Rhodes James, *The Apocryphal New Testament* (Oxford 1924; reprinted 1955), p. xx. See also p. 228 sq.

[3]On Ælfric's source see Richard Adelbert Lipsius, *Die apokryphen Apostelgeschichten und Apostellegenden*, 2 vols. (Braunschweig 1883–4), I, 138 ff., 175 f.; also Max Förster, *Über die Quellen von Ælfric's Homiliae Catholicae: I. Legenden* (Berlin [1892]), pp. 17 f.

Mellitus-text"—in all essentials the same as that used by Ælfric—in Bonantius Mombritius, *Sanctuarium, seu Vitae Sanctorum*, 2 vols. (Paris 1910), II, 55–61; we have occasionally quoted this version (with modernized spelling and punctuation) in our notes, when its readings serve to clarify Ælfric's syntax or meaning. Another modern printed version, which is sometimes closer verbally to Ælfric than the Mombritius version, is that of Johannes Albertus Fabricius, *Codex Apocryphus Novi Testamenti*. . . , 2nd ed. (Hamburg 1719), II, 531–90; as a sample of this we have included (unmodernized) the Latin corresponding to the famous passage 11. 127–49 of our homily: Ælfric's thoroughgoing rearrangement of his source material here is particularly interesting.

Though the present homily is one of Ælfric's earliest works, it shows his already highly developed and highly flexible style, and has often been cited "as an excellent example of Ælfric's manner at its best for . . . simple and dignified rhetoric" (Wrenn p. 231).

The homily survives today (in complete or nearly complete versions) in nine MSS.[4] Three of the most important of these are

A British Museum, Royal 7 C. xii (Ker 257);
K Cambridge, University Library Gg. 3. 28 (Ker 15);
Q Cambridge, Corpus Christi College 188 (Ker 65).

K, which contains both series of *Catholic Homilies*, was doubtless produced under Ælfric's supervision. It represents an advanced stage of recension, and contains a double set of Latin and Old English prefaces which are designed to introduce the book to the larger audience for which Ælfric now intended it.[5] Q represents an even later recension of the text on Ælfric's part.

The text in the present edition is based upon A, for the following two reasons:

(1) Recent investigation has established that A represents an earlier stage—in fact the earliest extant stage—in the development of the text of the First Series of *Catholic Homilies*. Moreover it seems highly likely that it was produced at Ælfric's own monastery of Cerne Abbas, and that it can be dated with considerable assurance to the first half of the year 990. Many of the corrections which it contains were undoubtedly made at Ælfric's direction, and some of them are in his own hand.[6]

(2) A collotype facsimile of MS A, edited by Norman Eliason and Peter Clemoes, has recently been published (*EEMSF*, XIII), and we hope that

---

[4]See Ker pp. 511 ff.

[5]K was adopted by Thorpe as the basis for his edition, *The Homilies of the Anglo-Saxon Church*, 2 vols. (London 1844–46). A new edition of the First Series of *Catholic Homilies*, based upon A, is forthcoming from EETS.

[6]Ælfric presumably wrote the first drafts of his homilies on wax tablets, and this text was subsequently transferred to parchment. A itself does not give evidence of being a transcription made directly from tablets; Clemoes' conclusions (*EEMSF*, XIII, 30) are that its scribes "had before them a parchment copy of the homilies—perhaps the first that had been made—which was not bound."

students will consult the facsimile when they are studying this selection. We give a highly diplomatic text—i.e. one which reproduces the peculiarities of the MS with great exactitude[7]—and hope that it will, used in conjunction with the facsimile, serve to ease the student's passage from highly edited texts (like most of those in this book) to direct confrontation with OE MSS themselves. Even students who do not consult the facsimile will get a good idea of the appearance and peculiarities of OE MSS by a study of this text.

Where the readings of A differ from those of K, the latter are reported in the notes, unless they are simply a matter of spelling.[8]

The following information is intended chiefly for students who wish to compare the text printed here with the facsimile.

In the MS the text of the homily begins at 19v11, i.e. the 19th folio (or leaf), verso (the backside of the leaf), line 11, and ends at 26r13, i.e. folio 26, recto (the foreside of the leaf), line 13. Our text is set up so as to correspond line for line to the MS, and the figures in square brackets in the right margin will guide the student quickly to the corresponding MS line. Note that we use the modern foliation (printed at the bottom of each facsimile page in *EEMSF*), not the sixteenth-century foliation (written in ink in the upper right-hand corner of each leaf [recto] and lagging four leaves behind the modern numbering throughout the text of this homily).[9] The numbers in our left-hand margin run consecutively throughout the text, and it is these numbers which are referred to in the notes and glossary.

The bulk of A was written by two scribes, though various other hands (including that of Ælfric himself)[10] have made additions and corrections. The first (and largest) part of the present homily was written by Scribe 1; Scribe 2 takes over at 25vl (our line 292), though his hand had appeared earlier in a number of corrections—notably the full-line addition after 24v7 (our line 248). According to Eliason (p. 19), Scribe 2 seems to have borne "the greater share of responsibility" in the production of the MS. For remarks on the work of these two scribes and the characteristic (and distinctive) features of their handwriting, see Eliason p. 19 f.

Four punctuation marks are used by the scribes. In our text these have been replaced by their modern "equivalents." This replacement is done mechanically, so that although the symbols themselves are different, their density and distribution remain the same as in the MS, and our text therefore represents the

---

[7]For a statement of the ideal in these matters, see N. Denholm-Young, *Handwriting in England and Wales* (Cardiff 1954), p. 7. Our text is not completely diplomatic: for ease in reading (and glossing) we have normalized word-division according to dictionary practice, and we have not reported all erasures.

[8]The corrected (not the original) readings of A are the basis here. Hence in all cases where A has been corrected, it may be assumed that the corrections agree with K. The readings of K are taken from Sweet[14].

[9]See Eliason, *EEMSF*, XIII, 17, 36.

[10]For Ælfric's contributions, see Eliason p. 19 n.8. None of them occurs in the present homily.

scribes' punctuation. The system of substitutions is as follows:

For the MS *punctus* ("point"), a simple dot placed above the line at about half the height of a letter [·], we substitute a comma. For the *punctus elevatus* [⁏] we use a semicolon. For the *punctus versus* [;] we use a period. And for the *punctus interrogativus* [∽] we use a question mark. According to Clemoes (p. 30) there is "every reason to suppose that [the punctuation of A] substantially represents Ælfric's own practice [and] brings us as close as we can get to the system of punctuation which Ælfric was using when he wrote the First Series of *Catholic Homilies*." The student will note that the punctuation is often extremely heavy by modern standards. It is now thought that its function was as much rhetorical as grammatical (on this whole question see Clemoes p. 24 f.).

In a few instances where the scribes' punctuation is likely to seriously confuse or mislead the modern student—generally by obscuring the relationship of clauses—an appropriate editorial punctuation is suggested between parentheses in the right margin (see further l. 8 n.).

The sign [⁊] for *and* is retained; so is the abbreviation [ꝥ] for *þæt*. We have reproduced the acute accent marks which occur in the MS. Eliason writes (p. 26) that they are "sporadically used to mark long vowels and diphthongs"—e.g. *wín* (1.9) or *éác* (1.65)—and that when "not used for this purpose they are evidently intended as a graphic device for distinguishing between homographs, particularly short words that might easily be misread as prefixes or suffixes," e.g. *ón* (1.6) or *t́o* (1.37). In the latter example the mark has been placed above the consonant preceding the vowel, and this occurs not infrequently.

Word-division (e.g. the treatment of compounds and prefixes) is editorial and corresponds to the practice of this edition as a whole. Our capitalization attempts to reproduce that of the MS, but only in a very general fashion, since the MS uses capitals of widely varying shapes and sizes. Eliason writes that in this MS capitals "are regularly used only at the beginning of sentences, and not consistently there. . . . Usually [proper] names begin with a capital only at the opening of a sentence. . . . The use of different shapes is often a matter of whim" (p. 22).

All of the corrections and insertions in the MS have been incorporated into the text, but printed in italics; this is true also of letters which have been written over erasures. Erasures as such are not indicated in our text,[11] though attention is called to most of them in the notes.

---

[11]"It is not easy to distinguish in a facsimile between a mark left by an erasure and an accidental stain or smudge of which there are a good many in [A]" (Clemoes p. 33).

VIª kł IANVARII
ASSVMPTIO SCĪ IOHANNIS APŁ.

Iohannes se godspellere cristes dyrling wearð on ðysum dæge
to heofenan rices myrhðe þurh godes neosunge genumen.
he wæs cristes modrian sunu, 7 he hine lufode synderlice,
na swa miclum for ðære mæglican sibbe swa for ðære
clænnysse his ansundan mægðhades. he wæs on mægðhade [19v15]
gode gecoren, 7 he ón ecnysse on ungewemmedū mæigðhade
þurhwunade. hit is geræd on gewyrdelicum racum
ꝥ he wolde wifian, 7 crist wearð to his gyftum gelaðod, (,[2]/;)
þa gelamp hitꝥ ðam gyftum wín ateorode. *Se* Hælend þa het
þa þenincm*e*nn afyllan six stænene fatu mid hlu*t*trū [19v20]
wætere; 7 he mid his bletsungeꝥ wæter to æþelum wíne

Title. This is the heading or "rubric" of the homily (so called because it is written in red ink [cf. Lat. *rubrica* "red ochre, red chalk"]). It consists of the date for which the homily was intended and its title. This heading is to be expanded to: *VIa kalendas ianuarii assumptio sancti iohannis apostoli*, i.e. "The sixth (day before the) calends (i.e. first day) of January: the Assumption of St. John the Apostle." St. John's Day is December 27th. This heading—like all the others in the MS—is the work of Scribe 2 and is written in rustic capitals. The rest of the homily is written in late Anglo-Saxon minuscule.

1 **cristes dyrling** Note that no punctuation is used to set off this appositional phrase. The disciple is called *cristes dyrling* on the basis of his references to himself in John 13:23, 19:26 and 21:20.

3 **cristes modrian sunu** For the notion—recurrent in Ælfric—that "the mother of James and John, the sons of Zebedee, was the Virgin Mary's sister," see Pope[3], I, 217–20.

hē[2] Christ.

5–20 **he wæs . . . wunade** On the ultimate source for much of this passage—the so-called Monarchian Preface to the Gospel of John—see Lipsius, I, 445 f. The fact that this Preface was often referred to as an *ecclesiastica historia* perhaps explains Ælfric's use of the phrase *on gewyrdelicum racum* in 1.7.

6 **gode** Lat. *a deo.*

ungewemmedū Final postvocalic *m* is often abbreviated in this fashion, and many instances of it will be found in this selection.

mæigð- For this spelling see 6/3 n.

8 **gelaðod,** The marginal notation—(,[2]/;)—means that according to modern notions of punctuation a semicolon would be more appropriate here than the scribe's second comma (actually, of course, his *punctus*).

9–13 Cf. John 2:1–11.

9 **ðam . . . ateorode** MS K reads *æt ðam gyftum win wearð ateorod*; either construction is idiomatic.

Se Note that this word was inserted later above the line, the place of its insertion being indicated by a *caret* (Lat. "it is lacking").

10 **þa þenincmenn** Scribe 1 originally wrote *þam þenincmannum*, dat. pl.; this was subsequently corrected to the acc. pl., which is *de rigeur* in acc. + inf. constructions of this sort. The correction was made by erasing the final *m* of *þam* and the *a* and *um* of *þenincmannum*; then an *e* was added above the erasure of *a*.

awende. þis is ꝥ forme tacn, þe he on his menniscnysse
openlice geworhte. þa wearð iohannes swa onbryrd þurh
ꝥ tacn, ꝥ he þærrihte his bryd on mægðhade forlet;
7 symle syððan drihtne folgode; 7 wearð þa hī inwerdlice [19v25]
gelufod, for ðan þe he hine ætbræd þam flæsclicum lustū.
Witodlice þisum leofan leorningcnihte befæste se hælend
his moder; þa ða he on rodehengene mancyn alysde; (; *bis*/,)
ꝥ his clæne lif þæs clænan mædenes marian, gymde; And
heo þa on hyre sweoster suna þenungum wunade. Eft ón [20r5]
fyrste æfter cristes upstige to heofenum, rixode sum
wælreow casere on romana ríce æfter nerone; se wæs
domicianus gehaten; cristenra manna ehtere; se hét
afyllan ane cyfe, mid weallendum ele, 7 þone mæran
godspellere þæron besceofon; ac he þurh godes gescyld [20r10]
nysse ungewemmed of þā hatum bæðe eode. eft þa ða
se wælreowa ne mihte þæs eadigan apostoles bodunge
alecgan, þa ásende he hine on wræcsið to anū *igeoðe*
þe is paðmas geciged, ꝥ he ðær þurh hungres scearp
nysse *ac wæle*. Ac se ælmihtiga hælend ne forlet to gyme
leaste his gelufedan apostol; ac geswutelode hī on ðam
wræcsiðe þa toweardan onwrigenysse; be ðære he
awrat þa bóc þe is gehaten apocalipsis; 7 se wælreowa

---

14 **bryd** MS K has *bryde*. Both forms were possible (see Campbell §604).
on mægðhade Construe with *he*.

15 **hī** "By him."

16 **he hine ætbræd** "He (had) snatched himself."

17–20 Cf. John 19:25–7.

25 **besceofon** MS K reads *het bescufan* here, so we may take this form in A to be an infinitive. There is considerable late confusion of final *-an*/*-on*/*-en* in verbal forms in this text. Note especially that subjunctive plurals regularly end in *-an*, less frequently in *-on*, never in historical *-en*.

25 f. **gescyld | nysse** A single word; cf. *scearp | nysse* in 29 f., *gyme | leaste* in 30 f., *ǵe | cyrde* in 37 f. etc. Scribe 2 sometimes uses dashes to indicate that a word has been split between lines: cf. 294 f., 300 f.

26 **hatum** Cf. 12/81b n.

28 sq. Cf. Revelation 1:9–11.

28 **wræcsið** Notice that Scribe 1 originally wrote the dat. sg. form *wræcsiðe*, incorrect in this situation of motion, and that the *-e* was later erased.
igeoðe This word appears to have been written over an erasure.

30 **acwæle** Scribe 1 wrote *acwele*, which he no doubt intended as preterite subjunctive: he often uses ē and ǣ indiscriminately (cf. *ber* 42, *þere* 78, *-bætende* 187, *fræced-* 327). In this case his spelling is ambiguous, however, since *acwele* is the normal form of the present subjunctive. Hence the word was later underlined (indicating that it was to be deleted) and *acwæle* written above it in another hand—which also altered the following *punctus elevatus* to a *punctus versus*. Eliason attributes this change to Scribe Y (p. 19, n. 6) who has made a number of other alterations in the MS (including the addition *ðæs* in l. 122).

32 **þa toweardan onwrigenysse** Lit. "the future revelation," i.e. a revelation of what was to come.

domicianus on ðam ylcan geare wearð acweald æt his
witena handum; 7 hi ealle ánmodlice ræddon ꝥ ealle [20r20]
his gesetnyssa aydlode wæron. þa wearð nerfa swiðe
arfæst ḿan ſo casere gecoren; be his geðafunge ǵe
cyrde se apostol ongéán mid miclū wurðmynte;
se ðe mid hospe to wræcsiðe asend wæs. hī urnon
ongéán weras 7 wif fægniende 7 cweðende; gebletsod is [20r25]
se ðe com on godes naman. Mid þam þe se apostol iohannes
stop Into ðære byrig efesum, þa ber man hī togeanes
anre wydewan lic to byrgenne; hyre nama wæs drusiana.
heo wæs swiðe gelyfed 7 ælmesgeorn, 7 þa ðearfan þe heo
mid cystigū mode eallung*a* afedde, dreorie mid [20v5]
wópe þam lice folgodon. Ðа het se ápostol þa bære
settan 7 cwæð. Min drih̄ hælend crist arære ðe drusiana;
aris 7 gecyr ham 7 gearca ús gereordunge on ðinum
huse. drusiana þa aras swilce of slæpe awreht; 7 car
ful be ðæs apostoles hæse hám gewende. on ðam oðrū [20v10]
dæge eode se apostol be ðære stræt þa ofseah he hwær (stræt;)
sum uðwita lædde twegen gebroðru, þe hæfdon be
hwyrfed eall heora yldran gestréón on deorwurðum
gymstanum, 7 woldon þa tocwysan on ealles folces
gesihðe, to wæfersyne; swilce *to* forsewennysse woruld (; /,) [20v15]
licera æhta. hit wæs gewunelic on ðam timan ꝥ ða
þe wolden woruldwisdom gecneordlice leornian,
ꝥ hi behwyrfdon heora are on gymstanum, 7 þa to
brǽcan; oððe on sumum gyldenum wecge, 7 þone on sæ
awurpan, þy læs þe seo smeagung *þæra* æhta hi æt þære lare [20v20]
hremde. þa clypode se apostol þone uðwitan graton
him to; 7 cwæð. *d*yslic bið ꝥ hwa woruldlice speda for
hogie for manna herunge; 7 beo on godes dome

---

34 f. **æt his witena handum** Lat. *a senatu romano.*

38 **ongéán . . . wurðmynte** Lat. *cum honore ad Ephesum* (whence he had been taken to Rome on Domitian's orders).

39 **hī** The object of *ongéán* in 1.40.

40 f. **gebletsod . . . naman** Quotations are not indicated by any special punctuation; they are generally preceded in this MS by a *punctus versus.*

42 **ber** For this spelling (cf. *bær* in MS K) see l. 30 n.

45 **eallunga** Scribe 1 wrote *eallunge*, which was later corrected.

47 **drih̄** Abbreviation for *drihten.*

arære Optative subjunctive.

49 f. **carful . . . hæse** Lat. *sollicita de iussione apostoli.*

51 **stræt** Uninflected forms of this word are not uncommon.

53 **yldran** K has *yldrena.* In LWS one occasionally finds *-an* as the gen. pl. inflection of weak adjs. (see Campbell ∫656).

54 **ealles folces** K has *ealles þæs folces.*

55 f. **swilce . . . æhta** "As if in contempt of worldly possessions."

58 **þa** I.e. the *gymstanas.*

62 **dyslic . . . hwa** "(It) is foolish that anyone" etc.

genyþerod. ydel bið se læcedóm þe ne mæg þone untruman
gehælan; swa bið éác ydel seo lár þe ne gehælð þære [20v25]
saule leahtras 7 unþeawas. Soðlice min lareow crist,
sumne cniht ðe gewilnode þæs ecan lifes þisū wordū
lærde; ꝥ he sceolde ealle his welan beceapian, 7 ꝥ wurð
þearfum dælan, gif he wolde fullfremed béón; 7 he syððan
hæfde his goldhord on heofenum, 7 þærtoeacan [21r5]
ꝥ ece lif. Gráton se uðwita him andwyrde. þas gym
stanas, sind tocwysede for idelum gylpe; ac gif þin lar
eow is sóð god, gefeg þas bricas to ansundnysse; ꝥ heora (; /,)
wurð mæge þearfum fremian. Iohannes þa gega
derode þæra gymstana bricas, 7 beseah to heofenum [21r10]
þus cweðende. drih̄ hælend, nis þe nan ð*in*g earfoðe;
þu geedstaðelodest þysne tobrocenan middaneard
on þinū geleaffullum, þurh tacen þere halgan rode;
geedstaðela nu þas deorwurðan stanas, þurh ðinra
engla handum, ꝥ ðas nytenan men þine mihta oncnawan, [21r15]
7 on ðe gelyfan. hwæt ða færlice wurdon þa gimstanas
swá ánsunde; ꝥ furðon nan tacn þære ærran tocwysed (del ;)
nysse næs gesewen. Þa se uðwita gratón samod mid
þā cnihtum feol to iohannes fotū, gelyfende ón ǵod.
Se apostol hine fullode mid eallum his hirede; 7 he [21r20]
ongann godes geleafan openlice bodian. þa twegen
gebroðra atticus 7 eugenius sealdon heora gym
stanas 7 ealle heora æhta, dældon wædlum; 7 filigdan
þam apostole 7 micel menigu geleaffulra him eac (apostole;)
togeðeodde. þa becom se apostol æt sumum sæle [21r25]
to ðære byrig pergamum þær ða foresædan cnihtas, *iu ǽr* (del ,)
eardedon. 7 gesawon heora þeowan mid godewebbe

66–71 **Soðlice . . . lif** See Matthew 19:16–22.
66 ff. MnE word order: *Soðlice min lareow crist lærde sumne cniht . . . þisū wordū.*
70 **hæfde** "Would have."
71 **Gráton se** K has *Graton ða se.*
77 f. **þu . . . rode** Lat. [*tu*] *fractum mundum per lignum crucis tuae in tuis fidelibus restaurasti* (but for the sense, see the fuller statement in Fabricius' version: [*tu*] *fractum mundum per lignum concupiscentiæ, rursus per lignum crucis tuæ in tuis fidelibus restaurasti*).
78 **þere** I.e. *þære* (cf. 1.30 n.).
79 **stanas** K has *gymstanas.*
80 **handum** K has *handa.* MSS K and A frequently disagree over the rection of prepositions. Scribe 1 of A, here and in 1. 161 f., prefers *þurh* + dat. to the *þurh* + acc. usage of K; he also prefers a dat. after *on*, as opposed to K's *on* + acc. usage: see 11. 165, 235, 254. Scribe 2 of A gives *wið* a dat. rection (11. 294, 301) where K gives it an acc.
82 **swá** Lat. *ita.*
91 **iu ǽr** These two words (and perhaps the *punctus* preceding them) were added later (by Scribe 2?).
92 A single letter has been erased before the first *e* of *eardedon*, and two or three letters between the *a* and *w* of *gesawon*.
gesawon Sc. *hi.*

gefrætewade, 7 on woruldlicum wuldre scinende. þa wurdon hi mid deofles flan þurhscotene, 7 dreorige on mode;ꝥ hi wædliende on anum waclicum wæfelse (del ;) ferdon, 7 heora þeowan on woreldlicū wuldre scinende wæron. þa undergeat se apostol þas deoflican facn 7 cwæð. Ic geseoꝥ eower mod is awend 7 eower andwlita; for ðan ðe ge (; /,) eowre speda þearfum dældon 7 mines drihtnes lare filigdon. gað nu for ði t*o* wuda 7 heawað incre byrðene gyrda; [21v10] 7 gebringað to me. hi dydon be his hæse 7 he on godes naman þa grenan gyrda gebletsode, 7 hi wurdon to readū golde awende. Eft cwæð se apostol iohannes. gað to ðære sǽ strande, 7 feccað me papolstanas. hi dydon swa, 7 Iohannes þa on godes mægenðrymme hi gebletsode, 7 hi wurdon ge [21v15] hwyrfde to deorwyrðum gymmū. þa cwæð se apostol. gað to smiððan 7 fandiað þyses goldes, 7 þyssera gymstana. hi ða eodon 7 eft comon, þus cweðende. ealle þas goldsmiðas secgað ꝥ hi næfre ǽr swa clæne gold ne swa read ne gesawon. Eac þas gymwyrhtan secgaðꝥ hi næfre swa [21v20] deorwyrðe gymstanas ne gemetton. þa cwæð se apostol hī to. Nimað þis gold 7 þas gimstanas, 7 farað 7 bicgað eow landáre; for ðan þe ge forlúron þa heofenlican speda. bicgað eow pællene cyrtlas,ꝥ ge to lytlere hwile scinan sẃa sẃa ŕosé,ꝥ ge hrædlice forweornian. [21v25] beoð blowende 7 welige hwilwendlice,ꝥ ge ecelice wædlian. Hwæt la ne mæg se ælmihtiga wealdend þurhteonꝥ he do his þeowan ŕice for worulde; genihtsume on welan, 7 unwið metenlice scinan? Ac he sette gecamp geleaffullum

---

94 **deofles flan** Cf. Ephesians 6:16.

100 **to** Scribe 1 wrote *te*, which suggests that the vowel of this lightly stressed preposition was [ə] in his pronunciation. Later the *e* was underdotted for omission and an *o* written above it in another hand.

100 f. **heawað . . . me** *Incre* is acc. fem. sg. of the possessive adj. which is formed from the genitive dual of the second person pronoun. The dual is probably used here (in contradistinction to the plural in the preceding two lines) in order to give the distributive sense required by *singulus* in the Latin: *deferte mihi virgas rectas in singulis fascibus*. Translate: "each of the two of you cut his load of twigs" etc.

107 **gað to smiððan** Lat. *per septem dies ite per aurifices et gemmarios*.

109 **ꝥ hi næfre** The scribe inadvertently wrote this phrase twice; the first occurrence has been struck through.

114 ff. **bicgað . . . wædlian** Lat. *Emite vobis sericas vestes, ut pro tempore fulgeatis sicut rosa, quæ cum odorem pariter et ruborem ostendit, repente marcescit. . . . Estote floridi, ut marcescatis; estote divites temporaliter, ut in perpetuum mendicetis*.

114 **lytlere** I.e. *lytelre*, dat. sg. fem. See another example of the same metathesis (*myclere* for *mycelre*) in 10/223, and cf. Campbell ∫459.(4).

119 **scinan** Note that this adjective is declined weak, even though it occurs in sequence with another adjective declined strong. No doubt Ælfric felt that if a quality is described as "incomparable," it is by definition unique, and probably,

saulum;ꝥ hi gelyfan to geagenne þa ecan welan, þa ðe [22r5]
for his naman þa hwilwendan speda forho*gia*ð ge gehældon (forho*gia*ð.)
untruman on *ðæs* hælendes naman; ge afligdon deoflu; ge for
geafon blindum gesihðe; 7 gehwilce uncoðe gehældon;
efne nu is þeos gyfu eow ætbroden, 7 ge sint earmingas
gewordene, ge ðe wæron mære 7 strange. swa micel ege stod [22r10]
deoflū from eow, ꝥ hi be eowere hæse þa ofsettan deoful
seoc*an* forlet*o*n; Nu ge ondrædað eow deoflu. þa h́eófan
lican æhta; synd us eallū ǵeḿæne. Nacode we wæron (del ;)
acennede 7 nacode we gewitað. þære sunnan beorht
nys 7 þæs monan leoht. 7 ealr*a* tungla sind gemæne (del .) [22r15]
þam rican, 7 þam héan*an*. Renscuras, 7 cyrcan duru, fulluht
7 synne forgyfenes, huselgang, 7 godes neosung, sind eallū
gemæne, earmū, 7 eadigum. Ac se ungesæliga gitsere

Amator enim pecuniæ, servus est Mamonæ. Mamona autem dæmonis nomen est, qvi lucris carnalibus præest, & dominator eorum qvi diligunt mundum. Ipsi autem amatores mundi non possident divitias, sed ipsi à divitiis possidentur. Absurdum enim est, cum sit unus venter, cui tot cibi reponantur, qvi mille ventribus satisfacerent: & uni corpori tot vestes, qvæ mille hominum corporibus præbere indumenta valeant. Sic frustra, qvod in usum non venit, custoditur: & cui custodiatur, omnino nescitur, dicente Sancto Spiritu per Prophetam: Vanè conturbatur omnis homo, qui thesaurizat, & ignorat cui congregat ea. Nudos nos fuderunt in lucem partus mulierum, egentes cibi & poculi: nudos nos recipiet terra, quos edidit. In communi possidemus cœli divitias, splendor solis diviti & pauperi æqualis est, similiter lunæ lumen &

---

therefore, "definite." (Lat. *Numquid valet manus domini ut faciat servos suos divitiis affluentes et incomparabiliter splendentes*?)

119 f. **Ac . . . ðe** "But he decreed (that) for faithful souls (life here on earth should be) a conflict, in order that those (individuals) might believe (themselves destined) to acquire eternal riches, who" etc. (Lat. *Sed certamen statuit animorum, ut credant se æternas habituros divitias, qui pro eius amore omnes temporales opes habere noluerint.*)

121 **forhogiað** A letter has been erased between o^2 and *g*, and the *i* has been written (by Scribe 2?) over Scribe 1's original *e*.

ge A new sentence begins here.

125 f. **swa . . . eow** "Devils were so afraid of you" (lit. "So much fear came to devils from you").

126 f. **deofulseocan forleton** Heavily corrected. Scribe 1's original entry seems to have been something like *deofulseoce forlætan*, with the adj. inflected strong, *ǣ* used characteristically for *ē* (see 1. 30 n.), and a 3 pl. pret indic. verb in *-an* (cf. *tobrǽcan* in 58 f., *filigdan* in 88).

127–49 **þa h́eófanlican æhta . . . þrowian** For purposes of comparison we have printed the Latin text of this passage in the middle of the page (Fabricius pp. 564–7).

128 f. Cf. Job 1:21.

129 f. **beorhtnys** Scribe 1 originally wrote *-nysse*, assuming that this word was in construction with *þære* ("of the sun's brightness"); the *-se* was later erased.

130 **ealra** Scribe Z's correction of Scribe 1's original *ealre*.

132 **godes neosung** Lat. *visitatio domini*. Fabricius (p. 566 n.) says this alludes to Jesus, *qui venit in terram, pro omnium salute mortem oppetiturus*.

133–49 **Ac . . . þrowian** With this whole passage compare Ecclesiastes 5:9–16.

wile mare habban þon̄ hī genihtsumað, þon̄ he furðon
orsorh ne brihð, his genihtsumnyssę. Se gitsere hæfð ænne (del ,) [22r20]
lichaman, 7 menigfealde scŕud. he hæfð ane wambe;
7 þusend manna bileofan. witodlice ꝥ he for gytsunge
uncyste, nanū oðrū syllan ne mæg, ꝥ he hordað 7 nat hwā;
swa swa se witega cwæð. On ydel byð ælc man gedrefed se ðe
hordað, 7 nat hwā he hit gegaderað. witodlice, ne bið he [22r25]
þæra æhta hlaford þon̄ he hi dælan ne mæg; ac he bið þæra
æhta þeow*a*, Þon̄ he hī ealung*a* þeowað. þærtoeacan him
wexað untrumnyssa on his lichaman; ꝥ he ne mæg ætes (; /,)
oððe wætes brucan. he carað dæges 7 nihtes ꝥ his feoh
gehealden sy; he gymð grædelice his teolunge, his gafo [22v5]
les, his gebytlu, he berypð þa wanspedigan, he fulgæð
his lustum, 7 his plegan. þon̄ færlice gewit he of þyssere

---

siderum. Aëris quoque temperies, & pluviarum guttæ: & Ecclesiæ janua, & fons sanctificationis, & remissio peccatorum, & participatio altaris, & esca corporis & potus sanguinis Christi, & chrismatis unctio, & gratia largitoris, & visitatio Domini, & indulgentia peccati: hæc omnia absque personæ acceptione æqualis est dispensatio conditoris. Neque aliter dives, aliter pauper his donis utitur. Sed miser & infelix homo, qvi vult plus aliqvid habere, qvam sufficit. Nascuntur enim hinc calores febrium, rigores frigorum, dolores varii in cunctis corporum membris. Et neqve esca cibari potest, neq: poculo satiari, ut cognoscat aviditas non sibi pecunias profuturas: qvæ repositæ, custodibus suis sollicitudinem diurnam nocturnamqve incutiunt, & nec unius horæ spatio quietos aut securos esse patiuntur. Nam dum custodiuntur, fures insidiantur, dum possessio colitur, dum aratris intendunt, dum solvunt fiscalia, dum ædificant promptuaria, dum lucris student, dum potentiorum impetus mitigare nituntur, dum minus potentes nudare contendunt, dum iras suas quibus possunt inferunt, & inlatas in se tolerare vix possunt, dum blandimenta carnis assentiunt [,] dum ludere tabulis & spectaculis non perhorrescunt, dum polluere & pollui non metuunt, subitò exeunt de isto sæculo, nudi, sola secum peccata portantes, pro quibus sunt pœnas passuri perpetuas.

---

134 **þon̄**[1,2] Abbreviation for *þonne*.

134 f. **þon̄**[2] **. . . genihtsumnysse** "Although he does not even enjoy his abundance without anxiety."

genihtsumnysse Note the caudal ("tailed") ę (and cf. Eliason p. 21 n. 2).

137 **ꝥ** I.e. *þæt þæt*, the first of these being correlative with ꝥ in l. 138. Translate the sentence: "Truly, that which because of the niggardliness of greed he is incapable of giving to others, he is hoarding up, and he knows not for whom."

139 **swa**[1] **. . . cwæð** This is to be connected with what follows rather than with what precedes. For the quotation cf. Psalm 39:6.

141 f. **þon̄**[1,2] Causal: "since."

142 **þærtoeacan** K has *and þærtoeacan*.

146 **gebytlu** This is probably a late inverted spelling of the gen. pl.; if it is acc. pl. (which is suggested by the fact that MS K has the same reading), then we have here a genuine example of mixed reaction with a verb (thus BTS s.v. *gīman* I.(4a)).

worulde nacod 7 forscyldgod; synna ana mid him
ferigende, for ðam ð*e* he sceal ece wite þrowian. Efne ða ða
se apostol þas lare sprecende wæs, ða bær sum wudewe [22v10]
hire suna lic to bebyrgenne; Se hæfde gewifod
þrittigū nihtū ær. Seo dreorige moder þa samod
mid þam licmannum rarigende hi astrehte æt þæs
halgan apostoles *fotum*, biddende ꝥ he hire sunu
on godes naman arærde, swa swa he dyde þa wyde [22v15]
wan drusianam. Iohannes þa ofhreow þære
meder 7 þæra licmanna dreorignysse, 7 astrehte
his lichoman to eorðan on langsumum gebede,
7 þa æt nehstan aras, 7 eft upahafenum handum langlice
bæd. þa ða he þus þriwa gedon hæfde, þa het he unwindan [22v20]
þæs cnihtes líc, 7 cwæð. eala ðu cniht, þe ðurh þines
flæsces luste hrædlice þine sawle forlure. eala ðu
cniht, þu ne cuþest þinne scyppend; þu ne cuðest manna
hælend, þu ne cuþest þone soðan freond, 7 for ði þu be
urne on ðam wyrstan fynd. Nu ic ageat mine tearas, [22v25]
7 for þinre nytennysse geor*n*lice bæd, ꝥ ðu of deaðe arise,
7 þysum twam gebroðrum, attico, 7 eugenio, cyþe hu micel
wuldor hi forluron; 7 hwilc wite hi geearnodon. Mid þā
þa aras se cniht stacteus; 7 feol to iohannes fotum, 7 began
to þreagenne þa gebroðra þe miswende wæron, þus cweðende.
Ic geseah þa englas þe éower gymdon dreorige wepan, 7 þa awyr
gedan sceoccan blissigende, on eowerum forwyrde. eow wæs
heofonan rice gearu, 7 scinende gebytlu, mid wistum afyllede, (del ,[2])
7 mid ecum leohte; þa ge forluron þurh unwærscipe; 7 ge be
geaton eow þeosterfulle wununga mid dracan afyllede, [23r10]
7 mid brastliendum ligum, mid unasecgendlicū witum

---

148 **synna ana** D.o. of *ferigende*.

149 **for ðam ðe** The ð*e* was added later above the line; note that the original reading answers better to the Latin (*pro quibus pœnas passuri sunt perpetuas*).

152 **þrittigū nihtū** Dat. of degree with the comp. adv. *ær*. It is corrected from Scribe 1's *þrittig nihta*, an acc. (extent of time) construction which would be improper here.

154 **halgan** Written *hal gan* in the MS to avoid a hole in the parchment.
fotum, Written by Scribe 2 above his erasure of Scribe 1's original *fet*; (dat. sg.).

161 **þe** MW suggest emending to *þu*, but this is not necessary.

162 **luste** K has *lust*; see 1.80 n.

164 f. **beurne on ðam wyrstan fynd** Lat. *hostem pessimum incurristi* (with which cf. the reading of Fabricius, *in insidias hostis pessimi incurristi*).

165 **on ðam wyrstan fynd** K has *on ðone wyrstan feond*; cf. 1. 80 n. Two later examples (11. 235 and 254) of this scribe's preference for *on* + dat. have been corrected in the MS; this example was not, and should have been, since the phrase here was clearly intended to stand in syntactical-rhetorical balance with *þone soðan freond* in the line before.

174 **þa** D.o. of *forluron*.

175 **dracan** K has *dracum*.

afyllede, 7 mid anþræcum stencum; on ðam ne ablinð granung, 7 þoterung dæges oððe nihtes. Biddað for ðy mid inweardre heortan þysne godes apostol eowerne lareow, ꝥ he eow fram ðā ecū forwyrde arære; swa swa (; /,) [23r15] he me fram deaðe arærde, 7 he eowre saula þe nu sind adylegode of þære liflican béc, gelæde eft to godes gyfe 7 miltsunge. Se cniht ða stacteus þe of deaðe aras samod mid þā gebroðrū astrehte hine to iohánnes fót swaðū, 7 ꝥ folc forð mid, ealle ánmodlice bi*d*dende, ꝥ he hī [23r20] to gode geþingode. Se apostol þa bebéád þā twā gebroðrū ꝥ hi þrittig daga behreowsunge dædbætende gode geoffrodon and on ðam fæce geornlice bædon ꝥ ða gyldenan gyrda eft to ðam ærran gecynde awendan; 7 þa gymstanas to heora wacnysse. æfter þrittig*ra* daga [23r25] fæce þa ða hi ne mihton mid heora benū ꝥ gold 7 þa gymstanas (fæce,) to heora gecynde awendan; þa comon hi mid wope to ðam (; /,) apostole þus cweðende. Symle þu tæhtest mildheortnysse, 7 ꝥ man oðrū miltsode. 7 gif man oðrum miltsað; hu micle swiðor wile god miltsian 7 arian mannū his handgeweorce? [23v5] ꝥ ꝥ we mid gitsiendum eagū agylton; ꝥ we nu mid wependū eagū behreowsiað. þa andwyrde se ápóstol. berað þa gyrda to wuda, 7 þa stanas to sǽstrande; hi sind gecyrrede to heora gecynde. þa ða hi ðis gedon hæfdon, þa underfengon hi eft godes gyfe; swa ꝥ hi adræfdon deoflu, 7 blínde 7 untru [23v10] me gehældon, 7 fela tacna on drihtnes naman gefre medon swa swa hí ær dydon. Se apostol ðá gebigde to gode ealne þone eard asiā se is geteald to healfan dæle middan (asiā,) eardes; 7 awrat þa feorðan cristes boc; Seo hrepað swiðost ymbe cristes godcundnysse. þa oðre þry god [23v15] spelleras, matheus, marcus, lucas, awriten æror be cristes menniscnysse; þa asprungon gedwolmen on godes gelaðunge, 7 cwædon, ꝥ crist nære ær he acenned wæs of marian. þa bædon ealle þa leodbiscopas þone halgan apostol, ꝥ he ða feorðan bóc gesette, 7 þæra gedwolmanna dyrstig [23v20]

---

180 **ecū** Cf. 12/81b n.

181 **7 he** I.e. *and þæt he* etc.

185 **forð mid** "Along with (them)," cf. BTS *forþ* (2a).

187 f. **ꝥ . . . geoffrodon** Word order: *ꝥ hi, dædbætende, geoffrodon gode behreowsunge þrittig daga.* The Lat. has: *ut per triginta dies Deo pœnitentiam offerrent* (Fabricius p. 571).

188 **ðam** Omitted in K.

194 f. **7 gif . . . mannū** *Et, si homo homini indulgere vult, quanto magis deus ipse . . . homini indulgit et parcit.*

203 **asiā** I.e. *Asiam*, a Lat. acc. sg.

healfan K has *healfum*. Cf. 12/81b n.

204–15 **Seo hrepað . . . ongan** For this long digression on the Gospel of John, Ælfric turns away from the apocryphal Acts. His ultimate sources for this passage will be found in Pope[3], I, 197 (notes to 11.17–26) and 221 (the same).

nysse adwæscte. Iohannes þa bead þreora daga fæsten
gemænelice, 7 he æfter þam fæstene wearð swa miclum
mid godes gaste afylled ꝥ he ealle godes englas 7 ealle
gesceafta mid healicū mode oferstah and mid þysum
wordū þa godspellican gesetnysse ongan. Im principio [23v25]
erat uerbum, et uerbum erat apud d̄m, et d̄s erat uerbū.
et reliqua. ꝥ is on englisc; on frymðe wæs word, 7 ꝥ word wæs
mid gode, 7 ꝥ word wæs god. þis wæs on frymðe mid gode.
ealle þing sind þurh hine geworhte, 7 nis nan þing buton hī
gesceapen. 7 swa forð on ealre þære godspellican gesetnysse, [24r5]
he cydde fela be cristes godcundnysse; hu he ecelice buton
angynne of his fæder acenned is; 7 mid him rixað on annysse
þæs halgan gastes, á butan ende. Feawa he awrát be his (,²/,)
menniscnysse; for ðan ðe ða þry oðre godspelleras
genihtsumlice be ðam heora bec setton. hit gelamp [24r10]
æt sumum sæle ꝥ ða deofulgyldan þe ða gyt ungeleaffùlle
wæron, gecwædon ꝥ hí woldon þone apostol to heora
hæþenscipe geneadian. þa cwæð se apostol to ðam hæðen
gyldum. Gað ealle endemes to godes cyrcan, 7 clypiað
to eowerum godum ꝥ seo cyrce afealle þurh heora mihte; [24r15]
þōn buge ic to eowerum hæþenscipe. gif ðōn eower godes
miht þa halgan cyrcan towurpan ne mæg; Ic towurpe (; /,)
eowerne tempel, þurh ðæs ælmihtigan godes mihte; 7 ic
tocwyse eower deofulgyld; 7 bið þōn rihtlic geþuht ꝥ ge ge
swicon eoweres gedwyldes, 7 gelyfan on ð*one* soðan god, [24r20]
se ðe ana ís ælmihtig. þa hæþengyldan þysum cwyde geþwær
læhton; 7 iohannes mid geswæsum wordum ꝥ folc tihte
ꝥ hi ufor eodon fram ðam deofles temple, 7 mid beorhtre
stemne ætforan him eallū clypode. On godes naman
ahreose þis tempel; mid eallū þā deofulgyldū þe hī on eardiað; (;¹,²/,) [24r25]
ꝥ ðeos meniu tocnáwe ꝥ ðis hæðengyld deofles biggencg is.
Hwæt ða færlice ahréás ꝥ tempel grundlung*a*, mid eallū
his anlicnyssum to duste awende. On ðam ylcan dæge wur

---

215 **Im** An error for *In*. For the quotation see John 1:1.

216 **d̄m, d̄s**. Abbreviations for *deum*, *deus* respectively.

217 **et reliqua** "And so forth" (lit. "and the rest").

224 **oðre** Scribe 1 wrote this word twice and the second occurrence was later erased.

225 sq. **hit gelamp** etc. Here Ælfric returns to the apocryphal Acts.

227 f. **gecwædon . . . geneadian** Lat. *ex quo factum est ut Iohannem traherent ad templum Dianæ, et urgerent eum ut ei fæditatem sacrificiorum offerret.*

229 **clypiað** K has *clypiað ealle*.

233 **eowerne** The acc. sg. masc. inflection is an error: note the gender of *tempel* in 11. 240 and 242. K has *eower* here.

235 **ðone soðan god** Altered from *ðam soðan gode*. Both rections are attested with *gelyfan on*, though acc. is much more common. Cf. 1.164 f. n.

242 **grundlunga** Altered from *grundlunge*.

243 **awende** If we supply an "and" before *mid* in 1.242, we can take this verb as

don gebigede twelf þusend hæþenra manna to cristes
geleafan, 7 mid fulluhte gehalgode. Ðа scorede þa gyt [24v5]
se yldesta hæðengylda mid micelre þwyrnysse, 7 cwæð
ꝥ he nolde gelyfan buton Iohannes attor drunce; (; /,)
7 þurh godes mihte þone cwelmbæran drenc oferswiðde.
þa cwæð se apostol. þeah þu me attor sylle; þurh godes (; /,)
naman hít mé né déraþ. Ðа cwæð se hæðengylda aristo
demús. þu scealt ærest oðerne geseon drincan 7 þær [24v10]
rihte cwelan; ꝥ huru þín heorte swa forhtige for ðā (; /,)
deadbærum drence. Iohannes hī andwyrde. gif þu
on god gelyfan wylt; ic únforhtmód þæs drences (; /,)
onfó. þa getengde se aristodemus to ðam heahgerefan;
7 genam on his cwearterne twegen þeofas 7 sealde hī þone
unlybban ætforan eallū *ðā* folce on Iohannes gesihðe, [24v15]
7 hi þærrihte æfter þam drence gewiton. Syððan se
hæþengylda eac sealde þone attorbæran drenc þam
apostole; 7 he mid rodetacne his muð 7 ealne his lichaman
gewæpnode, 7 þane unlybban on godes naman halsode,
7 syððan mid gebyldū mode, hine ealne gedranc. Aristo (del ,) [24v20]
demus þa 7 ꝥ folc beheoldon þone apostol þreo tida
dæges. 7 gesawon hine habban glædne andwlitan buton
blacunge 7 forhtunge, 7 hi ealle clypodon. An soð god ís;
se ðe iohannes wurðað. þa cwæð se hæðengylda to ðam
apostole. gyt me twynað; ac gif þu ðas deadan sceaðan *on* þines [24v25]
godes naman arærst, þon̄ bið min heorte geclænsod fram
ælcere twynunge. þa cwæð Iohannes. Aristodeme; Nim
mine tunecan 7 lege bufon þæra deadra manna lic, 7 cweð.
þæs hælendes cristes apostol mé ásende to eow, ꝥ ge on his
naman of deaðe arisan; 7 ælc man oncnawe ꝥ deað 7 lif (del ;) [25r5]
þeowiað minum hælende. he ða be ðæs apostoles hæse
bær his tunecan, 7 alede uppon þā twā deadan, 7 hi ðær
rihte ansunde arisan. þa ða se hæþengylda ꝥ geseah; (; /,)

---

3 sg. Otherwise we must take it as a past participle, though in that case we would expect it to be inflected either nom. sg. neut. with *tempel* or dat. pl. fem. with *anlicnyssum*. Perhaps it is nom. pl. neut., inflected *ad sensum* with both. The Lat. has: *omnia simul cum templo suo idola corruerunt, ut efficerentur sicut pulvis.*

246 **se yldesta hæðengylda** Lat. *Aristodemus vero qui erat pontifex idolorum.*

248 The entire line has been inserted by Scribe 2. Either Scribe 1 inadvertently omitted it, or it represents a later addition to the text by Ælfric. It occurs in the other MSS of this homily.

249 f. **þurh godes naman** Lat. *invocato nomine dei mei*; cf. Mark 16:17 f.

251 **drincan** Scribe 1 seems to have written *drihcan* at first; later the ascender of the *h* was erased.

254 **god** Altered from *gode*; cf. 1.164 f. n.

255 **to ðam heahgerefan** Lat. *ad Proconsulem.*

256 **twegen þeofas** Lat. *duos viros qui pro suis sceleribus erant decollandi.*

269 **Aristodeme** A Lat. vocative sg.

274 **deadan** K has *deadum*. Cf. 1.203 and n.

þa astrehte he hine to Iohannes fotū; 7 syþðan ferde [25r10]
to þā heahgerefan 7 hī þa wundra mid hludre stemne
cydde. hi ða begen þone apostol gesohton; his miltsunge (; /,)
biddende. Đa bead se apostol hī syfan nihta fæsten,
7 hi syððan gefullode, 7 hi æfter ðā fulluhte towurpon
eal hyra deofulgyld 7 mid heora maga fultume [25r15]
7 mid eallū cræfte arærdon gode mære cyrcan on þæs
apostoles wurðmynte. þa ða se apostol wæs nigon 7 hund
nigontig geara þa æteowede him driħ crist mid þā oðrū (geara,)
apostolū þe he of þysū life genumen hæfde; 7 cwæð. Iohannes;
cū to me tima ísꝥ ðu mid þinū gebroðrū wistfullige on (me:) [25r20]
minū gebeorscipe. Iohannes þa aras; 7 eode wið þæs
hælendes; ac he hī to cwæð. Nu on sunnandæg mines æ
ristes dæge þu cymst to me; 7 æfter þā worde driħ gewende
to heofenū. Se apostol miclū blissode on þā behate; 7 on þā
sunnanuhtan ærwacel to ðære cyrcan cō, 7 þā folce [25r25]
fram hancrede oð undern godes riht lærde, 7 him mæs
san gesang; 7 cwæð ðæt se hælend hine on þam dæge to heofe
num gelaðod hæfde. Het ða delfan his byrgene wið ðam weo-
-fode, 7 þæt greot ut awegan, 7 he eode cucu 7 gesund into his
byrgene; 7 astrehtum handum to gode clypode. drihten [25v5]
crist, ic þancige ðe þæt ðu me *ge*laðodest to þinum wistum;
þu wast þæt ic mid ealre heortan þe gewilnode. Oft ic þe
bædꝥ ic moste to þe faran; ac ðu cwæde þæt ic andbidode
þæt ic ðe mare folces gestrynde. ðu heolde mi*n*ne lic-
-haman wið ælcere besmitennysse; 7 þu symle mine [25v10]
sawle onlihtest, 7 me nahwar ne forlete. Đu settest
on minum muðe þinre soðfæstnysse word, 7 ic awrat
þa lare ðe ic of þinum muþe gehyrde, 7 þa wundra ðe ic
þe wyrcan geseah. Nu ic ðe betæce drihten þine bearn

---

279 **syfan nihta** Or perhaps this is the adj. *syfannihta* (see BTS s.v. *seofon-nihte*).

281 **eal** Originally *ealle*, with *-le* later erased.

282 **gode** Ind. object.

288 f. **Nu . . . me** Lat. *dominica resurrectionis meæ dei, qui post* [*q*]*uinque dies futurus est, ita venies ad me*.
sunnandæg, dæge Note the dat. in apposition to an acc. (When it is part of the name of a weekday, *-dæg* is generally acc. after *on*; standing alone it is often dat.)

291 **sunnanuhtan** A letter (*h*?) has been erased between n^3 and u^2.

292 With this line, which begins fol. 25v, Scribe 2 takes over.
riht lærde Corrected (by erasure) from *rihtalærde*. K has *gerihta lærde*, which suggests how the confusion arose and doubtless represents the original reading.

293 The punctuation mark here is either wholly or in part a later addition; similarly in 1.308 (after *broðrum*) and 1. 322 (after *gemet*).

294 f. **wið ðam weofode** K has *wið þæt weofod*. Cf. 1.80 n.

300 **mare folces** *Mare* is acc. sg. neut. of the comp. adj. (used substantivally); *folces* is partitive gen.; cf. BT s.v. *micel* IV.(a). K has *mare folc* here.

301 **ælcere** K has *ælce*. Cf. 1. 294 f. and n.

305 ff. **Nu . . . gestrynde** MnE word order: *Nu ic ðe betæce, drihten, þine bearn*

þa ðe þin gelaðung mæden 7 moder, þurh wæter, 7 þone [25v15] halgan gast þe gestrynde. Onfoh me to minum ge broðrum; mid þam ðe ðu come 7 me gelaðodest. Geope (del ;) na ongean me lifes geat, þæt ðæra ðeostra ealdras me ne gemeton. Ðu eart crist þæs li*fi*endan godes sunu, þu ðe be þines fæder hæse middaneard gehældest, [25v20] 7 us ðone halgan gast gesendest. Ðe we heriað 7 þan ciað þinra menigfealdra goda geond ungeendode worulde, amen. Æfter þysum gebede æteowde heofenlic leoht bufon þam apostole binnon þære byrgyne an*e* tid; swa beorhte scinende þæt nanes (; /,) [25v25] mannes gesihð þæs leohtes leoman sceawian ne mihte 7 he mid þam leohte his gast ageaf þam drihtne þe hine to his rice gelaðode. He gewat swa freoh fram deaðes sarnysse of þisum andwerdan life; swa swa he wæs ælfremed fram (; /,) lichamlicere gewemmednysse. Soðlice syððan wæs his [26r5] byrgen gemet; mid manna *a*fylled. Manna wæs gehaten (del ;) se heofonlica mete; þe feowertig geara afedde israhela (del ;) folc on westene. Nu wæs se bigleofa gemet on iohannes byr gene, 7 nan þing elles, 7 se mete is weaxende on hire; oð ðysne (del ;) andwerdan dæg. Ðær beoð fela tacna æteowede, 7 untrume ge [26r10] hælde; 7 fram eallum frecednyssum alysede, þurh ðæs (del ;) apostoles þingunge. ðæs him getiþað drihten cr*is*t; þam is wurð mynt 7 wuldor; mid fæder *and* halgum gaste, á buton ende, AM̅.

[pl.], *þa ðe þin gelaðung, mæden 7 moder, gestrynde þe þurh wæter* [i.e. baptism] *7 þone halgan gast*. Some letters have been erased between *l* and *g* in *halgan* and between *r* and *n* in *gestrynde*; the *y* of the latter has been written over the erasure.

308 **mid þam ðe** "Inasmuch as." But no doubt Ælfric originally wrote *mid þam*, "in whose company."

309 **ðæra ðeostra ealdras** Lat. *principes tenebrarum.*

310 **gemeton** Present subjunctive. Corrected (by erasure) from *gemetton.*

316 **ane tid** Corrected (by erasure and overwriting) from what looks like *anre tide*, i.e. a dative (point of time) construction where sense demands an acc. (extent of time).

319 ff. **swa . . . gewemmednysse** Lat. *tam a dolore mortis factus extraneus, quam a corruptione carnis noscitur alienus*; this derives once again from the Monarchian Preface (see 11. 5–20 n.).

321 f. **Soðlice . . . afylled** Lat. *postea vero inventa est et fovea illa plena, nihil aliud in se habens nisi mana, quod usque hodie gignit locus ille.*

322 **gemet** Past participle of *(ge)mētan*, nom. sg. fem.

mid manna afylled Something seems to have been erased between a^2 and *f*; a^3 is written over the erasure. K reads *mannan* here: the noun *manna* could be treated either as indeclinable or as weak masc.

327 **freced-** Corrected from *fræced-*; for this spelling compare *-bætende* in 1. 187; and see 1. 30 n.

328 f. **wurðmynt 7 wuldor** K reverses the order of these two nouns.

329 **AM̅** Abbreviation for *Amen.*

12 / homily on the death of saint oswald, king and martyr

(For August 5th)

The *Lives of Saints* is a collection of homilies issued by Ælfric between 992 and 1002. They are translated or adapted from standard authorities and celebrate saints who were particularly honored by monks.

Ælfric's version of the life and death of King Oswald is based directly upon Bede's account of this monarch in Book III, Chapters i–xiii of the *Historia Ecclesiastica*, but Ælfric rearranges the material to conform to his own conception of clear, consecutive narrative pattern. The bracketed Roman numerals printed to the right of our text indicate the relevant chapters in Bede.

Like the other *Lives of Saints*, Ælfric's homily on Oswald is written in "rhythmical prose." According to John C. Pope, this term

> as applied to Ælfric's compositions must be understood to refer to a loosely metrical form resembling in basic structural principles the alliterative verse of the Old English poets, but differing markedly in the character and range of its rhythms as in strictness of alliterative practice, and altogether distinct in diction, rhetoric and tone. It is better regarded as a mildly ornamental, rhythmically ordered prose than as a debased, pedestrian poetry. . . . So far as we know Ælfric invented the form, and none of his contemporaries . . . followed his example.[1]

Following the lead of Skeat, and latterly of Pope, we have arranged the text as verse, in the belief that so helpful a guide to Ælfric's phrasing and to his rhetorical and rhythmic intentions ought to be exploited as fully as possible.

Two complete MSS of the homily survive. The source of our text is MS Cotton Julius E. vii in the British Museum (Ker 162). It was written at the

[1] *Homilies of Ælfric: A Supplementary Collection*, EETS, 259 (1967), p. 105. The essay on "Ælfric's Rhythmical Prose" (pp. 105–36) furnishes a detailed and invaluable introduction to the subject.

beginning of the eleventh century and offers a rich assortment of confused spellings in inflectional syllables—reflecting the fact that in the spoken language of this time, *a*, *e*, *o* and *u* in final syllables had all been reduced to schwa [ə]. Some of these spellings are mentioned in the notes, but the student should be on his guard for the frequent appearance of *a* instead of *e* where the latter is expected, e.g. in the oblique cases in the sg. of fem. nouns (acc. sg. *þearfa* 244a) and strong adjectives (dat. sg. fem. *eallra* 267a); and conversely of *e* instead of *a* (e.g. acc. pl. fem. *gesetnysse* 86a, gen. pl. neut. *gēare* 149b).

At some point not long after it was written, parts of the MS were subjected to extensive review by a reviser. In the main he seems to have wanted to restore more conservative spellings—he has reversed the *a*/*e* spelling in all four of the above examples—but he was not averse to making more extensive alterations, some of which are deleterious to the rhythm, some to the alliteration, some to the sense.

The homily is most conveniently available in G. I. Needham's edition, *Lives of Three English Saints* (London 1966).

NONAS AUGUSTI. NATALE SANCTI OSWALDI REGIS ET MARTYRIS.

Æfter ðan ðe Augustīnus   tō Engla lande becōm
wæs sum æðel(e) cyning,   Ōswold gehāten,
on Norðhymbra lande,   gelȳfed swȳþe on God.
Sē fērde on his iugoðe   fram frēondum and māgum [i]
tō Scotlande on sǣ   and þǣr sōna wearð fullod
and his gefēran samod   þe mid him sīþedon.
Betwux þām wearð ofslagen   Ēadwine his ēam,
Norðhymbra cynincg,   on Crīst gelȳfed,
fram Brytta cyninge,   Cedwalla gecīged,
and twēgen his æftergengan   binnan twām gēarum.
And sē Cedwalla slōh   and tō sceame tūcode

Title. "(The) nones of August [i.e. August 5th]. (The) birth of Saint Oswald, King and Martyr." The rubric is erroneous and should read *PASSIO* ("martyrdom") instead of *NATALE* ("birth")—unless perhaps the scribe is thinking of the Saint's death as his "birth" into heaven.

2b **Ōswold** His father was King Æðelfrið of Bernicia, his maternal grandfather King Ælle of Deira (see 1/17 n.). During the reign of his mother's brother Eadwine (616–32), who united these two kingdoms of Northumbria, Oswald lived in exile in Scotland and absorbed Irish Christianity from the monks of Iona (cf. ll. 4 f.). He acceded to the Northumbrian throne in 633 and reigned eight years. See *A-SE* 81 f.

3b **gelȳfed** Adj. (past participle), "having faith, believing."

7a **Betwux þām** "Meanwhile."

wearð ofslagen Ēadwine October 12th, 632; see 1/182 n.

10a **twēgen his æftergengan** "His two successors." Eadwine was succeeded briefly in Deira by his cousin Osric and in Bernicia by his nephew Eanfrið (Oswald's brother). Oswald reunited the two kingdoms after his victory over the Welsh king Cadwallon (OE *Cedwalla*) at Rowley Burn, south of Hexham, late in 633 (the Battle of Heavenfield).

11b **tō sceame** "Shamefully."

þā Norðhymbran lēode   æfter heora hlāfordes fylle
oð þæt Ōswold se ēadiga   his yfelnysse ādwǣscte.
Ōswold him cōm tō   and him cēnlīce wiðfeaht [ii]
mid lȳtlum werode,   ac his gelēafa hine getrymde
and Crīst him gefylste   tō his fēonda slege.
Ōswold þā ārǣrde   āne rōde sōna
Gode tō wurðmynte   ǣr þan þe hē tō ðām gewinne cōme,
and clypode tō his gefērum: "Uton feallan tō ðǣre rōde
and þone Ælmihtigan biddan   þæt hē ūs āhredde
wið þone mōdigan fēond   þe ūs āfyllan wile.
God sylf wāt geare   þæt wē winnað rihtlīce
wið þysne rēðan cyning   tō āhreddenne ūre lēode."
Hī fēollon þā ealle   mid Ōswolde on gebedum
and syþþan on ōðerne mergen   ēodon tō þām gefeohte
and gewunnon þǣr sige,   swā swā se Wealdend him ūðe
for Ōswoldes gelēafan,   and ālēdon heora fȳnd,
þone mōdigan Cedwallan   mid his micclan werode,
þe wēnde þæt him ne mihte   nān werod wiðstandan.
Sēo ylce rōd siððan   þe Ōswold þǣr ārǣrde
on wurðmynte þǣr stōd,   and wurdon fela gehælde
untrumra manna   and ēac swilce nȳtena
þurh ðā ylcan rōde,   swā swā ūs rehte Bēda:
sum man fēoll on īse   þæt his earm tōbærst
and læg þā on bedde   gebrocod forðearle
oð þæt man him fette   of ðǣre foresǣdan rōde
sumne dǣl þæs mēoses   þe hēo mid beweaxen wæs,
and se ādliga sōna   on slǣpe wearð gehǣlẹd
on ðǣre ylcan nihte   þurh Ōswoldes geearnunga.
Sēo stōw is gehāten   "Heofonfeld" on Englisc,
wið þone langan weall   þe þā Rōmāniscan worhtan,
þǣr þǣr Ōswold oferwan   þone wælhrēowan cynincg.
And þǣr wearð siþþan ārǣred   swīðe mǣre cyrce
Gode tō wurðmynte,   þe wunað ā on ēcnysse.
Hwæt ðā Ōswold ongann   embe Godes willan tō smēagenne [iii]
sōna swā hē rīces gewēold,   and wolde gebīgan
his lēoda tō gelēafan   and tō þām lifigendan Gode.
Sende ðā tō Scotlande,   þǣr se gelēafa wæs ðā,
and bæd ðā hēafodmenn   þæt hī his bēnum getīþodon
and him sumne lārēow sendon   þe his lēoda mihte
tō Gode gewēman;   and him wearð þæs getīþod.

17a **ārǣrde** "(Had) erected."

25a **on ōðerne mergen** MS Ii. i. 33 has *on ǣrne mergen*, which agrees better with Bede's *incipiente diluculo* ("when it was just beginning to grow light").

29a **þe** Cedwalla is the antecedent.

48a **Sende** Sc. *hē*.

Scotlande I.e. Iona, where Aidan was a monk.

48b **þǣr . . . ðā** Northumbria itself had largely reverted to heathendom after the death of Eadwine; cf. 1.63.

51b **and . . . getīþod** I.e. *and hī getīþodon him þæs*. Note: verb maintains rections of its active form even when passive and part of an impersonal construction.

Hī sendon þā sōna   þām gesǣligan cyninge
sumne ārwurðne bisceop,   Aidan gehāten.
Sē wæs mǣres līfes man   on munuclicre drohtnung(e) [v]
and hē ealle woruldcara   āwearp fram his heortan,
nānes þinges wilnigende   būtan Godes willan.
Swā hwæt swā him becōm   of þæs cyninges gifum
oððe rīcra manna,   þæt hē hraðe dǣlde
þearfum and wǣdlum   mid welwillend(um) mōde.
Hwæt ðā Ōswold cyning   his cymes fægnode [iii]
and hine ārwurðlīce underfēng   his folce tō ðearfe,
þæt heora gelēafa wurde   āwend eft tō Gode
fram þām wiþersace   þe hī tō (ge)wende wǣron.
Hit gelamp þā swā   þæt se gelēaffulla cyning
gerehte his witan   on heora āgenum gereorde
þæs bisceopes bodunge   mid blīþum mōde
and wæs his wealhstod,   for þan þe hē wel cūþe Scyttysc
and se bisceop Aidan   ne mihte gebīgan his sprǣce
tō Norðhymbriscum gereorde   swā hraþe þā gīt.
Se biscop þā fērde   bodigende [v]
geond eall Norðhymbra land,   gelēafan and fulluht,
and þā lēode gebīgde   tō Godes gelēafan
and him wel gebysnode   mid weorcum symle,
and sylf swā leofode   swā swā hē lǣrde ōðrum.
Hē lufode forhæfednysse   and hālige rǣdinge
and iunge men tēah   georne mid lāre
swā þæt ealle his gefēran   þe him mid ēodon
sceoldon sealmas leornian   oððe sume rǣdinge,
swā hwider swā hī fērdon   þām folce bodigende.
Seldon hē wolde rīdan,   ac sīðode on his fōtum
and munuclīce leofode   betwux ðām lǣwedum folce
mid mycelre gesceādwīsnysse   and sōþum mægnum.
Þā wearð se cynincg Ōswold   swīðe ælmesgeorn [vi]
and ēadmōd on þēawum   and on eallum þingum cystig;
and man āhrǣrde cyrcan   on his rīce geond eall [iii]
and mynsterlice gesetnysse   mid micelre geornfulnysse.
Hit gelamp on sumne sǣl   þæt hī sǣton ætgædere, [vi]
Ōswold and Aidan,   on þām hālgan Ēasterdæge.
Þā bær man þām cyninge   cynelice þēnunga

---

56 **wilnigende, willan** Note the paronomasia (and cf. 89, 99, 140, 263 and 278).
58b **þæt** D.o. of *dǣlde* (and correlative with *Swā hwæt swā* in 57a).
62a **þæt** Introducing a purpose clause.
63b **tō** See 1/155 n.
68b **gebīgan his sprǣce** "Adapt what he wanted to say" (lit. "force his utterance").
81b **lǣwedum** Note this inverted spelling in *-um* for the expected *-an* of the weak adj. dat. sg. neut. (and compare the opposite phenomenon in *sylfrenan* 90a, where the strong adj. dat. sg. masc. ending *-um* is represented by *-an*).
85a **āhrǣrde** I.e. *ārǣrde*; cf. the opposite phenomenon in 229b (*rōfes* for *hrōfes*). See Campbell §61.

on ānum sylfrenan disce,   and sōna þā inn ēode
ān þæs cyninges þegna   þe his ælmyssan bewiste
and sǣde þæt fela þearfan   sǣtan geond þā strǣt,
gehwanon cumene   tō þæs cyninges ælmyssan.
Þā sende se cyning   sōna þām þearfum
þone sylfrenan disc,   mid sandum mid ealle,
and hēt tōceorfan þone disc   and syllan þām þearfum,
heora ǣlcum his dǣl;   and man dyde ðā swā.
Þā genam Aidanus   se æðela bisceop
þæs cyninges swȳþran hand   mid swīðlicre blysse
and clypode mid gelēafan,   þus cwæðende him tō:
"Ne forrotige on brosnung(e)   þ(ēos) gebletsode swȳðr(e)!"
And him ēac swā geēode—   swā swā Aidanus him bæd—
þæt his swīðr(e) hand   is gesundful oð þis.
Ōswoldes cynerīce   wearð gerȳmed þā swȳðe
swā þæt fēower þēoda   hine underfēngon tō hlāforde,
Peohtas and Bryttas,   Scottas and Angle,
swā swā se ælmihtiga God   hī geānlæhte tō ðām
for Ōswoldes geearnungum   þe hine ǣfre wurðode.
Hē fulworhte on Eferwīc   þæt ǣnlice mynster
þe his mǣg Ēadwine   ǣr begunnon hæfde,
and hē swanc for heofonan rīce   mid sing(ā)lum gebedum [xii]
swīþor þonne hē hogode   hū hē gehēolde on worulde
þā hwīlwendlican geþincðu   þe hē hwōnlīce lufode.
Hē wolde æfter ūhtsange   oftost hine gebiddan
and on cyrcan standan   on syndrigum gebedum
of sunnan ūpgange   mid swȳðlicre onbryrdnysse:
and swā hwǣr swā hē wæs   hē wurðode ǣfre God,
ūpāwendum handbredum   wiþ heofon(e)s weard.
On þām ylcan tīman   cōm ēac sum bisceop [vii]
fram Rōmebyrig,   Birinus gehāten,
tō Westsexena kyninge,   Cynegyls gehāten:
sē wæs ðā gīt hǣðen   and eall Westsexena land.
Birinus witodlīce   gewende fram Rōme
be ðæs pāpan rǣde   þe ðā on Rōme wæs

95b **mid[1] . . . ealle** "With all the food"; see 4/131 n.
101a **forrotige** Optative subjunctive.
102 **him[2]** "For him, on his behalf."
107b **tō ðām** "To that (extent)."
109 f. **Hē fulworhte . . . hæfde** See 1/178–82.
110b **begunnon** I.e. *begunnen*; cf. 232a.
111a **for** "In pursuit of."
118a **ūpāwendum handbredum** Dat. absolute: "palms turned upwards." Cf. the OE Bede: *swā hwǣr swa hē sæt, . . . his gewuna wæs þæt hē his honda ūpweard hæfde ofer his cnēo ond symle Drihtne Gode his gooda þanc sægde.*
118b **wiþ heofon(e)s weard** "Toward heaven."
119 sq. **On þam ylcan tīman** etc. According to the Anglo-Saxon Chronicle, Birinus' mission occurred in 634 and Cynegils' baptism the following year. Cynegils reigned from 611 to c642.
124a **ðæs pāpan** Honorius I (625–38).

and behēt þæt hē wolde   Godes willan gefremman
and bodian þām hǣþenum   þæs Hǣlendes naman
and þone sōðan gelēafan   on fyrlenum landum.
Þā becōm hē tō Westseaxan,   þe wæs ðā gȳt hǣþen,
and gebīgde þone cynincg   Kynegyls tō Gode
and ealle his lēode   tō gelēafan mid him.
Hit gelamp þā swā   þæt se gelēaffulla Ōswold,
Norðhymbra cyning,   wæs cumen tō Cynegylse
and hine tō fulluhte nam,   fægen his gecyrrednysse.
Þā gēafon þā cynegas,   Cynegyls and Ōswold,
þām hālgan Birine   him tō bisceopstōle
þā burh Dorcanceaster,   and hē þǣrbinnan wunode,
Godes lof ārǣrende   and gerihtlǣcende þæt folc
mid lāre tō gelēafan   tō langum fyrste,
oð þæt hē gesǣlig   sīþode tō Crīste.
And his līc wearþ bebyrged   on ðǣre ylcan byrig
oð þæt Hædde bisceop   eft his bān ferode
tō Wintanceastre   and mid wurðmynte gelōgode
binnan Ealdan Mynstre,   þær man hine wurðað gȳt.
Hwæt þā Ōswold cyning   his cynedōm gehēold [ix]
hlīsfullīce for worulde   and mid micclum gelēafan
and on eallum dǣdum   his Drihten ārwurðode,
oð þæt hē ofslagen wearð   for his folces ware
on þām nigoðan gēare   þe hē rīces gewēold,
þā þā hē sylf wæs on yld(e)   eahta and þrittig gēare.
Hit gewearð swā be þām   þæt him wann on Penda,
Myrcena cyning,   þe æt his mǣges slege ǣr,
Ēadwines cyninges,   Cedwallan fylste;
and sē Penda ne cūðe   be Crīste nān þincg
and eall Myrcena folc   wæs ungefullod þā gīt.

128a **Westseaxan** I.e. *Westseaxum*. Historically the word denotes the people themselves and is therefore pl. But here—as is shown clearly by the sg. verb which follows—it has come to be used of the territory which the people inhabited and is no longer thought of as pl. Cf. the MnE place name Hastings < OE *Hǣstingas* (pl.), the name of a tribe.

133a **hine . . . nam** I.e. was his sponsor (godfather).

134a **cynegas** I.e. *cyningas* (see Campbell ʃ474.(5)).

141 sq. Birinus died c649. His bones were translated from Dorchester-on-Thames to Winchester when the West Saxon see was moved there during the episcopate of Hædde (676–705).

143a **Ealdan Mynstre** The cathedral church of SS. Peter and Paul, founded by Cynegils' successor Cenwalh; it was so called in order to distinguish it from *Nīwe Mynster*, founded in 901 by Edward the Elder.

147a **ofslagen** August 5th, 641.

149b **gēare** The reviser has altered this to *gēara* (the historical spelling of the gen. pl.).

150a **be þām** "As regards that" (i.e. Oswald's death).

150b **Penda** King of Mercia from 632 to 654; see *A-SE* 81 ff.

Hī cōmon þā tō gefeohte   tō Maserfelda bēgen
and fēngon tōgædere   oð þæt þǣr fēollon þā Crīstenan
and þā hǣðenan genēalǣhton   tō þām hālgan Ōswolde.
Þā geseah hē genēalēcan   his līfes geendunge   [xii]
and gebæd for his folc   þe þǣr feallende sweolt
and betǣhte heora sāwla   and hine sylfne Gode
and þus clypode on his fylle: "God, gemiltsa ūrum sāwlum!"
Þā hēt se hæþena cynincg   his hēafod ofāslēan
and his swīðran earm,   and settan hī tō myrcelse.
    Þā æfter Ōswoldes slege   fēng Ōswīg his brōðor
tō Norðhymbra rīce,   and rād mid werode
tō þǣr his brōðor hēafod stōd   on stacan gefæstnod
and genam þæt hēafod   and his swīðran hand
and mid ārwurðnysse ferode   tō Lindisfarnēa cyrcan.
Þā wearð gefylled,   swā wē hēr foresǣdon,
þæt his swīðre hand   wunað hāl mid þām flǣsce
būtan ǣlcere brosnunge,   swā se bisceop gecwæð.
Se earm wearþ gel(ē)d   ārwurðlīce on scrīne,   [vi]
of seolfre āsmiþod,   on Sancte Pētres mynstre
binnan Bæbbanbyrig   be þǣre sǣ strande,
and līð þǣr swā andsund   swā hē ofāslagen wæs.
    His brōþor dohtor eft siððan   on Myrcan wearð cwēn   [xi]
and geāxode his bān   and gebrōhte hī tō Lindesīge
to Bar(d)anīge mynstre,   þe hēo micclum lufode;
ac þā mynstermenn noldon   for menniscum gedwylde

155b **Maserfelda** Lit. "Maplefield," generally identified with Oswestry (< *Ōswoldes trēo*), Shropshire.

158a **genēalēcan** I.e. *hit genēalēcan*, with omission of impersonal subject; cf. 9/27.

163b **and . . . myrcelse** "And (commanded) them (to be) raised (up) as a trophy."

164b **Ōswīg** King (of Bernicia only) from 641 to 654. In the latter year he defeated Penda and his legendary thirty legions in a great battle at the River *Winwæd* (unidentified; somewhere near Leeds) and after that he ruled united Northumbria until his death in 670.

168b **Lindisfarnēa** Gen. sg. ("of Lindisfarne"). On *-ēa* instead of historical *-ēg* see Campbell §238.(2) n. 2. *Lindisfarnēg* < *Lindisfarena ēg*, "the island of the travellers from Lindis" (Lindis being the old name for North Lincolnshire). Oswald had given Lindisfarne to Aidan as his see; it is located off the Northumbrian coast slightly to the north of Bamborough (OE *Bæbbanburg*), the fortified rock which served as the capitol of early Bernicia.

173b **Sancte** This form (instead of expected *Sanctes*) represents the normal OE development of the Lat. gen. sg. masc. *sancti* (see Sweet[14], n. ad loc.).

175b **swā** "As (when)."

176 **His . . . cwēn** Oswig's daughter Osþryð was married to Æðelræd, King of Mercia from 675 to 704. **Myrcan** See 128a n.

179 ff. **ac þā . . . līcræste** Bede says the monks refused to admit the bones into the monastery, even though they acknowledged Oswald's sanctity: "they pursued him even when dead with old grudges, since he had been born in a different province, yet had exercised kingship over them." As a result, the wagon containing the bones remained outside all night, covered with a large tent.

þone sanct underfōn,   ac man slōh ān geteld
ofer þā hālgan bān   binnan þǣre līcræste.
Hwæt þā God geswutelode   þæt hē hālig sanct wæs
swā þæt heofonlēoht,   ofer þæt geteld āstræht,
stōd ūp tō heofonum   swilce hēalic sunnbēam
ofer ealle ðā niht,   and þā lēoda behēoldon
geond ealle þā scīre,   swīðe wundrigende.
Þā wurdon þā mynstermen   micclum āfyrhte
and bǣdon þæs on mergen   þæt hī mōston þone sanct
mid ārwurðnysse underfōn,   þone þe hī ǣr forsōcon.
Þā ðwōh man þā hālgan bān   and bær intō þǣre cyrcan
ārwurðlīce on scrīne   and gelōgodon hī upp,
and þǣr wurdon gehǣlede   þurh his hālgan geearnunge
fela mettrume menn   fram mislicum coþum.
Þæt wæter þe man   þā bān mid āþwōh
binnan þǣre cyrcan   wearð āgoten swā
on ānre hyrnan,   and sēo eorðe siþþan
þe þæt wæter underfēng   wearð manegum tō bōte:
mid þām dūste wurdon āflīgde   dēofla fram mannum,
þā þe on wō(d)nysse ǣr   wǣron gedrehte.
Ēac swilce þǣr hē fēol,   on þām gefeohte ofslagen,   [ix]
men nāmon þā eorðan   tō ādligum mannum
and dydon on wæter   wanhālum tō þicgenne
and hī wurdon gehǣlede   þurh þone hālgan wer.
Sum wegfarende man   fērde wið þone feld:
þā wearð his hors gesīc(c)lod   and sōna þǣr fēol,
wealwigende geond ðā eorðan   wōdum gelīcost.
Mid þām þe hit swā wealweode   geond þone wīdgillan feld,
þā becōm hit embe lang   þǣr se cynincg Ōswold
on þām gefeohte fēoll,   swā swā wē ǣr foresǣdan,
and hit sōna ārās   swā hit hrepode þā stōwe,
hāl eallum limum,   and se hlāford þæs fægnode.
Se ridda þā fērde   forð on his weg
þider hē gemynt hæfde.   Þā wæs þǣr ān mæden
licgende on paralisyn   lange gebrocod.
Hē began þā tō reccenne   hū him on rāde getīmode,
and mann ferode þæt mǣden   tō þǣre foresǣdan stōwe.

183a **swā** "In such a way."

191b **gelōgodon** Pl. because its antecedent (the indefinite pron. *man*) is collective in sense.

198b **dēofla** Nom. pl. neut. (and showing the late confusion of unstressed *a* and *u*; cf. acc. pl. neut. *beboda* 244b, *wundra* 268b).

206b **wōdum gelīcost** "Very much like an insane (being)."

208a **embe lang** "After a considerable (time)."

210 **sōna . . . swā** "As soon as."

211a **eallum limum** Dat. of respect; similarly 218a.

215b **getīmode** Sc. *hit*.

heofonum swilce healic sunnbeam ofer ealle ða 154
niht. and þa leoda beheoldon geond ealle þa scire
wundrigende. Þa wurdon þa mynster men
micclum afyrhte. and bædon þæs on mergen þæt hi
moston þone sanct mid arwurðnysse underfon.
þone þe hi ær forsocon. Ða dwoh man þa halgan
ban. and bær into þære cyrcan arwurðlice on scrine.
and gelogodon hi upp. and þær wurdon gehælede þurh
his halgan geearnunge fela mettrume menn fram
mislicum coþum. Þæt wæter þe man þa ban mid
aþwoh binnan þære cyrcan wearð agoten swa
on anre hyrnan. and seo eorðe siððan þe þæt wæter
underfeng wearð manegum to bote. Mid þam
duste wurdon aflígde deofla fram mannum.
þa þe on wodnysse ær wæron gedrehte. Eac swil
ce þær he feol on þam gefeohte ofslagen. men
namon þa eorðan to adligum mannum. and dy
don on wæter wanhalum to þicgenne. and hi wur
don gehælede þurh þone halgan wer. Sum weg
farende man ferde wið þone feld. þa wearð
his hors geswicelod. and sona þær feol wealwigen
de geond ða eorðan wodum gelicost. mid þam
þe hit swa wealwode geond þone widgillan feld ferde.
þa becom hit embe lang þær se cyning oswold
on þam gefeohte feoll swa swa we ær sæ
dan. and hit sona aras swa hit hrepode þa stowe.
hal eallum limum. and se hlaford þæs fægnode.
Se ridda þa ferde forð on his weg þider he ge
mynt hæfde. þa wæs þær an mæden licgende
on paralisyn lange gebrocod. He began þa to
reccenne hu him on rade getimode. and mann fe
rode þæt mæden to þære stowe sædan. Heo

Miracles of St. Oswald. London, British Museum, ms *Cotton Julius E. vii*, fol. 156r. (See p. 239 f. and cf. 12/184a–217a)

Hēo wearð þā on slǣpe   and sōna eft āwōc,
(an)sund eallum limum   fram þām egeslican broce;
band þā hire hēafod   and blīðe hām fērde,
gangænde on fōtum   swā hēo gefyrn ǣr ne dyde.
Eft siððan fērde ēac   sum ǣrendfæst ridda [x]
be ðǣre ylcan stōwe   and gebaand on ānum clāþe
of þām hālgan dūste   þǣre dēorwurðan stōwe
and lǣdde forð mid him   þǣr hē fundode tō.
Þā gemētte hē gebēoras   blīðe æt þām hūse;
hē āhēng þā þæt dūst   on ǣnne hēahne post
and sæt mid þām gebēorum   blissigende samod.
Man worhte þā micel fȳr   tōmiddes ðām gebēorum,
and þā spearcan wundon   wið þæs rōfes swȳðe
oð þæt þæt hūs fǣrlīce   eall on fȳre wearð
and þā gebēoras flugon   āfyrhte āweg.
Þæt hūs wearþ ðā forburnon   būton þām ānum poste
þe þæt hālige dūst   on āhangen wæs:
sē post āna ætstōd   ansund mid þām dūste,
and hī swȳðe wundroden   þæs hālgan weres geearnunga,
þæt þæt fȳr ne mihte   þā moldan forbærnan.
And manega menn siððan   gesōhton þone stede,
heora hǣle feccende   and heora frēonda gehwilcum.
Þā āsprang his hlīsa   geond þā land wīde, [xiii]
and ēac swilce tō Īrlande   and ēac sūþ tō Franclande,
swā swā sum mæssepreōst   be ānum men sǣde.
Se prēost cwæð þæt ān wer   wǣre on Īrlande gelǣred
sē *ne* gȳmde his lāre,   and hē līthwōn hogode
embe his sāwle þearfa   oððe his Scyppendes beboda
ac ādrēah his līf   on dyslicum weorcum
oð ðæt hē wearð geuntrumod   and tō ende gebrōht.

217a **Hēo wearð þā on slǣpe** Bede writes: *At illa posita in loco obdormiuit parumper* ("Placed in the spot, she fell asleep for a little while").

219a **band . . . hēafod** Bede writes: *crines conposuit, caput linteo cooperuit* ("arranged her hair and covered her head with a linen kerchief").

219b **blīðe** Adj.

223a **of** Partitive usage: "(a portion) of." Similarly 260a, 263b.

225b **blīðe** Adj. modifying *gebēoras*.

229b **rōfes** Cf. 85a n.

232a **forburnon** I.e. *forburnen*; cf. the opposite confusion in 235a (where *wundroden* = *wundrodon*).

238 **heora[1] . . . gehwilcum** "Obtaining their (own) cure and (a cure) for each of their friends."

239b **þā land** "Those regions."

241a **sum mæssepreōst** St. Willibrord, who studied 12 years in Ireland before starting his famous mission to convert the Frisians (see further *A-SE* 166 ff.).

242b–3a **gelǣred . . . lār** Ælfric uses the rhetorical device known as *figura etymologica* to point up the antithesis which he found in Bede: *doctus quidem uir studio litterarum, sed erga curam perpetuae saluationis nihil omnino studii et industriae gerens* ("a man learned in the study of literature, but devoting abso-

Þā clypode hē þone prēost   þe hit cȳdde eft þus
and cwæð him tō sōna   mid sārlicre stemne:
"Nū ic sceall geendian   earmlicum dēaþe
and tō helle faran   for fracodum dǣdum,
nū wolde ic gebētan   gif ic ābīdan mōste,
and tō Gode gecyrran   and tō gōdum þēawum,
and mīn līf āwendan   eall tō Godes willan;
and ic wāt þæt ic ne eom   wyrðe þæs fyrstes
būton sum hālga mē þingie   tō þām Hǣlende Crīste.
Nū is ūs gesǣd   þæt sum hālig cyning
is on ēowrum earde,   Ōswold gehāten:
nū gif þū ǣnig þincg hæfst   of þæs hālgan reliquium,
syle mē, ic þē bidde."   Ðā sǣde se prēost him:
"Ic hæbbe of þām stocce   þe his hēafod on stōd,
and gif þū gelȳfan wylt,   þū wurþ(e)st hāl sōna."
Hwæt þā se mæsseprēost   þæs mannes ofhrēow
and scōf on hālig wæter   of þām hālgan trēowe;
sealde þām ādligan   of tō sūpenne
and hē sōna gewyrpte   and syððan leofode
lange on worulde   and gewende tō Gode
mid eallra heortan   and mid hālgum weorcum,
and swā hwider swā hē cōm   hē cȳdde þās wundra.
For þȳ ne sceall nān mann āwǣgan   þæt hē sylfwylles behǣt
þām ælmihtigan Gode   þonne hē ādlig bið,
þē lǣs þe hē sylf losige   gif hē ālīhð Gode þæt.
Nū cwæð se hālga Bēda,   þe ðās bōc gedihte, [ix]
þæt hit nān wundor nys   þæt se hālga cynincg
untrumnysse g(e)hǣle   nū hē on heofonum (leo)fað,
for ðan þe hē wolde gehelpan,   þā þā hē hēr on līfe wæs,
þearfum and wannhālum   and him bigwiste syllan.
Nū hæfð hē þone wurðmynt   on þǣre ēcan worulde
mid þām ælmihtigan Gode   for his gōdnysse.
Eft se hālga Cūðberht,   þā þā hē gīt cnapa wæs,
geseah hū Godes ænglas   feredon Aidanes sāwle,
þæs hālgan bisceopes,   blīðe tō heofonum,
tō þām ēcan wuldre   þe hē on worulde geearnode.
Þæs hālgan Ōswoldes bān   wurdon eft gebrōht
æfter mænegum gēarum   tō Myrcena lande
intō Glēawceastre,   and God þǣr geswutelode
oft fela wundra   þurh þone hālgan wer.
Sȳ þæs wuldor þām Ælmihtigan   ā tō worulde. Amen.

---

lutely no study or industry to concern with his everlasting salvation").

249a–51a **Nū . . . nū** Correlative.

249b **earmlicum dēaþe** Inst. dat.

269b **þæt** I.e. *þæt þæt.*

272b **ðās bōc** The *Historia Ecclesiastica.*

280b **feredon . . . sāwle** I.e. when Aidan died in 651. This story is told by Bede in the fourth chapter of his biography of St. Cuthbert.

287 **þæs** "For that, in return for that."

13 / The Preface to Genesis

Ælfric's paraphrases of the Old Testament are generally assigned to the period 992–1005, but precisely what portions of the surviving OE version are to be credited to him is a vexed question. To accompany these translations he wrote the present preface and a *Treatise on the Old and New Testament*, both of which deal with the nature and purpose of Holy Writ. In the Preface to Genesis we find not only some interesting remarks about Ælfric's theories of translation, but also a lengthy introduction to the allegorical and typological habit of reading scripture so dear to the Middle Ages.

A sample of Ælfric's paraphrase of Genesis will be found on pp. 290–95, accompanied by the Latin version of the Vulgate. On the general subject of Ælfric's Biblical paraphrases (canon and MSS), see Minnie Cate Morrell, *A Manual of Old English Biblical Materials* (Knoxville 1965), pp. 1–18; the best and most recent edition is that by S. J. Crawford, *The Old English Version of the Heptateuch, Ælfric's Treatise on the Old and New Testament, and His Preface to Genesis*, EETS, Original Series, 160 (1922 [for 1921]).

The Preface survives in three MSS, two from the eleventh and one from the twelfth century. The earliest of the three, British Museum Cotton Claudius B. iv (Ker 142), a splendidly illustrated codex from the first half of the eleventh century,[1] is now missing its first leaf, with the result that its text of the Preface only becomes available with *and sylð ūs* in l. 53. Up to that point, therefore, we have to print from Bodleian Library Laud Misc. 509 (Ker 344), which is from the second half of the century and derives either directly or indirectly from the Cotton MS.[2] However, the leaf now missing from Claudius B. iv was still intact in the sixteenth century, when it was transcribed as far as *weorcum* in l. 36 by the Elizabethan antiquary Robert Talbot (c1505–1558). We have consulted this transcript (now MS 379 in Corpus Christi College, Cambridge)

[1]One of its illustrations is reproduced as the frontispiece to this book.

[2]As an interesting confirmation of this, see p. 385, textual notes to Selection 15, n. on [7 f.].

and have reported all its substantive variants in the textual notes; furthermore we have used its readings to support a restoration (l. 26) and an emendation (l. 29).

INCIPIT PREFATIO GENESIS ANGLICE.

Ælfrīc munuc grēt Æðelwærd ealdormann ēadm(ōd)līce. Þū bǣde mē, lēof, þæt ic sceolde ðē āwendan of (Lȳ)dene on Englisc þā bōc Genesis. Đā þūhte mē hefigtīme þē tō tīþienne þæs, and þū cwǣde þā þæt ic ne þorfte nā mār(e) āwendan þǣre bēc būton tō Īsaace, Abrahames suna, for þām þe sum ōðer man þē hæfde āwend fram Īsaace þ(ā) bōc oþ ende.

Nū þincð mē, lēof, þæt þæt weorc is swīðe plēolic mē oððe ǣnigum men tō underbeginnenne, for þan þe ic ondrǣde, gif sum dysig man ðās bōc rǣt oððe rǣdan g(e)hȳrþ, þæt hē wille wēnan þæt hē mōte lybban nū, on þǣre nī(wan) ǣ, swā swā þā ealdan fæderas leofodon þā on þǣre tīde ǣr þan þe sēo ealde ǣ gesett wǣre, oþþe swā swā men leofodon under Moyses ǣ. Hwīlon ic wiste þæt sum mæsseprēost, sē þe mīn māgister wæs on þām tīman, hæfde þā bōc Genesis, and hē cūðe be dǣle Lȳden understandan; þā cwæþ hē be þām hēahfædere Iācobe, þæt hē hæfde fēower wīf, twā geswustra and heora twā þīnena. Ful sōð hē sǣde, ac hē nyste—ne ic þā gīt—hū micel tōdāl ys betweohx þǣre ealdan ǣ and þǣre nīwan. On anginne þisere worulde nam se brōþer hys swuster tō wīfe, and hwīlon ēac se fæder tȳmde be his āgenre dehter; and manega hæfdon mā wīfa tō folces ēacan, and man (ne mih)te þā æt fruman wīfian būton on his siblingum. Gyf hwā wyle nū swā lybban æfter Crīstes tōcyme swā swā men leofodon ǣr Moises ǣ oþþe under Moises ǣ, ne byð sē man nā Crīsten, ne hē furþo*n* wyrðe ne byð þæt him ǣnig Crīsten man mid ete.

Đā ungelǣredan prēostas, gif hī hwæt lītles understandað of þām Lȳdenbōcum, þonne þingð him sōna þæt hī magon mǣre lārēowas bēon; ac hī ne cunnon swā þēah þæt gāstlice andgit þǣrtō, and hū sēo ealde ǣ wæs getācnung tōweardra þ(i)nga, oþþe hū sēo nīwe gecȳþnis æfter Crīstes menniscnisse (w)æs gefillednys ealra þǣra þinga þe sēo ealde gecȳðnis getācnode tōwearde

---

1 **Æðelwærd ealdormann** See p. 137, n. 3.

4 **būton** "Than."

5 **þē . . . ende** I.e. *hæfde āwend þē þ(ā) bōc fram Īsaace oþ ende.*

8 f. **nū, on þǣre nī(wan) ǣ** "Now(adays), in (the era of) the New Law," i.e. the Christian dispensation of the New Testament. *Sēo ealde ǣ* of l. 9 f. and *Moyses ǣ* of l. 10 are identical.

12 **be dǣle** Adv. phrase, "in part; a little."

13 **hē . . . þīnena** Cf. Genesis 19:16–29.

17 **mā wīfa** I.e. than one.
on "From among."

20 **mid** Postposition governing *him.*

21 **hwæt lītles** "Some little thing" (lit. "something of a little," *lītles* being partitive gen.).

22 f. **ac hī . . . þǣrtō** "But they do not understand, however, the spiritual significance (pertaining) thereto"—i.e. to the *Lȳdenbōcum* of the Old Testament. The rest of the sentence explains the nature of this *gāstlice andgit.*

25 **getācnode tōwearde** "Portended to be in the future" (lit. "betokened coming").

be Crīste and be hys gecorenum. Hī cweþaþ ēac oft be *Pētre*, hwī hī ne mōton habban (w)īf swā swā Pētrus se apostol hæfde; and hī nellað gehīran (n)e witan þæt se ēadiga Pētrus leofede æfter Moises ǣ oþ (þ)æt Crīst, þe on þām tīman tō mannum cōm, | began (t)ō bodienne his hālige godspel and gecēas Pētrum ǣrest (h)im tō gefēran: þā forlēt Pētrus þǣrrihte his wīf, and ealle þā twelf apostolas—þā þe wīf hæfdon—forlēton ǣgþer ge wīf ge ǣhta and folgodon Crīstes lāre tō þǣre nīwan ǣ and clǣnnisse þe hē silf þā ārǣrde. Prēostas sindon gesette tō lārēowum þām lǣwedum folce: nū gedafnode him þæt hig cūþon þā ealdan ǣ gāstlīce understandan and hwæt Crīst silf tǣhte and his apostolas on þǣre nīwan gecȳðnisse, þæt hig mihton þām folce wel wissian tō Godes gelēafan and wel bisnian tō gōdum weorcum.

Wē secgað ēac foran tō þæt sēo bōc is swīþe dēop gāstlīce tō understandenne, and wē ne wrītaþ nā māre būton þā nacedan gerecednisse: þonne þincþ þām ungelǣredum þæt eall þæt andgit bēo belocen on þǣre ānfealdan gerecednisse—ac hit ys swīþe feor þām. Sēo bōc ys gehāten Genesis, þæt ys "Gecyndbōc," for þām þe hēo ys firmest bōca and spricþ be ǣlcum gecinde (ac hēo ne spricð nā be þǣra engla gesceapenisse). Hēo onginð þus: "In principio creauit Deus celum et terram," þæt ys on Englisc, "On annginne gesceōp God heofenan and eorþan." Hit wæs sōðlīce swā gedōn, þæt God ælmihtig geworhte on anginne, þā þā hē wolde, gesceafta; ac swā þēah æfter gāstlicum andgite þæt anginn ys Crīst, swā swā hē sylf cwæþ tō þām Iūdēiscum: "Ic eom angin, þe tō ēow sprece." Þurh þis angin worhte God Fæder heofenan and eorþan, for þan þe hē gesceōp ealle gesceafta þurh þone Sunu, sē þe wæs ǣfre of him āccenned, wīsdōm of þām wīsan Fæder. Eft stynt on þǣre bēc on þām forman ferse: "Et spiritus Dei ferebatur super aquas," þæt is on Englisc, "And Godes gāst wæs geferod ofer wæteru." Godes gāst ys se Hālga Gāst, þurh þone gelīffæste se Fæder ealle þā gesceafta þe hē gesceōp þurh þone Sunu. And se Hālga Gāst færþ geond manna heortan || and sylð ūs synna forgyfnysse, ǣrest ðurh wæter on ðām fulluhte and syððan ðurh dǣdbōte; and gyf hwā forsyhð ðā forgyfnysse ðe se Hālga Gāst sylð, ðonne bið his syn ǣfre unmiltsigendlic on ēcnysse.

---

26 **Hī . . . hī** etc. "Furthermore they often talk about Peter, (and ask) why they" etc. The word *Pētre* has been almost totally erased in the Laud MS, and *Paul* written above the erasure in a sixteenth- to seventeenth-century hand. But the Cotton MS once read *Pētre* here (as shown by Talbot's transcript), and that is also the reading of the third extant MS of this Preface, the twelfth-century MS Cambridge, University Library Ii. 1. 33 (Ker 18).

33 **nū gedafnode him** "(Therefore) it would befit them" etc. *Nū* here has almost no temporal force; see BTS s.v. I.(4–5b)).

37 **foran tō** "Beforehand; by way of introduction."

38 **þā nacedan gerecednisse** "The bare narrative," i.e. without any gloss supplying the *gāstlice andgit.* For a brief but masterful introduction to the allegorical method employed here by Ælfric, see Plummer[2], I, lvi–lxii.

þonne "Consequently."

40 **ac . . . þām** "But it (i.e. the truth of the matter) is quite different from that" (lit. "very far from that").

44 **Hit . . . gedōn** "It was literally done in this fashion."

48 **ǣfre . . . āccenned** "Ever-begotten of him."

49 **Eft** "Then again" (used here and in what follows to introduce further examples).

ferse Here "passage."

Oft is sēo hālige Đrȳnnys geswutelod on ðisre bēc, swā swā is on ðām worde ðe God cwæð: "Uton wyrcean mannan tō ūre anlīcnisse." Mid ðām ðe hē cwæð: "Uton wyrcean," is sēo Đrȳnnys gebīcnod; mid ðām ðe hē cwæð: "tō ūre anlīcnysse," is sēo sōðe Ānnys geswutelod. Hē ne cwæð nā menigfealdlīce: "tō ūrum anlīcnyssum," ac ānfealdlīce: "tō ūre anlīcnysse." Eft cōmon ðrȳ englas tō Abrahame and hē spræc tō him eallum ðrȳm swā swā tō ānum. Hū clypode Ābeles blōd tō Gode būton swā swā ǣlces mannes misdǣda wrēgað hine tō Gode būtan wordum? Be ðisum lȳtlan man mæg understandan hū dēop sēo bōc is on gāstlicum andgyte, ðēah ðe hēo mid lēohtum wordum āwriten sȳ!

Eft Iōsep, ðe wæs geseald tō Ēgypta lande—and hē āhredde ðæt folc wið ðone miclan hunger—, hæfde Crīstes getācnunge, ðe wæs geseald for ūs tō cwale and ūs āhredde fram ðām ēcan hungre hellesūsle. Đæt micele geteld ðe Moyses worhte mid wundorlicum cræfte on ðām wēstene, swā swā him God sylf gedihte, hæfde getācnunge Godes gelaðunge, ðe hē sylf āstealde ðurh his apostolas mid menifealdum frætewum and fægerum ðēawum. Tō ðām weorce brōhte ðæt folc gold and seolfor and dēorwurðe gimstānas and mænifealde mǣrða; sume ēac brōhton gātehǣr, swā swā sēo ǣ bebēad. Þæt gold getācnode ūrne gelēafan and ūre gōde ingehȳd ðe wē Gode offrian sceolon; ðæt seolfor getācnode Godes sprǣca and ðā hālgan lāre ðe wē habban sceolon tō Godes weorcum; ðā gimstānas getācnodon mislice fægernyssa on Godes mannum; ðæt gātehǣr getācnode ðā stīðan dǣdbōte ðǣra manna ðe heora synna behrēowsiað. Man offrode ēac fela cynna orf Gode tō lāce binnan ðām getelde, be ðām is swȳðe mænifeald getācnung; and wæs beboden ðæt se tægl sceolde bēon gehāl ǣfre on ðām nȳtene æt ðǣre offrungae, for ðǣre getācnunge ðæt God wile ðæt wē symble well dōn oð ende ūres līfes: ðonne bið se tægl geoffrod on ūrum weorcum.

Nū is sēo foresǣde bōc on manegum stōwum swȳðe nearolīce gesett, and ðēah swȳðe dēoplīce on ðām gāstlican andgyte; and hēo is swā geendebyrd swā swā God sylf hī gedihte ðām wrītere Moyse, and wē ne durron nā māre āwrītan on Englisc þonne ðæt Lēden hæfð, ne ðā endebyrdnysse āwendan būton ðām ānum ðæt ðæt Lēden and ðæt Englisc nabbað nā āne wīsan on ðǣre sprǣce fandunge: ǣfre sē ðe āwent oððe sē ðe tǣcð of Lēdene on Englisc, ǣfre hē sceal

---

56 **swā swā is** "As (it) is (for example)."

60 f. **Eft . . . ānum** Cf. Genesis 18:2–10. Ælfric cites this episode as his second example of how a *gāstlice andgit* about *sēo hālige Đrȳnnys* and its *sōðe Ānnys* can be perceived in a literal narrative from Genesis.

63 **Be ðisum lȳtlan** "By this little (series of examples)."

64 **lēohtum** Both the other MSS read *lēohtlicum.*

67 sq. See Exodus 35–8.

76 sq. See Leviticus 3.

77 **fela cynna orf** In this instance *fela* is an adj: "livestock of many kinds."

78 **and wæs beboden** Sc. *hit.*

79 **for ðǣre getācnunge** "In order to symbolize" (lit. "for the betokening").

80 **ðonne . . . weorcum** "Then will the tail (i.e. the latter part of our lives) be offered (to God) among our (other good) works." If Bede had read this passage he would have nodded with approval and murmured: *Quid utilitatis habebat hæc cauda si non mysticum aliquid tacite signaret?* (cf. Plummer[2], I, lviii, n. 1).

84 ff. **būton ðām ānum . . . fandunge** "Except in the one (circumstance) that the Latin and the English do not have a single manner when it comes to (lit. in) a test of the language." *Fandung* denotes "testing" or "assay" (cf. 11/107), and

gefadian hit swā ðæt ðæt Englisc hæbbe his āgene wīsan, elles hit bið swȳðe gedwolsum tō rǣdenne ðām ðe ðæs Lēdenes wīse ne can.

Is ēac tō witene ðæt sume gedwolmen wǣron ðe woldon āwurpan ðā ealdan ǣ, and sume woldon habban ðā ealdan and āwurpan ðā nīwan, swā ðā Iūdēiscean dōð. Ac Crīst sylf and his apostolas ūs tǣhton ǣgðer tō healdenne, ðā ealdan gāstlīce and ðā nīwan sōðlīce mid weorcum. God gesceōp ūs twā ēagan and twā ēaran, twā nosðyrlu, twēgen weleras, twā handa and twēgen fēt; and hē wolde ēac habban twā gecȳðnyssa on ðisre worulde gesett, ðā ealdan and ðā nīwan, for ðan ðe hē dēð swā swā hine sylfne gewyrð, and hē nǣnne rǣdboran næfð. Ne nān man ne ðearf him cweðan tō: "Hwī dēst ðū swā?" Wē sceolon āwendan ūrne willan tō his gesetnyssum, and wē ne magon gebīgean his gesetnyssa on ūrum lustum.

Ic cweðe nū ðæt ic ne dearr ne ic nelle nāne bōc æfter ðisre of Lēdene on Englisc āwendan, and ic bidde ðē, lēof ealdormann, ðæt ðū mē ðæs nā leng ne bidde, ðī lǣs ðe ic bēo ðē ungehȳrsum, oððe lēas gyf ic dō. God ðē sȳ milde ā on ēcnysse.

Ic bidde nū on Godes naman, gyf hwā ðās bōc āwrītan wille, ðæt hē hī gerihte wēl be ðǣre bysne, for ðan ðe ic nāh geweald, ðēah ðe hī hwā tō wōge gebringe ðurh lēase wrīteras—and hit bið ðonne his pleoh, nā mīn. Micel yfel dēð se unwrītere, gyf hē nele his gewrit gerihtan.

---

the text as it stands can be construed as saying that one must first "test" English—i.e. search through it for an exact equivalent of the Latin—and only if this procedure fails resort to looser methods of translation. The Laud MS agrees in reading *fandunge* here. However, MS Cambridge, University Library Ii. 1.33 has *fadunge* ("arrangement, order"), and the context suggests that this is probably the original reading: cf. *gefadian* in l. 87 and the emphasis in this entire paragraph on *endebyrdnys*.

88 **wīse** Possibly an error for *wīsan* (the reading of the other two MSS), though according to BT s.v. *wīse* Ia "the word is found with strong forms."

89 **witene** I.e. *witenne* (see SB ʃ231.4).

93 **nosðyrlu** Both the other MSS read *and* after this word: this may well be original, since it makes for more consistent parallelism.

101 **oððe lēas gyf ic dō** "Or untruthful (as regards my vow never to translate again) if I do (in fact do so, owing to your persuasions)."

103 **hī** I.e. the copy.

104 f. **ðēah ðe . . . gebringe** "In the event that someone introduces corruptions into the text" (lit. "even if someone should bring it into error").

104 **hī** D.o. of *gebringe*.

tō In the MS *t* has been altered to *g* in another hand and ink.

14 / Wulfstan's Sermo Lupi ad Anglos

The Benedictine monk Wulfstan became Bishop of London in 996 and Bishop of Worcester and Archbishop of York in 1002. He died at York on May 23rd, 1023 and is buried at Ely. Besides being a busy and important church official and the writer of a large collection of sermons and homilies, he was a jurist and political theorist of considerable stature: he drew up a number of legal codes for King Æðelred II, drafted the laws of King Cnut, and an important work of his on ecclesiastical and secular polity has come down to us.

All of Wulfstan's interests are reflected in the *Sermo Lupi ad Anglos*. Here, writing during a period of acute national anxiety and demoralization, at a time when his countrymen were suffering defeat after defeat at the hands of the Danes, he surveys the situation in England and interprets Viking enormities, social disorder and legal inequalities as God's judgment on a corrupt and sinful society. His welding of personal observation and wide reading is seamless and his style, always highly elaborated and very personal in his other sermons, frequently becomes incandescent here.

The *Sermo Lupi ad Anglos* survives in five MSS. The basis for our text is British Museum Cotton Nero A. i (Ker 164). This MS was probably written at one of Wulfstan's sees (York or Worcester) in the first quarter of the eleventh century, and a number of entries in it may well be in Wulfstan's own hand. We are much indebted in the present edition to Dorothy Whitelock's *Sermo Lupi ad Anglos*, 3rd ed. (London 1963); also to Dorothy Bethurum's *The Homilies of Wulfstan* (Oxford 1957); these two works are referred to in the notes as W and B respectively. Further material has come from *A-SE*, Chapter XI of which, "The Decline of the Old English Monarchy," should be read by the student for background.

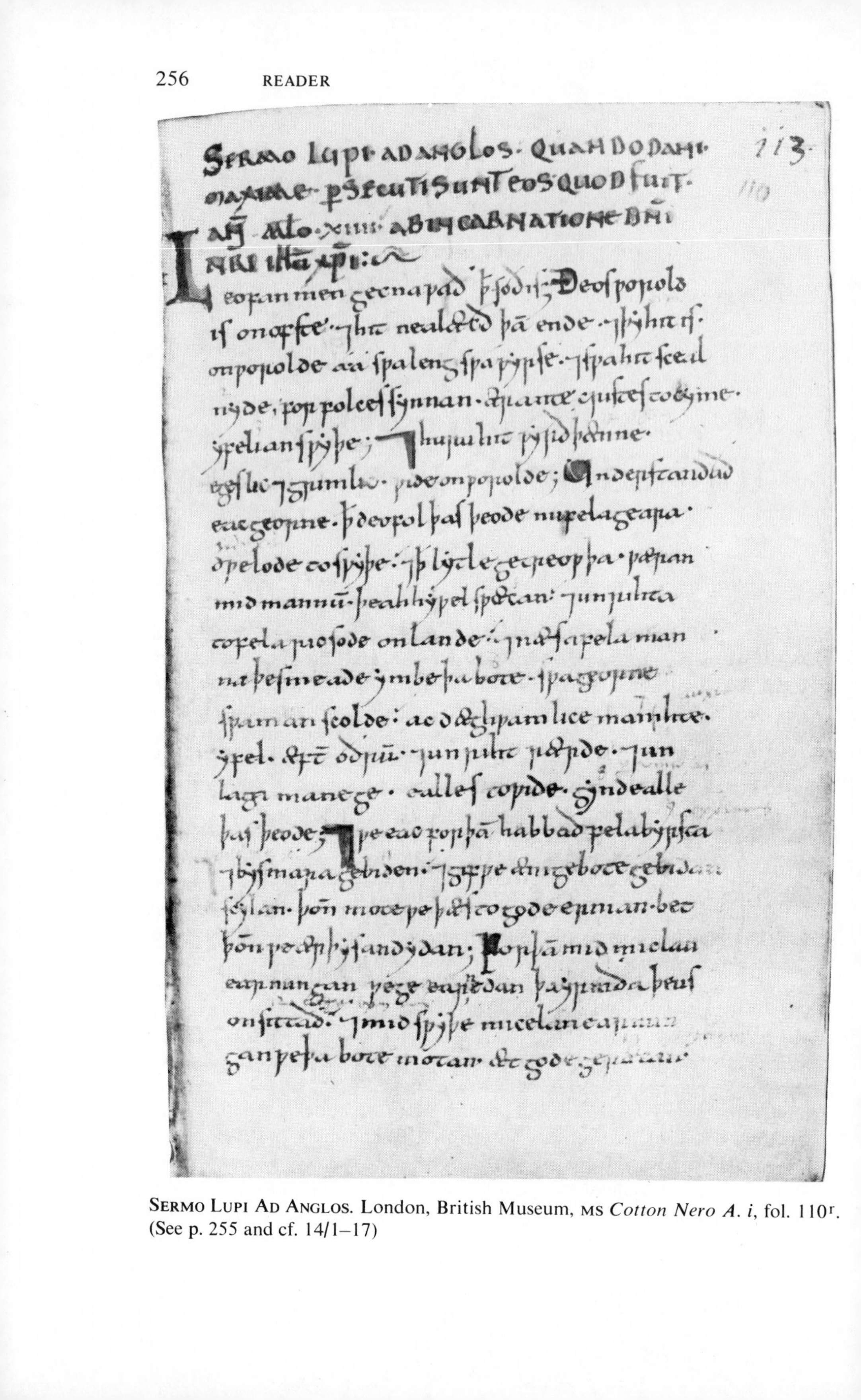

SERMO LUPI AD ANGLOS. London, British Museum, MS *Cotton Nero A. i*, fol. 110r.
(See p. 255 and cf. 14/1–17)

SERMO LUPI AD ANGLOS QUANDO DANI MAXIME PERSECUTI SUNT EOS, QUOD FUIT ANNO MILLESIMO XIIII AB INCARNATIONE DOMINI NOSTRI IESU CRISTI

Lēofan men, gecnāwað þæt sōð is! Ðēos worold is on ofste and hit nēalǣcð þām ende, and þȳ hit is on worolde aa swā leng swā wyrse; and swā hit sceal nȳde for folces synnan ǣr Antecrīstes tōcyme yfelian swȳþe. And hūru hit wyrð þænne egeslic and grimlic wīde on worolde. Understandað ēac georne þæt dēofol þās þēode nū fela gēara dwelode tō swȳþe and þæt lȳtle getrēowþa wǣran mid mannum, þēah hȳ wel *spǣcan*, and unrihta tō fela rīcsode on lande; and næs ā fela manna þe smēade ymbe þā bōte swā georne swā man scolde, ac dæghwāmlīce man īhte yfel æfter ōðrum and unriht rǣrde and unlaga manege ealles tō wīde gynd ealle þās þēode. And wē ēac for þām habbað fela byrsta and bysmara gebiden, and gif wē ǣnige bōte gebīdan scylan, þonne mōte wē þæs tō Gode ernian bet þonne wē ǣr þysan dydan. For þām mid miclan earnungan wē geearnedan þā yrmða þe ūs on sittað, and mid swȳþe micelan earnungan wē þā bōte mōtan æt Gode gerǣcan, gif hit sceal heonanforð gōdiende weorðan. Lā hwæt, wē witan ful georne þæt tō miclan bryce sceal micel bōt nȳde, and tō miclan bryne wæter unlȳtel, gif man þæt fȳr sceal tō āhte ācwencan. And micel is nȳdþearf man*n*a gehwilcum þæt hē Godes lage gȳme heonanforð georne and Godes gerihta mid rihte gelǣste. On hæþenum þēodum ne dear man forhealdan

---

Title. "(The) address of Wolf to the English when the Danes were most severely persecuting them, which was in the 1014th year from the incarnation of our Lord Jesus Christ." The Latin *Lupus* (= OE *Wulf*) was Wulfstan's *nom de plume*.

5 **þæt sōð is** Probably "that which is true" (with *þæt* = *þæt þæt*). Alternatively it is possible to take *þæt* as a conjunction and *sōð* as a noun: "that (the) truth is (as follows)," but 11.30 and 150 f. support the first suggestion.

hit Almost certainly a new impersonal subject (like the *hit*'s which follow) rather than a pronoun in false concord with the fem. antecedent *worold* (but cf. *bōte . . . þæs* in 1.14).

6 **aa . . . wyrse** "Continually the worse (in proportion as things go on) the longer." For the idea see 20/89 f. n.

7 **Antecrīste** For the patristic tradition of the Last Days and the reign of Antichrist, see B 278–82, also 282–93 passim.

9 **dēofol** "The use of this word without an article is one of the characteristic features of Wulfstan's style" (W).

nū fela gēara "(For) many years now."

lȳtle getrēowþa "Few loyalties" (for this use of *lȳtel* see BTS s.v. A.II.(3)).

17 **gif hit sceal . . . gōdiende weorðan** "If it (i.e. the situation) is to start improving."

18 **sceal** "Is required."

21 **Godes gerihta** These are "plough-alms, tithe of young livestock, tithe of the fruits of the earth, Peter's pence, light-dues and payment for the souls of the dead" (W). See further B 342 f.

gerihta mid rihte Cf. *fela ungelimpa gelimpð* in 1. 86. Wulfstan was enormously fond of various kinds of word play, one of his favorites being the balanced (or contrasted) use of two words with the same root but different meanings. See B 28.

lȳtel ne micel þæs þe gelagod is tō gedwolgoda weorðunge; and wē forhealdað ǣghwǣr Godes gerihta ealles tō gelōme. And ne dear man gewanian on hǣþenum þēodum inne ne ūte ǣnig þǣra þinga þe gedwolgodan brōht bið and tō lācum betǣht bið; and wē habbað Godes hūs inne and ūte clǣne berȳpte. And Godes þēowas syndan mǣþe and munde gewelhwǣr bedǣlde; and gedwolgoda þēnan ne dear man misbēodan on ǣnige wīsan mid hǣþenum lēodum, swā swā man Godes þēowum nū dēð tō wīde, þǣr Crīstene scoldan Godes lage healdan and Godes þēowas griðian.

Ac sōð is þæt ic secge, þearf is þǣre bōte, for þām Godes gerihta wanedan tō lange innan þysse þēode on ǣghwylcan ænde, and folclaga wyrsedan ealles tō swȳþe, and hālignessa syndan tō griðlēase wīde, and Godes hūs syndan tō clǣne berȳpte ealdra gerihta and innan bestrȳpte ǣlcra gerisena; and wydewan syndan fornȳdde on unriht tō ceorle, and tō mænege foryrmde and gehȳnede swȳþe; and earme men syndan sāre beswicene and hrēowlīce besyrwde and ūt of þysan earde wīde gesealde, swȳþe unforworhte, fremdum tō gewealde, and cradolcild geþēowede þurh wælhrēowe unlaga for lȳtelre þȳfþe wīde gynd þās þēode, and frēoriht fornumene and þrǣlriht genyrwde and ælmæsriht gewanode, and—hrædest is tō cweþenne—Godes laga lāðe and lāra forsawene. And þæs wē habbað ealle þurh Godes yrre bysmor gelōme, gecnāwe sē þe cunne. And se byrst wyrð gemǣne (þēh man swā ne wēne) eallre þysse þēode, būtan God beorge.

For þām hit is on ūs eallum swutol and gesēne þæt wē ǣr þysan oftor brǣcan þonne wē bēttan, and þȳ is þysse þēode fela onsǣge. Ne dohte hit nū lange

---

24 **bið** Sg. agreeing with *ǣnig*; but note that *lācum* is pl. agreeing with *þǣra þinga*.

25 **hūs** Pl., as shown by the inflection of the following past participle; cf. 1.32 f.

26 f. **þēowas, þēnan** Respectively Christian clerics, pagan priests.

32 **swȳþe** After this word Bodleian Library MS Hatton 113 (Ker 330) adds: *syððan Ēadgār geendode*. King Eadgar died July 8th, 975. On his life see *A-SE* 367–72, on Wulfstan's admiration for him B 82 f.

34 **fornȳdde . . . tō ceorle** "Forced to (marry) a man." "According to secular and canon law widows were permitted to marry after a year, though the church would not bless a second marriage, and to encourage them to remain chaste placed them under the special protection of the church and the king" (B).

35 f. **earme men . . . gesealde** Here Wulfstan disapproves of the selling of Christians to the heathen as slaves or sacrificial victims.

36 f. **cradolcild . . . þēode** A law (c694) of the West Saxon King Ine "states that if a man steal with the knowledge of his household, all are to go into slavery." A law of King Cnut tempers the severity of this: "It has been the custom up till now for grasping persons to treat a child which lay in the cradle, even though it had never tasted food, as being as guilty as though it were fully intelligent. But I strictly forbid such a thing henceforth" (W).

38 **ælmæsriht** "The right of receiving alms, implying the obligation to give alms" (B).

39 **þæs** "Therefore."

40 **gecnāwe** Optative subjunctive, a frequent construction in this selection.

41 **beorge** Sc. *ūs*.

43 **þysse . . . onsǣge** "(So) much (trouble) assailing this people." *Fela* is spelled out in the two sentences that follow.

inne ne ūte, ac wæs here and hunger, bryne and blōdgyte on gewelhwylcan ende oft and gelōme. And ūs stalu and cwalu, strīc and steorfa, orfcwealm and uncoþu, hōl and hete and rȳpera rēaflāc derede swȳþe þearle, and ungylda swȳðe gedrehtan, and ūs unwedera foroft wēoldan unwæstma, for þām on þysan earde wæs, swā hit þincan mæg, nū fela gēara unrihta fela and tealte getrȳ*w*ða æghwǣr mid mannum. Ne bearh nū foroft gesib gesibban þē mā þe fremdan, ne fæder his bearne, ne hwīlum bearn his āgenum fæder, ne brōþor ōþrum. Ne ūre ǣnig his līf fadode swā swā hē scolde: ne gehādode regollīce, ne lǣwede lahlīce. Ac worhtan lust ūs tō lage ealles tō gelōme, and nāþor ne hēoldan ne lāre ne lage Godes ne manna swā swā wē scoldan. Ne ǣnig wið ōþerne getrȳwlīce þōhte swā rihte swā hē scolde, ac mǣst ǣlc swicode and ōþrum derede wordes and dǣde; and hūru unrihtlīce mǣst ǣlc ōþerne æftan hēaweþ mid sceandlican onscytan, dō māre gif hē mæge. For þām hēr syn on lande ungetrȳwþa micle for Gode and for worolde, and ēac hēr syn on earde on mistlice wīsan hlāfordswican manege. And ealra mǣst hlāfordswice sē bið on worolde þæt man his hlāfordes sāule beswīce. And ful micel hlāfordswice ēac bið on worolde þæt man his hlāford of līfe forrǣde oððon of lande lifiendne drīfe. And ǣgþer is geworden on þysan earde: Ēadweard man forrǣdde and syððan ācwealde and æfter þām forbærnde. And godsibbas and godbearn tō fela man forspilde wīde gynd þās þēode, tōēacan *ōðran ealles* tō manega*n þe man* unscyld*ige* forfōr *ealles tō wīde*. And ealles tō mænege hālige stōwa wīde forwurdan þurh þæt

---

Ne dohte hit "Nothing has prospered" (lit. "it has not availed").

46 **ungylda** I.e. the Danegeld.

49 **Ne bearh** etc. Cf. Matthew 10:21.

52 **Ac . . . lage** "But (we) made pleasure our law."

54 f. **wordes and dǣde** Either inst. gen. or gen. of respect.

56 **syn** I.e. *synd*, with late simplification of the final consonant group. The form is repeated in the next line and occurs again later.

58 **And . . . þæt man** Word order: *And sē bið on worolde mǣst hlafordswice ealra, þæt man* etc.

60 **of līfe forrǣde** "Should kill by plotting" (lit. "should plot from life"; cf. ON *ráða af dǫgum*).

61 **Ēadweard** Eadward the Martyr succeeded his father Eadgar (see l. 32 n.) in 975. On March 18th, 978, he was treacherously murdered at Corfe in Dorset by the men of his half-brother Æðelred, who succeeded him on the throne. For details see *A-SE* 372 f.

62 **forbærnde** After this word two MSS (Cambridge, Corpus Christi College 419 [Ker 68] and Bodleian Library Bodley 343 [Ker 310]) add *and Æþelred man drǣfde ūt of his earde*, which is obviously necessary to complete the sense. Æðelred had fled to Normandy sometime after Christmas 1013, leaving King Sveinn tjúguskegg of Denmark (Swein Forkbeard) in possession of England. He returned after Sveinn's death (February 3rd, 1014). The omission of the clause about Æðelred's expulsion by Sveinn is understandable enough in MSS made during the reign of Cnut, Sveinn's son. See *A-SE* 384–6; W 6.

63 f. **tōēacan . . . wīde** This was added in the margin of the MS in a hand that has been thought by some to be Wulfstan's own. Later it was partly erased and partly cut by the binder. The restorations here are from MS Hatton 113 (see l.32 *swȳþe* n.).

64 ff. **þurh . . . wolde** "For this (reason), that (some)one (had), prior to that

þe man sume men ǣr þām gelōgode, swā man nā ne scolde, gif man on Godes griðe mǣþe witan wolde. And Crīstenes folces tō fela man gesealde ūt of þysan earde nū ealle hwīle; and eal þæt is Gode lāð, gelȳfe sē þe wille. And scandlic is tō specenne þæt geworden is tō wīde, and egeslic is tō witanne þæt oft dōð tō manege, þe drēogað þā yrmþe þæt scēotað tōgædere and āne cwenan gemǣnum cēape bicgað gemǣne and wið þā āne fȳlþe ādrēogað, ān æfter ānum and ǣlc æfter ōðrum, hundum gelīccast þe for fȳlþe ne scrīfað, and syððan wið weorðe syllað of lande fēondum tō gewealde Godes gesceafte and his āgenne cēap þe hē dēore gebohte.

Ēac wē witan georne hwǣr sēo yrmð gewearð þæt fæder gesealde bearn wið weorþe and bearn his mōdor, and brōþor sealde ōþerne fremdum tō gewealde; and eal þæt syndan micle and egeslice dǣda, understande sē þe wille. And gȳt hit is māre and ēac mænigfealdre þæt dereð þysse þēode. Mænige synd forsworene and swȳþe forlogene, and wed synd tōbrocene oft and gelōme; and þæt is gesȳne on þysse þēode þæt ūs Godes yrre hetelīce on sit, gecnāwe sē þe cunne.

And lā, hū mæg māre scamu þurh Godes yrre mannum gelimpan þonne ūs dēð gelōme for āgenum gewyrhtum? Ðēh þrǣla wylc hlāforde æthlēape and of Crīstendōme tō wīcinge weorþe, and hit æfter þām eft geweorþe þæt wǣpngewrixl weorðe gemǣne þegene and þrǣle, gif þrǣl þæne þegen fullīce āfylle, licge ǣgylde ealre his mǣgðe. And gif se þegen þæne þrǣl þe hē ǣr āhte fullīce āfylle, gylde þegengylde. Ful earhlice laga and scandlice nȳdgyld þurh Godes yrre ūs syn gemǣne, understande sē þe cunne. And fela ungelimpa gelimpð þysse þēode

---

(time), placed certain (unsuitable) men (there), as he never should have done, if he (had) wanted to show respect for God's sanctuary." According to W, "it is not certain whether this is a reference to foundations held by secular canons, instead of Benedictine monks, or merely to unsuitable admissions into monasteries." The idiom *mǣþe on* + dat. ("respect for [something]") seems to be peculiar to Wulfstan (cf. BT *mǣþ* V).

67–73 **And . . . gebohte** The word play and rhetorical patterning in this sentence will repay careful study. Note especially the stunning effect with which *cēape bicgað* in 1.70 is echoed by *cēap . . . gebohte* in 1.72 f.

68 **þæt**[1,2] I.e. *þæt þæt* ("what").

69 **þæt** Introducing a clause explaining *þā yrmþe*.

scēotað "Go in" (and sc. *hīe*). For the use of *scēotan* (lit. "contribute, pay") see BT s.v. VII.

69 f. **gemǣnum cēape** "As a joint purchase" (inst. dat.).

70 **gemǣne** Construe with *cwenan*; the disjunction is for rhetorical effect.

þā Acc. sg. fem.

71 **and syððan wið weorðe** "And then for a price."

72 **Godes gesceafte** I.e. the woman.

81 **for āgenum gewyrhtum** Supply *ūrum*.

wylc I.e. *hwylc* (see SB ∫217 Anm. 1).

82 f. **þæt . . . þrǣle** "That swordplay should become common to thane and thrall," i.e. that they should fight each other.

83 **fullīce** This intensification of *āfyllan* seems strange, but W calls attention to the verb *fullslēan* ("kill outright") in BTS. Mossé's reading *fūlīce* ("foully") is not supported by the immediate context, which is legal rather than moral.

85 **þegengylde** The *wergild* of a *þegen* was 1200 shillings (or £25). "Apparently the grievance here is the exaction by the Danes of the same price even when the slain man was a deserting English slave" (W); a slave's *wergild* was fixed by statute at £1.

oft and gelōme. Ne dohte hit nū lange inne ne ūte, ac wæs here and hete on gewelhwilcan ende oft and gelōme, and Engle nū lange eal sigelēase and tō swȳþe geyrigde þurh Godes yrre, and flotmen swā strange þurh Godes þafunge þæt oft on gefeohte ān fēseð tȳne and hwīlum lǣs, hwīlum mā, eal for ūrum synnum. And oft tȳne oððe twelfe, ǣlc æfter ōþrum, scendað tō bysmore þæs þegenes cwenan, and hwīlum his dohtor oððe nȳdmāgan, þǣr hē on lōcað, þe lǣt hine sylfne rancne and rīcne and genōh gōdne ǣr þæt gewurde. And oft þrǣl þæne þegen þe ǣr wæs his hlāford cnyt swȳþe fæste and wyrcð him tō þrǣle þurh Godes yrre. Wālā þǣre yrmðe and wālā þǣre woroldscame þe nū habbað Engle, eal þurh Godes yrre! Oft twēgen sǣmæn, oððe þrȳ hwīlum, drīfað þā drāfe Crīstenra manna fram sǣ tō sǣ ūt þurh þās þēode, gewelede tōgædere, ūs eallum tō wo*rol*dscame, gif wē on eornost ǣnige cūþon āriht understandan. Ac ealne þæne bysmor þe wē oft þoliað wē gyldað mid weorðscipe þām þe ūs scendað. Wē him gyldað singāllīce, and hȳ ūs hȳnað dæghwāmlīce. Hȳ hergiað and hȳ bærnað, rȳpaþ and rēafiað and tō scipe lǣdað; and lā, hwæt is ǣnig ōðer on eallum þām gelimpum būtan Godes yrre ofer þās þēode, swutol and gesǣne?

Nis ēac nān wundor þēah ūs mislimpe, for þām wē witan ful georne þæt nū fela gēara mænn nā ne rōhtan foroft hwæt hȳ worhtan wordes oððe dǣde, ac wearð þes þēodscipe, swā hit þincan mæg, swȳþe forsyngod þurh mænigfealde synna and þurh fela misdǣda: þurh morðdǣda and þurh māndǣda, þurh gītsunga and þurh gīfernessa, þurh stala and þurh strūdunga, þurh mannsylena and þurh hæþene unsida, þurh swicdōmas and þurh searacræftas, þurh lahbrycas and þurh ǣswicas, þurh mǣgrǣsas and þurh manslyhtas, þurh hādbrycas and þurh ǣwbrycas, þurh siblegeru and þurh mistlice forligru. And ēac syndan wīde, swā wē ǣr cwǣdan, þur*h* āðbricas and þurh wedbrycas and þurh mistlice lēasunga forloren and forlogen mā þonne scolde, and frēolsbricas and fæstenbrycas wīde geworhte oft and gelōme. And ēac hēr syn on earde apostatan ābroþene and cyrichatan hetole and lēodhatan grimme ealles tō manege, and oferhogan wīde godcundra rihtlaga and Crīstenra þēawa, and hōcorwyrde dysige ǣghwǣr on þēode, oftost o*n* þā þing þe Godes bodan bēodaþ, and swȳþost on þā þing þe ǣfre tō Godes lage gebyriað mid rihte. And þȳ is nū geworden wīde and sīde tō ful yfelan gewunan þæt menn swȳþor scamað nū for gōddǣdan þonne for misdǣdan, for þām tō oft man mid hōcere gōddǣda hyrweð and godfy*r*hte lehtreð ealles tō swȳþe, and swȳþost man tǣleð and mid olle gegrēteð ealles tō gelōme þā þe riht lufiað and Godes ege habbað be ǣnigum dǣle. And þurh þæt

---

87 f. **Ne . . . gelōme** Cf. 1.43 ff. Mossé calls attention to the way in which this passage piles up all of Wulfstan's favorite formulas and stylistic devices.

91 f. **þæs þegenes . . . þe** "Of that thane who."

94 **him** "For himself."

97 **gewelede** Acc. pl. fem., modifying *þā drāfe*.

98 **ǣnige** Sc. *scame* (which in fact occurs here in MS Corpus Christi College, Cambridge, 419).

101 f. **hwæt . . . ōðer** "What else is it."

111 **syndan** The subject is *mā þonne scolde*, "more (people) than should (have been)" in 1.113.

116 **dysige** Adj. used substantivally, like *gōdfyrhte* in 1.120, *dwǣsan* in 1.127.

117 **oftost** I.e. *oftost hōcorwyrde*.

122 **be ǣnigum dǣle** "To any degree."

þe man swā dēð þæt man eal hyrweð þæt man scolde heregian and tō forð lāðet þæt man scolde lufian, þurh þæt man gebringeð ealles tō manege on yfelan geþance and on undǣde, swā þæt hȳ ne scamað nā þēh hȳ syngian swȳðe and wið God sylfne forwyrcan hȳ mid ealle; ac for īdelan onscytan hȳ scamað þæt hȳ bētan heora misdǣda swā swā bēc tǣcan, gelīce þām dwǣsan þe for heora prȳtan lēwe nellað beorgan ǣr hȳ nā ne magan, þēh hȳ eal willan.

Hēr syndan þurh synlēawa, swā hit þincan mæg, sāre gelēwede tō manege on earde. Hēr syndan mannslagan and mǣgslagan and mæsserbanan and mynsterhatan; and hēr syndan mānsworan and morþorwyrhtan. And hēr syndan myltestran and bearnmyrðran and fūle forlegene hōringas manege. And hēr syndan wiccan and wælcyrian, and her syndan rȳperas and rēaferas and worolstrūderas, and, hrædest is tō cweþenne, māna and misdǣda ungerīm ealra. And þæs ūs ne scamað nā, ac ūs scamað swȳþe þæt wē bōte āginnan swā swā bēc tǣcan, and þæt is gesȳne on þysse earman forsyngodan þēode. Ēalā, micel magan manege gȳt hērtōēacan ēaþe beþencan þæs þe ān man ne mehte on hrædinge āsmēagan, hū earmlīce hit gefaren is nū ealle hwīle wīde gynd þās þēode. And smēage hūru georne gehwā hine sylfne and þæs nā ne latige ealles tō lange. Ac lā, on Godes naman utan dōn swā ūs nēod is, beorgan ūs sylfum swā wē geornost magan, þē lǣs wē ætgædere ealle forweorðan.

Ān þēodwita wæs on Brytta tīdum, Gildas hātte. Sē āwrāt be heora misdǣdum, hū hȳ mid heora synnum swā oferlīce swȳþe God gegræmedan þæt hē lēt æt nȳhstan Engla here heora eard gewinnan and Brytta dugeþe fordō*n* mid ealle. And þæt wæs geworden, þæs þe hē sǣde, þurh rīcra rēaflāc and þurh gītsunge wōhgestrēona; ðurh lēode unlaga and þurh wōhdōmas; ðurh biscopa āsolcen-

---

122 ff. **þurh þæt þe . . . þurh þæt** "Because . . . therefore."

127 **bēc** I.e. "the penitential books used in the Anglo-Saxon Church" (W).
tǣcan Subjunctive because the *swā swā* clause depends on the *þæt* clause and thus is felt to participate in its contrary-to-factness.

128 **lēwe** The d.o. of *beorgan*. "Wulfstan is comparing people who will not undergo penance with those who will not seek healing for their [bodily] infirmities until it is too late" (W).

133 **worolstrūderas** I.e. *woroldstrūderas;* the *d* was unvoiced before *s* and then lost (see Campbell ∫480.(3) and ∫477.(1)).

136 **micel . . . manege** Respectively the d.o. and the subject of *magan beþencan.*

137 **þæs** Partitive gen. dependent on *micel.*

138 f. **smēage, latige** Optative subjunctive.

139 **þæs** Gen. of respect: "as regards that (duty)."

142 **Gildas** The British cleric Gildas wrote, in the early or mid-sixth century, the *Liber Querulus de Excidio Britanniae*, a jeremiad against the sins of his countrymen, the Romanized Celts in England.

145 **þæs þe** "According to what."

145–50 **þurh . . . forwurdan** These lines are imitated "from a passage in a letter of Alcuin to Æthelheard, Archbishop of Canterbury, which claims, by the evidence of Gildas, that the English conquest of Britain was a divine punishment for the sins of the Britons, and fears that the English may similarly merit the Viking raids of his day" (W), i.e. those of 790–803. (B cites the relevant Latin: *Legitur vero in libro Gildi Brettonum sapientissimi, quod idem ipsi Brettones propter rapinas et avaritiam principum, propter iniquitatem et iniustitiam iudicum, propter desidiam et pigritiam praedicationis episcoporum,*

nesse and þurh lȳðre yrhðe Godes bydela, þe sōþes geswugedan ealles tō gelōme and clumedan mid ceaflum þær hȳ scoldan clypian. Þurh fūlne ēac folces gǣlsan and þurh oferfylla and mænigfealde synna heora eard hȳ forworhtan and selfe hȳ forwurdan. Ac wutan dōn swā ūs þearf is, warnian ūs be swilcan. And sōþ is þæt ic secge, wyrsan dǣda wē witan mid Englum þonne wē mid Bryttan āhwār gehȳrdan, and þȳ ūs is þearf micel þæt wē ūs beþencan and wið God sylfne þingian georne. And utan dōn swā ūs þearf is, gebūgan tō rihte and be suman dǣle unriht forlǣtan and bētan swȳþe georne þæt wē ǣr brǣcan. And utan God lufian and Godes lagum fylgean, and gelǣstan swȳþe georne þæt þæt wē behētan þā wē fulluht underfēngan, oððon þā þe æt fulluhte ūre forespecan wǣran. And utan word and weorc rihtlīce fadian, and ūre ingeþanc clǣnsian georne, and āð and wed wærlīce healdan, and sume getrȳwða habban ūs betwēonan būtan uncræftan. And utan gelōme understandan þone micla*n* dōm þe wē ealle tō sculon, and beorgan ūs georne wið þone weallendan bryne hellewītes, and geearnian ūs þā mǣrþa and þā myrhða þe God hæfð gegearwod þām þe his willan on worolde gewyrcað. God ūre helpe. Amen.

---

propter luxoriam et malos mores populi patriam perdiderunt. Caveamus, haec eadem nostris temporibus vitia inolescere; quatenus benedictio divina nobis patriam conservet in prosperitate bona, quam nobis in sua misericordia perdonare dignatus est.)

145 **rīcra rēaflāc** The corresponding Lat. indicates that *rēaflāc* is pl. and *rīcra* subjective gen.

158 **sume getrȳwða** If (as *āð* suggests) all the d.o.'s in the sentence are sg., then this is "a certain amount of loyalty."

162 **God ūre helpe** *Ūre* is the gen. object of *helpe*, which is optative subjunctive.

old english poetry

General Remarks

The purpose of this section is to introduce the student to the characteristic features of Old English poetry, to suggest a few of the problems that arise in connection with it, and to define some of the terms that are frequently used in discussing it.

Manuscript and Text

The great bulk of OE verse has survived in four MSS, which are described briefly in the headnotes to the selections which follow. At least one poem has been included from each of these MSS, and there is a sprinkling of other poems besides. With two exceptions,[1] the order of the selections follows the order in *ASPR*,[2] which is the standard edition of the entire corpus of OE verse.[3]

Most of the poems printed in this book survive only in single copies.[4] Consequently the editorial treatment of their texts involves problems quite different from those which must be faced in dealing with the prose. For example, in a passage where one MS of Wulfstan's *Sermo Lupi ad Anglos* reads

[1]Selection 5 (*The Battle of Brunanburh*) has been included among the prose readings, since it seemed unwise to dissociate it from the other Chronicle passages; Selections 15 and 16 (from *Genesis*) have been reversed in order.

[2]*The Anglo-Saxon Poetic Records*, ed. George Philip Krapp and Elliott Van Kirk Dobbie, 6 vols. (New York 1931–53).

[3]Consequently the order of the selections in this book offers no clue to their increasing difficulty. It is perhaps misleading to try to suggest such an order, since the complexities of some of the poems are syntactic (Selection 23), of others semantic or interpretational (19), but the grouping that follows is at least approximate: 25, 18, 24, 5, 15, 17, 21, 22, 19, 16, 23, 20.

[4]Cædmon's Hymn and *The Battle of Brunanburh* are the only exceptions.

nonsensically *manige fleardre*, the best MS contains the correct reading *manigfealdre* (see 14/77). Here, as is often the case, comparison of two or more prose MSS enables us to establish a sound text without any difficulty. An interesting example from the poem *The Battle of Brunanburh* (Selection 5) further illustrates the problem. This text survives in four MSS. In line 53b, three of them read correctly *nægledcnearrum*. The fourth contains the nonsensical corruption *dæg gled on garum*. Alistair Campbell suggests that this error can ultimately be traced to an Anglo-Saxon scribe's unfamiliarity with the second element of the compound, *cnearr*, which is not a native OE word but a loan from ON *knǫrr*. Campbell continues that we can only guess at the subsequent steps by which the corruption arose, "but it is instructive to consider how helpless any editor would be in the face of such an error preserved in one MS. only."[5] Since the lion's share of the poetry has in fact survived in unique copies, this difficulty is constantly presenting itself. The texts of OE poems are full of *cruces* ("crosses," i.e. problems) and *loci desperati* ("desperate places"). Sometimes it is possible to deduce, through knowledge of the sort of error that scribes were liable to make, how a given corruption arose and thus to restore the original reading. Sometimes a syntactical, verbal, metrical or formulaic pattern elsewhere in OE poetry suggests an emendation. Sometimes the editor simply relies on intuition and inspiration. The latter technique was very popular in the late nineteenth century, when editors would emend at the least provocation. The contemporary approach is more conservative: an editor first tries desperately to make some kind of sense out of the text as it stands and, if this proves impossible, he either (1) adopts an emendation that is endorsed by linguistic and paleographical arguments (not to mention common sense), or else (2) simply allows the corruption to stand and confesses that he finds it hopeless.

Punctuation

In the MSS, as is shown by the two facsimiles facing pp. 297 and 373, OE verse is not divided into lines but is written out continuously as if it were prose. The only mark of punctuation is the *punctus*,[6] which is used to separate metrical units which correspond to the halflines in modern printed editions. The scribes of the two MSS illustrated employ the *punctus* very regularly for this purpose; the two scribes who wrote out *Beowulf*, on the other hand, used it very sparingly.

It will be seen from this that whereas the MSS give modern editors some help in establishing the metrical punctuation of the OE poetic texts, the syntactical and rhetorical punctuation in modern editions—i.e. commas, periods, paragraphing, capitalization etc.—is editorial, and tends in the main to follow current stylistic and typographical conventions. The student should be constantly aware that the commas, semicolons and parentheses which facilitate his comprehension of a passage are due to editorial discretion, and that a dif-

[5] *The Battle of Brunanburh*, ed. Alistair Campbell (London 1938), p. 114.
[6] See p. 225.

ferent or a new interpretation of the passage might require that they be totally rearranged. Sometimes, indeed, punctuation which is introduced to expedite translation actually disguises the structure and movement of the verse. For example:

Gewitan him þā Normen   nægledcnearrum,
drēorig daraða lāf,   on Dinges mere,
ofer dēop wæter   Difelin sēcan. (5/53 ff.)

A form of the verb *gewītan* + a refl. dat. pronoun + the infinitive of a verb of motion is a frequently recurring syntactic pattern. The Anglo-Saxon, hearing or reading *Gewitan him*. . . , feels that the utterance is incomplete without the verb of motion (*sēcan* in this case), so he anticipates it all through the intervening swirl of complements and appositives. Hence there is for him in these three lines a sense of syntactic suspension which is resolved, when it finally and inevitably occurs, by the climactic verb of motion. The editorial commas inhibit any sense of this climax by diverting the reader's attention from the sweep of the sentence as a whole to the nervously compartmentalized complements and appositives.

The texts in this volume are punctuated as if they were modern English; the student should appreciate the short-range advantages and long-range disadvantages of such a procedure.

Diction: Enumeration and Variation

The "adding style"—the frequent use of parallelism (often asyndetic parallelism)—results in the characteristically long, non-periodic sentences of OE poetry. This technique is well illustrated in the first four lines of Cædmon's Hymn (printed here without punctuation);

Nū sculan herigean   heofonrīces Weard
Meotodes meahte   ond his mōdgeþanc
weorc Wuldorfæder   swā hē wundra gehwæs
ēce Drihten   ōr onstealde.

The first line contains a perfectly normal subject / verb / direct object sequence (with the subject, *wē*, in ellipsis). Lines 2a, 2b and 3a supply additional direct objects (*meahte*, *mōdgeþanc*, *weorc*) which are syntactically parallel to, but different in meaning from, the first one (*Weard*). This is called *enumeration*. Here it is used to suggest four things which should be praised when speaking about God. A fifth object of praise follows, in the form of a clause introduced by the conjunctive adverb *swā* ("how"). This clause has a more disjoined word order: the subject (*hē*) comes first, but the verb is at the end (*onstealde*), preceded by the direct object (*ōr*), whose genitive complement (*gehwæs*) and *its* genitive complement (*wundra*) are back in the preceding line. Between the genitive complement of the direct object and the direct object itself is inserted a halfline (*ēce Drihten*) which is in apposition to the subject (*hē*): this is called *variation*, since the phrase *ēce Drihten* merely amplifies the idea of *hē* and does not introduce a new referent.

As used by Cædmon, the techniques of enumeration and variation are very effective. In the nine lines of his hymn he is paraphrasing the simple factual statement contained in the first verse of the Bible: *In principio creavit Deus cælum et terram* ("In the beginning God created the Heaven and the Earth"). Out of this he creates a mood of static rapture ideally suited to a hymn: swirling patterns of variation concentrate the attention, intense and enraptured, on God in his various aspects.

In the hands of a hack, of course, the "adding style" could become a column of figures with no sum. A poem on the death of King Edgar (975) from the Anglo-Saxon Chronicle tells us how Earl Oslac of Northumbria was driven from the land

ofer ȳða gewealc,
ofer ganotes bæð, gamolfeax hæleð,
wīs and wordsnotor, ofer wætera geðring,
ofer hwæles ēðel. . . .

A bad poet, as Alistair Campbell remarks, "could keep such stuff up indefinitely."[7] But if the technique was liable to abuses, it was also capable of remarkable triumphs, as is shown by Cædmon's Hymn, by many of the poems in this book,[8] and by almost every page of *Beowulf*.

Diction: Figurative Language

The stuffed owlery about Oslac will serve as an introduction to the subject of metaphor in OE verse. There are very few similes in this verse, and the usual types of metaphoric statement are firmly conditioned by the nature and resources of OE as a compounding language. The technical terminology used in the following paragraphs is Old Norse, since the Scandinavians were the only Germanic people who subjected their vernacular poetry to a contemporary critical analysis—at least, to one that has survived.[9]

(1) *ókend heiti* ("uncharacterized terms"). The *ókent heiti*[10] is an unqualified base word denoting a person or thing. Thus in OE a ship may be called—with absolute literalness—*scip* "ship" or *bāt* "boat"; or it may be called—more figuratively—*flota* "floater" or *lid* "journeyer, sailor." *Ókend heiti* of the figura-

[7]Op. cit., p. 37.

[8]Note for example the cleverly contrived climax of 23/44a–6a.

[9]The terms are from *Skáldskaparmál* ("Poetic Diction"), the second section of the prose *Edda* of Snorri Sturluson. The paragraphs which follow are based upon (and often quote directly) Appendix A, "The Varieties of Poetic Appellation," in Arthur Gilchrist Brodeur's *The Art of Beowulf* (Berkeley 1960).

[10]In ON the noun *heiti* ("name, designation") is neuter; the adjectival form *ókent* (lit. "unkenn'd") is nom. sg. neut., whereas *ókend* is nom. pl. neut.

tive sort most frequently designate the referent in terms of one of its aspects or functions, of its material, or of one of its essential qualities: e.g. *freca* "(wolflike) warrior," *lind* "(lindenwood) shield," *æsc* "(ashwood) spear or boat."

(2) *kend heiti* ("characterized terms"). A base-word becomes "characterized" (in terms of some actual quality or relationship) when it is combined with some limiting word—e.g. *bēaga brytta* "giver of rings," *helmberend* "helmet-bearer." As these two examples suggest, this limiting word may be a genitive complement of the base-word (cf. the phrase *ȳða gewealc* "rolling of waves") or may be joined directly to it to form a compound (*ȳðgewealc* "wave-rolling"): as far as meaning goes the two structures are equivalent. Note also that these *kend heiti*, like the *ókend heiti*, may be either literal (*sǣbāt* "sea-boat") or figurative (*wēgflota* "wave-floater"): in either case the *kent heiti*, unlike the *kenning*, calls the referent something which it actually *is*.

(3) *kenning* ("a characterizing periphrasis"). The kenning is always figurative. It is a compound (or noun + genitive complement) in which the base-word identifies the referent as something which it is *not*, except in relation to the concept expressed in the limiting word. For example, a ship is not a horse; but in the kenning *merehengest* we find a ship (referent) called the horse (base-word) of the sea (limiting word): i.e. it carries men over the sea as a horse carries them over land. In *Judith* (Selection 23/222a) arrows are referred to as *hildenǣdran* "battle-adders." But an arrow (the referent) is not a snake (the base-word) except in the special situation of battle (limiting word): an arrow, in battle, looks like and stings like an adder. We may say then that a kenning is a metaphor in which the limiting word ("sea") supplies the context in which the tenor ("ship") and the vehicle ("horse") achieve their union; or that in all kennings (as in all metaphor) there is a tension between the concept and the base-word, and that the limiting word partially resolves the unreality of that relation. Some genuine kennings in OE are *rodores candel* "candle of the sky" for the sun, *beadolēoma* "battle-flame" for the sword (since it flashes in battle). Since a kenning is in reality a kind of metaphor, it is sometimes capable of extension beyond the boundaries of the two-element kenning itself. In these cases the result is the sort of metaphor with which we are more familiar: we are told in *The Rune Poem*, for example, that during storms at sea *se brimhengest brīdles ne gȳmeð*, "the sea-steed does not heed its bridle."

As a rule the kenning in OE verse is not intended to puzzle; in fact we generally find it introduced to "vary" a more ordinary designation of the referent: in the example from *Judith* the warriors shoot *flāna scūras, / hildenǣdran*, "showers of arrows, battle-adders." In this case we may think of the kenning as merely an imagistic increment to the idea expressed in *flānas*. Sometimes, however, the referent is unexpressed and must be deduced from the kenning—considerable help of course being furnished by the context. For example the otherwise unidentified *hamora lāfan* "leavings of hammers" of *The Battle of Brunanburh* (5/6b) are swords (which are shaped by hammer-blows); and *fugles wyn* "the bird's joy" (21/26/7b) turns out in context to be a goose-quill pen. In these instances the kenning clearly shows its affiliation with the riddle. What is "the waves' binding"? Probably ice. "The hillside's seaweed"? Grass. "The sea of beasts"? The earth. The last two examples are Scandinavian, and it is interesting to note that in the poetry of the Scandinavian skalds the riddling potentialities of the kenning developed at the expense of the poetic. Periphrasis was piled upon periphrasis, until half the joy of composition lay in seeing just how many veils of allusion one could wrap one's referent in. For example a runestone from the Swedish island of Öland, dating from about the year 1000, calls the man whom it commemorates "(the) chariot-Óðinn of (the) enormous land of Ondill" (*ræið-Wiðurr jarmungrundar Ondils*). Ondill was a legendary sea-king; his "enormous land" is therefore the sea itself; the "chariot of the sea" is of course a ship; and the Óðinn (i.e. the god) of a ship is its captain. Through such tortuous analysis the kenning of skaldic poetry yields up its meaning.

In the hands of a bad Anglo-Saxon poet, of course, traditional *kend heiti* and kennings could become lumber, nothing but grist for the mill endlessly turning out variations. The passage about Oslac (p. 267) piles up *kend heiti* and kennings in a perfectly mechanical fashion. There is no vitality in this verse. The successful OE poet demonstrates his awareness of the living tension in kennings either by coining new ones, or by substituting apt synonyms for elements in the frame of traditional ones, or by extending the metaphorical idea beyond the boundaries of the kenning proper: "The steeds of the surge stood ready along the ocean shoreline, sea-mares tethered next to the water" (*Elene* 226b–8b).

Diction: Synonyms

The student approaching OE verse will be struck by the large number of apparent synonyms for the objects and concepts which are the most frequent concern of the poetry. Such a situation is the inevitable outgrowth of the alliterative system: the stock commodities of the verse will have to be mentioned over and over under different alliterative conditions. Hence we find that a list of the synonyms for warrior (or boat, or sea) is remarkably redundancy-free as regards first letter, since obviously twenty words for "sea" beginning with *s* would be (from the point of view of the practicing poet) no more useful than *one* word beginning with *s*. What the student should realize is that these synonyms were in some cases certainly, in most cases probably, not absolutely equivalent in meaning: their denotations were the same but their connotations were not. Usually a glance at the etymology of the supposed "synonyms" will suggest their differing connotations to us. In the last five lines of Cædmon's Hymn, for example, God is referred to as *Scyppend*, *Weard*, *Drihten* and *Frēa*. Etymologically *Scyppend* is the Creator, *Weard* the Guardian, *Drihten* the Lord and Master, whereas *Frēa* is a word which is related to the name of the Germanic love-goddess Freyja (ON)—a name which survives into MnE as the first element in the word Friday.

Oral-Formulaic Theory

As long ago as 1912, H. M. Chadwick discussed *Beowulf* in terms of what was then known about Yugoslavian oral poetry and decried "the chimæra of a literary Beowulf."[11] He was politely ignored. Then in recent years two classical scholars at Harvard, Milman Parry and Albert B. Lord, investigated this Yugoslavian poetry intensively for the light which it might shed on the authorship and composition of the Homeric poems.[12] Their results were extended to OE verse in a very important article by Francis P. Magoun, Jr., which makes clear his debt to Parry and Lord.[13] According to this oral-formulaic theory, the oral poet does not first memorize by rote and then subsequently perform and reperform an unvarying text; rather he creates at every performance a fresh verbal realization of the skeletal and basically stable narrative pattern. He does this by having learned, over a long period of apprenticeship to his art, a number of what we may call "formula frames."

Each of these frames is an abstract verbal pattern whose metrical and syntactic contours are fixed, but whose constituent verbal elements may, in any concrete manifestation (an actual "formula" as it occurs in the verse), vary according to the demands of alliteration and/or context. This requires elaboration. Take the second halfline of *Beowulf*, *in geārdagum* "in days of yore." This is a formula, as indicated by the fact that we find precisely the same form of words in *The Wanderer* (Selection 19/44a). But in *Christ and Satan* (367a) we find *on geārdagum*, and in *The Phoenix* (384a) *æfter geārdagum*. These are not precisely the same formula as *in geārdagum* but clearly they are closely related. We can express the relationship of these concrete formulas by an abstract frame: "[preposition] + *geārdagum*." Notice that the variation permitted by this free substitution of prepositions enables the members of this frame to be used in different contextual situations. Glancing through the poetry we now come upon *on fyrndagum* (*Andreas* lb), *in ǣrdagum* (Christ 79a), *in ealddagum* (*Christ* 303a)—all of which mean precisely the same thing as *in geārdagum*. We can now adjust our abstract frame to the form: "[preposition] + x-*dagum*." The variation permitted by free substitution of first elements in the compound "x-*dagum*" enables the members of this frame to be used in different alliterative situations. All members of the frame "[preposition] + x-*dagum*" have the same rhythm (x–́| ύx; see p. 282) and the same syntax (prepositional phrase used adverbially); hence the definition at the beginning of this paragraph.

Language itself supplies a useful parallel. The child learns his language by abstracting recurrent patterns out of the apparent chaos he hears in the speech of adults. He learns how to substitute within grammatical "frames"—substitute

[11] H. Munro Chadwick, *The Heroic Age* (Cambridge 1912), p. 76.

[12] See Albert B. Lord, *The Singer of Tales* (Cambridge, Mass. 1960).

[13] "Oral-Formulaic Character of Anglo-Saxon Narrative Poetry," *Speculum*, XXVIII (1953), 446–67; reprinted in *An Anthology of Beowulf Criticism*, ed. Lewis E. Nicholson (Notre Dame 1963), pp. 189–221.

one noun for another, etc. The frames themselves remain constant. The oral poet learns, in a similar way, the grammar of formulaic substitution—and will ultimately be as flexible and spontaneous at oral poetical composition as we are at speaking our native language.

The development of this system of formula frames among the Germanic peoples must have been concurrent with the development of alliterative verse itself. It took place long before the Anglo-Saxons migrated to England. Hence we find the same frames and often the same formulas in the extant verse of all the Germanic languages—ON for example yields the by now familiar *í árdaga* "in days of yore."

The great question, of course, is this: how much, if any, extant OE poetry is directly oral in origin—i.e. a written record, taken down by dictation, of an oral performance by an unlettered *scop*? How much of it, on the other hand, is a literary reflex of earlier oral tradition—i.e. the written production of literate clerics and poets who used and imitated the ancient oral style simply because it was the only style in which poetry in the vernacular was known to exist? Sometimes external evidence strongly suggests oral composition—as for example Bede's account of Cædmon and the genesis of his hymn.[14] Bede himself on his deathbed, in addition to quoting a good deal of Latin, spoke *in nostra quoque lingua, ut erat doctus in nostris carminibus* ("also in our own language, seeing as how he was skilled in our vernacular songs")—which has been taken by many scholars to imply that he was composing rather than simply quoting. On the other hand, internal evidence often argues conclusively against oral origin. It was no illiterate oral singer who ended *The Phoenix* with what he conceived to be a fine macaronic climax: according to him, after death we shall all

geseōn sigora Frēan   sine fine
ond him lof singan   laude perenne
ēadge mid englum   Alleluia.

Nor could anyone trained only in the "formula frames" of oral composition, those syntactic units ready to hand for fitting into easy paratactic syntax, have come up with the Latinate disjunction and involution of *Judith* 52b–4a.

While recognizing, then, that the corpus of OE verse unquestionably includes some orally composed poetry along with some literary poetry written in imitation of the oral style (and possibly also some transitional pieces), at the present moment we have not developed techniques which will in every case enable us to distinguish between the different types.

Finally it is important to note that in the broader narrative, too, the oral-formulaic theory calls attention to the use of formulaic "themes," characterized and identified by their having conventional subject-matter and expressing conventional attitudes.[15] Neither the occurrence of a theme nor the point of its

[14]See Francis P. Magoun, Jr., "Bede's Story of Caedman: The Case History of an Anglo-Saxon Oral Singer," *Speculum*, XXX (1955), 49–63.

[15]See F. P. Magoun, Jr., "The Theme of the Beasts of Battle in Anglo-Saxon Poetry," *NM*,

appearance can be predicted, nor are any two presentations of the same theme identical; yet there is enough similarity from one version to another to justify (in a broad sense) the word "formulaic." We may feel certain both that an audience would have expected the oral poet to bring into his heroic narrative at appropriate points certain accustomed themes, and that the poet, while satisfying that expectation, would yet have been free to present the theme in his own way.

Authorship

The perfectly understandable desire to give every OE poem a local habitation and a name led early scholars to attribute all OE verse to the two major poets whose names have come down to us: Cædmon and Cynewulf. Thus the contents of the Junius MS were allotted to Cædmon and great chunks of the Exeter and Vercelli Books to Cynewulf. Massive metrical, syntactic and glossarial statistics were assembled to support or explode these attributions. More recently our expanding awareness of the wide and active literary culture of Anglo-Saxon England has discouraged the notion that several centuries of verse can be safely hung on two pegs, and the theory of oral-formulaic composition suggests that our ideas of literary originality and imitation—and thus our techniques for ascribing poems to one author or another—must be drastically revised in order to fit the realities of the OE situation. No one, at the moment, would feel comfortable about attributing to Cædmon more than the nine lines which are attributed to him in the OE period itself, or to Cynewulf anything other than the four poems (*Elene*, *Christ II*, *Juliana* and *The Fates of the Apostles*) into which he has cunningly woven his signature in runic characters. The vast bulk of OE poetry is firmly anonymous.

Dialect

Though the four great poetic MSS are all West Saxon, they contain a number of words or phonological forms that are Anglian (i.e. Northumbrian or Mercian).[16] Consequently it used to be thought that much of the poetry was Anglian in origin, that it had been written in the period of Bede when Northumbria flourished as the cultural center of England, and that it had preserved traces of this origin even after transcription and re-transcription by West Saxon scribes. Kenneth Sisam has recently argued, however, that there may well have been a general literary *koiné* or "Old English poetic dialect, artificial, archaic, and perhaps mixed in its vocabulary, conservative in inflexions that affect the verse structure, and indifferent to non-structural irregularities."[17] This poetic

---

LVI (1955), 81–90; also S. B. Greenfield, "The Formulaic Expression of the Theme of 'Exile' in Anglo-Saxon Poetry," *Speculum*, XXX (1955), 200–206.

[16]For example, the poetry uses exclusively the Anglian-Kentish form *mēce* ("sword"), whereas the West-Saxon form of the word would be *mǣce*.

[17]*Studies in the History of Old English Literature* (Oxford 1953), p. 138. Sisam's thesis has recently been challenged, at least in part, by Hans Schabram's *Superbia: Studien zum altenglischen Wortschatz*, I (Munich 1965).

koiné was familiar in all dialect areas and incorporated features from several dialects. The advantage of such a *koiné* in Anglo-Saxon times would have been that a new composition could attain currency throughout England without having to be "adjusted," metrically or linguistically, as it passed from one dialect region to another. According to Sisam, evidence for this theory is supplied by a comparison of the prose and poetry that may be reasonably attributed to King Ælfred: his poetry contains "Anglian" elements out of all proportion to his prose, yet both were written by one man. If Sisam's theory is correct, we must admit that linguistic evidence furnishes much less help than was formerly supposed in identifying the area of England in which a given poem was composed.

Poetic Syntax

The substantival use of adjectives seems more common in poetry than in prose. *Hwæðere þǣr fūse feorran cwōman / tō þām Æðelinge*, "Nevertheless eager (ones) came from afar to the Prince" (17/57a–8b); *for ðon dōmgeorne drēorigne oft / in hyra brēostcofan bindað fæste*, "therefore eager-for-glory (ones) often confine tight in their breast-locker a gloomy (thought)" (19/17a–8b). With some poets, e.g. the author of *Judith* (Selection 23), the substantival use of adjectives becomes a characteristic and highly personal stylistic feature.

In the examples cited above no noun is present, so the substantival status of the adjective is beyond question. When a noun *is* present, it is often difficult to tell whether the adjective is being used substantivally, or attributively and with disjunction. Take for example 24/7a–8b:

hē lēt him þā of handon   lēofne flēogan
hafoc wið þæs holtes   and tō þǣre hilde stōp.

Here the adjective *lēofne* seems attributive. But in 19/37a–8b one could argue that the adjective *lēofes* is being used appositionally, i.e. substantivally, and therefore that a comma should be introduced after *winedryhtnes*:

For þon wāt sē þe sceal   his winedryhtnes
lēofes lārcwidum   longe forþolian.

Though disjunction (i.e. the separation of two words whose logical place is next to each other, e.g. a noun and adjective) is possible in prose for stylistic or rhetorical reasons, it is much more common in the poetry. Often it is the "exigencies of meter" that are responsible for syntactic dislocation, sometimes (especially in the more complicated examples) a poet's sheer delight in this kind of artifice. An easy example comes from 17/37b–8a: *Ealle ic mihte / fēondas gefyllan*, "I could (have) fell(ed) all (the) enemies"; here the adjectival complement (*Ealle*) of the d.o. (*fēondas*) is separated from it by the subject and part of the verb. A much more complex example can be found in 23/52b–4a:

nymðe se mōdiga hwæne
nīðe rōfra him þē nēar hēte
rinca tō rūne gegangan.

Following the OE word order we arrive at this translation: "unless the arrogant (one) any in wickedness bold him nearer should summon of (the) warriors to council to come," which may be duly uncoded: "unless the arrogant (one) should summon any of (the) warriors bold in wickedness to come nearer him to council." Students of OE need not anticipate disjunctions of greater complexity than this. It is interesting to note, however, that in the verse of the later Scandinavian skalds disjunction as a stylistic principle is much more fully developed: often the elements of two separate sentences may be freely intermingled. Here, for example, is a literal translation (in MnE word order) of the first half of the *vísa* ("stanza") which Harald Hardrada is supposed to have composed before his defeat at Stamfordbridge in 1066 (see Selection 6): "In battle we creep not into the shelter of a shield because of the crashing of weapons: thus bade the word-true goddess of the hawk's ground." The word order of the original is as follows: "Creep we because of weapons (of the hawk's ground) the crashing not (thus bade the goddess) in battle (word-true) into the shelter of a shield." On first acquaintance one is reluctant to call this sort of thing poetry; but listen to a modern Icelander defending it: "I have always felt that having two or more sentences running at the same time gives a pleasant dilation of the attention that must have a certain aesthetic value."[18] Clearly, *de gustibus non est disputandum.*

Versification

All surviving OE verse has come down to us in written form, in MSS where it is not arranged in lines but runs continuously as if it were prose.[19] Scholars have had no real difficulty in establishing the line divisions of this verse, however, since the line-unit is identified by an alliterative pattern which is prominent and very regular; furthermore in some MSS halflines are carefully punctuated as such (see p. 265). The difficulties have arisen in knowing how to deal with the number of syllables, which varies considerably from as few as seven in a line to twice that number. If meter or a regular rhythm is to be

[18]Quoted by Margaret Ashdown, *English and Norse Documents Relating to the Reign of Ethelred the Unready* (Cambridge 1930), p. 261.

[19]It is important to note that in the Anglo-Saxon period itself a good deal of the verse may have been presented orally, i.e. sung or recited to the accompaniment of a harp or lyre, which was used not so much for melody as to furnish the rhythmic beat.

maintained, as the alliteration implies, what does one do to overcome this apparent irregularity? What of vowel length, the weight of syllables, the relative time allotted to each syllable? Are there places where the words need to be drawn out more slowly, others where they should be said quickly, so that time compensates for the unequal numbers?

Two chief "systems" have been worked out fully enough to demand presentation in this book, those of Eduard Sievers and John C. Pope. Sievers' system was first presented in 1885, won wide acceptance, and is still generally considered the "standard" one, though Sievers himself was never fully satisfied with it. Pope's system was first presented in 1942 and has gradually gained ground, though without displacing that of Sievers. Each has its attractions and its shortcomings. Sievers' system will be outlined in some fullness in the following pages;[20] Pope's will be very summarily sketched.[21]

Of both systems it may be said that the modern assumption of exact regularity as binding on the poet may not have applied to the Anglo-Saxon *scop*, especially under conditions of extempore composition. The scientific prosodist today feels the necessity of accounting for every least detail—and he must certainly describe and classify them all, noting recurrences and regularities. However, there is no way of proving—and it may be misleading to assume—that the Anglo-Saxon poet had any such concern for the minutiae. He is far more likely to have had his few broad rules, based on the structure of the language, and beyond these a considerable tolerance of variations. The prosodic system was firmly regular as regards stressed alliterating initial consonants and vowels; as to the number and type of unstressed elements there was more elasticity.

We metronome-minded moderns, influenced also by the regularity of machines, take for granted exactness of timing. Even if the *scop* used a harp to keep his rhythm regular there is no certainty that he did not use rhetorical pauses, prolongations for emphasis, and other devices which to a modern musician would seem quite irregular. Even a very sensitive musical notation, then, almost certainly imposes on OE verse the impression of a conscious complexity which it may not have had in the mind of the practitioner.

Sievers' System

GENERAL PRINCIPLES

1. **Line** Every line consists of two parts, the first halfline (or a-verse) and the second halfline (or b-verse). These halflines are separated by a caesura and

[20] For a more elaborate sketch of Sievers' system, see Jakob Schipper, *A History of English Versification* (Oxford 1910). A. J. Bliss' important reaffirmation and modification of this system, published in full form as *The Metre of Beowulf* (Oxford 1958), is handily abstracted for beginners in *An Introduction to Old English Metre* (Oxford 1962).

[21] The interested student should consult Pope's excellently condensed account in his *Seven Old English Poems* (Indianapolis 1966).

linked by alliteration (i.e. initial rhyme):[22]

wīcinga fela **wīges georne** (24/73)

2. Halfline Every halfline (or verse) has two rhythmic stresses, or accents, and consequently two rhythmic measures, or "feet"; it is a basic structural unit and has a scansion of its own, independent of that of its complementary halfline:

wī́ges / géorne

In contrast to the second halfline, the first halfline is more favorable to the expanded and heavier forms of the foot.

3. Foot The foot (or measure) in its simplest form consists of two parts, an accented and an unaccented part (arsis and thesis);

wī́ges

However, two additional forms are found, and are always used in conjunction: a foot of one part only (an arsis), and a foot of three parts, of which one is an arsis (having the chief rhythmic stress), another has a secondary stress, and the third is unaccented, e.g.:

Frḗa / ǣ́lmìhtig (2/37b)

4. Arsis The arsis (or rhythmic stress) requires a long syllable[23] or the equivalent of a long syllable. This equivalent is called a *resolved stress* and consists of two syllables, the first of which is short (but bears a word-accent), the second of which is light enough in accent to combine with the first to produce the metrical equivalent of a long syllable; thus *hæleð* "hero" is metrically equivalent to *hǣlð* "health." Furthermore there are certain special conditions under which the arsis may consist of a short syllable.

5. Thesis The thesis (or unstressed part of the foot) consists of a varying number of syllables, which are either unaccented or subordinate in emphasis.

[22] End rhyme is found occasionally, but only as an incidental ornament. Usually it occurs between halflines (e.g. 18/15 f., 54; 23/2, 29, 60 etc.), sometimes within a halfline (e.g. 21/28/4a–6a, 23/23b). It is often regarded as an indication of late date.

[23] A syllable is long if it contains a long vowel or diphthong (**cū**, **Frēa**, **gōd**, **bēag**, **ō-net-tan, on-*bēo*-dan**) or if it contains a short vowel or diphthong followed by more than one consonant (***sæp, sceap, nytt, weorð, hwyrft, web*-ba, *neal*-les, *swef*-len-nes, ge-*reor*-dung**). Syllables ending in short vowels or diphthongs are short (***fe*-la, *ceo*-le, wi-ðo-bend, ge-*ni*-ðe-rung**). Note that in syllabicating OE, a single medial consonant always belongs to the syllable which follows (**swe-*lan***), whereas at least one member of a medial consonant cluster always belongs to the syllable which precedes (***swel*-lan, *swel*-gan**).

No metrical distinction is made between long and short syllables in the thesis.

6. Alliteration Alliteration (initial rhyme) is used to unite the two halflines into the larger rhythmic unit of the complete line. Alliteration is restricted to syllables in the arsis and marks the most emphatic of these; any alliteration occurring in the thesis is without structural significance and may well be accidental. The alliterating syllables have the same initial consonant (but note that the treatment of the initial clusters **st-**, **sp-** and **sc-** is exceptional, each alliterating only with itself and not with any other initial **s-**), or they have an initial vowel sound, any vowel or diphthong alliterating either with itself or (more commonly) with any other vowel sound.[24]

The alliterating syllables are distributed as follows: (*a*) In the second halfline only the first arsis alliterates;[25] (*b*) in the first halfline both the first and the second arsis may alliterate, or the first alone, or (less frequently) the second alone.[26] Examples:

ofer *scíld scóten*, swilce *Scíttisc* éac (5/19)
***Nā́p níhtscūa*, *nórþan* sníwde** (20/31)
***Éall* is *éarfoðlic* *éorþan* ríce** (19/106)
and þis *déorce* líf *déope* geondþénceð (19/89)
***Ríncas* míne, *réstað* íncit** (15/2881)
***Éngle* ond Séaxe *úp* becōman** (5/70)
hwǣ́r is þæt *líber*, þæt þū *tórht* Góde (15/2891)[26]
Gewā́t him þā se *ǽðeling* ond his *ágen* súnu (15/2885)[26]

Furthermore there are sporadic examples of *transverse alliteration*, in which all four arses in a line alliterate in the pattern *ab|ab*:

þǣre *wítegan býrig* *wéallas blícan* (23/137)[27]

The art of versification declines toward the end of the Anglo-Saxon period, and consequently in a poem as late as *The Battle of Maldon* we find infringements of the strict rules of alliteration:

Mē *séndon* tō þé *sǣ́men snélle* (24/29)

[24]This indiscriminate alliteration of vowel sounds has sometimes been explained by suggesting that at the time when the Germanic metrical system first evolved, all the vowels were preceded by a glottal stop, and this was the real alliterating sound.

[25]Since it is the only arsis in the line that *always* alliterates, it is the key to the alliteration of any given line. In ON its alliterating letter was known as the *hǫfuðstafr* ("head-stave" or "chief letter"), whereas those of the first two arses in the line were called *stuðlar* ("studs" or "supporters").

[26]It is possible, however, that all examples of this latter sort are to be otherwise interpreted: see n. 28.

[27]Transverse alliteration of the pattern *ab|ba* is occasionally found, but only in lines where the first halfline is of the questionable type discussed in n. 28, e.g.:

Hǽbbe* ic *gefrúgnen* þætte is *féor héonan (18/1)

7. Rhythmic stress The rhythmic stress (or *ictus*) which characterizes the arsis coincides in general with the emphasis required by the sense. The four stresses of a complete line are therefore on the four most significant words or syllables of the line. These are not restricted to syllables with the primary word-accent, but may include syllables with a secondary word-accent, such as the radical syllable of the second member of a compound noun or adjective (e.g. **heorðge*nēa*tas**) and the more important formative and derivative syllables (e.g. **flō*wen*de**).

The words that are made prominent by the rhythmic stress, being logically or rhetorically the most significant words in the line, are chosen according to the gradation of sentence accent. Thus nouns, adjectives, infinitives and participles, intrinsically significant in a sentence, are used only with rhythmic stress (primary or secondary) and are excluded from the true thesis. Next in this order may be placed the adverbs, which have relatively strong sentence accent and are therefore usually found in the arsis. The finite forms of the verb normally have a weak accent in the principal clause but are more or less strongly accented in the subordinate clause, and this distinction is reflected to some extent in the gradations of the rhythmic stress: though the verb of the principal clause is not excluded from an emphatic arsis (with alliteration), it is very frequently placed in an arsis of weaker stress (such as the last arsis of the line), and is often relegated to the thesis. The remaining grammatical categories are subject to the usual exigencies of sentence accent, rhythm or emphasis. An ictus on a preposition, for example, or on a personal or demonstrative pronoun, must be warranted by special conditions (see respectively 15/2849b and n., 19/58b and n.).

RHYTHMIC TYPES

The structure of the halfline, the fundamental structural unit of Old English poetry, conforms to one of five basic types. These are treated in the pages that follow. We use the symbol –́ to represent the long syllable of an arsis, x to represent a syllable of the thesis (the quantity of which is in most cases disregarded), and ú͜x to represent a resolved stress. A secondary word-accent is indicated by the usual symbol (̀), but when it is raised to the function of a primary rhythmic stress it is represented accordingly (́).

1. Type A –́ x | –́ x In Type A the rhythm, in its simplest form, is trochaic:

stīðum wordum (15/2849a)	–́ x | –́ x
hlōh ond hlȳdde (23/23a)	–́ x | –́ x
heorðgenēatas (24/204a)	–́ x | –́ x
þancolmōde (23/172b)	–́ x | –́ x

With resolved stress:

eaforan þīnne (15/2916a) ⏑́x x | –́ x
salowigpāda (23/211a) ⏑́x x | –́ x
ofstum fetigan (23/35b) –́ x | ⏑́x x
feorh generede (5/36b) –́ x | ⏑́x x
ealdorduguðe (23/309b) –́ x | ⏑́x x

The second (or final) thesis (as also in Type C) never consists of more than one syllable. However the first thesis (as in Types B and C) can have a varying number of syllables. Generally it has either one or two syllables, occasionally three, on rare occasions four or five:

fȳsan tō fōre (15/2861a) –́ xx | –́ x
Efste þā swīðe (15/2873a) –́ xx | –́ x
Here wæs on lustum (23/161b) ⏑́x xx | –́ x
Fisc sceal on wætere (25/27b) –́ xx | ⏑́x x
līfes belidenne (23/280a) –́ xx | ⏑́x x
hlynede ond dynede (23/23b) ⏑́x xx | ⏑́x x
Ellen sceal on eorle (25/16a) –́ xxx | –́ x
Tungol sceal on heofenum (25/48b) –́ xxx | ⏑́x x
gierede mec mid golde (21/26/13a) ⏑́x xxx | –́ x

There is a limited use of *anacrusis*, i.e. the appearance of an unstressed syllable (or occasionally two), not required by the structural type, at the beginning of a halfline:

ne sunnan hǣtu (18/17a) x | –́ x | –́ x
gebiden in burgum (20/28a) x | ⏑́x x | –́ x
geslōgon æt sæcce (5/4a) x | –́ xx | –́ x
and ealle þā gāstas (25/59a) x | –́ xx | –́ x
Ābrægd þā mid þȳ bille (15/2932a) x | –́ xxx | –́ x
Ne forsæt hē þȳ sīðe (15/2860a) xx | –́ xx | –́ x

The thesis may be the second member of a substantive compound, which has a secondary word-accent, or it may be the second word of a substantive collocation which is accented like a compound (e.g. **brād swurd** in the fifth example below). This makes the foot "heavy," and if a heavy foot of this sort comes first in the halfline it may, in compensation, be followed by a foot which is "light" (i.e. which has a short arsis), as in the last two examples:

scildburh scǣron (23/304a) –́ –̀ | –́ x
gūðsceorp gumena (23/328a) –́ –̀ | ⏑́x x
segelgyrd seomian (25/25a) ⏑́x –̀ | ⏑́x x
fǣges feorhhūs (24/297a) –́ x | –́ –̀
bord and brād swurd (24/15a) –́ x | –́ –̀
heolfrig herereāf (23/317a) –́ x | ⏑́x –̀

druncen ond dolhwund (23/107a)   –́ xx | –́ –̀
mōdig ond medugāl (23/26a)   –́ xx | ú͜x –̀
ferðloca frēorig (19/33a)   –́ x̀x | –́ x
goldwine gumena (23/22a)   –́ x̀x | ú͜xx
brimcald brecað (18/67a)   –́ –̀ | úx
blāchlēor ides (23/128a)   –́ –̀ | úx

A notable form of Type A is often found in the first halfline. The alliteration is restricted to the second arsis because of the light character of the first arsis.[28] Furthermore the lightness of the first foot encourages a compensatory increase in the number of syllables in the thesis:

Þā þæs rinces (15/2846a)   –́ x | –́ x
Sindon þā bearwas (18/71a)   –́ xx | –́ x
Nis þǣr on þām londe (18/50a)   –́ xxx | –́ x
Gyf þū þat gerǣdest (24/36a)   –́ xxx | –́ x
Hæfde ðā gefohten (23/122a)   –́ xxx | –́ x
Hī lēton þā of folman (24/108a)   –́ xxxx | –́ x
Ne mihte þǣr for wætere (24/64a)   –́ xxxx | ú͜xx
Tō raþe hine gelette (24/164a)   –́ xxxxx | –́ x

With anacrusis:

Gewāt him þā se æðeling (15/2885a)   x | –́ xxx | ú͜xx

2. Type B   x –́ | x –́   In Type B the rhythm, in its simplest form, is iambic:

þīn āgen bearn (15/2852a)   x –́ | x –́
ne winterscūr (18/18b)   x –́ | x –́
þurh Meotudes meaht (18/6a)   xú͜x | x –́
ne hrīmes dryre (18/24a)   x –́ | xú͜x
ne dene ne dalu (18/24a)   xú͜x | xú͜x

There is considerable freedom in the number of syllables which make up the first thesis; in the second thesis the number is limited to one or two.

With one syllable in the second thesis:

ðonne sorg ond slǣp (19/39a)   xx –́ | x –́
Nis se foldan scēat (18/3b)   xx –́ | x –́

[28]Many scholars prefer the explanation that the first arsis has been "suppressed" in these halflines and that consequently they contain only a single rhythmic stress, which naturally bears the alliteration. They designate halflines of this kind as "Type a." It is interesting to note that almost all first halflines which seem to alliterate on the second arsis only are of this sort.

Is þæt æþele lond (18/20b)	xxúx | x–́
wið þæs fæstengeates (23/162a)	xx–́ | xúx
in ðām wlitegan træfe (23/255a)	xxúx | xúx
Đonne onwæcneð eft (19/45a)	xxx–́ | x–́
ond ðǣr genyðerad wæs (23/113b)	xxxúx | x–́
þæt hē ǣr fācen dyde (25/56b)	xxx–́ | xúx
ymbe hyra þēodnes træf (23/268a)	xxxx–́ | x–́
þæt hē in þæt būrgeteld (23/276b)	xxxx–́ | x–́
Ne biþ him tō hearpan hyge (20/44a)	xxxx–́ | xúx

With two syllables in the second thesis:

þā ēadigan mægð (23/35a)	x–́ | xx–́
hwider hreþra gehygd (19/72a)	xx–́ | xx–́
ofer waþema gebind (19/57a)	xxúx | xx–́
sē hit on frymþe gescōp (18/84b)	xxx–́ | xx–́
þe hyre sigores onlēah (23/124b)	xxxúx | xx–́
nymðe se mōdiga hwæne (23/52b)	xxx–́ | xxúx
Ful oft mec hēr wrāþe begeat (22/32b)	xxxx–́ | xx–́
hū hyre æt beaduwe gespēow (23/175b)	xxxxúx | xx–́
þe mec on þissum līfe begeat (22/41b)	xxxxx–́ | xx–́

3. **Type C** x–́ \| –́x The juxtaposition of the two stresses gives the rhythm of Type C an abrupt, arresting quality. Though double alliteration in the first halfline is not unusual, it is more common to find the alliteration restricted to the first arsis (which always has the stronger stress).

on flot fēran (24/41a)	x–́ | –́x
on lides bōsme (5/27a)	xúx | –́x
and gomol snoterost (25/11b)	xux | úxx

The first thesis can have a varying number of syllables, but the final thesis (as in Type A) never contains more than one syllable:

nemne dēað āna (22/22b)	xx–́ | –́x
þe for Gode hweorfað (25/59b)	xxúx | –́x
þǣr þā ceare seofedun (20/10b)	xxúx | úxx
þā þe him God sendeð (25/9b)	xxx–́ | –́x
sē þe on lagu fundað (20/47b)	xxxúx | –́x
For þon is mīn hyge geōmor (22/17b)	xxxxúx | –́x
þe hīe ofercuman mihton (23/235b)	xxxxxúx | –́x

In compensation for this juxtaposition of the two stresses, the second stress is often on a short syllable:

on flēam sceacan (23/291a)	x–́ | úx

ofer dēop wæter (15/2876b)	xx _́ | úx
Ic þis giedd wrece (22/1a)	xx _́ | úx
in þās woruld cuman (25/41b)	xxú͜x | úx
ongan his feax teran (23/281b)	xxx _́ | úx
þonne him þæt feorg losað (20/94b)	xxxx _́ | úx

Type C lends itself especially to the use of the adjacent word-accents of a substantive compound—i.e. its primary and secondary accents—as the two required rhythmic stresses. The syllable with the secondary word-accent may be long or short in quantity.[29]

ne sincaldu (18/17b)	x _́ | _́ x
ne stānclifu (18/22b)	x _́ | úx
in geārdagum (19/44a)	x _́ | úx
geond lagulāde (19/3a)	xú͜x | _́ x
on þīs ēiglande (5/66a)	xx _́ | _́ x
ne tō hrædwyrde (19/66b)	xx _́ | _́ x
æt ðām æscplegan (23/217a)	xx _́ | úx
and þȳ hygeblīþran (21/26/20b)	xxú͜x | _́ x
hæfde ic ūhtceare (22/7b)	xxx _́ | úx
and wið þæs bealofullan (23/248a)	xxxú͜x | _́ x

Just as the secondary word-accents of substantive compounds are available for ictus, so also are the secondary word-accents of significant syllables of formation and derivation (see General Principles, 7). Some of the most important of these syllables are: **-ende** (of the pres. participle); **-en** (of the past participle and other derivatives); **-ra** and **-est** (of the comparative and superlative adjectives); **-ig**, **-ing** (**-ung**), **-līce**, **-nes**, **-sum**; and the post-radical syllable of weak verbs of Class II.

þǣr cōm flōwende (24/65a)	xx _́ | _́ x
tō ðām wiggendum (23/283b)	xx _́ | _́ x
unbefohtene (24/57a)	xx _́ | úx
þām yldestan (23/242a)	x _́ | _́ x
slōgon eornoste (23/231b)	xx _́ | _́ x
on þā wīcingas (24/322b)	xx _́ | _́ x
hū hī fǣrlīce (19/61a)	xx _́ | _́ x
oððe gecunnian (23/259a)	xxx _́ | úx

[29]Many scholars prefer to think that in halflines of the sort discussed in this paragraph—as in those of a certain sub-type of A (see n. 28)—the first arsis has been suppressed, and that consequently they contain only one full rhythmic stress. They are designated as "Type d," since (thus interpreted) they are clearly more closely related to Type D than to Type C, e.g.:

ne sincaldu	[′] x | _́ _̀ x
þǣr cōm flōwende	[′] xx | _́ _̀ x
and swinsiað	[′] x | _́ ùx

and swinsiað (21/7/7b)	x –́ | úx
and mec longade (22/14b)	xx –́ | úx
ond gefeterode (15/2903a)	xxúx | úx

4. Type D (*a*) D¹ –́ | –́ x̀x; (*b*) D –́ | –́ xx̀ In Type D the first foot contains only an arsis. In compensation for this brevity, the second foot is "heavy": it consists of an arsis followed by a specially constituted thesis of two members, one of which has secondary stress. Although secondary word-accent usually supplies the secondary stress of the rhythm, it is also available for ictus (as in Type C). Type D, like Type E, is a heavy form, and when used in the first halfline is especially favorable to double alliteration. The type is subdivided according to which member of the thesis bears the secondary stress.

(*a*) D¹ –́ | –́ x̀x In D¹, which is the basic form of the type, secondary stress is on the first syllable of the thesis. The quantity of this syllable is variable, though it is most often long.

Frēa ælmihtig (23/300b)	–́ | –́ –̀ x
grim gūðplega (24/61a)	–́ | –́ ùx
wadan wræclāstas (19/5a)	úx | –́ –̀ x
weras wīnsade (23/71a)	úx | –́ ùx
lucon lagustrēamas (24/66a)	úx | úx –̀ x
sumor sunwlitegost (25/7a)	úx | –́ ùxx
hrīð hrēosende (19/102a)	–́ | –́ –̀ x
ealdhettende (23/320b)	–́ | –́ –̀ x
brimlīþendra (24/27b)	–́ | –́ –̀ x
medowērige (23/229a)	úx | –́ ùx
searoþoncelra (23/330b)	úx | –́ –̀ x
grið fæstnian (24/35b)	–́ | –́ ùx
hām sīðie (24/251b)	–́ | –́ ùx
leger weardiað (22/34b)	úx | –́ ùx
hand wīsode (24/141b)	–́ | –́ ùx
bord hafenode (24/309b)	–́ | úxùx

Occasionally we find a halfline consisting of three prominent words (cf. D², second group of examples):

Wit eft cumað (15/2882b)	–́ | –́ ùx
weras wīf somod (23/163a)	úx | –́ ùx

D¹ is often expanded by a syllable after the first arsis; such expansions are generally more frequent in the first halfline than in the second. There is a limited use of the form with three prominent words (as in the last example below):

beorna bēahgifa (5/2a)	–́ x | –́ ùx
atolne ecgplegan (23/246a)	úxx | –́ ùx
strǣlas stedehearde (23/223a)	–́ x | úx –̀ x

caldum cylegicelum (18/59a) ´– x | ´ᴗx ` ᴗx x
grēteð glīwstafum (19/52a) ´– x | ´– ` ᴗx
sōhte seledrēorig (19/25a) ´– x | ´ᴗx ` – x
wrǣtlic weorc smiþa (21/26/14a) ´– x | ´– ` ᴗx

With anacrusis:

bihongen hrīmgicelum (20/17a) x | ´– x | ´– ` ᴗx x
Ongietan sceal glēaw hæle (19/73a) x | ´ᴗxx | ´– ` ᴗx

Occasionally this expansion of D¹ after the first arsis consists of two or three syllables:

Eald is þes eorðsele (22/29a) ´– xx | ´– ` ᴗx
healdne his hordcofan (19/14a) ´– xx | ´– ` ᴗx
ferede in forðwege (19/81a) ´ᴗxxx | ´– ` ᴗx
hǣðenes heaðorinces (23/179a) ´– xx | ´ᴗx ` – x
Wōriað þā wīnsalo (19/78a) ´– xxx | ´– ` ᴗx
men on ðǣre medobyrig (23/167a) ´– xxx | ´ᴗx ` ᴗx

(*b*) D² ´– / ´– x` x In D² secondary stress is on the final syllable of the thesis:

hār hilderinc (24/169a) ´– | ´– x `–
wīs ealdorman (24/219a) ´– | ´– x `–
ides ellenrōf (23/109a) ´ᴗx | ´– x `–

In D² the form often consists of three prominent words, in most instances these three words alone. The last two of these words are more closely related to each other grammatically than the first two and thus constitute an accentual unit, resembling in accentuation a substantive compound; consequently the primary stress is on the first word of the unit and the secondary stress on the second:

wer wintrum geong (15/2889a) ´– | ´– x `–
earn ǣses georn (24/107a) ´– | ´– x `–
gār golde fāh (25/22a) ´– | ´– x `–
rūm recedes mūð (25/37a) ´– | ´ᴗxx `–
clufon cellod bord (24/283a) ´ᴗx | ´– x `–
hægl scūrum flēag (20/17b) ´– | ´– x `–
gǣst ellor hwearf (23/112b) ´– | ´– x `–
crēad cnear en flot (5/35a) ´– | ´– x `–

With anacrusis:

him an wuldres God (15/2916b) x | ´– | ´– x `–

Like D[1], D[2] is often expanded by a syllable after the first arsis:

wērig, wīges sæd (5/20a)	´— x | ´— x `—
drēorig daraða lāf (5/54a)	´— x | ´⏑x x `—
Wōd þā wīges heard (24/130a)	´— x | ´— x `—
Wyrd bið ful ārǣd (19/5b)	´— x | ´— x `—

The preceding forms of D[2] are sometimes found with two unstressed syllables after the second arsis:

eald enta geweorc (19/87a)	´— | ´— xx `—
fæst fingra gebeorh (25/38a)	´— | ´— xx `—
heard heortan geþōht (22/43a)	´— | ´— xx `—
atol ȳþa gewealc (20/6a)	´⏑x | ´— xx `—

5. Type E ´— `xx / ´— Type E is closely related to Type D[1], generally containing the same elements in inverse order. Thus it is now the second foot which contains only an arsis, and the first foot which consists of an arsis followed by a two-member thesis, the first member of which has secondary stress.

With substantive compounds in the first foot:

ondlongne dæg (5/21a)	´— `— x | ´—
hrīmcealde sǣ (19/4b)	´— `— x | ´—
fyrngēarum frōd (25/12a)	´— `— x | ´—
gylpwordum spræc (24/274b)	´— `— x | ´—
ēastdǣlum on (18/2a)	´— `— x | ´—
foremǣrne blǣd (23/122b)	´⏑x `— x | ´—
mægenēacen folc (23/292a)	´⏑x `— x | ´—
tōðmægenes trum (25/20a)	´— `⏑x x | ´—
ginfæstum gifum (15/2920a)	´— `— x | ´⏑x
winemǣga hryre (19/7b)	´⏑x `— x | ´⏑x
slegefǣge hæleð (23/247a)	´⏑x `— x | ´⏑x
byrnwigena brego (23/39a)	´— `⏑x x | ´⏑x

With the secondary stress on significant syllables of formation and derivation (cf. Types C and D):

flēotendra ferð (19/54a)	´— `— x | ´—
Scyppendes mægð (23/78a)	´— `— x | ´—
nergende Fæder (25/63a)	´— `— x | ´⏑x
hǣðenra hosp (23/216a)	´— `— x | ´—
blōdigne gār (24/154b)	´— `— x | ´—
ofstlīce scēat (24/143b)	´— `— x | ´—

When the form consists of three prominent words, the first two of these words are more closely related to each other grammatically than the last two and thus constitute an accentual unit, resembling in accentuation a substantive compound; consequently the primary stress is on the first word of the unit and the secondary stress on the second (cf. Type D[2]):

Wyn eal gedrēas (19/36b)	–́ –̀ x | –́
Godes condel beorht (5/15b)	⏑́x –̀ x | –́
dæges þriddan ūp (15/2876a)	⏑́x –̀ x | –́

The thesis may be expanded by an additional syllable:

ēadhrēðige mægð (23/135a)	–́ –̀ xx | –́
sinsorgna gedreag (22/45a)	–́ –̀ xx | –́
tīrfæstra getrum (25/32a)	–́ –̀ xx | –́
woruldstrenga binōm (21/26/2a)	⏑́x –̀ xx | –́
sigefolca gesetu (25/66a)	⏑́x –̀ xx | ⏑́x

There is an exceptional form of Type E in which an unaccented syllable appears immediately after the first arsis. But this syllable is generally one ending in **l**, **r**, **n** or **m** and is therefore easily slurred in the rhythm:

ealdorlangne tīr (5/3b)	–́ x –̀ x | –́
ēcan līfes blǣð (20/79b)	–́ x –̀ x | –́
Drihten āna wāt (25/62b)	–́ x –̀ x | –́
hrūsan heolstre biwrāh (19/23a)	–́ x –̀ xx | –́

6. Hypermetric Forms A special modification of the preceding types occurs when an extra foot is added at the beginning of a rhythmically normal halfline (most often a normal halfline of Type A). This extra foot may be preceded by anacrusis. In the first halfline the extra foot generally participates in the alliteration of the line; in the second halfline it more often does not. Usually hypermetric halflines are coupled to form hypermetric lines;[30] moreover these hypermetric lines tend to be clustered in groups, usually for no apparent reason, but sometimes at strategic points in the structure of a poem (e.g. the conclusions of Selections 19 and 23), or else to give emphasis to passages of particular emotive or narrative importance. In the present edition (except in Selection 16)[31] hypermetric lines are indicated typographically by extending their left margin beyond that of the normal lines.[32]

[30] There are only seven hypermetric halflines in the texts in this book which are not so coupled. 15/2857a, 17/40b, 19/65a, 20/23a, 23/62a and 96b, 25/47a.

[31] Indication of hypermetric lines is not feasible in this text, since in too many cases it is impossible to decide whether a halfline is in fact hypermetric or whether it is simply a normal line whose abnormal length and structure reflect the poem's OS origin.

[32] This practice is also followed in the seven cases where only one of the constituent halflines is hypermetric; see n. 30 above.

The following scansion for the cluster of hypermetric lines which concludes Selection 23 will serve to exemplify the foregoing principles (11.337–48):

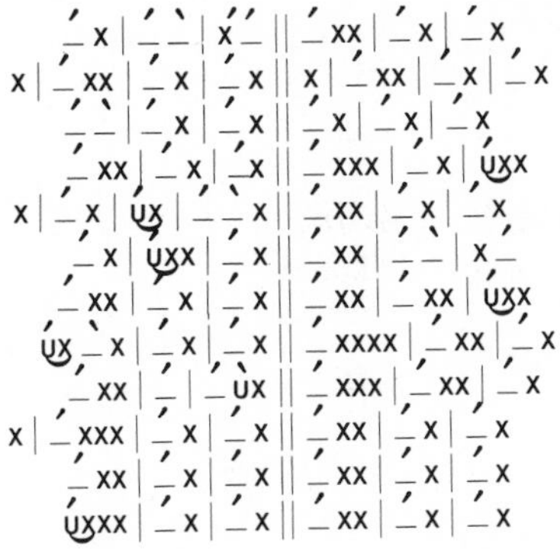

–x | –– | x– || –xx | –x | –x
x | –xx | –x | –x || x | –xx | –x | –x
–– | –x | –x || –x | –x | –x
–xx | –x | –x || –xxx | –x | uxx
x | –x | ux | ––x || –xx | –x | –x
–x | uxx | –x || –xx | –– | x–
–xx | –x | –x || –xx | –xx | uxx
ux –x | –x | –x || –xxxx | –xx | –x
–xx | – | –ux || –xxx | –xx | –x
x | –xxx | –x | –x || –xx | –x | –x
–xx | –x | –x || –xx | –x | –x
uxxx | –x | –x || –xx | –x | –x

Pope's System

Pope agrees with Sievers in recognizing the five basic types of halfline, though with some important differences of detail. His innovations consist chiefly in assuming that the verse was isochronous, and in scoring the lines in musical notation indicating the duration of each syllable within 4/8 time. As in musical scores, he allows for rests, arguing that the harp was often struck at places calling for stress where no word was being said or sung. All normal lines are considered to have alternating primary and secondary stresses (duple rhythm) in each verse. Also, some measures are heavy (ʹʹ and ˋˋ) and some light (ʹ and ˋ). Rests come at the beginning and ends of halflines.

Examples of the five types, taken from *Beowulf*, are:

Type A **gomban gyldan** (11a)
torht getǣhte (313a)
waca wið wrāþum (660a)
(These are only three of the 107 sub-types.)

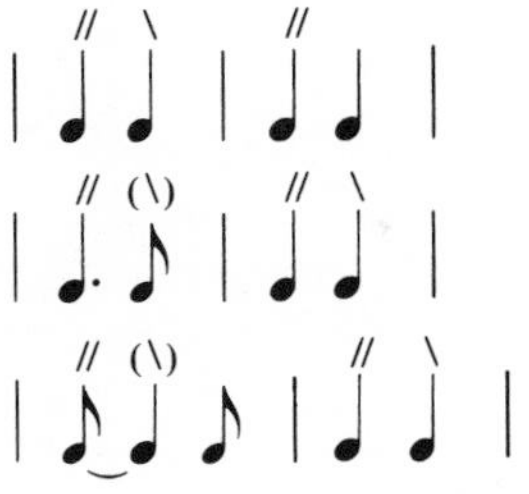

Type B **on sīdne sǣ** (507a)
(There are 58 sub-types.)

Type C **of brȳdbūre** (921a)
(There are 39 sub-types.)

Type D **heardhicgende** (394a)
(There are 58 sub-types.)

Type E **flōdȳþum feor** (542a)
(There are 17 sub-types.)

The hypermetric lines are treated as having doubled time (4/4). The range of quantities remains the same as in normal verses.

Examples:

þū scealt geōmor hweorfan (*Genesis* 1018b)
Geseah ðā swīðmōd cyning (*Daniel* 268a)

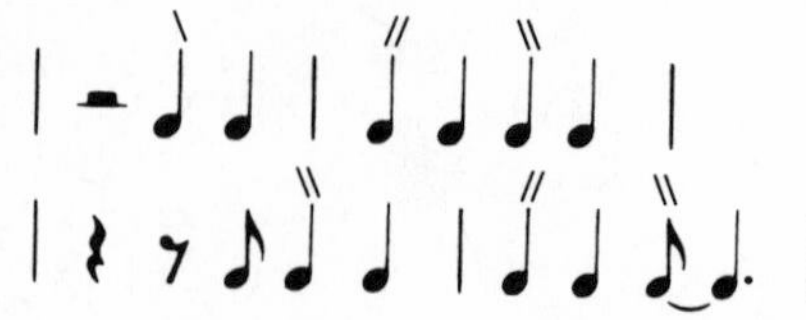

15 / The Sacrifice of Isaac
(From *Genesis A*)

MS Junius 11 (Ker 334) is named after its last private owner, Franciscus Junius (1589–1677), an early scholar of Old English who donated it to the Bodleian library at Oxford. It was he who first attributed its contents to Cædmon (see Selection 2), and though modern scholarship no longer accepts this ascription, the codex is still sometimes referred to as "The Cædmon Manuscript" and is regarded as containing poetry of the "Cædmonian School" (see Wrenn 97–102). It was written about A.D. 1000, perhaps at Christ Church, Canterbury, and great care was taken in its production; consequently it is the most handsome of all the OE poetic MSS. Halflines are punctuated (consistently and fairly accurately) with lozenge-shaped dots, sections begin with elaborate zoomorphic ("animal form") capitals, and there are a number of highly interesting line-drawings in the style of the "Winchester school." It is a fascinating experience to page through the sumptuous facsimile edition of this MS by Sir Israel Gollancz, *The Cædmon Manuscript* (Oxford 1927); we have included one plate facing p. 297.

The MS contains four OE poems, *Genesis*, *Exodus*, *Daniel* and *Christ and Satan*. The first of these, a long narrative of 2936 lines, begins with the creation and ends with the sacrifice of Isaac (our selection), thus paraphrasing the first twenty-two chapters of the Old Testament. Its date is as uncertain as its authorship, though since the time of Junius scholars—influenced by Bede's famous account of how Cædmon sang *eal þæt stǣr Genesis* (*þæt is sēo ǣreste Moyses booc*)—have felt the attraction of assigning it to him and thus dating its composition in the late seventh century. Lines 235a–851b of *Genesis* (or *Genesis B*; see p. 299) have been edited several times in recent years; except for Krapp's edition in *ASPR*, I, however, much the greater part of the poem (*Genesis A*) has not been edited since Ferdinand Holthausen's *Die ältere Genesis* (Heidelberg 1914).

The story of Abraham and Isaac, with its absolute, arbitrary God and its unquestioning, obedient human protagonist, is rich in natural drama. And it must have been particularly effective for an Anglo-Saxon audience, since it shows that devotion to God must override even the ties of kinship, which constituted the strongest social bond in the Germanic world. Its popularity is attested by another telling of the same story in the OE poem *Exodus* (384–446).

For purposes of comparison we have printed the Vulgate version of Genesis 22:1–19 beneath the poem, and beneath this Latin text we have printed Ælfric's paraphrase of it in OE prose.[1] We have also included, as the frontispiece to this volume, an Anglo-Saxon artist's interpretation of this popular story: it is reproduced from MS British Museum Cotton Claudius B. iv (see p. 250), where it adorns the text of Ælfric's paraphrase.

[1]For general remarks about Ælfric's Biblical paraphrases, see the headnote to Selection 13.

Þā þæs rinces   se rīca ongan
Cyning costigan,   cunnode georne
hwilc þæs æðelinges   ellen wǣre,
stīðum wordum   spræc him stefne tō:
"Gewīt þū ofestlīce,   Abraham, fēran,
lāstas lecgan,   ond þē lǣde mid
þīn āgen bearn.   Þū scealt Īsaac mē
onsecgan, sunu ðīnne,   sylf tō tībre,
siððan þū gestīgest   stēape dūne,

Quæ postquam gesta sunt, tentavit Deus Abraham, et dixit ad eum: "Abraham!" Ille respondit: "Adsum." Ait illi: "Tolle filium tuum unigenitum, quem diligis, Isaac, et vade in terram visionis: atque offer eum ibi in holocaustum super unum montium quem monstravero tibi." Igitur Abraham de nocte consurgens, stravit

---

God wolde þā fandian Abrahames gehȳrsumnysse and clypode hys naman and cwæð him ðus tō: "Nym ðīnne āncennedan sunu Īsaac, þe ðū lufast, and far tō þām lande 'Uisionis' hraðe, and geofra hyne þǣr uppan ānre dūne." Abraham

---

2849b **him stefne tō** *Stefne* is inst. and *tō* governs *him*: "to him with (his) voice." Cf. similar postpositions in 2851b (*mid*), 2869a (*mid*), 2912a (*tō*). Postposition always confers full stress.

2851b **ond** On the several occasions when this conjunction is written out in full by the scribe (*Genesis* 625b, 1195a, 1335a) it has the form *ond*. Consequently we have expanded the usual abbreviation ⁊ to *ond* (rather than *and*) in this selection and the selection from *Genesis B* which follows.

lǣde Probably a byform of the imperative sg. (see Campbell §752, last paragraph), though possibly a hortative subjunctive used in sequence with the preceding imperative (*Gewīt*) and equivalent to it in function (see Frank Behre, *The Subjunctive in Old English Poetry* [Göteborg 1934], p. 16).

2852b, 53b **Þū . . . sylf** "You yourself."

hrincg þæs hēan landes,   þe ic þē heonon getǣce,
ūp þīnum āgnum fōtum.   Þǣr þū scealt ād gegærwan,
bǣlfȳr bearne þīnum,   ond blōtan sylf
sunu mid sweordes ecge,   ond þonne sweartan līge
lēofes līc forbærnan   ond mē lāc bebēodan."
Ne forsæt hē þȳ sīðe,   ac sōna ongann
fȳsan tō fōre.   Him wæs Frēa engla
wordondrysne,   ond his waldende lēof.
Þā se ēadga   Abraham sīne
nihtreste ofgeaf.   Nalles Nergendes
hǣse wiðhogode,   ac hine se hālga wer
gyrde grǣgan sweorde,   cȳðde þæt him gāsta Weardes
egesa on brēostum wunode.   Ongan þā his esolas bǣtan,
gamolferhð goldes brytta,   heht hine geonge twēgen
men mid sīðian.   Mǣg wæs his āgen þridda,
ond hē fēorða sylf.   Þā hē fūs gewāt
from his āgenum hofe   Īsaac lǣdan,
bearn unweaxen,   swā him bebēad Metod.
Efste þā swīðe   ond ōnette
forð foldwege,   swā him Frēa tǣhte
wegas ofer wēsten,   oð þæt wuldortorht
dæges þriddan ūp   ofer dēop wæter
ord ārǣmde.   Þā se ēadega wer
geseah hlīfigan   hēa dūne,
swā him sægde ǣr   swegles Aldor.

---

asinum suum, ducens secum duos juvenes et Isaac, filium suum. Cumque concidisset ligna in holocaustum, abiit ad locum quem præceperat ei Deus. Die autem

---

ðā ārās on þǣre ylcan nihte and fērde mid twām cnapum tō þām fyrlenum lande, and Īsaac samod, on assum rīdende. Þā on ðone ðriddan dæg, þā hī ðā dūne

---

2856a **ūp** Adv. with *gestīgest* 2854a.

2861b f. **Him . . . lēof** The passage is usually emended and arranged as follows:

Him wæs Frēa*n* engla
word ondrysne,   ond his Waldend, lēof,

i.e. "(the) word of (the) Lord of angels was awesome to him, and his Ruler dear (to him)." But we prefer to let the MS stand. For the phrase *Frēa engla* cf. *Genesis A* 2837b. The compound *wordondrysne* "awesome of word" is not otherwise attested, but is comparable to *word-* compounds like *-fæst*, *-glēaw*, *-snotor*, *-wīs*. L. 2862b may be translated in three ways: (1) "and, (even when) governing him (in such a matter as this), beloved"; (2) "and (he was) dear to his Lord" (cf. *Genesis A* 2598b); (3) "and his Lord (was) dear (to him)"—in this case taking *Waldende* as nom. sg. and exemplifying the confusion which is common in OE with nom. sg. *Hǣlend(e)*.

2866b **him** Possessive dat. with *on brēostum* 2867a.

2867a **brēostum** Cf. 17/63b (n. on *hēafdum*).

2875b **wuldortorht** This modifies *ord* (2877a), of which *dæges þriddan* (2876a) is a gen. complement. *Dæges ord* = daybreak, dawn.

Ðā Abraham spræc tō his ombihtum:
"Rincas mīne, restað incit
hēr on þissum wīcum. Wit eft cumað,
siððan wit ǣrende uncer twēga
Gāstcyninge āgifen habbað."
Gewāt him þā se æðeling ond his āgen sunu
tō þæs gemearces þe him Metod tǣhte
wadan ofer wealdas. Wudu bær sunu,
fæder fȳr ond sweord. Ðā þæs fricgean ongann
wer wintrum geong wordum Abraham:
"Wit hēr fȳr ond sweord, frēa mīn, habbað;
hwǣr is þæt tīber, þæt þū torht Gode
tō þām brynegielde bringan þencest?"
Abraham maðelode (hæfde on ān gehogod,
þæt hē gedǣde swā hine Drihten hēt):
"Him þæt Sōðcyning sylfa findeð,
moncynnes Weard, swā him gemet þinceð."
Gestāh þā stīðhȳdig stēape dūne
ūp mid his eaforan, swā him se ēca bebēad,
þæt hē on hrōfe gestōd hēan landes,
on þǣre *stōwe* þe him se stranga tō,
wǣrfæst Metod, wordum tǣhte.

---

tertio, elevatis oculis, vidit locum procul: dixitque ad pueros suos: "Exspectate hic cum asino: ego et puer illuc usque properantes, postquam adoraverimus, revertemur ad vos." Tulit quoque ligna holocausti, et imposuit super Isaac filium suum: ipse vero portabat in manibus ignem et gladium. Cumque pergerent duo simul, dixit Isaac patri suo: "Pater mi!" At ille respondit: "Quid vis, fili?" "Ecce," inquit, "ignis et ligna: ubi est victima holocausti?" Dixit Abraham: "Deus providebit sibi victimam holocausti, fili mi." Pergebant ergo pariter: veneruntque ad locum quem ostenderat ei Deus, in quo ædificavit altare, et desuper

---

gesāwon, ðǣr ðǣr hī tō sceoldon tō ofslēane Īsaac, ðā cwæð Abraham tō þām cnapum ðus: "Anbidiað ēow hēr mid þām assum sume hwīle; ic and þæt cild gāð unc tō gebiddenne, and wē syððan cumað sōna eft tō ēow." Abraham þā hēt Īsaac beran þone wudu tō þǣre stōwe and hē sylf bær hys swurd and fȳr. Īsaac ðā āxode Abraham hys fæder: "Fæder mīn, ic āxige hwǣr sēo offrung sȳ? Hēr ys wuda and fȳr." Him andwyrde se fæder: "God forescēawað, mīn sunu, him sylf ðā offrunge." Hī cōmon þā tō ðǣre stōwe þe him geswutelode God, and hē

2882a **wīcum** The pl. of *wīc* is frequently used with sg. meaning.

2891 f. **hwǣr . . . þencest** I.e. *hwǣr is þæt torht tīber þæt þū þencest bringan Gode tō þām brynegielde?*

2893b **hæfde on ān gehogod** Either "had resolved on one thing" (BTS s.v. *ān* I.(1)(a)(ß)), or "had continuously intended" (ibid. XII), or "had determined at once" (ibid. s.v. *on* B.I.(4)) or even "had determined once and for all." See further GK s.v. *ān* 8.

2894a **gedǣde** On the form see Campbell ∫768.(b), last paragraph.

2895a **Him** Refl. (see BTS *findan* II.(2a)); *þæt* is the d.o.

2900a **stōwe** Not in the MS. But something is obviously needed, and this tradi-

Ongan þā ād hladan,   ǣled weccan,
ond gefeterode   fēt ond honda
bearne sīnum,   ond þā on bǣl āhōf
Īsaac geongne,   ond þā ǣdre gegrāp
sweord be gehiltum: wolde his sunu cwellan
folmum sīnum,   fȳre scencan
mǣges drēore.   Þā Metodes ðegn
ufan, engla sum,   "Abraham!" hlūde
stefne cȳgde.   Hē stille gebād
āres sprǣce   ond þām engle oncwæð.
Him þā ofstum tō,   ufan of roderum,
wuldorgāst Godes   wordum mǣlde:
"Abraham lēofa,   ne sleah þīn āgen bearn,
ac þū cwicne ābregd   cniht of āde,
eaforan þīnne!   Him an wuldres God!
Mago Ebrēa,   þū mēdum scealt
þurh þæs Halgan hand,   Heofoncyninges,
sōðum sigorlēanum   selfa onfōn,
ginfæstum gifum.   Þē wile gāsta Weard

---

ligna composuit: cumque colligasset Isaac filium suum, posuit eum in altare super struem lignorum. Extenditque manum, et arripuit gladium, ut immolaret filium suum. Et ecce angelus Domini de cœlo clamavit dicens: "Abraham! Abraham!" Qui respondit: "Adsum." Dixitque ei: "Non extendas manum tuam super puerum, neque facias illi quidquam: nunc cognovi quod timeas Deum, et non

---

ðǣr wēofod ārǣrde on ðā ealdan wīsan, and þone wudu gelōgode swā swā hē hyt wolde habban tō hys suna bærnette syððan hē ofslagen wurde. Hē geband þā hys sunu and hys swurd ātēah þæt hē hyne geoffrode on þā ealdan wīsan. Mid ðām ðe hē wolde þæt weorc begynnan, ðā clypode Godes engel ardlīce of heofonum: "Abraham!" Hē andwyrde sōn(a). Se engel him cwæð tō: "Ne ācwel ðū þæt cild, ne þīne hand ne āstrece ofer hys swuran: nū ic oncnēow

---

tional emendation is confirmed by alliteration, by the Latin source of this passage (*locum*), and by Ælfric's translation of it (*stōwe*).

2907b–8a **fȳre . . . drēore** "Give drink to (the) fire with (his) son's blood." *Scencan* is Bright's emendation of MS *sencan* (which could perhaps mean "submerge, flood," but which, along with its compounds, normally appears to govern the acc.).

2910b–11a **Hē . . . oncwæð** "Motionless, he heard (lit. experienced) the angel's salutation (lit. utterance)." Or *stille* could be an adv. Note that Abraham's reply, given in the Latin ("*Adsum*"), is not reported in either the OE poem or in Ælfric's paraphrase.

2916b **Him . . . God** This could mean either "God grants him glory" or "(the) God of glory is pleased with him," and probably means both, with *wuldres* functioning simultaneously in two constructions (a device known as apo koinou); cf. 5/76–8a and n.

2921b **lēofra** I.e. *lēofre*, nom. sg. fem. The form exemplifies the typical late confusion in the spelling of the vowels of weakly stressed syllables.

lissum gyldan   þæt þē wæs lēofra his
sibb ond hyldo   þonne þīn sylfes bearn."
  Ād stōd onǣled.   Hæfde Abrahame
Metod moncynnes,   mǣge Lōthes,
brēost geblissad,   þā hē him his bearn forgeaf,
Īsaac cwicne.   Ðā se ēadega bewlāt
rinc ofer exle,   ond him þǣr rom geseah
unfeor þanon   ǣnne standan,
brōðor Ārones,   brembrum fæstne.
Þone Abraham genam   ond hine on ād āhōf
ofestum miclum   for his āgen bearn.
Ābrægd þā mid þȳ bille,   brynegield onhrēad,
rēccendne wēg   rommes blōde,
onblēot þæt lāc Gode,   sægde lēana þanc
ond ealra þāra   þe hē him sīð ond ǣr
gifena Drihten   forgifen hæfde.

---

pepercisti unigenito filio tuo propter me." Levavit Abraham oculos suos, viditque post tergum arietem inter vepres hærentem cornibus suis, quem assumens obtulit holocaustum pro filio suo. Appellavitque nomen loci illius, "Dominus videt."

---

sōðlīce þæt ðū swȳðe ondrǣtst God, nū þū þīnne āncennedan sunu ofslēan woldest for him." Ðā beseah Abraham sōna under bæc and geseah ðǣr ǣnne ram betwux þām brēmelum be ðām hornum gehæft, and hē āhefde ðone ram tō ðǣre offrunge and hyne þǣr ofsnāð Gode tō lāce for hys sunu Īsaac. Hē hēt þā þā

2927b **him** Refl. with *gesēon* (see Farr p. 12, Voges p. 370).

2932b **onhrēad** "Adorned." But comparison with *Exodus* 413 f. and *The Meters of Boethius* 8/34 strongly suggests that we should read *onrēad* "reddened" (for the intrusive *h* see 12/85a n.). Or perhaps a grisly pun on these two words is intended both here and in *Beowulf* 1151b–2a (*Ðā wæs heal hroden / fēonda fēorum*).

2933a **rēccendne wēg** Undoubtedly "the smoking altar," even though this means (1) that we must take *rēccendne* as an error for *rēocendne* (confusion of *c* and *o* being quite common) or else as a very perverse spelling of it, and (2) that we must take *wēg* as an unexampled spelling of *wīh*—which in any event ought not to mean "altar" but "idol." The alternative, taking MS *reccendne weg* to mean "the guiding path," i.e. the path which had guided Abraham to this place and upon which he had erected the altar, is just too bizarre (even granting the slight support given by *Beowulf* 320b and *Andreas* 985b).

2935 f. **ond . . . hæfde** There is no alliteration in the first of these lines, but the lack could easily be remedied by reversing the order of *sīð* and *ǣr*: both word orders are frequently attested, and a scribe's unconscious substitution of one for the other is easily understandable. *Gifena* is probably dependent on *þanc* (either as variation of *ealra þāra* "all those (things)" [cf. 2/38, 20/50a], or as part of the unitary but awkwardly disjunct phrase *ealra þāra gifena*). It could also, however, be construed as the gen. complement of *Drihten* (i.e. "the God of gifts"), and in fact the suggestion of an apo koinou construction is probably deliberate, and the elaborate and involved structure of the last lines is intended to finish off the poem with a climactic flourish (reinforced at the very end by the echoing of *gifena* and *forgifen*,

Unde usque hodie dicitur: "In monte Dominus videbit." Vocavit autem angelus Domini Abraham secundo de cœlo, dicens: " 'Per memetipsum juravi,' dicit Dominus: 'quia fecisti rem hanc, et non pepercisti filio tuo unigenito: benedicam tibi, et multiplicabo semen tuum sicut stellas cœli, et velut arenam quæ est in littore maris: possidebit semen tuum portas inimicorum suorum, et benedicentur in semine tuo omnes gentes terræ, quia obedisti voci meæ.' " Reversus est Abraham ad pueros suos, abieruntque Bersabee simul, et habitavit ibi.

---

stōwe "Dominus uidit," þæt ys, "God ı gesyhð," and gȳt ys gesǣd swā: "In monte Dominus uidit," þæt ys, "God ı gesyhð on dūne." Eft clypode se engel Abraham and cwæð: " 'Ic swerige ðurh mē sylfne,' sǣde se Ælmihtiga, 'nū ðū noldest ārian þīnum āncennedan suna, ac ðē wæs mīn ege māre þonne hys līf: ic ðē nū bletsige and ðīnne ofspringc gemenigfylde swā swā steorran on heofonum and swā swā sandceosel on sǣ; þīn ofspringc sceal āgan heora fēonda gata, and on þīnum sǣde bēoð ealle ðēoda gebletsode, for þan ðe þū gehȳrsumodest mīnre hǣse ðus'." Abraham ðā gecyrde sōna tō hys cnapum and fērde him hām swā mid heofonlicre bletsunge.

---

a device known as *figura etymologica*). For the sentiment and syntax and rhetoric of the passage as a whole compare the following exhortation from Blickling Homily VIII: *On eallum tīdum secggan wē* [*Gode*] *þanc ealra his miltsa and his ēaðmōdnessa and his geofena þe hē ūs forgeaf.*

SATAN REBELS. Oxford, Bodleian Library, MS *Junius 11*, p. 14 (See p. 289 and cf. 16/246a–270b)

Note that the text is given metrical punctuation by dots, positioned slightly higher than the modern period, which divide it into units corresponding exactly to our typographical halflines. (One dot has been omitted by the scribe, after *ongan* in 1.20 of the MS.)

Note the large number of accent marks added over vowels. These "are not so systematically employed as the metrical marks, and indeed the purpose of them is often far from clear. They are not used consistently to mark long vowels, for short vowels frequently have accent marks, nor to mark the alliterating or metrically stressed syllables of the lines, nor to make emphatic logically or rhetorically important words in a passage. Apparently they were used for any of these purposes, when it struck the fancy of the scribe so to use them" (*ASPR*, I, xxiii).

Note finally that the elements of compounds are often written separately (e.g. *engel cynna* [1.1 of MS], *for geaf* [1.5], *gylp word* [1.22]) and that metrically insignificant words are often crammed together (e.g. *nemihte* [1.19], *nemeah|tehe* [1.23 f.]).

The first number represents the line of the MS page, the second that of the corresponding passage in the edited text which follows.

1 246a An elaborate capital *H* in zoomorphic ("animal form") style begins the page. The way in which the left margin of the first six lines of text is determined by the contours of this *H* shows that the illustrator drew his capital first, and then the scribe entered the text.

" " The unbroken form *alwalda* of poetic *koiné* has been normalized to strict WS *ealwalda* by addition of a superscript *e* and a subscript tag (the latter, exactly like the modern caret, indicating place of insertion). On the "correctors" and their normalizations, see p. 385.

2 248a Anglian *tene* has been normalized to WS *tyne* by placing a dot under e^1 (indicating that it should be omitted) and adding *y* above it (and slightly to the left, probably to avoid the accent mark). Note that this *y* is in a different hand from the superscript *y* in 1. 20 of the MS: since both of these *y*'s are normalizations which cannot be attributed to the original scribe, there must have been *two* "correctors" at work.

" " The *i* of *getrimede* has been altered to *y* by the addition of a diagonal stroke; according to Timmer, the change shows the purely orthographic "late WS. preference of *y* for *i* in the neighbourhood of *m*."

3 249a Note the usual abbreviation ꝥ = *þæt*.

5 250b *him* corrected to *heom*.

" 251a Note the usual abbreviation ⁊ = *and/ond*. See 15/2851b n.

10 255a MS *wæwtm* (the scribe's error for *wæstm*) results from dittography ("double writing"), the unintentional repetition of a recently used letter.

15 258b The horizontal stroke above *n* in MS *þon̄* is an abbreviation for *-ne*. Such abbreviations are usually expanded in modern printed texts (i.e. to *þonne* in this case).

16 " The scribe originally wrote *læte*, which later, by erasing the first loop of the graph *æ*, was corrected to *lete*, the normal 3 sg. pret. subj. of this verb. This erasure could equally well have been made by the original scribe or by one of the correctors.

16,17 259 Original *wende*, *hebban* altered to *awende*, *ahebban* by a corrector. Note that his added *a*'s lack the small horn (in the upper left-hand corner) which is characteristic of this letter in the script of the original scribe.

18 260a *waldend* normalized to *wealdend* (see above, second n. on 1. 1 of the MS).

" 260b MS *þā* is an abbreviation for *þam*.

19 261a Original *ure* (gen. pl. of the pers. pron.) is altered to *urum* (dat. sg. masc. of the possessive adj.) by underdotting the *e* and adding *v̄* (a contraction for *-um*) above.

20 261b Dots below *e* and *o* in *weorðan* indicate that they are to be replaced by *y*, which is written above in a late hand (see above, first n. on line 2 of the MS). This is a change from WS to LWS.

21 263a MS *herran* normalized to *hearran*. Timmer thinks the *herran* spelling is OS, but it is a common enough OE variant of *hearran*.

24 267a It would simplify matters to attribute the addition of (the obviously needed) *he* to the original scribe; but the *e* seems to be in the handwriting of the corrector of *waldend* in 1.18 of the MS, and not in the handwriting of the scribe.

16 / Satan in Hell
(From *Genesis B*)

As early as 1826 it was realized that ll. 235–851 of the OE poetical paraphrase of the first part of the Book of Genesis were radically unlike their context, and in 1875 the great German scholar Eduard Sievers argued from internal evidence that these lines (which he called *Genesis B* to distinguish them from the rest of the poem, or *Genesis A*) were a translation into OE from an Old Saxon original. This theory received astonishing confirmation in 1894 when K. Zangemeister, another German scholar, discovered in the Vatican Library three fragments of an OS poem on Genesis, one of which corresponded unequivocally to ll. 791–817a of the OE poem. It is now thought that the OS original was written c840 and the OE adaptation done c900. Sievers was of the opinion that the adaptor was an Anglo-Saxon, but Timmer thinks he was an Old Saxon, resident in England, who had only a shaky knowledge of OE, and that this explains why so many traces of OS origin remain in the poem as he left it. A number of OS words seem to have been imported into the OE version simply because they stood in alliterating position in the original and no legitimate OE synonym could be found that met the alliterative requirements. There are other OS borrowings, and OS influence on idiom, syntax and formula is frequent. The extraordinarily long halflines, the very heavy use of variation, the repetitiveness and the lack of color in figurative language are also a reflex of the poem's OS origin.

The present extract shows the poet's love of contrast, his psychological insight and dramatic power, as well as the familiar superficial Germanization of Christian narrative: Satan's followers are a *comitatus*, he is their treasure-giver, etc.

Fr. Klaeber's *The Later Genesis and Other Old English and Old Saxon Texts Relating to the Fall of Man* (Heidelberg 1913) is still valuable. The most recent published edition of the poem is B. J. Timmer's thorough (if often careless) *The Later Genesis* (Oxford 1948; 2nd ed. [with additions and corrections] 1954), but serious students will want to consult the excellent unpublished work of John Frederick Vickrey, Jr., "*Genesis B*: A New Analysis and Edition" (Indiana diss. 1960). Both of the latter works contain extensive bibliographies.

[VI]

Hæfde se Alwalda   engelcynna
þurh handmægen,   hālig Drihten,
tēne getrimede,   þǣm hē getruwode wel
þæt hīe his giongorscipe   fyligan wolden,
wyrcean his willan;   for þon hē him gewit forgeaf
ond mid his handum gesceōp,   hālig Drihten.
Gesett hæfde hē hīe swā gesǣliglice;   ǣnne hæfde hē swā swīðne geworhtne,
swā mihtigne on his mōdgeþōhte;   hē lēt hine swā micles wealdan,
hēhstne tō him on heofona rīce;   hæfde hē hine swā hwītne geworhtne;
swā wynlic wæs his wæstm on heofonum   þæt him cōm from weroda Drihtne;
gelīc wæs hē þām lēohtum steorrum.   Lof sceolde hē Drihtnes wyrcean,
dȳran sceolde hē his drēamas on heofonum,   ond sceolde his Drihtne þancian
þæs lēanes þe hē him on þām lēohte gescerede: þonne lǣte hē his hine lange wealdan.

[VI] In the division of the text into sections ("fits") and the restoration of the section numbers we have followed Gollancz (*The Cædmon Manuscript*, pp. xxx ff., cix f.).

246b **engelcynna** Gen. complement of *tēne* in 248a. According to Ælfric there were *nigon engla werod* which remained faithful to God, while *ðæt tēoðe werod ābrēað and āwende on yfel*.

248 sq. **tēne** etc. The first two words are no doubt acc. pl. neut., taking their gender from *-cynna*; but *þǣm* and the pronouns which follow are probably masc. pl. and have the *engel-* element of the compound as their antecedent; at any rate the last pronoun in the series (*hīe* 252a) *must* refer to "angels" in order for 252b to make any sense.

249b **fyligan** This word gives poor sense here and furthermore it does not alliterate. It probably represents a miscopying of *fulgangan*: the latter verb is stressed on the second syllable (thus alliterating), it is common in OS, and it occurs elsewhere in *Genesis B* (783a).

251a **ond** See 15/2851b n.

252a **swā** "Exceedingly, very"; an emphatic use of the adv. which continues in the following passage.

gesǣliglice Judging from the construction of the following lines, this is probably an adj. modifying *hīe* and not an adv.

253b **micles** Gen. object of *wealdan*.

254a **tō** "Next to, after."

255a **wæstm** Probably neuter here (as suggested by the gender of the following rel. pron. *þæt*), though elsewhere in *Genesis B* it is masc.

258a **lēanes** Vickrey emends to *lǣnes*, arguing that its meaning ("gift that may be recalled," more precisely here "fief") suits the context better than *lēan* ("reward").

258b **þonne . . . wealdan** "Then he would have let him possess it for a long time"; *his* is gen. object of *wealdan*.

Ac hē wende hit him tō wyrsan þinge,   ongan him winn ūphebban
wið þone hēhstan heofnes Waldend,   þe siteð on þām hālgan stōle.
Dēore wæs hē Drihtne ūre;   ne mihte him bedyrned weorðan
þæt his engyl ongan   ofermōd wesan,
āhōf hine wið his Herran,   sōhte hetespræ̅ce,
gylpword ongēan,   nolde Gode þēowian,
cwæð þæt his līc wæ̅re   lēoht ond scēne,
hwīt ond hīowbeorht.   Ne meahte hē æt his hige findan
þæt *hē* Gode wolde   geongerdōme,
Þēodne þēowian.   Þūhte him sylfum
þæt hē mægyn ond cræft   māran hæfde
þonne se hālga God   habban mihte
folcgestælna.   Feala worda gespæc
se engel ofermōdes: þōhte þurh his ānes cræft
hū hē him strenglicran   stōl geworhte,
hēahran on heofonum;   cwæð þæt hine his hige spēone
þæt hē west ond norð   wyrcean ongunne,
trymede getimbro;   cwæð him twēo þūhte
þæt hē Gode wolde   geongra weorð*an*.
"Hwæt sceal ic winnan?" cwæð hē.   "Nis mē wihtæ þearf
hearran tō habbanne.   Ic mæg mid handum swā fela
wundra gewyrcean.   Ic hæbbe geweald micel
tō gyrwanne   gōdlecran stōl,
hēarran on heofne.   Hwȳ sceal ic æfter his hyldo ðēowian,
būgan him swilces geongordōmes?   Ic mæg wesan God swā hē.

---

259 **him**[1,2] The first *him* is a dat. of interest ("for himself"); the second is refl. with *ongan* (cf. 17/65b, 67b n.).

264a **ongēan** I.e. *ongēan his Herran*.

267b **geongerdōme** Inst. dat., "in discipleship," "with allegiance."

269a–71a **mægyn ond cræft . . . folcgestælna** Probably "greater strength and power as regards allies" (gen. of respect), although "a greater troop and host of allies" would also be possible.

272a **ofermōdes** This noun as been interpreted as variation of *worda*, as a gen. complement of *worda*, and as an adv. gen. ("in his pride"). But it is easiest to take it simply as the gen. complement of *engel* and to regard the phrase *se engel ofermōdes* as a learned imitation of innumerable phrases in the Vulgate like *judex iniquitatis* ("the unjust judge") Luke 18:7 etc. See further Albert S. Cook, *The Christ of Cynewulf* (Boston 1909), p. 148 f.; see also 1. 328a and n. below.

272b sq. **þōhte** etc. With this passage compare Isaiah 14:12–16.

þurh his ānes cræft "By means of his own strength" (lit. "through the strength of him alone"). This adv. phrase is to be construed with the following *hū* clause rather than with *þōhte*.

275a **west ond norð** In 1. 667b, God is said to dwell *sūð ond ēast*. For the medieval cosmographical tradition which underlies these directions, see *Anglia*, 87 (1969), 303–11.

278a **cwæð hē** The use of this phrase as a tag is common in OS verse but rare in OE.

282a **hēarran** Mossé calls attention to the word-play on *hēahran* 274a, *hearran* 279a, *hēarran* here, and *hearran* 285b.

283a **būgan . . . geongordōmes** "Bow down to him in such servitude." Probably

Bigstandað mē strange genēatas,   þā ne willað mē æt þām strīðe geswīcan,
hæleþas heardmōde.   Hīe habbað mē tō hearran gecorene,
rōfe rincas;   mid swilcum mæg man rǣd geþencean,
fōn mid swilcum folcgesteallan.   Frȳnd synd hīe mīne georne,
holde on hyra hygesceaftum.   Ic mæg hyra hearra wesan,
rǣdan on þis rīce.   Swā mē þæt riht ne þinceð,
þæt ic ōleccan   āwiht þurfe
Gode æfter gōde ǣnegum.   Ne wille ic leng his geongra wurþan."
  Þā hit se Allwalda   eall gehȳrde,
þæt his engyl ongan   ofermēde micel
āhebban wið his Hearran   ond spræc hēalic word
dollīce wið Drihten sīnne,   sceolde hē þā dǣd ongyldan,
worc þæs gewinnes gedǣlan,   ond sceolde his wīte habban,
ealra morðra mǣst.   Swā dēð monna gehwilc
þe wið his Waldend   winnan ongynneð,
mid māne wið þone mǣran Drihten.   Þā wearð se Mihtiga gebolgen,
hēhsta heofones Waldend,   wearp hine of þan hēan stōle.
Hete hæfde hē æt his Hearran gewunnen,   hyldo hæfde his ferlorene;
gram wearð him se gōda on his mōde.   For þon hē sceolde grund gesēcean
heardes hellewītes,   þæs þe hē wann wið heofnes Waldend.
Ācwæð hine þā fram his hyldo   ond hine on helle wearp,
on þā dēopan dala,   þǣr hē tō dēofle wearð,
se fēond mid his gefērum eallum.   Fēollon þā ufon of heofnum
þurhlonge swā,   þrēo niht ond dagas,
þā englas of heofnum on helle,   ond hēo ealle forsceōp
Drihten tō dēoflum.   For þon hēo his dǣd ond word
noldon weorðian,   for þon hē hēo on wyrse lēoht
under eorðan neoðan,   ællmihtig God,
sette sigelēase   on þā sweartan helle.
Þǣr hæbbað hēo on ǣfyn   ungemet lange,

---

swilces geongordōmes is adv. gen., though Sweet[15] suggests that the OS original "may have had some such verb as *gehan* 'avow', which takes the genitive, in place of *būgan*."

285b **gecorene** I.e. *gecorenne* acc. sg. masc.; for the spelling see Campbell ʃ457, SB ʃ231.4.

287a **fōn** Probably parallel to *geþencean*, governing the same d.o., and with some such contextual sense as "execute." It could also, however, be intransitive (BTS s.v. II), "reach out, grasp, take control."

291b **wurþan** The use of this word rather than *wesan* or *bēon* reflects the preferred fashion of expressing futurity in OS.

295b **sceolde hē** The inverted word order strongly suggests that this is a main clause having zero correlation (i.e. omission of *þā* "then") with the dependent *Þā* "when" clause beginning in 292a.

296a **worc . . . gedǣlan** "(He must) receive pain as his share in return for that warfare," perhaps in ironic comparison with the loyal retainer who receives a share in positive rewards by fighting on his lord's behalf; cf. 301a.

301b **ferlorene** On the spelling see 5/43b and n.

307a **þurhlonge swā** "For a very long time in this fashion."

309 f. **For þon . . . for þon** Correlative.

ealra fēonda gehwilc, fȳr ednēowe;
þonne cymð on ūhtan ēasterne wind,
forst fyrnum cald: symble fȳr oððe gār,
sum heard ge*þwing* habban sceoldon.
Worhte man hit him tō wīte (hyra woruld wæs gehwyrfed),
forman sīð*e* fylde helle
mid þām andsacum. Hēoldon englas forð
heofonrīces hēhðe, þe ǣr Godes hyldo gelǣston.

[VII]

Lāgon þā ōðre fȳnd on þām fȳre, þe ǣr swā feala hæfdon
gewinnes wið heora Waldend. Wīte þoliað,
hātne heaðowelm helle tōmiddes,
brand ond brāde līgas, swilce ēac þā biteran rēcas,
þrosm ond þȳstro, for þon hīe þegnscipe

313a–6a It was a commonplace of medieval hell lore that the damned alternated between punishments of heat and cold, forever condemned

> To bathe in fiery floods, or to reside
> In thrilling region of thick ribbed ice,

as Claudio puts it in Shakespeare's *Measure for Measure*. The conception derives ultimately from Job 24:19 (*Ad nimium calorem transeat ab aquis nivium*, lit. "let him pass from the waters of snows into excessive heat") as interpreted by St. Jerome, *Commentarius in Librum Job*, *PL*, XXVI, col. 685.

316b **gār** The significance of this word is much disputed. Krapp suggests that it may be taken literally since prodding with spears is one of the traditional torments of hell (and moreover the association of fire with the torture implements of hell is not unusual: in Blickling Homily IV a dilatory priest is assigned *tō þǣre fȳrenan ēa and tō þǣm īsenan hōce*). Stylistically, however, one would like the opposed *fȳr* and *gār* pair to parallel the opposed *fȳr* and *wind/forst* pair of the last few lines. "Is *gār* meant for 'piercing cold'?" (Klaeber). Or could *gār* mean " 'icicle,' that is, 'a spear of ice'?" (Vickrey). Or could it mean "storm, tempest" (Malone)—presumably an icy storm like that in 19/101–5? It is not inconceivable, finally, that the poem originally read *īs* ("ice") here, which at some point in the transmission of the text became confused with *īsen* ("an instrument or weapon of iron"), from which the transition to *gār* would have been easy enough.

317a **geþwing** The MS form *gewrinc*, though possibly connected with the verb *wringan*, is unexampled in OE, anð Sisam's emendation *geþwing* is now generally accepted. The phrase *hard helleo gethuing*, which is very close to our halfline, occurs in the OS poem *Heliand* (2145a) and strongly supports the emendation.

318a **Worhte man hit** Equivalent to a passive construction; similarly [*man*] *fylde helle* in the next line.

321b **gelǣston** We begin a new section after this word. The numbering and capitalization in the MS show the new section beginning with *brand ond brāde līgas* in 325a, but Gollancz argues convincingly (p. xxx f.) that this is the result of an error on the part of the artist who illustrated the codex.

322a **þā ōðre fȳnd** Not "the other fiends," of course, but "the others, (the) fiends."

Godes forgȳmdon. Hīe hyra gāl beswāc,
engles oferhygd, noldon Alwaldan
word weorþian, hæfdon wīte micel,
wǣron þā befeallene fȳre tō botme
on þā hātan hell þurh hygelēaste
ond þurh ofermētto, sōhton ōþer land,
þæt wæs lēohtes lēas ond wæs līges full—
fȳres fǣr micel. Fȳnd ongēaton
þæt hīe hæfdon gewrixled wīta unrīm
þurh heora miclan mōd ond þurh miht Godes
ond þurh ofermētto ealra swīðost.
Þā spræc se ofermōda cyning þe ǣr wæs engla scȳnost,
hwītost on heofne ond his Hearran lēof,
Drihtne dȳre, oð hīe tō dole wurdon,
þæt him for gālscipe God sylfa wearð,
mihtig on mōde yrre, wearp hine on þæt morðer innan,
niðer on þæt nīobedd, ond sceōp him naman siððan,
cwæð se hēhsta hātan sceolde
Sātan siððan, hēt hine þǣre sweartan helle,
grundes gȳman, nalles wið God winnan.
Sātan maðelode, sorgiende spræc,
sē ðe helle forð healdan sceolde,
gīeman þæs grundes, wæs ǣr Godes engel,
hwīt on heofne, oð hine his hyge forspēon,
ond his ofermētto ealra swīðost,
þæt hē ne wolde wereda Drihtnes
word wurðian. Wēoll him oninnan
hyge ymb his heortan, hāt wæs him ūtan
wrāðlic wīte. Hē þā worde cwæð:

328a **engles oferhygd** On the assumption that OE usage does not "allow us to take the singular as generic, translating 'angelic arrogance' " (Sisam p. 30), this phrase is generally either emended or else interpreted as referring to the pride of Satan when he had been an angel (*RES*, V [1954], 55–8). But it is possible that this is another imitation of the learned idiom for which we have argued in 272a. And the fact that a phrase like *se āttres ord* (*Christ* 768a) or *āttres ord* (*Juliana* 471a) is interchangeable with *ǣtterne ord* (24/146a) is strong support for arguing that *engles oferhygd* can in fact mean *engellic oferhygd*. Cf. further 17/146b and n.

330b **fȳre** An OS construction; in OE the possessive dat. is normally found only with animate objects. Cf. 361b.

331a **hell** The acc. sg. without *-e* reflects OS usage.

333 It was a commonplace of hell lore that *ðæt hellice fȳr hæfþ unāsecgendlice hǣtan and nān lēoht* (Ælfric).

340b **hīe tō dole wurdon** "They turned to folly"? "They became too foolish"? (The antecedent of *hīe* is *engla* in 338b).

344a **cwæð** Sc. *þæt* (which has in fact been inserted into the MS at this point by one of its later correctors).

353b–4a **Wēoll . . . heortan** It is interesting to note that in the OS *Heliand* (= OE *Hǣlend*) there is a passage which corresponds word for word:

"Is þæs ænga styde   ungelīc swīðe
þām ōðrum   þe wē ǣr cūðon,
hēan *on* heofonrīce,   þe mē mīn Hearra onlāg.
Þēah wē hine for þām Alwaldan   āgan ne mōston,
rōmigan ūres rīces,   næfð hē þēah riht gedōn
þæt hē ūs hæfð befælled   fȳre tō botme,
helle þǣre hātan,   heofonrīce benumen;
hafað hit gemearcod   mid moncynne
tō gesettanne.   Þæt mē is sorga mǣst,
þæt Ādam sceal,   þe wæs of eorðan geworht,
mīnne stronglican   stōl behealdan,
wesan him on wynne,   ond wē þis wīte þolien,
hearm on þisse helle!   Wālā, āhte ic mīnra handa geweald
ond mōste āne tīd   ūte weorðan,
wesan āne winterstunde,   þonne ic mid þȳs werode—
ac licgað mē ymbe   īrenbenda,
rīdeð racentan sāl.   Ic eom rīces lēas;
habbað mē swā hearde   helle clommas
fæste befangen.   Hēr is fȳr micel

---

uuel imu aninnen
hugi um is herte.   (3687b–8a)

The comparison of OE and OS here brings out the close relationship of the two languages and shows how we have, in *Genesis B*, not so much a "translation" as an adaptation from one dialect to another, often maintaining precisely the same word order.

356a **ænga** Cramped quarters were one of the traditional features of hell, *ðæs ængestan ēðelrīces* (*Solomon and Saturn* 106).

357a **þām ōðrum** This verse is short a syllable. The putative OS original **thesero oðrun* would have been metrically adequate.

359a–60b **Þēah . . . þēah** Correlative.

359a **hine** The *styde* of 356a.

359b **mōston** Subjunctive; see 399b n.

364b sq. It was widely held during the Middle Ages that mankind had been created to fill the gap left by the fallen order of angels.

365a sq. **sceal** etc. QW ∫134 explain the construction as showing the parallel use of analytical subjunctive (*sceal behealdan*, *sceal wesan*) and inflected subjunctive (*þolien*).

367a **him** Reflexive with *wesan*. This usage probably reflects the OS original: it is rare (though not unattested) in OE.

369a–70a **ond . . . winterstunde** "And (if I) could get outside just once, stay (there) for just a winter's hour." The translation follows Vickrey (who interprets *āne tīd* as signifying uniqueness of opportunity) and Sweet[15] (which points out that since "the day was divided into twelve hours from sunrise to sunset, the length of an hour varied with the season").

370b **werode** There is nothing missing after this word: the poet is using the rhetorical figure of aposiopesis to convey Satan's sudden realization of the futility of his plans.

373a **hearde** This could be either an adj. modifying *clommas* or an adv. parallel to *fæste*. Cf. 24/33a and n.

ufan ond neoðone: ic ā ne geseah
lāðran landscipe. Līg ne āswāmað,
hāt ofer helle. Mē habbað hringa gespong,
slīðhearda sāl, sīðes āmyrred,
āfyrred mē mīn fēðe; fēt synt gebundene,
handa gehæfte; synt þissa heldora
wegas forworhte: swā ic mid wihte ne mæg
of þissum lioðobendum. Licgað mē ymbe
heardes īrenes hāte geslægene
grindlas grēate. Mid þȳ mē God hafað
gehæfted be þām healse, swā ic wāt hē mīnne hige cūðe;
ond þæt wiste ēac weroda Drihten,
þæt sceolde unc Ādam yfele gewurðan
ymb þæt heofonrīce, þǣr ic āhte mīnra handa geweald!

VII [I]

"Ac ðoliaþ wē nū þrēa on helle: þæt syndon þȳstro ond hǣto,
grimme, grundlēase. Hafað ūs God sylfa
forswāpen on þās sweartan mistas. Swā hē ūs ne mæg ǣnige synne gestǣlan,
þæt wē him on þām lande lāð gefremedon, hē hæfð ūs þēah þæs lēohtes bescyrede,
beworpen on ealra wīta mǣste. Ne magon wē þæs wrace gefremman—
gelēanian him mid lāðes wihte— þæt hē ūs hafað þæs lēohtes bescyrede.
Hē hæfð nū gemearcod ānne middangeard, þǣr hē hæfð mon geworhtne
æfter his onlīcnesse, mid þām hē wile eft gesettan
heofona rīce mid hlūttrum sāulum. Wē þæs sculon hycgan georne,
þæt wē on Ādame, gif wē ǣfre mægen,
ond on his eafrum swā some andan gebētan,
onwendan him þǣr willan sīnes, gif wē hit mægen wihte āþencan.
Ne gelȳfe ic mē nū þæs lēohtes furðor þæs þe hē him þenceð lange nīotan,
þæs ēades mid his engla cræfte. Ne magon wē þæt on aldre gewinnan,
þæt wē mihtiges Godes mōd onwǣcen. Uton oðwendan hit nū monna bearnum

---

377b **hringa gespong** Lit. "joinings of rings," probably a kenning for "chain."

384b **Mid þȳ** "Since," loosely correlative with *swā* ("therefore") in 385b.

387 **þæt . . . gewurðan** "That Adam and I should agree badly." *Gewurðan* is used impersonally with an acc. object; *unc Ādam* is literally "us two, (me and) Adam"—an elliptical pronominal construction which is common in ON with both dual and plural but is limited in OE usage to the dual.

388b **þǣr** "If."

391b **Swā** "Although" (correlative with *þēah* in 392b); this concessive use of *swā* is well attested (see Ericson p. 62 f.).

393b **þæs** "In return for that," correlative with *þæt* in 394b.

399b, 400a **gebētan, onwendan** Subjunctive; cf. *mōston* 359b. There are a number of pres. and pret. pl. subjunctives in this text with the late spellings *-on* or *-an* instead of historical *-en*. Cf. 405a *onwendon*.

400a **onwendan . . . sīnes** Both the meaning and syntax of *onwendan* are uncertain. Probably we should translate: "change (it) for the worse for them there with respect to their joy," though Mossé's interpretation also has a good deal to recommend it: "frustrate him (God) of his intention in this matter."

401 **mē . . . him** "For myself . . . for himself."

þæt heofonrīce, nū wē hit habban ne mōton, gedōn þæt hīe his hyldo forlǣten,
þæt hīe þæt onwendon þæt hē mid his worde bebēad: þonne weorð hē him wrāð on mōde,
āhwēt hīe from his hyldo; þonne sculon hīe þās helle sēcan
ond þās grimman grundas; þonne mōton wē hīe ūs tō giongrum habban,
fīra bearn on þissum fæstum clomme! Onginnað nū ymb þā fyrde þencean.
Gif ic ǣnegum þegne þēodenmādmas
geāra forgēafe, þenden wē on þan gōdan rīce
gesǣlige sǣton ond hæfdon ūre setla geweald,
þonne hē mē nā on lēofran tīd lēanum ne meahte
mīne gife gyldan, gif his gīen wolde
mīnra þegna hwilc geþafa wurðan,
þæt hē ūp heonon ūte mihte
cuman þurh þās clūstro, ond hæfde cræft mid him
þæt hē mid feðerhoman flēogan meahte,
windan on wolcne, þǣr geworht stondað
Ādam ond Ēue on eorðrīce
mid welan bewunden— ond wē synd āworpene hider
on þās dēopan dalo! Nū hīe Drihtne synt
wurðran micle ond mōton him þone welan āgan
þe wē on heofonrīce habban sceoldon,
rīce mid rihte; is se rǣd gescyred
monna cynne. Þæt mē is on mīnum mōde swā sār,
on mīnum hyge hrēoweð, þæt hīe heofonrīce
āgan tō aldre. Gif hit ēower ǣnig mæge
gewendan mid wihte þæt hīe word Godes,
lāre forlǣten, sōna hīe him þē lāðran bēoð.
Gif hīe brecað his gebodscipe, þonne hē him ābolgen wurðeþ;
siððan bið him se wela onwended ond wyrð him wīte gegarwod,
sum heard hearmscearu. Hycgað his ealle,
hū gē hī beswīcen! Siððan ic mē sēfte mæg
restan on þyssum racentum, gif him þæt rīce losað.
Sē þe þæt gelǣsteð, him bið lēan gearo

404a **nū** "Now that."

409a–21a **Gif ic . . . dalo** Satan's rhetorical powers are nowhere more evident than in this extremely elaborate periodic sentence.

412b **lēanum** Inst. dat., "by means of favors."

413b–5b **his . . . geþafa wurðan, þæt hē . . . mihte** "Assent to it (lit. be an assenter to it) that he might . . ."

416b **ond hæfde** "And (if he) had" etc.

418b **þǣr** "To (the place) where."
geworht Neut. pl., since Adam and Eve are of mixed gender.

422b **him** "For themselves."

426a **hrēoweð** Sc. *mē* as the object of this impersonal verb.

432b **Hycgað . . . ealle** "Give thought to it, all (of you) . . ."

433b **mē** Refl. acc. with *restan*.
sēfte A curious hybrid form: the usual positive of this adv. is *sōfte*, the comparative *sēft*.

435b–7b **lēan . . . þæs wē hērinne magon . . . fremena gewinnan** "A reward (consist-

æfter tō aldre   þæs wē hērinne magon
on þyssum fȳre forð   fremena gewinnan.
Sittan lǣte ic hine wið mē sylfne,   swā hwā swā þæt secgan cymeð
on þās hātan helle,   þæt hīe Heofoncyninges
unwurðlīce   wordum ond dǣdum
lāre"

---

ing) of that (portion) of benefits (which) we may achieve here." Satan's statement, though seriously intended, has the effect of irony, since there are few "benefits" to be attained in hell.

441a **lāre** Sc. *forlǣten* (as in 429a). After *lāre* four pages (i.e. two leaves) are missing from the MS. This lacuna probably contained more speechifying, at the end of which one of Satan's followers accepted the mission to earth. When the text resumes he is just getting ready to set out on the fateful expedition.

17 / The Dream of the Rood

The sublime paradoxes of the Crucifixion—the fact that it was at once triumph and tragedy, splendor and suffering, action and passion, *mysterium* and *supplicium*—have never been more concisely or effectively explored than in the first half of *The Dream of the Rood*. Here Christ's cross, originally fashioned as a shameful torment for criminals, becomes a spectacle gazed at by the whole creation, spanning the sky, streaming with blood one moment, gleaming with gold and precious stones the next. Yet this cross is more than a lustrously ambivalent cosmic emblem, as the second half of the poem goes on to show: it is the vehicle of each individual's personal salvation, for the way of the Christian lies *per crucem ad lucem*.

No single source has been discovered for *The Dream of the Rood* and it is unlike any other extant dream vision. The Crucifixion section is based ultimately on Matthew 27 (which the student would do well to read), though the poet has also drawn upon the passion gospels and apocalypses of the New Testament apocrypha, as well as the immense body of devotional and doctrinal literature which had grown up around the cross. Furthermore there are scattered echoes of the hymns and responses and liturgical offices of the Anglo-Saxon church. The second half of the poem, finally, shows considerable influence from the apocryphal story of the crucifixion of St. Andrew.

The poet's vision of the cross in the sky may owe something to the notion that such a phenomenon will indeed occur at the Day of Judgment when—as Blickling Homily VII puts it—*sēo rōd ūres Drihtnes bið ārǣred on þæt gewrixle þāra tungla*. Visions of a great cross in the sky are common enough in early Christian literature—prototypical is the cross which appeared to the emperor Constantine, bearing the legend *In hoc signo vinces*—though it is quite unusual to find these crosses speaking. On the other hand, prosopopoeia of this sort is common enough in the OE riddles of the Exeter Book (see p. 338 sq.), and their technique has often been adduced in explanation. It is also worth noting, when we assess the role of the native OE poetic tradition in this poem, that although its picture of Christ as an active, heroic warrior rather than a passive sufferer is widespread in the literature and iconography of the early period,[1] it blends particularly well in this poem with the Germanic conception of the hero and the language in which this conception was traditionally expressed.

The Dream of the Rood is one of six OE poems scattered in among the twenty-three homilies of the Vercelli Book, a MS from the second half of the tenth century, now Codex CXVII in the chapter library of the cathedral at Vercelli near Milan (Ker 394).[2] How the MS found its way to northern Italy is still a matter for speculation. A slightly different version of some of the lines of the poem is found carved in runes on the late seventh- or early eighth-century sandstone cross at Ruthwell [rɪvl], Dumfriesshire, and this suggests a very early date for at least part of the poem. A more distant echo is graven in silver on the Brussels Cross, a famous reliquary cross now preserved in the sacristy of the Cathedral of SS. Michel and Gudule in Brussels.

A. S. Cook's edition of the poem (Oxford 1905) contains excellent notes, introduction and glossary; the more recent edition of Bruce Dickins and Alan S. C. Ross (4th ed., London 1954; reprinted with further additions and corrections 1963) has an up-to-date bibliography and an especially full treatment of the Ruthwell and Brussels Crosses. For interpretation of the poem and important commentary on its literary, doctrinal and iconographical background, see especially Howard R. Patch, "Liturgical Influence in 'The Dream of the Rood'," *PMLA*, XXIV (1919), 233–57; Rosemary Woolf, "Doctrinal Influences on *The Dream of the Rood*," *MÆ*, XXVII (1958), 137–53; J. A. Burrow, "An Approach to the Dream of the Rood," *Neophilologus*, XXXXIII (1959), 123–33; John V. Fleming, " 'The Dream of the Rood' and Anglo-Saxon Monasticism," *Traditio*, XXII (1966), 43–72.

[1]The poet may be particularly indebted to a passage in St. Ambrose (*PL*, XV, col. 1830 ff.).

[2]There is a reduced facsimile edition by Massimiliano Foerster (i.e. Max Förster), *Il Codice Vercellese con Omelie e Poesie in Lingua Anglosassone* (Rome 1913), and a collotype facsimile (ed. Celia Sisam) is forthcoming in the *EEMSF* series.

Hwæt, ic swefna cyst secgan wylle,
h*w*æt mē gemǣtte tō midre nihte,
syðþan reordberend reste wunedon.
Þūhte mē þæt ic gesāwe syllicre trēow

3b **reste wunedon** The verb may be either intransitive with a dat. complement ("in bed") or transitive with an acc. object.

4b **syllicre trēow** In this "absolute" use of the comparative—for which cf. Latin usage and *Beowulf* 915a, 3038b—the comparison is implicit: "a more marvellous tree (than any other tree)."

on lyft lǣdan   lēohte bewunden,
bēama beorhtost.   Eall þæt bēacen wæs
begoten mid golde;   gimmas stōdon
fægere æt foldan scēatum,   swylce þǣr fīfe wǣron
uppe on þām eaxlgespanne.   Behēoldon þǣr engel Dryhtnes ealle,
fægere þurh forðgesceaft.   Ne wæs ðǣr hūru fracodes gealga,
ac hine þǣr behēoldon   hālige gāstas,
men ofer moldan   ond eall þēos mǣre gesceaft.
Syllic wæs se sigebēam,   ond ic synnum fāh,
forwunded mid wommum.   Geseah ic wuldres trēow
wǣdum geweorðod,   wynnum scīnan,
gegyred mid golde;   gimmas hæfdon
bewrigen, weorðlīce   Weald*end*es trēow.

5a **on lyft lǣdan** "Extend into the air" (cf. *The Phoenix* 178b, where all trees are characterized as *ūplǣdende*, "extending upwards").

8a **foldan scēatum** Probably "(the) surface of (the) earth," i.e. the ground at the foot of the cross; cf. 1. 37a and especially 43a. But Patch's suggestion—"the corners of the earth, to which the cross reaches as it spreads over the sky"—is also tempting.

9a **eaxlgespanne** The meaning is not certain. "Shoulder beam or shoulder joint, intersection" (Pope[2]); "the beam of a cross which passes behind the shoulders" (BTS).

9b **engel Dryhtnes ealle** MS *engel dryht* | *nes ealle*. A famous crux involving both grammar and meter. Attempts to solve it have been very instructive and fall into three categories:

(I) Retention of the reading in the MS, either (A) translating as "all (beheld) God's angel (i.e. either Christ [Krapp] or the cross itself, conceived of as a *nuntius* "messenger" [Bolton]) or (B) taking *engel* as a peculiar nom. pl. without inflection [Grein].

(II) Regularization of the grammar through (A) emendation of MS *engel* to either (1) *englas* nom. pl. [Cook] or (2) *engla* gen. pl. [Krapp], or (B) emendation of *engel drihtnes* to *engeldryhte* [Fowler].

(III) Regularization of both grammar and meter through (A) omission of *ealle* and either (1) emendation II.A.1 [Sievers] or (2) emendation of MS *engel dryhtnes* to *engeldryhte* "angel hosts" [Dickins-Ross], or (B) omission of *dryhtnes* and emendation II.A.1 [Mossé], or (C) emendation of the whole phrase to *engeldryhta feala* "many angel hosts" [Pope].

None of the suggestions of types I or II solves the metrical problems, and all of the emendations of type III do considerable violence to the MS reading, hence it is impossible to arbitrate among them.

10a **þurh forðgesceaft** Either "through the future" or "by virtue of eternal decree."

15a **wǣdum** Probably a metaphor for the gold casing and precious stones which adorn the cross (cf. 22a).

17b **Wealdendes** MS *wealdes*. Although *wealdes trēow*, "a (mere) tree of the forest," is difficult metrically, it makes excellent sense. Furthermore, if we were to take it as standing in deliberate opposition to *wuldres trēow* in 14b, then this contrast would embody a notion which occurs frequently in this poem (4b, 27b, and especially 90 f.), and elsewhere in literature connected with the cross: cf. Venantius Fortunatus' *Crux fidelis, inter omnes / Arbor una nobilis* ("Faithful cross, the one noble tree among the rest"). On the other hand, 25b supports the usual emendation.

Hwæðre ic þurh þæt gold   ongytan meahte
earmra ǣrgewin,   þæt hit ǣrest ongan
swǣtan on þā swīðran healfe.   Eall ic wæs mid sorgum gedrēfed,
forht ic wæs for þǣre fægran gesyhðe.   Geseah ic þæt fūse bēacen
wendan wǣdum ond blēom: hwīlum hit wæs mid wǣtan bestēmed,
beswyled mid swātes gange,   hwīlum mid since gegyrwed.
Hwæðre ic þǣr licgende   lange hwīle
behēold hrēowcearig   Hǣlendes trēow,
oð ðæt ic gehȳrde   þæt hit hlēoðrode;
ongan þā word sprecan   wudu sēlesta:
"Þæt wæs geāra iū—   ic þæt gȳta geman—
þæt ic wæs āhēawen   holtes on ende,
āstyred of stefne mīnum.   Genāman mē ðǣr strange fēondas,
geworhton him þǣr tō wǣfersȳne,   hēton mē heora wergas hebban.
Bǣron mē ðǣr beornas on eaxlum   oð ðæt hīe mē on beorg āsetton;
gefæstnodon mē þǣr fēondas genōge.   Geseah ic þā Frēan mancynnes
efstan elne mycle   þæt hē mē wolde on gestīgan.
Þǣr ic þā ne dorste   ofer Dryhtnes word
būgan oððe berstan,   þā ic bifian geseah
eorðan scēatas.   Ealle ic mihte
fēondas gefyllan,   hwæðre ic fæste stōd.
"Ongyrede hine þā geong Hæleð—   þæt wæs God ælmihtig—,
strang ond stīðmōd;   gestāh hē on gealgan hēanne,
mōdig on manigra gesyhðe,   þā hē wolde mancyn lȳsan.
Bifode ic þā mē se Beorn ymbclypte;   ne dorste ic hwæðre būgan tō eorðan,
feallan tō foldan scēatum,   ac ic sceolde fæste standan.

19a **earmra ǣrgewin** "The dreamer associates the blood not only with Christ but, typically, with the many wretches who have endured this form of punishment" (Pope[2]). In 31b and 87a–8a, too, the rood typefies all crosses, while still remaining uniquely the cross of Christ.

20a **swīðran healfe** According to early post-Biblical tradition, the wound given Christ by the centurion (John 19:34) was on his right side.

22a **wǣdum, blēom** Dat. of respect.

31a **geworhton . . . wǣfersȳne** "Made (me) there into a spectacle for themselves." This halfline probably refers to the fashioning of the felled tree into a cross, while the next halfline (with which compare the OE words *weargrōd* and *weargtrēow* "gallows, gibbet") explains semi-parenthetically just what sort of a *wǣfersȳn* the *fēondas* intended it to be. There is plainly some connection between this line and 10b f., where the gallows has turned into a *wǣfersȳn* that would have astonished its builders.

37b **mihte** "Could (have)."

39a **Ongyrede . . . Hæleð** Originally it was St. Andrew and not Christ who *exspolauit se et uestimenta sua tradidit carnificibus* ("stripped himself and gave his garments to the executioners"). This and the following quotations from the *Passio Sancti Andreae Apostoli* are cited (repunctuated) from the text and variants in M. Bonnet, *Acta Apostolorum Apocrypha,* II, I (Leipzig 1898), 1–37.

42a **ymbclypte** St. Andrew in his address to the cross says: *amator tuus semper fui et desideraui amplecti te* ("I have always been your lover and desired to embrace you").

Rōd wæs ic āræ̅red; āhōf ic rīcne Cyning,
heofona Hlāford; hyldan mē ne dorste.
Þurhdrifan hī mē mid deorcan næglum: on mē syndon þā dolg gesīene,
opene inwidhlemmas. Ne dorste ic hira ǣnigum sceððan.
Bysmeredon hīe unc būtū ætgædere. Eall ic wæs mid blōde bestēmed,
begoten of þæs Guman sīdan siððan hē hæfde his gāst onsended.
Feala ic on þām beorge gebiden hæbbe
wrāðra wyrda: geseah ic weruda God
þearle þenian. Þȳstro hæfdon
bewrigen mid wolcnum Wealdendes hrǣw,
scīrne scīman; sceadu forðēode,
wann under wolcnum. Wēop eal gesceaft,
cwīðdon Cyninges fyll: Crīst wæs on rōde.
"Hwæðere þǣr fūse feorran cwōman
tō þām Æðelinge: ic þæt eall behēold.
Sāre ic wæs mid *sorgum* gedrēfed, hnāg ic hwæðre þām secgum tō handa,
ēaðmōd, elne mycle. Genāmon hīe þǣr ælmihtigne God,
āhōfon hine of ðām hefian wīte. Forlēton mē þā hilderincas
standan stēame bedrifenne; eall ic wæs mid strǣlum forwundod.
Ālēdon hīe ðǣr limwērigne, gestōdon him æt his līces hēafdum;
behēoldon hīe ðǣr heofenes Dryhten, ond hē hine ðǣr hwīle reste,
mēðe æfter ðām miclan gewinne. Ongunnon him þā moldern wyrcan
beornas on banan gesyhðe, curfon hīe ðæt of beorhtan stāne,
gesetton hīe ðǣron sigora Wealdend; ongunnon him þā sorhlēoð galan,

---

48b–9b **Eall . . . onsended** Cf. John 19:33 f.

49a **begoten . . . sīde** "Covered (with blood) from that Man's side."

51a **wrāðra wyrda** Construe with *Feala* in 50 a.

52a **þenian** "A passive infinitive was usually expressed with the active form" (QW ∫131).

55b–6b **Wēop . . . rōde** According to a Greek version of the apocryphal Apocalypse of Paul, "when the Jews hanged the son of God upon the cross, all the angels and archangels, and the righteous and the whole creation of things in heaven, and things in earth, and things under the earth, lamented and mourned with a great lamentation" (*The Ante-Nicene Fathers* [see p. 204, n. 5], VIII, 580 f.).

56a **cwīðdon** Pl. because *gesceaft* is collective in force.

57a **fūse** Adj. used substantivally. These *fūse* were Joseph of Arimathea and Nicodemus, cf. John 19:38 f.

59a **sorgum** Not in the MS, but supplied on the basis of the text of this passage on the Ruthwell Cross.

62b **strǣlum** Cf. 46a.

63b **gestōdon him** "Took up their stand"; *him* is reflexive with *gestandan*.
hēafdum Cf. *brēostum* in 118a. These are pl. forms with sg. meaning (see Hermann Hirt, *Handbuch des Urgermanischen* [Heidelberg 1934], III, 13 f.).

64b–5a **ond hē . . . gewinne** "Following St. Ambrose on Luke, the poet has described the Crucifixion in the mood of an athletic contest, violent and incidentally exhausting" (Fleming).

65b, 67b **him** Probably reflexive with *onginnan*; cf. 16/259b (and also *Genesis A* 1880a, *The Descent into Hell* 1a).

66a **banan** The cross (as the agent of Christ's death).

earme on þā ǣfentīde. Þā hīe woldon eft sīðian
mēðe fram þām mǣran Þēodne; reste hē ðǣr mǣte weorode.
Hwæðere wē ðǣr *grēotende* gōde hwīle
stōdon on staðole, syððan *stefn* ūp gewāt
hilderinca. Hrǣw cōlode,
fæger feorgbold. Þā ūs man fyllan ongan
ealle tō eorðan; þæt wæs egeslic wyrd!
Bedealf ūs man on dēopan sēaþe; hwæðre mē þǣr Dryhtnes þegnas,
frēondas gefrūnon,
gyredon mē golde ond seolfre.
"Nū ðū miht gehȳran, hæleð mīn se lēofa,
þæt ic bealuwara weorc gebiden hæbbe,
sārra sorga. Is nū sǣl cumen
þæt mē weorðiað wīde ond sīde
menn ofer moldan ond eall þēos mǣre gesceaft,
gebiddaþ him tō þyssum bēacne. On mē Bearn Godes
þrōwode hwīle; for þan ic þrymfæst nū
hlīfige under heofenum, ond ic hǣlan mæg
ǣghwylcne ānra þāra þe him bið egesa tō mē.
Iū ic wæs geworden wīta heardost,
lēodum lāðost, ǣr þan ic him līfes weg

67b–8a **ongunnon . . . ǣfentīde** For the extended lamentations of Mary and Mary Magdalene at the tomb of Jesus, see the Greek version of the apocryphal Acts of Pilate (*The Ante-Nicene Fathers*, VIII, 431).

69b **mǣte weorode** In 124a, where this phrase varies *āna*, it is clearly litotes for "no one at all," and the meaning is presumably the same here.

70a **wē** The three crosses.

71b **stefn** Not in the MS; but the lack of alliteration shows that something is missing. *Stefn* is the likeliest emendation and picks up the idea of 67b.

75b sq. **hwæðre mē** etc. Alluding to the Invention (i.e. discovery) of the True Cross by St. Helena, the mother of Constantine the Great. Cynewulf's *Elene* is a treatment of this story.

76b A passage from Cynewulf's poem suggests the substance of the missing halfline: *āhōf*[*on*] *of foldgræfe* (*Elene* 843b–4a). But the loss here may well be more extensive than that of a single halfline.

78a **Nū ðū miht** etc. The homiletic second half of the poem, which begins here, is regarded as a later accretion by many scholars, who adduce its (supposed) artistic inferiority and its radically different tone and metric. The most recent critics, however, regard the poem as a unified work, whether or not it is by a single poet.

78b **hæleð . . . lēofa** Cf. 10/23.

79a–80a **þæt ic . . . sorga** "That I have experienced (the) work of dwellers in bale, (the pain) of sore sorrows." *Weorc* is used zeugmatically (i.e. in a different sense vis-à-vis each of its two genitive complements).

86 **ǣghwylcne . . . mē** "Everyone who feels awe towards me" (lit. "each of ones of those to whom is fear of me").

87a–9a **Iū ic . . . gerȳmde** Cf. St. Andrew's address to the cross: *Antequam te ascenderet Dominus, timorem terrenum habuisti, modo uero amorem caelestem obtinens pro uoto susciperis* ("Before the Lord ascended upon you, you had earthly terror [i.e. the terror of earthdwellers]; but now, since you have heavenly love, you will receive me according to my wish").

rihtne gerȳmde,   reordberendum.
Hwæt, mē þā geweorðode   wuldres Ealdor
ofer hol*t*wudu,   heofonrīces Weard,
swylce swā hē his mōdor ēac,   Mārian sylfe,
ælmihtig God   for ealle menn
geweorðode   ofer eall wīfa cynn.
  "Nū ic þē hāte,   hæleð mīn se lēofa,
þæt ðū þās gesyhðe   secge mannum:
onwrēoh wordum   þæt hit is wuldres bēam,
sē ðe ælmihtig God   on þrōwode
for mancynnes   manegum synnum
ond Ādomes   ealdgewyrhtum.
Dēað hē þǣr byrigde;   hwæðere eft Dryhten ārās
mid his miclan mihte   mannum tō helpe.
Hē ðā on heofenas āstāg.   Hider eft fundaþ
on þysne middangeard   mancynn sēcan
on dōmdæge   Dryhten sylfa,
ælmihtig God,   ond his englas mid,
þæt hē þonne wile dēman,   sē āh dōmes geweald,
ānra gehwylcum   swā hē him ǣrur hēr
on þyssum lǣnum   līfe geearnaþ.
Ne mæg þǣr ǣnig   unforht wesan
for þām worde   þe se Wealdend cwyð:
frīneð hē for þǣre mænige   hwǣr se man sīe,
sē ðe for Dryhtnes naman   dēaðes wolde
biteres onbyrigan,   swā hē ǣr on ðām bēame dyde.
Ac hīe þonne forhtiað   ond fēa þencaþ
hwæt hīe tō Crīste   cweðan onginnen.
Ne þearf ðǣr þonne ǣnig   *a*nforht wesan
þe him ǣr in brēostum bereð   bēacna sēlest,
ac ðurh ðā rōde sceal   rīce gesēcan
of eorðwege   ǣghwylc sāwl,
sēo þe mid Wealdende   wunian þenceð."
  Gebæd ic mē þā tō þan bēame   blīðe mōde,
elne mycle,   þǣr ic āna wæs

93b **for** "On behalf of, for the benefit of." Pope[2] explains: "In choosing Mary for his mother God honored her above all womankind, and he did this for the sake of all men, in that his ultimate purpose was their redemption."

94 **geweorðode . . . cynn** A reference to the Annunciation, cf. Luke 1:28.

108b–9b **ǣrur . . . geearnaþ** "Shall have earned." Just as *ǣr* (or *ǣror*) + pret. is often equivalent to a pluperfect, so here *ǣrur* + future is equivalent to a future perfect. Similarly *ǣr . . . bereð* in 118a.

115b–6b **ond fēa . . . onginnen** "And few will conceive what they should undertake to say to Christ."

117b **anforht** For MS *unforht*, which makes no sense.

119a–21b **ac ðurh . . . þenceð** Cf. Andrew's address to the cross: *O crux beata, sine amore tuo ad illam regionem nullus adtingit, nullus ingreditur* ("Oh blessed cross, without your love no one reaches that place, no one enters it").

mǣte werede.   Wæs mōdsefa
āfȳsed on forðwege,   feala ealra gebād
langunghwīla.   Is mē nū līfes hyht
þæt ic þone sigebēam   sēcan mōte
āna oftor   þonne ealle men,
well weorþian: mē is willa tō ðām
mycel on mōde,   ond mīn mundbyrd is
geriht tō þǣre rōde.
                    Nāh ic rīcra feala
frēonda on foldan,   ac hīe forð heonon
gewiton of worulde drēamum,   sōhton him wuldres Cyning,
lifiaþ nū on heofenum   mid Hēahfædere,
wuniaþ on wuldre,   ond ic wēne mē
daga gehwylce   hwænne mē Dryhtnes rōd,
þe ic hēr on eorðan   ǣr scēawode,
on þysson lǣnan   līfe gefetige
ond mē þonne gebringe   þǣr is blis mycel,
drēam on heofonum,   þǣr is Dryhtnes folc
geseted tō symle,   þǣr is singāl blis,
ond *mē* þonne āsette   þǣr ic syþþan mōt
wunian on wuldre,   well mid þām hālgum

124b–6a **Wæs mōdsefa . . . langunghwīla** Cf. Andrew's address: *O bona crux quae decorem et pulchritudinem de membris Domini suscepisti, diu desiderata, sollicite amata, sine intermissione quaesita et aliquando iam concupiscenti animo praeparata, accipe me ab hominibus et redde me magistro meo, ut per te me recipiat qui per te redemit me* ("Oh good cross, you who received grace and beauty from the limbs of the Lord; oh long desired, earnestly loved, sought without respite and now at last prepared for my yearning soul, take me away from men and restore me to my master, so that through you he may receive me who through you has redeemed me").

125b–6a Although taking *ealra* here in the rare adv. sense "in all, all told" (Dickens-Ross) would make the passage less awkward, it is almost certainly wrong to dissociate it from *langunghwīla*; cf. 19/63a.

136b **mē** Object of *gefetige* 138b.

138a–44a **on þysson . . . brūcan** This passage seems to reflect St. Andrew's words both substantially and stylistically: *Accipe me ab hominibus et redde me magistro meo. . . . Iam enim regem meum uideo, iam adoro, iam in conspectu eius consisto, ubi sunt angelorum cori ubique solus imperator regnat, ubi lux sine nocte est, ubi flores nunquam marcescunt, ubi dolor nunquam scitur nec nomen tristiciae auditum est, ubi leticia et exultatio finem non habent* ("Take me away from men and restore me to my master. . . . For already I see my king, already I worship him, already I stand in his sight, where there are choirs of angels and where he reigns as sole ruler, where there is light without night, where flowers never wither, where grief is never known nor the name of sorrow heard, where joy and exultation have no end").

142a **mē** The MS has *he*, which is of course possible syntactically. But it is not very attractive stylistically, and the argument from rhetoric, admittedly often dangerous, seems overpowering in this case: the rising climax embodied in the progression *mē . . . gefetige, mē . . . gebringe*, demands that *mē . . . āsette* be the last member.

drēames brūcan.   Sī mē Dryhten frēond,
sē ðe hēr on eorþan   ǣr þrōwode
on þām gealgtrēowe   for guman synnum:
hē ūs onlȳsde   ond ūs līf forgeaf,
heofonlicne hām.   Hiht wæs genīwad
mid blēdum ond mid blisse   þām þe þǣr bryne þolodan;
se Sunu wæs sigorfæst   on þām sīðfate,
mihtig ond spēdig,   þā hē mid manigeo cōm,
gāsta weorode,   on Godes rīce,
Anwealda ælmihtig,   englum tō blisse
ond eallum ðām hālgum   þām þe on heofonum ǣr
wunedon on wuldre,   þā heora Wealdend cwōm,
ælmihtig God,   þǣr his ēðel wæs.

144b **Sī . . . frēond** Cf. 131b–2a.

146b **for guman synnum** Cf. l. 99. *Guman* has been interpreted as generic sg. ("for man's sins") and as a LWS spelling for *gumena,* gen. pl.

148b sq. **Hiht wæs** etc. The poem concludes with a brief allusion to Christ's harrowing of hell, followed by a fuller account of his triumphal entry into heaven.

18 / neorxnawang: the earthly paradise

(From *The Phoenix*)

Among the donations of Leofric, Bishop of Cornwall and Devon (d. 1072), to Exeter Cathedral was *i mycel Englisc bōc be gehwilcum þingum on lēoðwīsan geworht*. This MS, today known as the Exeter Book (Ker 116), is still in the cathedral library. It is now thought to be a copy, made about 970–90, of a poetical miscellany originally compiled in the time of Ælfred or of his successors Eadweard and Æðelstan. An excellent facsimile edition is available in *The Exeter Book of Old English Poetry* (London 1933).

The first of the selections which we print from this MS, the radiant description of *neorxnawang* ("paradise") which follows, comprises the opening section of the 677-line OE poem *The Phoenix*. The first 380 lines of this work are a free adaptation of the *Carmen de Ave Phoenice*, a Latin poem generally ascribed to the Christian apologist L. Caecilius Firmianus Lactantius (c250–c340); the remaining 296 lines furnish a multi-level allegorical interpretation in which, quite traditionally, the immolation and rebirth of the phoenix symbolize the death and resurrection of man. Noteworthy in the following description of the phoenix's habitat are the poet's frequent use of the *nis . . . ac* construction, his fondness for rhyme and assonance, and his conception of paradise largely in terms of the absence of precisely those unpleasant aspects of life and nature whose presence is so heavily stressed in the three elegiac poems which follow. For purposes of comparison we have printed the relevant part of the Latin text beneath the OE.

The handy edition by N. F. Blake, *The Phoenix* (Manchester 1964), does not supersede the learned treatment of A. S. Cook in *The Old English Elene, Phœnix, and Physiologus* (New Haven 1919).

Hæbbe ic gefrugnen   þætte is feor heonan
ēastdǣlum on   æþelast londa,
fīrum gefrǣge.   Nis se foldan scēat
ofer middangeard   mongum gefēre
folcāgendra,   ac hē āfyrred is
þurh Meotudes meaht   mānfremmendum.
Wlitig is se wong eall,   wynnum geblissad
mid þām fægrestum   foldan stencum;
ǣnlic is þæt īglond,   æþele se Wyrhta,
mōdig, meahtum spēdig,   sē þā moldan gesette.
Ðǣr bið oft open   ēadgum tōgēanes,
onhliden hlēoþra wyn,   heofonrīces duru.
Þæt is wynsum wong,   wealdas grēne,
rūme under roderum.   Ne mæg þǣr rēn ne snāw,
ne forstes fnǣst,   ne fȳres blǣst,
ne hægles hryre,   ne hrīmes dryre,
ne sunnan hǣtu,   ne sincaldu,
ne wearm weder,   ne winterscūr
wihte gewyrdan,   ac se wong seomað
ēadig ond onsund.   Is þæt æþele lond
blōstmum geblōwen.   Beorgas þǣr ne muntas
stēape ne stondað,   ne stānclifu
hēah hlīfiað,   swā hēr mid ūs,
ne dene ne dalu   ne dūnscrafu,
hlǣwas ne hlincas,   ne þǣr hleonað oo
unsmēþes wiht,   ac se æþela feld
wrīdað under wolcnum   wynnum geblōwen.
Is þæt torhte lond   twelfum hērra,

Est locus in primo felix oriente remotus,
Qua patet aeterni maxima porta poli,
Nec tamen aestivos hiemisve propinquus ad ortus,
Sed qua sol verno fundit ab axe diem.
Illic planities tractus diffundit apertos,

1b **þætte is** "That (there) is. . . ."

5b–6b **ac . . . mānfremmendum** In Irish tradition the terrestrial paradise was a place *in quo nullis, nisi crimine mundis, patet introitus* ("into which an entry lies open to none but those free of crime"); see *Vitae Sanctorum Hiberniae*, ed. Carolus Plummer (Oxford 1910), II, 271.

9a **īglond** Here "land beyond the water; remote land."

12a **hleoþra wyn** "(The) delight of voices," i.e. the delight of hearing the angels singing.

22a **stēape** Adj. (and so too *hēah* 23a, *beorhte* 31b, *hēa* 32a and *grēne* 36a).

25b–6a **ne þǣr . . . wiht** "Nor does aught of unsmooth ever lie (or lean) there"; presumably this means "nor does any rugged ground lie outstretched (or jut out) there." This summarizes 21b–5a and leads directly into the contrast with *feld* (26b), a word which implies flat ground.

folde fæðmrīmes,   swā ūs gefreogum glēawe
wītgan þurh wīsdōm   on gewritum cȳþað,
þonne ǣnig þāra beorga   þe hēr beorhte mid ūs
hēa hlīfiað   under heofontunglum.
Smylte is se sigewong;   sunbearo līxeð,
wuduholt wynlic.   Wæstmas ne drēosað,
beorhte blēde,   ac þā bēamas ā
grēne stondað,   swā him God bibēad:
wintres ond sumeres   wudu bið gelīce
blēdum gehongen;   nǣfre brosniað
lēaf under lyfte,   ne him līg sceþeð
ǣfre tō ealdre,   ǣr þon edwenden
worulde geweorðe.   Swā iū wætres þrym
ealne middangeard,   mereflōd þeahte
eorþan ymbhwyrft,   þā se æþela wong
ǣghwæs onsund   wið ȳðfare
gehealden stōd   hrēora wǣga,
ēadig, unwemme,   þurh ēst Godes;
bīdeð swā geblōwen   oð bǣles cyme,
Dryhtnes dōmes,   þonne dēaðræced,
hæleþa heolstorcofan,   onhliden weorþað.
Nis þǣr on þām londe   lāðgenīðla,
ne wōp ne wracu,   wēatācen nān,
yldu ne yrmðu   ne se enga dēað,
ne līfes lyre,   ne lāþes cyme,
ne synn ne sacu   ne sārwracu,

Nec tumulus crescit nec cava vallis hiat;
Sed nostros montes, quorum iuga celsa putantur,
Per bis sex ulnas imminet ille locus.
Hic Solis nemus est et consitus arbore multa
Lucus, perpetuae frondis honore virens.
Cum Phaethonteis flagrasset ab ignibus axis,
Ille locus flammis inviolatus erat,
Et cum diluvium mersisset fluctibus orbem,
Deucalioneas exsuperavit aquas.
Non huc exsangues morbi, non aegra senectus,
Nec mors crudelis nec metus asper adest;
Nec scelus infandum nec opum vesana cupido
Cernitur aut ardens caedis amore furor;
Luctus acerbus abest et egestas obsita pannis

28b–9a **twelfum hērra . . . fæðmrīmes** "Twelve cubits higher" (lit. "higher by twelve of fathom-measure"); *folde* 29a is variation of *lond* 28a.

29b–30b **swā ūs . . . cȳþað** Word order: *swā wītgan, glēawe gefreogum, cȳþað ūs þurh wīsdōm on gewritum.*

37a **wintres ond sumeres** Adverbial gen.

41b **Swā** "When," correlative with *þā* 43b; a variant of the more usual *þā . . . þā* construction.

ne wǣdle gewin, ne welan onsȳn,
ne sorg ne slǣp ne swār leger,
ne wintergeweorp, ne wedra gebregd
hrēoh under heofonum; ne se hearda forst
caldum cylegicelum cnyseð ǣnigne.
Þǣr ne hægl ne hrīm hrēosað tō foldan,
ne windig wolcen, ne þǣr wæter fealleþ
lyfte gebysgad, ac þǣr lagustrēamas,
wundrum wrǣtlice wyllan onspringað
fægrum foldwylmum, foldan leccaþ,
wæter wynsumu of þæs wuda midle,
þā mōnþa gehwām of þǣre moldan tyrf
brimcald brecað, bearo ealne geondfarað
þrāgum þrymlīce: is þæt Þēodnes gebod
þætte twelf sīþum þæt tīrfæste
lond geondlāce laguflōda wynn.
Sindon þā bearwas blēdum gehongne,
wlitigum wæstmum; þǣr nō w*a*niað ō,
hālge under heofonum, holtes frætwe,
ne feallað þǣr on foldan fealwe blōstman,
wudubēama wlite, ac þǣr wrǣtlīce
on þām trēowum symle telgan gehladene,

Et curae insomnes et violenta fames.
Non ibi tempestas nec vis furit horrida venti
Nec gelido terram rore pruina tegit,
Nulla super campos tendit sua vellera nubes,
Nec cadit ex alto turbidus umor aquae.
Sed fons in medio est, quem "vivum" nomine dicunt,
Perspicuus, lenis, dulcibus uber aquis,
Qui semel erumpens per singula tempora mensum
Duodecies undis inrigat omne nemus.
Hic genus arboreum procero stipite surgens
Non lapsura solo mitia poma gerit.

41b–9b Note in this passage how familiar Christian themes have been substituted for Phaeton's fire and Deucalion's flood in the Latin.

60b **hrēosað** I.e. *hrēoseð* 3 sg., an example of late spelling confusion in the vowels of weakly stressed syllables (cf. Blake p. 6).

64a **foldwylmum** Usually emended to *flōdwylmum* since the word *foldwylmas* occurs nowhere else and *fold-* seems otiose here in the light of the following *foldan*. But *foldwylmas* is a perfectly transparent compound (cf. *Elene* 1132a), it is entirely apt as a description of *wyllan*, and furthermore it is precisely the fact that this *folde* is watered by *foldwylmum* which serves to contrast it with the natural world watered from the skies (cf. 60a– 62a).

68a **þrāgum þrymlīce** "At (appointed) times with a mighty current" (lit. "mightily").

69a **twelf sīþum** "Twelve times (a year)."

ofett ednīwe   in ealle tīd,
on þām græswonge   grēne stondaþ,
gehroden hyhtlīce   Hāliges meahtum,
beorhtast bearwa.   Nō gebrocen weorþeð
holt on hīwe,   þǣr se hālga stenc
wunaþ geond wynlond.   Þæt onwended ne bið
ǣfre tō ealdre,   ǣr þon endige
frōd fyrngeweorc   sē hit on frymþe gescōp.

75b–78b **ac þǣr . . . stondaþ** "But wondrously there on the trees ever laden boughs (and) fruit renewed throughout all time stand green in that grassy plain." In what follows, we can regard *beorhtast bearwa* (with its modifying participial phrase *gehroden hyhtlīce Hāliges meahtum*) as standing in apposition to (and summarizing) *telgan* and *ofett*. (Or else we can take 79a–80a as an absolute participial construction in the nominative: "since the brightest of groves is gaily adorned by the powers of the holy [one]").

19 / the wanderer

This poem, *The Seafarer* and *The Wife's Lament* are often referred to as "elegies" or "elegiac lyrics." All three support S. B. Greenfield's definition of the Old English elegy as "a relatively short reflective or dramatic poem embodying a contrasting pattern of loss and consolation, ostensibly based upon a specific personal experience or observation, and expressing an attitude towards that experience."[1] All three share an emphasis on isolation, lack of opportunity for communication and intense suffering. And they are all difficult: they have been interpreted and re-interpreted, punctuated this way and that; the only thing upon which scholars find themselves in agreement is that they are very complex and very moving.

According to Dorothy Whitelock, *The Wanderer* "poignantly describes the desolation of a lordless man and of a ruined city in order to contrast it with the security of trust in the eternal Lord."[2] One might go a step farther and still be on relatively safe ground: the evanescence of dreams on the one hand, and of the men of past times and their works on the other, are not only symbols of the progressive decay of the phenomenal world, but closely related symbols: *Sege hwār synd cyningas, hwār ealdras, hwār waldendras, hwār welige þinga, hwār mihtige worulde? Gewislīce swylce sceadu gewitan, swylce swefen fordwinan* (Bede). With these two symbols of mutability is contrasted the stability of God; the pattern is very reminiscent of Spenser's Mutability Cantos.

The cultural background of the poem has been intensively studied. In summary, "*The Wanderer* appears to contain a blend of traditional Germanic themes and images and themes derived from Boethius and the Christian Latin literature emanating from Irish writers, or writers influenced by the traditions, techniques and interests of Irish Christianity" (Leslie).

[1] In *Continuations and Beginnings: Studies in Old English Literature*, ed. Eric Gerald Stanley (London 1966), p. 143.

[2] *The Beginnings of English Society* (Harmondsworth 1952), p. 212.

It is not possible to decide with finality whether there are one or two speakers in the poem, nor where individual speeches begin and end, and there is no general agreement on these points. For the sake of simplicity we have assumed that "the wanderer" speaks everything except eight lines (1–7, 111) of authorial comment; furthermore that 92–96 are a speech within his speech. But this is theory only. Our paragraphing (like that of Dunning and Bliss) conforms to the use of small capitals in the MS, but it is well for the student to remember that the rhetorical structure of the poem is by no means self-evident and is far from being a matter of common agreement. While the student may adjust the quotation marks and paragraphing as his understanding of the poem prompts him, he should bear in mind the probability that arguments about the precise tailoring of these elegies to modern editorial conventions (and therefore preconceptions) are *īdel ond unnyt*, reminiscent of nothing so much as Procrustes' bed.

R. F. Leslie's edition, *The Wanderer* (Manchester 1965), contains a thorough treatment of most of the problems and has an excellent bibliography; the complementary edition of T. P. Dunning and A. J. Bliss, *The Wanderer* (London 1969), is particularly helpful on semantic and syntactic matters, as well as on larger questions of theme and structure. Serious students will also want to consult P. L. Henry, *The Early English and Celtic Lyric* (London 1966).

Oft him ānhaga   āre gebīdeð,
Metudes miltse,   þēah þe hē mōdcearig
geond lagulāde   longe sceolde
hrēran mid hondum   hrīmcealde sǣ,
wadan wræclāstas.   Wyrd bið ful ārǣd!
Swā cwæð eardstapa,   earfeþa gemyndig,
wrāþra wælsleahta,   winemǣga hryre:
"Oft ic sceolde āna   ūhtna gehwylce
mīne ceare cwīþan.   Nis nū cwicra nān
þe ic him mōdsefan   mīnne durre

1b **gebīdeð** Whether the word means "expects, awaits, seeks" or "experiences" is still a moot point (see *NM*, LXIX [1968], 172–75), though the distinction is crucial for our understanding of "the wanderer's" situation.

4a **hrēran mid hondum** A circumlocution for "to row."

6a **Swā** Both *The Wanderer* and *The Seafarer* exhibit the nonconjunctive use of *swā* and *for þon* which is characteristic of the homiletic rhetoric of the Blickling Homilies. In these homilies *swā* is often used to introduce quotations; cf. 9/7 n. and the examples in Ericson p. 9. We have followed this hint in punctuating the present passage, taking 1–5 as an authorial preface and 6 f. as introducing the quotation which follows.

7b **hryre** It is simplest to take this as acc. sg., the d.o. of *cwæð*, though it is also possible to regard it as a comitative dat. complement of *wælsleahta* ("battles accompanied by the fall of kinsmen").

10a **þe ic him** "To whom I. . . ."

sweotule āsecgan.   Ic tō sōþe wāt
þæt biþ in eorle   indryhten þēaw
þæt hē his ferðlocan   fæste binde,
healdne his hordcofan,   hycge swā hē wille.
"Ne mæg wērig mōd   wyrde wiðstondan,
ne se hrēo hyge   helpe gefremman:
for ðon dōmgeorne   drēorigne oft
in hyra brēostcofan   bindað fæste,
swā ic mōdsefan   mīnne sceolde—
oft earmcearig,   ēðle bidǣled,
frēomǣgum feor—   feterum sǣlan,
siþþan geāra iū   goldwine mīn*ne*
hrūsan heolstre biwrāh   ond ic hēan þonan
wōd wintercearig   ofer waþe*ma* gebind,
sōhte seledrēorig   sinces bryttan,
hwǣr ic feor oþþe nēah   findan meahte
þone þe in meoduhealle   mīn*ne* wisse,
oþþe mec frēondlēas*ne*   frēfran wolde,
wēman mid wynnum.   Wāt sē þe cunnað
hū slīþen bið   sorg tō gefēran
þām þe him lȳt hafað   lēofra geholena:
warað hine wræclāst,   nales wunden gold,

12a **þæt** I.e. *þæt þæt*.

14a **healdne** The usual emendation *healde* is satisfactory both contextually and stylistically, but the MS reading can be defended as a highly syncopated spelling of *healdenne*, past participle (for the syntax cf. 20/115a, for the word-order 24/240a).

14b **hycge . . . wille** "Let him think as he will," i.e. "whatever he may be thinking."

15a **wērig mōd** Sometimes printed as a compound, though taking it as two words gives better parallelism with 16a.

17a **dōmgeorne** Nom. pl. masc., used substantivally.

17b **drēorigne** Modifying *hyge*, understood from the previous line.

19 **mōdsefan mīnne** Object of *sceolde . . . sǣlan* (19b, 21b).

22a–3a **siþþan . . . biwrāh** The meaning at least is clear: his lord has died and been buried. The problem is to find a subject for *biwrāh*. The most tempting solution is to assume that *heolstor* can have a byform *heolstre*, nom. sg. (see BTS s.v.). Alternatively one can emend *heolstre* to *heolstor*, *hrūsan* to *hrūse*, or regard *ic* (19a) as being still in force. This last alternative is very doubtful.

24b **waþema gebind** (1) "The binding of the waves"—a kenning for ice? Cf. *Beowulf* 1133a. (2) "The collective mass of waves"—i.e. the ocean's surface?

27 **þone . . . mīnne** The idea of *sinces bryttan* remains in force with both: "that (treasure-giver) who in (his) meadhall might be familiar with my (treasure-giver)"—and who thus might be expected to feel receptively disposed towards me. Alternatively (and avoiding emendation of MS *mine*) one could read in 27b: *mīne* [sc. *þēod* fem.] *wisse*, "might be familiar with my (people)."

31 **lȳt . . . lēofra geholena** Litotes.

ferðloca frēorig, nalæs foldan blǣd;
gemon hē selesecgas ond sincþege,
hū hine on geoguðe his goldwine
wenede tō wiste. Wyn eal gedrēas.
For þon wāt sē þe sceal his winedryhtnes
lēofes lārcwidum longe forþolian,
"ðonne sorg ond slǣp somod ætgædre
earmne ānhogan oft gebindað,
þinceð him on mōde þæt hē his mondryhten
clyppe ond cysse ond on cnēo lecge
honda ond hēafod, swā hē hwīlum ǣr
in geārdagum giefstōlas brēac.
"Đonne onwæcneð eft wineléas guma,
gesihð him biforan fealwe wēgas,
baþian brimfuglas, brǣdan feþra,
hrēosan hrīm ond snāw, hagle gemenged.
Þonne bēoð þȳ hefigran heortan benne,
sāre æfter swǣsne: sorg bið genīwad
þonne māga gemynd mōd geondhweorfeð,
grēteð glīwstafum, georne geondscēawað.
Secga geseldan swimmað oft onweg,
flēotendra ferð nō þǣr fela bringeð
cūðra cwidegiedda. Cearo bið genīwad
þām þe sendan sceal swīþe geneahhe

34–57 It has recently been suggested that this moving evocation of the wanderer's haunted memories, dreams and fantasies is under heavy debt to a passage in St. Ambrose' *Hexaemeron* (*PL*, XIV, col. 275); see further Peter Clemoes, "*Mens absentia cogitans* in *The Seafarer* and *The Wanderer*," in *Medieval Literature and Civilization: Studies in Memory of G. N. Garmonsway*, ed. D. A. Pearsall and R. A. Waldron (London 1969), pp. 62–77.

37a–41a **wāt sē . . . ðonne . . . þinceð him** "He knows . . , (that) when . . , it seems to him." The syntax of this passage has caused much discussion, but this solution of Leslie's seems to take care of most of the problems.

42b–3a **ond on cnēo . . . hēafod** An ancient gesture of submission and homage; see *Íf*, II, 179 and n.

43b **swā** "Just as (when)."

44b **giefstōlas** For the late gen. sg. in *-as*, see SB ∫237 Anm. 1.

47b **brǣdan feþra** Either "preening their feathers" or "spreading their wings."

49a–55a **Þonne bēoð . . . cwidegiedda** A very perplexing passage which has been interpreted and punctuated in a number of ways. Students will find a convenient summary of the problem and the many solutions in Leslie's notes to these lines.

50a **sāre æfter swǣsne** "Painful (from longing) for the beloved (one)."

51a **gemynd** This is the d.o. of the three verbs which follow, *mōd* being the subject.

53a **Secga geseldan** This is best taken as a further reference to the *brimfuglas* of 47a. On their ironic role as "men's companions," cf. 20/19b–22b.

53b **oft** Frequently emended to *eft*.

54a **flēotendra ferð** "The minds (lit. mind) of the floating ones"—another allusion to the birds.

ofer waþema gebind   wērigne sefan.
"For þon ic geþencan ne mæg   geond þās woruld
for hwan mōdsefa,   mīn ne gesweorce,
þonne ic eorla līf   eal geondþence,
hū hī fǣrlīce   flet ofgēafon,
mōdge maguþegnas,   swā þes middangeard
ealra dōgra gehwām   drēoseð ond fealleþ.
For þon ne mæg wearþan wīs   wer, ǣr hē āge
wintra dǣl in woruldrīce.   Wita sceal geþyldig:
"ne sceal nō tō hātheort,   ne tō hrædwyrde,
ne tō wāc wiga,   ne tō wanhȳdig,
ne tō forht, ne tō fægen,   ne tō feohgīfre,
ne nǣfre gielpes tō georn   ǣr hē geare cunne:
beorn sceal gebīdan,   þonne hē bēot spriceð,
oþ þæt collenferð   cunne gearwe
hwider hreþra gehygd   hweorfan wille.
"Ongietan sceal glēaw hæle   hū gǣstlic bið
þonne eal*re* þisse worulde wela   wēste standeð,
swā nū missenlīce   geond þisne middangeard
winde biwāune   weallas standaþ,
hrīme bihrorene,   hryðge þā ederas.
Wōriað þā wīnsalo,   waldend licgað
drēame bidrorene;   duguþ eal gecrong,
wlonc bī wealle: sume wīg fornōm,
ferede in forðwege;   sumne fugel oþbær
ofer hēanne holm;   sumne se hāra wulf

58b **þās woruld** As opposed to the eternal world of God. Note that *þās* alliterates and is heavily stressed.

59a **for hwan** "Why."

61b **flet ofgēafon** I.e. "died."

65b **Wita** etc. A gnomic passage begins here. Ellipsis of *bēon* or *wesan* after *sceal* is a characteristic feature of gnomic style; cf. Selection 25.

66a–72b It has recently been urged (*NM*, XLIX [1968], 191–98) that the poet, far from counseling moderation in the qualities listed here, is suggesting—through understatement—that they should be avoided altogether.

67a **wiga** MW and Pope[2] suggest *wīga*, gen. (pl.) of reference: "in war." Stylistically this is perhaps superior: it makes the polysyndetic sequence (*ne* . . . *ne* . . . *ne* etc.) wholly adjectival and it is supported by the syntax of 69a.

69 **gielpes . . . cunne** "Too eager for vaunting (i.e. making heroic pledges), before he really knows" the whole situation and what his vaunt will entail. A man was expected to fulfill any vow he had made, even an irresponsible one uttered while he was drunk.

72a **hreþra** Cf. 17/63b (n. on *hēafdum*).

73b **bið** "(It) will be."

76a **winde biwāune** "Windswept, wind-beaten."

80b **sume** As the text stands it is best to take this as collective and the following three *sumne*-clauses as distributive, spelling out the various ways in which the bodies of those who fell in battle *bī wealle* were disposed of.

81b **fugel** "An actual bird would of course remove a body piecemeal" (Leslie). The bird is probably the Gray Sea Eagle; see 5/63a n.

dēaðe gedǣlde;   sumne drēorighlēor
in eorðscræfe   eorl gehȳdde.
Ȳþde swā þisne eardgeard   ælda Scyppend
oþ þæt burgwara   breahtma lēase
eald enta geweorc   īdlu stōdon.
"Sē þonne þisne wealsteal   wīse geþōhte
ond þis deorce līf   dēope geondþenceð,
frōd in ferðe,   feor oft gemon
wælsleahta worn   ond þās word ācwið:
'Hwǣr cwōm mearg? Hwǣr cwōm mago?   Hwǣr cwōm māþþumgyfa?
Hwǣr cwōm symbla gesetu?   Hwǣr sindon seledrēamas?
Ēalā beorht būne!   Ēalā byrnwiga!
Ēala þēodnes þrym!   Hū sēo þrāg gewāt,
genāp under nihthelm,   swā hēo nō wǣre!'
"Stondeð nū on lāste   lēofre duguþe
weal wundrum hēah,   wyrmlīcum fāh.
Eorlas fornōman   asca þrȳþe,
wǣpen wælgīfru,   wyrd sēo mǣre—
ond þās stānhleoþu   stormas cnyssað;
hrīð hrēosende   hrūs*an* bindeð,
wintres wōma,   þonne won cymeð,
nīpeð nihtscūa,   norþan onsendeð

83b **drēorighlēor** Construe with *eorl.*

86 **burgwara breahtma lēase** "Deprived of the noises of (their) inhabitants." Or this might be asyndetic parataxis: "deprived of citizens, of noises." *Lēase* qualifies *geweorc.*

87a **enta geweorc** Cf. 25/1b–3a and n.

88a **Sē** "He (who)."

88b **wīse geþōhte** Usually taken to mean "(has) wisely pondered," but "with a wise mind" (instrumental) is just as likely and does not raise the troublesome issue of a change of tense (*geþōhte . . . geondþenceð*).

92a **Hwǣr cwōm** "What has become of" (cf. 9/79 f. and BTS *cuman* II, *hwǣr* I.(2)). The passage which begins here is an imitation in OE of the *ubi sunt* sequences frequent in Latin homiletic literature.

93a **cwōm . . . gesetu** Probably analogy with the preceding phrases is responsible for the lack of agreement between subject and verb, though such a construction "is not infrequently found in Old English poetry, especially when the predicate precedes the subject" (Leslie).

96b **swā** "As (if)."

98b **wyrmlīcum fāh** "Decorated with serpent(ine) forms." It has recently been suggested (*Speculum*, XLV [1970], 287) that this phrase is nothing more than a close rendering of the Latin term *vermiculatus* ("inlaid so as to resemble the tracks of worms, vermiculated").

99a–107b **Eorlas . . . heofonum** The punctuation of this passage is very uncertain.

99b **asca þrȳþe** "Hosts of spears" (BT).

103b **won** Usually taken as an adj. with *nihtscūa*, though this raises syntactic difficulties. Dunning and Bliss take it as an adj. used substantivally: "the dark one" (i.e. night). Perhaps it is the rare noun *wan/won* ("want, lack, dearth").

hrēo hæglfare   hæleþum on andan.
  "Eall is earfoðlic   eorþan rīce;
onwendeð wyrda gesceaft   weoruld under heofonum.
Hēr bið feoh lǣne,   hēr bið frēond lǣne,
hēr bið mon lǣne,   hēr bið mǣg lǣne:
eal þis eorþan gesteal   īdel weorþeð!"
Swā cwæð snottor on mōde,   gesæt him sundor æt rūne:
"Til biþ sē þe his trēowe gehealdeþ,   ne sceal nǣfre his torn tō rycene
beorn of his brēostum ācȳþan,   nemþe hē ǣr þā bōte cunne,
eorl mid elne gefremman.   Wel bið þām þe him āre sēceð,
frōfre tō Fæder on heofonum,   þǣr ūs eal sēo fæstnung stondeð."

104a–5a **nīpeð . . . hæglfare** In his *Vita Beatorum Abbatum* (II.xiv), Bede quotes an unidentified Latin verse which seems very close to this: *Nox ruit hibernis algida flatibus* ("Night falls, cold with wintry blasts"). It occurs in a passage contrasting the night of human life with the day of eternity.

105b **hæleþum on andan** "As a vexation for men."

106a **Eall** This could be the subject (in which case *eorþan rīce* = "in the kingdom of earth") or *rīce* could be the subject, with *Eall* either an adj. or an adv.

107a **wyrda gesceaft** "The ordained course of events."

108a–10b Extraordinarily close in language and sentiment are some lines at the end of the *Hákonarmál*, a poem written by the court poet Eyvindr skáldaspillir to commemorate the death (c966) of the Norwegian king Hákon the Good:

Deyr fé,
deyia frændr,
eyðisk land ok láð

("Cattle die, friends and relatives die, land and sea are laid waste").

109b **mǣg** "Kinsman." Pope[2] would read *mæg*, "maiden, woman," but see Campbell p. 260 n. 1.

111a **Swā cwæð . . . mōde** With regard to the wise man's thoughts throughout this poem, cf. 25/54b–5a. With *Swā* begins a new paragraph and a series of hypermetric lines.

111b **gesæt . . . rūne** Cf. Eadwine's behavior in the passage cited on p. 110.

112b **torn** Object of *ācȳþan*. The subject of *sceal* is *beorn* in 113a.

113b **þā bōte** Object of *gefremman* (which is itself dependent on *cunne*).

114b **Wel bið þām þe** "(It) will turn out well for the one who" etc.

115b **ūs** "For us."

20 / the seafarer

Though the pages in the Exeter Book which contain this poem are undamaged, it is evident that the text has suffered much corruption at some point in its transmission. This fact, coupled with its idiosyncratic and sometimes clumsy syntax, makes it one of the most difficult of OE poems.

Earlier criticism regarded everything after 1.64a as a Christian addition and considered the "genuine" part of the poem to be either a dialogue between an old sailor and a young one (Rieger) or else a dialogue in the mind of one man (Lawrence). Recent and more organic interpretation regards the seafaring imagery of 1–33a as an allegorical representation of the hardships of human life; 33b–64a as voicing the speaker's desire to set forth on another and different voyage, the voyage to eternity; and the rest of the poem as homiletic development of traditional themes of *contemptus mundi* (Anderson). Another theory argues that "the seafarer" is a *peregrinus* like those described in 4/118 sq., i.e. a pilgrim-hermit who seeks salvation by submitting himself to the trials and loneliness of self-imposed exile from kin and country (Whitelock). A complementary, allegorical interpretation takes the poem to exemplify the patristic notion that the true Christian is a *peregrinus* on earth and must voyage through life and death to the *elþēodigra eard*, the real homeland of such strangers, heaven (Smithers). As Blickling Homily II puts it:

> Wē synd on þisse worlde ælþēodige, and swā wǣron siþþon se ǣresta ealdor þisses menniscan cynnes Godes bebodu ābræc; and for þon gylte wē wǣron on þysne wræcsīþ sende, and nū eft sceolon ōþerne ēþel sēcan, swā wīte, swā wuldor, swā wē nū geearnian willaþ.

Recently, however, it has been suggested that the strictly allegorical interpretations are too confining and that the poem is rather "an imaginative evocation of physical and emotional experiences that are used to illuminate a symbolic spiritual truth" (Gordon).

Date and provenance are uncertain; various considerations, including similarity to Welsh elegy, suggest that "we have in the West Midland region of the mid-tenth century, and possibly a little earlier, an environment, both poetic and homiletic, in which *The Seafarer* might well have had its origin" (Gordon).

Mrs. I. L. Gordon's edition, *The Seafarer* (London 1960), contains an excellent introduction and a full bibliography. There is a helpful translation of the poem by W. S. Mackie, EETS, Original Series, 194 (1934 [for 1933]), and a curious imitation by Ezra Pound.

Mæg ic be mē sylfum　　sōðgied wrecan,
sīþas secgan,　　hū ic geswincdagum
earfoðhwīle　　oft þrōwade,
bitre brēostceare　　gebiden hæbbe,
gecunnad in cēole　　cearselda fela,
atol ȳþa gewealc.　　Þǣr mec oft bigeat
nearo nihtwaco　　æt nacan stefnan,
þonne hē be clifum cnossað.　　Calde geþrungen
wǣron mīne fēt,　　forste gebunden
caldum clommum,　　þǣr þā ceare seofedun
hāt ymb heortan;　　hungor innan slāt
merewērges mōd.　　Þæt se mon ne wāt,
þe him on foldan　　fægrost limpeð,
hū ic earmcearig　　īscealdne sǣ
winter wunade　　wræccan lāstum,
winemǣgum bidroren,
bihongen hrīmgicelum;　　hægl scūrum flēag.
Þǣr ic ne gehȳrde　　būtan hlimman sǣ,
īscaldne wǣg.　　Hwīlum ylfete song
dyde ic mē tō gomene,　　ganetes hlēoþor
ond huilpan swēg　　fore hleahtor wera,

2b　**geswincdagum**　Temporal dat.

8a　**be clifum cnossað**　"Dashes (or beats) along (beneath) the cliffs." *Be* cannot mean "against."

11a　**hāt**　I.e. *hāte*, with elision (and scribal omission) of final *e* before a following vowel. The word could be either a (nom. pl. fem.) adj. modifying *ceare* or an adv. With 11. 8b–12a cf. 16/353b–5a.

12b　**Þæt**　Object of *wāt*; it anticipates the *hū*-clause (14a sq.).

13　**þe . . . limpeð**　Lit. "to whom on land most fairly (it) happens," more freely "whom it befalls in fairest manner on land" (Gordon). Or *on foldan* could mean "on earth."

14b–15a　**sǣ . . . wunade**　*Sǣ* is d.o. of (transitive) *wunian*; *winter* is temporal acc.: "during the winter."

15b　**wræccan lāstum**　"In the paths of exile," lit. "in the tracks of an exile." Pope[2] finds this halfline contextually inappropriate and suggests throwing it out "as a stock phrase that has been carelessly added." The present 1. 16 would then become 15b, thus regularizing the meter.

18　**ic ne gehȳrde būtan**　"I heard nothing but."

20a　**dyde . . . gomene**　"I took for my entertainment."

mǣw singende   fore medodrince.
Stormas þǣr stānclifu bēotan;   þǣr him stearn oncwæð,
īsigfeþera;   ful oft þæt earn bigeal,
ūrigfeþra;   n*e* ǣnig hlēomǣga
fēasceaftig ferð   frē*f*ran meahte.
For þon him gelȳfeð lȳt,   sē þe āh līfes wyn
gebiden in burgum,   bealosīþa hwōn,
wlonc ond wīngāl,   hū ic wērig oft
in brimlāde   bīdan sceolde.
Nāp nihtscūa;   norþan snīwde;
hrīm hrūsan bond;   hægl fēol on eorþan,
corna caldast.   For þon cnyssað nū
heortan geþōhtas   þæt ic hēan strēamas,
sealtȳþa gelāc   sylf cunnige:
monað mōdes lust   mǣla gehwylce
ferð tō fēran,   þæt ic feor heonan
elþēodigra   eard gesēce.

---

21 f. **fore**[1,2] This preposition governs first an acc. (*hleahtor*) and then a dat. (*medodrince*). Examples of mixed rection are not uncommon in OE verse and prose, and the device sometimes seems to have been used deliberately in order to achieve a stylistic effect.

23b **him** I.e. the storms.

24b Generally interpreted as acc. sg. neut., object of *bigeal* (transitive). But what does it refer to? *Stormas* and *stearn* are masc. and the *stānclifu* are pl. Furthermore the verb occurs nowhere else, so it is impossible to decide whether the *bi*-prefix gives the sense of "around" (i.e. "screamed round about *þæt*") or merely intensifies ("screamed *þæt* out"). If we could take *begiellan* as intransitive, two alternative solutions present themselves: (1) *þæt* is a scribal error for *þǣr* (the fourth and climactic member of the *þǣr*-sequence begun in 18a and intensified in 23); (2) *ful oft þæt* = "full often (it happens) that" etc. (see 1/181 and note, also BT s.v. *þæt* conj. V. (1) and (3)).

25 f. **ūrigfeþra . . . meahte** The inelegant occurrence of *ūrigfeþra* so soon after *īsigfeþera*, plus the fact that both *ne ǣnig* and *frēfran* are emendations (MS *nænig* gives no alliteration and MS *feran* no sense), suggest that there is extensive corruption in these lines.

27b **āh** The use of forms of *āgan* (instead of *habban*) as perfect auxiliaries is very rare; it occurs again in one of the MSS of Wulfstan's *Sermo Lupi ad Anglos* (see Dorothy Whitelock's 3rd ed. of the latter, p. 53). It is more common in ON (cf. CVC s.v. *eiga* A.III.ß).

31b **snīwde** "(It) snowed."

33b–5b **For þon . . . cunnige** MW translate: "Now, indeed, thoughts urge (lit. beat on) my heart to (lit. that I myself should) try out the high seas, the tumult of the salt waves." This is perhaps the meaning of the passage, although in the light of the formula *heortan geþōht(as)* "thought(s) of the heart" (cf. 22/43a, *Christ* 1047b) one is tempted to take *cynssað* intransitively and translate: "now the thoughts of (my) heart impel that I should" etc.

37a **ferþ** This is probably d.o. of *monað* (though it might vary *mōdes lust*; in which case cf. 53a for a comparable intransitive use of *monian*).

tō fēran This stands for the inflected infinitive *tō fēranne*.

For þon nis þæs mōdwlonc   mon ofer eorþan,
ne his gifena þæs gōd,   ne in geoguþe tō þæs hwæt,
ne in his dǣdum tō þæs dēor,   ne him his dryhten tō þæs hold,
þæt hē ā his sǣfōre   sorge næbbe,
tō hwon hine Dryhten   gedōn wille.
Ne biþ him tō hearpan hyge   ne tō hringþege,
ne tō wīfe wyn,   ne tō worulde hyht,
ne ymbe ōwiht elles   nefne ymb ȳða gewealc;
ac ā hafað longunge   sē þe on lagu fundað.
Bearwas blōstmum nimað,   byrig fægriað,
wongas wlitigað;   woruld ōnetteð;
ealle þā gemoniað   mōdes fūsne,
sefan tō sīþe,   þām þe swā þenceð,
on flōdwegas   feor gewītað.
Swylce gēac monað   geōmran reorde;
singeð sumeres weard,   sorge bēodeð

---

39 **nis . . . mon** "There is no man so proud."

40a **gifena . . . gōd** Either "generous with his presents" or "happy in his gifts" (i.e. his abilities, talents, etc.); context suggests the latter. *Gifena* is gen. of respect, parallel to the *in*-phrases which follow.

41b **ne . . . hold** "Nor (is there a man) to whom his (temporal [or possibly heavenly]) lord (is) so gracious. . . ."

42 **ā . . . næbbe** "Has not always," i.e. "never has."

sǣfōre "On (or concerning) his sea-voyage," (inst.) dat. or gen. of respect.

43 **tō . . . wille** "[As to] what the Lord will bring him to" (Gordon). For the idea, see the quotation in the headnote.

44a **him** Possessive dative with *hyge*; it continues in force with *wyn* and *hyht* in the next line (cf. *Andreas* 1113b–4a, 1162b; *Guðlac* 98b). Translate *tō* as "on" in this line, as "in" in the next.

46a **ymbe** This preposition probably depends more immediately on *hyge* than on *wyn* or *hyht*. Translate the line: "Nor concerned with anything else than (the) tossing of waves."

48a **nimað** This verb is not recorded governing the dat. Either it is used intransitively here in some such sense as "to take to flourishing, to come alive," or else we have an imitation of the construction with dat. object which is possible with the nearly synonymous *fōn*.

48b, 49a **byrig, wongas** These are the d.o.'s of their respective verbs, *bearwas* continuing as the subject.

49b **ōnetteð** Not "is quickened" (as it is frequently glossed), but "hastens onward." For this poet the flourishing of nature immediately suggests its decay. Cf. Blickling Homily V: *Hwæt wē witon þæt ǣlc wlite and ǣlc fægernes tō ende efsteþ and ōnetteþ þisse weorlde līfes.* See further *MÆ*, XXVIII (1959), 104–6.

50a **ealle þā** "All those (things)."

51a **sefan** Object of *gemoniað*, parallel to *fūsne* (adj. used substantivally).

51b **þām þe** "In one who, for the one who."

52b **gewītað** Usually emended to the infinitive *gewītan*. But *-að* for the 3 sg. pres. indic. ending *-eð* is not at all unusual in the Exeter Book, and it is best to take 51b as an utterance complete in itself (cf. *Beowulf* 289b).

54b–5a **sorge . . . brēosthord** "Inspires bitter sorrow into (the) breast." For the

bitter in brēosthord. Þæt se beorn ne wāt,
ēstēadig secg, hwæt þā sume drēogað
þe þā wræclāstas wīdost lecgað.
For þon nū mīn hyge hweorfeð ofer hreþerlocan,
mīn mōdsefa mid mereflōde
ofer hwæles ēþel hweorfeð wīde,
eorþan scēatas, cymeð eft tō mē
gīfre ond grǣdig, gielleð ānfloga,
hweteð on wælweg hreþer unwearnum
ofer holma gelagu. For þon mē hātran sind
Dryhtnes drēamas þonne þis dēade līf,

---

idiom cf. *Juliana* 404 f. Analogy with 17/113b–4a suggests that *bitter* here is acc. sg. fem. qualifying *sorge*. For the form see 11a n.

56a **ēstēadig** MS *eft ēadig*, taken as a compound, has been defended as meaning "repeatedly blessed"; but it is doubtful whether *eft-* can suggest frequent repetition. Of possible emendations, *ēstēadig* is the most convincing paleographically (since confusion of *f* and *s* is widespread in OE MSS); *sēftēadig* is better metrically.

56b **þā sume** "Those ones."

58a–64a **For þon . . . gelagu** Cf. 19/55b sq. For this description of the escape of the mind (*hyge*) from the confining body (*ofer hreþerlocan*) and its subsequent wide ranging across sea and land, the poet is probably indebted to two passages in Alcuin's *De Animae Ratione Liber* (*PL*, CI, col. 642 f., 647). The passages in Alcuin themselves go back to a passage in St. Ambrose' *Hexaemeron* (*PL*, XIV, col. 275). The second of the Alcuin passages speaks of the intelligent soul,

Quæ mare, quæ terras, cœlum quæ pervolat altum,
Quamvis sit carnis carcere clausa suæ

("Which flies across the sea, the lands and the lofty sky, even though it is shut in the prison of its body"). The transition from Alcuin's suggestive but colorless *pervolat* to the Old English poet's fully developed image of the wandering mind as *ānfloga*, a solitary bird, is natural enough, and need not have been mediated by any other sources. Still, it is not out of the way to recall the raven Huginn from Scandinavian mythology: his name means "Thought" and is cognate with OE *hyge*. Huginn, along with his comrade Muninn ("Memory"), symbolizes the omniscience of Óðinn. Every dawn the god sends his two ravens out to fly over the whole earth; they return at breakfast, perch on his shoulders and report everything they have seen and heard. (See further—on Alcuin and Ambrose—Peter Clemoes, "*Mens absentia cogitans* in *The Seafarer* and *The Wanderer*," in *Medieval Literature and Civilization: Studies in Memory of G. N. Garmonsway*, ed. D. A. Pearsall and R. A. Waldron [London 1969], pp. 62–77. On Óðinn and his birds see *Essays in Criticism*, XVII [1967], 211 ff.)

61a **scēatas** Parallel to *ēþel*.

63a **wælweg** This probably stands for *hwælweg* (the spelling *w-* for *hw-* occurs elsewhere in the Exeter Book), though the whale's reappearance here so soon after 60a is certainly otiose. Smithers argues (*MÆ*, XXVI [1957], 137–40) that we have here a different word, **wælweg*, "road taken by the dead; road to the abode of the dead," but this is considerably less likely metrically and contextually.

65b **þis dēade līf** Note the oxymoron. Heaven is *lifgendra lond*, "(the) land of (the) living," in *Christ* 437.

lǣne on londe: ic gelȳfe nō
þæt him eorðwelan ēce stondeð;
simle þrēora sum, þinga gehwylce,
ǣr his tīdege tō twēon weorþeð:
ādl oþþe yldo oþþe ecghete
fǣgum fromweardum feorh oðþringeð.
For þon þæt eorla gehwām æftercweþendra
lof lifgendra lāstworda betst,
þæt hē gewyrce, ǣr hē onweg scyle,
frem*um* on foldan wið fēonda nīþ,
dēorum dǣdum dēofle tōgēanes,
þæt hine ælda bearn æfter hergen,
ond his lof siþþan lifge mid englum
āwa tō ealdre, ēcan līfes blǣð,
drēam mid dugeþum. Dagas sind gewitene,
ealle onmēdlan eorþan rīces;
n*ea*ron nū cyningas ne cāseras
ne goldgiefan swylce iū wǣron,
þonne hī mǣst mid him mǣrþa gefremedon
ond on dryhtlicestum dōme lifdon.
Gedroren is þēos dugð eal, drēamas sind gewitene;
wuniað þā wācran ond þās woruld healdaþ,
brūcað þurh bisgo. Blǣd is gehnǣged;

---

67 **þæt . . . stondeð** "That earthly riches last forever for it" (i.e. *līf*). For the sentiment and syntax of this line, cf. Pope Gregory's warning in the OE version of the *Liber Regulae Pastoralis: þes middangeard . . . ēow ne mæg ealneg standan.* Alternatively one can take *him* in 67a as a refl. pronoun with *standeð* (an unusual construction), or as a pronoun referring back vaguely to a hypothetical person who lives *þis dēade līf* (in which case cf. 19/115b for the syntax).

eorðwelan . . . stondeð Taking *stondeð* as sg., we can interpret *eorðwelan* as sg. (for the late spelling with *-n* in this MS cf. *Christ* 1042a, *The Phoenix* 251a). Taking *eorðwelan* as pl., we can interpret *stondeð* as pl. (cf. 21/28/10 f.). In any event there is no need to emend.

68 f. **simle . . . weorþeð** "One of three (destinies) always, (and) invariably, proves to be a matter of uncertainty before its (appointed) time." Presumably *tīdege* (MS *tide ge*) = *tīddæge*; for the word see *Genesis* 1165b, for the meaning cf. *mǣldæg* (*Genesis* 1632a, 2341b) and ON *máldagi*.

68b **þinga gehwylce** "Invariably" (lit. "in each of cases"); this adv. phrase parallels *symle*.

71 **fǣgum fromweardum** "(The man who is) fated to die and about to depart."

72a **þæt** Sc. *bið* (which is often added by editors). The *þæt* not only anticipates *lof* in 73a ("that, i.e. the praise of after-speakers, of the living, [is] the best of posthumous reputations"), but is correlative with *þæt* in 74a ("that [is] the best of posthumous reputations for each man that he bring [it] about" etc.).

75a **fremum** Instrumental dat.

79b **blǣð** I.e. *blǣd*. Confusion of ð/þ and *d* is common in late MSS.

82 **nearon** Mrs. Gordon explains MS *næron* as "a scribal error due to the proximity of *wæron* in the next line."

84a **mid him** "Among themselves."

88a **brūcað þurh bisgo** " 'Occupy it in toil and trouble'. Þ*urh* with an abstract

eorþan indryhto ealdað ond sēarað
swā nū monna gehwylc geond middangeard:
yldo him on fareð, onsȳn blācað,
gomelfeax gnornað, wāt his iūwine,
æþelinga bearn, eorþan forgiefene.
Ne mæg him þonne se flǣschoma, þonne him þæt feorg losað,
ne swēte forswelgan ne sār gefēlan
ne hond onhrēran ne mid hyge þencan.
Þēah þe græf wille golde strēgan
brōþor his geborenum, byrgan be dēadum
māþmum mislicum þæt hine mid wille,
ne mæg þǣre sāwle þe biþ synna ful
gold tō gēoce for Godes egsan,
þonne hē hit ǣr hȳdeð þenden hē hēr leofað.
Micel biþ se Meotudes egsa, for þon hī sēo molde oncyrreð;
sē gestaþelade stīþe grundas,
eorþan scēatas ond ūprodor.
Dol biþ sē þe him his Dryhten ne ondrǣdeþ: cymeð him se dēað unþinged.
Ēadig bið sē þe ēaþmōd leofaþ: cymeð him sēo ār of heofonum.
Meotod him þæt mōd gestaþelað, for þon hē in his meahte gelȳfeð.
Stīeran mo*n* sceal strongum mōde, ond þæt on staþelum healdan,
ond gewis werum, wīsum clǣne.
Scyle monna gehwylc mid gemete healdan

---

noun is a frequent method of expressing the adverbial of manner or state" (Gordon).

89 f. **eorþan . . . middangeard** "*S. Augustine* I remember hath an excellent meditation, comparing the severall ages of the world to the ages of man; . . . making the *infancie* thereof from *Adam* to *Noah*, the *Childhood* from *Noah* to *Abraham*, the *Youth* from *Abraham* to *David*, the *mans estate* from *David* to *Christ*, the *old age* from *Christ* to the *end* of it" (George Hakewill, *An Apologie or Declaration of the Power and Providence of God in the Government of the World*, 2nd ed. [Oxford 1630], p. 23).

97a–102b **Þēah þe . . . leofað** Cf. Psalm 48:4 f. (Vulgate). As the passage stands it may be translated very tentatively: "Though a brother will strew with gold a grave for his born (brother), bury (him) among the dead with various treasures which (he) wants (to be in the grave) with him, gold cannot (be) a help, in the presence of God's awful power, to the soul that is full of sins, (not even) when he (i.e. the dead man himself) has hidden it while he lives here (on earth)." Adopting Sisam's emendation [*nille;*] for [*wille,*] in 99b would make the sequence of thought more coherent and would also clear up the strange syntax of 99b (by making *þæt* = the burial goods).

103b **for þon . . . oncyrreð** "Before which the earth turns itself aside"—an allusion to Revelation 20:11, *a cujus conspectu fugit terra et caelum* ("from whose face the earth and the heaven flee away"). Cf. 10/264 f.

109b **ond . . . healdan** "And hold it on (its) foundations," i.e. keep it under control.

110a **ond** Sc. *wesan.*

werum The MS form could represent either *wĕrum* or *wērum*, hence the halfline could mean "reliable among men" or "stedfast in his pledges." The latter is preferable rhetorically.

wiþ lēofne ond wiđ lāþne bealo,
þēah þe hē hine wille fȳres fulne
oþþe on bǣle forbærnedne
his geworhtne wine. Wyrd biþ swīþre,
Meotud meahtigra þonne ǣnges monnes gehygd.
Uton wē hycgan hwǣr *wē* hām āgen,
ond þonne geþencan hū wē þider cumen,
ond wē þonne ēac tilien þæt wē tō mōten
in þā ēcan ēadignesse
þǣr is līf gelong in lufan Dryhtnes,
hyht in heofonum. Þæs sȳ þām Hālgan þonc,
þæt hē ūsic geweorþade, wuldres Ealdor,
ēce Dryhten, in ealle tīd. Amen.

111b–5a **mid gemete . . . wine** Extensive textual corruption makes the form and meaning of these lines very uncertain. Translate: "govern with moderation (his) malice against friend and against foe, even though he (i.e. the foe) might want him (to be) full of fire or (might want) the friend he has made (to be) burned up on a pyre." Holthausen's addition of *lufan* after *lēofne* in 112 gives better sense ("his love for a loved one and his malice towards a foe"), and his juggling of *wille* in 113 to the end of the line gives tolerable meter. There seems to be no point in dividing 112 f. into half-lines, since we cannot be certain where the losses occurred.

113 **fȳres fulne** *Christ* 1562a reports that a damned soul in hell is *fȳres āfylled*, "filled with fire."

119b **þæt wē tō mōten** "That we may (go) thither."

21 / Riddles

Kennings like *hildenǣdre* or *merehengest* are riddles in embryo, and if their implicit metaphor is given the barest explicit extension—as for example by saying that during a storm *se brimhengest brīdles ne gȳmeð* (*The Rune Poem*, 1.66)—then one is well on the way to the sort of extended enigmatic composition which is exemplified in the selections that follow. It was Aristotle, after all, who first noticed the intimate connection between riddles and metaphor. But the ninety-five OE riddles of the Exeter Book are not accounted for simply by certain inbuilt mechanisms of the OE poetic system. Riddles have always been enormously popular among the "folk," and in Anglo-Saxon England—as on the continent—this lowbrow form secured the extensive approval of intellectuals: the writing of literary riddles in Latin, set afoot at a very uncertain date by the poet Symphosius, seems to have been a favorite pastime of English clerics of the eighth century. Such men as Aldhelm, Tatwine, Eusebius and Alcuin practised the form diligently, and it is not unlikely that the vernacular riddles of the Exeter Book belong to roughly the same period.

These riddles, formerly assigned to Cynewulf, are now thought to be by a variety of hands. Some of them seem to imitate Latin models directly, others to give independent expression to the same traditional material. Some are perfectly transparent; in others the writer seems to forget obfuscation and yield himself up to an impulse that is primarily poetic; in yet others the obliquely allusive language has put the subject of the riddle beyond the reach even of German scholarship. Some of the riddles of this latter class still await their Oedipus. Yet these often difficult poems are invaluable as a window upon the daily life and occupations of the Anglo-Saxons, since they are stocked with a God's plenty of creatures who in their different voices howl, warble, creak, clink, bellow and crow the common demand for identification: *Saga hwæt ic hātte*! Furthermore, in the variety of their subject-matter and treatment these enigmas appeal to all tastes: the "romantic" quality of 7 is Wordsworthian; Cowper would have been delighted by the fine mock-heroics of 47; the mysterious, semi-mythical 29 would have entranced Yeats; and Chaucer's monk, worn out by reading the object described in 26, would—while sipping 28—have found instruction and delight in the manly strains of 44.

The standard editions are those of Frederick Tupper, Jr., *The Riddles of the Exeter Book* (Boston 1910)—a very elaborate study, bulging with antiquarian lore—and A. J. Wyatt's more ingratiating (but less full) *Old English Riddles* (Boston 1912). There is a translation by Paull F. Baum, *Anglo-Saxon Riddles of the Exeter Book* (Durham [North Carolina] 1963).

7

Hrægl mīn swigað þonne ic hrūsan trede
oþþe þā wīc būge oþþe wado drēfe.
Hwīlum mec āhebbað ofer hæleþa byht
hyrste mīne ond þēos hēa lyft,
ond mec þonne wīde wolcna strengu
ofer folc byreð. Frætwe mīne
swōgað hlūde ond swinsiað,
torhte singað, þonne ic getenge ne bēom
flōde ond foldan, fērende gǣst.

8

Ic þurh mūþ sprece mongum reordum,
wrencum singe, wrixle geneahhe
hēafodwōþe, hlūde cirme,
healde mīne wīsan, hlēoþre ne mīþe,
eald ǣfensceop, eorlum bringe
blisse in burgum, þonne ic būgendre
stefne styrme, stille on wīcum
sit*te* ð*in*gende. Saga hwæt ic hātte,
þā swā scīrenīge sceāwendwīsan
hlūde onhyrge, hæleþum bodige
wilcumena fela wōþe mīnre.

7/5b **wolcna strengu** A kenning for the wind.

7/6b–8a **Frætwe . . . singað** No kind of swan actually produces aeolian music with its plumage, though medieval birdlore often credited them with this ability.

Solution: Perhaps the wild (or whistling) swan, *Cygnus ferus*.

8/4a **healde . . . wīsan** "Am true to my nature."

8/5a **eald** The adj. here (as often in MnE) suggests long familiarity rather than literal old age.

8/7b **on wīcum** "In (my) abode," cf. 15/2882a n.

8/9a **þā . . . scīrenīge** "When (I), so bright-eyed" etc.

Solution: Probably the nightingale, though the frog also fits all the terms. The riddle may in fact be playing on a traditional association of these two night-singers: three Anglo-Saxon glossaries render Lat. *luscinius* "nightingale" by the OE word *forsc* (*frox*, *frocx*) "frog," and the frog is even today known by such names as the "Dutch nightingale" or the "rossignol des marais." See Herbert Dean Meritt, *Some of the Hardest Glosses in Old English* (Stanford 1968), p. 8.

26

Mec fēonda sum   fēore besnyþede,
woruldstrenga binōm;   wǣtte siþþan,
dȳfde on wætre;   dyde eft þonan,
sette on sunnan,   þǣr ic swīþe belēas
hērum þām þe ic hæfde.   Heard mec siþþan
snāð seaxses ecg, ,   sindrum begrunden;
fingras fēoldan;   ond mec fugles wyn
geond spēddropum   spyrede geneahhe,
ofer brūnne brerd   bēamtelge swealg,
strēames dǣle,   stōp eft on mec,
sīþade sweartlāst.   Mec siþþan wrāh
hæleð hlēobordum,   hȳþe beþenede
gierede mec mid golde;   for þon mē glīwedon
wrǣtlic weorc smiþa,   wīre bifongen.
Nū þā gerēno   ond se rēada telg
ond þā wuldorgesteald   wīde mǣre
dryhtfolca Helm,   nales dol wīte.
Gif mīn bearn wera   brūcan willað,
hȳ bēoð þȳ gesundran   ond þȳ sigefæstran,
heortum þȳ hwætran   ond þȳ hygeblīþran,
ferþe þȳ frōdran;   habbaþ frēonda þȳ mā,
swǣsra ond gesibbra,   sōþra ond gōdra,
tilra ond getrēowra,   þā hyra tȳr ond ēad
ēstum ȳcað   ond hȳ ārstafum,
lissum bilecgað,   ond hī lufan fæþmum
fæste clyppað.   Frige hwæt ic hātte
niþum tō nytte.   Nama mīn is mǣre,
hæleþum gifre,   ond hālig sylf.

26/3b **dyde . . . þonan** "Took (me) out again."

26/7b **mec** Object of *geond*; *spēddropum* is inst. dat.

fugles wyn I.e. one of his feathers: this is a kenning for a quill pen.

26/9a **brerd** I.e. of the inkhorn.

26/12b **hȳþe beþenede** "Stretched leather over (them)," or more literally "stretched over (them) by means of hide." *Hȳþe* = *hȳde* (cf. 20/79b n.).

26/13b–4a **for þon . . . smiþa** "Indeed splendid objects wrought by smiths adorned me." But since *glīwian* is not elsewhere attested in this sense, Trautmann's suggestion *forþ on mē glisedon* ("thenceforth glistened on me") is very attractive. The poet is here talking about the binding of the book.

26/16b–7b **wīde . . . wīte** A controversial passage. Taking *mǣre* as optative subj. 3 pl. (for the form see 1/150 f. n. and Campbell §472), we can translate: "may they (i.e. the ornaments listed in 15a–6a) glorify far and wide the protector of noble peoples (i.e. God), may they not be entrusted to a fool (lit. may a foolish [person] not at all take care of [them])." Taking *mǣre* as an adj. and assuming an anacoluthon we can translate: "(these ornaments) famous far and wide—let a protector of noble peoples, not a foolish (person), take care of (them)."

Solution: A splendid Bible codex.

28

Biþ foldan dǣl   fægre gegierwed
mid þȳ heardestan   ond mid þȳ scearpestan
ond mid þȳ grymmestan   gumena gestrēona,
corfen, sworfen,   cyrred, þyrred,
bunden, wunden,   blǣced, wǣced,
frætwed, geatwed,   feorran lǣded
tō durum dryhta.   Drēam bið ininnan
cwicra wihta,   clengeð, lengeð,
þāra þe ǣr lifgende   longe hwīle
wilna brūceð   ond nō wið spriceð,
ond þonne æfter dēaþe   dēman onginneð,
meldan mislīce.   Micel is tō hycganne
wīsfæstum menn,   hwæt sēo wiht sȳ.

29

Ic wiht geseah   wundorlīce
horn*um* bitwēonum   hūþe lǣdan,
lyftfæt lēohtlic,   listum gegierwed,
hūþe tō þām hām   of þām heresīþe;
walde hyre on þǣre byrig   būr ātimbra*n*,
searwum āsettan,   gif hit swā meahte.
Ðā cwōm wundorlicu wiht   ofer wealles hrōf,
sēo is eallum cūð   eorðbūendum:
āhredde þā þā hūþe   ond tō hām bedrǣf
wreccan ofer willan;   gewāt hyre west þonan
fǣhþum fēran,   forð ōnetteð.
Dūst stonc tō heofonum,   dēaw fēol on eorþan,
niht forð gewāt.   Nǣnig siþþan
wera gewiste   þǣre wihte sīð.

28/10a **brūceð** This and the following two verbs are pl.; *-eð* for *-að* reflects the late OE spelling confusion in the vowels of weakly-stressed syllables.

28/10b **ond . . . spriceð** "And don't speak against (them)." Does life = sobriety and death = drunkenness (during which one says irresponsible things, 11b–2a)? Or does life = drunkenness and death = the besotted sleep which follows it (after waking from which one blames the drink, 11b–2a)?

28/12b **Micel . . . hycganne** "(It) will be hard to figure out."

Solution: Barley and the liquor (beer or ale) made from it.

29/4a **hām** For the form cf. 8/20 and n.

29/5a **hyre** "For herself."

29/6b **gif . . . meahte** "If it might so (be)," i.e. "if possible."

29/10b **gewāt** The subject is understood from *wreccan*.

29/11b **ōnetteð** Usually emended to preterite *ōnette*, but the momentary switch to historical present is not particularly disturbing.

Solution: The conflict of moon and sun. A few days before new moon the moon rises shortly before dawn. A thin sunlit crescent half-encircles the rest of its surface, which is earth-lit and clearly if dimly visible (11.2–3). Before the moon

44

Wrǣtlic hongað   bī weres þēo,
frēan under scēate.   Foran is þȳrel.
Bið stīþ ond heard,   stede hafað gōdne
þonne se esne   his āgen hrægl
ofer cnēo hefeð,   wile þæt cūþe hol
mid his hangellan   hēafde grētan
þæt hē efe*n*lang ǣr   oft gefylde.

47

Moððe word frǣt;   mē þæt þūhte
wrǣtlicu wyrd,   þā ic þæt wundor gefrægn,
þæt se wyrm forswealg   wera gied sumes,
þēof in þȳstro,   þrymfæstne cwide
ond þæs strangan staþol.   Stælgiest ne wæs
wihte þȳ glēawra   þē hē þām wordum swealg.

57

Ðēos lyft byreð   lȳtle wihte
ofer beorghleoþa: þā sind blace swīþe,
swearte, salopāde.   Sanges rōpe
hēapum fērað,   hlūde cirmað,
tredað bearonæssas,   hwīlum burgsalo
niþþa bearna,   nemnað hȳ sylfe.

---

can rise to the zenith (5–6), dawn appears on the horizon (7–8) and the earthlit portion of the moon fades to invisibility (9a). She pursues her westward course (9b–11). A wind comes up (12a; cf. 16/315) and dew falls (12b) as night yields to morning (13a). During the next few days (new moon) the moon will be entirely invisible (13b–14).

44/1a **Wrǣtlic** "A curious (object)."
Solution: A key.

47/5a **ond . . . staþol** "And (the very) foundation of that mighty (utterance)"—i.e. the vellum upon which it was written.
Solution: A bookworm, bookmoth.

57/6b **nemnað hȳ sylfe** "They name themselves."
Solution: Probably the jackdaw, the smallest member of the family *Corvidae*, who "names itself" to an Anglo-Saxon by crying **cā* (*PMLA*, LXII [1947], 1–8). Cf. mod. Scots dial. *kae*.

22 / the Wife's Lament

Suppose that Hamlet's soliloquy, "How all occasions do inform against me" (IV.iv.32–66), had survived, and nothing else of the play. We would be moved by the bursts of powerful emotion, would be tantalized by the brief allusions to persons and situations unknown, but could make only the wildest guesses as to the full experiential context that had prompted such utterances.

Scholars are now pretty much agreed that the so-called *Wife's Lament* is a dramatic monologue spoken by a woman. They agree about little else. Textual and semantic problems abound and punctuation and glossing inevitably support one parti pris or another. Are there one or two men in the poem? The woman and her husband (*if* it is her husband) have been separated by her kin. Why? Have they (the kin) also succeeded in turning him against her? He has sent her (or has he?) to her present dismal abode—is it a refuge or a prison? Do we have here simply masterful psychological elaboration of what an Anglo-Saxon would have regarded as a stock elegiac situation? Is this the explanation of the vagueness? Or did the actors once have names and were their deeds and sorrows registered in a heroic or legendary story that has not survived—or has not been recognized?

R. F. Leslie has recently edited the poem, along with *The Husband's Message* and *The Ruin*, in *Three Old English Elegies* (Manchester 1961; reprinted with corrections and supplementary bibliography 1966). Mackie's translation (see above p. 331) is very helpful.

Ic þis giedd wrece bī mē ful geōmorre,
mīnre sylfre sīð. Ic þæt secgan mæg,
hwæt ic yrmþa gebād, siþþan ic ūp wēox,

1b **geōmorre** Dat. sg. fem., modifying *mē*. The fem. form of this adj. (and of the phrase *mīnre sylfre* in the next line) confirm that the speaker is a woman and not, as several critics have wanted to argue, a man.

2a **sīð** Direct object, parallel to *giedd*.

nīwes oþþe ealdes,   nō mā þonne nū;
ā ic wīte wonn   mīnra wræcsīþa.
  Ǣrest mīn hlāford gewāt   heonan of lēodum
ofer ȳþa gelāc;   hæfde ic ūhtceare
hwǣr mīn lēodfruma   londes wǣre.
Đā ic mē fēran gewāt   folgað sēcan,
winelēas wræcca,   for mīnre wēaþearfe.
Ongunnon þæt þæs monnes   māgas hycgan
þurh dyrne geþōht,   þæt hȳ tōdǣlden unc,
þæt wit gewīdost   in woruldrīce
lifdon lāðlīcost,   ond mec longade.
Hēt mec hlāford mīn   hēr heard niman;
āhte ic lēofra lȳt   on þissum londstede,
holdra frēonda.   For þon is mīn hyge geōmor.
Đā ic mē ful gemæcne   monnan funde(,)
heardsǣligne,   hygegeōmorne,
mōd mīþendne,   morþor hycgend*ne*.
Blīþe gebǣro   ful oft wit bēotedan
þæt unc ne gedǣlde   nemne dēað āna,
ōwiht elles;   eft is þæt onhworfen,
is nū   swā hit nō wǣre,
frēondscipe uncer.   S*c*eal ic feor ge nēah
mīnes felalēofan   fǣhðu drēogan.

4a **nīwes oþþe ealdes** Adv. genitive.

5 **ā . . . wræcsīþa** "I (have) always got pain in return for my exile-journeys"; *mīnra wræcsīþa* is gen. of compensation, used here with bitter irony. Another possible translation: "always I suffered (the) torment of my miseries."

8 **hwǣr . . . londes** "(As to) where on earth" (cf. ON *hvar lands* [CVC s.v. *hvar* II.3]). *Londes* is independent gen. of place (with adv. function); cf. 47a.

11a **þæt** A pronoun, object of *hycgan*; the next *þæt* (12b) is correlative with it and introduces an explanatory clause (hypothetical, hence in the subjunctive); the third *þæt* (13a) introduces a result clause in the indicative.

15b **hēr heard** Is it the speaker's *hlāford* who is *heard*? Or is *heard* semi-adv.? Or should we emend (as some editors do) to *hēr eard* and translate the line: "My lord ordered me to take up residence here"?

16a **lēofra lȳt** See 19/31a and n.

18b **funde**(,) Whether or not one punctuates with a comma is of critical importance for the interpretation of the poem. With a comma: she found a man who was *gemæc* precisely because he was *heardsǣlig* etc. Without the comma: only after she had committed herself to the man she considered *gemæc* did she discover that in reality he was *heardsǣlig* etc.

20a–1b **mōd . . . bēotedan** Or should the period follow *gebǣro* rather than *hycgendne* (thus beginning a new sentence with *Ful*)? Yet another alternative: note that the MS has not *hycgendne*, the usual emendation, but *hycgende*; if we retain the latter, then the period must follow *mīþendne* and the sense of what follows (and of the whole poem) is much altered: "Contemplating crime (or: considering [our] injury), (and yet) cheerful of demeanour, full often we two vowed" etc.

22a–3a **ne . . . ōwiht** I.e. *nāwiht* (for purposes of translation).

24a **is nū** Some such participle as *geworden* or *fornumen* must be supplied to complete the halfline.

Heht mec mon wunian   on wuda bearwe,
under āctrēo   in þām eorðscræfe.
Eald is þes eorðsele,   eal ic eom oflongad,
sindon dena dimme,   dūna ūphēa,
bitre burgtūnas   brērum beweaxne,
wīc wynna lēas.   Ful oft mec hēr wrāþe begeat
fromsīþ frēan.   Frȳnd sind on eorþan,
lēofe lifgende,   leger weardiað,
þonne ic on ūhtan   āna gonge
under āctrēo   geond þās eorðscrafu.
Þǣr ic sitta*n* mōt   sumorlangne dæg,
þǣr ic wēpan mæg   mīne wræcsīþas,
earfoþa fela;   for þon ic ǣfre ne mæg
þǣre mōdceare   mīnre gerestan,
ne ealles þæs longaþes   þe mec on þissum līfe begeat.
Ā scyle geong mon   wesan geōmormōd,
heard heortan geþōht,   swylce habban sceal
blīþe gebǣro,   ēac þon brēostceare,
sinsorgna gedreag.   Sȳ æt him sylfum gelong
eal his worulde wyn,   sȳ ful wīde fāh
feorres folclondes   þæt mīn frēond siteð
under stānhliþe,   storme behrīmed,
wine wērigmōd   wætre beflōwen
on drēorsele,   drēogeð sē mīn wine
micle mōdceare;   hē gemon tō oft
wynlicran wīc.   Wā bið þām þe sceal
of langoþe   lēofes ābīdan.

27a–8b **Heht mec . . . eorðscræfe** Tantalizing, because it suggests the possible legendary affiliations of this poem, is a passage in the ON *Helreið Brynhildar* (*Brunhild's Funeral Journey*). Brunhild says:

Lét mic af harmi   hugfullr konungr
Atla systor,   undir eic búa

("Out of sorrow the courageous king made me, the sister of Attila, dwell beneath an oak"). Unfortunately the quotation is—in its context—almost as enigmatic as *The Wife's Lament*.

33b **Frȳnd** "Lovers" (cf. 25a; also 25/44a).

35a **þonne ic** "While I (on the other hand)."

42a–5a **Ā scyle . . . gedreag** These are probably generalized (gnomic) statements suggesting correct behavior. The switch from *scyle* (42a) to *sceal* (43b) is somewhat disconcerting (but cf. 20/109a, 111a).

43a **heard** Sc. *scyle wesan*.

45b–51a **Sȳ . . . mōdceare** Adopting Leslie's punctuation and interpretation: the two *sȳ*'s introduce balanced concessive clauses, the second of which is impersonal ("Whether is . . . or whether it is . . ."); *þæt . . . drēorsele* is a complete clause, part of the second hypothesis (it amplifies *ful wīde fāh*); *drēogeð . . . mōdceare* is the principal clause. But the syntax of this passage is very ambiguous and a number of alternative explanations are possible.

47a **feorres folclondes** Cf. *londes* 1. 8 and n.

53a **of langoþe** Probably "on account of longing." But this is a very strange use of *of*, hence Grein's suggestion (endorsed by BT) that it be emended to *on*.

23 / Judith

Judith is a remarkably successful account of the devotion and derring-do of a saint militant, whose success is in direct proportion to the strength of her faith. The author, probably writing in Wessex in the tenth century, has followed quite freely the Vulgate version of the Book of Judith,[1] amplifying the story into a Christian epic which frequently embodies not only the language of the older Germanic heroic style, but sometimes even the attitudes and institutions to which this style was subservient. He prunes away non-narrative elements in his source, for example Judith's long song of praise to God, and expands scenes which lend themselves to the techniques of OE poetry, e.g. Holofernes' banquet and the battle scenes. He reduces the figures whose names are given to two, thus focussing attention strongly and effectively on the opposed characterizations of Holofernes and Judith. The poem is galvanized throughout by its author's remarkable rhetorical and metrical dexterity: he is in fact one of the most mannered of OE poets, and delights in nothing so much as arresting the reader's attention by vivid metaphorical usages or by introducing unexpected words into stereotyped phrases. He is very fond of rhyme and transverse alliteration and is a master of the artistic and dramatic use of the hypermetric line.

The *Expositio in Librum Judith* which Hrabanus Maurus of Fulda wrote in 834 does not seem to have had any direct influence on our poem, though the author may be presumed to have been aware of intensive allegorical exegesis of this type. Ælfric concludes his metrical homily on Judith with a very similar interpretation, which illuminates a number of features in the OE poem:

Hēo ēadmōd and clǣne   and ofercōm þone mōdigan,
lȳtel and unstrang   and ālēde þone micclan,

[1]Timmer (pp. 14–16) cites most of the relevant passages from the Vulgate and gives the numbers of the lines in the OE poem to which they correspond.

for ðan þe hēo getācnode · untwēolīce mid weorcum
þā hālgan gelaðunge þe gelȳfð nū on God:
þæt is Crīstes cyrce on eallum Crīstenum folce,
his ān clǣne brȳd, þe mid cēnum gelēafan
þām ealdum dēofle offorcearf þæt hēafod,
ǣfre on clǣnnysse Crīste þeowigende.

Ælfric's homily[2] and *Judith* seem to be completely independent treatments of the same subject, and it is fascinating to compare them. Ælfric's eye is much more closely focussed on the Latin text, he takes very few liberties with the narrative. Although he too creates a spare story by drastic condensation, by dropping the name of a minor character (Vagao) and by soft-pedaling the non-narrative elements (Judith's song), his version lacks the poetic additions which are the lifeblood of the OE poem.

Attempts to identify the heroine of the poem with an actual Anglo-Saxon woman—such as King Ælfred's stepmother Judith, or Queen Æðelflæd of Mercia—are very dubious, but it is certainly not impossible that one of the author's purposes was to encourage his countrymen in their struggle against the Viking invaders. At least Ælfric, in his *Treatise on the Old and New Testament,* maintained that the Book of Judith was useful *ēow mannum tō bysne, þæt gē ēowerne eard mid wǣ*[*p*]*num bewerian wið onwinnendne here.*

Extrapolation on the basis of the fit numbers and the relationship of our fragment to the Book of Judith suggests that *Judith* was originally a poem of 1200–1300 lines and that only slightly more than the last quarter has survived. Recently, however, this view has been challenged and it has been argued that the poem is virtually complete (*MLR*, L [1955], 168–72).

Judith follows *Beowulf* in the Nowell Codex, British Museum Cotton Vitellius A. xv, ff. 94–209 (Ker 216), which has recently been edited in facsimile by Kemp Malone (*EEMSF*, XII). This MS was damaged in the Cottonian fire of 1731 and we must now rely for a number of readings on a seventeenth-century transcript by Fransiscus Junius (Bodleian MS Junius 105). B. J. Timmer's recent edition of the poem (2nd ed., London 1961) does not entirely supersede the earlier edition of Albert S. Cook (Boston 1888 and 1904 [abridged, but with notes added]) and the very careful study by T. Gregory Foster, "Judith, Studies in Metre, Language and Style," *Quellen und Forschungen* LXXI (Strassburg 1892). Elliot Van Kirk Dobbie's edition in *ASPR*, IV, is also excellent.

[2]It is published in Grein-Wülker, *Bibliothek der Angelsächsischen Prosa*, III, 102–16.

[IX]

tweōde
gifena in ðȳs ginnan grunde. Hēo ðǣr gearwe funde
mundbyrd æt ðām mǣran Þēodne, þā hēo āhte mǣste þearfe,
hyldo þæs hēhstan Dēman, þæt hē hīe wið þæs hēhstan brōgan
gefriðode, frymða Waldend. Hyre ðæs Fæder on roderum
torhtmōd tīðe gefremede, þe hēo āhte trumne gelēafan
ā tō ðām Ælmihtigan. Gefrægen ic ðā Hōlofernus
wīnhātan wyrcean georne ond eallum wundrum þrymlic
girwan ūp swǣsendo; tō ðām hēt se gumena baldor
ealle ðā yldestan ðegnas. Hīe ðæt ofstum miclum
ræfndon, rondwiggende, cōmon tō ðām rīcan þēodne
fēran, folces rǣswan. Þæt wæs þȳ fēorðan dōgore
þæs ðe Iūdith hyne glēaw on geðonce,
ides ælfscīnu, ǣrest gesōhte.

X

Hīe ðā tō ðām symle sittan ēodon,
wlance tō wīngedrince, ealle his wēagesīðas,
bealde byrnwiggende. Þǣr wǣron bollan stēape
boren æfter bencum gelōme, swylce ēac būnan ond orcas
fulle fletsittendum; hīe þæt fǣge þēgon,
rōfe rondwiggende, þēah ðæs se rīca ne wēnde,

1b sq. Holofernes, general of the Assyrian king Nabuchodonosor, has invaded Judea with a vast army and besieged Bethulia. The widow Judith, accompanied by a female servant, goes to the Assyrian camp; she hopes to save the city, using her great beauty to ensnare Holofernes. She has just uttered a prayer asking for God's support when the fragment opens. Probably *twēode* was originally preceded by a negative (cf. 345b–6a).

4b **hēhstan brōgan** In obvious contrast with *hēhstan Dēman*. The phrase, like many others in the poem, suggests the association of Holofernes with the Devil.

5b–6b **Hyre . . . þe** "(The) glorious father in (the) heavens made her (this) grant (i.e. granted her prayer), because" etc.; *ðæs . . . þe* = *ðæs þe*.

7a **ðām Ælmihtigan** Substantival use of adjectives is a characteristic stylistic feature of this poem.

7b **Hōlofernus** Thus spelled throughout, though it always alliterates with vowels. See *Andreas*, ed. Kenneth R. Brooks (Oxford 1961), p. 88 (n. to 1.756).

8b **þrymlic** Probably acc. pl. neut. modifying *swǣsendo* (though *þrymlicu* would be more normal).

12a **rǣswan** Probably nom. pl. (parallel to *Hīe* and *rondwiggende*), but possibly dat. sg. (parallel to *þēodne*).

16b **wēagesīðas** The ambiguity of this word (which could mean either "companions in crime" or "companions in misery") stands the poet in good stead. It is twice applied by Wulfstan to Satan's comrades, the fallen angels in hell.

20b **ðæs** Gen. object of *wēnan*. Its referent is the fact that Holofernes' men (and he himself) are *fǣge*.

egesful eorla dryhten.   Đā wearð Hōlofernus,
goldwine gumena,   on gytesālum:
hlōh ond hlȳdde,   hlynede ond dynede,
þæt mihten fīra bearn   feorran gehȳran
hū se stīðmōda   styrmde ond gylede
mōdig ond medugāl,   manode geneahhe
bencsittende   þæt hī gebǣrdon wel.
Swā se inwidda   ofer ealne dæg
dryhtguman sīne   drencte mid wīne,
swīðmōd sinces brytta,   oð þæt hīe on swīman lāgon,
oferdrencte his duguðe ealle,   swylce hīe wǣron dēaðe geslegene,
āgotene gōda gehwylces.   Swā hēt se gumena baldor
fylgan fletsittendum,   oð þæt fīra bearnum
nēalæhte niht sēo þȳstre.   Hēt ðā nīða geblonden
þā ēadigan mægð   ofstum fetigan
tō his bedreste   bēagum gehlæste,
hringum gehrodene.   Hīe hraðe fremedon,
anbyhtscealcas,   swā him heora ealdor bebēad,
byrnwigena brego: bearhtme stōpon
tō ðām gysterne,   þǣr hīe Iūdithðe
fundon ferhðglēawe,   ond ðā fromlīce
lindwiggende   lǣdan ongunnon
þā torhtan mægð   tō træfe þām hēan
þǣr se rīca hyne   reste on symbel
nihtes inne,   Nergende lāð,
Hōlofernus.   Þǣr wæs eallgylden
flēohnet, fæger   ond ymbe þæs folctogan

24a **þæt mihten** If we take *mihten* as pret. subj. (with Cook and Timmer), then we must regard *þæt* as a conjunction introducing a purpose clause. But *mihten* may well = *mihton* (cf. 54b *gebrōhton*, 150b *forlǣton*, both corrected in the MS from *-en*, apparently by the original scribe himself); if so, *þæt* could be either a conj. introducing a result clause, or else a pronoun—d.o. of *gehȳran*—beginning a new sentence.

27b **gebǣrdon wel** "Should behave themselves appropriately;" cf. *Beowulf* 1012b.

31a **oferdrencte** It is best to take this as a past participle modifying *ealle* (nom. pl. masc.) and *duguðe* as a partitive gen.; otherwise (taking *oferdrencte* as 3 sg. pret. and *duguðe ealle* as acc. sg.) the halfline becomes clumsily parenthetical.
The paradoxical antithesis between this halfline and 32a—Holofernes' men are simultaneously "flooded" (with liquor) and "drained" (of vitality)—is typical of this poet.

32b **baldor** In the MS the *b* of this word has been imperfectly erased.

34b **nīða geblonden** "The one corrupted by (lit. mixed together with) evils"; *nīða* is inst. gen. (see BTS *geblandan* V).

44a, 45a **þǣr . . . inne** "Wherein."

47a **flēohnet** Hrabanus Maurus interprets this as symbolizing the *insidias . . . dolosæ cogitationis* ("the snares of deceitful thought").

47b **ond** Omitted by most editors; but this poet was certainly capable of the stylistic extravagance of making *āhongen* a predicate adj.

bed āhongen,   þæt se bealofulla
mihte wlītan þurh,   wigena baldor,
on ǣghwylcne   þe ðǣrinne cōm
hæleða bearna,   ond on hyne nǣnig
monna cynnes,   nymðe se mōdiga hwæne
nīðe rōfra   him þē nēar hēte
rinca tō rūne gegangan.   Hīe ðā on reste gebrōhton
snūde ðā snoteran idese;   ēodon ðā stercedferhðe
hæleð heora hearran cȳðan   þæt wæs sēo hālige mēowle
gebrōht on his būrgetelde.   Þā wearð se brēma on mōde
blīðe, burga ealdor,   þōhte ðā beorhtan idese
mid wīdle ond mid womme besmītan.   Ne wolde þæt wuldres Dēma
geðafian, þrymmes Hyrde,   ac hē him þæs ðinges gestȳrde,
Dryhten, dugeða Waldend.   Gewāt ðā se dēofulcunda,
gālferhð gumena ðrēate,
bealofull his beddes nēosan,   þǣr hē sceolde his blǣd forlēosan
ǣdre binnan ānre nihte: hæfde ðā his ende gebidenne
on eorðan unswǣslicne,   swylcne hē ǣr æfter worhte,
þearlmōd ðēoden gumena,   þenden hē on ðysse worulde
wunode under wolcna hrōfe.   Gefēol ðā wīne swā druncen
se rīca on his reste middan   swā hē nyste rǣda nānne
on gewitlocan.   Wiggend stōpon
ūt of ðām inne   ofstum miclum,
weras wīnsade,   þe ðone wǣrlogan,
lāðne lēodhatan,   lǣddon tō bedde
nēhstan sīðe.   Þā wæs Nergendes
þēowen þrymful   þearle gemyndig
hū hēo þone atolan   ēaðost mihte
ealdre benǣman   ǣr se unsȳfra,
womfull, onwōce.   Genam ðā wundenlocc,
Scyppendes mægð,   scearpne mēce,
scūrum heardne,   ond of scēaðe ābrǣd
swīðran folme;   ongan ðā swegles Weard
be naman nemnan,   Nergend ealra
woruldbūendra,   ond þæt word ācwæð:
"Ic ðē, frymða God   ond frōfre Gǣst,
Bearn Alwaldan,   biddan wylle
miltse þīnre   mē þearfendre,

52b–4a **nymðe . . . gegangan** For the translation see p. 274. *Nīðe* is dat. of respect.

54b **on . . . gebrōhton** "Put into"; similarly 57a and 125b–7a. Perfective *gebringan* was treated as a verb of rest, therefore the preposition governs the dative.

65b **swylcne . . . worhte** "(Just) such (a one) as he had striven after."

67b, 68b **swā . . . swa** "So . . . as if."

73a **nēhstan sīðe** "On that last occasion," or perhaps "for the last time."

79a **scūrum heardne** "Hard (or perhaps hardened) in storms (of battle)."

85b **mē** "For me."

Ðrȳnesse ðrym.   Þearle ys mē nū ðā
heorte onhǣted   ond hige geōmor,
swȳðe mid sorgum gedrēfed.   Forgif mē, swegles Ealdor,
sigor ond sōðne gelēafan,   þæt ic mid þȳs sweorde mōte
gehēawan þysne morðres bryttan;   geunne mē mīnra gesynta,
þearlmōd Þēoden gumena.   Nāhte ic þīnre nǣfre
miltse þon māran þearfe.   Gewrec nū, mihtig Dryhten,
torhtmōd tīres Brytta,   þæt mē ys þus torne on mōde,
hāte on hreðre mīnum."   Hī ðā se hēhsta Dēma
ǣdre mid elne onbryrde,   swā hē dēð ānra gehwylcne
hērbūendra   þe hyne him tō helpe sēceð
mid rǣde ond mid rihte gelēafan.   Þā wearð hyre rūme on mōde,
hāligre hyht genīwod;   genam ðā þone hǣðenan mannan
fæste be feaxe sīnum,   tēah hyne folmum wið hyre weard
bysmerlīce,   ond þone bealofullan
listum ālēde,   lāðne mannan,
swā hēo ðæs unlǣdan   ēaðost mihte
wel gewealdan.   Slōh ðā wundenlocc
þone fēondsceaðan   fāgum mēce,
heteþoncolne,   þæt hēo healfne forcearf
þone swēoran him,   þæt hē on swīman læg,
druncen ond dolhwund: næs ðā dēad þā gȳt,
ealles orsāwle.   Slōh ðā eornoste
ides ellenrōf   ōðre sīðe
þone hǣðenan hund,   þæt him þæt hēafod wand

86a **Ðrȳnesse ðrym** Here Judith addresses collectively the three members of the Trinity whom she has just mentioned individually.

86b–7b **Þearle . . . geōmor** Cf. Psalm 54:5, *Cor meum conturbatum est in me* ("My heart is sore pained within me"); 6:4, *anima mea turbata est valde* ("My soul is . . . sore vexed").

90a **morðres bryttan** In contrast with 93a. In *Andreas* 1170b it is the Devil who is *morþres brytta*—which pretty succinctly suggests Holofernes' associations.

90b **geunne . . . gesynta** Probably "grant me success."

93b–4a **þæt mē ys . . . mīnum** "(Avenge it) that my soul is thus distressed, my breast (thus) heated." *Torne on mōde* is an imitation of the frequent construction *weorce on mōde* and is equivalent in meaning; *torne* is an inst. sg. used adverbially. In 94a the poet builds the parallel phrase *hāte on hreðre mīnum* on the same pattern.

96b **him tō helpe** "As a help for himself."

97b **Þā . . . mōde** "Then her soul grew enlarged" (lit. "then [it] became expansively for her in [her] soul"): a description of the expanding consciousness of divine inspiration. Cf. Judith 12:18 (*magnificata est anima mea hodie prae omnibus diebus meis*). For the impersonal adverbial construction here see BT *weorþan* II.(4)(b), esp. *Genesis B* 676b: *Wearð mē on hige lēohte*. Cf. also an ON phrase like *þér varð heimskliga*, and see further CVC *verða* A.II.3.

98a **hāligre** "For the holy (one)."

99b **wið hyre weard** "Toward her(self)."

106a **him** Possessive dat.

forð on ðā flōre.   Læg se fūla lēap
gēsne beæftan,   gǣst ellor hwearf
under neowelne næs   ond ðǣr genyðerad wæs,
sūsle gesǣled   syððan ǣfre,
wyrmum bewunden,   wītum gebunden,
hearde gehæfted   in hellebryne
æfter hinsīðe.   Ne ðearf hē hopian nō,
þȳstrum forðylmed,   þæt hē ðonan mōte
of ðām wyrmsele,   ac ðǣr wunian sceal
āwa to aldre   būtan ende forð
in ðām heolstran hām,   hyhtwynna lēas.

XI

Hæfde ðā gefohten   foremǣrne blǣd
Iūdith æt gūðe,   swā hyre God ūðe,
swegles Ealdor,   þe hyre sigores onlēah.
Þā sēo snotere mægð   snūde gebrōhte
þæs herewǣðan   hēafod swā blōdig
on ðām fǣtelse   þe hyre foregenga,
blāchlēor ides,   hyra bēgea nest,
ðēawum geðungen,   þyder on lǣdde,
ond hit ðā swā heolfrig   hyre on hond āgeaf,
higeþoncolre,   hām tō berenne,
Iūdith gingran sīnre.   Ēodon ðā gegnum þanonne
þā idesa bā   ellenþrīste,
oð þæt hīe, becōmon,   collenferhðe,
ēadhrēðige mægð,   ūt of ðām herige,
þæt hīe sweotollīce   gesēon mihten
þǣre wlitegan byrig   weallas blīcan,
Bēthūliam.   Hīe ðā bēahhrodene
fēðelāste   forð ōnettan
oð hīe glædmōde   gegān hæfdon
tō ðām wealgate.   Wiggend sǣton,
weras wæccende   wearde hēoldon
in ðām fæstenne,   swā ðām folce ǣr
geōmormōdum   Iūdith, bebēad,
searoðoncol mægð,   þā hēo on sīð gewāt,

111b **lēap** "(Wicker) basket," i.e. the body (as container of the soul). This bold metaphor is an extension of such body-kennings as *eorðfæt*, *lāmfæt* (*Soul and Body I*, 8a, 131a). Holofernes' *lēap* was *gēsne* ("empty") as soon as his *gǣst ellor hwearf* (112b); cf. 279b and *Andreas* 1083a–5a.

118b **mōte** Sc. *faran*.

129b **on** To be taken with *þe* in 127b; see 1/155 n.

132b **þanonne** For the spelling see SB ∫231.4 Anm. 1.

134a **hīe** MS *hie hie*. It is just possible that both *hīe*'s ought to be retained, though a refl. pron. in the acc. would be we odd with *(be)cuman*; cf. Voges p. 339.

ides ellenrōf.   Wæs ðā eft cumen
lēof tō lēodum,   ond ðā lungre hēt
glēawhȳdig wīf   gumena sumne
of ðǣre ginnan byrig   hyre tōgēanes gān
ond hī ofostlīce   in forlǣton
þurh ðæs wealles geat,   ond þæt word ācwæð
tō ðām sigefolce: "Ic ēow secgan mæg
þoncwyrðe þing,   þæt gē ne þyrfen leng
murnan on mōde.   Ēow ys Metod blīðe,
cyninga Wuldor;   þæt gecȳðed wearð
geond woruld wīde,   þæt ēow ys wuldorblǣd
torhtlic tōweard   ond tīr gifeðe
þāra lǣðða   þe gē lange drugon."
Þā wurdon blīðe   burhsittende,
syððan hī gehȳrdon   hū sēo hālige spræc
ofer hēanne weall.   Here wæs on lustum,
wið þæs fæstengeates   folc ōnette,
weras wīf somod,   wornum ond hēapum,
ðrēatum ond ðrymmum   þrungon ond urnon
ongēan ðā Þēoðnes mægð   þūsendmǣlum,
ealde ge geonge: ǣghwylcum wearð
men on ðǣre medobyrig   mōd ārēted
syððan hīe ongēaton   þæt wæs Iūdith cumen
eft tō ēðle,   ond ðā ofostlīce
hīe mid ēaðmēdum   in forlēton.
Þā sēo glēawe hēt,   golde gefrætewod,
hyre ðīnenne   þancolmōde
þæs herewǣðan   hēafod onwrīðan
ond hyt tō bēhðe   blōdig ætȳwan
þām burhlēodum,   hū hyre æt beaduwe gespēow.
Spræc ðā sēo æðele   tō eallum þām folce:
"Hēr gē magon sweotole,   sigerōfe hæleð,
lēoda rǣswan,   on ðæs lāðestan,
hǣðenes heaðorinces,   hēafod starian,
Hōlofernus   unlyfigendes,
þe ūs monna mǣst   morðra gefremede,

150b **forlǣton** An infinitive; cf. *tōbrēdon* 247b.

158a **þāra lǣðða** "In return for the injuries."

165a **þēoðnes** I.e. *þēodnes*; for the form see 20/79b n.

170a **hīe** Acc. sg. fem. (referring to Judith). Perhaps it doubles as the subject (nom. pl. masc.); otherwise 169b–70b are anacoluthon.

174a–5b **ond . . . hū** Word order: *ond ætȳwan hyt, blōdig, þām burhlēodum tō bēhðe hū* etc.

178b **lāðestan** Probably an adj. used substantivally, with *hǣðenes heaðorinces* and *Hōlofernus* [gen. sg.] *unlyfigendes* in apposition to it. Cf. 314b–5b, 248a–50a.

181 **þe ūs . . . gefremede** This sounds like a parody of *Beowulf* 2645a–6a, where the hero is praised in these terms: *hē manna mǣst mǣrða gefre-*

sārra sorga, ond þæt swȳðor gȳt
ȳcan wolde; ac him ne ūðe God
lengran līfes, þæt hē mid læððum ūs
eglan mōste: ic him ealdor oðþrong
þurh Godes fultum. Nū ic gumena gehwæne
þyssa burglēoda biddan wylle,
randwiggendra, þæt gē recene ēow
fȳsan tō gefeohte, syððan frymða God,
ārfæst Cyning, ēastan sende
lēohtne lēoman: berað lindé forð,
bord for brēostum ond byrnhomas,
scīre helmas in sceaðena gemong,
fyllan folctogan fāgum sweordum,
fǣge frumgāras. Fȳnd syndon ēowere
gedēmed tō dēaðe, ond gē dōm āgon,
tīr æt tohtan, swā ēow getācnod hafað
mihtig Dryhten þurh mīne hand."
Þā wearð snelra werod snūde gegearewod,
cēnra tō campe. Stōpon cynerōfe
secgas ond gesīðas, bǣron *sige*þūfas,
fōron tō gefeohte forð on gerihte,
hæleð under helmum of ðǣre hāligan byrig
on ðæt dægred sylf. Dynedan scildas,
hlūde hlummon. Þæs se hlanca gefeah
wulf in walde, ond se wanna hrefn,
wælgīfre fugel: w*i*stan bēgen
þæt him ðā þēodguman þōhton tilian
fylle on fǣgum; ac him flēah on lāst
earn ǣtes georn, ūrigfeðera,
salowigpāda sang hildelēoð,
hyrnednebba. Stōpon heaðorincas,
beornas tō beadowe bordum beðeahte,
hwealfum lindum, þā ðe hwīle ǣr
elðēodigra edwīt þoledon,
hǣðenra hosp: him þæt hearde wearð
æt ðām æscplegan eallum forgolden,
Assȳrium, syððan Ebrēas

---

mede, / dǣda dollicra. The syntax of both passages is very ambiguous. It seems most likely that *mǣst* (superlative of the adv. *micle* "greatly") participates in two constructions by apo koinou: first adverbially in the construction *þe monna mǣst gefremede* "who, most (vigorously) of men, perpetrated" (cf. ON *mest manna* in a sentence like *Gekk Þorfinnr mest manna fyrir sekð þeira* [*Íf*, VII, 62]); second nominally, d.o. (acc. sg. neut.) of *gefremede* and with dependent gen. pls. *morðra* and *sārra sorga*: "who perpetrated against us the greatest number of crimes, grievous woes."

190b **sende** Pres. subj. (with fut. perfect sense). Cf. Judith 14:2, *cum exierit sol* ("when the sun shall have risen").

194a **fyllan** "In order to cut down."

208a **him** Indirect object of *tilian*.

under gūðfanum gegān hæfdon
tō ðām fyrdwīcum. Hīe ðā fromlīce
lēton forð flēogan flāna scūras,
hildenǣdran, of hornbogan,
strǣlas stedehearde; styrmdon hlūde
grame gūðfrecan, gāras sendon
in heardra gemang. Hæleð wǣron yrre,
landbūende, lāðum cynne,
stōpon styrnmōde, stercedferhðe
wrehton unsōfte ealdgenīðlan
medowērige; mundum brugdon
scealcas of scēaðum scīrmæled swyrd,
ecgum gecoste, slōgon eornoste
Assīria ōretmæcgas,
nīðhycgende, nānne ne sparedon
þæs herefolces, hēanne ne rīc*ne*
cwicera manna þe hīe ofercuman mihton.

XII

Swā ðā magoþegnas on ðā morgentīd
ēhton elðēoda ealle þrāge,
oð þæt ongēaton ðā ðe grame wǣron,
ðæs herefolces hēafodweardas,
þæt him swyrdgeswing swīðlic ēowdon
weras Ebrisce. Hīe wordum þæt
þām yldestan ealdorþegnum
cȳðan ēodon, wrehton cumbolwigan
ond him forhtlīce fǣrspel bodedon,
medowērigum morgencollan,
atolne ecgplegan. Þā ic ǣdre gefrægn
slegefǣge hæleð slǣpe tōbrēdon
ond wið þæs bealofullan būrgeteldes,
weras *wērig*ferhðe, hwearfum þringan,

220a **fyrdwīcum** Both *fyrdwīc* and *herewīc* gloss Latin *castra* and generally appear in the pl., probably on the analogy of the Latin word. But cf. 15/2882a n.

223a **stedehearde** Cf. the compound *ecgheard* (*Andreas* 1181a), applied to a sword. It is likely that the first element of *stedeheard* is the familiar OE word *stede* "a fixed place or position, site," and that it designates the iron socket in the arrowhead (*strǣl, flān*) into which the shaft (*sceaft*) was fitted: cf. *Beowulf* 985a (unemended) and *The Rune Poem* 82b.

231a **ecgum gecoste** "Tested as to their edges," i.e. proven to be good.

239b **hēafodweardas** "Sentinels" (see BTS s.v.), here apparently rendering Lat. *exploratores* "scouts" (Judith 14:3, 8).

245 **medowērigum** This word is parallel to *him*, *morgencollan* to *fǣrspel*.

246b–50a **þā ic . . . Hōlofernus** Word order: *Þā ic gefrægn slegefǣge hæleð ǣdre tōbrēdon* [infinitive] *slǣpe ond, wērigferhðe, þringan hwearfum wið būrgeteldes þæs bealofullan, Hōlofernus.*

Hōlofernus: hogedon āninga
hyra hlāforde h*i*ld*e* bodian
ǣr ðon ðe him se egesa onufan sǣte,
mægen Ebrēa. Mynton ealle
þæt se beorna brego ond sēo beorhte mægð
in ðām wlitegan træfe wǣron ætsomne,
Iūdith sēo æðele ond se gālmōda,
egesfull ond āfor. Næs ðēah eorla nān
þe ðone wiggend āweccan dorste
oððe gecunnian hū ðone cumbolwigan
wið ðā hālgan mægð hæfde geworden,
Metodes mēowlan. Mægen nēalǣhte,
folc Ebrēa, fuhton þearle
heardum heoruwǣpnum, hæfte guldon
hyra fyrngeflitu, fāgum swyrdum,
ealde æfðoncan; Assȳria wearð
on ðām dægeweorce dōm geswiðrod,
bælc forbīged. Beornas stōdon
ymbe hyra þēodnes træf þearle gebylde,
sweorcendferhðe; hī ðā somod ealle
ongunnon cohhetan, cirman hlūde
ond gristbitian, Gode orfeorme,

249a **weras wērigferhðe** Of the several possible emendations of the meaningless *weras ferhðe* of the MS, this is the easiest to justify paleographically and is supported by the poet's treatment of 71a, 142a and 163a.

251b **hilde** While MS *hyldo* ("loyalty, devotion") is not impossible contextually, comparison of this line with Judith 14:3 (*ad principem suum excitandum ad pugnam* ["in order to arouse their leader to battle"]) strongly supports the usual emendation.

259b–60b **hū . . . geworden** *Geweorðan* here is construed impersonally with the acc.: "how the warrior had decided (to act) toward the holy maid" (Dobbie), or perhaps "how (it had) pleased the warrior (to behave) in the company of the holy maiden."

263b **hæfte** "With the haft," i.e. "with the sword." Synecdochic usage of *ord* and *ecg* is extremely common in OE verse (e.g. 24/60a) and furnished the poet with the pattern upon which he rung this highly original change; cf. his analogous innovations in 92b–4a, 111b. It is not particularly surprising to find dat. sg. *hæfte* inserted into a variation sequence which otherwise consists of dat. plurals, since such synecdochic usages often have a collective sense (cf. *Elene* 1186a, and more specifically 24/124a, 126a, where *mid wǣpnum* varies *mid orde*).

268b–9a **þearle gebylde, sweorcendferhðe** Cf. Judith 14:17 *et turbati sunt animi eorum valde* ("and their souls are exceedingly disturbed"). The poet seems to have extended the meaning of *byldan* from "embolden, encourage" to "excite, agitate." (Cosijn suggested emending to *geblȳde* [= *geblygde*] "dismayed.")

271b **Gode orfeorme** Or should we read *gōde orfeorme*? Both interpretations of this formula are attested elsewhere: in *Vainglory* 49b the reading *Gode* is indicated by the variation *Wuldorcyninge* in the next line, whereas in *Andreas* 406b we clearly have *gōde* (see Brooks' note ad loc.). Since the

mid tōðon torn þoligende. Þā wæs hyra tīres æt ende,
ēades ond ellendǣda. Hogedon þā eorlas āweccan
hyra winedryhten; him wiht ne spēow.
Þā wearð sīð ond late sum tō ðām arod
þāra beadorinca þæt hē in þæt būrgeteld
nīðheard nēðde, swā hyne nȳd fordrāf:
funde ðā on bedde blācne licgan
his goldgifan gǣstes gēsne,
līfes belidenne. Hē þā lungre gefēoll
frēorig tō foldan, ongan his feax teran,
hrēoh on mōde, ond his hrægl somod,
ond þæt word ācwæð tō ðām wiggendum
þe ðǣr unrōte ūte wǣron:
"Hēr ys geswutelod ūre sylfra forwyrd,
tōweard getācnod, þæt þǣre tīde ys
mid nīðum nēah geðrungen þe wē sculon *nȳde* losian,
somod æt sæcce forweorðan. Hēr līð sweorde gehēawen,
behēafdod healdend ūre." Hī ðā hrēowigmōde
wurpon hyra wǣpen ofdūne, gewitan him wērigferhðe
on flēam sceacan. Him mon feaht on lāst,
mægenēacen folc, oð se mǣsta dǣl
þæs heriges læg hilde gesǣged
on ðām sigewonge, sweordum gehēawen,
wulfum tō willan ond ēac wælgīfrum
fuglum tō frōfre. Flugon ðā ðe lyfdon,
lāðra lindwīg. Him on lāste fōr
swēot Ebrēa sigore geweorðod,
dōme gedȳrsod; him fēng Dryhten God
fægre on fultum, Frēa ælmihtig.

---

context in *Judith* supports either reading, we may well have a deliberate pun here: a "paper" pun only, of course, since the two words were pronounced differently. Compare the play on these same two words in 16/291a.

272b **Þā . . . ende** "Then (it) was all over (lit. at an end) as regards their glory." *Wæs* is used impersonally and *tīres* is gen. of respect.

275b–6a **sum . . . beadorinca** Word order: *sum þāra beadorinca arod tō ðām. Tō ðām* "to such an extent."

286a **getācnod** This participle appears to function simultaneously in two constructions: *Hēr ys ūre sylfra forwyrd getācnod tōweard,* i.e. "portended (to be) imminent," and *Hēr ys getācnod þæt* etc.

286b–7b **þæt . . . losian** Translate: "that it has arrived (lit. pressed forward, constricted) with troubles (or should we read *mid nĭðum* "among men"?) nearly to that time when we must of necessity perish."

297a **lindwīg** This is Malone's reading of the MS, which is severely damaged at this point.

299b–300a **him . . . fultum** "The Lord God gave them generous help," lit. "seized splendidly upon help for them" (see BTS *fōn* III.(I)(c)(α) and Wülfing ʃ788). The phrase is perhaps calculated upon Psalm 69:2, *Deus, in adju-*

Hī ðā fromlīce   fāgum swyrdum,
hæleð higerōfe,   herpað worhton
þurh lāðra gemong,   linde hēowon,
scildburh scǣron;   scēotend wǣron
gūðe gegremede,   guman Ebrisce,
þegnas on ðā tīd   þearle gelyste
gārgewinnes.   Þǣr on grēot gefēoll
se hȳhsta dǣl   heafodgerīmes
Assīria   ealdorduguðe,
lāðan cynnes: lȳthwōn becōm
cwicera tō cȳððe.   Cirdon cynerōfe,
wiggend on wiðertrod,   wælscel oninnan,
rēocende hrǣw.   Rūm wæs tō nimanne
londbūendum   on ðām lāðestan,
hyra ealdfēondum   unlyfigendum,
heolfrig hererēaf,   hyrsta scȳne,
bord ond brād swyrd,   brūne helmas,
dȳre mādmas.   Hæfdon dōmlīce
on ðām folcstede   fȳnd oferwunnen
ēðelweardas,   ealdhettende
swyrdum āswefede: hīe on swaðe reston,
þā ðe him tō līfe   lāðost wǣron
cwicera cynna.   Ðā sēo cnēoris eall,
mǣgða mǣrost,   ānes mōnðes fyrst,
wlanc, wundenlocc,   wǣgon ond lǣddon
tō ðǣre beorhtan byrig,   Bēthūliam,
helmas ond hupseax,   hāre byrnan,
guðsceorp gumena   golde gefrætewod,
mǣrra mādma   þonne mon ǣnig
āsecgan mæge   searoþoncelra,
eal þæt ðā ðēodguman   þrymme geēodon,

---

torium meum intende ("God, endeavor to help me," lit. "stretch forth in my aid").

311b sq. **Cirdon** etc. The Jews turn back from pursuing fugitives in order to plunder the corpses of the Assyrian dead.

314a **londbūendum** A dat. of interest dependent on *rūm* ("an opportunity for the natives," i.e. the Jews); *lāðestan* is dat. pl. (object of *on*, "from"); observe that the direct objects of *tō nimanne* do not start appearing until 316a.

319b **fȳnd** The d.o.; *ēðelweardas* in 320a is the subject.

320b–1a **ealdhettende . . . āswefede** "Ancient enemies (who had been) put to sleep by swords"; the phrase varies *fȳnd*. *Āswefede* is a predicate adj. (acc. pl. masc.) modifying *ealdhettende*.

329a **mǣrra mādma** "Of more famous treasures." The phrase can be taken (without emendation) as a descriptive gen. complement of *gūðsceorp* or *golde*, or as a partitive gen. complement of *eal* in 331a: in the latter case the syntax would be the same as in 338b–40a, only with more extreme disjunction.

330b **searoþoncelra** Adj. used substantivally, dependent here on *mon ǣnig*.

cēne under cumblum ond compwīge,
þurh Iūdithe glēawe lāre,
mægð mōdigre. Hī tō mēde hyre
of ðām sīðfate sylfre brōhton,
eorlas æscrōfe, Hōlofernes
sweord ond swātigne helm, swylce ēac sīde byrnan
gerēnode rēadum golde, ond eal þæt se rinca baldor
swīðmōd sinces āhte oððe sundoryrfes,
bēaga ond beorhtra māðma, hī þæt þǣre beorhtan idese
āgēafon gearoþoncolre. Ealles ðæs Iūdith sægde
wuldor weroda Dryhtne, þe hyre weorðmynde geaf,
mǣrðe on moldan rīce, swylce ēac mēde on heofonum,
sigorlēan in swegles wuldre, þæs ðe hēo āhte sōðne gelēafan
ā tō ðām Ælmihtigan; hūru æt þām ende ne twēode
þæs lēanes ðe hēo lange gyrnde. Þæs sȳ ðām lēofan Dryhtne
wuldor tō wīdan aldre, þe gesceō*p* wind ond lyfte,
roderas ond rūme grundas, swylce ēac rēðe strēamas
ond swegles drēamas, þurh his sylfes miltse!

332b **ond** Editors usually emend to *on,* but there is no reason why *compwīge* cannot be an independent locative dat., parallel to *under cumblum*; cf. *Beowulf* 1656a.

334b–5b **hyre . . . sylfre** It is not clear whether this highly disjunct phrase is possessive dat. with *mēde* (so Mossé §158.2) or the ind. object of *brōhton*; the suggestion of a double construction may well be deliberate. See further Wülfing §931 *bringan* 2.

338b–9b **ond eal . . . sundoryrfes** Word order: *ond eal sinces oððe sundoryrfes* [partitive genitives dependent on *eal*] *þæt se swīðmōd rinca baldor āhte. . . .*

345a **ā** Most editors are agreed to add the word *ā* at the beginning of this halfline, in order to make it hypermetric (like the lines preceding and following), and in conformance with 7a.

346b–7a **Þæs sȳ . . . aldre** Cf. 12/287 and n.

349a Pope[1] (p. 100) suggests adding the word *sǣs* at the beginning of this halfline. However it seems to us inadvisable to secure, at the expense of somewhat dubious sense (*sǣs . . . drēamas*), a metrical regularity which the poet may have deliberately tried to avoid in his climactic last line: compare the way in which the ninth section ends with two normal lines (13 f.) after an extended hypermetric passage.

24 / the Battle of maldon

The Parker MS of the Anglo-Saxon Chronicle opens its annal for the year 991 with the following notice:

> Hēr on ðissum gēare cōm Unlāf mid þrim and hundnigontigon scipum to Stāne and forhergedon þæt on ȳtan, and fōr ðā ðanon tō Sandwīc and swā ðanon tō Gipeswīc and þæt eall oferēode, and swā tō Mældūne. And him ðǣr cōm tōgēanes Byrhtnōð ealdorman mid his fyrde and him wið gefeaht, and hȳ þone ealdorman þǣr ofslōgon and wælstōwe geweald āhtan.

This engagement occurred on August 10th or 11th. It was "not an important failure" in terms of the overall military situation during the feeble reign of Æðelred the Unready, and the historical sources treat it accordingly. But it stimulated an unknown poet to write one of the finest battle poems in the English language, a stirring expression of the Germanic heroic ethos, always more attractive in defeat than in victory.

Though the text of the poem is defective at both ends, and was so even in 1705 when Humfrey Wanley described it as *fragmentum capite et calce mutilum, sex foliis constans* ("a fragment maimed at head and heel, consisting of six leaves"), its account of the battle seems virtually complete. Hence most scholars are agreed that not a great deal of text has been lost.

The Old English MS containing the poem (British Museum Cotton Otho A. xii [Ker 172]) was almost totally destroyed in the Cottonian fire of 1731; the six folios holding *The Battle of Maldon* perished utterly. But fortunately a transcription of them had been made c1724 by John Elphinston, under-keeper of the Cottonian Library, and it is upon this MS (Rawlinson B. 203 in the Bodleian Library at Oxford) that modern editions are directly or indirectly based. The best and most convenient of these is E. V. Gordon's *The Battle of Maldon* (London 1937), where all the information bearing on the battle is marshalled and the characters of the poem identified as thoroughly as our historical knowledge permits. Serious students will consult E. D. Laborde's *Byrhtnoth and Maldon* (London 1936) and Margaret Ashdown's *English and Norse Documents Relating to the Reign of Ethelred the Unready* (Cambridge 1930). There is an excellent translation (by W. P. Ker) in R. W. Chambers' *England before the Norman Conquest* (London 1926). For critical interpretation and attempts to locate the poem in the spectrum of heroic poetry, see Ker's *Epic and Romance* (London 1908), C. M. Bowra's *Heroic Poetry* (London 1952), Edward B. Irving, Jr.'s "The Heroic Style in *The Battle of Maldon*," *SP*, LVIII (1961), 457–67, and George Clark's "*The Battle of Maldon*: A Heroic Poem," *Speculum*, XLIII (1968), 52–71.

brocen wurde.
Hēt þā hyssa hwæne   hors forlǣtan,
feor āfȳsan   and forð gangan,
hicgan tō handum   and tō hige gōdum.
Þā þæt Offan mǣg   ǣrest onfunde,
þæt se eorl nolde   yrhðo geþolian,
hē lēt him þā of handon   lēofne flēogan
hafoc wið þæs holtes   and tō þǣre hilde stōp:
be þām man mihte oncnāwan   þæt se cniht nolde
wācian æt þām wigge   þā hē tō wǣpnum fēng.
Ēac him wolde Ēadrīc   his ealdre gelǣstan,
frēan tō gefeohte,   ongan þā forð beran
gār tō gūþe.   Hē hæfde gōd geþanc
þā hwīle þe hē mid handum   healdan mihte
bord and brād swurd;   bēot hē gelǣste
þā hē ætforan his frēan   feohtan sceolde.

Ðā þǣr Byrhtnōð ongan   beornas trymian,

2a **Hēt** The subject is Byrhtnoð, *se eorl* of 6a. The title *eorl* is reserved for Byrhtnoð in the poem.
hwæne Probably "some one, a certain one" (referring to the *Offan mǣg* of 5a), cf. 23/52b; though possibly "each one" (=*gehwæne*).

4a **tō handum** I.e. upon what he would accomplish with his *handum* in the forthcoming engagement.

5a **þā** "When," correlative with *þā* "then" in 7a. The pronoun *þæt* (d.o. of *onfunde*) anticipates the clause beginning with *þæt* (conjunction) in 6a.

7a **him** Possessive dat.
handon Cf. *handum* 4a. The late spelling *-on* is frequent in this poem not only for *-um* of the dat. pl. (e.g. 23a, 129a etc.) but also for *-en* of the subj. pl. (e.g. 20b, 21b, 32b etc.).

11a **Ēac** Preposition.
Ēadrīc The names of the combatants are not included in the Glossary; see Gordon's edition of the poem for identification and discussion.

14a **þā hwīle þe** "As long as" (lit. "for the time that"): *þā hwīle* is temporal acc.

17–24 From horseback Byrhtnoð marshals and exhorts the recruits of the *fyrd*

rād and rǣdde, rincum tæhte
hū hī sceoldon standan and þone stede healdan,
and bæd þæt hyra randa*s* rihte hēoldon
fæste mid folman and ne forhtedon nā.
Þā hē hæfde þæt folc fægere getrymmed,
hē līhte þā mid lēodon þǣr him lēofost wæs,
þǣr hē his heorðwerod holdost wiste.
Þā stōd on stæðe, stīðlīce clypode
wīcinga ār, wordum mǣlde,
sē on bēot ābēad brimlīþendra
ǣrænde tō þām eorle þǣr hē on ōfre stōd:
"Mē sendon tō þē sǣmen snelle,
hēton ðē secgan þæt þū mōst sendan raðe
bēagas wið gebeorge; and ēow betere is
þæt gē þisne gārrǣs mid gafole forgyldon
þon wē swā hearde *hi*lde dǣlon.
Ne þurfe wē ūs spillan, gif gē spēdaþ tō þām;
wē willað wið þām golde grið fæstnian.
Gyf þū þat gerǣdest þe hēr rīcost eart,
þæt þū þīne lēoda lȳsan wille,
syllan sǣmannum on hyra sylfra dōm
feoh wið frēode and niman frið æt ūs,
wē willaþ mid þām sceattum ūs tō scype gangan,

---

or East Saxon shire levies (*beornas*, *folc*), then alights to fight on foot among his personal retainers (*heorðwerod*).

23b **þǣr . . . wæs** Impersonal. "where (it) was most pleasing for him (to be)."

25a **stæðe** The Vikings had sailed up the estuary of the river *Pante* in Essex and established themselves on the island of Northey, about two miles east of the fortified town (*burh*) of Maldon. The island is joined to the west bank of the river by a narrow causeway some eighty yards long. This causeway is dry at low tide but submerged at high; hence the poet can accurately call it both a *bricg* (74b, 78b) and a *ford* (81a, 88a). Presumably the Viking herald shouts his demands from the shore of the island near the east end of this causeway.

29–41 Notice the herald's alternating use of 2 sg. and pl. according to whether he is thinking of Byrhtnoð individually or the English as a group.

31a **wið** "In exchange for"—as also in 35a, 39a.

33a **þon** A spelling variant of *þonne*: "than (that)."

33 **wē . . . dǣlon** Whether one translates this as "we (Vikings and English) should share" or "we (Vikings) should deal out" depends upon one's interpretation of *hearde*, the syntax of which is highly ambiguous: it is generally taken to be an adj. modifying *hilde*, but it could just as well be an adj. modifying *wē* (cf. *Andreas* 1137a, *Beowulf* 347a, *Judith* 130a) or even an adv. (cf. *Genesis B* 652, *Elene* 939a–40a). The latter possibility is strongly supported by the balance between this line and l. 59.

34a **þurfe wē** Cf. *sceole gē* in 59a. For this reduction of 1 and 2 pl. endings to *-e* when the pronoun follows immediately, see Campbell ∫730.

34b **gif gē spēdaþ tō þām** "If you are rich enough" (lit. "to that [extent]").

38b "According to their own judgment"; cf. 3/23 *hiera āgenne dōm* n.

40b **ūs** Reflexive with *gangan*.

on flot fēran   and ēow friþes healdan."
  Byrhtnōð maþelode,   bord hafenode,
wand wācne æsc,   wordum mǣlde
yrre and ānrǣd,   āgeaf him andsware:
"Gehȳrst þū, sǣlida,   hwæt þis folc segeð?
Hī willað ēow tō gafole   gāras syllan,
ǣttrynne ord   and ealde swurd,
þā heregeatu   þe ēow æt hilde ne dēah.
Brimmanna boda,   ābēod eft ongēan,
sege þīnum lēodum   miccle lāþre spell,
þæt hēr stynt unforcūð   eorl mid his werode,
þe wile gealgean   ēþel þysne,
Æþelredes eard,   ealdres mīnes
folc and foldan: feallan sceolon
hǣþene æt hilde!   Tō hēanlic mē þinceð
þæt gē mid ūrum sceattum   tō scype gangon
unbefohtene,   nū gē þus feor hider
on ūrne eard   in becōmon.
Ne sceole gē swā sōfte   sinc gegangan:
ūs sceal ord and ecg   ǣr gesēman,
grim gūðplega,   ǣr *wē* gofol syllon."

  Hēt þā bord beran,   beornas gangan
þæt hī on þām ēasteðe   ealle stōdon.
Ne mihte þǣr for wætere   werod tō þām ōðrum:
þǣr cōm flōwende   flōd æfter ebban,
lucon lagustrēamas.   Tō lang hit him þūhte
hwænne hī tōgædere   gāras bēron.

  Hī þǣr Pantan strēam   mid prasse bestōdon,
Ēastseaxena ord   and se æschere.
Ne mihte hyra ǣnig   ōþrum derian
būton hwā þurh flānes flyht   fyl genāme.
  Se flōd ūt gewāt.   Þā flotan stōdon gearowe,

41b "And leave you in peace" (lit. "and treat you peacefully," see BTS *healdan* A.VI.(1)). The adv. gen. *friþes* is unusual; normally *healdan* takes a dat. (inst.) complement in this idiom.

46a **tō gafole** Cf. 8/41 for the normal meaning and context of this word, here used with heavy irony.

47a **ǣttrynne** Probably only by way of metaphor.

48a **heregeatu** Literally "war-gear," but probably used here—with high irony—in its legal sense of "heriot": "a feudal service originally consisting of weapons, horses and other military equipments, restored to a lord on the death of his tenant" (*MLR*, XXII [1927], 260).

50b **miccle lāþre spell** I.e. than the one they had been expecting.

52a **gealgean** A late form of *ealgian*.

64b **werod tō þām ōðrum** "(One) band (get) to the other."

66a **lucon lagustrēamas** When the tide comes in the water rises on both sides of the causeway until it is awash.

\+

fleā geƿyrcan ac hi fæstlice ƿið ða fynd Fo. 8.
ƿeredon þa hƿile þe hi ƿæpna ƿealdan
moston. þa hi ꝥ ongeaton 7 georne ge
saƿon. ꝥ hi þær bricg ƿeardas bitere
fundon. ongunnon lytegian þa laðe
gystas. bædon ꝥ hi upgangan agan
moston. ofer þone ford faran feran
lædan. Ða se eorl ongan for his a-
fermode alyfan landes to fela la þere
ðeode. ongan ceallian þa ofer cald ƿa-
ter byrhtelmes bearn beornas gehlyston. nu eoƿ is gerymed gað ricene
to us guman to guþe. god ana ƿat hƿa
þære ƿæl stoƿe ƿealdan mote. Ƿodon
þa ƿæl ƿulfas for ƿætere ne murnon
ƿicinga ƿerod ƿest ofer Pantan ofer
scir ƿæter scyldas ƿegon lidmen to
lande linde bæron þær ongean gramū
gearoƿe stodon. Byrhtnoð mid beornum he mid bordū het ƿyrcan þone
ƿihagan. 7 ꝥ ƿerod healdan fæste. ƿið
feondū. þa ƿæs feohte neh tir æt ge
tohte ƿæs seo tid cumen ꝥ þær fæge
men feallan sceoldon þær ƿearð hre-
am ahafen hremmas ƿundon. earn æses
georn.

THE VIKINGS CROSS THE PANTE. Oxford, Bodleian Library, MS *Rawlinson B. 203*, p. 8b. (See p. 360 and cf. 24/81b–107a)

wīcinga fela   wīges georne.
Hēt þā hæleða hlēo   healdan þā bricge
wigan wīgheardne—   sē wæs hāten Wulfstān—
cāfne mid his cynne: þæt wæs Cēolan sunu,
þe ðone forman man   mid his francan ofscēat
þe þǣr baldlīcost   on þā bricge stōp.
Þǣr stōdon mid Wulfstāne   wigan unforhte,
Ælfere and Maccus,   mōdige twēgen,
þā noldon æt þām forda   flēam gewyrcan
ac hī fæstlīce   wið ðā fȳnd weredon
þā hwīle þe hī wǣpna   wealdan mōston.
Þā hī þæt ongēaton   and georne gesāwon
þæt hī þǣr bricgweardas   bitere fundon,
ongunnon lytegian þā   lāðe gystas,
bǣdon þæt hī ūpgangan   āgan mōston,
ofer þone ford faran,   fēþan lǣdan.
  Ðā se eorl ongan   for his ofermōde
ālȳfan landes tō fela   lāþere ðēode.
Ongan ceallian þā   ofer cald wæter
Byrhtelmes bearn—   beornas gehlyston—:
"Nū ēow is gerȳmed.   Gāð ricene tō ūs,
guman tō gūþe.   God āna wāt
hwā þǣre wælstōwe   wealdan mōte."
  Wōdon þā wælwulfas,   for wætere ne murnon,
wīcinga werod,   west ofer Pantan,
ofer scīr wæter   scyldas wēgon,
lidmen tō lande   linde bǣron.
Þǣr ongēan gramum   gearowe stōdon
Byrhtnōð mid beornum.   Hē mid bordum hēt
wyrcan þone wīhagan   and þæt werod healdan
fæste wið fēondum.   Þā wæs feohte nēh,
tīr æt getohte.   Wæs sēo tīd cumen
þæt þǣr fǣge men   feallan sceoldon.
Þǣr wearð hrēam āhafen,   hremmas wundon,
earn ǣses georn.   Wæs on eorþan cyrm.
  Hī lēton þā of folman   fēolhearde speru,
gegrundene   gāras flēogan.
Bogan wǣron bysige,   bord ord onfēng.

76a **mid** "Along with" (i.e. like all the rest of them).

82a **hī** Refl. acc. with *werian*; cf. 283b.

86a **lytegian** This word is usually glossed "to use guile," and it is certainly possible that the poet has let his chauvinism run away with him here. But the related adj. *lytig* can have the positive sense "prudent" (BTS), hence some such meaning as "to act prudently," "to behave in an appropriate pragmatic way" is not out of the question for *lytegian* here. See further *Speculum*, XLIII (1968), 68.

2a **Byrhtelmes bearn** Byrhtnoð.

2b **and þæt werod healdan** "And (ordered) the army to hold (that formation)" (cf. BTS s.v. *healdan* B.II).

Biter wæs se beaduræ̅s,   beornas fe̅ollon
on gehwæðere hand,   hyssas la̅gon.
Wund weard Wulfmæ̅r,   wælræste gece̅as,
Byrhtno̅ðes mæ̅g: he̅ mid billum wearð,
his swuster sunu,   swi̅ðe forhe̅awen.
Þæ̅r wærd wi̅cingum   wiþerle̅an a̅gyfen:
gehy̅rde ic þæt E̅adweard   a̅nne slo̅ge
swi̅ðe mid his swurde,   swenges ne wyrnde,
þæt him æt fo̅tum fe̅oll   fæ̅ge cempa;
þæs him his ðe̅oden   þanc gesæ̅de,
þa̅m bu̅rþe̅ne,   þa̅ he̅ byre hæfde.
Swa̅ stemnetton   sti̅ðhicgende
hysas æt hilde,   hogodon georne
hwa̅ þæ̅r mid orde   æ̅rost mihte
on fæ̅gean men   feorh gewinnan,
wigan mid wæ̅pnum.   Wæl fe̅ol on eorðan;
sto̅don stædefæste.
Stihte hi̅ Byrhtno̅ð,
bæd þæt hyssa gehwylc   hogode to̅ wi̅ge
þe on Denon wolde   do̅m gefeohtan.

Wo̅d þa̅ wi̅ges heard,   wæ̅pen u̅p a̅ho̅f,
bord to̅ gebeorge,   and wið þæs beornes sto̅p.
E̅ode swa̅ a̅nræ̅d   eorl to̅ þa̅m ceorle:
æ̅gþer hyra o̅ðrum   yfeles hogode.
Sende ðа̅ se sæ̅rinc   su̅þerne ga̅r
þæt gewundod wearð   wigena hla̅ford;
he̅ sce̅af þa̅ mid ða̅m scylde   þæt se sceaft to̅bærst
and þæt spere sprengde   þæt hit sprang onge̅an.
Gegremod wearð se gu̅ðrinc: he̅ mid ga̅re stang
wlancne wi̅cing   þe him þa̅ wunde forgeaf.
Fro̅d wæs se fyrdrinc;   he̅ le̅t his francan wadan
þurh ðæs hysses hals,   hand wi̅sode

113a **weard** I.e. *wearð*: an example of the confusion of *ð*/*þ* and *d* which is characteristic of late MSS. There are four other examples in this excerpt (*wærd* 116a, *æ̅gder* 224a, *od* 324b, and *gu̅de* 325b).

116a **wærd** I.e. *wearð*: on *d* for ð see 113a n.; on *æ* for *ea* see Campbell ∫329.(2) and n. 2.

126a **wigan** Generally taken to be nom. pl. (parallel to *hysas*) but quite possibly dat. sg. (and parallel to *men*).

126b–7a **fe̅ol . . . sto̅don** The same contrast occurs again in 301b–3b.

130a **wi̅ges heard** A Viking, the *ceorl* of 132b. *Wi̅ges* is descriptive gen.

134b **su̅þerne** The Vikings placed a high value on weapons of southern (i.e. Frankish and English) manufacture.

136 f. "Then he thrust with (the rim of) his shield in such a way that the shaft broke and (he thereby) made the spear(point) spring in such a way that it sprang back (out of the wound)." The Icelandic sagas contain accounts of similar dexterity in the use of the shield.

þæt hē on þām fǣrsceaðan   feorh geræ̅hte.
  Ðā hē ōþerne   ofstlīce scēat
þæt sēo byrne tōbærst;   hē wæs on brēostum wund
þurh ðā hringlocan,   him æt heortan stōd
ǣtterne ord.   Se eorl wæs þē blīþra,
hlōh þā mōdi man,   sǣde Metode þanc
ðæs dægweorces   þe him Drihten forgeaf.
  Forlēt þā drenga sum   daroð of handa
flēogan of folman,   þæt sē tō forð gewāt
þurh ðone æþelan   Æþelredes þegen.
  Him be healfe stōd   hyse unweaxen,
cniht on gecampe,   sē full cāflīce
brǣd of þām beorne   blōdigne gār,
Wulfstānes bearn,   Wulfmǣr se geonga,
forlēt forheardne   faran eft ongēan:
ord in gewōd   þæt sē on eorþan læg
þe his þēoden ǣr   þearle geræ̅hte.
Ēode þā gesyrwed   secg tō þām eorle:
hē wolde þæs beornes   bēagas gefecgan,
rēaf and hringas   and gerēnod swurd.

  Þā Byrhtnōð brǣd   bill of scēðe,
brād and brūneccg,   and on þā byrnan slōh.
Tō raþe hine gelette   lidmanna sum
þā hē þæs eorles   earm āmyrde.
Fēoll þā tō foldan   fealohilte swurd:
ne mihte hē gehealdan   heardne mēce,
wǣpnes wealdan.   Þā gȳt þæt word gecwæð
hār hilderinc,   hyssas bylde,
bæd gangan forð   gōde gefēran.
Ne mihte þā on fōtum leng   fæste gest*a*ndan.
Hē tō heofenum wlāt:
"Geþanc*ie* þē,   ðēoda Waldend,
ealra þǣra wynna   þe ic on worulde gebād.
  "Nū ic āh, milde Metod,   mǣste þearfe
þæt þū mīnum gāste   gōdes geunne,
þæt mīn sāwul tō ðē   sīðian mōte,
on þīn geweald,   Þēoden engla,
mid friþe ferian.   Ic eom frymdi tō þē
þæt hī helsceaðan   hȳnan ne mōton."
  Ðā hine hēowon   hǣðene scealcas
and bēgen þā beornas   þe him big stōdon:

143a **ōþerne** I.e. *fǣrsceaðan*, not *francan*.
144b **brēostum** Cf. 17/63b *hēafdum* n.
159 **gesyrwed secg** Yet another Viking.
173a **Geþancie þē** Sc. *ic* (for the omission of which cf. MnE "Thank you").
182a **and . . . beornas** We associate this phrase with *hine* as part of the d.o. of *hēowon*; most eds. take it as the subject of *lāgon*.

Ælfnōð and Wulmǣr   bēgen lāgon,
ðā onemn hyra frēan   feorh gesealdon.
  Hī bugon þā fram beaduwe   þe þǣr bēon noldon.
Þǣr wurdon Oddan bearn   ǣrest on flēame,
Godrīc fram gūþe,   and þone gōdan forlēt
þe him mænigne oft   mēar gesealde—
hē gehlēop þone eoh   þe āhte his hlāford,
on þām gerǣdum   þe hit riht ne wæs—
and his brōðru mid him   bēgen ær*n*don,
God*w*ine and Godwīg,   gūþe ne gȳmdon,
ac wendon fram þām wīge   and þone wudu sōhton,
flugon on þæt fæsten   and hyra fēore burgon,
and manna mā   þonne hit ǣnig mǣð wǣre,
gyf hī þā geearnunga   ealle gemundon
þe hē him tō duguþe   gedōn hæfde.
Swā him Offa on dæg   ǣr āsǣde,
on þām meþelstede,   þā hē gemōt hæfde,
þæt þǣr mōdelīce   manega sprǣcon
þe eft æt þ*earf*e   þolian noldon.

  Þā wearð āfeallen   þæs folces ealdor,
Æþelredes eorl: ealle gesāwon
heorðgenēatas   þæt hyra heorra læg.
Þā ðǣr wendon forð   wlance þegenas,
unearge men   efston georne,
hī woldon þā ealle   ōðer twēga:
līf forlǣt*an*   oððe lēofne gewrecan.
  Swā hī bylde forð   bearn Ælfrīces,
wiga wintrum geong,   wordum mǣlde,
Ælfwine þā cwæð,   hē on ellen spræc:
"Gemun*aþ* þ*āra* mǣla   þe wē oft æt meodo sprǣcon,
þonne wē on bence   bēot āhōfon,
hæleð on healle,   ymbe heard gewinn.
  "Nū mæg cunnian   hwā cēne sȳ!

186a **wurdon . . . bearn** Pl., since the poet is thinking not only of Godric but his brothers (cf. 191 f.).

190b **þe . . . wæs** "Which it was not right (for him to mount on)." It has been suggested (*MLN*, LXIX [1954], 466 f.) that we have here not the relative particle *þe* but the conjunction *þē* (i.e. *þēah*; for the spelling cf. *Andreas* 507a, 630b), but the rhetorical patterning of ll. 189 f. militates strongly against this.

198a **on dæg** "That (very) day."

200a **mōdelīce** For the form see Campbell ∫371.

212a **mǣla** Generally translated "speeches"—the only occurrence of this meaning in OE. Perhaps we ought to take it in its more usual sense of "times," regarding *þe* 212b as semi-conjunctive ("when"): cf. 23/286b–7b. This would bring the whole passage more firmly into line with *Beowulf* 2633 sq., with which it seems formulaically associated.

215a "Now (one) can find out."

Ic wylle mīne æþelo   eallum gecȳþan,
þæt ic wæs on Myrcon   miccles cynnes;
wæs mīn ealda fæder   Ealhelm hāten,
wīs ealdorman,   woruldgesǣlig.
Ne sceolon mē on þǣre þēode   þegenas ætwītan
þæt ic of ðisse fyrde   fēran wille,
eard gesēcan,   nū mīn ealdor ligeð
forhēawen æt hilde.   Mē is þæt hearma mǣst:
hē wæs ǣgder mīn mǣg   and mīn hlāford."
Þā hē forð ēode,   fǣhðe gemunde,
þæt hē mid orde   ānne gerǣhte
flotan on þām folce,   þæt sē on foldan læg
forwegen mid his wǣpne;   ongan þā winas manian,
frȳnd and gefēran,   þæt hī forð ēodon.
Offa gemǣlde,   æscholt āsceōc:
"Hwæt þū, Ælfwine,   hafast ealle gemanode
þegenas tō þearfe.   Nū ūre þēoden līð,
eorl on eorðan,   ūs is eallum þearf
þæt ūre ǣghwylc   ōþerne bylde
wigan to wīge,   þā hwīle þe hē wǣpen mæge
habban and healdan,   heardne mēce,
gār and gōd swurd.   Ūs Godrīc hæfð,
earh Oddan bearn,   ealle beswicene:
wēnde þæs formoni man,   þā hē on mēare rād,
on wlancan þām wicge,   þæt wǣre hit ūre hlāford;
for þan wearð hēr on felda   folc tōtwǣmed,
scyldburh tōbrocen.   Ābrēoðe his angin,
þæt hē hēr swā manigne   man āflȳmde!"
Lēofsunu gemǣlde   and his linde āhōf,
bord tō gebeorge;   hē þām beorne oncwæð:
  "Ic þæt gehāte,   þæt ic heonon nelle
flēon fōtes trym,   ac wille furðor gān,
wrecan on gewinne   mīnne winedrihten.
Ne þurfon mē embe Stūrmere   stedefæste hælæð
wordum ætwītan,   nū mīn wine gecranc,
þæt ic hlāfordlēas   hām sīðie,
wende fram wīge,   ac mē sceal wǣpen niman,
ord and īren."   Hē ful yrre wōd,
feaht fæstlīce,   flēam hē forhogode.
Dunnere þā cwæð,   daroð ācwehte,
unorne ceorl,   ofer eall clypode,

217b **miccles cynnes** Descriptive gen.; similarly 266b.
218a **ealda fæder** "Grandfather."
235b **mæge** Subjunctive by attraction (to *bylde* 234b).
239a **þæs** Gen. object of *wēnan*, and correlative with *þæt* 240b.
242b **Ābrēoðe** Optative subjunctive.
256b **ofer eall** "Over all" (i.e. "louder than all else and to all parts: so all could hear" [Pope[2]]).

bæd þæt beorna gehwylc Byrhtnōð wrǣce:
"Ne mæg nā wandian sē þe wrecan þenceð
frēan on folce, ne for fēore murnan."
Þā hī forð ēodon, fēores hī ne rōhton:
ongunnon þā hīredmen heardlīce feohtan,
grame gārberend, and God bǣdon
þæt hī mōston gewrecan hyra winedrihten
and on hyra fēondum fyl gewyrcan.
Him se gȳsel ongan geornlīce fylstan;
hē wæs on Norðhymbron heardes cynnes,
Ecglāfes bearn; him wæs Æscferð nama.
Hē ne wandode nā æt þām wīgplegan,
ac hē fȳsde forð flān genehe;
hwīlon hē on bord scēat, hwīlon beorn tǣsde,
ǣfre embe stunde hē sealde sume wunde
þā hwīle ðe hē wǣpna wealdan mōste.

Þā gȳt on orde stōd Ēadweard se langa,
gear*o* and geornful, gylpwordum spræc
þæt hē nolde flēogan fōtmǣl landes,
ofer bæc būgan, þā his betera leg.
Hē bræc þone bordweall and wið þā beornas feaht,
oð þæt hē his sincgyfan on þām sǣmannum
wurðlīce wrec ǣr hē on wæle lǣge.
Swā dyde Æþerīc, æþele gefēra,
fūs and forðgeorn, feaht eornoste,
Sībyrhtes brōðor, and swīðe mænig ōþer:
clufon cellod bord, cēne hī weredon.
Bærst bordes lærig and sēo byrne sang
gryrelēoða sum. Þā æt gūðe slōh
Offa þone sǣlidan þæt hē on eorðan fēoll,
and ðǣr Gaddes mǣg grund gesōhte.
Raðe wearð æt hilde Offa forhēawen;
hē hæfde ðēah geforþod þæt hē his frēan gehēt,
swā hē bēotode ǣr wið his bēahgifan,
þæt hī sceoldon bēgen on burh rīdan,
hāle tō hāme, oððe on here crin*c*gan,
on wælstōwe wundum sweltan:
hē læg ðegenlīce ðēodne gehende.
Ðā wearð borda gebræc. Brimmen wōdon,
gūðe gegremode; gār oft þurhwōd

---

265 sq. Cf. 3/17 and n.

277 Eadweard "broke the Danish line and fought hand to hand with individual Danes" (Gordon).

279b **on wæle** "Among the slain."

283 Pope[2] suggests that after this line there has dropped out a passage in which a Viking initiates an attack upon Offa.

287a **Gaddes mǣg** Offa.

fǣges feorhhūs. Forð ðā ēode Wīstān,
Þurstānes suna, wið þās secgas feaht;
hē wæs on geþrang*e* hyra þrēora bana,
ǣr him Wīgelines bearn on þām wæle lǣge.
Þǣr wæs stīð gemōt. Stōdon fæste
wigan on gewinne; wīgend cruncon
wundum wērige, wæl fēol on eorþan.
Ōswold and Ēadwold ealle hwīle,
bēgen þā gebrōþru, beornas trymedon,
hyra winemāgas wordon bǣdon
þæt hī þǣr æt ðearfe þolian sceoldon,
unwāclīce wǣpna nēotan.
Byrhtwold maþelode, bord hafenode—
sē wæs eald genēat—, æsc ācwehte;
hē ful baldlīce beornas lǣrde:
"Hige sceal þē heardra, heorte þē cēnre,
mōd sceal þē māre þē ūre mægen lȳtlað.
Hēr līð ūre ealdor eall forhēawen,
gōd on grēote. Ā mæg gnornian
sē ðe nū fram þīs wīgplegan wendan þenceð.
Ic eom frōd fēores; fram ic ne wille,
ac ic mē be healfe mīnum hlāforde,
be swā lēofan men licgan þence."
Swā hī Æþelgāres bearn ealle bylde,
Godrīc tō gūþe. Oft hē gār forlēt,
wælspere windan on þā wīcingas;
swā hē on þām folce fyrmest ēode,
hēow and hȳnde, od þæt hē on hilde gecranc.
Næs þæt nā sē Godrīc þe ðā gūde forbēah

297b–300b **Forð . . . lǣge** Since Wistan cannot have two fathers, most scholars take *Þurstān* and *Wīgelin* to be two names for the same man. Gordon suggests that *Wīgelines bearn* is Offa.

300a **him** Reflexive; cf. the same usage in 318 f.
Wīgelines Usually emended to *Wīgelmes* (< *Wīghelmes*), but it probably ought to be retained as a legitimate late byform of that name: see William George Searle, *Onomasticon Anglo-Saxonicum* (Cambridge 1897), p. xxx.

313b **mægen** Either the (diminishing) English troop or their (waning) bodily strength.

324b, 325b **od, gūde** See 113a n.

CYNINC SCEAL RICE HEALDAN
ceastra beoð feorran gesyne· orðanc enta geweorc· þa þe on
þysse eorðan syndon· wrætlic weall stana geweorc· wind byð on
lyfte swiftust· þunar byð þragū hludast· þrymmas syndan
cristes myccle· wyrd byð swiðost· winter byð cealdost· lenc
ten hrimigost· he byð lengest ceald· sumor sun wlitegost· swe
gel byð hatost· hærfest hreð eadegost· hæleðum bringeð· geares
wæstmas· þa þe him god sendeð· soð bið switolost· sinc byð deo
rost· gold gumena gehwam· ⁊ gomol snoterost· fyrn gearū
frod· se þe ær feala gebideð· wea bið wundrum clibbor· wolc
nu scriðað· geongne æþeling sceolan gode gesiðas byldan to bea
duwe· ⁊ to beah gife· ellen sceal on eorle· ecg sceal wið hell
me hilde gebidan· hafuc sceal on glofe· wilde gewunian· wulf
sceal on bearowe· earm anhaga· eofor sceal on holte· toð mæ
genes trum· til sceal on eðle· domes wyrcean· daroð sceal on
handa· gar golde fah· gim sceal on hringe· standan steap ⁊
geap· stream sceal on yðum· mecgan mere flode· mæst sceal
on ceole· segel gyrd seomian· sweord sceal on bearme· driht
lic isern· draca sceal on hlæwe· frod frætwum wlanc· fisc
sceal on wætere· cynren cennan· cyning sceal on healle·
beagas dælan· bera sceal on hæðe eald ⁊ egesfull· ea of dune
sceal flod græg feran· fyrd sceal æt somne· tir fæstra ge
trum· treow sceal on eorle· wisdom on were· wudu sceal on
foldan· blædum blowan· beorh sceal on eorþan grene standan·
god sceal on heofenū dæda demend· duru sceal on healle·
rum recedes muð· rand sceal on scylde· fæst fingra gebeorh·

GNOMES. London, British Museum, MS *Cotton Tiberius B. i*, fol. 115r. (See p. 136 and cf. 25/1a–38a)

25 / MAXIMS II

In addition to many gnomic and aphoristic passages scattered throughout OE poetry, there survive from the Anglo-Saxon period two lengthy compilations of sententious wisdom. The longer of these, *Maxims I* (also known as *The Exeter Gnomes*), is found in the Exeter Book (see p. 318). The other, *Maxims II* (or *The Cotton Gnomes*), occurs in the British Museum MS Cotton Tiberius B. i (Ker 191), where it is part of the introductory material to a version of the Anglo-Saxon Chronicle (see p. 136).

Maxims II probably reached its present form in the tenth century or slightly earlier, though some of the material in it may be much older. Some scholars have regarded it as little more than a metrical exercise: there is no discernible organic structure, and frequently the only connection between two maxims is alliteration. On the other hand, there is a (perhaps merely fortuitous) progression from *byð* maxims (lb–13a) through *sceal* maxims (14a–57a) to a solemn and impressive concluding passage (57b–66b) about "that undiscovered country from whose bourn / No traveller returns." Furthermore, the insertion of the collection into a Chronicle MS, apparently as part of the prefatory material, strongly suggests that it struck Anglo-Saxons as a solemn, profound and fittingly sententious prologue to a serious historical work.

Blanche Coulton Williams' *Gnomic Poetry in Anglo-Saxon* (New York 1914) contains a full introduction to the study of the poem, now somewhat dated, and provides text, notes and glossary for both *Maxims I* and *II*.

Cyning sceal rīce healdan.   Ceastra bēoð feorran gesӯne,
orðanc enta geweorc,   þā þe on þysse eorðan syndon,
wrǣtlic weallstāna geweorc.   Wind byð on lyfte swiftust.
Þunar byð þrāgum hlūdast.   Þrymmas syndan Crīstes myccle.
Wyrd byð swīðost.   Winter byð cealdost,
lencten hrīmigost   (hē byð lengest ceald),
sumor sunwlitegost   (swegel byð hātost),
hærfest hrēðēadegost   (hæleðum bringeð
gēres wæstmas,   þā þe him God sendeð).
Sōð bið swi*t*olost.   Sinc byð dēorost,
gold gumena gehwām,   and gomol snoterost,
fyrngēarum frōd,   sē þe ǣr feala gebīdeð.
Wēa bið wundrum clibbor.   Wolcnu scrīðað.
Geongne æþeling sceolan   gōde gesīðas
byldan tō beaduwe   and tō bēahgife.
Ellen sceal on eorle.   Ecg sceal wið hellme
hilde gebīdan.   Hafuc sceal on glōfe
wilde gewunian.   Wulf sceal on bearowe,
ear*m* ānhaga.   Eofor sceal on holte,
tōðmægenes trum.   Til sceal on ēðle
dōmes wyrcean.   Daroð sceal on handa,
gār golde fāh.   Gim sceal on hringe
standan stēap and gēap.   Strēam sceal on ӯðum
mecgan mereflōde.   Mæst sceal on cēole,
segelgyrd seomian.   Sweord sceal on bearme,
drihtlic īsern.   Draca sceal on hlǣwe,
frōd, frætwum wlanc.   Fisc sceal on wætere
cynren cennan.   Cyning sceal on healle
bēagas dǣlan.   Bera sceal on hǣðe,

1b–3a **Ceastra . . . geweorc** The loan-word *ceastra* (< Lat. *castra*) was often used in OE to refer to Roman cities. The earliest Anglo-Saxon invaders built exclusively of wood, hence were astonished by the Roman masonry which they found in England.

9 **gēres, him** In the MS these two words have been altered to *gēares* and *hiom* by the addition of letters in a later hand and different ink.

10a **switolost** The MS has *swicolost*, not a very appropriate epithet for *sōð*! The emendation is suggested by common sense and supported by the fact that scribal confusion of *c* and *t* is widespread: a comparison of the forms of these two letters on the accompanying facsimile will show why.

12a **fyrngēarum** Inst. dat.

12b **ǣr . . . gebīdeð** "Has experienced."

13a **Wēa . . . clibbor** "Misfortune is amazingly clinging."

16a **sceal** Sc. *wesan* (as often subsequently).

20b **Til** "(The) good (man)."

24a **mecgan mereflōde** "Mix with the sea-tide." MS *mecgan* is often emended to *mencgan*, but this is not necessary: see BT s.v. *mecgan*, where two other occurrences are cited.

25a **segelgyrd seomian** "(And the) sailyard hang (from it)."

27a **frætwum** I.e. those in the burial mound which he inhabits.

eald and egesfull.   Ēa ofdūne sceal
flōdgrǣg fēran.   Fyrd sceal ætsomne,
tīrfæstra getrum.   Trēow sceal on eorle,
wīsdōm on were.   Wudu sceal on foldan
blǣdum blōwan.   Beorh sceal on eorþan
grēne standan.   God sceal on heofenum,
dǣda Dēmend.   Duru sceal on healle,
rūm recedes mūð.   Rand sceal on scylde,
fæst fingra gebeorh.   Fugel uppe sceal
lācan on lyfte.   Leax sceal on wǣle
mid scēote scrīðan.   Scūr sceal on heofenum,
winde geblanden,   in þās woruld cuman.
Þēof sceal gangan þȳstrum wederum.   Þyrs sceal on fenne gewunian,
āna innan lande.   Ides sceal dyrne cræfte,
fǣmne hire frēond gesēcean,   gif hēo nelle on folce geþēon
þæt hī man bēagum gebicge.   Brim sceal sealte weallan,
lyfthelm and laguflōd   ymb ealra landa gehwylc
flōwan, firgenstrēamas.   Feoh sceal on eorðan
tȳdran and tȳman.   Tungol sceal on heofenum
beorhte scīnan,   swā him bebēad Meotud.
Gōd sceal wið yfele;   geogoð sceal wið yldo;
līf sceal wið dēaþe;   lēoht sceal wið þȳstrum,
fyrd wið fyrde,   fēond wið ōðrum,
lāð wið lāþe   ymb land sacan,
synne stǣlan.   Ā sceal snotor hycgean
ymb þysse worulde gewinn,   wearh hangian,
fægere ongildan   þæt hē ǣr fācen dyde
manna cynne.   Meotod āna wāt
hwyder sēo sāwul sceal   syððan hweorfan,
and ealle þā gāstas   þe for Gode hweorfað
æfter dēaðdæge,   dōmes bīdað
on Fæder fæðme.   Is sēo forðgesceaft
dīgol and dyrne;   Drihten āna wāt,
nergende Fæder.   Nǣni eft cymeð
hider under hrōfas   þe þæt hēr for sōð
mannum secge,   hwylc sȳ Meotodes gesceaft,
sigefolca gesetu,   þǣr hē sylfa wunað.

40a **scēote** This could mean either "rapid motion" or "trout."
40b **on** Often emended to *of*, which gives better sense.
43b **dyrne cræfte** "Clandestinely."
44b–5a **gif . . . gebicge** Ironic: "If, (while) among (her) people, she doesn't want to bring it about that someone buys her (from her father) with rings." I.e. girls who have secret lovers never get married. But this is rather naïve, and one would like to think that a moralizing scribe has juggled with folk wisdom, leaving us with *nelle* (44b) where pragmatism wrote *wille*.
50a sq. **Gōd sceal wið yfele** etc. Cf. Ecclesiasticus 33:15.
54a **synne stælan** "Institute sin," i.e. "enter into conflict."
59b **for Gode hweorfað** Probably "go into the presence of God."
65b **hwylc . . . gesceaft** "What (sort of thing) God's establishment is," i.e. what heaven looks like.

textual notes

As a general principle we emend only when the text of the MS we have chosen to print does not make sense. When a work survives in multiple MSS, this means that we will accept our chosen MS—as long as its reading is at all plausible—over the others, even if they are unanimous in supporting a different reading. (Usually we report this different reading in the explanatory notes.) We make no attempt, in other words, to reconstruct the text of the archetype, but put the modern student in the position of the Anglo-Saxon reader who has a single MS in his hands. Only when this text is so disturbed that our hypothetical Anglo-Saxon would have paused in confusion or bemusement do we feel justified in tampering with it.

Abbreviations are silently expanded and ę is represented by *æ*. MS corrections which can reasonably be attributed to the original scribe are silently accepted. Except in Selection 11, where the procedure is different (see the headnote to it), a letter which is added to the MS text, or which replaces a letter or group of letters in the MS text, is italicized; omission of a letter or group of letters is indicated by a subscript sign (ͺ) at the point where the omission occurs.

1, 2.

For the sigla see p. 107 f. Texts and variants are from the MSS (except for variants in B, which are from Miller and Schipper).

The Latin text is based upon Plummer². Since, however, the OE translation was made from a Latin MS of the Cotton Tiberius C. ii type and not of the Moore type (see Plummer², I, cxxviii f.; *PBA*, XLVIII [1962], 86, n. 123; and *NM*, LXX [1969], 370 f.), we have introduced the readings of Tiberius C. ii from Plummer's variants into his text in the two places in Selection 2 where the OE translation manifestly reflects a Latin MS of this type (i.e. *mihi* is omitted in the Latin corresponding to *þū meaht singan* in l. 25 [see further the explanatory n. ad loc.], and we read *Deo* instead of *Domino* corresponding to *Godes* in l. 94).

1.

7 þ*æt* *Thus B O Ca (7* ꝥ *N); T has* þa.

10 f. *ge . . . won* *Not in T; supplied from O.*

14 *on*wrignesse Onwrigenesse *O Ca* (ónwringe nesse *N*), onwrigennesse *B; T has* wrignesse.

50 ānͺlēpnesse Anlypnesse *B,* anlipnesse *(with* i *altered from* e*) O,* anlepnesse *Ca; T has* onslæpnesse, *N* anlefnesse.

52 nē*a*hͺnesse Neahnysse *B,* neahnesse *N; cf. Lat.* proximo. *T has* nihtnesse, *O* ehtnesse *(altered from* nehnesse?*), Ca* ehtnysse.

56 ætēcte   Æticte *B*, æt ecte *N*, ætycte *O* (ge ycte *Ca*); *T has* gyt ecte.
66 ˌelde   Ylde *B N O Ca; T has* helde.
86 dēorwyrðre eallum māðmum.   *Lat.* omnibus ornamentis pretiosior. *B* deorwyrðre 7 máre þonne ealle madmas; *O* dyrwyrþe 7 mare eallum maþmum; *N* deorwyrðre 7 mare eallum maðmum *(similarly Ca).*
86 Hwæ*t*   *From B N O Ca; T has* hwæs.
113 Þā *through 149* wig-   *Not in T; text from O.*
115 *mid*   *From B Ca; not in O (or N).*
137 hrine*n*   *See explanatory n.*
150 *ðe*   Ðe *B*, þe *N O Ca; T has* ða.
156 *ic*   *Thus N O Ca; T has* eac.
157 biseˌne   Bysene *N O* (bysne *Ca*); *T has* bisencenne.
168 forbærn*an*   *Thus B N O Ca; T has* forbærndon.

2.

16 scalde   *See explanatory n.*
17 forˌ   For for *T*.
39 Gode ˌwyrðes   Gode wyrðes *B*, gode wyrþes *C O*, góde wýrðes *Ca; T has* godes wordes.
81 *ne* wǣre   *Thus B O Ca; N* nære. *T has simply* wære.
97 o*n*hylde   *Thus B N O Ca; T has* ohylde.

3, 4, 5.

Texts from the EETS facsimile of A (see p. 136); variants in B from Thorpe, in C from Rositzke, in D from Classen and Harmer, and in E from the *EEMSF* facsimile.

4.

3 *wiþ*   *Not in A. Emendation based upon B C; D E have the word order* hi him wið frið namon *(D).*
90 tuel*f*tan   *MS* tueltan.
91 *ond* micel þæs folcesˌ   *See explanatory n.*
100 cōm*on*   *See explanatory n.*
113 ān   *See explanatory n.*
126 s*u*me   *See explanatory n.*
132 micla*n*   *See explanatory n.*
144 *Ond*   *See explanatory n.*
148 hīˌ mon   *MS* hī mon.
181 Bˌēamflēote   *MS* bleam fleote.
198 þǣr*e* ē   *MS* þær é.
203 þegn*as . . . geslegen*   *See explanatory n.*
253 wīcger*ē*fa   *See explanatory n.*

5.

13a seggaˌ *swāte*   *See explanatory n.*
25a heˌardes   *MS* he eardes; heardes *B C D and Otho B. xi.*
26a þǣ*ra þe*   *MS* þæ; þara ðe *B C*, þæra þe *D*.
49b c*u*mbo*l*gehnā*st*es   *See explanatory n.*
56a ˌIra   *MS* hira; ira *B*, yra *C D. See explanatory n.*
66b ǣf*re*   *MS* æfer; æfre *B C D.*
72b Wēˌaˌles   *MS* weealles; wealas *B C D.*

6.

Text from C and D (see p. 136); variants in E from the *EEMSF* facsimile.

Millesimo lxvi *Not in C; supplied from E.*

1 *O*n O *not in C; supplied from D E.*

2 -wintr*e* *C* wintran; *emendation from D.*

wǣron *Not in C; supplied from D.*

6 steorra*n* *C* steorra *followed by a vellum repair which probably covers the* n; *restoration from D.*

10 þano*n* *C* þano.

28 Lund*ene* *C* lunde.

32 ǣ*r* *C* æ *followed by a vellum repair.*

33 Ūsa*n* *C* us *followed by what looks like* a *followed by a vellum repair.*

35 hē *C* h *followed by a vellum repair.*

44 hi*m* mon *C* himon *(by haplology).*

62 fa*r*an *D* fafan.

7.

Text from the *EEMSF* facsimile of H (see p. 179). Variants in C are as reported by Sweet; those in D U as reported by Magoun. In restoring the original scribe's readings we follow Ker in doubtful cases (p. 24 f. of the *EEMSF* volume). Note that the first *d* in *woruldcundre* (l. 3) and the *i* in *andgiete* (l. 57) were inserted above the line by the original scribe.

8.

Text and variants from the MSS (see p. 185). The several corrections by the original scribe of the Tollemache MS are silently incorporated into the text.

28 hors̹hwælum *See explanatory n.*

66 þon̹e *MS* þonne.

80 *on* *See explanatory n.*

94 E̹stlande *MS* eastlande.

97 E̹stland *MS* eastland.

125 E̹stum *MS* eastum.

9.

Text from the *EEMSF* facsimile (see p. 196 f.). Paragraph divisions correspond to capitals in the MS (except for the paragraph beginning in l. 11, which is editorial), and the MS punctuation has often guided ours. All substantive variants (i.e. everything except spelling differences) from MS Corpus Christi College, Cambridge, 198 are reported; this MS is referred to as C.

14 ungecyn*d*elice *MS* ungecynelice.

39 fulwiht *and* hādas *MS* fulwiht | hadas.

56 dōm*e*s *MS* domos.

59 is mycel *C* is þonne mycel.

60 ūs . . . geðencean *C* þencean us sylfe.

61 gehȳron *C* gehyrað.

ūs . . . rǣdan *C* rædan 7 reccean.

63 þon . . . beteran *C* þam þe betere.

64 for *Omitted C.*

66 þæt þæt *C* ꝥ.

ne . . . ne *C* oððe forhwon sculan we.

68 Gesēo . . . forgeorne *C* geseoð we fulgeorne.

tō ðæs *C* to ðam.

68 f. nafað . . . ðon *C* hafað ne to ðam.

69 worlde *C* middangearde.

70 ǣr hēr *C* her ær.

71 man nǣfre *C* man sylf næfre.

ðon *C* þam.

72 ff. ne heora . . . unfæger *For C's reading see the explanatory n.*

76 wyrma *C* wyrmes.

77 wista *C* wlenca.

wlencea *C* wista.

78 anmēdlan *C* idelnys.

his . . . gescyrplan *C* þa . . . gegyrlan.

79 hē . . . frætwode *C* hi . . . frætewedon.

80 hēr *C* ær.

81 āgyldan *C* awyrcean 7 agyldon.

83 Magon wē *C* we magon.

secggean be *sumum welegum men* *C has* secgan be sumum welegan men. *In the Blickling MS only the tops of the* s *and* g *of* secg-, *the* l *of* welegum *and the* e *of* men *are visible.*

84 þysse *C* þissere.

mōdelico *C* modiglicum.

89 leng . . . mihte *C* ne mihte lengc on þam lande gewunian.

89 f. cȳþþe . . . earde *C* earde 7 of his cyþþe gewat.

90 on *For C's reading see the explanatory n.*

91 gehyrde *C* hyrde.

ongan hine *C* hine ongan.

92 for þon *C* to þam.

hwylc *C* 7 hwilc.

93 oft *C* ful oft.

fægerne *For C's reading see the explanatory n.*

mid man*num* *Thus C. In the Blickling MS the tops of the letters in* mid *are clearly visible, and what follow look like the tops of an* m, a *and* n *in this scribe's hand.*

94 For *C* to.

96 mid *Omitted C.*

þǣr þǣr *C* þær.

97 sēonne *C* geseonne.

98 þū . . . þis *C* for þam þu freond and mæg man [=mægman?] min gemune me.

99 nū eom *C* eom nu.

101 onwend *C* onwen.

tō *C* on.

102 gecyr *C* gecyrre.

Gode . . . andfenge *C* andfencge þam ælmihtigan gode.

103 gnorngende *C* gnornful.

þā *Omitted C.*

104 þisse *C* ðissere.

104 f. leornian . . . lǣran *C* læran . . . leornian.

105 him þā gife *C* godes miltse 7 god him forgeaf þa gife.

106 ēac *C* eac swilce.

generede *C* gefriþade.

110 þe *Omitted C.*

gedrorenlic *C* gehrorenlic.

111 þēos . . . gewiten *For C's reading see the explanatory n.*
113 ealre fægernesse *C* ealra fægernyssa.
114–8 And . . . wynsumnesse *Omitted C.*
117 wy*n*sumlic *MS* wymsumlic.
118 þon *C* þam.
118–21 And þā . . . gedafen *ne* is *For C's reading see the explanatory n.*
119 f. *nū hē is . . . is hē* *MS* is nu; *see explanatory n.*
121 *ne* *Not in MS.*
hrēam *C* hearm.
ǣghwonon[2] *C* æghwono.
tōlēsnes *C* to lyt.
122 yfel *C* fyll.
123 him . . . fylgeaþ *C* hine fleondne fylgeat.
feallendne *C* feallende.
125 þæs C ꝥ.
128 wiþ *Omitted* C.
129 þǣm . . . leofað *For C's reading see the explanatory n.*
on . . . world *C* in ealra woruld aworuld.

10.

Text from the MS (see p. 205); variants in B from the *EEMSF* facsimile. Erased letters have been restored in parentheses (1) when it is not likely that the erasure is by the original scribe and (2) when usage elsewhere in the text makes it fairly certain what letter(s) should be restored. There is naturally a good deal of doubt in individual cases.

2 apostol(as) *MS* apostoli, *with the* i *written over an erasure of two letters.*
5 hī(e) *MS* hi *followed by an erasure of one letter.*
8 geblanden *The second* n *is written over an erasure and in another hand (originally* geblanded*?).*
12 carcerne *B* carcern.
13 tōlēsed *B* to lysedu.
mōd *B adds* næs.
13 f. tō Drihtne biddende *B* hine todrihtne gebiddende.
15 cnēorisse *B* cneorisne.
18 þe *Omitted B.*
19 Hǣlend(e) *MS* hælend *followed by an erasure of one letter. B* hælende.
ne[1] *B adds* þu.
20 dēaþ *B adds* 7.
22 beorht *B* frea beorht *(i.e.* frēabeorht*).*
22 wæs *For B's addition, see the explanatory n.*
23 mē *B adds* Se eadiga.
hē *Omitted B.*
24 Drihtnes stefn *B* drihten.
25 ne[2] *Omitted B.*
26 nalæs . . . simle *Omitted B.*
27 on[2] *Omitted B.*
oþ *B* on.
xxvii *B* seofon 7 twentig.
and *Omitted B.*
29 syndon *B adds* 7.
31 Māthēus *B adds* he.
and *B* wæs.
32 in[2] *B* on.

35 III *B* þry.

37 sē *B* þa.

Hǣlend(e) *MS* hælend *followed by an erasure of one letter. B* hælend.

38 tō *B adds* ðæm halgan.

39 Marmadonia *B* mermedonia *here and subsequently.*

ālǣd *B* alǽde.

40 Māthēus *B* matheum þinne broþor ofþæm car cerne.

þon *B adds* þenu gít.

iii *B* þry.

tō (h)lāfe *MS* to lafe, *with an erasure of one letter between the two words; see explanatory n.*

41 gedōn *B* dón.

42 Hǣlend(e) *MS* hælend *followed by an erasure of one letter. B* hælende.

44 gefaran *B* geferan.

45 hrædlīce gefaran *B* hrædlicor þider geferan.

þon *B adds* þemin drihten.

46 ic þone weg *B* þone weg ic.

47 Drihten *B adds* crist.

gehēr *B* gehyre.

48 sīð *B* siþfæt.

sǣ*s* *MS* sæ; *B* sǽs.

49 waroðe *B adds 7.*

50 discipulum *B adds the long passage in OE and Latin quoted in the explanatory n.*

52 iii *B* þry.

53 mid micle *B* myclum.

54 willað gē faran *B* wille feran.

55 Hǣlend *B* hælende crist.

swā (se) *MS* swa *followed by an erasure of two letters. B* swase.

56 him² *B adds* þa.

58 hē *Omitted B.*

60 willað *B* wille.

61 fēran *B* faran.

62 Nēdmycel *B* med my | cel. *See explanatory n.*

63 hit *B adds* þeh.

64 Hǣlend *B* hælende crist.

65 færsceat *B* fersceat *(so too in l. 66 f.).*

66 nabbað *B* nehabbað.

70 mid *Omitted B.*

gecȳð *B* gecyþe.

þone *MS* þonn̄ *(abbreviation for* þonne*); B* swa þeah þone.

71 Hǣlend *Omitted B.*

72 Andrēas *B adds* þa.

73 scip *B adds* mid his discipulum.

beforan *B* be; *cf. Cas* iusta.

stēorrēþran *B adds* þæs scipes.

75 Hǣlend *B adds* crist.

for þon þe *B* ꝥ.

76 lande *B* eorþan.

77 þǣre *B* adds þe.

eart sended *B* sended eart.

78 þū *B adds* þonne.

79 Mīne *B* mín.

79 wille *B* willaþ.
tō lande faran *B* astigan | oneorðan.
81 discipulī (him) *MS* discipuli *followed by an erasure of two letters. B* discipuli hī.
hīe *Omitted B.*
82 wē¹ *B adds* fremde; *see explanatory n.*
gearwodest *B* ge gearwodest.
83 hwǣr *B* hwyder.
84 hālgan Andrēa *Omitted B.*
85 spec *B* sprec.
86 þæt *B* þ̄te.
gebletsod *An attempt has been made to change* e² *to* i *by erasure. B has* geblissad *here; Cas* letetur corda eorum.
ofergieton *B* sýn ofer gytende.
88 Andrēas *B adds* þa.
89 scip *B adds* 7.
90 hrēoge þā sǣ *B* hreonesse | ðære sæwe.
91 þā¹ *Added, probably by the original hand. It occurs here in B.*
andrǣdon *The* æ *has been altered to* e; *B* ondŕedon.
93 and *B* ða.
hīe *B* 7hihine.
94 mīne *B* mín.
96 hē sette *B* asette.
97 discipul *B* discipula.
slēp *B* he onslep.
Hǣlend *B* hælende crist.
99 h*weorf*að *MS* hrowað; *B* hweorfað.
100 And þā englas *B* þa englas þa.
102 þā² . . . wæs *Omitted B.*
104 Ārīsað *B adds* ge.
105 wē witon *B* witon we; *see explanatory n.*
107 swā *B* swa swa.
108 tō heofonum *B* on | heofenas.
110 swā tō *B* swto.
111 onȳwe *B* æteowe.
112 þā² *Omitted B.*
113 geseoh *B* gefeoh.
114 mīn *Omitted B.*
115 And *Omitted B.*
115 f. ic þē ne *B* þeic þe.
117 nǣnigwuht þū gefirnodest *B* negefyrenodest þu nán | wuht.
117 f. ic swā dyde, for þon *Omitted B.*
118 swā² *Omitted B.*
meahtes *B* mihte.
iii *B* ðrim.
118 f. þider gefēran *B* hider gefaran.
119 ætēow*de* *MS* æteowe; *B* æteow | de *(supported by Gr. "I have showed thee," Val* hostendi, *Cas* ostendi*).*
mihtig *B adds* mid worde.
dōn*ne* *MS* done; *B* dónne.
120 swā swā *B* swa hwæt | swa.
gā *B* gang.
121 lǣt *B* alæde.

124 þæt *B* þte.
flōwð *B* flewþ.
swā *B* swa swa.
dēaþeˌ hīe *Emendation from B (see explanatory n.).*
125 gel*ǣ*dan *MS* geladan; *B* ge | lǽdan.
ac . . . magon *Not in MS; supplied from B (see explanatory n).*
127 Gemune . . . earfoðnesse *Omitted B; cf. Cas* Recordare mei.
128 þā *Omitted B.*
spǣtton *B* spæt lædon.
mīne onsȳne *B* minne ondwleotan.
129 hwylce *B* hwylcum.
142 tō (h)lāfe *MS* to lafe, *with an erasure of one letter between the two words; see explanatory n. to l. 40.*
155 andg*ie*t *MS* andgeat.
166 Andrēas [. . .] and *See explanatory n. There is no gap here in the MS.*
171 anbīdende *MS* án bi dende, *with an erasure of one letter* (d?) *between* i *and* d^1 (Cas expectantem autem quid accideret de eo*)*.
172 gelǣd*an* . . . hi*m* *MS* gelæddon ⁊ hie *(see explanatory n.).*
175 *n*ǣnige *MS* mænige *(Gr. "we found nobody," Cas* non invenimus quemquam*).*
179 *ālȳsde þā* þe *MS* þy.
187 unriht*n*esse *MS* unrihtesse.
Hǣlend(e) *MS* hælend *followed by an erasure of one letter.*
232 ondrǣdon *Original* æ *has been altered to* e.
hine *Not in MS; see the explanatory n.*
233 þeˌ ǣr *hē* *MS* þe he ær.
240 Hǣlend(e) *MS* hælend *followed by an erasure of one letter.*
241 genihtsumiað *With* i^2 *added above, apparently by the original scribe.*
Hǣlend(e) *MS* hælend *followed by an erasure of one letter.*
246 locc *With* c^2 *partially erased.*
247 þī *mīn* līchamaˌ *MS* þinum lichaman.
251 Driht(e)nes *MS* Driht nes, *with an erasure of one letter between* t *and* n. *Cf. ll. 72, 284, and esp. 285 (and the textual note to the latter).*
253 ne *Added above, probably by the original hand.*
267 swā *MS* swa swa, *with* swa^1 *erased (see explanatory n.).*
269 st*ǣn*ene *MS* stefne.
270 hi*t* *MS* hie.
man*na* *MS* mana.
274 geneˌˌsan *MS* geneosian.
284 gehwyrfede *MS* gehwerfede, *with* y *written above* e^2, *probably by the original scribe.*
285 Drihtenes *With* e^1 *added above by the original scribe.*
289 tō hlāfe *An attempt has been made to erase* h; *see explanatory n. to l. 40.*
294 ondrǣdon *An attempt has been made to alter* æ *to* e *by erasure.*
298 þus geworden *Erasure between these two words.*
301 Hǣlend(e) *MS* hælend *followed by an erasure of one letter.*
305 Hǣlendesˌ *MS* hælendest.
310 gedēfra*n* *MS* gedefra.
316 Hǣlend(e) *MS* hælend *followed by an erasure of one letter.*
318 ofer *The* er *is added in the hand of the original scribe.*
319 hwyrf(e) *MS* hwyrf, *followed by an erasure of one letter (see explanatory n.).*
322 Hǣlend(e) *MS* hælend *followed by an erasure of one letter.*

328 Hǣlendes *Erasure of one letter after this word, probably* t *(see textual n. to l. 305).*
330 (Mar)madonia *MS* madonia *preceded by an erasure of three letters.*
332 Hǣlend(e) *MS* hælend *followed by an erasure of one letter.*
333 (A)men *MS* men, *the* a *no longer visible as a consequence of the erasure of the rest of the MS page, which contained the beginning of a new text (see Ker p. 81).*

11.

The text is fully discussed in the headnote to this selection (p. 223 ff.) and in the explanatory notes.

12.

Text and variants from the MSS (see p. 239 f.). Additions and corrections which seem to be by the original scribe are silently incorporated; additions or corrections which are not his are ignored. When the original scribe's text has been erased and rewritten, or otherwise altered, it is silently restored if the original letters seem fairly certain; otherwise the alteration is printed (but in parentheses). Erasures which remain blank have not been noted. For more careful discriminations than are possible in this edition, see Needham's textual notes.

71a Norðhymbra land ˌ *MS* norhymbra lande; *MS Ii. l. 33, University Library, Cambridge, has* norð humbra land.
243a *ne* *Added by the reviser.*

13.

Text and variants from the MSS (see p. 250 f.). Parentheses are used to indicate restorations which are necessary because of the damaged condition of the first leaf of the Laud MS. T = Talbot's transcript of the beginning of the now missing first leaf of the Cotton MS.

6 f. tō underbeginnenne *T* to beginnen *(with* n[3] *crossed out).*
12 and hē cūðe *T* ⁊ cuðe.
19 oþþe under Moises ǣ *Omitted T.*
20 furþo*n* *MS* furþo.
26 *Pētre* *T* Petre*; see explanatory n.*
29 cōm,ˌ began *MS* com ⁊ began*; T* com began.
31 hæfdon—forlēton *T* hæfdon ⁊ forleton.
56 *O*ft *is* . . . geswutelod ˌ on *MS* eft seo halige ðrynnys geswutelode. *The Laud MS has* oft ys . . . geswutelod*; MS Cambridge, University Library Ii. 1. 33 has* oft is . . . geswutolod.

14.

Text from the MS (see p. 255). The many corrections in this MS are accepted in the text but not reported here; this information is readily available in W and B (who are often in disagreement). MS punctuation and capitalization have generally guided ours.

10 s*p*ǣcan *MS* swæcan.
20 man*n*a *MS* mana.
48 getrȳ*w*ða *MS* getryða.
63 f. tōēacan . . . *wīde* See explanatory n.
79 gecn*ā*we *MS* gecnewe.
98 wor*o*ldscame *MS* wolodscame.

112 þur*h* *MS* þur.
117 o*n* *MS* of.
120 godfy*r*hte *MS* godfyhte.
144 fordō*n* *MS* fordom.
159 micla*n* *MS* miclam.

15.

Text from Gollancz' facsimile (see p. 289). The Latin text is from *PL*, XXVIII, col. 188 f., with the punctuation slightly modified.

2900a *stōwe* *Not in MS; see explanatory n.*
2907b s*c*encan *MS* sencan.

The text of Ælfric's paraphrase is from MS British Museum Cotton Claudius B. iv (see p. 250).

[7 f.] tō þāmˌ cnapum *MS* to þā mcnapum. *MS Bodleian Library Laud Misc. 509 (see p. 250) shows its pedigree clearly here by reproducing exactly this reading. (A later reader of the Laud MS erased the third limb of* m[1], *thus producing the admirable reading* to þā ii cnapum*!)*
[18] sōn(a) *The* a *is over an erasure and in a different hand.*
[24, 25] Godˌ gesyhð *MS* godes gesyhð, *with* s[1] *erased, in both places.*

16.

Text from Gollancz' facsimile (see p. 289). The MS contains a large number of corrections, some made by the original scribe himself, some made by (an)other person(s)—"the corrector(s)"—who had a strong normalizing bent. In general we have incorporated the corrections of the original scribe into our text and ignored the normalizations of the "corrector(s)." There is bound to be a certain arbitrariness about this procedure, since the handwriting of all the scribes involved is so similar that scholars are not agreed what changes to attribute to whom. Examination of the MS reproduction facing p. 297, and the accompanying commentary, will make the nature of the problem clear. The following notes report neither corrections nor normalizations, only modern emendations (and corrections made in the MS by someone other than the original scribe which we have accepted as emendations). The other corrections and normalizations can be studied with profit only in Gollancz' facsimile, or in Krapp, Timmer and Vickry (where they are reported in detail and discussed with considerable disagreement).

255a wæ*s*tm *MS* wæwtm.
267a *hē* *Added by a corrector.*
277b weorð*an* *MS* weorð *(with* an *added by a corrector).*
317a ge*þwing* *MS* gewrinc.
319a sīð*e* *MS* sið *(with* e *added by a corrector).*
358a *on* *Added in the margin by "a later hand" (Timmer).*

17.

Text from Förster's facsimile (see p. 310, n. 2).

2a h*w*æt *MS* hæt.
9a eaxlˌgespanne *MS* eaxle ge spanne.
15a geweorðodˌ *MS* geweorðode.
17a bewrigenˌ *MS* bewrigene.
17b Weald*end*es *MS* wealdes.

20b sorgum *MS* surgum.
47b ˌǣnigum *MS* nænigum.
59a *sorgum* *Not in MS.*
70a grēotende *MS* reotende.
71b *stefn* *Not in MS.*
91a hol*t*wudu *MS* holmwudu.
117b *a*nforht *MS* unforht.
142a *mē* *MS* he.

18.

Text from the facsimile (see p. 318).

15a fnǣ*s*t *MS* fnæft.
72b w*a*niað *MS* wuniað.

19.

Text from the facsimile (see p. 318).

22b mīn*n*e *MS* mine.
24b waþe*m*a *MS* waþena.
27b mīn*n*e *MS* mine.
28a frēondlēas*n*e *MS* freond lease.
59a mōdsefaˌ *MS* mod sefan.
74a eal*r*e *MS* ealle.
89a deorˌce *MS* deornce.
102b hrūs*an* *MS* hruse.

20.

Text from the facsimile (see p. 318).

25b n*e* ǣnig *MS* nænig.
26b fr*ē*fran *MS* feran.
56a ē*s*tēadig *MS* eft eadig.
75a frem*um* *MS* fremman.
82a n*ea*ron *MS* næron.
109a mo*n* *MS* mod.
115b swī*þ*re *MS* swire.
117b *wē* *MS* se.

21.

Text from the facsimile (see p. 318).

8/8a sit*t*e ð*in*gende *MS* siteð nigende.
26/6a ecgˌ *MS* ecge.
29/2a horn*um* bitwēonum *MS* horna abit·weonū.
29/5b ātimbra*n* *MS* atimbram.
44/7a efe*n*lang *MS* efe lang.

22.

Text from the facsimile (see p. 318).

20b hycgend*n*e *MS* hycgende.
25b S*c*eal *MS* seal.
37a sitta*n* *MS* sittam.

23.

Text from the *EEMSF* facsimile (see p. 347). Readings derived from MS Junius 105 are not distinguished in the present edition: this information is available in Dobbie, Timmer and (most accurately) Malone.

85b þearfˌendre *MS* þearf | fendre.
87a heorteˌ on- *MS* heorte ys on-.
134a hīeˌ be- *MS* hie hie be-.
144b Iūdithˌ be- *MS* iudithe be-.
179b staria*n* *MS* stariað.
201b *sige-* *Not in MS.*
207b w*i*stan *MS* westan.
234b rīc*n*e *MS* rice.
249a *wērig-* *Not in MS.*
251b h*i*ld*e* *MS* hyldo.
287b *nȳde* *Not in MS.*
345a *ā* *Not in MS.*
347b gesceō*p* *MS* ge sceow.

24.

Text from Elphinston's transcript (see p. 360). The paragraphing (except before *Byrhtnōð* 101a) follows the capitalization there (see Gordon pp. 35, 40).

4b t*ō* MS t.
5a þ*ā* *MS* þ.
10a w*i*gge *MS* w. . . .ge, *indicating the omission of two or three letters between* w *and* g.
20a randa*s* *MS* randan.
33b *hi*lde *MS* . .ulde.
61b *wē* *MS* þe.
86b l*ā*ðe *MS* luðe.
103b f*e*ohte *MS* fohte.
171b gest*a*ndan *MS* ge stundan.
173a Geþanc*ie* *MS* ge | þance.
191b ær*n*don *MS* ærdon.
192a God*w*ine *MS* godrine.
201a þ*earf*e *MS* þære.
208a forlǣt*an* *MS* for lætun.
212a Gemun*aþ* þā*ra* *MS* ge | munu þa.
274a gear*o* *MS* gearc.
292b crin*c*gan *MS* crintgan.
297b Forð*ðā* *MS* forða.
299a geþrang*e* *MS* geþrang.

25.

Text from the MS (see p. 373).

10a swi*t*olost *MS* swicolost.
19a ear*m* ānhaga *MS* earn án haga.

GLOSSARY

Citation is by text number and line, e.g. 7/48 means Selection 7, line 48. Cross-reference is frequently made to the paradigms in the Grammar, the reference being to chapter and paragraph (e.g. §13.4). In view of the amplitude of this cross-referencing, extensive exemplification of inflectional variants was not considered necessary. Nor, in the light of the heterogeneous nature of the reading material, would a full concordance have served any useful purpose. The vocabulary of the brief reading selections in the Grammar is omitted by design.

The following abbreviations are used:

a	a-halfline	inst	instrumental
acc	accusative	interj	interjection
adj	adjective	interr	interrogative
adv	adverb	Lat	Latin
Æ	Selection 15, Ælfric's prose	lit	literally
		m	masculine
anom	anomalous	n	neuter *or* note
art	article	nom	nominative
b	b-halfline	obj	object
cf	compare	pers	person
comp	comparative	pl	plural
conj	conjunction	pple	participle
dat	dative	prep	preposition
def	definite	pres	present
dem	demonstrative	pret	preterit
f	feminine	pron	pronoun
gen	genitive	refl	reflexive
h	headnote	rel	relative
imper	imperative	sb	substantive
impers	impersonal	sg	singular
indecl	indeclinable	st	strong
indef	indefinite	subjunc	subjunctive
indic	indicative	sup	superlative
indir	indirect	vb	verb
inf	infinitive	wk	weak

The class of all verbs is indicated, Arabic numerals being used for strong verbs and Roman numerals for weak.

Parts of both weak and strong verbs which have a base that is spelled differently from that of the infinitive are cross-referenced (e.g. *worhte* is cross-referenced to its infinitive *wyrcan, bād* to *bīdan*). Noun forms which have a base that is spelled differently from that of the nominative singular are treated in the same way (e.g. *frīend* is cross-referenced to its nominative singular *frēond*).

Headwords are printed in boldface type. They are arranged in alphabetical order and their spelling reflects the spelling of the texts (except that *þ* and *ð* are normalized to *þ* initially and *ð* medially and finally). In the case of words which occur in the texts in more than one spelling, the headword spelling conforms to that in Clark Hall's *Dictionary,*[1] and all variants which are likely to give the student difficulty (e.g. those in which the spelling of the root syllable differs) are cross-referenced to it. On the other hand words which show variation between a double and single final consonant are given a headword form which reflects this variability (e.g. *man(n)*, *hālignes(s)*).

The letters *þ* and *ð* are alphabetized following *t*; *æ* and *œ* are alphabetized as if they were spelled *ae* and *oe*. When it occurs initially, the prefix *ge-* is ignored for purposes of alphabetization and is printed in italic type to distinguish it from the alphabetized portion of the headword (e.g. the verb *gewītan* is to be found under *w,* and the headword has the form *ge***wītan**). For words which occur both with and without the prefix, and in which its presence or absence does not substantially affect the meaning, the symbol (*ge*) is used (i.e. both *fyllan* and *gefyllan* are found under *f* with the headword form (*ge*)**fyllan**). If, however, the prefixed and non-prefixed form are sometimes substantially different in meaning, then they are entered separately. All words in which *ge-* is not a prefix are alphabetized regularly (e.g. *geond*).

We have not supplied etymologies. Students interested in information of this sort should consult BT/BTS and F. Holthausen, *Altenglisches etymologisches Wörterbuch,* 2nd ed. (Heidelberg 1963). It was particularly hard to restrain ourselves from supplying etymologies for place-anmes—but we did. The interested student will find this fascinating information in Eilert Ekwall's *Concise Oxford Dictionary of English Place Names*, 4th ed. (Oxford 1960). (Incidentally we base our indications of vowel-length in place names on Ekwall's etymologies.) The student interested in OE personal names should consult William George Searle, *Onomasticon Anglo-Saxonicum* (Cambridge 1897).

---

[1]John R. Clark Hall, *A Concise Anglo-Saxon Dictionary*, 4th ed. (with a Supplement by Herbert D. Meritt) (Cambridge 1962).

A

ā adv *ever, always* 6/95; 8/21; 9/129; 10/333; 11/223 etc; 12/44 etc; 13/101; 14/6 etc; 16/375; 18/25, 35, 72; 20/42, 47; 22/5 etc; 23/7 etc; 24/315; 25/54: see also **woruld**

aa = ā

ā–bād pret 1 and 3 sg of **ā–bīdan**

abbod, –ud m (§13.3) *abbot* 6/92

abbudisse f (§14.7) *abbess* 2/1, 42

ā–bēad pret 1 and 3 sg of **ā–bēodan**

Ābel personal name *Abel* 13/62

ā–belgan 3 *anger, enrage* 16/430

ā–bēodan 2 *announce* 24/27, 49

ā–bīdan 1 with gen obj *wait for, await* 6/22; 22/53: *continue living* 12/251

ā–bisgian II *occupy, engage* 4/188

ā–blinnan 3 *cease, abate* 11/177

ā–bolgen past pple of **ā–belgan**

ā–bræc pret 1 and 3 sg of **ā–brecan**

ā–brǣcon pret pl of **ā–brecan**

ā–brǣd = **ā–brægd** (pret 1 and 3 sg of **ā–bregdan**)

ā–brægd pret 1 and 3 sg of **ā–bregdan**

Abraham personal name *Abraham* 13/4 etc; 15/2850 etc

ā–brēað pret 1 and 3 sg of **ā–brēoðan**

ā–brecan 4 *take by storm, capture* 4/136, 174 etc: *break* 20/h

ā–bregdan 3 *draw* 23/79: *snatch* 15/2915: *strike, slash* 15/2932

ā–brēoðan 2 *fall away, degenerate* 14/114; 16/246n: *fail, come to naught* 24/242

ā–broðen past pple of **ā–brēoðan**

ac conj *but* 1/13 etc; 2/10 etc; 3/17; etc

āccennan = **ā–cennan**

ā–cēgan I *call* 1/31

ā–cennan I *bear* (a child) 11/129, 208: *beget* 9/53; 11/222; 13/48

Āchāia see 10/38n

ācsian = **āscian**

āc–trēo n (§13.6) *oak tree* 22/28 etc

ā–cwælde = **ā–cwealde** (pret 1 and 3 sg of **ā–cwellan**)

ā–cwǣlon pret pl of **ā–cwelan**

ā–cwæð pret 1 and 3 sg of **ā–cweðan**

ā–cweald past pple of **ā–cwellan**

ā–cwealde pret 1 and 3 sg of **ā–cwellan**

ā–cwealdon pret pl of **ā–cwellan**

ā–cweccan I *shake, brandish* 24/255 etc

ā–cwehte pret 1 and 3 sg of **ā–cweccan**

ā–cwelan 4 *die* 11/30: past pple **ā–cwolen** *dead* 4/200

ā–cwellan I *kill, destroy* 1/h; 10/35, 40, 142 etc; 11/34; 15/Æ; 14/61

ā–cwencan I *extinguish, quench* 14/19

ā–cweðan 5 *speak, utter* 19/91; 23/82 etc: *renounce, banish* 16/304

ā–cwið pres 3 sg of **ā–cweðan**

ā–cwolen past pple of **ā–cwellan**

ā–cȳðan I *make known, disclose* 19/113

ād m (§13.2) *funeral pile, pyre* 8/108; 15/2856 etc

Ādam personal name *Adam* 16/365 etc; 17/100

ā–dīlegian II *destroy, devastate* 4/h: *blot out, erase, expunge* 11/182

ā–dīligian = **ā–dīlegian**

ādl f (§14.1) *disease, sickness* 20/70: *plague* 9/18

ādlig adj *sick* 12/38 etc

Ādom = **Ādam**

ā–drǣfan I *drive, drive away* 4/63, 91: *drive out, banish* 3/3, 7; 11/200

ā–drāf pret 1 and 3 sg of **ā–drīfan**

ā–drēah pret 1 and 3 sg of **ā–drēogan**

ā–drencan I *drown* 6/41

ā–drēogan 2 *spend, pass* 12/245: *practice* 14/70

ā–drīfan 1 *drive* 6/20

ā–drifon pret pl of **ā–drīfan**

ā–drincan 3 *be drowned* 6/57

ā–druncen past pple of **ā–drincan**

ā–dwǣscan I *extinguish* 1/57; 11/211; 12/13

ā–dȳlegian = **ā–dīlegian**

ǣ f (§14.6) *law* 7/40; 13/9 etc

Æbbe personal name *Æbbe* 4/275

ā–ebbian II *ebb, ebb away* 4/272

ǣce = **ēce**

ǣdre adv *quickly, instantly* 15/2905; 23/64 etc

ǣ–fæst adj *religious, pious* 2/8, 13 etc

ǣ–fæstnes(s), –nis(s) f (§14.2) *religion, piety* 1/h, 123; 2/3, 12

ǣfen(n) m n (§13.3, 5) *eve, evening* 2/78; 6/6; 10/211, 257; 16/313

ǣfen–sceop m (§13.2) *evening–singer, evening poet* 21/8/5

ǣfen–tīd f (§14.6) *evening time* 17/68

ǣfre adv *always* 6/61, 75; 9/129; 12/108 etc; 13/78 etc; 23/h: *ever* 1/64; 5/66; 7/36; 9/h; 10/25; 16/398; 13/48, 55, 78; 22/39; 23/114: **ǣfre embe stunde** *ever and anon, repeatedly* 24/271: see also **ealdor II.**

æftan adv *from behind* 5/63: *from behind, in the back* 14/55

æfter prep with acc, dat and inst **I.** (local) *along, through* 4/93, 147; 23/18: *behind* 7/30; 10/253: **II.** (temporal) *after* 1/97; 2/4; 4/46; 6/2 etc; 8/86 etc; 9/99; 10/153, 181, 304; 11/212 etc; 12/12 etc; 13/99; 14/12; 17/65; 24/65: **æfter þām (þǣm, þan, þon)** adv *after that, afterwards* 1/21; 4/h, 138, 215; 10/28, 148; 14/62 etc: **æfter þām þe (þan þe, þon þe, þon þæt)** conj *after* 1/81, 182n; 10/1; 12/1: **III.** (causal) *according to, in accordance with* 1/95; 9/97; 40/126, 216; 13/28, 45: *in* 16/396: **IV.** (object) *in pursuit of* 4/85, 104 etc; 16/282 etc; 23/65: *for, on account of* 19/50

æfter adv *afterwards, subsequently* 2/36; 16/436; 20/77: *behind* 6/94

æftera comp adj *second* 1/24: *next, following* 1/h

æfter–cweðend m (§15.5) *"after speaker":* pl *those speaking afterwards* (i.e. speaking of a man after his death) 20/72

æfter–fylgan I with dat obj *succeed* 1/97

æfter–fylgend m (§15.5) *successor* 1/182

æfter–genga m (§14.7) *successor* 12/10

æf–þonca m (§14.7) *grudge* 23/265

ǣfyn(n) = **ǣfen(n)**

ǣgder = **ǣgðer** = **ǣg–hwæðer**

Ægel–nāð personal name *Ægelnað* 6/92

ǣg–hwǣr adv *everywhere* 6/10 etc; 14/23, 48f etc

ǣg–hwæs adv (gen sg of **ǣg–hwā** pron *each*) *in every respect, entirely* 18/44

ǣg–hwæðer I. pron *either* 4/146: *each* 8/46; 24/133: *both* 13/91; 14/60: **II.** adj *each* 6/69: **III.** conj **ǣghwæðer (. . .) ge . . . ge** *both . . . and* 1/27f, 114; 4/190, 216f, 259 etc; 6/9, 55; 7/3, 5f etc; 8/24f; 13/31: **ǣghwæðer . . . and** *both . . . and* 24/224

ǣg–hwār = **ǣg–hwǣr**

ǣg–hwilc I. pron (often with partitive gen) *each, everyone* 8/43; 17/86; 23/50; 24/234: **II.** adj *each, every* 9/58; 10/6, 186f; 14/31; 17/120; 23/166

ǣg–hwonan, –on adv *on all sides* 1/h; 9/121 etc

ǣg–hwylc = **ǣg–hwilc**

ǣgðer = **ǣg–hwæðer**

ǣgwār = **ǣg–hwǣr**

ǣ–gylde adj *unpaid for, without wergild* 14/84

Ǣgypte = **Ēgypte**

ǣht f (§14.6) *possessions* 8/35; 11/56 etc; 13/31: *riches* 11/128

ǣigðer = **ǣg–hwæðer**

ǣlc I. pron *each* 4/149; 7/63; 8/116 etc; 12/97; 14/70 etc: see also **mǣst II.**: **II.** adj *every* 4/127, 193 etc; 7/61; 8/67 etc; 11/139, 269 etc; 13/41 etc; 20/49n: *any* 4/118, 157; 8/123; 12/171: *all* 14/33

aelde = **ælde**

ælde m pl (§14.5) *men* 19/85; 20/77

ǣled m (§13.3) *fire* 15/2902

Ælf–red personal name *Ælfred* 4/16 etc; 7/1; 8/1

æl–fremed adj *exempt, free* 11/320

Ælf–rīc personal name *Ælfric* 13/1

ælf–scīne adj *beautiful as an elf* 23/14

æll–mihtig = **æl–mihtig**

Ælle personal name *Ælle* 4/7

ælmæs–riht n pl (§13.4) *rights of receiving alms* 14/38

ælmes–georn adj *charitable* 9/30; 11/44; 12/83

æl–mihteg, –ig adj *almighty* 2/37; 7/16; 9/45, 81; 11/30 etc; 12/20 etc; 13/44; 15/Æ; 16/311; 17/39 etc; 23/7 etc

ælmysse f (§14.7) *alms, alms–giving* 12/91 etc

æl–þēodig = **el–þēodig**

æl–þēodisc adj *foreign, strange* 10/6

geǣmetigan II with refl pron and gen obj *disengage (oneself) from* 7/18

ænde = **ende**

ænge = **enge**

ængel = **engel**

ǣnges = **ǣniges**

ǣnig I. pron *any, any one* 14/53; 17/110

etc; 18/59: with partitive gen 1/64; 14/24 etc; 16/427; 17/47; 18/31; 20/25; 24/70: with partitive phrase 10/192: **II.** adj *any* 1/127, 150; 2/84; 4/146; 6/90; 7/16; 8/7 etc; 9/33; 12/258; 13/6 etc; 14/14 etc; 16/291 etc; 20/116; 23/329; 24/195

ǣnlic adj *peerless, noble* 12/109; 18/9

ǣnne m acc sg of **ān**

ā–ēode pret 1 and 3 sg of **ā–gān**

ǣr I. adj *early* 12/25n: see also **ǣrra** (comp), **ǣrest** (sup): **II.** adv (§24.5) *before, formerly, previously, earlier* 1/25 etc; 2/74 etc; 3/21; etc: *first* 4/277; 19/113; 24/60: see also **ǣror** (comp), **ǣrest** (sup): see also **gefyrn, gēo, sīð: III.** conj *before* 3/10; 4/86, 153, 179, 210, 242, 277, 284, 286; 6/23, 28; 8/78 etc; 10/233; 11/208; 14/93 etc; 19/64, 69; 20/74; 23/76; 24/61, 279: **IV.** prep with dat and inst *before* 1/17; 7/53; 13/19; 14/7, 15 etc; 20/69: **ǣr þǣm þe (þām þe, þan þe, þon, þon þe)** conj *before* 1/180; 6/37f, 88; 7/23; 12/18; 13/9; 17/88; 18/40, 83; 23/252: **V.** sb = **ēar**

ǣrænde = **ǣrende**

ærce–bisce(o)p = **arce–biscop**

ærce–biscpe = **ærce–biscope** (dat sg of **ærce–biscop**)

ǣren adj *brazen* 10/170

ǣrend n *message* 1/h

ǣrende n (§13.6) *message* 1/h; 15/2883; 24/28: *errand, mission* 10/62

ǣrend–fæst adj *bound on an errand* 12/221

ǣrend–gewrit n (§13.4) *letter* 7/13

ǣrendian II *negotiate for* 1/89

ǣrend–wreca m (§14.7) *messenger, minister, representative* 1/22, 24, 89; 7/5

ǣrest I. sup adj (see **ǣr I.**) *first* 1/h; 8/117; 2/61; 20/h: **II.** sup adv (see **ǣr II.**) *first* 1/35, 155; 2/33, 59; 4/h, 152; 6/6; 7/40; 8/68 etc; 9/113; 11/251; 13/30 etc; 17/19; 22/6; 23/14; 24/5, 124 etc

ǣr–gewin(n) n (§13.4) *ancient struggle, former agony* 17/19

ǣrist m n f *resurrection* 9/56; 11/288f

ǣrist = **ǣrest**

ærmðu = **iermðu**

ærnan I *gallop* 8/115 etc; 24/191

geærnan I *reach by galloping* 8/117

ǣror comp adv (see **ǣr II.**) *sooner* 6/84: *earlier* 11/206; 17/108

ǣrost = **ǣrest**

ǣrra comp adj (see **ǣr I.** and §12.8) *earlier, former, previous* 11/82, 189

ǣr–wacel adj *awake early, rising early* 11/291

ǣs n (§13.4) *food* (usually of creatures of prey), *carrion* 5/63; 24/107

æsc m (§13.2) *spear* (of ashwood) 19/99; 24/43 etc: *warship* (ON *askr*) 4/256 etc

Æsces–dūn f (§14.1) *Ashdown* (Berkshire) 4/33

æsc–here m (§13.6) *Viking army* (lit. a *here* which comes from *æscas,* q.v.) 24/69

æsc–holt n (§13.4) *spear* (of ashwood) 24/230

æsc–plega m (§14.7) *spear–play, battle* 23/217

æsc–rōf adj *brave, warlike* 23/336

æstel m (§13.3) *book marker, pointer* 7/62 etc

ǣ–swic m (§13.2) *deception, offense* 14/110

æt prep with acc and dat **I.** (local) *at, near, next to, by, in, on, to* 1/93; 2/21, 59; 3/4, 34; 4/13, 109; 5/4, 8; 11/60; 12/225; 16/266, 284; 19/111: **II.** (temporal) *at, on, in* 6/25, 76; 11/90: **æt nīehstan, æt nȳhstan** adv *at last, at length, finally* 1/11, 18; 11/159; 14/144: **III.** (source) *from* 1/126; 7/58; 14/17; 16/301; 23/3; 24/39

ǣt I. sb n (§13.4) *food, prey* 11/143; 23/210: **II.** pret 1 and 3 sg of etan

æt–brǣd pret 1 and 3 sg of **æt–bregdan**

æt–bregdan 3 *take away, withdraw* 11/124: with refl acc *refrain from* 11/16

æt–brōden past pple of **æt–bregdan**

æt–ēawan = **æt–īewan**

æt–ēcan I *add to, augment* 1/56

æt–ēowan = **æt–īwan**

æt–foran prep with dat **I.** (local) *before, in the presence of* 11/239, 257: *in front of* 24/16: **II.** (temporal) *before* 6/90

æt–gæd(e)re adv *together* 2/82; 4/190;

12/87; 14/141; 17/48: see also **samod**

æt–hlēapan 7 with dat obj *escape from, run away from* 14/81

æt–īewan I *appear* 1/139; 4/125; 6/6; 11/314: with indir obj 1/12, 73; 10/89, 119, 120, 181 etc; 11/284: *show, manifest* 1/14, 37; 10/107, 112, 129, 147 etc; 11/326; 23/174: *point out* 1/64, 169: *disclose* 9/12

æt–īwan = æt–īewan

ǣton pret pl of **etan**

æt–samne, –somne adv *together* 1/116; 2/77; 5/57; 10/2; 23/255; 25/31

æt–standan 6 *remain standing* 12/234

æt–stōd pret 1 and 3 sg of **æt–standan**

ǣtterne, ǣttryn(n) adj *poisonous, deadly* 24/47, 146

ǣttrian I *poison* 1/h

æt–wītan with dat obj *reproach* 24/220 etc

æt–ȳwan = æt–īewan

Æðel–bryht personal name *Æðelbryht* 4/1

æðele adj *noble, fine, excellent, glorious* 1/83; 5/16; 8/29; 11/11; 12/2 etc; 18/2 etc; 23/176 etc; 24/151 etc

*ge***æðele** adj *inborn in, natural for* 5/7

Æðel–ferð personal name *Æðelferð* 4/275

Æðel–frið personal name *Æðelfrið* 1/17 etc

Æðel–here personal name *Æðelhere* 4/275

æðeling m (§13.3) *prince* 1/74; 3/7 etc; 5/3 etc; 15/2848 etc; 17/58; 20/93: *noble* 1/173; 25/14

Æðeling(g)aēig(g) f (§14.2) *Athelney* (Somerset) 4/97 etc

æðelnes(s) f (§14.2) *nobility, excellence* 9/116

Æð–elm personal name *Æðelm* 4/192, 284

Æðel–nōð personal name *Æðelnoð* 4/192

Æðel–rēd personal name *Æðelred* (the Unready) 14/62n

Æðel–stān personal name *Æðelstan* (King of Wessex 924–939) 5/1

æðelu n pl (§13.6) *noble origin, descent* 24/216

Æðel–wærd personal name *Æðelwærd* 13/1

Æðel–wulf personal name *Æðelwulf* 4/27

Æðel–wulfing patronymic *the son of Æðelwulf* 4/50, 286

Æðe–red personal name *Æðered* 4/1 etc

ǣw–bryce m (§14.5) *adultery* 14/111

ǣwisc–mōd adj *ashamed in spirit* 5/56

afara = eafora

ā–faran 6 *go, go away, depart* 4/172; 6/49

ā–faren past pple of **ā–faran**

ā–feallan 7 *fall* 24/202: *fall down, collapse* 11/230: *fall off, decay* 7/53

ā–feallen past pple of **ā–feallan**

ā–fēdan I *sustain, support* 11/45, 323

ā–flieman I *put to flight* 10/221; 24/243

ā–fligan I *drive out, put to flight* 11/122; 12/198

ā–flȳman = ā–flieman

āfor adj *bitter, fierce* 23/257

ā–fyllan I **I.** *fill* 11/10, 24, 173 etc; 20/113n: **II.** *strike down, kill* 12/21; 14/83

ā–fyrhtan I *frighten, terrify* 12/187 etc

ā–fyrran I *deprive* (someone, acc) *of* (something, dat) 16/379: *make remote, remove* 18/5

ā–fyrsan II *remove, withdraw* 10/283

ā–fȳsan I *urge forward, impel* 17/125: *drive away* 24/3

(*ge*)**āgan** pret–pres vb (§23.3) *have, possess, own* 4/44; 9/71, 83; 13/104; 14/84; 15/Æ; 16/359, 368 etc; 17/107, 131; 19/64; 20/117; 22/16; 23/3 etc; 24/h, 175 etc: *obtain* 4/31, 45 etc; 6/41 etc; 23/196; 24/87: *acquire* 11/120: as auxiliary used to indicate perfect tense *have* 20/27

ā–gān anom vb (§7.7) *go* 4/266: *go by, pass* 9/h; *occur, befall* 6/15: *exhaust* 6/26

ā–geaf pret 1 and 3 sg of **ā–giefan**

ā–gēafon pret pl of **ā–giefan**

ā–gēat pret 1 and 3 sg of **ā–gēotan**

ā–gef = ā–geaf (pret 1 and 3 sg of **ā–giefan**)

ā–gēfon = ā–gēafon (pret pl of **ā–giefan**)

āgen adj *own* 3/23; 7/27 etc; 8/19 etc; 9/28; 12/65; 13/16 etc; 14/50 etc; 15/2852 etc; 21/44/4

ā–gēotan 2 *pour out* 12/195: *shed* 11/165: past pple with gen *drained* 23/32

ā–gētan I *destroy* (by shedding blood) 5/18

ā–giefan 5 *give, deliver* 1/23, 54; 7/h; 15/2884; 23/130 etc; 24/44 etc: *give back, restore* 2/50; 4/178: *give up* 11/318.

ā–gifan = **ā–giefan**

ā–gifen past pple of **ā–giefan**

ā–ginnan = **on–ginnan**

ā–goten past pple of **ā–gēotan**

ā–gyfen = **ā–gifen** (past pple of **ā–giefan**)

ā–gyldan 3 *pay, render* 9/81

ā–gyltan I *commit as a sin* 11/196

ah = **ac**

āh pres 1 and 3 sg of **āgan**

ā–hafen past pple of **ā–hebban**

ā–hangen past pple of **ā–hōn**

ā–hēawan 7 *cut down* 17/29

ā–hēawen past pple of **ā–hēawan**

ā–hebban 6 *lift up, raise* 15/2904 etc; 15/Æ; 16/294; 17/44 etc; 21/7/3; 24/106 etc: *elevate, exalt* 1/109: *rear* 16/263: *stir up* 10/91

ā–hebbian = **ā–ebbian**

ā–hefde pret 1 and 3 sg (wk) of **ā–hebban**

ā–hēng pret 1 and 3 sg of **ā–hōn**

ā–hof pret 1 and 3 sg of **ā–hebban**

ā–hōfon pret pl of **ā–hebban**

ā–hōn 7 *hang* 4/280; 12/226 etc; 23/48

ā–hongen = **ā–hangen** (past pple of **ā–hōn**)

ā–hrǣran = **ā–rǣran**

ā–hrēas pret 1 and 3 sg of **ā–hrēosan**

ā–hreddan I *rescue* 4/156; 21/29/9: *save, deliver* 12/20 etc; 13/65 etc

ā–hrēosan 2 *fall down, collapse* 11/240 etc

āhsian = **āscian**

*ge***āhsian** = *ge***āscian**

āhtan = **āhton** (pret pl of **āgan**)

āhte I. dat sg of **ā–wiht: II.** pret 1 and 3 sg of **āgan**

āhton = pret pl of **āgan**

ā–hwǣtan 7 (see *EGS*, IV [1951–2], 80–4) *expel, banish* 16/406

ā–hwār = **ǣg–hwǣr**

ā–hwēt = **ā–hwǣt** (pret 1 and 3 sg of **ā–hwǣtan**)

Aidan(us) personal name *Aidan* 12/53 etc

ā–īdli(g)an II *profane* 1/155: *invalidate, abrogate* 11/36

ā–lǣdan I *lead, conduct* 1/33; 10/28, 39 etc: *bring away* 4/240

ā–lǣtan 7 *let* 10/149

ald = **eald**

aldor = **ealdor**

aldor-bold n (§13.4) *chief residence, court* 1/h

aldor–man(n), –mon(n) = **ealdor–man(n)**

aldor–men(n) dat sg and nom and acc pl of **ealdor–man(n)**

Ald-red = **Eald-red**

ā–lecgan I *lay, place* 11/274: *lay down* 8/110 etc; 17/63; 23/101: *lay low* 12/27; 23/h: *suppress, put an end to* 11/28

ā–lēd past pple of **ā–lecgan**

a–lēde pret 1 and 3 sg of **ā–lecgan**

a–lēdon pret pl of **ā–lecgan**

ā–lēogan 2 *deny* (something, acc) *to* (someone, dat) 12/271

ā–lēsan = **ā–līesan**

ā–līesan I *free, release, deliver* 1/53; 9/107; 10/179; 11/327: *redeem* 11/18

ā–līhð pres 3 sg of **ā–lēogan**

al(l) = **eal(l)**

alle = **ealle**

all–mectig = **æl–mihtig**

all–walda m (§14.7) *ruler of all, God* 16/246 etc; 23/84

Alor m *Aller* (Somerset) 4/108

al–walda = **all–walda**

a–lȳfan I *allow, permit, grant, give* 1/91, 161; 24/90

ā–lȳsan = **ā–līesan**

ā–mang prep with dat *among, during*: **āmang þissan** adv *meanwhile* 6/47

amber f (§14.1) *measure* 8/45

am–byre adj *suitable, favorable, opportune* (see Pope[3], I, 257 f) 8/67

ā–myrran I *wound, maim, cripple* 24/165: with gen *hinder from, obstruct from* 16/378

an pres 1 and 3 sg of **unnan**

ān (m acc sg st generally **ǣnne**) **I.** numeral and pron *one* 3/31; 4/76, 268; 7/62[1]; 10/306, 331; 12/91; 13/61; 14/70[2,3] etc; 16/252; 24/117: gen pl **ānra** (cf Lat. *singulorum*) *individuals* 9/3; 10/120; 17/86, 108: see also **nealles**:

II. adj and indef article *a, a certain* 1/136; 3/4, 7; 4/66, 113 etc; 7/62²; 8/16, 65; 11/24, 28 etc; 14/69; 15/Æ; 16/395; 24/226: *one* 4/51, 74, 102 etc; 7/15; 8/44, 67 etc; 10/96; 11/265, 316; 12/232; 13/85; 23/324: *a single* 1/138; 3/17; 4/131; 7/13; 8/124; 10/242, 246; 11/95, 135, 136; 13/85; 16/369, 370; 23/64: *one and only, unique* 23/h: *one and the same* 8/27; 14/70¹: *alone* 1/h, 40, 47, 74 etc; 2/12; 9/36, 81; 10/139; 11/236; 12/234; 13/85; 15/2928; 16/272; 17/123, 128; 19/8; 22/22 etc; 24/94; 25/43 etc: *only* 7/21; 11/148: gen pl **ānra** (cf Lat. *singulorum*) *individual* 9/1; 23/95

ana = **heonu**

an–bīdan = **on–bīdan**

(*ge*)**an–bidian** II *wait* 11/299; 15/Æ (with refl pron): *wait to see* 6/78

anbyht–scealc m (§13.2) *attendant, retainer* 23/38

ān–cenned adj (past pple) *only begotten* 15/Æ

and conj *and* 1/8; etc

anda m (§14.7) *injury, spite, malice* 16/399; 19/105

and–bidian = **an–bidian**

and–efn f (§14.1) *amount* 8/110

andettan I *confess, acknowledge* 1/122, 147; 9/52

and–fenge adj *acceptable* 9/102

and–get, –giet, –git, –gyt n (§13.4) *mind* 1/5: *understanding* 10/155: *knowledge* 9/7: *meaning* 7/57; 13/23, 39 etc

and–git–fullīce adv *intelligibly* 7/60

and–lang prep with gen *along* 6/33

an–drǣdan = **on–drǣdan**

Andred see 3/3n

Andredes–weald m (§15.2) see 3/3n

and–saca m (14.7) *apostate, enemy* 16/320

and–sund = **an–sund**

and–swarian II *answer, reply* 1/49; 2/23; 10/42 etc

and–swaru f (§14.1) *answer, reply* 1/69; 2/26; 24/44

and–weard, –werd adj *present* 1/132; 2/44; 11/320 etc

and–wlita m (§14.7) *face, countenance, visage* 1/45, 77; 11/98 etc

and–wyrdan I (often with indir obj) *answer* 7/36; 11/71, 197 etc; 15/Æ

ane = **heonu**

ān–feald adj *simple* 13/39

ān–fealdlīce adv *singly, in the singular* 13/60

ān–floga m (§14.7) *lone flyer, solitary flyer* 20/62

an–forht adj *very frightened* 17/117

ān–for–lǣtan 7 *leave behind, give up* 2/53: *abandon* 9/22

ān–for–lēt pret 1 and 3 sg of **ān–for–lǣtan**

Angel *Angeln* 8/75

Angel–cyn(n) n (§13.6) *the English people* or *nation, the English* 4/h, 2, 65 etc; 7/3 etc

Angel–þēod f (§14.1) *the people of the English, England* 1/182n; 2/8

an–gin(n), –gyn(n) n (§13.4) *beginning* 11/222; 13/15 etc: *undertaking, action* 24/242

Angle m pl (§14.5) *the English* 12/106

ān–haga, –hoga m (§14.7) *"lone–dweller," solitary, recluse* 19/1, 40; 25/19

āninga adv *at once* 23/250

*ge*ā**n–lǣcan** I *unite* 12/107

*ge*ā**n–lǣhte** pret 1 and 3 sg of *ge*ā**n–lǣcan**

An–lāf personal name *Óláfr Guðfriðarson* (King of Dublin 934–941) 5/26 etc

ān–lēpe adj *solitary, single* 7/15

ān–lēpnes(s) f (§14.2) *solitude, loneliness* 1/50

an–līcnes(s), –nis(s), –nys(s) = **on–līcnes(s)**

ān–līpig adj *solitary, single, individual* 4/55

an–mēdla m (§14.7) *splendor, glory, pomp* 9/78; 20/81

ān–mōdlīce adv *unanimously* 11/35: *steadfastly, resolutely* 11/185

ann–gin(n) = **an–gin(n)**

ānnys(s) f (§14.2) *oneness, unity* 11/222; 13/59

ān–rǣd adj *resolute* 24/44 etc

an–sī(e)n f (§14.6) *form* 10/56, 316: *face* 10/128, 229 etc: *presence* 10/112: *appearance* 20/91

ān–streces adv *at one stretch, continuously, directly* 4/208
an–sund adj *whole* 11/82; 12/175: *perfect* 11/5: *unharmed, safe and sound* 11/275; 12/234; 18/20 etc: *cured* 12/218
an–sundnys(s) f (§14.2) *wholeness* 11/72
Antecrīst m (§13.2) *Antichrist* 14/7
an–þrǣce adj *horrible* 11/177
an–wealda m (§14.7) *ruler, the Lord* 17/153
An–wynd personal name *Anwynd* 4/73
apostata m (§14.7) *apostate* 14/114
apostol m (§13.3) *apostle* 1/176; 2/64; 10/2, 38, 167; 11/27, 31 etc; 13/27, 31 etc
apostolæ = apostole (dat sg of **apostol**)
apostolic adj *apostolic* 1/1
Apuldor *Appledore* (Kent) 4/139 etc
apuldre f (§14.7) *apple–tree* 6/67
ār **I.** m (§13.2) *messenger* 15/2911; 24/26: **II.** f (§14.1) *oar* 4/258: **III.** f (§14.1) *honor, glory* 1/109: *mercy, favor, grace* 9/10; 19/1, 114; 20/107: *wealth, income* 8/41; 11/58
ā–rǣdan I *read* 7/51 etc: *determine, fix* 19/5
ā–ræfnan I *endure* 10/126, 128 etc
ā–rǣman I *rise* 15/2877
ā–rǣran I *raise up* 11/47, 155 etc; 12/137: *erect* 11/282; 12/17 etc; 15/Æ; 17/44: *establish* 13/32
ā–rās pret 1 and 3 sg of **ā–rīsan**
arce–biscep, –biscop m (§13.3) *archbishop* 4/24, 25, 32; 6/73 etc; 7/58
ardlīce adv *quickly* 15/Æ
ā–reccean I *translate* 7/13: *interpret* 7/61
ā–refnan = ā–ræfnan
ā–rētan I *cheer, gladden* 23/167
ār–fæst adj *honorable, virtuous* 11/37: *merciful* 23/190
ār–fæstnes(s), –nis(s) f (§14.2) *goodness, grace* 1/4, 10: *virtue* 2/3
ār–hwæt adj *glorious* 5/73
ār–hwate m nom pl of **ār–hwæt**
ārian II with dat obj *pardon* 11/95: *spare* 15/Æ: used absolutely *show mercy, spare* 10/285
ā–riht adv *aright, properly* 14/98
ā–rīsan 1 *rise, arise* 1/78; 2/17, 94; 9/15; 10/51, 92 etc; 11/48 etc; 12/210; 15/Æ; 17/101; etc
ā–rison pret pl of **ā–rīsan**
Aristodēmus personal name *Aristodemus* 11/250f etc
ār–lēas adj *impious, wicked, foul* 1/181
arn pret 1 and 3 sg of **iernan**
arod adj *daring, bold* 23/275
Āron personal name *Haran* 15/2929
ār–stæf m (§13.2) *kindness, honor* 21/26/24
ār–stafas nom and acc pl of **ār–stæf**
ār–wurð, –wyrð adj *venerable, reverend* 12/53
ār–wurðian II *honor* 12/146
ār–wurðlīce adv *honorably, with honor* 12/61 etc
ār–wurðnys(s) f (§14.2) *honor, reverence* 12/168 etc
ā–sǣde = ā–sægde (pret 1 and 3 sg of **ā–secgan**)
ā–sǣton pret pl of **ā–sittan**
ā–scān pret 1 and 3 sg of **ā–scīnan**
Ascan–mynster n (§13.5) *Axminster* (Devonshire) 3/34
ascas nom and acc pl of **æsc**
asce f (§14.7) *ash* 10/313f n
ā–sceacan 6 *shake, brandish* 24/230
ā–sceōc pret 1 and 3 sg of **ā–sceacan**
āscian II *ask* 1/102, 154; 10/76; 15/Æ
*ge*āscian II *learn of, find out about* 9/14, 18, 19; 12/177: *discover* 1/21; 3/8; 6/16
ā–scīnan 1 *shine* 10/313
ā–scūfan II *shove, push, launch* 4/277
ā–scȳran I *make clear, make transparent* 9/48
ā–secgan III *tell, express* 19/11; 23/330; 24/198
ā–sendan I *send* 11/28, 39 etc
ā–seten past pple of **ā–sittan**
ā–settan I *set, place* 8/127
Asia *Asia* 11/203
ā–singan 3 *sing, recite* 2/50
ā–sittan 5 *run aground* 4/269 etc
ā–smēagan II *devise, treat of* 14/137
ā–smiðian II *make* : past pple *wrought* 12/173
ā–solcennes(s) f (§14.2) *laziness, sloth, indolence, inactivity* 14/146

ā–song pret 1 and 3 sg of **ā–singan**
ā–spendan I *spend* 8/120
ā–sprang pret 1 and 3 sg of **ā–springan**
ā–springan 3 *spring up* 11/207: *spread* 12/239
ā–sprungon pret pl of **ā–springan**
assa m (§14.7) *ass* 15/Æ
Asser personal name *Asser* 7/58
Assīrias = **Assӯrias**
Assӯrias m pl *Assyrians* 23/218 etc
ā–stāh = **ā–stāg** (pret 1 and 3 sg of **ā–stīgan**)
ā–stāg pret 1 and 3 sg of **ā–stīgan**
ā–standan 6 *stand up, rise* 1/h; 9/47
ā–stealde pret 1 and 3 sg of **ā–stellan**
ā–stellan I *establish, create* 2/29 sq n; 13/69
ā–stīgan 1 *ascend* 10/1, 100 etc; 17/103: *descend* 10/275: *come up* 10/64, 72¹: *go up* 10/49, 72², 76 etc
ā–stigon pret pl of **ā–stīgan**
ā–stingan 3 *stab, thrust:* **āstingan ūt** *put out* 10/7, 11
ā–stōd pret 1 and 3 sg of **ā–standan**
ā–stræht = **ā–streht** (past pple of **ā–streccan**)
ā–streccan I *prostrate* 11/153, 157 etc: *stretch out, extend* 11/296; 12/183; 15/Æ
ā–streht past pple of **ā–streccan**
ā–strehte pret 1 and 3 sg of **ā–streccan**
ā–stungon pret pl of **ā–stingan**
ā–styrian I *move, remove* 17/30
ā–swāmian II *abate, cease* 16/376
ā–swebban I *put to sleep, kill* 5/30; 23/321
ā–swefed past pple of **ā–swebban**
ā–tēah pret 1 and 3 sg of **ā–tēon**
ā–tēon 3 *draw* 2/68; 15/Æ
ā–tēorian II *be used up, run out* 11/9
ā–timbran I *build* 21/29/5
atol adj *terrible* 20/6; 23/75 etc
Atticus personal name *Atticus* 11/87 etc
āttor n (§13.4) *poison* 1/h; 10/7, 12; 11/246 etc; 16/328n
āttor–bǣre adj *poisonous* 11/259
ā–tugon pret pl of **ā–tēon**
āð m (§13.2) *oath* 4/67, 78 etc; 6/61 etc; 14/157
āð–brice m (§14.5) *oath–breaking, perjury* 14/112
ā–þencan I *contrive, devise* 16/400
ā–þenian II *stretch out* 10/259, 264
āðer conj: **āðer oððe . . . oððe** *either . . . or* 8/49
ā–þiestrian II *become dark, be eclipsed* 4/114
Aðulfing = **Æðel–wulfing**
ā–þwēan 6 *wash* 12/194
ā–þwōh pret 1 and 3 sg of **ā–þwēan**
Augustīnus personal name *Augustine* 12/1
āwa = **ā**
ā–wæcnan 6 *wake up* 12/217
ā–wǣgan I *repudiate, go back on* 12/269
ā–weahte pret 1 and 3 sg of **ā–weccan**
ā–wearp pret 1 and 3 sg of **ā–weorpan**
ā–weccan I *wake, rouse* 10/104, 301; 23/258 etc: *excite, incite* 2/69
ā–weg = **on–weg**
ā–wegan 5 *carry* 11/295
ā–wehte pret 1 and 3 sg of **ā–weccan**
ā–wendan I *turn* 11/12, 103 etc; 12/62; 16/246n: *change* 11/98, 189; 13/84; *restore* 11/192: *translate* 7/61; 13/2, 86 etc: *direct* 12/253: *subdue, bend* 13/97
ā–went pres 3 sg of **ā–wendan**
ā–weorpan 3 *throw, cast* 1/159; 11/60; 12/55; 16/420: *depose* 4/6: *reject, discard, throw away* 13/89 etc
ā–wiht indef pron (with partitive gen) *anything, aught* 9/48: acc sg used as adv *at all* 16/290: **tō āhte** adv *at all* 14/19
ā–wōc pret 1 and 3 sg of **ā–wæcnan**
ā–worpen past pple of **ā–weorpan**
ā–wrāt pret 1 and 3 sg of **ā–wrītan**
ā–wreccan I *awaken* 11/49
ā–wreht past pple of **ā–wreccan**
ā–wrītan 1 *write* 7/27; 11/33, 204 etc; 13/64 etc; 14/142: *write down* 11/303: *copy* 13/103
ā–writon pret pl of **ā–wrītan**
ā–writen past pple of **ā–wrītan**
ā–wunian I *last, abide* 9/20
ā–wurpan = **ā–weorpan**
ā–wurpon pret pl of **ā–weorpan**
ā–wyrgan I *curse, damn* 11/171f
āxian = **āscian**
*ge***āxian** = *ge***āscian**
ā–ӯdlian = **ā–īdli(g)an**

B

bā f nom and acc dual *both* 23/128, 133
Bāch–secg personal name *Bachsecg* 4/34 etc
bād pret 1 and 3 sg of **bīdan**
*ge***bād** pret 1 and 3 sg of *ge***bīdan**
Bæbban–burg f (§15.7) *Bamborough* (Northumbria) see 12/168b n
bæc n (§13.4) *back:* **ofer bæc** adv *backwards, to the rear* 24/276: **under bæc** adv *backwards, behind* 15/Æ
bæc–bord n (§13.4) *larboard, port* 8/9 etc
bæd pret 1 and 3 sg of **biddan**
*ge***bæd** pret 1 and 3 sg of *ge***biddan**
bǣdon pret pl of **biddan**
*ge***bǣdon** pret pl of *ge***biddan**
bǣl n (§13.4) *fire, pyre* 15/2904; 18/47; 20/114
bælc m (§14.5) *pride* 23/267
bǣl–fȳr n (§13.4) *funeral fire* 15/2857
bær pret 1 and 3 sg of **beran**
bǣr f (§14.1) *bier* 11/46
*ge***bǣran** I *behave, conduct oneself* 23/27
*ge***bǣre** n (§13.6) *outcry, behavior* 3/14: *demeanor, bearing* 22/21 etc
bærnan I *burn* 14/101
bærnet(t) n (§13.6) *burning* 15/Æ
*ge***bǣro** = *ge***bǣre**
bǣron pret pl of **beran**
bærst pret 1 and 3 sg of **berstan**
bǣtan I *bridle* 15/2867
bæð n (§13.4) *bath, immersion* 1/174; 11/26
Bāg–secg = **Bāch–secg**
bald = **beald**
baldlīce adv *boldly* 24/78 etc
baldor = **bealdor**
bān n (§13.4) *bone* 8/124; 9/94, 96; 12/141 etc: *ivory* 8/29, 42
bana m (§14.7) *slayer* 3/26; 17/66; 24/299
(*ge*)**band** pret 1 and 3 sg of (*ge*)**bindan**
*ge***bannan** 7 *call up, summon* 1/89
Bardan–īg f (§14.2) *Bardney* (Lincolnshire) 12/178
barn = **bearn**
Basengas m pl (§13.3) *Basing* (Hampshire), lit "the people of *Basa*" (see 4/2n, 12/128a n) 4/41
bastard m *bastard* 6/14f n
bāt m (§13.2) *boat* 4/118 etc
baðian II *bathe* 19/47
be prep with dat **I.** (local) *along, by* 4/71, 113, 147, 157 etc; 6/10, 25; 8/5, 8 etc; 11/51; 12/174; 19/80; 20/8; 24/152, 318: *near, next to* 1/h; 10/170; 12/222; 20/98; 21/44/1; 24/182: *past* 8/18: **II.** (means) *by, by means of, with* 2/22; 7/57; 11/37; 13/16; 14/150; 15/2906; 23/81 etc; 24/9: *to the accompaniment of* 2/16: **III.** (reference) *about, concerning* 1/75, 144; 2/59; 9/23, 83; 11/32, 50, etc; 12/150 etc; 13/12, 26 etc; 14/142; 18/h; 20/1; 22/1: **IV.** (casual) *according to, in accordance with, by* 8/42; 11/101, 126 etc; 12/124; 13/63, 104: **bī þǣm þe** conj *according to what* 1/81: see also **dǣl, ēastan, ful(l), sūð(an), norðan, westan**
be adv *therefrom* 7/67
bēacen n (§13.5) *sign* 17/6 etc
(*ge*)**bēad** pret 1 and 3 sg of (*ge*)**bēodan**
beado–rinc m (§13.2) *warrior* 23/276
beadowe = **beaduwe** (dat sg of **beadu**)
beadu f (§14.3) *battle* 23/175 etc; 25/15
beadu–rǣs m (§13.2) *rush of battle, onslaught* 24/111
beaduwe dat sg of **beadu**
beadu–weorc n (§13.4) *warlike deed, fighting* 5/48
be–æftan I. adv *behind* 23/112: **II.** prep with dat *behind* 3/19, 21
bēag I. sb m (§13.2) *ring, armlet* 4/78; 23/36 etc; 24/31 etc; 25/29 etc: **II.** pret 1 and 3 sg of **būgan I.**
bēah = **bēag II.** (pret 1 and 3 sg of **būgan I.**)
bēah–gifa m (§14.7) *ring–giver, lord* 5/2; 24/290
bēah–gifu f (§14.1) *ring–giving, generosity* 25/15
bēah–hroden adj (past pple) *ring–adorned* 23/138
beald adj *bold, confident, assured* 1/59; 9/41; 23/17
bealdor m (§13.2) *lord, master* 23/9 etc
bealo–ful(l) adj *baleful, wicked* 23/48 etc
bealo–sīð m (§13.2) *"harm journey," bitter experience, adversity* 20/28
bealu n (§13.6) *wickedness* 9/41: *malice* 20/112
bealu–ware m pl (§14.5) *dwellers in iniq-*

uity, evil men 17/79
bealwes gen sg of **bealu**
bēam m (§13.2) *tree* 17/6 etc; 18/35
Bēam–flēot m (§13.2) *Benfleet* (Essex) 4/170 etc
bēam–telg m (§13.2) *"tree–dye," ink* (made from oak–gall) 21/26/9
bearh = **bearg** (pret 1 and 3 sg of **beorgan**)
bearhtm m (§13.2) *din, clamor* 23/39
bearm m (§13.2) *bosom, lap* 25/25
bearn n (§13.4) *child, son* 2/33; 4/175; 9/32; 10/79, 184 etc; 11/305; 14/50 etc; 15/2852 etc; 16/403 etc; 17/83; 20/77 etc; 21/26/18; 21/57/6; 23/24 etc; 24/155 etc
bearn–myrðra, –e m, f (§14.7) *child–killer, infanticide* 14/132
bearo m (§13.6) *grove, wood, forest* 18/67, 71, 80; 20/48; 22/27; 25/18
bearo–næs(s) m (§13.2) *wooded headland* 21/57/5
bear(o)we dat sg of **bearo**
bēatan 7 *beat* 20/23
be–bēad pret 1 and 3 sg of **be–bēodan**
be–bēodan 2 often with indir obj *bid, enjoin, command* 2/48, 81; 7/17, 63; 9/31, 36, 38; 10/92, 100, 163, 330; 11/186; 13/72 etc; 15/2872 etc; 16/405; 18/36; 23/38 etc; 25/49: *offer* 15/2859: *entrust* 2/20: *commend* 2/102
be–bīodan = **be–bēodan**
be–bod n (§13.4) *commandment* 1/108; 10/305; 12/244; 20/h: *command* 10/68
be–boden past pple of **be–bēodan**
be–budon pret pl of **be–bēodan**
be–bycgan I *sell* 1/85
be–byrgan I *bury* 11/151; 12/140
bēc dat sg and nom and acc pl of **bōc**
be–cēapian II *sell* 11/68
be–cōm pret 1 and 3 sg of **be–cuman**
be–cōman = **be–cōmon**
be–cōmon pret pl of **be–cuman**
be–cuman 4 *come* 2/100; 5/70; 6/11; 9/86; 11/90; 12/1 etc; 23/134 etc; 24/58: *attain* 1/15, 88: *come upon, befall* 7/20
be–cwōm pret 1 and 3 sg of **be–cuman**
Bēda personal name *Bede* 12/33 etc
be–dǣlan I *deprive* 14/26
bēdan I *compel* 5/33
bed(d) n (§13.6) *bed* 12/35; 23/48 etc
*ge***bed(d)** n (§13.4) *prayer* 1/10; 10/21, 31, 153; 11/158 etc; 12/24 etc
be–dealf pret 1 and 3 sg of **be–delfan**
be–delfan 3 *bury* 17/75
be–dīglian II *conceal* 9/48
be–drǣf = **be–drāf** (pret 1 and 3 sg of **be–drīfan**)
bed–rest f (§14.2) *bed* 23/36
be–drīfan 1 *drive, compel, force* 6/41; 21/29/9: *sprinkle* 17/62: see also **flēam**
be–drifen past pple of **be–drīfan**
be–dyrnan I *conceal* 16/261
be–ebbian II *strand* (by the ebb tide) 4/273
be–ēode pret 1 and 3 sg of **be–gān**
be–ēodon pret pl of **be–gān**
be–fællan I *throw down* 16/361
be–fæstan I *secure, make secure* 4/207, 241: *apply, use* 7/19: *entrust* 11/17
be–fangen past pple of **be–fōn**
be–feallan 7 *fall* 16/330
be–feallen past pple of **be–feallan**
be–fēolan 3 with dat obj *apply oneself to* 7/49
be–flōwan 7 *flow around, surround, encompass* 22/49
be–flōwen past pple of **be–flōwan**
be–fōn 7 *seize, grasp* 16/374: *encircle, cover* 21/26/14
be–foran prep with dat **I.** (local) *before, in front of* 1/h, 41; 9/61; 10/73, 99 etc; 19/46: **II.** (temporal) *before, prior to* 5/67
be–gān anom vb (§7.7) *surround* 3/10: *practise* 1/124, 154, 159; 9/22, 80: *worship* 1/146, 157
be–gang m (§13.6) *worship* 1/120, 125, 147 etc: *concern, affair* 9/104
be–gan(n) pret 1 and 3 sg of **be–ginnan**
bēgea gen pl of **bā**
be–geat pret 1 and 3 sg of **be–gietan**
be–gēatan = **be–gēaton**
be–gēaton pret pl of **be–gietan**
bēgen m nom and acc dual *both* 4/11, 38 etc; 5/57; 6/35; 11/278; 12/155; 23/207; 24/182 etc

be–geondan prep with dat *beyond* 1/170; 6/8 etc; 7/14

be–gēotan 2 *cover* (with a liquid, or metaphorically with a solid) 17/7 etc

be–gēton = **be–gēaton** (pret pl of **be–gietan**)

be–gietan 5 *get, find, obtain* 4/245 (with refl dat); 5/73; 6/9 etc; 7/10: *acquire* 7/29; 11/174f: *occupy, hold* 20/6: *oppress* 22/32 etc

be–ginnan 3 *begin* 11/169; 12/110 etc; 13/29; 15/Æ

be–giondan = **be–geondan**

be–gitan = **be–gietan**

be–giten past pple of **be–gietan**

be–goten past pple of **be–gēotan**

be–grindan 3 *remove by grinding, grind free, polish clean* 21/26/6

be–grunden past pple of **be–grindan**

be–gunnen past pple of **be–ginnan**

be–gynnan = **be–ginnan**

be–gytan = **be–gietan**

be–hǣt pres 3 sg of **be–hātan**

be–hāt n (§13.4) *promise* 11/290

be–hātan 7 *promise* 6/50 etc; 12/125; 14/155

be–hāten past pple of **be–hātan**

be–hēafdian II *behead* 23/289

be–healdan 7 *behold, see* 10/16, 109 etc; 16/366; 17/25 etc: *look* 10/23, 253: *watch, observe, gaze at* 11/263; 12/185; 17/9 etc: *look around* 10/193

be–hēold pret 1 and 3 sg of **be–healdan**

be–hēoldon pret pl of **be–healdan**

be–heonan prep with dat *on this side of* 4/101; 7/12

be–hēt pret 1 and 3 sg of **be–hātan**

be–hētan = **be–hēton**

be–hēton pret pl of **be–hātan**

be–hindan **I.** adv *behind* 4/162: *behind his back* 10/212: **II.** prep with dat *behind* 5/60

be–hinon = **be–heonan**

be–hionan = **be–heonan**

be–hrēowsian II *repent* 11/197; 13/76

be–hrēowsung f (§14.1) *penitence* 11/187

be–hrīman I *cover with rime* (i.e. hoarfrost) 22/48

bēhð f (§14.1) *sign, proof* 23/174

be–hwyrfan I *convert* 11/53, 58

be–iernan 3 *run* 11/164f

be–lēas pret 1 and 3 sg of **be–lēosan**

be–lēosan 2 with dat obj *lose* 21/26/4

belgan 3 *be angry:* past pple *angry* 16/299

be–liden past pple of **be–līðan**

be–līfan 1 *remain, be left* 6/94

be–lifen past pple of **be–līfan**

be–lifon pret pl of **be–līfan**

be–limpan 3 *belong* 8/91: *be proper, be adapted* 2/3, 12

be–līðan 1 with gen obj *deprive of* 23/280

be–locen past pple of **be–lūcan**

be–lūcan 2 *lock, shut up* 3/22: *contain, comprise* 13/39

be–lumpon pret pl of **be–limpan**

bēn f (§14.6) *request* 1/28; 12/49: *prayer* 9/9, 102; 11/191

be–nǣman I *deprive* (someone, acc) *of* (something, dat) 23/76

be–nam pret 1 and 3 sg of **be–niman**

benc f (§14.6) *bench* 23/18; 24/213

benc–sittend m (§15.5) *"bench–sitter," guest* 23/27

Benedict personal name *Benedict*

be–neoman = **be–niman**

be–niman 4 *deprive* (someone, acc) *of* (something, gen or dat) 1/h; 3/1; 4/216; 8/94; 16/362; 21/26/2

ben(n) f (§14.2) *wound* 19/49

be–numen past pple of **be–niman**

bēo see **wesan** (§7.2)

(*ge*)**bēodan** 2 *offer* 3/16, 23, 26, 27: *command* 14/117: *enjoin upon* 11/279: *proclaim* 11/211: *announce, forbode* 20/54

bēom = **bēo** (see **wesan** §7.2)

bēon anom vb (§7.2) *be* 1/42, 110; etc: *stay* 10/320: **bēon on** *consist in* 8/35 etc

*ge***bēon** pret 1 and 3 sg of *ge***bannan**

*ge***bēor** m (§13.2) *drinker, drinking companion* 12/225 etc

beorg m (§13.2) *hill, mountain* 17/32 etc; 18/21 etc; 25/34

*ge***beorg** n (§13.4) *protection, defense* 24/31 etc; 25/38

beorgan 3 *protect* (something, dat) *against* (something, acc) 1/39; with dat obj only *protect, save* 14/140, 160; 24/194: *spare* 14/41, 49 etc: *seek a cure for* 14/128

beorg–hleoð n (§13.4) *hill–slope* 21/57/2

beorh = **beorg**

*ge***beorh** = *ge***beorg**

Beorh–hām–stede m (§14.5) *Great Berkhamstead* (Hertfordshire) 6/81

beorht adj *bright, shining, lustrous* 5/15; 10/22; 17/6 etc; 18/31 etc; 19/94; 23/58 etc: *clear* 11/238

beorhte adv *brightly* 11/316; 25/49

beorhtnys(s) f (§14.2) *brightness, radiance* 11/129f

Beorht–ulf personal name *Beorhtulf* 4/251

Beormas m pl (§13.2) *Karelians* 8/22

beorn m (§13.2) *man, warrior* 5/2 etc; 17/32 etc; 19/70, 113; 20/55; 23/213 etc; 24/17 etc

Beorn–ulf personal name *Beornulf* 4/253

*ge***bēor–scipe** m (§14.5) *beer drinking party* 2/15, 19, 24: *banquet* 11/287

bēot n (§13.4) *vow, promise, boast* 19/70; 24/15 etc: **on bēot** adv *threateningly* 24/27

bēotian II *vow* 22/21; 24/290

bēoton pret pl of **bēatan**

bēotung f (§14.1) *threat* 1/27

bēoð see **bēon** (§7.2)

ber = **bær** (pret 1 and 3 sg of **beran**)

bera m (§14.7) *bear* 8/45; 25/29

be–rād pret 1 and 3 sg of **be–rīdan**

beran 4 *bear, carry* 8/61 etc; 10/255; 11/42, 150 etc; 15/2887; 15/Æ; 17/32, 118; 21/7/6; 21/57/1; 23/18 etc; 24/12 etc: *bring* 2/86; 12/89 etc: *take* 11/274: past pple as sb *one born in the same family, brother* 20/98

beren adj *bear–skin* 8/45

be–rīdan 1 *overtake* (by riding) 3/9

bēron = **bǣron** (pret pl of **beran**)

be–rōwan 7 *row past* 4/279

berstan 3 *burst, break* 17/36; 24/284

be–rȳpan I *rob, strip* 11/146; 14/25 etc

be–sæt pret 1 and 3 sg of **be–sittan**

be–sǣton pret pl of **be–sittan**

be–scēofon = **be–scūfan**

be–scūfan 2 *thrust* 11/25

be–scyrian I *deprive* (someone, acc) *of* (something, gen) 16/392 etc

be–seah pret 1 and 3 sg of **be–sēon**

be–sēon 5 *look* 11/75; 15/Æ

be–seten past pple of **be–sittan**

be–settan I *surround, besiege* 4/18n

be–sittan 5 *surround, besiege* 4/157, 186 etc

be–slagen past pple of **be–slēan**

be–slēan 6 *strike, smite* 5/42

be–smītan 1 *defile, pollute* 23/59

be–smitennys(s) f (§14.2) *defilement* 11/301

be–snyðian I *rob* (someone, acc) *of* (something, dat) 21/26/1

be–stæl pret 1 and 3 sg of **be–stelan**

be–stǣlon pret pl of **be–stelan**

be–standan 6 *stand on both sides of, stand around* 24/68

be–stelan 4 with refl pron *move with stealth, steal, slip, sneak* 4/77, 80, 90, 119

be–stēman I *make wet, suffuse* 17/22 etc

be–stōdon pret pl of **be–standan**

be–strȳpan I *strip, plunder* 14/33

be–swāpan 7 *sweep* 1/54

be–swīcan 1 *betray, deceive, seduce, delude* 14/35, 59; 16/327, 433; 24/238

be–swicen past pple of **be–swīcan**

be–swician II *escape, escape from* 1/106: with dat obj *survive* 1/15

be–swyllan I *drench* 17/23

be–syrwan I *deceive, defraud* 14/35

bet comp adv *better* 14/15

be–tǣcan I *commend, commit* 11/305; 12/160: *offer* 14/25

be–tǣhte pret 1 and 3 sg of **be–tǣcan**

be–tǣht past pple of **be–tǣcan**

(*ge*)**bētan** I *amend, make better* 6/84: *atone* 14/43: *atone for* 8/125; 9/44; 14/127, 154: *make amends* 12/251: *obtain compensation for, get satisfaction for* 16/399

betera = **betra**

Bēthūlia *Bethulia* 23/138 etc

betra comp adj (§12.10) *better* 1/63, 129; 5/48; 7/45; 9/63; 24/31: as sb *lord* 24/276

betst I. sup adj (§12.10) *best* 1/84; 2/50; 4/124; 8/32: *of highest rank, chief* 6/82f: as sb with gen *best* 20/73: **II.**

sup adv *best, in the best manner* 6/90
bēttan = **bētton** (pret pl of **bētan**)
be–tuh = **be–twux**
be–tux = **be–twux**
be–tweoh adv *in between* 1/h
be–tweohx = **be–twux**
be–twēonan, –on = **be–twēonum**
be–twēonum prep with dat *among* 8/100; 9/31; 10/2, 35 etc; 14/158: *between* 21/29/2
be–tweox = **be–twux**
be–twih = **be–twux**
be–twuh = **be–twux**
be–twux prep with dat or acc *between* 4/144; 8/69, 75; 13/14: *among* 4/5; 12/81; 15/Æ: **betwux þām** adv *meanwhile* 12/7
be–twȳnum = **be–twēonum**
be–tȳnan I *close, end, conclude* 2/72, 103: *shut* 10/33, 195, 220 etc: *shut up, imprison* 10/179, 279
be–þeaht past pple of **be–þeccan**
be–þeccan I *cover* 23/213
be–þencan I *call to mind* 14/137: with refl acc *bethink* 14/152
be–þenian I *stretch over, cover* 21/26/12
be–urnon pret pl of **be–iernan**
be–weaxan 7 *overgrow* 12/37; 22/31
be–weaxen past pple of **be–weaxan**
be–weorpan 3 *cast out, hurl* 16/393
be–werian II *defend* 23/h
be–windan 3 *surround* 16/420: *encircle, envelop* 17/5; 23/115
be–wiste pret 1 and 3 sg of **be–witan**
be–witan pret-pres vb (§23.2) *be in charge of, administer* 12/91
be–wlāt pret 1 and 3 sg of **be–wlītan**
be–wlītan 1 *look* 15/2926
be–worpen past pple of **be–weorpan**
be–wrāh pret 1 and 3 sg of **be–wrēon**
be–wrēon 1 *cover* 17/17 etc; 19/23
be–wrigen past pple of **be–wrēon**
be–wunden past pple of **be–windan**
bī = **be**
bi–bēad = **be–bēad**
*(ge)***bicgan** I *buy* 11/112 etc; 14/70, 73; 25/45
*ge***bīcnian** II *betoken, signify* 13/58
bi–dǣlan I with dat or inst obj *separate from, deprive of* 19/20
bīdan 1 intrans *remain, continue* 18/47; 20/30: trans with gen obj *wait for, await* 2/96; 8/12 etc; 9/44; 25/60
*ge***bīdan** 1 intrans *wait* 19/70: trans with gen or acc obj *experience* 14/14[2]; 15/2910; 17/50 etc; 19/1 (see n); 20/4, 28; 22/3; 24/174; 25/12, 17: *endure* 14/14[1]: *reach, attain* 23/64
biddan 5 with acc of person (or refl dat) and gen or acc of thing (or clause) *ask, entreat, implore* 1/19, 21, 159; 2/78, 80 etc; 4/15; 9/10; 10/17, 111 etc; 11/154, 166, 178, 185, 209 etc; 12/49 etc; 13/1, 100 etc; 23/84 etc; 24/20 etc: *pray* 10/14; 11/160, 188; 12/20, 102
*ge***biddan** 5 usually with refl acc or dat *pray* 2/96; 10/114, 135 etc; 12/114 etc; 15/Æ; 17/83, 122
*ge***biden** past pple of *ge***bidan**
bi–drēosan 2 with dat *deprive of, bereave of* 19/79; 20/16
bi–droren past pple of **bi–drēosan**
bi–ēodon = **be–ēodon** (pret pl of **be–gān**)
bi–fangen = **be–fangen** (past pple of **be–fōn**)
bifian II *tremble* 9/8; 17/36 etc
bi–foran = **be–foran**
*(ge)***bīg(e)an** I *convert* 11/202 etc; 12/46, 72 etc: *bend, force, adjust* 12/68; 13/97
big = **be**
bī–gang = **be–gang**
bi–geal(l) pret 1 and 3 sg of **bi–giellan**
big–gencg m (§13.6) *worship, cult* 11/241
bi–giellan 3 see 20/24b n
big–leofa = **bī–leofa**
bī–gong = **be–gang**
big–standan 6 with dat obj *stand by, support* 16/284
big–wist f (§14.6) *sustenance, food* 12/276
bi–hōn 7 with dat *hang around with* 20/17
bi–hongen past pple of **bi–hōn**
bi–hrēosan 2 *cover* 19/77
bi–hroren past pple of **bi–hrēosan**
bii = **bī** = **be**
bi–lecgan I *surround* 21/26/25

bī–leofa m (§14.7) *sustenance, food* 11/137, 324

bil–gesleht n (§13.4) *sword clash, battle* 5/45

bil(l) n (§13.4) *sword* 15/2932; 24/114 etc

bil–wit adj *honest, sincere* 2/98

*ge***bind** n (§13.4) *binding, fastening; band; that which is bound together to form an aggregate whole* 19/24, 57

(*ge*)**bindan** 3 *bind* 10/183; 12/219; 16/379; 19/13, 18, 40, 102; 20/9, 32; 31/28/5; 23/115: *tie* 10/211; 12/222; 15/Æ

binnan, –on I. adv *inside, within* 4/10, 174; 11/315: **II.** prep with dat *within, inside, in* 4/241; 6/63; 12/10 etc; 13/77; 23/64

bi–nōm pret 1 and 3 sg of **bi–niman** (=**be–niman**)

bīon=**bēon**

Birinus personal name *Birinus* 12/120 etc

bisce(o)p=**biscop**

bisceop–rīce n (§13.6) *bishopric* 4/12

biscep–stōl m (§13.2) *episcopal see* 7/61; 12/135

biscop m (§13.3) *bishop* 1/6, 98 etc; 4/12, 24 etc; 6/59; 7/1 etc; 9/37; 10/307; 12/53 etc; 14/147: *high priest* 1/153, 161, 171

biscop–seðl n (§13.4) *episcopal seat* 1/178

bisen f (§14.1) *example* 1/157; 9/108; 23/h: *exemplar, model* 13/104

bisgu f (§14.1) *occupation, care* 7/55; *toil, affliction* 20/88

bismer m n f (§13.3, 5; 14.1) *mockery, scorn* 10/223: *disgrace, insult, shame* 14/14, 40, 99: **tō bysmore** adv *disgracefully* 14/91

bism(e)rian II *mock* 10/223; 17/48

(*ge*)**bisnian** II *set* (someone, dat) *an example* 12/73; 13/36

bist see **bēon** (§7.2)

bi–swician=**be–swician**

biter adj *bitter, fierce, sharp, painful* 10/19; 16/325; 17/114; 20/4, 55; 22/31; 24/85 etc

biternes(s) f (§14.2) *grief, anguish* 9/123

bitter=**biter**

bi–twēonum=**be–twēonum**

bið see **bēon** (§7.2)

bi–wāun past pple of **bi–wāwan**

bi–wāwan 7 *blow upon* or *against* 18/76

bi–wrāh=**be–wrāh**

blāc adj pale 23/278

blace nom pl fem st of **blæc**

blāc–hlēor adj *bright cheeked* 23/128

blācian II *grow pale* 20/91

blācung f (§14.1) *pallor* 11/265

blæc adj *black* 21/57/2

blǣcan I *bleach* 21/28/5

blǣd I. sb m (§14.5) *glory* 19/33; 20/79, 88; 23/122: *blessing* 17/149: *prosperity, fame* 23/63: **II.**=**blēd I.**

blǣst m (§14.5) *blast, blaze* 18/15

blǣstan I with refl acc *hurl* 10/228

blǣð=**blǣd I.**

*ge***bland** n (§13.4) *blending, confusion, commotion, tumult* 5/26

blandan 7 *mix* 10/8; 25/41: *infect, corrupt* 23/34

*ge***blanden** past pple of **blandan**

blanden–feax adj *grizzle–haired, grey–haired* 5/45

Blēcinga ēg see 8/87n

blēd I. sb f (§14.1) *fruit, flower* 18/35 etc; 25/34: **II.**=**blǣd I.**

blēo n (§13.6) *color* 17/22

(*ge*)**bletsian** II *bless* 10/276, 325; 11/40, 102, 105; 12/101; 15/Æ: *cheer* 10/86

bletsung f (§14.1) *blessing* 11/11; 15/Æ

blīcan 1 *shine, gleam* 23/137

blind adj *blind* 10/191; 11/123, 200: *dark, secret* 1/43

blis(s) f (§14.2) *bliss, merriment* 2/16: *joy* 12/99; 17/139 etc; 21/8/6

blissian II *rejoice* 11/172, 290; 12/227: *gladden, make happy* 15/2925; 18/7

blīðe adj *blithe, cheerful, joyful, glad* 1/77; 12/66 etc; 17/122; 22/21 etc; 23/58 etc; 24/146: *making merry* 12/225: *kindly disposed, gracious* 2/88, 90; 23/154

blīðe–mōd adj *kindly disposed, friendly* 2/84, 91

blōd n (§13.4) *blood* 10/6, 124 etc; 13/62; 15/2933; 17/48

blōd–gyte m (§14.5) *bloodshed* 14/44

blōdig adj *bloody* 23/126 etc; 24/154

*ge***blonden**=*ge***blanden** (past pple of

blandan)
blōstma m (§14.7) *blossom, flower* 18/21 etc; 20/48
blōtan 7 *sacrifice* 15/2857
blōwan 7 *flower* 9/52, 114, 120: *flourish* 11/116; 25/34: past pple *flowering, blooming* 10/255; 18/21, 27, 47
*ge***blōwen** past pple of **blōwan**
bōc f (§15.7) *book* 2/61 etc; 5/68; 6/88; 7/title, 25 etc; 9/61; 11/33, 182 etc; 12/272; 13/2 etc; 14/127 etc; 18/h
bōcere m (§13.6) *scholar, scribe* 2/4
bōc–lǣden n (§13.5) *Latin* 4/126
*ge***bod** n (§13.4) *command* 10/71, 215; 18/68
boda m (§14.7) *messenger* 14/117; 24/49
*ge***boden** past pple of *(ge)***bēodan**
bodian II *announce, proclaim* 1/98, 110 etc; 21/8/10; 23/244 etc: *preach* 11/86; 12/70 etc; 13/29
*ge***bodscipe** m (§14.5) *command, commandment* 16/430
bodung f (§14.1) *preaching* 11/27; 12/66
boga m (§14.7) *bow* 24/110
*ge***bohte** pret 1 and 3 sg of *ge***bicgan**
*ge***bolgen** past pple of **belgan**
bolla m (§14.7) *bowl, flagon* 23/17
bolster m n (§13.2, 4) *bolster, pillow* 2/97
bond = **bạnd** (pret 1 and 3 sg of **bindan**)
Bonefātius personal name *Boniface* 1/1
booc = **bōc**
bord n (§14.4) *shield* 23/192 etc; 24/15 etc
bord–weal(l) m (§13.2) *shield–wall, wall of shields* 5/5; 24/277
*(ge)***boren** past pple of **beran**
bōsm m (§13.2) *bosom, womb* 5/27
bōt f (§14.1) *remedy* 12/197; 14/11, 14, 30; 19/113: *atonement* 14/18, 135
botm m (§13.2) *bottom* 16/330 etc
brād adj *broad, wide* 4/134; 5/71; 8/52 etc; 16/325; 23/317; 24/15 etc
bræc pret 1 and 3 sg of **brecan**
*ge***bræc** n (§13.4) *clash* 24/295
brǣcan = **brǣcon** (pret pl of **brecan**)
brǣcon pret pl of **brecan**
brǣd = **brægd** (pret 1 and 3 sg of **bregdan**)
brǣdan I *spread* 19/47
brǣdra comp adj *broader, wider* 8/53
brand m (§13.2) *fire* 16/325
brastlian II *roar, crackle* 11/176
brēac pret 1 and 3 sg of **brūcan**
breahtm m (§13.2) *noise, clamor* 19/86
brecan 4 *break* 4/9; 14/154; 16/430; 24/1, 277: *burst forth* 18/67: *fade* 18/80: *transgress* 14/42
brēgan I *alarm, frighten, terrify* 1/27; 4/h
bregd n (§13.4) *deceit, fraud* 9/41
*ge***bregd** n *change, vicissitude* 18/57
bregdan 3 *draw* 23/229; 24/162: *pull, pluck out* 24/154
brego, –u m (§15.2) *ruler, prince, chief* 5/33; 23/39 etc
brember = **brēmel**
brēme adj *famous* 23/57
brēmel m (§13.3) *briar, bramble* 15/2929; 15/Æ
brengan I *bring* 1/141; 4/234 etc
brēost m n f (§13.2, 4; 14.1) pl often with sg meaning *breast* 15/2867 etc; 17/118; 19/113; 23/192; 24/144
brēost–cearu f (§14.1) *"breast–care," grief of heart* 20/4; 22/44
brēost–cofa m (§14.7) *"breast–chamber," heart* 19/18
brēost–hord n (§13.4) *"breast–treasure," breast, thought, inmost feelings* 20/55
Breoton = **Bryten**
brēowan 2 *brew* 8/101
brēr m *briar* 22/31
brerd m *rim, brim* 21/26/9
Brettas = **Bryttas**
Bret–wālas m pl (§13.2) *Britons* 3/6
brēðer dat sg of **brōðor**
brice m (§14.5) *fragment* 11/73, 75
bricg = **brycg**
bricg–weard m (§13.2) *bridge guard* 24/85
brīdel m (§13.3) *bridle, rein* 21/h
brīhð pres 3 sg of **brūcan**
brim n (§13.4) *sea* 5/71; 25/45
brim–cald adj *"sea–cold," cold as the sea* 18/67
brim–fugol m (§13.2) *sea–bird* 19/47
brim–lād f (§14.1) *sea–way, ocean path* 20/30
brim–līðend m (§15.5) *seafarer, Viking* 24/27
brim–man(n) m (§15.7) *seaman, Viking* 24/49 etc

brim–men(n) dat sg and nom and acc pl of **brim–man(n)**

(*ge*)**bringan** 3 *bring* 4/175 etc; 6/51; 8/29; 11/101; 13/70 etc; 14/24 etc; 12/177 etc; 15/2892; 17/139; 19/54; 21/8/5; 23/335; 25/8: *inflict* 10/123, 125, 160: *put, place* 23/54, 57 etc

broc n (§13.4) *affliction, sickness* 12/218

(*ge*)**brocen** past pple of **brecan**

brocian II *afflict* 4/247 etc; 12/35 etc

brōga m (§14.7) *terror* 23/4

(*ge*)**brōht** past pple of (*ge*)**bringan**

(*ge*)**brōhte** pret 1 and 3 sg of (*ge*)**bringan**

(*ge*)**brōhton** pret pl of (ge)**bringan**

brosnian II *moulder* 9/101: *wither* 18/38

*ge***brosnodlic** adj *as if mouldered away* 9/111

brosnung f (§14.1) *corruption, decay* 12/101

brōðer, –or, –ur m (§15.4) *brother* 2/1, 91 etc; 3/8; 4/1, 16 etc; 5/2; 6/12 etc; 10/28, 53 etc; 12/164 etc; 13/15; 14/50 etc; 15/2929; 20/97; 24/191 etc

*ge***brōðer, –or, –ra, –ru** m pl (§15.4) *brothers, brethren* 5/57; 11/52, 87 etc; 24/305

*ge***browen** past pple of **brēowan**

brūcan 2 with gen *enjoy* 5/63; 11/135, 144; 17/144; 19/44; 21/28/10: *use, make use of, avail oneself of* 21/26/18: *possess* 20/88

brugdon pret pl of **bregdan**

brūn adj *shining, bright* 23/317: *brown, dark* 21/26/9

Brūnan–burh f (§15.7) "*the fort of* Bruna" (unidentified) 5/5

brūn–eccg adj *bright–bladed* 24/163

bryce m (§14.5) *offense, violation, breach* 14/18

brycg f (§14.2) *bridge* 6/52; 24/74 etc

brȳd f (§13.6) *bride* 11/14; 23/h

bryhtm m (§13.2) *blink, wink, twinkling* 1/138

bryne m (§14.5) *burning, fire, conflagration* 14/19, 44 etc; 17/149

bryne–gield n (§13.4) *burnt offering* 15/2892 etc

Bryten f *Britain* 1/39; 5/71

brytta m (§14.7) *dispenser, giver* 15/2868; 19/25; 23/30 etc

Bryttas m pl (§13.6) *the Britons; the Welsh* 1/182n; 12/9 etc; 14/142 etc

bryttian II *dispose of, enjoy* 5/60

Bryttisc adj *British* 3/17

būan irregular vb *dwell, live* 4/163; 8/2, 64, 65: *cultivate, settle* 8/18, 19, 22: *live in, inhabit* 21/7/2

budon pret pl of **bēodan**

bufan, –on prep with dat and acc *above* 4/228; 8/105; 11/315: *upon, over* 11/270

(*ge*)**būgan I.** st vb 2 *bend down* 17/36 etc: *bow down, submit* 6/78, 83; 11/231; 14/153; 16/283: *curve, bend* 8/11 etc: *turn, retreat* 24/185, 276: *warble* 21/8/6: **II.** = **būan**

bugon pret pl of **būgan I.**

(*ge*)**bunden** past pple of (*ge*)**bindan**

(*ge*)**bundon** pret pl of (*ge*)**bindan**

būne f (§14.7) *cup, beaker* 19/94; 23/18

Bunne f (§14.7) *Boulogne–sur–Mer* 4/130

būr n (§13.4) *private apartment, "bower," chamber* 3/9; 21/29/5

burg f (§15.7) *fortress, stronghold, enclosure* 3/22; 4/149 etc; 21/29/5: *town, city* 4/186, 232; 6/45; 8/97 etc; 11/42, 91; 12/136 etc; 20/28, 48; 21/8/6; 23/58 etc; 24/291

Burgenda land see 8/86n

būr–geteld n (§13.4) *pavilion, tent* 23/57 etc

burg–lēod m (§14.5) *citizen* 10/195, 206; 23/175 etc

burgon pret pl of **beorgan**

Burg–ræd personal name *Burgræd* 4/15 etc

burg–sæl n (§13.4) *city dwelling, hall* 21/57/5

burg–salo nom and acc pl of **burg–sæl**

burg–tūn m (§13.2) *"fortress–enclosure," habitation, mansion* 22/31

burg–ware m pl (§14.5) *citizens, inhabitants* 4/169, 223 etc; 19/86

burh = **burg**

burh–lēod = **burg–lēod**

burh–sittend m (§15.5) *city–dweller* 23/159

burh–waru f (§14.1) *citizenry* 6/73

būr–þēn m (§13.2) *"bower–thane," chamberlain* 24/121

būtan I. adv *outside, without* 4/10, 211: **II.** conj *except* 13/17, 62: *except that* 8/4, 12: *but* 4/260; 20/18: *than* 13/4, 38: *unless* 7/66; 11/247; 12/255; 14/41; 24/71: **III.** prep with dat (and occasionally acc) *except* 1/162; 3/31; 8/23; 9/75 etc; 12/56: *except for* 3/2, 17; 4/92, 151, 167, 268, 287; 8/20; 12/232; 13/84; 14/102: *without* 1/78, 150; 2/87; 4/118, 157; 9/59, 130; 10/317, 333; 11/219, 222 etc; 12/171; 13/63; 14/158; 23/120: *outside, outside of* 4/212: *not subject to* 4/midnote: **būtan þām þe** conj *aside from the fact that* 4/54

būte = **būtan**

būton = **būtan**

būtsa–carl = **būtse–karl**

būtse–karl m (§13.2) *shipman* (see 6/17n)

Butting–tūn (§13.2) *Buttington* (Montgomery [Wales]) 4/196

būtū m n f nom and acc dual *both* 4/43; 17/48

bydel m (§13.2) *officer, messenger* 14/147

byht m (§14.5) *habitation, dwelling* 21/7/3

byldan I *encourage, exhort* 24/169, 209 etc; 25/15: *excite, agitate* 23/268: past pple *confident* 11/262

b͞yne adj *cultivated* 8/51 etc

*ge***byrd** f (§14.6) *birth, rank* 8/44

byrde adj *of high birth, of high rank:* sup *highest ranking* 8/44

byre m (§14.5) *opportunity* 24/121

byreð pres 3 sg of **beran**

byrgan I *bury* 11/43; 20/98

byrgen(n) f (§14.2) *grave* 9/92; 11/294 etc

byrig dat sg and nom and acc pl of **burg**

*ge***byrian** I *belong, pertain* 14/118: impers with dat *be fitting, behoove* 9/53; 14/118

byrigan I *taste* 17/101

byrne f (§14.7) *coat of mail* 23/325 etc; 24/144 etc

byrn–hom(m) m (§13.2) *coat of mail* 23/192

byrn–sweord n (§13.4) *flaming sword* 9/46

byrn–wiga m (§14.7) *mailed warrior* 19/94; 23/39

byrn–wiggend m (§15.5) *mailed warrior* 23/17

byrst m (§14.5) *loss, calamity, disaster* 14/13 etc

byrð pres 3 sg of **beran**

byrðen(n) f (§14.2) *load* 11/100

bysen = **bisen**

*ge***bysgian** II *trouble, agitate* 18/62

bysig adj *busy* 24/110

bysmar, –or = **bismer**

bysmerian = **bism(e)rian**

bysmerl͞ice adj *shamefully* 23/100

(*ge*)**bysnian** = (*ge*)**bisnian**

byst = **bist**

*ge***bytlu** n pl *buildings* 11/146: *mansions, palaces* 11/173

byð = **bið**

C

Cǣfi = **Cēfi**

cāf adj *valiant* 24/76

cāfl͞ice adv *valiantly* 24/153

cald = **ceald**

(*ge*)**camp** m (§13.2) *battle, conflict, warfare* 5/8; 11/119; 23/200; 24/153

campian II with dat obj *fight for, campaign for* 1/182n

camp–stede m (§14.5) *battlefield* 5/29 etc

can(n) pres 1 and 3 sg of **cunnan**

Cant–uare–burg f (§15.7) *Canterbury* (Kent): dat sg **Cantuareberi** 4/25

carcern n (§13.5) *prison* 10/12, 22, 29 etc

car–ful(l) adj *solicitous* 11/49f

carian II *be concerned, be anxious* 11/144

cāsere m (§13.6) *emperor* 11/22, 37; 20/82

castel m (§13.3) *fort, castle* 6/65 etc

Ceadwealla = **Cedwalla**

ceafl m (§13.2) *jaw, chop* 14/148

ceald I. sb n (§13.2) *cold* 20/8, 33: **II.** adj *cold* 16/316; 18/59; 20/10; 24/91;

25/5, 6

ceallian II *call, shout* 24/91

cēap m (§13.2) *cattle* 4/211 etc: *purchase* 14/70, 72

cearo f (§14.1) *care, sorrow, anxiety* 19/9, 55; 20/10

cear–seld n (§13.4) *"care–seat"* or *"care–hall," abode of care, sorrow-(ful) place* 20/5

*ge*cēas pret 1 and 3 sg of *ge*cēosan

ceaster f (§14.1) *city, walled town* 4/208; 10/4 etc; 25/1

Cedmon personal name *Cedmon* 2/22

Cedwalla personal name *Cedwalla* 1/182n; 12/9 etc

Cēfi personal name *Cefi* 1/121 etc

cellod adj, meaning not known 24/283

cempa m (§14.7) *warrior* 24/119

cēne adj *keen, strong, brave* 23/h, 200 etc; 24/215, 283 etc

cēnlīce adv *bravely, valiantly* 12/14

cennan I *bring forth, propagate* 25/28

Cent indecl f *Kent* 4/132 etc

cēol m (§13.2) *ship* 20/5; 25/24

Cēol–ferð personal name *Ceolferð* p. 105

Cēol–mund personal name *Ceolmund* 4/251

Cēol–nōð personal name *Ceolnoð* 4/24

Cēol–wulf personal name *Ceolwulf* 4/89

ceorfan 3 *cut* 21/28/4: *carve* 17/66

ceorl m (§13.2) *freeman of lowest rank, man* 24/132 etc: *man, husband* 14/34

(*ge*)**cēosan** 2 *choose* 10/67; 11/6, 37; 13/29; 16/285; 24/113: *elect* 4/25: *decide* 2/45

Cerdic personal name *Cerdic* 3/34

cerdon = **cierdon**

*ge***cerran** = *ge***cierran**

cīegan I *cry out* 10/92, 240 etc; 15/2909: *call, name* 11/29; 12/9

(*ge*)**cierran** I *turn* 4/7; 8/17; 9/5, 7; 12/252; 21/28/4: *return* 1/89; 11/37f, 48; 15/Æ; 23/311: *make subject, subjugate* 4/92: *submit* 4/midnote: *convert* 1/7: *incline* 9/102: *restore* 11/198

cīgan = **cīegan**

cild n (§15.6) *child* 10/112, 316, 318: as title *princeling, young nobleman* 6/74 etc

*ge***cind** = *ge***cynd**

cining(c) = **cyning(c)**

cing(c) = **cyning(c)**

Cippan–ham(m) m (§13.2) *Chippenham* (Wiltshire) 4/90 etc

Ciren–ceaster f (§14.1) *Cirencester* (Gloucestershire) 4/112 etc

cirice f (§14.7) *church* 1/176, 177, 179 etc; 4/h, 65; 7/24; 9/54; 10/304; 11/131, 229 etc; 12/43 etc; 23/h

cirlisc adj *peasant* 4/136

cirm m (§13.2) *outcry* 10/319: *uproar, cry* 24/107

cirman I *cry out, shout, scream* 21/8/3; 21/57/4; 23/270

cirr m (§14.5) *time, occasion* 8/6; 4/262

(*ge*)**cirran** = (*ge*)**cierran**

Cisse–ceaster f (§14.1) *Chichester* (Sussex) 4/223

clǣne I. adj *clean* 2/57: *pure* 11/19 etc; 20/110; 23/h: **II.** adv *completely, entirely* 7/11; 14/25

clænnis(s), –nys(s) f (§14.2) *purity* 11/5; 13/32; 23/h

clǣnsian II *cleanse, purge* 11/268; 14/157

clāð m (§13.2) *cloth* 12/222

clengan I *adhere, remain* 21/28/8

clēofan 2 *cleave, split* 5/5; 24/283

cleopian = **clipian**

clibbor adj *clinging, sticky* 25/13

clif n (§13.4) *cliff* 8/75n; 20/8

clipian II *call* 11/61; 12/247; 15/Æ: *call out* 11/229; 12/19; 24/25, 256: *cry out, exclaim* 1/145; 9/10, 94; 11/239, 265 etc; 12/100 etc; 13/61; 14/148

clom(m) m (§13.2) *bond, chain, fetter* 16/373; 20/10: *enchainment, durance* 16/408

clūdig adj *rocky* 8/50

clufan = **clufon**

clufon pret pl of **clēofan**

clumian II *mumble* 14/148

clūstor n (§13.4) *barrier* 16/416

clypian = **clipian**

clyppan I *embrace, clasp* 2/52; 19/42; 21/26/26

cnapa m (§14.7) *boy, youth* 12/279; 15/Æ

*ge***cnāwan** 7 *know* 14/5: *understand* 7/46; 9/124: *acknowledge, recognize* 14/40, 79 etc

cnear m (§13.2) *ship* 5/35
cnēo n (§13.6) *knee* 12/118a n; 19/42; 21/44/5
cnēo–mǣg m (§13.2 footnote 1) *kinsman, ancestor* 5/8
*ge***cneordlīce** adv *earnestly, assiduously* 11/57
cnēoris(s) f (§14.2) *family, kin* 10/15: *tribe, nation* 23/323
cniht m (§13.2) *boy* 4/181; 15/2915: *young man, youth* 10/181; 11/67, 84 etc; 24/9 etc
cnossian II *dash, beat, drive, pitch* 20/8
cnyssan I *beat against, batter* 19/101: *afflict, trouble* 18/59: *urge, impel* 20/33
cnyttan I *bind* 14/94
cohhetan I *bluster, shout, cough* 23/270
cōlian II *cool, grow cold* 9/21; 17/72
collen–ferð adj *bold–spirited* 19/71; 23/134
Colun *the R. Colne* (Hertfordshire, Middlesex, Buckinghamshire) 4/157
cōm pret 1 and 3 sg of **cuman**
cōman = **cōmon**
cometa m (§14.7) *comet* 4/126; 6/5
cōmon pret pl of **cuman**
compian = **campian**
comp–wīg n (§13.4) *battle* 23/332
condel f (§14.1) *candle* 5/15
con(n) = **can(n)** (pres 1 and 3 sg of **cunnan**)
*ge***coren** past pple of *(ge)***cēosan**
corfen past pple of **ceorfan**
corn n (§13.4) *grain* 4/212 etc: *kernel* 20/33
Corn–wālas m pl (§13.2) *the Britons in Cornwall*, also the region they inhabited: *Cornwall* (see 4/2n, 12/128a n) 4/122
corōna f *crown* 6/89
*ge***cost** adj *tried, proven* 23/231
costi(g)an II with gen or acc obj *try, make trial of, prove* 10/90, 107; 15/2847
Costontīnus personal name *Constantine III*, King of Scots 5/38
coðu f (§14.1) *disease* 12/193
cradol–cild n (§15.6) *child in the cradle, infant* 14/36
cræft m (§13.2) *physical strength, might, power* 11/282; 16/269 etc: *skill* 13/68: *cunning, artifice* 25/43: *host* 16/402
*ge***cranc** = *ge***crang** (pret 1 and 3 sg of *ge***cringan**)
Crēacas m pl (§13.2) *the Greeks* 7/41
crēad pret 1 and 3 sg of **crūdan**
*(ge)***cringan** 3 *fall dead, fall in battle, perish* 5/10; 19/79; 24/250, 292 etc
crism–līsing f (§14.1) *"chrisom–loosing"* (see 4/109n)
Crīst m (§13.2) *Christ* 1/2, 8 etc; 2/63; etc
Crīsten adj *Christian* 4/202, 277; 7/21 etc; 11/23; 12/156; 13/19 etc; 14/66 etc: as sb 14/28
Crīsten–dōm m (§13.2) *Christendom, Christianity* 14/82
*ge***crīstnian** II *anoint with chrism* (as a catechumen) 1/177
*ge***crong** pret 1 and 3 sg of *ge***cringan**
crūdan 2 *crowd, press* 5/35
cruncon = **crungon** (pret pl of **cringan**)
crungon pret pl of **cringan**
crungun = **crungon** (pret pl of **cringan**)
cuǣdon = **cwǣdon** (pret pl of **cweðan**)
cucu archaic form of **cwic**
cuman 4 *come* 1/h, 18, 46 etc; 2/45; 4/h, 2, 26 etc; 6/10 etc; 7/2; 8/70 etc; 9/15, 70; etc: *make one's way* 1/h; 4/280; 5/38: *go* 1/72; 2/41; 6/19; 8/23; 9/80; 11/291; 12/18; 19/92: *mount* 1/160: **cuman onweg** *get away* 4/204, 269: **cuman ūp** *come about, happen* 10/278
cumb(o)l m (§13.4) *standard, banner* 23/332
cumbol–gehnāst n (§13.4) *clash of battle–standards* 5/49
cumbol–wiga m (§13.2) *warrior* 23/243 etc
Cumbra personal name *Cumbra* 3/5 etc
cumen past pple of **cuman**
cum–pæder m (§13.3) *co–sponsor* (at baptism) 4/183
cunnan pret–pres vb (§23.3) *know* 1/49, 140; 7/39; 10/46; 11/163 etc; 12/67 etc; 13/23, 34, 88; 16/357 etc; 19/69 etc: *be able, know how to* 2/23; 7/12 etc; 13/12, 34; 14/40 etc; 19/113
cunnian II *try, experience, have experience (of)* 19/29; 20/5, 35: *seek to know, investigate* 15/2847: *find out*

23/259; 24/215
cunnon pres pl of **cunnan**
cunnun = **cunnon**
cuōm = **cwōm**
cuōmon = **cwōmon**
curfon pret pl of **ceorfan**
cūð adj *well–known, familiar* 19/55; 21/29/8; 21/44/5
Cūð–berht personal name *Cuthbert* 12/279
cūðe pret 1 and 3 sg of **cunnan**
cūðlic adj *certain* 1/141
cūðlīce adv *certainly, for certain, clearly* 1/51, 122: *in a familiar* or *friendly fashion* 1/104
cūðon pret pl of **cunnan**
cwacian II *quake* 9/8
cwǣdan = **cwǣdon**
*(ge)***cwǣdon** pret pl of *(ge)***cweðan**
*(ge)***cwæð** pret 1 and 3 sg of *(ge)***cweðan**
cwæðan = **cweðan**
cwalu f (§14.1) *slaying, killing, destruction, death* 1/23, 25 etc; 13/67; 14/45
Cwat–brycg f (§14.2) *Bridgnorth* (Shropshire) 4/238 etc
cweartern n (§13.5) *prison* 11/256
*(ge)***cweden** past pple of *(ge)***cweðan**
cwelan 4 *die* 11/252
cwellan I *kill* 15/2906
cwellere m (§13.6) *executioner* 10/34
cwelm–bǣre adj *deadly* 11/248
cwēn f (§14.6) *queen* 1/82; 12/176
Cwēnas m pl (§13.2) see 8/57ff n
cwene f (§14.7) *woman* 14/69, 92
(*ge*)**cweðan** 5 *say* 1/32 etc; 2/23 etc; 3/25 etc; etc: *call* 10/85
cwic adj *living, alive* 11/295; 15/2915 etc: 19/9; 21/28/8; 23/235 etc
Cwic–helm personal name *Cwichelm* 1/h
cwide m (§14.5) *saying, utterance, language* 21/47/4: *proposal* 11/236
cwide–gied(d) n (§13.6) *spoken utterance* 19/55
cwild f (§14.6) *death* 4/248
cwist pres 2 sg of **cweðan**
cwīðan I *lament, bewail* 17/56; 19/9
cwōm pret 1 and 3 sg of **cuman**
cwōman = **cwōmon**
cwōmon pret pl of **cuman**
cwyde = **cwide**
cwyð pres 3 sg of **cweðan**
*ge***cȳdd** past pple of **cȳðan**
cȳdde pret 1 and 3 sg of **cȳðan**
cȳf f (§14.6) *tub, vat* 11/24
cȳgan = **cīegan**
cyle m (§14.5) *cold* 8/125 etc
cyle–gicel m (§13.2) *icicle* 18/59
cyme I. sb m (§14.5) *coming, arrival, advent* 2/64; 12/60; 18/47 etc: **II.** pres 1 sg of **cuman**
cym(e)ð pres 3 sg of **cuman**
cymst pres 2 sg of **cuman**
*ge***cynd** n f *nature* 1/h; 9/97: *natural state* 11/189, 192, 199: *origin* 13/40, 41
*ge***cynd–bōc** f (§15.7) *book of origin* (translating "Genesis") 13/40
*ge***cynde** adj *due by birth, proper* 6/74
cyne–dōm m (§13.2) *royal dignity, kingdom* 1/182n: *kingdom* 12/144
cyneg = **cyning(c)**
Cyne–gyls personal name *Cynegyls* 12/121 etc
Cyne–heard personal name *Cyneheard* 3/7 etc
cynelic adj *royal, kingly* 1/7; 12/89
cyne–rīce n (§13.6) *kingdom* 1/15, 57; 4/53; 7/55; 12/104: *dominion* 1/68
cyne–rōf adj *royally brave* 23/200 etc
Cyne–wulf personal name *Cynewulf* 3/1 etc
cyng(c) = **cyning(c)**
cynincg = **cyning(c)**
cyning(c) m (§13.3) *king* 1/h, 4 etc; 3/9 etc; 4/6; etc
cyning–cyn(n) n (§13.6) *royal race, royal line* 1/182n
cyn(n) n (§13.6) *race* 20/h; 23/52 etc; 25/57: *family, kindred* 24/76, 217, 266: **manna cyn(n)** *mankind* 10/187; 16/425: **wīfa cyn(n)** *womankind* 17/94
cynning = **cyning(c)**
cynren n (§13.5) *kind, progeny* 25/28
cyr(i)ce = **cirice**
cyric–hata m (§14.7) *church–hater, persecutor of the church* 14/115
cyrm = **cirm**
(*ge*)**cyrran** = (*ge*)**cierran**
*ge***cyrrednys(s)** f (§14.2) *conversion* 12/133

cyrtel m *tunic, coat* 8/45; 11/114

cyssan I *kiss* 10/140; 19/42

cyst f (§14.6) *best, choicest* 17/1

cystig adj *liberal, generous* 11/45; 12/84

(*ge*)**cȳðan** I *make known, reveal, declare, inform* 1/32; 2/43; 3/24; 6/11, 35 etc; 7/2; 9/129; 10/22, 70; 11/167, 221 etc; 12/247; 18/30; 23/155; 24/216: *announce, proclaim* 9/62; 15/2866; 23/56 etc: intrans with dat *appear to* 10/197

*ge***cyðnis(s)** f (§14.2) *testament* 13/24, 25 etc

cȳðð f (§15.3) *native land, home* 5/38, 58; 9/89, 92; 23/311

D

dǣd f (§14.6) *deed, action* 2/69; 3/2; 9/16; 12/146 etc; 14/54 etc; 16/295 etc; 20/41, 76; 23/181n; 25/36

dǣd–bētan I *make atonement* 11/187

dǣd–bōt f (§14.1) *penitence, atonement* 13/54, 76

*ge***dǣde** = *ge***dyde**

dæg m (§13.2) *day* 1/101; 2/65; 4/68, 114 etc; 5/21; 6/3 etc; 8/9 etc; 10/35, 213 etc; 11/51; etc: **dæges** adv (*by*) *day* 4/208; 6/37; 11/144, 178: **on dæg** adv *that day* 24/198: **tō dæge** adv *today* 1/170: **lange on dæg** adv *far on into the day, until late in the day* 4/44, 52; 6/53

dæg(e)–weorc n (§13.4) *day's work* 23/265; 24/148

dæg–hwāmlic adj *daily* 14/12

dæg–hwāmlīce adv *daily* 14/12, 100

dæg–red n (§13.4) *dawn* 23/204

dæig = **dæg**

dæl n (§13.4) *dale, valley* 16/305 etc; 18/24

dǣl m (§14.5) *part, portion* 4/92, 99, 101 etc; 7/35, 44; 8/110, 112 etc; 9/75; 11/203; 12/37; 21/28/1; 23/292 etc: *share* 12/97: *large number* 19/65: *large quantity, abundance* 21/26/10: *bit* 9/95: *particular, respect* 9/33: *region* 10/156: **be dǣle** adv *partially, to some extent* 13/12: **be ǣnigum dǣle** adv *to any extent* 14/122: **be sumum dǣle** adv *in some measure* 14/153f

dǣlan I *part, separate* 9/73: *distribute* 10/205; 11/69, 87 etc; 12/58; 24/33 (see n); 25/29: *share* 24/33 (see n)

*ge***dǣlan** I *part, separate* 22/22: *share out* 4/81, 89, 115: *obtain, receive as a share* 16/296: with dat *share with* 19/83

dǣl–neoman 4 *take part, participate*: pres pple *participant, partaker* 1/111

dænede see 5/12b n

*ge***dafen** adj *fitting, appropriate* 9/120

*ge***dafenian** II with dat or acc obj *befit, beseem, suit* 1/83; 2/13; 13/33

dagan = **dagum** (dat pl of **dæg**)

dagas nom and acc pl of **dæg**

dala, –o, –u nom and acc pl of **dæl**

darað, –oð m (§13.3) *spear, javelin* 5/54; 24/149 etc; 25/21

dēad adj *dead* 8/102 etc; 9/47; 10/136, 174 etc; 11/267 etc; 20/65; 23/107: as sb *the dead* 20/98

dēad–bǣre adj *deadly* 11/253

dēagolnes(s) f (§14.2) *secrecy, privacy* 1/82

dēah pres 1 and 3 sg of **dugan**

dear(r) pres 1 and 3 sg of **durran**

dēað m (§13.2) *death* 1/h, 37; 2/99; 9/14; 10/20, 295; 11/166 etc; 12/249; 17/101 etc; 18/52; etc

dēað–dæg m (§13.2) *day of death* 25/60

dēað–ræced n (§13.5) *"death–house," grave* 18/48

dēaw m n (§13.6) *dew* 21/29/12

*ge***dēfe** adj *confirmed* (in faith) 10/310

Def(e)na–scīr f (§14.1) *Devonshire* 4/95, 165

Def(e)ne m pl (§14.7) *the men of Devon,* also the region they inhabited: *Devon* (see 4/2n, 12/128a n) 4/199 etc

dehter dat sg of **dohtor**

delfan 3 *dig* 11/294

dēma m (§14.7) *judge* 23/4 etc

dēman I *judge, condemn* 21/28/11; 23/196: *decide* 2/16: with dat *judge, pass judgment on* 17/107

dēmend m (§15.5) *judge* 25/36

Dena–mearc f (§14.1) *Denmark* 8/77 etc

Dene m pl (§14.5) *the Danes* 4/287; 8/76; 24/129

Dene–mearc = **Dena–mearc**

Denisc adj *Danish* 4/h, 260 etc: **þā Deniscan** *the Danes* 4/22, 31 etc

denu f (§14.1) *glen, valley* 18/24; 22/30
*ge***deofanian** = *ge***dafenian**
dēoflic adj *devilish* 11/97
dēofol m n (§13.3, 5) *devil* 10/221, 226 etc; 11/122, 126 etc; 12/198; 16/305 etc: *Devil, the Devil* 10/181, 186 etc; 11/94 etc; 14/9; 20/76; 23/h
dēofol–cund adj *devilish, fiendish, diabolical* 23/61
dēofol–geld, –gild, –gyld n (§13.4) *idolatry* 1 /152: *idol* 1/155, 160, 164 etc; 11/234, 240, 281
dēoful–gylda m (§14.7) *devil–worshipper, idolater* 11/226
dēoful–sēoc adj *devil–possessed, insane* 11/126f
dēop I. sb n (§13.4) *deep* (water), *channel* 4/270: **II.** adj *deep* 5/55; 15/2876; 16/305 etc; 17/75: *profound* 13/37 etc
dēope adv *deeply, profoundly* 19/89
dēoplīce adv *deeply, profoundly* 13/82
dēor I. sb n (§13.4) *animal* 5/64; 8/36 etc: **II.** adj *brave, valiant* 20/41, 76
deorc adj *dark* 17/46; 19/89
dēore I. adj *dear* 16/261 etc: *precious* 8/38; 25/10: *costly, valuable* 8/119; 23/318: **II.** adv *dearly, at great cost* 14/73
Deorwente f (§14.7) *the R. Derwent* (Yorkshire) 1/h, 170
deor–wurð, –wyrð adj *precious, valuable* 1/85; 11/53, 79 etc; 12/223; 13/71
derian I with dat obj *hurt, injure* 10/162; 11/250; 14/46, 54 etc; 24/70
dēst pres 2 sg of **dōn**
dēð pres 3 sg of **dōn**
*ge***dēð** pres 3 sg of *ge***dōn**
Difelin *Dublin* 5/55
dīgol adj *hidden, obscure, unknown* 25/62
(*ge*)**dihtan** I *compose, write* 12/272: *dictate* 13/83: *direct* 13/69
dim(m) adj *dark, gloomy*
Dinges mere m (§14.5) unidentified (see 5/h)
disc m (§13.2) *dish* 12/90 etc
discipul m (§13.3) *disciple* 10/39, 49, 50 etc
dōgor m n (§15.6) *day* 19/63; 23/12
dohte pret 1 and 3 sg of **dugan**
dohtor f (§15.4) *daughter* 12/176; 13/16; 14/92
dol I. sb n (§13.4) *folly, presumption* 16/340 (see n): **II.** adj *foolish, presumptuous* 16/340 (see n); 20/106: as sb *a foolish person* 21/26/17
dolg n (§13.4) *wound* 17/46
dolh–wund adj *wounded* 23/107
dollic adj *audacious, daring* 23/181n
dollīce adv *in a foolhardy fashion, audaciously, rashly* 16/295
dōm m (§13.2) *judgment* 2/45, 65 etc; 9/h, 56; 11/63; 14/159;.17/107; 18/48; 25/60: *choice, assessment* 3/23; 24/38: *glory, renown* 20/85; 23/196 etc; 24/129; 25/21
dōm–dæg m (§13.2) *judgment day* 17/105
dōm–georn adj *eager for renown, anxious to achieve* **dōm** (i.e. a favorable judgment by one's contemporaries and posterity) 19/17
Domiciānus personal name *Domitian* 11/23, 34
dōmlīce adv *gloriously* 23/319
dōn anom vb (§7.6) *do* 1/h, 20; 2/9; 4/235; 6/90; 7/17; 10/100, 119 etc; 11/101, 155, 160; 12/97 etc; 13/44 etc; 14/15 etc; 23/95: *act* 1/32; 2/71; 6/84; 10/118, 126, 216; 13/80: *perform* 10/86: *inflict* 6/10, 83; 10/18, 296: *treat* 10/17, 202, 217, 290: *show, give* 1/61; 10/70: *make* 10/90; 11/117: *bring* 7/52: *take* 7/63; 20/20; 21/26/3: *fight* 6/77: *convert* 10/311: *put* 12/202: *commit* 25/56: **dōn on** *treat* 10/291: **dōn tō mete** *make into food* 10/33: **dōn þancas** with dat *thank* 10/262: **dōn þoncunc** *give thanks to* (someone, dat) *for* (something, gen) 1/61
*ge***dōn** anom vb (§7.6) *do* 1/54, 79 etc; 4/263: *bring* 20/43: *make* 1/111; 10/165, 310: *bring it to pass* 7/47; 8/128; 16/404: *arrive* 4/191, 208, 230, 238: **gedōn tō mete** *make into food* 10/35f, 41, 143 etc
Dorcan–ceaster = **Dorce–ceaster**
Dorce–ceaster f (§14.1) *Dorchester–on–Thames* (Oxfordshire) 4/252; 12/136
dorste pret 1 and 3 sg of **durran**
dorston pret pl of **durran**

dōð pres pl of **dōn**
draca m (§14.7) *dragon* 4/h; 25/26: *serpent* 11/175
drǣfan I *drive* 14/62n
drāf I. sb f (§14.1) *drove, band* 14/97: **II.** pret 1 and 3 sg of **drīfan**
*ge***dranc** pret 1 and 3 sg of *ge***drincan**
*ge***dreag** n (§13.4) *multitude, host* 22/45
drēam m (§13.2) *joy* 16/257; 17/133 etc; 19/79; 20/65, 80 etc; 21/28/7; 23/349
*ge***drēas** pret 1 and 3 sg of *ge***drēosan**
(*ge*)**dreccan** I *afflict, harass* 4/255; 12/199; 14/47
drēfan I *trouble, disturb* 11/139; 17/20 etc; 23/88: *stir up, make turbid* 21/7/2
*ge***dreht** past pple of (*ge*)**dreccan**
*ge***drehtan** = *ge***drehton** (pret pl of *ge***dreccan**)
drehton pret pl of **dreccan**
drenc m (§14.5) *drink, potion* 10/8; 11/248 etc
drencan I *drench, soak* 23/29
dreng m (§13.2) *Viking warrior* 24/149
drēogan 2 *suffer, undergo* 14/69; 20/56; 22/26 etc; 23/158: *commit, perpetrate* 14/69
drēor m (§13.2) *blood* 15/2908
drēorig adj *sad, mournful, dejected* 5/54; 11/45, 94 etc; 19/17
drēorig–hlēor adj *with tear–stained cheeks, sad faced* 19/83
drēorignys(s) f (§14.2) *grief, sorrow* 11/157
drēor–sele m (§14.5) *dreary hall* 22/50
(*ge*)**drēosan** 2 *fall* 18/34: *perish, come to an end, vanish* 9/100; 19/36, 63; 20/86
drīfan 1 *drive, force* 4/h; 14/60, 97: *sail* 6/28
drihten = **dryhten**
drihtlic = **dryhtlic**
drincan 3 *drink* 8/99 etc; 10/5, 6, 8 etc; 11/247 etc: past pple *drunk* 23/67 etc
*ge***drincan** 3 *drink down* 11/262
drinccan = **drincan**
drohtnung f (§14.1) *way of life, state* 12/54
*ge***droren** past pple of (*ge*)**drēosan**
*ge***drorenlic** adj *as if perished* 9/110
drugon pret pl of **drēogan**
druncen past pple of **drincan**
druncon pret pl of **drincan**
Drūsiāna personal name *Drusiana* 11/43 etc
dryctin = **dryhten**
drȳge adj *dry* 9/96: **on drȳgum** *on dry land* (cf Lat *super aridam*) 4/266
dryht f (§14.5) pl *men* 21/28/7
dryhten m (§13.3) *lord* 5/1; 20/41; 23/21: *Lord, the Lord, God* 2/32, 36 etc; 5/16; 9/52; 10/1; etc
dryht–folc n (§13.4) *noble people, nation* 21/26/17
dryht–guma m (§14.7) *retainer* 23/29
dryhtlic adj *lordly, magnificent* 20/85; 25/26
*ge***drync** n (§13.4) *drinking* 8/106 etc
dryre m (§14.5) *fall, downpour* 18/16
Dubslane personal name *Dubslane* 4/123
dugan pret–pres vb *avail* 24/48; 14/43, 87
dugeð = **duguð**
duguð f (§14.1) *company of noble warriors, host, nobility* 14/144; 19/79, 97; 20/86; 23/31: *heavenly host* 20/80; 23/61: *benefit, advantage* 24/197
dūn f (§14.1) *hill, mountain* 10/166; 15/2854 etc; 15/Æ; 22/30
dunnian II *grow dark* see 5/12b n
dūn–scræf n (§13.4) *mountain cave* 18/24
dūn–scrafu nom and acc pl of **dūn–scræf**
durran pret–pres vb (§23.3) *dare* 8/17f etc; 10/229; 13/83, 99; 14/21 etc; 17/35 etc; 19/10; 23/258
duru f (§15.2) *door* 1/136; 3/11; 10/134, 137 etc; 11/131; 18/12; 21/28/7; 25/36
dūst n (§13.4) *dust* 9/96; 11/243; 12/198 etc; 21/29/12
dūst–scēawung f (§14.1) *contemplation of dust* 9/103
dwǣs adj *foolish, stupid:* used as sb 14/127
dwelian II *lead astray, deceive* 14/9
*ge***dwol–god** m n (§13.2, 4) *false god* 14/22 etc
*ge***dwol–man(n)** m (§15.7) *heretic* 11/207, 210; 13/89
*ge***dwol–men(n)** dat sg and nom and acc pl of *ge***dwol–man(n)**
*ge***dwolsum** adj *misleading* 13/88
*ge***dwyld** n (§13.4) *error* 11/235; 12/179
dydan = **dydon**
dyde pret 1 and 3 sg of **dōn**

*ge***dyde** pret 1 and 3 sg of *ge***dōn**
dydon pret pl of **dōn**
*ge***dydon** pret pl of *ge***dōn**
dȳfan I *dip, plunge* 21/26/3
dynian II *clamor* 23/23: *clash, ring out* 23/204
dȳran I *glorify* 16/257
dȳre = **dēore**
dȳrling m (§13.3) *favorite* 11/1
dyrne adj *secret, hidden* 22/12; 25/43 etc
dȳrsian II *exalt* 23/299
dyrstignys(s) f (§14.2) *presumption* 11/210f
dysig adj *foolish, ignorant* 13/7: used as sb 14/116
dysignes(s) f (§14.2) *folly, foolishness* 1/157, 159
dyslic adj *foolish* 12/245: *absurd* 11/62

E

ē = **ēa**
ēa f (§15.7) *river* 1/h, 93, 170; 4/71, 134 etc; 8/17 etc; 16/316n; 25/30: gen sg **ēas** 4/235; 8/19: dat sg **ēæ** 4/233 (see Campbell §628.(4))
ēac I. prep with dat and inst *in addition to, besides* 4/254; 24/11: **ēac þon** adv *in addition to that, moreover* 22/44: **II.** adv *also, moreover* 1/h, 10; 4/105 etc; 5/2; 6/13 etc; 7/6 etc; 11/65 etc; 12/102 etc; 13/16 etc; 14/8 etc; 16/386 etc; 17/92; 20/119; etc: *even* 7/20: *too* 5/19: **ēac swā** adv *also* 4/180f, 229: **ēac swelce (swilce, swylce)** adv *also* 1/1; 2/7f, 99 etc; 12/32 etc
ēaca m (§14.7) *reinforcement* 4/190: *increase* 13/17
ēad n (§13.4) *prosperity, success, happiness* 16/402; 21/26/23; 23/273
Eād–gār personal name *Eadgar* 6/73 etc; 14/32n
ēad–hrēðig adj *triumphant* 23/135
ēadig adj *blessed, happy* 10/3, 10 etc; 11/27; 12/13; 13/28; 15/2863 etc; 18/11 etc; 20/107; 23/35: *wealthy* 11/133
ēadignes(s) f (§14.2) *blessedness, beatitude, happiness* 1/148; 20/120
*ge***ēad–mēdan** I with refl acc *humble, debase* 10/106
ēad–mōd = **ēað–mōd**
ēad–mōdlice adv *humbly* 13/1
Ēad–mund personal name **I.** *Eadmund* 4/22: **II.** *Eadmund* (King of Wessex 939–946) 5/3
Ēad–ulf personal name *Eadulf* 4/253
Ēad–w(e)ard personal name **I.** *Eadweard* (the Elder; King of Wessex 899–924; son and successor of Ælfred the Great) 4/288; 5/7, 52: **II.** *Eadweard* (the Martyr) 14/61: **III.** *Eadweard* (the Confessor) 6/14
Ēad–wine, –wini personal name *Eadwine* 1/h, 2 etc; 6/19, 38; 12/7, 110 etc
ēæ dat sg of **ēa**
eafora m (§14.7) *offspring, descendant, child* 5/7, 52; 15/2898 etc; 16/399
ēage n (§14.7) *eye* 1/138; 10/7, 17, 33 etc; 11/196; 13/92 etc
eahta numeral *eight* 8/32; 10/163; 12/149
eal = **eal(l)**
ēa–lā interj *oh! alas!* 9/65, 98; 11/161, 162; 14/136; 19/94 etc
ealað gen sg of **ealo**
Ealch–stān personal name *Ealchstan* 4/12
eald adj *old* 4/37; 5/46 etc; 9/2; 12/143; 13/9 etc; 14/33; 19/87; 21/8/5; 22/29; 23/h, 166 etc; 24/47 etc; 25/30: *ancient* 15/Æ: gen sg used as adv *long ago* 22/4: **ealda fæder** *patriarch* 13/9: *grandfather* 24/218
eald–fēond m (§15.5) *ancient enemy* 23/315
eald–genīðla m (§14.7) *ancient enemy* 23/228
eald–gewyrht n f (§13.4, 14.6) *deed of old, former action* 17/100
eald–hettend m (§15.5) *ancient enemy* 23/320
ealdian II *grow old* 20/89
ealdor I. sb m (§13.3) *lord, prince* 11/309; 15/2879; 17/90; 19/h; 20/h, 123; 23/38 etc; 24/11 etc: **II.** sb n (§13.4) *life* 23/76, 185: **on ealdre** adv *ever* 16/402: **(ǣfre, āwa) tō ealdre** adv *forever* 16/427, 436; 18/40, 83; 20/79; 23/120: **tō wīdan aldre** adv *forever* 23/347
ealdor–bisceop m (§13.3) *chief priest, high priest* 1/121

ealdor–duguð f (§14.1) *chief nobility* 23/309

ealdor–lang adj *age–long, eternal* 5/3

ealdor–man(n), –mon(n) m (§15.7) *"alderman," nobleman* (of the highest rank), *noble* 1/131, 134 etc; 3/2, 4 etc; 4/37, 30 etc; 13/1, 100; 24/h, 219: *chief man* 10/306: *superior* 2/41; 10/174f, 177

ealdor–þegn m (§13.2) *chief thane, retainer* 23/242

Eald–red personal name *Ealdred* 6/73 etc

ealgian II *defend* 5/9; 24/52

Ealh–heard personal name *Ealhheard* 4/252

eal(l) I. adj *all* 1/55 etc; 2/16 etc; 3/12 etc; 4/23; etc: *every* 9/113; 10/26: *the whole* 4/143, 152; 18/43, 67; 23/28, 237; 24/304: neut used as sb *all, everything* 4/174, 175, 211 etc; 6/86; 8/48; 10/119; 14/123; 24/256: **ealles** adv *all, entirely, quite, at all* 4/247; 14/13, 23 etc; 23/108: *of all* 4/248: **ealra** adv *of all* 14/58; 16/337: see also **geond, mid, weg: II.** adv *all, entirely, completely, thoroughly* 9/110, 111; 12/253; 14/88, 90 etc; 17/20, 48, 62; 22/29; 24/314: **eall swā** conj *just as, exactly as* 6/15, 32f, 71f etc

eall–gylden adj *all–golden* 23/46

eallinga = eallunga

eallon = eallum

eallunga adv *entirely, completely, absolutely* 1/123; 11/45, 142

ealneg = ealne weg

ealo n (dental stem, see Campbell §637) *ale* 8/101, 127

ealunga = eallunga

eam = eom

ēam m (§13.2) *maternal uncle* 12/7

ēar m *wave, sea* 5/26

eard m (§13.2) *country, homeland, home* 5/73; 9/90; 12/257; 14/36 etc; 20/38; 23/h; 24/53 etc: *region* 11/203: *residence* 20/15n

eard–geard m (§13.2) *habitation, city* 19/85

eardian II *dwell, live* 8/51 etc; 11/92, 240

eard–stapa m (§14.7) *"land–stepper," wanderer* 19/6

eardung f (§14.1) *precincts*

ēare n (§14.7) *ear* 13/93

earfeðe n (§13.6) *hardship, trouble, adversity* 1/109; 19/6; 22/39

earfoðe adj *difficult, hard* 11/76

earfoð–hwīl f (§14.1) *time of hardship* 20/3

earfoðlic adj *difficult, full of hardship* 19/106

earfoðnes(s) f (§14.2) *affliction, tribulation, torture* 9/23; 10/125, 127, 233 etc

ēar–gebland n (§13.4) *"wave–mingling," commotion of the sea* 5/26n

earh adj *cowardly* 24/238

earhlic adj *base* 14/85

earm I. sb m (§13.2) *arm* 12/34 etc; 24/165: **II.** adj *wretched, miserable, poor* 6/95; 9/30; 11/133; 14/35, 136; 17/19 etc; 19/40; 25/19

earm–cearig adj *wretched(ly) sorrowful, distraught with anxiety* 20/14

earming m (§13.3) *contemptible creature* 11/124

earmlic adj *wretched, miserable* 12/249

earmlīce adv *miserably, wretchedly, sorely, badly* 4/h; 14/138

earn m (§13.2) *eagle* 5/63; 20/24; 23/210; 24/107

(*ge*)**earnian** II *earn, deserve, merit* 9/50, 102, 105; 11/168; 12/282; 14/16, 160; 17/109; 20/h: with gen obj 14/15

(*ge*)**earnung** f (§14.1) *merit* 12/39, 108 etc: *favor* 24/196: *deserts* 14/15, 16

earon pres pl of **wesan** (see **SB** §427) *are* 20/82

eart see **wesan** (§7.2)

ēast adv *east, eastward* 4/169; 8/13: *to the east* 1/169

ēastan adv *from the east* 5/69; 8/92 etc; 23/190: **be ēastan** prep with dat *east of* 4/100, 194 etc: **wið ēastan** adv *to the east* 8/50

ēast–dǣl m (§14.5) *eastern quarter* (of a city) 10/166: *eastern region* (of the earth) 18/2: **æt ēastdǣle** *to the east* 1/93

ēast–ende m (§13.6) *eastern end* 4/132

Ēast–engle m pl (§14.5) *East Anglians*, also the region they inhabited: *East Anglia* (see 4/2n, 12/128a n) 1/4, 18;

4/2, 4 etc

Ēaster–dæg = Ēastor–dæg

ēasterne adj *eastern* 16/315

ēa–steð n (§13.4) *river–bank* 24/63

easte–we(a)rd I. adj *the eastern part of* 4/132, 168, 220: **II.** adv *in the east* 8/52

ēaste–weardes adv *eastwards* 4/168n

ēast–healf f (§14.1) *east side* 4/201

ēast–lang adv *to the east* 4/133

Ēastor–dæg m (§13.2) *a day in Easter week:* **se ǣresta (hālgesta, hālga) Ēastordæg** *Easter Sunday* 1/h, 176; 12/88

Ēastran f pl (§14.7) *Easter* 4/48, 97 etc; 6/1 etc

ēast–rīce n (§13.6) *eastern kingdom* (of the Franks), *Austrasia* 4/130, 140

ēast–ryhte adv *due east* 8/11

Ēast–seaxan, –e m pl (§14.7, 5) *East Saxons,* also the region they inhabited: *Essex* (see 4/2n, 12/128a n) 4/155 etc; 24/69

ēast–weard = ēaste–we(a)rd

ēað comp adv (see **ēaðe**) *more easily, more appropriately* 1/156

ēaðe adv *easily* 7/47; 14/137; 23/75 etc

ēað–mēdu f (§14.1) *reverence, humility* 23/170

ēað–mōd adj *humble, meek* 9/7; 12/84; 17/60; 20/107; 23/h

ēað–mōdlīce adv *humbly* 2/70

ēað–mōdnes(s) f (§14.2) *humility* 1/7: *act of humility* 9/128

eaxl f (§14.1) *shoulder* 15/2927; 17/32

eaxl–gespan(n) n (§13.4) see 17/9a n

ebba m (§14.7) *ebb–tide* 24/65

Ebrēas m pl *Hebrews* 15/2917; 23/218 etc

Ebr(ē)isc adj *Hebrew* 10/252; 23/241 etc

Ebrisc–geþīode n (§13.6) *the Hebrew language* 7/40

ēce I. adj *eternal, everlasting* 1/8; 2/32; 5/16; 9/56, 75; 11/67, 120 etc; 12/277 etc; 13/67; 15/2898; 20/79 etc: **II.** adv *eternally, forever* 20/67

ēcelīce adv *forever, for eternity* 9/66; 11/116: *eternally* 11/221

ecg f (§14.2) *edge* 5/4 etc; 15/2858; 21/26/6; 23/231; 24/60; 25/16

Ecg–bryhtes–stān m (§13.2) unidentified (see 4/100n)

ecg–hete m (§14.5) *"edge–hate," violence of the sword* 20/70

ecg–plega m (§14.7) *"edge–play," battle* 23/246

Ecg–ulf personal name *Ecgulf* 4/254

ēci = ēce

ēcnes(s),–nys(s) f (§14.2) *eternity:* **on (oð) ēcnesse** adv (= Lat. *in aeternum*) *forever, perpetually* 9/130; 10/27; 11/6; 12/44; 13/55, 102

eder m (§13.3) *building, dwelling* 19/77

ednēowe, –nīwe adj *renewed* 16/314; 18/77

*ge***ed–staðelian II** *restore* 11/77, 79

ed–wenden f (§14.2) *change, end* 18/40

ed–wīt n (§13.4) *insolence, abuse* 23/215

ee = īeg

efen–lang adj *just as long, of equal length* 21/44/7

efen–nēah adj *equally near* 4/213n

efen–nīehðu f (§15.3) (place of) *equal nearness* 4/213

Efer–wīc = Eofor–wīc

efes f (§14.1) *side, edge* 4/148

Efesum *Ephesus* 11/42

efne adv *even, precisely, just, indeed* 1/156; 2/12; 9/h; 11/124, 149

efn–ēce adj with dat *co–eternal with* 9/53

efstan I *hasten* 9/26; 10/184, 330; 15/2873; 17/34; 20/49n; 24/206

eft adv *again, afterwards, back, in turn* 1/24 etc; 2/24 etc; 4/20 etc; 5/55; 7/36 etc; 9/91 etc; 10/24 etc; 11/20 etc; 12/62 etc; 13/49; 14/82; 15/Æ; 16/396; 17/68; etc: **eft ongēan** adv *back again* 6/77f; 24/156: *in reply* 24/19: **eft siððan** adv *afterwards* 12/176

eft–fylgan I *follow upon, follow in turn, come after* 1/140

ege m (§14.5) *fear, terror* 10/87; 11/125; 14/122; 15/Æ

ēg = īeg

eg(e)sa m (§14.7) *fear, terror, awe* 9/32n; 15/2867; 17/86: *awful power* 20/101, 103: *menace* 23/252

egesful(l) adj *fearful, terrible* 23/21 etc; 25/30

egeslic adj *terrible, frightful* 12/218; 14/8, 68 etc; 17/74

eglan I with dat obj *plague, molest, grieve* 23/185

Ēgypte m pl (§14.5) *the Egyptians* 2/61; 13/65

ēhtan I *pursue, assail* 23/237: *persecute* 1/16

ēhtere m (§13.6) *persecutor* 1/19; 11/23

ēi = ēa

ēig–land = īg–land

elcor adv *otherwise, in any other fashion* 1/162

eldan = ieldan

ele m (§14.5) *oil* 11/24

ellen n (§13.5) *courage, zeal* 15/2848; 23/95; 25/16: inst sg **elne micle** adv *with great zeal* 17/34 etc: **on ellen** adv *courageously* 24/211: **mid elne** adv *valiantly, vigorously* 19/114

ellen–dǣd f (§14.6) *deed of courage* 23/273

ellen–rōf adj *daring, brave* 23/109 etc

ellen–þrīste adj *courageous* 23/133

ellen–wōdnis(s) f (§14.2) *zeal* 2/71f

elles adv *else* 9/75; 20/46; 22/23: *besides* 11/325: *otherwise* 13/87

ellor adv *elsewhere* 23/112

eln f (§14.1) *ell* (a unit of length, roughly 1½ to 2 feet, originally the distance between the elbow and the tip of the middle finger) 8/31 etc

el–þēod f (§14.1) *foreign people* 23/237

el–þēodig adj *foreign* 10/182, 282: used as sb *foreigner, stranger, alien* 10/279, 291; 20/h, 38; 23/215

el–þēodignes(s) f (§14.2) *pilgrimage* 4/120

emb = ymb

embe = ymbe

emb–gangan 7 *surround* 10/274

emn–lang adj with dat *co–extensive with, parallel to* 8/51

en = on

end = ond

enda m (§14.7) *end* 1/183

ende m (§13.6) *end* 2/72; 6/25 etc; 9/h, 12; 10/333; 11/223 etc; 12/246; 13/5 etc; 14/6; 20/49n; 23/64 etc: *district, region* 4/182; 6/80; 14/31 etc: *edge* 17/29

ende–byrdan I *arrange, organize* 13/82

ende–byrdnes(s) f (§14.2) *order, succession* 2/16, 28: (word) *order* 13/84

endemes adv *together* 11/229

(*ge*)**endian** II *end, finish, complete* 1/181, 182; 2/98; 9/86: *put an end to* 18/83: *die* 12/249; 14/32n

end–lyfta adj *eleventh* 1/174

*ge***endung** f (§14.1) *ending* 12/158

enge adj *narrow, confined* 16/356 and n: *painful, cruel* 18/52

engel m (§13.3) *angel* 10/44 etc; 11/80, 171 etc; 12/280; 13/42 etc; 15/2861; etc

engel–cyn(n) n (§13.6) *order of angels* 16/246

engel–dryht f (§14.6) *host of angels* 17/9n

engellic adj *angelic* 16/328n

Engla–feld m (§15.2) *Englefield* (Berkshire) 4/27

Engle m pl (§14.5) *the Angles* 5/70; 8/79: *the English* 6/4, 47 etc; 12/1; 14/88 etc

Englisc adj *English* 4/126, 276; 6/40 etc; 7/51 etc; 11/217; 12/40: as neuter sb (the) *English* (language) 7/13 etc; 11/217; 12/40; 13/2 etc; 18/h

Englisc–gereord n (§13.4) *the English language* 2/5

engyl = engel

ent m (§14.5) *giant* 19/87; 25/2

ēodan = ēodon

ēode pret 1 and 3 sg of **gān**

geēode pret 1 and 3 sg of *gegān*

ēodon pret pl of **gān**

geeōdon pret pl of *gegān*

eodorcan I *chew the cud, ruminate* 2/57

Eofer–wīc = Eofor–wīc

eofor m (§13.3) *boar* 25/19

Eofor–wīc n (§13.4) *York* 6/1, 34 etc; 12/109

Eofor–wīc–ceaster f (§14.1) *York* 1/169, 175; 4/4, 8f etc

eoh m (§13.2) *war–horse, charger* 24/189

eolet n *voyage*

eom see **wesan** (§7.2)

Ēomǣr personal name *Eomær* 1/h

eorl(l) m (§13.2) *earl* (Danish *jarl* or English *ealdormann*) 4/27, 34 etc; 5/31; 6/8 etc; 24/6 etc: in poetry *warrior, nobleman, man* 5/1, 73; 19/12, 60 etc; 21/8/5; 23/21 etc; 25/16 etc

eorl–dōm m (§13.2) *earldom* 6/39

eornost f (§14.1) *earnestness, seriousness*: **on eornost** adv *in earnest, seriously*

14/98

eornoste adv *resolutely, fiercely* 23/108 etc; 24/281

ēorod–cist m f (§14.5, 6) *troop* 5/21

eorð–būend m (§15.5) *earth–dweller, man* 21/29/8

eorðe f (§14.7) *earth* 1/132; 2/33; 8/105; 9/115; 10/124, 209 etc; 11/158; 13/44 etc; 16/311 etc; 17/37 etc; 18/43; 19/106 etc; 20/32, 39 etc; 21/29/12; 22/33; 23/65; 24/107 etc; 25/2 etc: *ground* 8/106; 12/206: *soil* 12/196 etc

eorð–rīce n (§13.6) "*earth–kingdom*," *earth* 16/419

eorð–scræf, –scraf n (§13.4) "*earth–cave*," *grave* 9/44; 19/84: *underground room, cave* 22/28

eorð–sele m (§14.5) "*earth–hall*," *cave, barrow* 22/29

eorð–weg m (§13.2) *earthly way, earth* 17/120

eorð–wela m (§14.7) *earthly riches, worldly goods* 20/67

ēow see **þū** (§6.2) *you, yourselves*

ēowan I *show* 23/240

ēower I. see **þū** (§6.2) *you, of you*: **II.** possessive adj *your* 3/29; 10/65, 236; 11/98, 172 etc; 23/195

Eow–land m (§13.4) *Öland* 8/88

erede pret 1 and 3 sg of **erian**

ergende pres pple of **erian**

erian I *plow* 4/81; 8/40 etc

ermðu = **iermðu**

ernian = **earnian**

Escan–ceaster f (§14.1) *Exeter* (Devonshire) 4/80 etc

esne m (§13.6) *man, youth* 1/182n; 21/44/4

esol m (§13.3) *ass* 15/2867

ēst f (§14.6) *grace, favor* 18/46; 21/26/24

Este m pl (§14.5) see 8/91n

ēst–ēadig adj "*favor–blessed*," *fortunate* 20/56

Est–land n (§13.4) *the land of the* Este 8/94 etc

Est–mere m (§14.5) "*the sea of the* Este", see 8/91n

etan 5 *eat* 10/5, 12 etc; 13/20

ettan I *graze* 8/49

Ēðan–dūn f (§14.1) *Edington* (Wiltshire) 4/103

ēðel m (§13.3) *home, homeland, native land* 19/20; 20/h, 60; 23/169; 24/52; 25/20: *territory* 7/7

ēðel–rīce n (§13.6) *realm* 16/356n

ēðel–weard m (§13.2) *protector of the country* 23/320

Ēue personal name *Eve* 16/419

Eugenius personal name *Eugenius* 11/87 etc

Exan–ce(a)ster = **Escan–ceaster**

exl = **eaxl**

F

fāc(e)n n (§13.4) *crime* 25/54: *wile* 11/97

*(ge)***fadian** II *arrange, order* 13/87; 14/51, 157

fadung f (§14.1) *arrangement, order* 13/85n

fæc n (§13.4) *space of time, time, period* 1/138; 9/99; 11/188, 191: **medmicel fæc** *a little while* 1/139; 2/4, 97; 10/309

fæder m (§15.4) *father* 9/32n, 54; 10/242; 11/222 etc; 13/9 etc; 14/50 etc; 15/2888; 15/Æ; 19/115; 23/5; 25/61 etc: see also **eald**

fæge adj *fated to die, doomed* 5/12 etc; 20/71; 23/19 etc; 24/105 etc

*(ge)***fægen** adj *happy, elated* 19/68: with gen *glad of, happy about* 12/133: *glad to see* 4/102

fæger adj *fair, lovely, beautiful, attractive* 2/72; 9/17, 93, 97 etc; 10/112, 316; 13/70; 17/8 etc; 18/8 etc; 23/47

fæg(e)re adv *fairly, pleasantly* 9/93n; 20/13; 21/28/1: *splendidly, generously* 23/300: *properly* 24/22: *justly* 25/56

fægernes(s) f (§14.2) *loveliness* 9/113, 118; 20/49n: *excellence, fine quality* 13/75

fægrian II *adorn, deck* 20/48

fægnian II *rejoice* 11/40: with gen obj *rejoice in* 12/60 etc

fǣhð(u) f (§15.3) *feud, state of feud, hostility* 22/26; 24/225: dat pl used as adv *vengefully* 21/29/11

fǣmne f (§14.7) *woman, girl* 25/44

fær n (§13.4) *journey, way* 4/160

fǣr m (§13.2) *sudden onset, peril* 16/334

færest pres indic 2 sg of **faran**
fǣrlic adj *sudden* 9/86
fǣrlīce adv *suddenly* 11/81, 147 etc; 12/230; 19/61
fær–sceat(t) m (§13.2) *passage–money, fare* 10/65, 66f
fǣr–sceaða m (§14.7) *sudden attacker* 24/142
fǣr–spel(l) n (§13.4) *sudden and horrible news* 23/244
færð = **fareð** (pres 3 sg of **faran**)
fæst adj *fast, firm, secure* 16/408; 25/38: *caught fast* 15/2929
fæste adv *fast, firmly* 1/166; 2/38; 9/50; 14/94; 16/374; 17/38 etc; 19/13, 18; 21/26/26; 23/99; 24/21 etc
fæsten–bryce m (§14.5) *non–observance of fasts* 14/113
fæsten–geat n (§13.4) *stronghold gate* 23/162
fæsten(n) m (§13.6) **I.** *stronghold, fortress* 4/86, 136n; 23/143: *"fastness," a place naturally strong against attack, safe place* 4/197; 24/194: **II.** *fast* 11/211 etc
fæstlīce adv *firmly* 1/152: *stoutly, resolutely* 24/82, 254
(*ge*)**fæstnian** II *fasten, make fast* 12/166; 17/33: *confirm* 24/35
fæstnung f (§14.1) *stability, permanence, fixity, security* 19/115
fæt n (§13.4) *vessel* 11/10
fǣtels m n (§13.3, 5) *vessel* 8/127: *bag, pouch* 23/127
fæðm m (§13.2) *embrace* 21/26/25; 25/61
fæðm–rīm n (§13.4) *number of fathoms* (i.e. cubits), *"fathom–measure"* 18/29
fāg adj *stained* 17/13 (with a pun on **fāh** **I.**?): *decorated* 19/98; 23/104 etc; 25/22
*ge***fāgian** II *variegate, embroider* 9/96
fāh adj **I.** a person who is *fāh* is in a state of liability to punishment for a crime or fault that he has committed; hence he is *guilty*, perhaps *outlawed*, very probably *hostile* 22/46: **II.** = **fāg**
Falster *Falster* 8/85
fandian II with gen obj *test, assay* 11/107; 15/Æ: *find out* 8/6
fandung f (§14.1) *test, examination, assay* 13/85
*ge***fangen** past pple of **fōn**
faran 6 *go, travel, march* 1/90; 4/4, 14 etc; 6/10, 36 etc; 8/7 etc; 10/161, 315; 15/Æ; 12/250; 23/202 etc; 24/h, 88 etc: *pass* 13/53: **faran on** with dat *overtake* 20/91
*ge***faran** 6 *go, travel* 4/89, 138; 10/43, 44: *set out* 8/82: *pass away, die* 4/12, 24 etc: **gefaran tōsomne** *engage in battle* 1/92: **bēon gefaren** *have come about, have happened* 14/138
*ge***faren** past pple of (*ge*)**faran**
fatu nom and acc pl of **fæt**
fēa adj *few* 7/12, 14, 22; 17/115: *a few* 4/136; 8/4: *few things* 11/223
*ge***fēa** m (§14.7) *joy* 10/53, 72, 327 etc
fēa–gītsung f (§14.1) *avarice, greed* 1/85
*ge***feah** pret 1 and 3 sg of *ge***fēon**
feaht pret 1 and 3 sg of **feohtan**
*ge***feaht** pret 1 and 3 sg of *ge***feohtan**
feala = **fela**
fealdan 7 *fold* 21/26/7
(*ge*)**feallan** 7 *fall* 1/104; 5/12; 11/84, 169; 12/205 etc; 16/306; 17/43; 18/61 etc; 20/32; 21/29/12; 23/67 etc; 24/54 etc: *fall in battle* 12/156 etc: *fall in ruin* 9/123; 19/63: *kneel* 12/19, 24: *flow, run* 8/71
feallendlic adj *as if falling in ruin* 9/111
fealo adj *fallow* (i.e. the light color of the sea in sandy shallows), *brown, yellowish–green, dusky* 5/36; 19/46: *withered* 18/74
fealo–hilte adj *"fallow–hilted," gold–hilted* 24/166
fēa–lufu f (§14.7) *love of money* 1/15
Fearn–ham(m) m (§13.2) *Farnham* (Surrey) 4/156
fēa–sceaftig adj *poor, destitute* 20/26
fēawa (see Campbell §653.(2)) = **fēawe**
fēawe m n f nom and acc pl of **fēa**
fēawum dat pl of **fēa**
feax n (§13.4) *hair* 23/99 etc
feaxed adj (past pple) *long–haired* 4/126; 6/6
(*ge*)**feccan** II *fetch, take, carry off, bring* 4/239; 11/104; 12/36; 17/138; 23/35; 24/160: *obtain* 12/238
*ge***fecgan** = *ge***feccan**

fēdan I *raise, bring up*
ge**fēgan** I *join together* 11/73
fela I. indecl sb, usually with gen *many* 4/38, 46 etc; 6/71; 8/24 etc; 11/201 etc; 12/31 etc; 14/9, 10 etc; 16/271 etc; 17/50, 125, 131; 19/54; 20/5; 21/8/11; 22/39; 24/73: *much* 14/43; 16/322; 24/90: *much, many things* 11/221; 25/12: **II.** indecl adj *many* 13/77; 14/62
fela–lēof adj *much beloved, dearly beloved* 22/26
ge**fēlan** I *feel* 20/95
feld m (§15.2) *flat open country, plain, field, battlefield* 4/146; 5/12; 12/204 etc; 18/26; 24/241
fel(l) n (§13.4) *skin, pelt* 8/42 etc
ge**fellan** = ge**fyllan**
(ge)**fēng** pret 1 and 3 sg of (ge)**fōn**
(ge)**fēngon** pret pl of (ge)**fōn**
fen(n) n (§13.6) *fen, marsh* 4/136; 25/42
fēo dat sg of **feoh**
feoh n (§13.4) *money, property, treasure* 1/23, 25; 3/16, 23; 4/111, 174 etc; 6/9; 8/108, 110 etc; 10/69; 11/144; 19/108; 24/39: *cattle* 25/47
ge**feoh** imper sg of ge**fēon**
feoh–gīfre adj *"wealth–greedy," avaricious* 19/68
feoh–lēas adj *without property, moneyless* 4/245
ge**feoht** n (§13.4) *fight, battle* 1/26, 94, 182n; 3/6; 4/46 etc; 5/28; 6/42 etc; 12/25 etc; 14/90; 23/189 etc; 24/12: *fighting* 4/18: *war* 9/15
feohtan 3 *fight* 3/13, 17 etc; 4/22, 39 etc; 6/53 etc; 10/187; 23/262 etc; 24/16 etc
ge**feohtan** 3 *fight* 1/92; 4/16, 28 etc; 6/40; 24/h: *gain by fighting, win, achieve* 23/122; 24/129
(ge)**feohte** f (§14.7) *battle* 24/103; 14/90
fēolan 3 *penetrate* 3/30
fēoldan = **fēoldon**
fēoldon pret pl of **fealdan**
fēol–heard adj *hard as a file* 24/108
(ge)**fēol(l)** pret 1 and 3 sg of (ge)**feallan**
fēollan = **fēollon**
fēollon pret pl of **feallan**
ge**fēon** 5 *rejoice* 1/74; 2/82; 10/53, 113n, 327: with gen obj *rejoice in* 1/167; 23/205
fēond m (§15.5) *enemy* 1/29, 54, 57 etc; 11/165; 12/16 etc; 14/72; 15/Æ; 17/30 etc; 20/75; 21/26/1; 23/195 etc; 24/82 etc; 25/52: *fiend* 16/306 etc
fēond–sceaða m (§14.7) *injurious foe* 23/104
feor = **feor(r)**
fēore, fēores dat and gen sg of **feorh**
feorg = **feorh**
feorg–bold n (§13.4) *"life–dwelling," body* 17/73
feorh m n (§13.2, 4) *life, soul, spirit* 3/16, 32; 5/36; 15/2932n; 20/71, 94; 21/26/1; 24/125 etc
feorh–hūs n (§13.4) *"soul–house," body* 24/297
feor(h)–hyrde m (§13.6) *"life–guardian," protector* 1/20, 80
feor(r) I. adj *far, distant* 22/47: **II.** adv *far, far away* 1/59, 169; 2/95; 8/9 etc; 10/109; 18/1; 19/26; 20/37, 52; 22/25; 24/3, 57: *from long ago* 19/90: with dat *far from* 13/40; 19/21
feorran adv *from afar* 17/57; 21/28/6; 23/24; 25/1
feorða adj *fourth* 1/182n; 11/204, 210; 15/2870; 23/12
fēorum dat pl of **feorh**
fēos gen sg of **feoh**
fēower numeral *four* 4/231; 8/13; 12/105; 13/13
fēowertig numeral *forty* 1/182n; 4/164; 8/32; 10/164; 11/323
fēowertȳne numeral *fourteen* 2/73f
ge**fēra** m (§14.7) *companion* 1/168; 3/27, 29; 4/110; 12/6 etc; 16/306; 19/30; 24/170 etc: *associate, follower* 13/30
fēran I *go* 1/164; 4/17; 10/61, 162, 330; 11/96, 276; 12/4 etc; 24/41, 221: *journey, travel* 15/2850; 15/Æ; 20/37; 21/7/9; 21/29/11; 21/57/4; 22/9; 23/12: *flow* 25/31
ge**fēran** I *journey* 10/119: *come to pass, happen* 6/76
fēre adj *able to move on, fit for service* 6/65
ge**fēre** adj *accessible* 18/4

fer–grunden past pple of **for–grindan**
ferhð–glēaw adj *wise, prudent* 23/41
ferian I *carry, transport* 4/154, 163; 12/168, 216 etc; 13/51; 19/81: *take* 11/149: *translate* 12/141: *go, depart* 24/179
fer–loren = **for–loren**
*ge***ferod** past pple of **ferian**
fers n (§13.4) *verse* 2/27; 13/49
fersc adj *fresh–water* 8/61
ferð m n (§13.2, 4) *mind, soul, spirit* 19/54, 90; 20/26, 37; 21/26/21
ferð–loca m (§14.7) *"soul–enclosure," breast* 19/13, 33
fēsan I *drive away* 14/90
fēt dat sg and nom and acc pl of **fōt**
feter f (§14.1) *fetter* 19/21
*ge***feterian** II *bind* 15/2903
(*ge*)**feti(g)an** = (*ge*)**feccan**
fette pret 1 and 3 sg of **feccan**
fēða m (§14.7) *foot–troop* 24/88
fēðe n (§13.6) *power of walking, ability to move* 16/379
fēðe–lāst m (§13.2) *"walking–track," footpath* 23/139
feðer f (§14.1) *feather* 8/42 etc (*eider-down*); 19/47
feðer–homa m (§14.7) *feather–coat* or *–covering*: *wings* 16/417
fexed = **feaxed**
fic–trēow n (§13.6) *fig–tree* 10/156
(*ge*)**fiellan** I *fell, strike down, slay* 5/41 etc; 17/38; 23/194: *cut down* 17/73
fierd f (§14.6) *army* 1/26, 90; 4/8, 17 etc; 6/37 etc; 24/h, 221; 25/31 etc: *expedition, campaign* 16/408
fierdian II *campaign* 4/160
fierd–lēas adj *undefended by the* **fierd** 4/148
fif numeral *five* 4/268; 5/28; 6/63; 8/16 etc; 17/8
fifteg, –ig numeral *fifty* 7/62; 8/33
fif–tēn, –tȳn numeral *fifteen* 8/44 etc
fihtest pres 2 sg of **feohtan**
filigan = **fylgan**
*ge***fillednys(s)** f (§14.2) *fulfillment* 13/25
findan 3 *find* 8/124; 15/2895 (with refl dat); 16/266; 19/26; 22/18; 23/2, 41 etc; 24/85: *devise* 7/40: pret 1 and 3 sg **funde** 22/18; 23/2
finger m (§13.2) *finger* 21/26/7; 25/38
Finnas m pl (§13.2) *Lapps* see 4/4n
fiorm f (§14.1) *sustenance, benefit, profit* 7/26
firas m pl (§13.6) *men* 2/37; 16/408; 18/3; 23/24 etc
fird = **fierd**
firgen–strēam m (§13.2) *"mountainous stream," mighty stream* 25/47
firmest = **fyrmest**
*ge***firnian** II *sin* 10/115, 117
firrest sup adv *farthest* 8/10
first m n (§14.5) *time, space of time* 7/50; 9/69, 91; 12/138; 23/324: *interval, respite* 12/254: **on firste** adv *in the course of time* 11/20f
fisc m (§13.2) *fish* 25/27
fiscað m (§13.3) *fishing* 8/5 etc
fiscere m (§13.6) *fisher* 8/20 etc
flǣsc n (§14.5) *flesh* 9/75; 11/162; 12/170
flǣsc–homa m (§14.7) *"fleshly covering," body* 20/94
flǣsclic adj *fleshly* 9/97; 10/45: *carnal* 11/16
flān m (§13.2) *arrow* 11/94; 23/221; 24/71 etc
flēag pret 1 and 3 sg of **flēogan**
flēah = **flēag**
flēam m (§13.2) *flight* 4/204; 5/37; 23/291; 24/186 etc: **bedrīfan on flēam** *put to flight*: **weorðan on flēame** *flee, take to flight* 6/56: **gewyrcan flēam** *flee, take to flight* 24/81
flēman = **flieman**
flēogan 2 *fly* 4/h; 16/417; 20/17; 23/209 etc; 24/7 etc: *flee* 24/275
flēoh–net(t) n (§13.6) *fly–net, curtain* 23/47
flēon 2 *flee* 1/38; 4/157; 9/122, 123; 10/60, 230 etc; 12/231; 23/296; 24/194 etc
fleosewian II *dissemble* 1/h
flēotend m (§15.5) *floating one, swimming one* 19/54
flēow pret 1 and 3 sg of **flōwan**
flet–sittend m (§15.5) *"hall–sitter," guest* 23/19 etc
flet(t) n (§13.6) *hall* 19/61

(ge)flīeman I *put to flight, rout* 1/182n; 4/38, 43f, 52, 76 etc; 5/32

floc(c) m (§13.2) *band, detachment* 4/148

floc–rād f (§14.1) *mounted detachment* 4/147

flōd m (§13.2) *flood, sea* 5/36; 21/7/9: *flood–tide* 4/277; 24/65 etc

flōde f (§14.7) *channel* 3/4

flōd–grǣg adj *sea–grey* 25/31

flōd–weg m (§13.2) *"sea–way," ocean path* 20/52

flōd–wylm m (§14.5) *flowing stream* 18/64n

flōr f (§14.1, 15.2) *floor* 23/111

flot n (§13.4) *water, sea* 5/35; 24/41

flota m (§14.7) *sailor* 5/32; 24/72, 227: *fleet* 5/32n

flot–man(n) m (§15.7) *sailor, pirate* 14/89

flot–men(n) dat sg and nom and acc pl of **flot–man(n)**

flōwan 7 *flow* 10/124, 210; 24/65; 25/47

flugon pret pl of **flēon**

flyht m (§14.5) *flight* 24/71

flȳhð pres 3 sg of **flēon**

flȳma m (§14.7) *fugitive, exile* 1/18, 39

flȳman = **flīeman**

fnǣst m (§14.5) *breath, blast* 18/15

gefohten past pple of **(ge)feohtan**

folc n (§13.4) *people* 1/164; 2/61; 4/h, 91, 230; 5/67; 6/54, 72, 95; 7/5; 9/35; 10/193, 199 etc; 11/54, 185 etc; 12/61 etc; 13/17 etc; 14/7 etc; 17/140; 21/7/6; 23/h, 12 etc; 24/45, 54, 202; 25/44: *army* 4/168; 6/40, 44, 67; 24/22, 227, 241, 259, 323: *commoners* 1/174

folc–āgend m (§15.5) *ruler of a people, chieftain*; *man* 18/5

folc–gefeoht n (§13.4) *pitched battle, general engagement* 4/53; 6/63

folc–gestælla, –gestealla m (§14.7) *war–companion, comrade* 16/270 etc

folc–lagu f (§14.1) *people's law, public law* 14/31

folc–lond n (§13.4) *"folk–land," country* 22/47

folc–stede m (§14.5) *battlefield* 5/41; 23/319

folc–toga m (§14.7) *leader of a people, general* 23/47 etc

folde f (§14.7) *earth* 2/37; 17/8 etc; 18/3 etc; 19/33; 20/13, 75; 21/7/9; 21/28/1; 23/281; 24/166 etc; 25/33: *country* 18/29; 24/54

fold–græf n (§13.4) *earth–grave* 17/76n

fold–weg m (§13.2) *"earth–way," path* 15/2874

fold–wylm m (§14.5) *"earth–welling"* (a surge of water emanating from the earth) 18/64

folgað m (§13.3) *service* (i.e. either the state of being in service with a lord, or the service owed to a lord by a retainer) 22/9

folgian II with dat obj *follow* 3/26; 11/15, 46; 13/31

folm(e) f (§14.1, 7) *hand* 15/2907; 23/80 etc; 24/31 etc

(ge)fōn *seize, capture* 4/76, 154 etc; 23/299: *catch* 8/38: *execute* 16/287: **fōn tō rīce** *succeed to the kingdom* 4/1, 50, 288; 7/15f; 12/164f: **fōn tō þǣre sprǣce** *take up the discussion* 1/131f: **fōn tō wǣpnum** *take up arms* 24/10: **fōn tōgædere** *join battle* 6/53; 12/156

for prep with dat and inst **I.** (local) *before, in front of, in the sight of, in the presence of* 7/20; 9/29, 59; 11/118; 12/145; 14/57; 17/112; 23/192; 25/59: **II.** (causal) *for, because of, on account of, for the sake of* 1/85 etc; 2/6 etc; 3/1 etc; 4/119 etc; 6/72 etc; 7/37; 8/18 etc; 9/64, 215 etc; 11/63, 121, 137 etc; 12/27 etc; 14/7, 37 etc; 16/341, 359; 17/21, 93; 20/h, 103; 22/10; 24/64: **for þǣm, for þām, for þan, for þon, for þȳ** adv *therefore* 1/128f, 140, 149; 2/11, 15, 23 etc; 4/278; 7/17, 30, etc; 8/95 etc; 9/27, 48; 11/100, 164 etc; 12/269; 14/42; 16/250, 302 etc; 17/84; 19/17, 58; 22/17; 24/241: *for that reason* 14/13: *indeed, assuredly* 19/37, 64; 20/27, 33, 39, 58, 64, 72; 21/26/13; 22/39: **for þǣm (þe), for þām (þe), for þon (þe), for þon (þæt), for þȳ (þe), for þȳ . . . þe** conj *because, since* 1/91, 128, 146 etc; 2/2, 9, 24 etc; 4/119,

127, 162, 178, 216; 6/13f etc; /l26 etc; 8/14, 17 etc; 9/6, 53, 92 etc; 10/12f, 14f, 25 etc; 11/16, 98 etc; 12/67, 275; 13/4, 7, 47 etc; 14/47, 104 etc; 15/Æ; 16/309, 326; 20/108; 23/h: *for* 1/88, 124; 2/9, 69, 73; 14/15, 30, 56: *that* 10/75, 97, 122, 145, 256, 258, 282: **for þon . . . þæt** *so that* 10/298f: **for þon . . . for þon** *for that reason . . . that* 10/117f, 119: **for hwon** interr adv *why* 9/94; 10/230, 242, 317: conj *why* 1/46, 51; 2/80; 19/59: see also **sōð**: **III.** (other) *in place of, instead of* 15/2931; 15/Æ

fōr I. sb f (§14.1) *journey, trip, expedition* 15/2861: **II.** pret 1 and 3 sg of **faran**

*ge***fōr** pret 1 and 3 sg of *ge***faran**

foran adv *from in front* 4/155, 212, 264: *in front* 21/44/2: **foran tō** adv *beforehand* 13/37

fōran = **fōron** (pret pl of **faran**)

for–bærnan I *burn* 4/176, 212; 7/24; 8/107, 120 etc: *burn down* 1/168: *burn up, consume* 12/236; 14/62; 15/2859; 20/114: *burn to death* 6/57

for–bēah = **for–bēag** (pret 1 and 3 sg of **for–būgan**)

for–beornan 3 *burn down* 12/232

for–bīgan I abase, humiliate 23/267

for–būgan 2 *flee from* 24/325

for–burnen past pple of **for–beornan**

for–cearf pret 1 and 3 sg of **for–ceorfan**

for–ceorfan 3 *cut through* 23/105

ford m (§15.2) *ford* 4/157; 24/81 etc

for–dōn anom vb (§7.6) *destroy, ruin* 1/171; 14/144

for–drāf pret 1 and 3 sg of **for–drīfan**

for–drīfan 1 *impel, compel* 23/277

for–dwīnan 1 *vanish, evanesce* 19/h

for–dwinon pret pl of **for–dwīnan**

for–dyde pret 1 and 3 sg of **for–dōn**

fore prep with dat and acc *for, for the sake of* 1/8: *at the head of, in charge of* 1/9, 182n: *in place of, instead of* 20/21, 22

fore–bēcen n (§13.4) *portent* 4/h

fore–cweðan 4 *predict* 1/63

fore–cwið pres 3 sg of **fore–cweðan**

fore–gangan 7 *go before, precede* 1/139f

fore–genga m (§14.7) *"one who goes before," attendant* 23/127

fore–gīsl m (§13.2) see 4/87n

fore–mǣre adj *very illustrious* 23/122

fore–sǣd adj (past pple) *aforesaid* 11/91; 12/36 etc; 13/81

fore–sǣdon pret pl of **fore–secgan**

fore–secēawian II *provide, see to* 15/Æ

fore–secgan III *mention before* 12/169 etc

fore–speca m (§14.7) *sponsor, advocate* 14/156

fore–sprecen adj (past pple) *aforesaid, previously mentioned* 1/77, 153; 4/228

fore–þingian II *intercede* 1/11

fore–we(a)rd adj *early, early in the* 1/31; 4/225n

for–faran 6 *destroy* 6/57; 14/63: *blockade* 4/264

for–faren past pple of **for–faran**

for–geaf pret 1 and 3 sg of **for–giefan**

for–gēafon pret pl of **for–giefan**

for–gēfon = **for–gēafon**

for–georne adv *very clearly* 9/68

for–giefan 5 *give, grant* 1/60, 178; 2/47; 10/17; 11/122f; 15/2936; 16/250 etc; 17/147; 20/93; 23/88; 24/139 etc: *give back* 15/2925: *forgive* 10/114

for–gi(e)fen past pple of **for–giefan**

for–gieldan 3 *repay, requite* 23/217

for–gifan = **for–giefan**

for–golden past pple of **for–gieldan**

for–grindan 3 *grind to pieces, destroy* 5/43

for–gyfenes(s) f (§14.2) *forgiveness, remission* 11/132; 13/53, 54

for–gyfnys(s) = **for–gyfenes(s)**

for–gyldan 3 *pay* (someone, dat) *back for* (something, acc) 10/202: *buy off* 24/32

for–gȳman I *neglect* 16/327

for–hæfednys(s) f (§14.2) *temperance, continence* 12/75

for–healdan 7 *hold back, withhold* 14/21, 22

for–heard adj *very hard* 24/156

for–hēawan 7 *hew down, cut down* 24/115 etc

for–hēawen past pple of **for–hēawan**

for–hergian II *ravage* 7/24; 24/h

for–hogdnis(s) f (§14.2) *contempt* 2/7
forhtlīce adv *in terror, in alarm* 23/243
for–hogian II *scorn, disdain* 9/9; 24/254: *despise* 11/62f, 121
forht adj *afraid, frightened, terrified* 1/46, 103; 7/21: *fearful, apprehensive* 19/68
forhtian II *fear, apprehend* 1/52; 8/8: *be afraid* 11/252; 17/115; 24/21: *tremble* 10/265
forhtung f (§14.1) *apprehension* 11/265
for–hwaga adv *approximately* 8/110 etc
for–lǣtan 7 *let* 10/281, 326; 17/61; 23/150 etc; 24/149 etc: *leave* 1/182; 2/18, 100; 5/42; 10/312; 11/14, 127: *abandon* 4/237; 24/2, 187: *forsake* 10/15, 19 etc; 11/30, 302; 13/30 etc; 14/154; 16/429: *violate* 1/36: *lose* 7/30; 9/66, 70; 16/404; 24/208: *leave undone, neglect* 7/38
for–lǣten past pple of **for–lǣtan**
for–lǣtnes(s) f (§14.2) *remission* 9/55
for–legen adj (past pple) *adulterous* 14/132
for–lēogan 2 *commit perjury:* past pple *perjured* 14/78, 113
for–lēosan 2 *lose, throw away* 1/85; 11/113, 162 etc; 16/301; 23/63: *destroy* 1/150: *lose, ruin* 14/113
for–lēt pret 1 and 3 sg of **for–lǣtan**
for–lētan = **for–lǣtan**
for–lēton pret pl of **for–lǣtan**
for–liger n (§13.4) *fornication* 14/111
for–logen past pple of **for–lēogan**
for–loren past pple of **for–lēosan**
for–luron pret pl of **for–lēosan**
forma sup adj (§12.9) *first* 11/12; 13/49; 16/319; 24/77
for–moni adj *very many a, too many a* 24/239
for–niman 4 *carry off, destroy* 19/80, 99; 22/24n: *take away* 14/38
for–nōm pret 1 and 3 sg of **for–niman**
for–nōman = **for–nōmon**
for–nōmon pret pl of **for–niman**
for–numen past pple of **for–niman**
for–nȳdan I *compel, force* 14/34
for–oft adv *very often* 14/47, 49 etc
fōron pret pl of **faran**
*ge***fōron** pret pl of *ge***faran**
for–rād pret 1 and 3 sg of **for–rīdan**
for–rǣdan I *betray* 14/61: **forrǣdan of līfe** *kill treacherously* 14/60
for–rīdan 1 *cut off* (by riding), *intercept* (on horseback) 4/155, 212
for–rotian II *rot away, decay* 12/101
for–sacan 6 *abandon, forsake* 6/16–21n: *reject* 12/189
for–sæt pret 1 and 3 sg of **for–sittan**
for–sawen past pple of **for–sēon**
for–scēop pret 1 and 3 sg of **for–scieppan**
for–scieppan 6 *transform* 16/308
for–scyldgod adj (past pple) *guilty* 11/148
for–sēon 5 *reject, disdain, scorn* 9/9; 13/54: *despise* 14/39
for–sewennys(s) f (§14.2) *contempt* 11/55
for–sittan 5 with inst obj *defer, delay* 15/2860
for–sōcan = **for–sōcon**
for–sōcon pret pl of **for–sacan**
for–spanan 6 *seduce, mislead* 16/350
for–spendan I *squander, consume* 8/121
for–spēon pret 1 and 3 sg of **for–spanan**
for–spillan I *destroy, kill* 14/62
forst m (§13.2) *frost* 16/316; 18/15 etc; 20/9
for–standan 6 *avail, be of use* 6/25: *understand* 7/60
for–stōd pret 1 and 3 sg of **for–standan**
for–stōdon pret pl of **for–standan**
for–swāpan 7 *sweep off, drive away* 16/391
for–swāpen past pple of **for–swāpan**
for–swealg, –swealh pret 1 and 3 sg of **for–swelgan**
for–swelgan 3 *swallow up* 10/293: *devour, eat* 20/95; 21/47/3
for–swerian II *forswear, swear falsely* 14/77
for–swīðe adv *very seriously* 4/247
for–sworen past pple of **for–swerian**
for–syhð pres 3 sg of **for–sēon**
for–syngod adj (past pple) *corrupt, ruined by sin* 14/106, 136
for–tēon II *fore–ordain, predestine* 1/185
forð adv *forth, forward, onward, away* 4/168; 5/20; 8/18; 12/212, 224; 15/2847; 17/132; 21/29/11, 13; 23/111 etc; 24/3 etc: *from now on* 1/109; 16/437: *from then on* 16/320, 348; 23/120: *from there on* 11/220: **forð**

mid adv *along with, besides* 11/185: **tō forð** *too much* 14/123: *too (far) forward, too deeply* 24/150

forð–brengan I *produce* 1/6

forð–brōhte pret 1 and 3 sg of **forð–brengan**

for–þearle adv *very badly, greatly* 12/35

forð–ēode pret 1 and 3 sg of **forð–gān**

forð–fēran I *depart, die* 4/250, 383 etc; 6/2

forð–fōr f (§14.1) *going forth, departure, death* 2/73 etc: **æt forðfōre** adv *at the point of death* 2/77

forð–gān anom vb (§7.7) *go forth* 17/54

forð–gelǣdan I *bring* 1/68

forð–georn adj *eager to advance* 24/281

forð–gesceaft f (§14.6) *future* 25/61: *future; eternal decree* 17/10

Forð–here personal name *Forðhere* 1/h

*ge***forðian** II *carry out, accomplish* 24/289

forðlīce adv *in a state of forwardness* 6/75

for–þolian II with dat obj *do without, forgo* 19/38

for–þylman I *enwrap, envelop* 23/118

for–wearð pret 1 and 3 sg of **for–weorðan**

forð–weg m (§13.2) *the way forth, the journey ahead* (into the hereafter) 17/125; 19/81

for–wegan 5 *carry off, destroy, kill* 24/228

for–wegen past pple of **for–wegan**

for–weornian II *wither* 11/115

for–weorðan 3 *perish* 10/246, 281; 14/141, 150; 23/288: *be lost* 4/84, 282; 6/28; 14/150: *deteriorate* 14/64

for–wiernan I with dat (of person) and gen (of thing) *deny* 4/233

for–wordenlic adj *as if undone* 9/110

for–worht past pple of **for–wyrcan**

for–worhtan = **for–worhton** (pret pl of **for–wyrcan**)

for–wundian II *badly wound* 4/281; 17/14 etc

for–wurdan = **for–wurdon**

for–wurdon pret pl of **for–weorðan**

for–wyrcan I *obstruct, block, close up* 4/234; 16/381: *forfeit* 14/149: with refl acc + **wio** (and acc) *commit wrongs against* (someone); *ruin* or *undo oneself with* (someone) 14/126

for–wyrd f (§14.6) *destruction* 11/172, 180; 23/285

for–wyrð pres 3 sg of **for–weorðan**

for–yrman I *impoverish, bring low* 14/34

fōt m (§15.7) *foot* 1/104; 10/289; 11/84 etc; 12/80 etc; 13/93; 15/2856 etc; 16/379; 19/9; 24/119 etc

fōt–mǣl n (§13.4) *foot's length* 24/275

fōt–swæð n (§13.4) *footprint* 11/184f

fōt–swaðu nom and acc pl of **fōt–swæð**

fracod adj *bad, wicked* 12/250: used as sb *evil man, criminal* 17/10

frǣcnes(s) = **frēc(e)n(n)es(s)**

*ge***frǣge** adj *well–known, famous* 18/3

frægn pret 1 and 3 sg of **frignan**

*ge***fræg(e)n** pret 1 and 3 sg of *ge***frignan**

Frǣna personal name *Fræna* 4/38

frǣt pret 1 and 3 sg of **fretan**

fræt(e)we f pl (§14.3) *trappings, ornaments, adornments, treasures* 13/70; 18/73; 21/7/6; 25/27

frætewian = **frætwian**

frætwian II *adorn, deck* 9/79; 11/93; 21/28/6; 23/171 etc

fram **I.** adj *bold, valiant* 1/182n: **II.** adv *away* 3/27; 24/317: **III.** prep with dat and inst **A.** (point of departure) *from* 1/40 etc; 2/17 etc; 3/25; etc: **B.** (reference) *of* 1/119; 11/268; 12/193, 218: **C.** (agent) *from, by* 1/175; 10/71, 90, 296; 12/9

franca m (§14.7) *spear, javelin* 24/77 etc

Franc–land n (§13.4) *the Frankish empire* 4/116; 12/240

frēa m (§14.7) *lord, master* 15/2890; 21/44/2; 22/33; 24/12 etc: *the Lord, God* 2/37; 15/2861 etc; 17/33; 23/300

frēcednys(s) f (§14.2) *harm* 11/327

frēc(e)n(n)es(s) f (§14.2) *peril, danger* 9/12, 23f; 10/26

frēfran I *comfort, console* 19/28; 20/26

fremde adj *unrelated* 8/122: *estranged* 10/82n: as sb *stranger* 14/36, 49 etc

fremian II with dat obj *benefit* 11/74

(*ge*)**fremman** I *bring about, achieve* 19/114: *commit, perpetrate* 9/4, 82; 23/181: *make* 23/6: *provide, furnish* 19/16: *perform* 11/201f: *do* 16/392; 23/37: *carry out* 12/125: *wreak* 16/393: *fight* 6/63

frem–sumnes(s) f (§14.2) *benefit, kindness, favor* 1/55f, 60, 126; 2/67; 9/128

fremu f (§14.1) *benefit, profit, gain*

16/437: *beneficial action, good deed* 20/75

Frencysc adj *French*: **þā Frencyscan** *the French* 6/71

frēod f (§14.1) *peace* 24/39

*ge***freoge** n *learning, knowledge, information* 18/29

frēo(h) adj *free* 7/48; 11/319

frēols–brice m (§14.5) *non–observance of church festivals* 14/113

*ge***frēolsian** II *set free, deliver* 10/25, 224 etc

frēo–mǣg m (§13.2) *noble kinsman* 19/21

frēond m (§15.5) *friend* 1/30, 77 etc; 5/41; 8/103; 9/98; 11/164; 12/4 etc; 16/287; 17/76 etc; 19/108; 21/26/21; 22/17; 24/229: *lover* 22/33, 47; 25/44

frēondlēas adj *friendless* 19/28

frēondlīce adv *in a friendly fashion, amicably* 7/1f

frēondscipe, –scype m (§14.5) *friendship* 6/61f: *friendship, love* 22/25

frēorig adj *cold, chilled, frozen* 19/33: *chilled by fear* 23/281

frēo–riht n pl (§13.4) *rights of freemen* 14/38

Frēsisc adj *Frisian* 4/260 etc

fretan 5 *eat up, devour* 4/200; 21/47/1

freten past pple of **fretan**

frettan I *graze up, graze to ruin* 4/213

fricg(e)an 5 *find out* 21/26/26: with gen *ask about* 15/2888

Frīesa m (§14.7) *a Frisian* 4/274 etc

frige imper sg of **fricg(e)an**

frignan 3 *ask, inquire* 1/46, 47, 119; 2/83, 87 etc; 17/112: **frignan fram** *inquire of* 1/119

*ge***frignan** 3 *learn* (by asking), *hear of, hear about, discover* 17/76; 18/1; 21/47/2; 23/7 etc

frignes(s) f (§14.2) *questioning, interrogation* 1/60

frīnan = **frignan**

frīo = **frēo(h)**

frīð m (§13.2) *peace* 4/3, 11 etc; 6/46 etc; 24/39, 179: gen sg used as adv *peacefully* 24/41: see also **niman**

*ge***friðian** II *protect, defend* 23/5

frōd adj *old, wise, experienced* 5/37; 18/84; 19/90; 21/26/21; 24/140, 317; 25/12, 27

frōfor f (§14.1) *consolation, comfort, help* 1/75; 19/115; 23/83 etc

from = **fram**

fromian II *accomplish* 1/24

fromlīce adj *promptly, boldly* 23/41 etc

from–sīð m (§13.2) *journey away, departure* 22/33

from–weard adj *about to depart away, on the way out* 20/71

Fronc–lond = **Franc–land**

fruma m (§14.7) *origin, beginning* 2/60; 9/113; 13/17

frum–gār m (§13.2) *leader, chief* 23/195

frum–sceaft f (§14.6) *original shaping* (of the world), *creation* 2/26

*ge***frugnon** pret pl of *ge***frignan**

*ge***frūnon** = *ge***frugnon**

frymdi adj *suppliant* 24/179

frymð(u) f (§14.1) *beginning, origin* 11/217, 218; 18/84; 23/5 etc

frȳnd nom and acc pl of **frēond**

fryð = **frið**

fugel m (§13.2) *bird* 8/42; 19/81; 21/26/7; 23/207 etc; 24/38

fugelere m (§13.6) *fowler* 8/21 etc

fuhton pret pl of **feohtan**

*ge***fuhton** pret pl of *ge***feohtan**

ful see **ful(l)**

fūl adj *foul, vile* 14/132, 148; 23/111

ful–gǣð pres 3 sg of **ful–gān**

ful–gān anom vb (§7.7) with dat obj *devote oneself to* 11/146

ful–gangan 7 *attend to, perform* 16/249n

fulgon pret pl of **fēolan**

fūlian II *rot* 8/126

ful(l) **I.** adj *full* 1/183: *full, brimming* 23/19: *complete* 6/45: with gen *full of* 8/127; 9/41, 113; 16/133; 20/100, 113: **be fullan** adv *completely, thoroughly* 7/34: see also **sōð** **I.** **II.** adv *fully, wholly, completely* 14/59; 19/5: *full, very* 14/18, 59, 85 etc; 20/24; 22/18 etc; 24/153 etc

Fullan–ham(m), –hom(m) m (§13.2) *Fulham* (Middlesex) 4/113 etc

full–fremman I *perfect* 11/69

(*ge*)**fullian** = (*ge*)**fulwian**

fullīce adv *fully, completely* 14/83 etc

fulluht = **ful–wiht**

ful–nēah adv *"full near," very nearly, almost* 4/258

fultom, –um m (§13.3) *help, support, aid* 1/182n, 184; 4/169; 7/47; 10/16; 11/281; 23/186 etc: **wesan on fultome** with dat *support* 1/182n

(*ge*)**fultumian** II with dat or acc obj *help, assist* 1/h, 5; 2/10f; 4/16

(*ge*)**fulwian** II *baptize* 1/175, 178, 185; 10/307; 11/85, 280; 12/5

ful–wiht m n f *baptism* 1/174; 4/106 etc; 9/39; 11/131 etc; 12/71 etc; 13/54; 14/156 etc: see also **niman, onfōn**

ful–worhte pret 1 and 3 sg of **ful–wyrcan**

ful–wyrcan I *complete* 12/109

funde pret 1 and 3 sg of **findan** (see Campbell §741)

funden past pple of **findan**

fundian II *direct one's course, set out, go, come* 12/224; 17/103; 20/47

fundon pret pl of **findan**

furlang n (§13.5) *furlong* 4/272

furðon = **furðum**

furðor, –ur adv *further* 7/51 etc; 24/247: *any more* 16/401

furðum adv *even* 7/13 etc; 9/h; 13/20: *indeed, in fact* 11/82, 134: *just* 4/236

fūs adj *ready, eager* 20/50; 24/281: *hastening* 15/2870; 17/57: *brilliant, shining* 17/21

*ge*fylce n (§13.6) *army* 6/49: *troop, division* 4/33, 43

fylcian I, II *marshal, array, set in order* (for fighting) 6/48, 68

*ge*fylcium dat pl of *ge***fylce**

fylg(e)an I with dat obj *follow* 4/h; 10/15, 246, 313 etc; 11/88, 100; 14/155; 16/249: *pursue* 9/49, 123: *adopt* 1/141: *serve* 23/33

fylian = **fylgan**

fyligan = **fylgan**

fyl(l) m (§14.5) *fall, death* 12/12 etc; 17/56; 24/71, 264

(*ge*)**fyllan I.** wk vb I *fill* 7/25; 16/319; 21/44/7: *fulfill* 1/14; 12/169: *perform* 1/71: *complete* 1/181; 10/37, 63, 77, 329: with gen *fill with* 7/35: **II.** = (*ge*)**fiellan**

fyllu f (§15.3) *fill, feast* 23/209

(*ge*)**fylstan I** with dat obj *aid, help, support* 6/21, 45; 12/16, 152; 24/265

fylð pres 3 sg of **feallan**

fȳlð f (§14.1) *filth, foul sin* 14/70, 71

fȳnd dat sg and nom and acc pl of **fēond**

fȳr n (§13.4) *fire* 1/44, 135, 151; 12/228 etc; 14/19; 15/2888 etc; 15/Æ; 16/314 etc; 18/15; 20/113

fyrd = **fierd**

fyrd–rinc m (§13.2) *warrior* 24/140

fyrd–wīc n (§13.4) pl *camp* 23/220

fyren f (§14.1) *sin, crime*: dat pl used as adv *"wickedly," very, intensely* 16/316

fȳren adj *fiery* 4/h; 10/273, 275; 16/316n

fyren–lust m (§13.2) *sinful desire* 9/80

fyrhtu f (§15.2) *horror, terror* 2/65

fyrlen adj *distant* 12/127; 15/Æ

fyrmest numeral (§25.2.7) *foremost, first* 13/41; 24/323

*ge***fyrn** adv *before, previously* 4/129: **gefyrn ǣr** adv *formerly* 12/220

fyrn–gēar n (§13.4) *former year, bygone year* 25/12

fyrn–geflit n (§13.4) *old strife, ancient quarrel* 23/264

fyrn–geweorc n (§13.4) *ancient work* 18/84

fyrst I. = **first**: **II.** sup adj (§12.8) *first, chief* 8/39

fȳsan I *impel, send forth rapidly, shoot* 24/269: *get oneself ready* 15/2861; 23/189 (with refl acc)

G

gā imper sg of **gān**

(*ge*)**gad(e)rian** II *gather, assemble, muster* 4/8, 113 etc; 6/12 etc: *gather, collect* 11/74f, 140

*ge***gadorian** = *ge***gad(e)rian**

gǣlsa m (§14.7) *pride, luxury, wantonness* 14/148

*ge***gærwan** = *ge***gierwan**

gǣst I. = **gāst**: **II.** pres 2 sg of **gān**

gǣstlic adj *ghastly, awesome, terrible* 19/73

gǣð pres 3 sg of **gān**

gafol n (§13.4) *tribute* 8/41 etc; 24/32 etc: *tax* 11/145f

gāl n (§13.4) *lust, wantonness, foolish arrogance* 16/327

galan 6 *sing* 17/67
gāl–ferhð adj *lustful, lascivious* 23/62
gāl–mōd adj *wanton, licentious* 23/256
gālscipe m (§14.5) *wantonness, folly, evil* 16/341
gamol–feax adj *"hoary–haired," grey headed* 20/92
gamol–ferhð adj *aged* 15/2868
gān anom vb (§7.7) *go* 1/13; 2/18; 3/11, 34; etc: *come* 12/90; 23/140, 149, 219: *advance* 24/247: *go away* 10/317: *flow* 10/287: *emerge* 11/26
*ge***gān** anom vb (§7.7) *conquer, subdue* 4/23, 64 etc; 6/15, 46: *win* 23/331: impers with dat *befall* 12/102
ganet = **ganot**
gang m (§13.2) *path* 9/33: *flow* 17/23
gangan 7 *go* 1/78; 2/19, 78; etc: *come* 1/44: *walk* 10/168; 12/220; 22/35: *move about* 2/75; 25/42
*ge***gangan** 7 *go, advance* 23/54: *get hold of, obtain* 24/59
gang–dæg m (§13.2) *Rogation Day*, i.e. one of the three processional days before Ascension Day (see p. 196): **gangdagas** pl *Rogation Days* 4/125; 9/h
ganot m (§13.3) *gannet* 20/20
gār m (§13.2) *spear* 5/18; 16/316 (see n); 23/224; 24/13 etc; 25/22
gār–berend m (§15.5) *spear–bearer, warrior* 24/262
gār–gewin(n) n (§14.5) *battle with spears* 23/307
gār–mitting f (§14.1) *meeting of spears* 5/50
gār–rǣs m (§13.2) *spear–rush, battle* 24/32
(*ge*)**garwian** = (*ge*)**gear(e)wian**
gāst m (§13.2) *spirit* 1/11, 73; 11/213; 13/50 etc; 15/2866 etc; 17/11, 49, 152; 21/7/9; 23/83 etc; 25/59: *soul* 2/102; 9/73; 10/244; 11/318; 24/176: **Hālig Gāst, se Hālga Gāst** *the Holy Ghost* 2/64; 9/53, 106; 10/301, 332; 11/223 etc; 13/51 etc
gāst–cyning m (§13.3) *king of souls, God* 15/2884
gāstlic adj *spiritual* 9/105; 13/23 etc
gāstlīce adv *spiritually* 13/34 etc

gata = **gatu**
gāte–hǣr n (§13.6) *goat's hair* 13/72, 75
gatu nom and acc pl of **geat**
ge conj *and* 1/h; 4/194; 8/104; 22/25; 23/166: **ge . . . ge** *both . . . and* 1/h, 9f, 51; 2/75; 4/149, 175; 13/31: see also **ǣghwæðer**
gē see **þū** (§7.2) *you*
gēac m (§13.2) *cuckoo* 20/53
geaf pret 1 and 3 sg of **giefan**
gēafon pret pl of **giefan**
geald pret 1 and 3 sg of **gieldan**
gealga m (§14.7) *gallows, cross* 17/10 etc
gealgean = **ealgian**
gealg–trēow n (§13.6) *gallows tree, cross* 17/146
gēap adj *convex, curved* 25/23
gēar m n (§13.2, 4) *year* 1/h, 17, 174, 183; 4/h, 1, 7 etc; 6/1; 8/105; 11/284 etc; 12/10; etc: *summer* 25/9
gēara adv *formerly* 16/410: **gēara iū** adv *a long time ago* 17/28; 19/22
gearcian II *prepare* 11/48
gēar–dagas m pl (§13.2) *days of yore, old times* 19/44
geare = **gearwe**
gēare = **gēara**
gearelīce adv *readily, clearly* 9/11
gearo adj *ready* 3/15; 4/68; 10/307; 23/2; 24/72, 100 etc: with dat *ready for* 4/67; 11/173; 16/435
gearo–þoncol adj *ready–witted* 23/341
gear(o)we f acc sg, m nom pl st of **gearo**
gearwe adv *well, clearly, thoroughly, entirely* 1/145; 12/22; 19/69 etc
(*ge*)**gear(e)wian** II *prepare* 2/79, 93; 14/161; 16/431; 23/199: *provide* 10/82: *do, perform* 10/289
geat n (§13.4) *gate* 3/22, 30; 10/195; 11/309; 15/Æ; 23/151
geatwan I *prepare, equip* 21/28/5
gēfon = **gēafon** (pret pl of **giefan**)
gefu = **giefu**
gegnum adv *straight, directly* 23/132
gelpan 3 with gen *boast about* 5/44
gēman = **gīeman**
gēn adv *yet, still* 1/170; 16/413: **þā gēn** adv *still, further, moreover* 1/143
gēna adv *yet, still* 1/h
Gend *Ghent* 4/117

gēo adv *once, formerly* 1/3, 12, 169; 7/2 etc; 9/99; 17/87; 18/41; 20/83: **gēo ǣr** adv *once, formerly* 11/91: see also **gēara**

gēoc f (§14.1) *help, succor, comfort* 20/101

geofu = **giefu**

geogoð, –uð f (§14.1) *youth* 12/4; 19/35; 20/40; 25/50: *male children* 7/48

gēomor adj *sad, mournful, troubled* 9/103; 20/53; 22/1 etc; 23/87

gēomor–mōd adj *sad–hearted, sober–minded* 22/42; 23/144

gēomrung f (§14.1) *sorrow* 9/88

geond prep with acc *through* 10/123, 208; 13/53: *throughout* 6/4 etc; 7/3 etc; 8/61; 9/14; 11/313; 12/71 etc; 14/13 etc; 18/82; 19/3, 58 etc; 20/90; 21/26/8; 22/36; 23/156: **geond eall** adv *everywhere* 12/85

geond–faran 6 *pass through, traverse* 18/67

geond–hweorfan 3 *visit every part of, rove through, canvass* 19/51

geond–lācan 7 *flow through* 18/70

geond–scēawian II *examine every part of, scrutinize* 19/52

geond–þencan I *ponder every aspect of, meditate on* 19/60, 89

geong adj *young* 1/74; 4/37; 5/29 etc; 9/2; 12/76; 15/2868 etc; 17/39; 22/42; 23/166; 24/155 etc; 25/14

geonger–dōm = **geongor–dōm**

geongor–dōm m (§13.2) *discipleship, allegiance* 16/267, 283

geongra m (§14.7) *subordinate, follower, servant* 16/277 etc: *disciple* 9/24

georn adj (usually with gen) *eager* 9/41; 16/287; 19/69; 23/210; 24/73 etc: *enthusiastic* 7/8

georne adv *eagerly* 12/76; 19/52; 23/8; 24/123 etc: *earnestly* 9/28, 60, 63 etc; 14/11, 18, 139, 153 etc; 16/397: *fully, exactly* 14/20; 15/2847: *well, clearly* 14/8, 18, 74 etc; 24/84

geornes(s) (= **georn–nes(s)**) f (§14.2) *exertion, energy, zeal*

georn–ful(l) adj *eager* 24/274: with gen *eager for* 9/26

georn–fulnes(s) f (§14.2) *eagerness, zeal* 2/69; 12/86

geornlīce adv *earnestly, intently* 1/75, 100, 128 etc; 2/68; 9/112; 11/166, 188: *eagerly, willingly* 24/265

gēr = **gēar**

gēsne adj *empty* 23/112: with gen *emptied of* 23/279

gied(d) n (§13.6) *word, utterance* 21/47/2: *song, poem, tale* 22/1

giefan 5 *give* 1/29; 6/59; 12/134; 23/342

gief–stōl m (§14.2) *"gift–seat," throne; the ceremony of gift–giving* 19/44

giefu f (§14.1) *gift* 1/25, 27, 28 etc; 2/42; 9/127; 11/124; 12/57; 15/2920 etc; 16/413; 20/40; 23/2: *grace* 1/105, 106; 2/1, 11, 47, 52; 9/105; 11/182, 200: *favor* 1/126

gieldan 3 *yield, give* 6/9: *pay* 8/41 etc; 14/85, 100: *reward, requite* 15/2921: *repay* 14/99; 16/413; 23/263

giellan 3 *cry out, scream* 20/62

gielp m n (§13.2, 4) *boasting, vaunting, boast, vaunt* 10/224; 19/69: **īdel gielp** *vainglory, ostentation* 11/72

gīeman I with gen or acc obj *heed, pay heed to, care for* 12/243; 21/h; 24/192: *observe, obey* 14/20: *take care of, supervise, look after* 11/19, 145, 171; 16/346 etc: *take care, see to it* 2/68

gīen = **gēn**

(*ge*)**gierwan** I *adorn, array* 17/16 etc; 21/26/13; 21/28/1; 21/29/3: *prepare* 15/2856: *build* 16/281: **girwan ūp** *serve up* 23/9

gīet adv *yet, still* 1/169; 2/93; 7/29; 10/309; 11/267; 12/143; 14/77; 15/Æ; 17/28; 23/182: **þā gīet** adv *yet, still* 1/32, 56, 74 etc; 8/10 etc; 11/226, 245; 12/69, 122 etc; 13/14; 23/107; 24/168 etc

gīeta adv *yet* 5/66

gif conj *if* 1/h, 14, 109; 3/23; etc

gīfernes(s) f (§14.2) *greed* 14/108

gifeðe adj *granted* 23/157

gifre adj *useful, salutary, beneficial* 21/26/28

gīfre adj *ravenous, voracious, eager* 20/62

gifu = **giefu**

Gildas personal name *Gildas* see 14/142n

gilp = **gielp**
gīmen f (§14.2) *care, solicitude, concern*
gim(m) m (§13.2) *gem* 11/106; 17/7 etc; 25/22
gim–stān m (§13.2) *gem, jewel* 11/54, 58 etc; 13/71 etc
gin–fæst adj *ample, substantial* 15/2920
gingre f (§14.7) *handmaiden* 23/132
gin(n) adj *spacious, wide* 23/2, 149
gioguð = **geoguð**
gioncg = **geong**
giond = **geond**
giongorscipe m (§14.5) *service* 16/249
giongra = **geongra**
giorn = **georn**
Gipes–wīc n (§13.4) *Ipswich* (Suffolk) 24/h
girwan = **gierwan**
gīsl m (§13.2) *hostage* 3/17; 4/67, 78n, 180; 6/51; 24/265
gīslian II *give hostages* 6/44, 85
gīt = **gīet**
gītsere m (§13.6) *avaricious man, miser* 11/133, 135
gītsian II *desire, covet* 11/196
gītsung f (§14.1) *avarice, greed, covetousness* 11/138; 14/107, 145
gīu = **gēo**
giung = **geong**
glād pret 1 and 3 sg of **glīdan**
glæd adj *cheerful, joyous* 11/264
glædlīce adv *gladly, joyfully* 2/86
glæd–mōd adj *glad–hearted* 23/140
(*ge*)**glængan** = (*ge*)**glengan**
glæs n (§13.4) *glass* 9/48
Glæstinga–burg f (§15.7) *Glastonbury* (Somerset): dat sg **Glæstingabiri** 6/92
glēaw adj *wise, intelligent* 1/h; 18/29; 19/73; 21/47/6; 23/13 etc
Glēaw–ceaster f (§14.1) *Gloucester* (Gloucestershire) 12/285
glēaw–hȳdig adj *wise, prudent* 23/148
gleng m *ornament, bauble* 9/79: *splendor* 9/109
(*ge*)**glengan** I *adorn, embellish* 2/5, 50
glēowian II *joke, jest* 2/83
glīdan 3 *glide* 5/15
glisian II *glisten, glitter* 21/26/13n
glīwian II *adorn* 21/26/13
glīw–stæf m (§13.2) *joyful salutation:* dat pl used as adv *joyfully* 19/52
glīw–stafas nom and acc pl of **glīw–stæf**
glōf f (§14.1) *glove* 25/17
gnorngan = **gnornian**
gnornian II *grieve, mourn* 1/51; 9/103; 20/92; 24/315
god n (§13.4) *god* 1/125, 127; 11/230, 231
God m (§13.2) *God* 1/98 etc; 2/11 etc; 4/119; etc
gōd I. sb n (§13.4) *goods* 1/55; 2/54: *good* 23/271n; 24/176; 25/50: *benefit, good thing* 10/82; 11/313; 16/291; 23/32: *gift* 12/118a n: **II.** adj *good* 2/69; 4/46 etc; 6/19 etc; 7/33; 8/30; 9/20, 57; 12/252; 13/36 etc; 16/302 etc; 17/70; 21/26/22; 21/44/3; 24/4 etc; 25/14: *firm* 4/111; 24/13: *happy, well–endowed* 20/40: *generous* 20/40n: *great* 14/93
god–bearn n (§13.4) *godchild* 14/62
god–cund adj *divine, sacred* 1/3f, 10; 2/1, 3, 48 etc; 14/116: *religious, spiritual* 7/3, 8
god–cundlīce adv *divinely* 2/10
god–cundnes(s), –nys(s) f (§14.2) *divinity, Godhead* 1/120; 11/205, 221
gōd–dǣd f (§14.6) *good deed* 14/119 etc
gode–web(b) = **god–web(b)**
god–fyrht adj *godfearing:* used as sb 14/120
god–gesprǣce, –sprēce n *divine message* 1/3, 16, 95
gōdian II *improve, get better* 14/17
gōdlec adj *goodly, splendid, magnificent* 16/281
Gōd–mundinga–hām m (§13.2) *Goodmanham* (Yorkshire) 1/170
gōdnes(s) f (§14.2) *good thing; goodness* 12/278
God–rum personal name Godrum 4/72
god–sib(b) m (§13.6) *sponsor* 14/62
god–spel(l) n (§13.4) *gospel* 9/61; 10/68; 13/29
god–spellere m (§13.6) *evangelist* 11/1, 25, 205f etc
god–spellic adj *gospel* 11/215, 220
god–sunu m (§15.2) *godson* 3/31; 4/178

god–web(b) n (§13.6) *fine cloth* 9/96; 11/92

gofol = **gafol**

gold n (§13.4) *gold* 1/85; 9/96; 11/103 etc; 13/71 etc; 15/2868; etc

gold–gi(e)fa m (§14.7) *gold–giver, lord* 20/83; 23/279

gold–hord n (§13.4) *treasure* 11/70

gold–smið m (§13.2) *goldsmith* 11/108

gold–wine m (§14.5) "*gold–friend,*" *generous lord* 19/22, 35; 23/22

gomel–feax = **gamol–feax**

gomen n (§13.5) *pleasure, pastime, entertainment* 20/20

gomol adj *old* 25/11

gong = **gang** (imper sg of **gangan**)

gongan = **gangan**

good = **gōd**

Got–land n (§13.4) *Gotland* 8/88

Gōt–land n (§13.4) *Jutland* 8/72 etc

grǣdelīce adv *greedily, covetously* 11/145

grǣdig adj *greedy* 5/64; 20/62

græf n (§13.4) *grave* 20/97

grǣg adj *grey* 5/64; 15/2866

græs–wong m (§13.2) *grass(y) plain* 18/78

gram adj *angry* 16/302; 23/224, 238 etc: *fierce* 24/100

*ge***græmian** II *anger, provoke, enrage* 14/143

Grante–brycg f (§14.2) *Cambridge* (Cambridgeshire) 4/73

grānung f (§14.1) *groaning* 11/178

*ge***grāp** pret 1 and 3 sg of *ge***grīpan**

Graton personal name *Graton* 11/61 etc

grēat adj *great, thick* 16/384

gremian I *enrage, madden* 23/305; 24/138 etc

grēne adj *green, living* 11/102; 18/13 etc; 25/35

grēot n (§13.4) *earth* 11/295; 23/307; 24/315

grēotan 2 *weep* 17/70

(*ge*)**grētan** I *greet* 1/46, 78; 2/22; 7/1; 13/1; 19/52: *say goodbye to* 10/312: *visit* 21/44/6: *attack* 14/121

grēting f (§14.1) *greeting* 1/2

Grim–bold personal name *Grimbold* 7/58f

grimlic adj *horrible, grim* 14/8

grim(m) adj *grim, fierce, cruel* 14/115; 16/390 etc; 21/28/3; 24/61

grindel m (§13.3) *bar, bolt* 16/384

grindan 3 *grind, sharpen* 24/109

*ge***grīpan** 1 *grasp, seize* 15/2905

grist–bitian II *gnash the teeth* 23/270

grið n (§13.4) *quarter* 6/59: *truce, peace* 14/66; 24/35

griðian I *take under one's protection, protect* 6/21; 14/29

griðlēas adj *violated* 14/32

grōwan 7 *grow* 9/51

grund m (§13.2) *ground, earth, land* 5/15; 23/2, 349; 24/287: *foundation* 20/104: *bottom, depth, abyss* 16/302 etc

*ge***grunden** past pple of **grindan**

grundlēas adj *bottomless, limitless, immense* 16/390

grundlunga, –e adv *from the foundations, completely* 11/242

grym(m) = **grim(m)**

gryre–lēoð n (§13.4) *terrible song* 24/285

gryð = **grið**

gū = **gēo**

gūd = **gūð**

guldon pret pl of **gieldan**

guma m (§14.7) *man* 5/18 etc; 17/49 etc; 19/45; 21/28/3; 23/9 etc; 24/94; 25/11

gūð f (§14.1) *battle* 5/44; 23/123 etc; 24/13 etc

gūð–fana m (§14.7) *battle–standard* 4/96n; 23/219

gūð–freca m (§14.7) *warrior* 23/224

gūð–hafoc m (§13.3) *war–hawk* 5/64

gūð–plega m (§14.7) *battle–play* 24/61

gūð–rinc m (§13.2) *warrior* 24/138

gūð–sceorp n (§13.4) *war–apparel, armor* 23/328

gyf = **gif**

gyfte f pl (§14.6) *marriage, nuptials* 11/8, 9

gyfu = **giefu**

gyld n (§13.4) *tax* 6/91

gyldan = **gieldan**

gylden adj *gold, of gold* 11/59, 189

gylian I *yell* 23/25

gylp = gielp

gylp–word n (§13.4) *vaunting word, boast* 16/264; 24/274

gylt I. sb m (§14.5) *sin* 9/4; 20/h: **II.** pres 3 sg of **gieldan**

gȳman = gīeman

gȳme–lēast f (§14.6) *heedlessness, inattention, neglect*: **tō gȳmelēaste** adv *carelessly* 11/30f

gym(m) = gim(m)

gym–stān = gim–stān

gym–wyrhta m (§14.7) *jeweller* 11/110

gynd = geond

gyrd f (§14.2) *twig* 11/100, 102 etc

gyrdan I *gird* 1/163; 15/2866

*ge***gyr(e)la** m (§14.7) *dress, attire, garb* 1/45: *trappings* 9/79

gyrnan I *yearn for, desire* 23/346

Gyrð personal name *Gyrð* 6/70

(*ge*)**gyrwan = (***ge***)gierwan**

Gyrwas, Gyrwe m pl (§13.2, 14.5) *Jarrow* (Durham); lit *the fen dwellers*, a tribal name (see 4/2n, 12/128a n)

gȳsel = gīsl

gȳslian = gīslian

gyst m (§14.5) *stranger* 24/86

gyst–ern n (§13.4) *guest hall, guest chamber* 23/40

gȳt = gīet

gȳta = gīeta

gyte–sǣl m f (§14.5, 6) *joy at wine pouring*: **on gytesālum** *in his cups* 23/22

gȳtsung = gītsung

H

habban III *have* 1/h, 105 etc; 2/38 etc; 3/13; etc: *have, hold, possess* 1/124; 3/2; 4/12; 9/100; 11/134: *get, obtain* 3/7; 4/63: *keep* 6/24; 13/87, 90: *contain* 13/84

hād m (§13.2, 15.2) *order, rank, position, office* 7/3, 8, 52: *station* 9/37, 39

hād–bryce m (§14.5) *injury to one in holy orders* 14/110

hādian II *consecrate*: past pple used as sb (pl) *those in holy orders, ecclesiastics* 14/51

hæbban = habban

hæbbe pres indic 1 sg, pres subjunc 1–3 sg of **habban**

hæbben pres subjunc 1–3 pl of **habban**

Hædde personal name *Hædde* 12/141

hæfdan = hæfdon (pret pl of **habban**)

hæfde pret 1 and 3 sg of **habban**

hæfdon, –un pret pl of **habban**

hæfst pres 2 sg of **habban**

hæft n (§13.4) *haft, handle* (of a sword) 23/263

hæftan I *chain, imprison* 16/380 etc; 23/116: *catch* 15/Æ

hæft–nīed f (§14.6) *bondage* 4/midnote

hæfð pres 3 sg of **habban**

hægl = hagol

hægl–faru f (§14.1) *shower of hail, hailstorm* 19/105

(*ge*)**hǣlan** I *heal, cure* 11/65, 122 etc; 12/31 etc: *save* 11/311; 17/85: adj (pres pple) **Hǣlende** *Savior* 10/57 etc

hæle = hæleð

Hælend m (§15.5) *Savior* 9/21, 53; 10/1; etc

hælæð = hæleð

hæleð m (dental stem, see Campbell §637) *man, hero* 5/25; 16/285; 17/39 etc; 18/49; 19/73 etc; 21/7/3; 21/8/10; 21/26/12, 28; 23/51 etc; 24/74 etc; 25/8

hǣlu f (§15.3) *cure* 12/238: *salvation* 1/8 etc; 9/22

hærfest m (§13.3) *harvest season, autumn* 4/88 etc; 6/24; 25/8

hǣs f (§14.6) *order, command* 11/50, 101 etc; 15/2865; 15/Æ

Hǣ–stēn personal name *Hæsten* 4/138, 170 etc

Hǣstinga–port m n (§13.2, 4) *Hastings* (Sussex) 6/65

Hǣstingas m pl *Hastings* (Sussex), lit "the people of *Hǣsta*" (see 4/2n, 12/128a n) 6/78

hǣt pres 3 sg of **hātan**

hǣte f (§14.7) *heat* 16/333n

hǣtu f (§15.3) *heat, ardor* 1/41; 16/389; 18/17

hǣð m n (§14.5) *heath* 25/29

hǣðen adj *heathen, pagan* 4/h, 34; 11/244; 12/122 etc; 14/21 etc; 23/98 etc; 24/55 etc

hǣðen–gyld n (§13.4) *idolatry* 11/241

hǣðen–gylda m (§14.7) *idolater* 11/228f, 236 etc
hǣðenscipe m (§14.5) *"heathenship," paganism, idolatry* 11/228, 231
Hǣð–feld m (§15.2) *Hatfield* (Yorkshire) 1/182n
Hǣðum see 8/75n
hafast pres 2 sg of **habban**
hafað pres 3 sg of **habban**
hafenian 2 *raise aloft, lift* 24/42 etc
hafoc, hafuc m (§13.3) *hawk* 24/8; 25/17
hagol m (§13.2) *hail* 18/16, 60; 19/48; 20/17, 32
(*ge*)**hāl** adj *whole* 9/6; 12/211; 13/78: *sound* 9/115: *unharmed* 24/292: *undecayed* 12/170: *well* 12/261
haldan = healdan
hāleg = hālig
hālettan I *hail* 1/77; 2/21
Half–dene personal name *Halfdene* 4/34 etc
hālg– see **hālig**
hālga m (§14.7) *saint* 12/255 etc; 17/143 etc
(*ge*)**hālgian** II *consecrate* 1/150, 117, 172; 11/245: past pple *holy* 9/54
Hālgo–land n (§13.4) *Helgeland* 8/64
hālig adj *holy, sacred, saintly* 1/176; 2/34; 4/78; 9/h; 10/42, 51 etc; 11/73 etc; 12/75 etc; 13/29 etc; 14/64; 18/73 etc; 20/122; 21/26/28; 23/h, 56 etc: used as sb *saint* 4/286; 9/119; 10/192: see also **gāst**
hālignes(s) f (§14.2) *religion* 1/154, 161: *sanctuary* 14/32
hals = heals
hālsian II *adjure, exorcise* 11/261
hālwende adj *saving, salvific* 1/5f, 65: *salutary* 2/101: *healthful* 9/115
hām I. sb m (§13.2) *home, dwelling* 4/150 etc; 5/10; 8/20; 17/148; 20/117; 21/29/4 etc; 23/121; 24/292: **II.** adv *home* 1/89; 2/18; 6/27 etc; 11/48 etc; 12/219; 15/Æ; 23/131; 24/251
hamor m (§13.2) *hammer* 5/6
Ham–tūn–scīr f (§14.1) *Hampshire* 3/2; 4/101 etc
hām–weard adv *homeward* 4/222
hām–weardes adv *on the way home* 4/161
han–cred m *cock–crow* 11/292
hand f (§15.2) *hand* 1/h, 69; 2/87; 10/153, 154 etc; 11/35 etc; 12/99 etc; 15/2903 etc; 15/Æ; 16/251 etc; 17/59; etc: *side* 4/30, 45; 24/112: **sellan on hand** *make a pledge, promise* 6/88
hand–bred n (§13.4) *palm* (of the hand) 12/118
hand–geweorc n (§13.4) *"handiwork," creation* 11/195
hand–mægen n (§13.5) *strength of hand* 16/247
hand–seax n (§13.4) *dagger* (lit *hand–knife*) 1/h
hangelle f (§14.7) *a dangling object, an instrument or appendage that hangs* 21/44/6
hangian II *hang* 21/44/1; 25/55
hār adj *grey* 19/82: *hoary, old* 5/39; 24/169: *ancient* 6/68; 23/327
Hareld personal name *Hareld* 4/38
Harold personal name *Harold* 6/1 etc
hasewan–pāda m (§14.7) *dun–coated one* 5/62
hāt adj *hot* 11/26; 16/324 etc; 20/11; 25/7: comp *warmer, more glowing* 20/64
*ge***hāt** n (§13.4) *promise, vow* 1/13, 80
hātan 7 *command, order* 1/25, 144, 168; 2/43, 44, 55; 4/257; 7/1 etc; 10/12, 244 etc; 11/10, 23 etc; 12/96 etc; 15/2868 etc; 15/Æ; 16/345; etc: *name, call* 1/h, 95, 121; 3/8; 4/126, 133 etc; 6/6; 8/37, 66, 75, 87 etc; 11/23, 33 etc; 12/2 etc; 13/40; 15/Æ; 24/75 etc: *be called* 16/344
*ge***hātan** 7 *promise* 1/14, 20, 28 etc; 4/105; 9/57; 24/246, 289
hāte adv *hotly* 16/383 (or is this inst sg of the sb **hāt** *heat, fire*?); 23/94
hāten past pple of **hātan**
*ge***hāten** past pple of (*ge*)**hātan**
*ge***hāt–land** n (§13.4) *promised land* 2/62
hāt–heort adj *"hot–hearted," irascible* 19/66
hāt–heorte f (§14.7) *anger, fury* 10/326
hātte passive pres and pret of **hātan** *am called, was called* 6/66; 14/142; 21/h; 21/8/8; 21/26/26
*ge***hāwian** II *look to see, examine* 4/233f

he = **hīe**

hē personal pron (§6.2, 4) *he*

hēa = **hēah**

hēaf m (§13.2) *wailing, mourning* 9/121

hēafod n (§13.5) *head* 1/70, 102; 2/97; 6/89; 10/96, 246 etc; 12/162 etc; 19/43; 21/44/6; 23/h, 110 etc: pl with sg meaning 17/63

hēafod–gerīm n (§13.4) *head–count, number of heads* 23/308

hēafod–mon(n) m (§15.7) *"head–man," leader* 4/96n; 12/49

hēafod–weard m (§13.2) *sentinel* 23/239

hēafod–wōð f (§14.1) *"head–eloquence," eloquent speech or song produced in the head* 21/8/3

hēah adj *high* 12/226; 15/2855 etc; 16/300, 358; 17/40; 18/23 etc; 19/98; 21/7/4; 23/43 etc: *deep* 19/82; 20/34

hēah–dīacon m (§13.3) *archdeacon* 9/37

hēah–fæder m (§15.4) *patriarch* 13/12; *God the Father* 17/134

hēah–gerēfa m (§14.7) *"high reeve," chief official, proconsul* 11/255, 277

Hēah–mund personal name *Heahmund* 4/45

hēahra = **hīer(r)a**

Hēah–stān personal name *Heahstan* 4/285

hēah–þungen adj *high–ranking* 8/104

hēal = **hāl**

(*ge*)**healdan** 7 *hold, keep, maintain* 1/h, 80, 108; 3/2; 4/67, 88 etc; 6/27, 62, 89; 7/6; 9/39, 53; 12/112 etc; 13/91; 14/28, 52 etc; 19/112; 20/109; 21/8/4; 23/142; 24/14 etc; 25/1: *govern* 20/111: *inhabit* 7/28; 16/320 etc; 20/87: *keep safe* 11/145: *guard, protect* 11/300; 18/45; 19/14: *treat, deal with* 24/41: intr *hold out* 24/102

healdend m (§15.5) *guardian, protector* 23/289

healf I. sb f (§14.1) *side* 4/127, 128 etc; 6/69; 8/19 etc; 17/20; 24/152 etc: *behalf* 4/144: **II.** numeral and adj *half* 4/120, 150 etc; 8/105; 11/203; 23/105

Healf–dene = **Half–dene**

hēalic adj *exalted, sublime* 11/214: *lofty* 12/184: *proud, haughty* 16/294

heal(l) f (§14.1) *hall, palace* 1/41, 135; 15/2932n; 24/214; 25/28 etc

heals m (§13.2) *neck* 16/385; 24/141

hēan adj *poor* 11/131; 23/234: *wretched, downcast* 19/23

hēanlic adj *disgraceful, humiliating* 24/55

hēa(n)nes(s), –nis(s) (= **hēah–nes(s), –nis(s)**) f (§14.2) *height* 1/180: *loftiness* 1/7, 15, 68

hēap m (§13.2) *crowd* 23/163: *flock* 21/57/4

heard adj *hard, fierce, bitter* 5/25; 10/186; 16/303 etc; 17/87; 18/58; 21/26/5; 21/28/2; 21/44/3; 22/15 etc; 23/79 etc; 24/33 etc

hearde adv *grievously, fiercely, bitterly* 23/116, 216; 24/33

heardlīce adv *fiercely, bitterly* 6/53 etc; 24/261

heard–mōd adj *stout–hearted, bold* 17/285

heard–sǣlig adj *unfortunate, unlucky, unblessed* 22/19

hearm m (§13.2) *damage, injury* 6/10, 83: *affliction* 16/368: *grief, sorrow* 24/223

hearm–scearu f (§14.1) *affliction, punishment* 16/432

hearpe f (§14.7) *harp, lyre* 2/16, 17; 20/44

hearra m (§14.7) *lord, master* 16/263 etc; 23/56; 24/204

hēarra = **hīer(r)a**

hēarsum adj with dat *obedient to* 1/65, 67, 110

heaðo–lind f (§14.1) *"war–linden," linden–wood shield* 5/6

heaðo–rinc m (§13.2) *warrior* 23/179 etc

heaðo–welm m (§14.5) *"battle–surge"* (of flame), *fierce flame* 16/324

(*ge*)**hēawan** 7 *cut, hew* 5/6; 11/100; 23/303; 24/324: *cut down, slay* 5/23; 23/90, 288 etc; 24/181: *stab* 14/55

*ge***hēawen** past pple of (*ge*)**hēawan**

hebban 6 (§21.3) *raise, lift up* 1/104; 17/31; 21/44/5

heben = **heofon**

hefaen–rīcae = **heofon–rīce**

hefelic adj *heavy, serious* 4/18

hefeð pres 3 sg of **hebban**

hefgian II *weigh down, burden* 2/74
hefig adj *heavy, grievous, bitter* 1/182n; 17/61; 19/49
hefig–tīme adj *burdensome* 13/3
hege m (§14.5) *hedge, enclosure* 1/155
hēhst sup adj (§12.7) *highest* 9/29; 16/254 etc; 23/4 etc: *greatest* 23/308
heht pret 1 and 3 sg of **hātan**
*ge***heht** pret 1 and 3 sg of *ge***hātan**
hēhðu f (§14.1) *height* 16/321
hel–dor n (§13.4) *"hell–door," gate of hell* 16/380
hel(l) f (§14.2) *hell* 10/188; 12/250; 16/304 etc
helle–bryne m (§14.5) *hell–fire* 23/116
helle–sūsl f (§13.4) *hell–torment* 13/67
helle–wīte n (§13.6) *hell–torment* 14/160; 16/303
hellic adj *hellish, of hell* 16/333n
hel(l)m m (§13.2) *helmet* 23/193 etc; 25/16: *protector* 21/26/17
help f (§14.1) *help* 17/102; 19/16; 23/96
(*ge*)**helpan** 3 with gen or dat obj *help* 12/275; 14/162
hel–sceaða m (§14.7) *"hell–enemy," fiend* 24/180
*ge***hende** prep with dat *near* 24/294
hēo see **hē** (§6.2, 4) *she; they, them*
heofanlic = **heofonlic**
heofen(e) = **heofon(e)**
heofenlic = **heofonlec, –lic**
heofon m (§13.3) *heaven* 1/112; 2/34; 6/4; 9/h; etc
heofon–cyning m (§13.3) *king of heaven* 15/2918; 16/439
heofone f (§14.7) *heaven* 11/2, 173; 12/111; 13/43 etc: **heofonan rīce** 11/2, 73; 12/111 = **heofonrīce**
Heofon–feld m (§15.2) *"Heavenfield,"* near Rowley Burn (Northumberland); see 12/10a n
heofonlec, –lic adj *heavenly* 1/3, 12 etc; 2/7, 46 etc; 9/56, 129; 11/113, 127f etc; 15/Æ; 17/148
heofon–lēoht n (§13.4) *heavenly light* 12/183
heofon–rīce n (§13.6) *heavenly kingdom* 2/29; 16/321 etc; 17/91; 18/12
heofon–tungl n (§13.4) *heavenly body, star* 18/32
(*ge*)**hēold** pret 1 and 3 sg of (*ge*)**healdan**
hēoldan = **hēoldon**
(*ge*)**hēoldon** pret pl of (*ge*)**healdan**
heolfrig adj *gory* 23/130 etc
heolstor, heolstre m n (§13.2, 4) *darkness, concealment* 19/23
heolstor adj *dark* 23/121
heolstor–cofa m (§14.7) *"darkness chamber," grave* 18/49
heom = **him**
heonan = **heonon**
heonan–forð = **heonon–forð**
heonon adv *hence, from here* 15/2855; 16/415; 17/132; 18/1; 20/37; 22/6; 24/246
heonon–forð adv *henceforth, in the future* 14/17, 20
heonon–ward adj *passing away* 9/124
heonu adv and interj *moreover, ah* 1/62, 105, 151, 182n: *lo!* 10/22, 186 etc
heora = **hira, hire** (see **hē̜**, §6.2, 4)
heord f (§14.1) *watching, surveillance, care* 2/19
heorra = **hearra**
heorte f (§14.7) *heart* 1/h, 79; 9/8, 51, 101 etc; 10/9; etc
heorð–genēat m (§13.2) *"hearth–sharer," household retainer* 24/204
heorð–werod n (§13.5) *"hearth–band," body of household retainers* 24/24
heoru–wǣpen n (§13.4) *bloody weapon, sword* 23/263
hēow pret 1 and 3 sg of **hēawan**
hēowan = **hēowon**
hēowon pret pl of **hēawan**
heowum = **hegum**
hēr I. sb n *hair* 21/26/5: **II.** adv *here, in this place, in this year* 3/1; 4/1, 4; etc
hera = **hira** (see **hē**, §6.2, 4)
*ge***hēran** = *ge***hīeran**
hēr–būend m (§15.5) *dweller here* (on earth) 23/96
here m (§13.6) *army, enemy army* (frequently used in the Chronicle of the Scandinavian invaders) 4/2, 4, 7 etc; 5/31; 6/40, 79; 14/144; 23/h, 135 etc: *army* (in general) 6/66; 14/144; 23/161; 24/292: *war, devastation* 14/43, 87
here–flēma m (§14.7) *fugitive* (from bat-

tle) 5/23

here–folc n (§13.4) *army* 23/234 etc

here–geatu f (§14.1) *war–gear, heriot* (see 24/48a n)

heregian = herian

here–hȳð(ð) f (§14.6) *war–spoil, booty, plunder* 4/154 etc

here–lāf f (§14.1) *remnant of an army, group of survivors* 5/47

herenes(s) f (§14.2) *praise* 2/27, 102

here–rēaf n (§13.4) *plunder, booty* 23/316

here–sīð m (§13.2) *military expedition, raid* 21/29/4

Hereða–land n (§13.4) ON *Hǫðaland* (see p 143 n 1)

here–wǣða m (§14.7) "*war–hunter*" (i.e. a hunter whose game is the enemy), *warrior* 23/126 etc

here–wīc n (§13.4) *dwelling, mansion* 9/100

herg m (§13.2) *sanctuary, fane* 1/154, 166 etc

hergan = herian

hergas nom and acc pl of **here**

hergað m (§13.3) *raid, expedition* 4/173, 183

hergian II *raid, plunder, ravage* 4/182, 217, 223; 6/18, 80 etc; 14/101: *make raids* 4/72; 8/59 etc

hergung f (§14.1) *ravaging, raid* 4/h

herian I *praise, extol* 2/29; 11/312; 12/123; 20/77

herig = herg

her(i)ge dat sg of **here**

herigean = herian

heriges gen sg of **here**

hēr–inne adv *herein* 16/436

her–pað m (§13.2) *war–path, passage for the army* 23/303

herra = hearra

hērra = hīer(r)a

hērsumian = hīersumian

hēr–tō–ēacan adv *besides, in addition* 14/137

herung f (§14.7) *praise* 11/63

hēt pret 1 and 3 sg of **hātan**

*ge***hēt** pret 1 and 3 sg of *ge***hātan**

hete m (§14.5) *hate, hatred, hostility* 1/39; 14/46 etc; 16/301

hetelīce adv *fiercely, violently* 6/56; 14/79

hete–sprǣc f (§14.1) *hostile speech* 16/263

hete–þoncol adj *hostile–minded* 23/105

hetol adj *hostile, violent* 14/115

hēton pret pl of **hātan**

*ge***hēton** pret pl of *ge***hātan**

hettend m (§15.5) *enemy, adversary* 5/10

hēðen = hǣðen

hī see **hē** (§6.2, 4) *they, them, themselves*

Hibernia *Ireland* 4/119

hicgan = hycgan

hider adv *hither, here, to this place* 2/24; 4/214 etc; 5/69; 6/15; 7/10; 8/79; 9/94; 16/420; 17/103; 24/57; 25/64

hīe = hī (see **hē**, §6.2, 4)

hieder = hider

hiene = hine (see **hē**, §6.2, 4)

hieora = hira (see **hē**, §6.2, 4)

hiera = hira (see **hē**, §6.2, 4)

hīera = hīer(r)a

hīeran I *hear* 4/166: with dat obj *obey, serve* 1/128; 9/127: **hīeran in on** with acc, **hīeran tō** with dat, *belong to* 8/76, 80f, 85, 88: **hīeran secgan** hear tell 2/104

*ge***hīeran** I *hear* 1/30, 113, 144 etc; 2/28, 58; 3/19; 9/10, 61; 10/47, 66, 129 etc; 11/304; 13/8, 27; 16/292; 17/26 etc; 20/18; 23/24 etc; 24/45: *hear of* 1/64; 14/152: **gehīeran secgan** *hear tell* 9/83: *hear told of* 9/16: *obey* 10/47

hierde–bōc f (§15.7) "*shepherd–book*" 7/56

hiere = hira, hire (see **hē**, §6.2, 4)

hīer(r)a comp adj (§12.7) *higher, loftier* 1/179; 4/259; 7/52; 16/274, 282; 18/28

*(ge)***hīersumian** II with dat obj *obey, be obedient to* 7/5; 10/234; 15/Æ

hig = hī (see **hē**, §6.2, 4)

hige = hyge

hige–rōf adj *valiant* 23/302

hige–þoncol adj *wise, thoughtful* 23/131

hiht = hyht

hild f (§14.2) *battle* 23/251 etc; 24/8 etc; 25/17

*ge***hild** n (§14.5) *observance*

hilde–lēoð n (§13.4) *battle–song* 23/211

hilde–nǣdre f (§14.7) "*battle–adder,*" *arrow* 23/221

hilde–rinc m (§13.2) *warrior* 5/39; 17/61 etc; 24/169
*ge***hilte** n f (§14.7) pl with sg meaning *hilt* 15/2906
him see **hē** (§6.2, 4) *him, himself; them, themselves; it, itself*
hindan adv *from behind, from the rear* 4/86, 196 etc; 5/23; 6/56
hine see **hē** (§6.2, 4) *him, himself, it* etc
hin–sīð m (§13.2) *journey hence, death* 23/117
hīo = **hēo** (see **hē**, §6.2, 4)
hīo = **hī** (see **hē**, §6.2, 4)
*(ge)***hīoldon** = *(ge)***hēoldon**
hiora = **hira, hire** (see **hē**, §6.2, 4)
hīow–beorht adj *bright of hue, radiant, beautiful* 16/266
hira see **hē** (§6.2, 4) *them, themselves, of them*
hira possessive adj *their* 3/25; etc
*ge***hīran** = *ge***hīeran**
hire see **hē** (§6.2, 4) *her, of her, to her* etc
hīred m (§13.3) *retinue* 4/96n; 11/85
hīred–man(n) m (§15.7) *household retainer* 24/261
hīred–men(n) dat sg and nom and acc pl of **hīred–man(n)**
his see **hē** (§6.2, 4) *him, of it* etc
his possessive adj *his, its* 1/80; etc
hit see **hē** (§6.2, 4) *it* etc
hīw n (§13.4) *form* 10/113: *hue, color, appearance* 18/80
hladan 6 *lade, load* 18/76: *heap, build up* 15/2906
*ge***hladen** past pple of **hladan**
hlæstan I *load, adorn* 23/36
hlǣw m (§13.2) *mound, barrow* 18/25; 25/26
hlāf I. sb m (§13.2) *bread* 10/5, 69: **II.** = **lāf**
hlāford m (§13.3) *lord, master* 1/h; 3/26; 6/86; 8/1; 11/141; 12/12 etc; 14/59 etc; 17/45; 22/6 etc; 23/251; 24/135 etc
hlāfordleas adj *lordless* 24/251
hlāford–swica m (§14.7) *traitor* (to one's lord) 14/57f
hlāford–swice m (§14.5) *treachery* 14/58, 59
hlanc adj *lean* 23/205
hleahtor m (§13.2) *laughter* 20/21
hlēapan 7 *leap, spring* 1/163
*ge***hlēapan** 7 *leap upon, mount* 24/189
*ge***hlēat** pret 1 and 3 sg of *ge***hlēotan**
hlehhan = **hliehhan**
hlēo n (§13.6) *protector, lord* 24/74
hlēo–bord n (§13.4) *protective board* 21/26/12
hlēo–mǣg m (§13.2) *protecting kinsman* 20/25
hleonian II *lean, incline* 18/25
hlēop pret 1 and 3 sg of **hlēapan**
gehlēop pret 1 and 3 sg of *ge***hlēapan**
gehlēotan 2 *receive by lot*: **gehlēotan tō** with dat *be allotted* 10/3
hlēoðor n (§13.4) *voice* 18/12: *cry* 20/20: *sound* 21/8/4
hlēoðrian II *speak* 17/26
hliehhan 6 *laugh* 5/47; 23/23; 24/147
hlīfi(g)an II *tower* 15/2878; 17/85; 18/23 etc
hlimman 3 *resound, roar* 20/18; 23/205
hlinc m (§13.2) *slope, hill* 18/25
hlīsa m (§14.7) *fame* 12/239
hlīsfullīce adv *gloriously* 12/145
hlōh pret 1 and 3 sg of **hliehhan**
hlot(t) n (§13.4) *lot* 10/2
hlōð f (§14.1) *band* 4/113, 147
hlūd adj *loud* 11/277; 25/4
hlūde adv *loudly* 15/2909; 21/7/7; 21/8/3, 10; 21/57/4; 23/205 etc
hlummon pret pl of **hlimman**
hlūttor adj *pure* 2/98; 11/10; 16/397
hlȳdan I *bellow, shout, whoop* 23/23
hlynnan I *roar* 23/23
*ge***hlystan** I *listen* 24/92
*ge***hnǣde** pret 1 and 3 sg of *ge***hnǣgan**
*ge***hnǣgan** I *humble, cast down, bring low* 10/188; 20/88
hnāg pret 1 and 3 sg of **hnīgan**
hnīgan 1 bow down 17/59
hōc m (§13.2) *hook* 16/316n
hocer n (§13.4) *scorn, derision* 14/120
hocor–wyrde adj *scornful in speech, derisive* 14/116
hof n (§13.4) *house, hall* 15/2871
hōf pret 1 and 3 sg of **hebban**
hogian II *think, consider* 12/112 etc; 15/2893; 24/123 etc: *plan, intend* 23/250 etc: with gen *be intent on, intend* 24/133
hol n (§13.4) *hole* 21/44/5

hōl n (§13.4) *malice* (?) 14/46
*ge***hola** m (§14.7) *confidant* 19/31
hold adj *kind, friendly, gracious* 6/86; 20/41: *loyal, devoted* 1/h; 6/90; 16/288; 22/17; 24/24
holm m (§13.2) *sea* 19/82; 20/64
Hōlofernus personal name *Holofernes* 23/7 etc
holt n (§13.4) *forest, wood* 17/29; 18/73 etc; 25/19
holt–wudu m (§15.2) *trees of the forest* 17/91
hōn 7 *hang* 18/38, 71
hond = **hand**
hond–plega m (§14.7) *"hand–play," fighting* 5/25
*ge***hongen** past pple of **hōn**
hongian = **hangian**
hopian 2 *hope* 23/117
hord m n (§13.2, 4) *hoard, treasure* 5/10
hord–cofa m (§14.7) *"treasure–chamber," heart* 19/14
hordian II *hoard, hoard up* 11/138, 140
hōring m (§13.3) *fornicator* 14/132
horn m (§13.2) *horn* 15/Æ; 21/29/2
horn–boga m (§14.7) *bow tipped with horn* (or curved like a horn?) 23/222
hors n (§13.4) *horse* 4/131, 200 etc; 8/41 etc; 12/205; 24/2
hors–hwæl m (§13.2) *walrus* 8/28
horsian II *provide with horses* 4/3; *mount* 4/80, 85
hors–þegn m (§13.2) *"horse–thane," marshal* 4/254, 283
hosp m (§13.2) *insult, contempt* 11/39; 23/216
hrǣ = **hrǣw**
hræd adj *rapid, quick* 1/176; 14/39, 134
hræding f (§14.1) *haste*: **on hrædinge** adv *quickly* 14/137
hrædlīce adv *swiftly, quickly* 1/136; 4/79; 9/4; 10/44, 45, 70; 11/115, 162
hræd–wyrde adj *hasty of speech* 19/66
hræfn m (§13.2) *raven* 4/96n; 5/61; 23/206; 24/106
hrægl n (§13.4) *clothing, raiment* 8/121; 10/69; 21/7/1; 23/282: *garment* 21/44/4: see also **twī–feald**
hrætlīce = **hrædlīce**
hrǣw n (§13.4) *corpse* 5/60; 17/53 etc; 23/313
hrān m (§13.2) *reindeer* 8/37 etc
hraðe adv *swiftly, quickly, rapidly, straightway* 1/150; 3/15; 6/37; 10/9, 10, 136, 138, 147 etc; 12/58 etc; 15/Æ; 23/37; 24/30 etc
hrēam m (§13.2) *clamor, outcry* 9/121; 24/106
hrefn = **hræfn**
hrēman I with dat *exult about* 5/39
hrēmig adj with gen *exulting in* 5/59
hremm = **hræfn**
hremman I *hinder, impede* 11/61
hrēo = **hrēoh**
hrēodan 2 *adorn* 15/2932n; 18/79; 23/37
hrēog = **hrēoh**
hrēoh adj *rough, stormy, turbulent* 10/90; 18/45, 58; 19/105: *troubled, turbulent* 19/16; 23/282
hrēora gen pl of **hrēoh**
hrēohnes(s) f (§14.2) *roughness, turbulence* 10/76
Hreope–dūn f (§14.1) *Repton* (Derbyshire) 4/62 etc
hrēosan 2 *fall* 18/60; 19/48, 102
hrēowan 2 impersonal *grieve, distress* 16/426
hrēow–cearig adj *sorrowful, troubled* 17/25
hrēowig–mōd adj *sad at heart, disconsolate* 23/289
hrēowlīce adv *cruelly* 14/35
hrepian II *deal, be concerned* 11/204: *touch* 12/210
hrēran I *stir, stir up* 19/4
hrēð–ēadeg adv *glorious, triumphant* 25/8
hreðer m n (§13.3, 5) pl often with sg meaning *breast, heart* 19/72; 20/63; 23/94
hreðer–loca m (§14.7) *"breast–enclosure," breast* 20/58
hrīm m (§13.2) *rime, hoarfrost* 18/16, 60; 19/48, 77; 20/32
hrīm–ceald adj *"rime–cold," ice–cold* 19/4
hrīm–gicel m (§13.2) *icicle* 20/17
hrīmig adj *frosty* 25/6
hrīnan I *touch, reach, harm* 1/137
hrincg = **hring**
hrinen past pple of **hrīnan**

hring m (§13.2) *ring* 16/377; 23/37; 24/161; 25/22: *rim, border* 15/2855

hring–loca m (§14.7) *linked ring* (in mail) 24/145

hring–þegu f (§14.1) *receiving of rings* 20/44

hrīð f (§14.1) *snowstorm* 19/102

(*ge*)**hroden** past pple of **hrēodan**

hrōf m (§13.2) *roof* 2/34; 12/229; 23/67; 25/64: *top, summit* 15/2899; 21/29/7

Hrōfes–ceaster f (§14.1) *Rochester* (Kent) 4/176f etc

hrūse f (§14.7) *earth* 19/23, 102; 20/32; 21/7/1

hrȳman I *cry out, lament* 10/313

hryre m (§14.5) *fall* 18/16; 19/7

hrȳðer n (§13.4) *cow* 8/39

hrȳðig adj *storm–beaten, snow–swept* 19/77

hū I. interr adv *how* 10/43; 11/194 etc; 13/61 etc; 14/80: intensive 7/3, 64; 19/95: **II.** conj *how* 1/32; 2/93; 7/4 etc; 12/112 etc; 13/23; 14/137 etc; 19/30, 35, 61, 73; 20/2, 14, 29 etc; 23/25 etc; 24/19

*gi***huaes** = *ge***hwæs**

huilpe f (§14.7) *curlew* 20/21

Humbre f (§14.1) *the R. Humber* 6/16–21n, 30–34n; 7/12 etc

Humbre–mūða m (§14.7) *the estuary of the R. Humber* 4/4

hund I. sb m (§13.2) *dog* 14/71; 23/110: **II.** numeral, sb n with gen *hundred* 4/132, 164, 224; 8/37 etc; 10/163

hund–nigontig numeral (§25.1) *ninety* 11/283f; 24/h

hund–twelftig numeral (§25.1) *a hundred and twenty* 4/133

hunger, hungor m (§13.2) *hunger* 11/24; 20/11: *starvation* 4/200: *famine* 4/h; 9/19; 13/66 etc; 14/43

hunig m (§13.3) *honey* 8/98

hunta m (§14.7) *hunter* 8/21 etc

huntoð m (§13.3) *hunting* 8/4

hup–seax n (§13.4) *short sword worn at the hip* 23/327

hūru adv *indeed, certainly* 8/92; 9/66; 11/252; 14/7 etc; 17/10; 23/345: *at least* 8/92

hūs n (§13.4) *house* 2/18, 19, 76 etc; 11/49; 12/225 etc; 14/25 etc: *dwelling* 8/106: *building* 1/136

hūsel–gang m (§13.2) *receiving the Eucharist, Holy Communion* 11/132

hūsl n (§13.4) *Eucharist* 2/84, 85 etc

hūð f (§14.6) *spoil, plunder, booty* 21/29/2 etc

hwā m f, **hwæt** n, interr pron (§6.5) *who, what: who* 1/154, 156; 11/138, 140; 24/95, 124, 215: indef *someone* 7/67; 13/104; 24/71: *some one, a certain one* 23/52; 24/2: *anyone* 11/62; 13/18, 54, 103: **swā hwā swā** *whoever* 16/438

*ge***hwā** pron *each, each one, everyone* 14/139: with partitive gen 2/31; 5/9; 18/66; 19/63; 23/186; 25/11

hwæl m (§13.2) *whale* 8/30 etc; 20/60: *walrus* 8/42, 43

hwæl–hunta m (§14.7) *whale hunter* 8/9

hwæl–huntað m (§13.3) *whale hunting, whaling* 8/32

hwǣm dat sg of **hwā, hwæt** (§6.5): see also **tō**

hwæne acc sg of **hwā**

*ge***hwæne** acc sg of *ge***hwā**

hwænne = **hwonne**

hwǣr adv *where* 4/120; 9/77; 10/224; 17/112; 19/92 etc: used as conj *where* 1/72; 4/234; 10/190; 14/74; 15/Æ; 17/112; 19/26; 20/117; 22/8: *somewhere* 7/66: **swā hwǣr swā** *wherever* 10/83; 12/117

*ge***hwæs** gen sg of *ge***hwā**

hwæt I. adj *brave, active, vigorous* 20/40; 21/26/20: **II.** neuter of **hwā** *what* 1/h, 42, 48 etc; 2/26; 4/h; 8/26; 10/254; 13/34; 14/101 etc; 17/2, 116; 20/56; 21/h; 21/8/8; 21/26/26; 21/28/13; 22/3; 24/45: indef *something* 13/21: **swā hwæt swā** indef pron *whatsoever, whatever* 2/3; 9/3; 12/57: adv *why* 16/278: interj *lo! behold! see! look!* 1/105, 127 etc; 9/1, 65, 124; 11/81 etc; 12/45 etc; etc

hwæt–hwugu indef pron *something* 2/22

hwæðer I. indef adj: **swā hwæðer . . . swā** *whichever* 4/147f: **II.** pron *which* (of the two) 8/12, 15: conj *whether* 1/48; 2/84; 6/78; 8/7; 10/76 *ge***hwæðer** adj *either* 4/30, 44; 24/112

hwæð(e)re adv *however, yet, nevertheless, but* 1/23; 2/9; 10/126; 17/8 etc

hwalas nom and acc pl of **hwæl**

hwan = **hwon**

hwanon adv *whence, from where* 1/76; 2/45

*ge***hwanon** adv *from all sides, from everywhere* 12/93

hwār = **hwǣr**

hwaðer = **hwæðer**

hwealf adj *hollow, concave* (?) 23/214

hwearf I. sb m (§13.2) *crowd* 23/249: **II.** pret 1 and 3 sg of **hweorfan**

hwelc = **hwilc**

*ge***hwelc** = *ge***hwilc**

hwēne adv *slightly* 8/53

hweorfan 3 *turn, go* 19/72: *return* 10/99: *pass, journey, depart* 20/58, 60; 23/112; 25/58 etc

*ge***hwerfan** = *ge***hwierfan**

hwettan I *whet, incite, urge* 20/63

hwī = **hwȳ**

hwider adv *whither, where* 1/38; 10/2; 19/72; 25/58: **swā hwider swā** *whithersoever, wherever* 12/79 etc

(*ge*)**hwierfan** I *return* 10/78, 155, 174, 319 etc: *turn, change, transform, alter* 2/49, 58; 10/56; 11/105f; 16/318: *convert* 10/284, 325

hwīl f (§14.1) *while, time* 8/68 etc; 11/115; 15/Æ; 17/24 etc; 21/28/9; 23/214; 24/203: dat pl used as adv **hwīlum** *sometimes, at times* 4/127; 7/57; 8/59 etc; 13/16; 14/50 etc; 17/22 etc; 20/19; 21/7/3; 21/57/5; 24/270: *in times past, once* 13/10; 19/43: **nū hwīle** adv *just now* 9/23: **þā hwīle þe** conj *while, as long as* 4/158, 232; 7/50; 9/125; 24/14 etc

hwilc I. adj *what* 1/h, 12, 51f; 2/42, 84; 7/19; 10/129; 11/168; 25/65: *of what sort* 1/119: *what sort of* 7/2: *some* 10/178: **swā hwelce dæge swā** *on whatsoever day as* 4/67f: **II.** interr pron *what* 1/22; 9/93; 10/224; 15/2848: **III.** indef pron *any such one* 1/53: with partitive gen *some* 14/81: *anyone* 16/414: **swā hwelc swā** *whoever, whosoever* 3/15

*ge***hwilc I.** adj *every* 11/123: *many, various* 18/h: **II.** pron with partitive gen *each* 3/16; 9/1; 10/3, 120; 12/238; 14/20; 16/297 etc; 17/108, 136; 19/8; 20/36, 68 etc; 23/32 etc; 24/127 etc; 25/46

hwīlon = **hwīlum** (dat pl of **hwīl**)

hwīl–wendlice adv *for a time, temporarily* 11/116

hwīl–wende adj *transitory, temporal* 11/121

hwīl–wendlic adj *temporal, transitory* 12/113

hwirfan = **hwierfan**

hwīt adj *white* 5/63: *shining, radiant* 16/254 etc

hwon inst of **hwā** (§6.5) *what*: see also **for**

hwōn I. pron with partitive gen *little, a few* 20/28: **II.** adv *slightly* 8/13

hwonan = **hwanon**

hwōnlīce adv *only moderately, only a little* 12/113

hwonne conj *when* 9/h, 45: *the time when* 17/136: *until the time when* 24/67

hwonon = **hwanon**

hwȳ I. interrog adv (§6.5) *why* 13/96; 16/282: **II.** conj *why* 13/26

hwyder = **hwider**

hwȳl = **hwīl**

hwylc = **hwilc**

*ge***hwylc** = *ge***hwilc**

(*ge*)**hwyrfan** = (*ge*)**hwierfan**

hȳ = **hī** (see **hē**, §6.2, 4)

hycg(e)an III *think, consider* 19/14; 20/117; 21/28/12; 22/11, 20; 24/4; 25/54: with gen *think about, give thought to* 16/397 etc

hȳd f (§14.6) *hide* 4/121; 8/30 etc; 21/26/12

(*ge*)**hȳdan** I *hide, bury* 19/84; 20/102

*ge***hygd** n f (§14.5, 6) *thought, intention* 19/72: *conception* 20/116

hyge m (§14.5) *mind, thought, heart* 16/266 etc; 19/16; 20/44, 58 etc; 22/17; 23/87: *courage* 24/4, 312

hyge–blīðe adj *glad in spirit* 21/26/20

hyge–gēomor adj *depressed in mind, melancholy* 22/19

hygelēast f (§14.6) *want of wisdom, folly* 16/331

hyge–sceaft m (§13.2) *mind, heart* 16/288

hȳhst = **hēhst**
hyht m (§14.5) *hope, joyous expectation, bliss* 10/225; 20/45, 122; 23/98: *joy* 17/126 etc
*ge*h**yhtan** I *trust* 9/54
hyhtlīce adv *gaily* 18/79
hyht–wyn(n) f (§14.6) *joy of hope* 23/121
hyldan I *bend, bow* 17/45 (with refl acc)
hyldo f (§15.3) *favor, grace* 15/2922; 16/282 etc; 23/4: *allegiance, loyalty* 16/321; 23/251n
hym = **him**
(*ge*)**hȳnan** I *humiliate, abuse* 14/34, 100; 24/180: used absolutely *lay low* 24/324
hyne = **hine**
hyra = **hira**
hȳran = **hīeran**
*ge*h**ȳran** = *ge*h**īeran**
*ge*h**yrdan** I *oppress* 9/91
hyrde m (§13.6) *guard, guardian* 10/135, 173 etc; 23/60
hyre = **hire**
hyrne f (§14.7) *corner* 12/196
hyrned–nebba m (§14.7) *horny–beaked one* 5/62; 23/212
*ge*h**ȳrnes(s)** f (§14.2) *hearing* 2/56
hȳrra = **hīer(r)a**
hyrst f (§14.6) *ornament, trappings* 21/7/4; 23/316
(*ge*)**hȳrsumian** = (*ge*)**hīersumian**
*ge*h**ȳrsumnys(s)** f (§14.2) *obedience* 15/Æ
hyrwan I *deride, abuse* 14/120, 123
hys = **his**
hyse m (§13.6, 14.5) *young man, young warrior* 24/2 etc
hyss– base for inflected forms of **hyse**
hyt = **hit**
hȳð = **hȳd**

I

Iācob personal name *Jacob* 13/13
ic personal pron (§7.2) *I*
īdel adj *idle* 19/h: *worthless, vain* 9/78; 11/64, 72; 14/126: *empty, desolate* 19/87, 110: **on īdel** adv *in vain* 11/139: see also **gielp**
ides f (§14.6) *woman* 23/14 etc; 25/43
Īdle f (§14.7) *the R. Idle* (Nottinghamshire and Lincolnshire) 1/93
īecan I *add, increase* 14/12
īeg f (§14.2) *island* 8/87
ieldan I *delay* 1/71: *hesitate* 1/66, 99: *postpone* 1/13
ieldest sup adj (§12.7) *chief, most important* 11/246; 23/10 etc
ieldran comp of **eald**, used as pl sb *ancestors* 1/58, 64: *parents* 11/53: *predecessors* 7/28
ieldu f (§15.3) *age* 12/149; 25/50: *old age* 2/14; 18/52; 20/70, 91
iermð(u) f (§14.1) *misery, hardship* 1/15, 67; 14/16, 74, 95; 18/52; 22/3: *crime, enormity* 14/69, 74
iernan 3 *run* 3/15; 8/83; 10/195, 201; 11/49; 23/164
īgeoð = **iggað**
iggað m (§13.3) *small island, islet* 4/157; 11/28
īg–land, –lond n (§13.4) *island* 4/220; 5/66; 8/69 etc: *land beyond the water, remote land* 18/9
Īg–lēa f (§14.1) see 4/102n
īhte pret 1 and 3 sg of **īecan**
ilca m, **ilce** n f, adj, usually wk (§12.4) *same* 1/94, 182; 2/39; 3/27; 4/h, 1, 12 etc; 8/107; 10/213; 11/34 etc; 12/30 etc; 15/Æ
Ilfing *the R. Elbing* 8/92
in prep with acc, dat and inst **I.** (local) *in, into, among* 1/11 etc; 2/15 etc; etc; **II.** (temporal) *in, at, during* 1/46: *for* 18/77; 20/124: **III.** (causal) *by, by means of, in*: **in þon** adv *thereby* 1/72: **IV.** (manner) *in, consisting in, in the form of*: **V.** (reciprocal) *for, in exchange for* 1/85
in adv = **in(n)**
in–bryrdnes(s) = **on–bryrdnes(s)**
inca m (§14.7) *grievance, grudge* 2/87, 88
incer possessive adj (§10.8) *your* (i.e. belonging to two of you) 11/100
incit see **þū** (§6.2) *you, yourselves*
in–dryhten adj *noble, excellent* 19/12
in–dryhto f (§15.3) *nobility* 20/89
in–gehygd n f (§14.5, 6) *intent, intention, conscience* 13/73
in–geþanc m n (§13.2, 4) *inner mind, conscience* 14/157
in–gong m (§13.2) *entry* 2/62, 93

in–gongan 7 *go in, enter* 1/101
in–innan adv *indoors* 21/28/7
in–lǣdan I *bring in* 2/77
in(n) **I.** sb n *room, chamber* 1/30; 23/70: **II.** adv *in* 1/h, 136; 4/201; 10/10, 32, 133 etc; 12/90; 23/150 etc; 24/58 etc: **in on** prep *into, in among, in upon* 4/155, 215; 8/11, 15, 17, 71 etc
innan **I.** prep with acc *in, in among* 4/241: *into, in among* 4/14, 17 etc: *among* 14/31: *in the interior of* 25/43: **II.** adv *from within* 20/11: *inside* 14/33: **on . . . innan** *into, inside* 16/342
innan–bordes adv *within the country, at home* 7/6
inne adv *inside, within* 1/30; 2/83; 4/9, 210; 14/24 etc; 23/45: *indoors* 8/102, 106, 122: *at home* 14/44: **inne on** prep with dat *in the depths of* 4/136
inn–gehygd f (§14.6) *intention, purpose* 1/82
inne–weard adj *inward, inner* 1/h
in–stæpe adv *at once, immediately* 1/69
in–tinga m (§14.7) *cause* 1/50; 2/16
in–tō prep with dat or acc *into* 4/77, 80, 175; 6/8 etc; 11/42, 295; 12/190: *toward* 6/62
In–wær personal name *Inwær* 4/94
in–weard adj *sincere* 11/179
in–werdlīce adv *sincerely, deeply* 11/15
in–widda m (§14.7) *malicious* or *deceitful one* 5/46; 23/28
in–wid–hlemm m (§13.2) *malicious wound* 17/47
in–wit n (§13.4) *guile, deceit* 9/41
in–wit–weorc n (§13.4) *works of malice* 9/49
īo = **gēo**
Iōhannes personal name *John* 11/1 etc
Iōsep personal name *Joseph* 13/65
īow = **ēow**
Īr(a)land n (§13.4) *Ireland* 8/69 etc; 12/240 etc
Īras m pl (§13.2) *the Irish* 5/56
īren n (§13.6) *iron* 16/383; 24/253; 25/26
īren–bend f (§14.2) *iron bond* 16/371
is see **wesan** (§7.2)
īs n (§13.4) *ice* 12/34
Isaac personal name *Isaac* 13/4 etc; 15/2852 etc
īs–cald, –ceald adj *ice–cold* 20/14, 19
īsen adj *iron* 16/316n
īsern = **īren**
īsig–feðera m (§14.7) *icy–feathered one* 20/24
Israhēlas m pl (§13.2) *Israelites* 2/61; 11/323
iū = **gēo**
Iūdēas m pl *the Jews* 10/127
Iūdēisc adj *Jewish*: **þā Iūdēiscan** *the Jews* 13/46 etc
Iūdith(ð) personal name *Judith* 23/13 etc
iugoð = **geoguð**
iung = **geong**
iū–wine m (§14.5) *friend of former days, old friend* 20/92

K

Kyne–gyls = **Cyne–gyls**
kyne–rīce = **cyne–rīce**
kyng(c) = **cyning(c)**
kyning = **cyning(c)**
kyrtel = **cyrtel**

L

lā interj *lo! see! behold! indeed!* 1/38; 9/75; 11/117; 14/80 etc: **lā hwæt** *look what! indeed look!* 14/18
lāc n (§13.4) *sacrifice* 13/77; 14/25; 15/2859 etc; 15/Æ
*ge*l**āc** n (§13.4) *"play," rolling, tumult* 20/35; 22/7
lācan 7 *play, sport* 25/39
lǣce–dōm m (§13.2) *medicine, remedy* 9/5; 11/64
(*ge*)**lǣdan** I *lead, bring, carry, take* 2/42; 4/279; 10/32, 59, 125 etc; 11/182; 12/224; 14/101; 15/2851 etc; 21/28/6; 21/29/2; 23/129, 325; 24/88: *conduct, escort* 10/331; 11/52; 23/42 etc: *extend* 17/5
Lǣden n (§13.5) *Latin* 7/13 etc; 13/2 etc
Lǣden–geþīode n (§13.6) *the Latin language* 7/51 etc
Lǣden–ware m pl (§14.5) *the Romans* 7/42
lǣfan I *leave* 3/21: with dat *leave to* 7/29
læg pret 1 and 3 sg of **licgan**
lǣgon, lǣgun = **lāgon** (pret pl of **licgan**)

Læ–land n (§13.4) *Lolland* 8/84

lǣn n f (§14.5, 6) *loan* 16/259n: **tō lǣne** adv *on loan* 7/67

lǣne adj *transitory, fleeting* 9/86; 17/109 etc; 19/108 etc; 20/66

lǣran I with acc or dat obj *teach* 1/98; 2/10; 9/32, 105; 10/3, 39, 328; 11/292; 12/74: *instruct* 7/51, 52; 11/68: *preach* 10/68: *advise, urge* 1/35, 83, 149; 2/53; 9/1, 32n; 24/311

*ge***lǣred** adj (past pple) *learned* 2/43; 7/64; 12/242

lǣrēow = **lārēow**

lærig m *rim* (?) 24/284

lǣs comp adv (§24.5) *less, fewer* 1/147; 4/282, 288: indecl sb *fewer* 14/90: **þē lǣs, þȳ lǣs þe** conj *lest* 10/33, 159, 234 etc; 11/60; 12/271; 13/101; 14/140f: **nōht þon lǣs** adv *nonetheless* 1/125

lǣssa comp adj (§12.10) *smaller* 8/31

lǣs(s)t sup adj (§12.10) *smallest, littlest, least* 1/138; 8/112 etc

(*ge*)**lǣstan** I *carry out, perform* 1/107; 4/106; 14/155; 16/321: *accomplish* 16/435: *fulfill* 24/15: *practise* 9/58: *pay* 14/21: with dat obj *follow, stick by, support* 4/69; 6/69; 24/11

læt adj *slow, tardy*; *slack, lax, negligent* 6/76

lǣtan 7 *let* 5/60; 6/62; 14/143; 16/253 etc; 23/221; 24/7 etc: *keep* 8/8: *release* 10/121: *consider* 14/93

lǣton = **lēton** (pret pl of **lǣtan**)

lǣððu f (§14.2) *affliction, injury* 23/158 etc

lǣwede adj *lay, unlearned* 1/81; 13/33: used as sb 14/51

lāf f (§14.1) *remainder, remnant* 4/11, 206; 5/54; 9/76: *leaving* 9/95: *thing left, product* 5/6: **tō lafe** *left* 6/55 etc; 8/108; 10/35, 40, 141 etc

*ge***lagian** II *ordain, appoint by law* 14/22

lāgon pret pl of **licgan**

lagu I. sb f (§14.1) *law* 14/20, 28 etc: *district governed by the same laws* 4/midnote: **II.** sb m (§15.2) *sea, water* 20/47

*ge***lagu** n pl (§13.4) *stretches, tracts, expanse* 20/64

lagu–flōd m (§13.2) "*water–flood,*" *ocean* 18/70; 25/46

lagu–lād f (§14.1) "*water–way,*" *sea* 19/3

lagu–strēam m (§13.2) *water stream* 18/62; 24/66

lah–bryce m (§14.5) *lawbreaking* 14/109

lahlīce adv *lawfully* 14/51

*ge***lamp** pret 1 and 3 sg of *ge***limpan**

land n (§13.4) *land, country* 2/61; 4/2, 23 etc; 5/9 etc; 6/4 etc; 7/38; 8/2 etc; 9/89; 12/1 etc; 13/65; 14/10 etc; 15/2855 etc; 15/Æ; 16/332; etc: *landed property* 3/23: *region, territory* 6/20; 12/239

land–ār f (§14.1) *landed property* 11/13

land–būend m (§15.5) "*land–dweller,*" *native* 23/226, 314

land–fyrd f (§14.6) *land force, army* 6/13 etc

landscipe m (§14.5) *region, country* 16/376

lane f (§14.7) *street* 10/123, 204 etc

lan–ferd = **land–fyrd**

lang adj *long* 4/127, 133, 257 etc; 6/23; 8/31 etc; 10/46; 11/41; 12/138; 17/24; 21/28/9; 24/66: *far* 8/3: *tall* 24/273: **embe lang** adv *after a long time* 12/208

*ge***lang** adj with **æt** or **in** *comprehended in, dependent on* 20/121

Langa–land n (§13.4) *Langeland* 8/84

lange adv *long, for a long time* 1/h, 43, 157; 7/64; 8/126; 9/49; 12/214 etc; 14/31, 43 etc; 16/258 etc; 19/3, 38; 23/158 etc: *far* 4/44, 52; 8/6: see also **dæg**

langian II impers with acc of person *long, desire* 9/91; 22/14

langlīce adv *for a long time* 11/159

langoð m (§13.3) *longing, desire* 22/41 etc

langsum adj *long, protracted* 11/158

langung f (§14.1) *grief* 9/88, 90: *longing, restless desire, anxiety* 20/47

langung–hwīl f (§14.1) *time of longing* or *desire* 17/126

lār f (§14.1) *teaching, doctrine* 1/6, 67, 119 etc; 2/47, 65; 7/8; 11/65, 99 etc; 12/76 etc; 13/32, 74; 16/429 etc: *study* 11/60: *knowledge* 7/10 etc: *instruction* 9/64: *precept* 14/39, 52: *advice* 1/179; 23/333: *admonition* 11/150

lār–cwide m (§14.5) *counsel, advice* 19/38

lārēow m (§13.6) *teacher* 1/175, 178; 2/59; 4/124; 7/16; 10/86; 11/66 etc; 12/50; 13/22, 33 etc

lāst m (§13.2) *track, footprint* 20/15: **lāstas lecgan** "make tracks," go 15/2851: **lecgan on lāst** with dat *pursue*: **on lāst** with dat *on the track of, behind, after* 19/97; 23/209 etc

lāst–word n (§13.4) *"the word on one's trail," reputation left behind after death, posthumous reputation* 20/73

late adv *late* 4/7; 23/275

latian II *delay, hesitate* 14/139

lāð I. sb n (§13.4) *harm, injury* 1/54, 79; 16/392; 18/53: *enmity, hostility* 1/36: **II.** adj *hateful, hated* 5/22; 14/39, 67; 16/376; 20/112; 23/72 etc; 24/50: with dat *hateful to, hated by* 14/67; 16/429; 17/88; 23/45: used as sb *foe* 5/9; 25/53

lāðettan I *loathe, hate* 14/123

lāð–genīðla m (§14.7) *hostile enemy, foe* 18/50

*(ge)***lāðian** II *invite* 11/8, 294, 297 etc

lāðlic adj *repulsive* 9/74

lāðlīce adv *horribly, unpleasantly*: sup *in most wretched fashion* 22/14

*ge***laðung** f (§14.1) *congregation, church* 11/207, 306; 13/69; 23/h

lēaf n (§13.4) *leaf* 18/39

*(ge)***lēafa** m (§14.7) *faith, belief* 1/2, 108, 114, 153 etc; 9/50, 57, 59; 10/310, 321 etc; 11/86 etc; 12/15 etc; 13/36, 73; 23/h, 6 etc

*ge***leaffulnes(s)** f (§14.2) *faith, belief* 9/52

*ge***leafful(l)** adj *faithful, believing, Christian* 9/35; 11/78, 89, 119; 12/64 etc

leahtor m (§13.2) *crime, fault; disease* 11/66

lēan n (§13.4) *reward, favor* 15/2934; 16/258 etc; 23/346

*ge***lēanian** I *repay, requite* 16/394

lēap m (§13.2) *wicker basket; container; carcass* 23/111

lēas I. adj *untruthful, forsworn* 13/101: *untrustworthy, unreliable* 13/105: **II.** adj with gen *bereft of, destitute of, without* 16/333 etc; 19/86; 22/32; 23/121

lēase adv *lyingly, deceitfully* 1/h

lēasung f (§14.1) *vanity, frivolity* 2/12: *lying, falsehood* 14/112

leax m (§13.2) *salmon* 25/39

leccan I *water, irrigate* 18/64

lecgan I *lay, place* 11/270; 12/172; 15/2851; 19/42: *impose* 6/91: see also **(wræc)lāst**

*ge***lēd** past pple of **lecgan**

Lēden = **Lǣden**

lēfan = **līefan**

*ge***lefan** = *ge***līefan**

leg = **læg** (pret 1 and 3 sg of **licgan**)

Lēga–ceaster f (§14.1) *Chester* (Cheshire) 4/209

legde pret 1 and 3 sg of **lecgan**

legdon, legdun pret pl of **lecgan**

lege imper sg of **lecgan**

leger n (§13.4) *lying* 8/121: *bed* 22/34: *illness* 18/56

lehtrian II *blame, revile* 14/120f

leide = **legde**

lencg = **leng**

lencten m (§13.3) *spring* 6/91; 25/6

*ge***lend** past pple of **lendan**

lendan I *go* 4/183

leng comp adv (§24.5) *longer* 1/13, 38; 6/27; 8/104; 9/89; 13/100; 14/6; 16/291; 23/153; 24/171

lengan I *be prolonged, linger* 21/28/8

lengest sup adv *longest* 3/3; 4/158; 25/6

lengra comp adj *longer* 4/134; 8/31; 23/184

lengten = **lencten**

lēod–biscop m (§13.3) *provincial bishop, suffragan* 11/209

lēode f pl (§14.6) *people* 5/11; 12/12 etc; 14/146; 17/88; 22/6; 23/147 etc; 24/23 etc

lēod–fruma m (§14.7) *"people–leader," lord* 22/8

lēod–hata m (§14.7) *"people–hater," tyrant* 14/115; 23/72

lēof adj *dear, beloved* 2/91; 9/1, 42, 65; 10/23 etc; 11/18; 13/100; 14/5; 15/2859 etc; 17/78 etc; 19/31, 38, 97; 20/112; 22/16 etc; 23/147; etc: *pleasant, pleasing* 9/70, 115; 24/23: with dat *dear to, loved by* 3/25; 9/17, 71; 15/2921; 16/349: in addressing persons *sir, dear sir* 13/1 etc: comp *better* 16/412: with dat *preferable to* 1/37

*ge***lēofan** = *ge***līefan**

leofian = **libban**

leofað pres 3 sg of **libban**

Lēof–wine personal name *Leofwine* 6/70

lēoht I. sb n (§13.4) *light* 10/21, 314; 11/130 etc; 16/333; 17/5; 25/51: *sight* 10/17: *world* 16/258 etc: **II.** adj **A.** *bright* 16/256 etc; 23/191: **B.** *light, light–weight* 8/63: *easy* 13/64

lēohtlic adj **I.** *bright, shining, radiant* 21/29/3: **II.** *easy* 13/64n

lēoma m (§14.7) *ray* (of light) 4/127; 11/317; 23/191

leomu nom and acc pl of **lim**

leornere m (§13.6) *scholar* 2/44

*(ge)***leornian** II *learn* 1/11, 122; 2/4, 10, 56, 59; 7/34 etc; 9/105; 12/78: *study* 11/57

leorning–cniht m (§13.2) *disciple* 11/17

lēoð n (§13.4) *song, poem, poetry* 2/2, 8 etc

lēoð–cræft m (§13.2) *art of poetry* 2/10

lēoð–song m (§13.2) *poem, song* 2/6, 48

lēoð–wīse f (§14.7) *verse, poetry* 18/h

lēt pret 1 and 3 sg of **lǣtan**

lētan = **lēton**

lēton pret pl of **lǣtan**

*ge***lettan** I *hinder, stop* 24/164

lēw f *injury, blemish* 14/128

lēwian II *blemish* 14/129

libban III *live* 9/29, 33, 85 etc; 10/298; 11/310; 12/47 etc; 13/8 etc; 14/60; 17/134; 20/78, 85 etc; 21/28/9; 22/14

līc n (§13.4) *body* 3/33; 4/13, 49; 8/106; 11/43, 46 etc; 12/140; 15/2859; 16/265; 17/63

*ge***līc** adj with dat *like, similar to* 1/142; 14/71 (sup), 127; 16/256

*ge***līccast** sup adj (see *ge***līc**)

liccetan I *feign, dissimulate* 1/h

*ge***līce** adv *alike* 18/37: with dat *like* 2/9; 12/206

licgan 5 *lie* 3/22, 33; 4/13, 49 etc; 5/17; 6/24; 8/49 etc; 10/102, 174; 12/35 etc; 16/322 etc; 17/24; 19/78; 23/30 etc; 24/222 etc: *lie dead* 3/17; 5/28; 24/112, 157 etc: with refl dat *lie down* 24/300, 319: *flow* 4/134; 8/91, 95: *extend, stretch* 8/7, 16, 50, 73: *remain* 14/83

līc–hama, –homa m (§14.7) *body* 1/h, 78; 9/40, 43, 79; 10/5; etc

līc–hamlic, –homlic adj *bodily* 2/74; 11/321

līcian II with dat obj *be pleasing to* 9/35; 10/207: impers 10/120, 203

līc–man(n) m (§15.7) *pall–bearer* 11/153, 157

līc–ræst f (§14.2) *bier, hearse* 12/181

lid n (§13.4) *ship* 5/27 etc

lid–man(n) m (§15.7) *shipman, sailor* 24/99 etc

lid–men(n) dat sg and nom and acc pl of **lid–man(n)**

līefan I *allow, permit* 6/27; 7/21

*ge***līefan** I *believe* 1/99, 185; 7/17; 9/56; 10/16, 27, 130, 282 etc; 11/81, 84, 120 etc; 14/67; 20/27 (with refl dat), 66; 23/h: *believe in* 9/55: *have faith* 12/261; 20/108: with gen *expect, feel sure of* 16/401: past pple **gelīefed** adj *faithful, pious, devout* 11/44: *believing* 12/3, 8

līf n (§13.4) *life* 1/h, 19, 116 etc; 2/7, 93 etc; etc: *manner of living* 11/14: **tō līfe** adv *in life, while living* 23/322

līfæs = **līfes**

lifde pret 1 and 3 sg of **libban**

lifdon pret pl of **libban**

līf–fæst adj *living, vivifying* 1/8

*ge***līf–fæstan** I *quicken, bring alive* 13/51

lifgend m (§15.5) *one who is alive*: pl *living ones, the living* 20/65n, 73; 22/34

lifg(i)an, lifi(g)an = **libban**

līflic adj *vital*: **sēo līflice bōc** *the book of life* 11/182

līg m (§14.5) *flame, fire* 11/176; 15/2858; 16/325 etc; 18/39

ligeð pres 3 sg of **licgan**

līg–ræsc m (§13.2) *flash of lightning* 4/h

līhtan I *alight* 24/23

Lilla personal name *Lilla* 1/h

lim n (§13.4) *limb* 2/20; 9/97; 12/211 etc

Limene–mūða m (§14.7) *the estuary of the R. Lympne* (Kent) 4/131 etc

*ge***limp** n (§13.4) *occurrence, happening* 14/102

(*ge*)**limpan** 3 *happen* 11/9, 225; 12/64 etc: with dat *befall, happen to* 10/171; 14/80, 86: impersonal with dat *befall, happen to* 9/86; 20/13: **limpan tō** *concern* 1/48

*ge***limplic** adj *suitable, appropriate, convenient* 1/100; 2/20

lim–wērig adj *weary of limb* 17/63

lind f (§14.1) *shield* (of lindenwood) 23/191 etc; 24/99 etc

Lindes–ēg f (§14.2) *Lindsey* (the old name of North Lincolnshire, see 12/168b n) 4/60, 62; 6/18

Lindes–īg = Lindis–ēg

Lindess–ē = Lindes–ēg

Lindis–farena ee f (§14.2) *Lindisfarne* (Northumberland) see 12/168b n

Lindis–farn–ēa = Lindisfarena ee

lind–wīg n (§13.4) *shield–armed force* 23/297

lind–wiggend m (§15.5) *shield–warrior* 23/42

*ge***liornian** = *ge***leornian**

liornung f (§14.1) *learning* 7/8 etc

lioðo–bend f (§14.2) *"limb–bond," fetter* 16/382

liss f (§14.2) *favor* 15/2921; 21/26/25

list f (§14.6) *skill:* dat pl used as adv *skilfully, cunningly, artfully* 21/29/3; 23/101

lītel = lȳtel

līt–hwōn adv *hardly at all* 12/243

lið n (§13.4) *fleet* 6/9, 22 etc: *army* 6/48

līð pres 3 sg of **licgan**

līxan I *shine, gleam, glisten* 18/33

loc(c) m (§13.2) *lock, hair* 10/246, 247 etc

lōcian II *look* 3/12; 10/23, 108 etc; 14/92

lof n (§13.4) *praise* 2/94, 101; 9/104; 10/31; 12/137; 16/256; 20/73 etc

*ge***lōgian** II *lodge, put* 14/65: *arrange* 15/Æ: *deposit, inter* 12/142: **gelōgian upp** *lay up, inter* 12/191

*ge***lōme** adv *frequently, often* 9/16; 14/23, 40 etc; 23/18

*ge***lōmlīcian** II *grow common* 9/19

lond = land

lond–būend = land–būend

lond–stede m (§14.5) *country* 22/16

lone = lane

long = lang

*ge***long** = *ge***lang**

longað = langoð

longe = lange

losian II *perish, be lost* 12/271; 23/287: with dat *be lost to* 16/434; 20/94

Lōth personal name *Lot* 15/2924

lūcan 2 *lock, lock together* 24/66

Lūcas personal name *Luke* 11/206

lucon pret pl of **lūcan**

Lucu–mon personal name *Lucumon* 4/274

lufigean = lufian

lufian II *love* 2/52; 7/20 etc; 9/65, 72, 105 etc; 10/306; etc: past pple *beloved* 11/31

luflīce adv *lovingly, affectionately* 7/1

lufu f (§14.1) often declined wk *love* 2/68, 69; 4/119; 9/21, 59; 20/121; 21/26/25: *kindness* 1/35

lumpon pret pl of **limpan**

Lunden *London* 4/285; 6/11 etc

Lunden–burg f (§15.7) *London* 4/58, 168 etc

lungre adv *immediately, forthwith, quickly* 23/147 etc

lust m (§13.2) *lust, desire* 11/16, 147 etc; 13/98: *pleasure, desire* 14/52: *desire, longing* 20/36: *ecstasy* 23/161

*ge***lustfullīce** adv *joyfully, heartily* 1/124

lustlīce adv *willingly, gladly* 1/20, 67

lybban = libban

lyb–cræft m (§13.2) *skill in the use of drugs, witchcraft* 10/8

Lȳden = Lǣden

Lȳden–bōc f (§15.7) *Latin book* 13/21f

lȳfan = līefan

*ge***lȳfan** = *ge***līefan**

lyfdon = lifdon (pret pl of **libban**)

*ge***lȳfed** adj *advanced* 2/14

lyft m n f (§13.2, 4; 14.6) *air* 4/h; 21/7/4; 21/57/1; 23/347; 25/3 etc: *sky* 18/39: *wind* 18/62: **on lyft** adv *aloft, on high* 17/5

lyft–fæt n (§13.4) *"air–vessel," bowl* or *cup in the sky* 21/29/3

lyft–helm m (§13.2) *mist, cloud* 25/46

Lȳge f (§14.7) *the R. Lea* (Bedfordshire, Hertfordshire, Essex, Middlesex) 4/226 etc

lyre m (§14.5) *loss* 18/53

lȳsan I *redeem, ransom* 17/41; 24/37: *break, mangle* 10/212

*ge***lȳstan** I impers vb with acc of person and gen of thing *desire* 23/306

lȳt indecl sb *few* 6/58: with partitive gen 19/31; 22/16: used as adv *little* 1/h; 20/27

lytegian II *use guile, be crafty; be prudent* 24/86

lȳtel I. adj *little, small* 3/9; 4/51, 93, 97; 5/34; 6/31; 7/26; 8/62; 12/15; 14/9; 21/57/1; 23/h: *petty* 14/37: neuter used as sb *little, a small part* 8/40; 13/21, 63; 14/22: **II.** adv *a little, slightly* 4/h

lȳt–hwōn pron with gen *few* 23/310

lȳtlian II *diminish, wane, dwindle* 24/313

lȳðre adj *wicked, vile* 14/147

M

mā I. indecl comp used as sb (usually with gen) and adj *more* 4/258; 6/32; 7/38; 13/17; 14/90, 113; 8/39, 109; 10/43; 13/17; 14/90, 113; 21/26/21; 22/4; 24/195: **II.** comp of **micle** adv *more, further* 1/86, 128: *rather* 1/80: *any more* 10/286, 287: **þē mā, þon mā, þȳ mā** *the more, any more* 3/29; 5/46; 14/49

Maccbethu personal name *Maccbethu* 4/123

mādm = māðm

maect = miht I.

*ge***mæc** adj with dat *suitable to, well–matched with* 22/18

mǣce = mēce

mǣden n (§13.5) *virgin* 11/19, 306: *maiden, girl* 12/213 etc

mæg pres 1 and 3 sg of **magan**

mǣg m (§13.2 footnote 1) *kinsman, relation* 1/64; 3/24, 25 etc; 5/40; 6/15; 8/103; 9/98; 11/281; 12/4 etc; 15/2924; 19/51, 109; 22/11; 24/5 etc: *son* 15/2869 etc

mægen I. sb n (§13.5) *strength, might, power* 9/26; 10/198, 285 etc; 16/269; 24/313: *virtue* 9/105; 12/82: *efficacy* 1/123: *miracle* 10/85: *force, army* 23/253 etc: **II.** pres subj 1–3 pl of **magan**

mægen–ēacen adj *mighty* 23/292

mægen–þrym(m) m (§14.5) *great majesty, grandeur* 11/105

mǣglic adj *familial* 11/4

mægon = magon (pres pl of **magan**)

mǣg–rǣs m (§13.2) *attack on a kinsman* 14/110

mæg–slaga m (§14.7) *kinsman slayer* 14/130

mægð f (dental stem, see Campbell §637) *maiden* 23/35 etc

mǣgð f (§14.1) *tribe, clan* 8/125; 23/324: *kin, family* 14/84: *province, country* 1/h, 33, 184

mægð–hād m (§15.2, 13.2) *virginity* 11/5, 6 etc

mægyn = mægen

mæigð–hād = mægð–hād

mǣl n (§13.4) **I.** *time, occasion* 20/36; 24/212 (see n): **II.** *speech* 24/212 (but see n)

(*ge*)**mǣlan** I speak 15/2913; 24/26 etc

Mǣl–dūn f (§14.1) *Maldon* (Essex) 24/h

Maelinmun personal name *Maelinmun* 4/124

*ge***mǣne** adj *owned in common, shared, joint* 5/40; 14/69, 70: with dat *common to* 11/128, 130 etc; 14/41, 83 etc: *common among* 14/86

mæneg = manig

*ge***mǣnelīce** adv *generally, universally* 11/212

mæni(g)feald = manigfeald

mænig = manig

mænigu = menigu

mænn = menn (dat sg and nom and acc pl of **man(n)**)

mǣran I *make famous* 2/2: *glorify* 21/26/16 (see n)

mǣre adj *famous, glorious, illustrious, sublime, splendid* 5/14; 11/24, 125 etc; 12/43 etc; 13/22; 16/299; 17/12 etc; 19/100 (*mighty*?); 21/26/16 (see n), 27; 23/3 etc

*ge***mǣre** n *boundary, border* 1/93

mǣrðu f (§14.1) *glory* 14/161; 20/84; 23/181n, 343: *glorious thing, splendid thing* 13/71

mæsse f (§14.7) *mass* 4/286; 11/292f

mæsse–ǣfen(n) m n (§13.3, 5) *the eve of a church festival* 6/64f

mæsse–prēost, –prīost m (§13.2) *priest* 7/59; 9/37; 12/241 etc; 13/11

mæsser–bana m (§14.7) *priest–slayer* 14/130

mæst m (§13.2) *mast* 25/24

mǣst I. sup adj (§12.10) *most* 4/149; 9/h: *greatest* 2/5; 4/92; 14/58; 23/3, 292; 24/175, 223: *largest* 8/33, 110 etc: neut used as sb 6/83: with partitive gen 16/297, 364, 393; 20/84; 23/181n: **II.** sup adv *mostly* 8/41: *most vigorously* 23/181n: **mǣst ǣlc** *almost everyone* 14/54, 55

*ge***mǣtan** I impers with dat *dream* 17/2

mǣte adj *small* 17/69 etc

mǣð f (§14.6) *measure: honor, respect* 14/26, 66: *fitness, appropriateness* 24/195

mǣw m (§14.5) *mew, seagull* 20/22

magan pret–pres vb (§23.3) *be able, may, can* 1/6 etc; 2/9 etc; 4/87 etc; etc: **magan tō** with dat *be capable of* 7/50

māgas nom and acc pl of **mǣg**

māgister m *master, teacher* 13/11

mago m (§15.2) *man, youth, warrior* 15/2917; 19/92

mago–þegn, magu–þegn m (§13.2) *young retainer* 19/62; 23/236

*ge***man** pres 1 and 3 sg of *ge***munan**

mān n (§13.4) *crime, wickedness* 14/134; 16/299

mancess m (§13.3) *mancus* (a gold coin worth 30 silver pence) 7/62

mān–dǣd f (§14.6) *evil deed* 2/69; 14/107

*ge***māne** = *ge***mǣne**

maneg = **manig**

mān–fremmend m (§15.5) *evil–doer* 18/6

mān–ful(l) adj *wicked, abominable* 1/h

*ge***mang** n (§13.4) *troop* 23/193 etc

(*ge*)**manian** II *admonish* 1/13, 83; 2/53; 9/28: *urge, exhort, prompt* 20/36, 50, 53; 23/26; 24/228 etc

manig adj *many* 1/17; 2/6; 4/224 etc; 6/18 etc; 7/14 etc; 8/73; 9/12; 12/197 etc; 13/16; 14/12, 34 etc; 17/41 etc; 18/4; 21/8/1; 24/200 etc: *many a* 1/h; 5/17; 8/97; 9/19; 24/188, 243

manig(e)o = **menigu**

manigfeald adj *manifold, abundant* 9/84, 114; 13/78: *numerous* 7/55; 11/136, 313; 13/70, 71; 14/104, 149: *various* 14/77

man(n) I. sb m (§15.7) *man* 1/h, 10 etc; 2/6 etc; 3/10; etc: *servant* 2/92; 8/49; 13/75: *vassal* 6/30–34n: see also **cyn(n)**: **II.** indef pron *one* 1/32 etc; 4/55, 87; etc: *one man* 11/194

manna I. sb m (§14.7) *man* 10/296; 13/57; 22/18; 23/98 etc: **II.** sb m (§14.7 and indecl) *manna* 11/322

man(n)–cyn(n) n (§13.6) *mankind* 2/35, 60; 11/18; 15/2896 etc; 16/363; 17/33 etc

mann–slaga m (§14.7) *man–slayer* 14/130

man–sleht, –slyht m (§14.5) *manslaughter, murder* 4/h; 14/110

mann–sylen f (§14.2) *selling of men* (into slavery) 14/108

mān–swora m (§14.7) *perjurer* 14/131

māra comp adj, see **micel** (§12.10) *more* 1/126; 7/38; 8/104; 11/134; 14/77 etc; 23/92: *greater* 1/25; 5/65; 15/Æ; 16/269; 24/313: *larger* 1/179: used as sb *more* 13/38, 83; 14/56: with partitive gen 11/300; 13/3: **þȳ māra . . . þȳ** *the more . . . in proportion as*

Marcus personal name *Mark* 11/206

Māria f (§14.7) *Mary* 4/65; 11/19, 208; 17/92

Marmadonia see 10/4n

Maser–feld m (§15.2) see 12/155b n

Mathēus personal name *Matthew* 11/206

maðelian II *speak, make a speech* 15/2893; 16/347; 24/42 etc

māðm m (§13.2) *treasure, jewel, ornament* 1/86; 7/25; 20/99; 23/318 etc

māððum–gyfa m (§14.7) *treasure–giver* 19/92

mē see **ic** (§6.2) *me, myself, to me, for me*

meaht I. sb = **miht**: **II.** pres 2 sg of **magan**

meahte pret 1 and 3 sg of **magan**

meahtes pret 2 sg of **magan**

meahtig = **mihtig**

meahton pret pl of **magan**

mēar = **mearh**

*ge***mearc** n (§13.4) *designated place*: **tō**

þæs gemearces þe *in the direction which* 15/2886
mēare dat sg of **mearh**
*ge***mearcian** II *mark out, fix the boundaries of, design* 16/363 etc
mearg = mearh
mearh m (§13.2) *horse, steed* 19/92; 24/188 etc
mearð m (§13.2) *marten* 8/44
mec see **ic** (§6.2) *me* etc
mēce m (§13.6) *sword* 5/24, 40; 23/78 etc; 24/167 etc
mecgan I *mingle, commingle, mix* 25/24
mēd f (§14.1) *reward* 1/52, 55; 15/2917; 23/334 etc
mēder dat and (LWS) gen sg of **mōdor**
med–micel adj *little* 1/139; 2/4, 97; 9/69; 10/54, 309: *venial* 9/4: see also **fæc**
med–myccel = med–micel
medo m (§15.2) *mead* 8/100 etc; 24/212
medo–burg f (§15.7) *"mead–city," rejoicing city* 23/167
medo–byrig dat sg and nom and acc pl of **medo–burg** 23/167
medo–drinc m (§13.2) *"mead–drink," mead* 20/22
medo–wērig adj *"mead–weary," sleepy with mead* 23/229 etc
medu–gāl adj *flushed with mead* 23/26
mehte pret 1 and 3 sg of **magan**
mehton pret pl of **magan**
meldan I *announce, declare; accuse* 21/28/12
mengan I *mingle* 10/209, 248; 19/48
mengeo = menigu
meni(g)–feald = manig–feald
menig–fealdlīce adv *manifoldly, in the plural* 13/59
*ge***menigfyldan** I *multiply* 15/Æ
meni(g)u f (§15.3) *multitude* 7/25; 10/313; 11/89, 241; 17/112, 151
men(n) dat sg and nom and acc pl of **man(n)**
mennisc adj *human* 10/244; 12/179; 20/h
menniscnes(s), –nys(s) f (§14.2) *incarnation* 2/63; 11/12; 13/24: *humanity* 11/207, 224
meodo = medo
meodu–heal(l) f (§14.1) *mead–hall* 19/27
meolc f (§15.7) *milk* 8/99
Mēore see 8/87n
mēos m (§13.2) *moss* 12/37
Meotod, Meotud = Metod
mēowle f (§14.7) *maiden, woman* 23/56 etc
Meran–tūn m *Merton* see 3/9n
Mercan = Miercan
mere m (§14.5) *lake* 8/60 etc: *body of water* 8/95
mere–flōd m (§13.2) *"sea–flood," ocean* 18/42; 20/59; 25/24
mere–hengest m (§13.3) *"sea–horse," ship* 21/h
Meres–īg f (§14.2) *Mersea Island* (Essex) 4/221 etc
Mere–tūn m (§13.2) *Merton* see 4/43n
mere–wērig adj *sea–weary* 20/12
mergen = morgen
*ge***met I.** sb n (§13.4) *measure, meter* 2/39: *nature* 1/16: *manner* 10/129: *measure, moderation, temperance* 20/111: **II.** adj *fit, proper* 15/2896
(*ge*)**mētan** I *meet, find* 1/34, 147; 3/22; 4/18; 6/30–34n; 10/49, 135, 156 etc; 11/310; 12/225: *encounter* 4/27; 11/111: *discover* 11/322, 324: *come upon* 4/84; 8/19
mete m (§14.5) *food* 4/121, 158 etc; 9/76; 11/323 etc: see also **dōn**
metelīest f (§14.6) *lack of food* 4/199
*ge***metlīce** adj *moderately* 2/75
Metod m (§13.3) *Creator, God* 2/30; 15/2872 etc; 18/6; 19/2; 20/103 etc; 23/154 etc; 24/147 etc; 25/49 etc
metsung f (§14.1) *provisions* 6/10 etc
met–trum adj *sick* 12/193
Metud = Metod
mēðe adj *weary, exhausted* 17/65 etc
meðel–stede m (§14.5) *meeting–place* 24/199
mic(c)el adj *great* 1/19, 36, 60 etc; 2/71; 3/6; 4/2 etc; 6/9 etc; 7/25; 8/17; 9/37; 10/93, 306 etc; 11/89 etc; 12/28 etc; 14/16 etc; 16/280 etc; 17/34; etc: *large* 4/60; 6/39, 44; 8/60; 18/h: *much* 1/23; 4/154; 8/98, 100; 9/68; 10/267; 11/125, 168; 16/253, 374; 21/28/12: *many* 1/174: *capital* 9/4: *splendid* 9/79: neuter used as sb, with partitive gen *much, a great part* 4/91, 203;

6/41; 14/22, 137

micle adv *much, by much* 1/146; 4/248; 8/30, 104; 11/194; 16/422; 24/50: see also **swā**

mic(c)lum adv (§24.4) *greatly, much* 3/12; 4/110; 8/125; 11/4, 213 etc; 12/178 etc

mid prep with acc, dat and inst **I.** (comitative) *with, along with, in the company of, among* 1/4, 22, 111 etc; 2/82; 3/10, 24; 4/68, 110 etc; 5/26; 8/38, 101, 120; 9/81; 10/70, 327; 11/83; 12/6 etc; etc: **mid þām** adv *with that, thereupon* 11/168: **mid þām þe** conj *when* 11/41; 12/207; 13/57 etc; 15/Æ: **mid þȳ (þe)** conj *when* 1/h, 6, 16, 36 etc; 2/81; 10/8, 21, 29 etc: *since, because* 1/h; 16/384: **II.** (causal) *by, by means of, by virtue of, through, with* 1/2, 9, 27 etc; 2/1, 71; 4/110, 248; 5/37; 6/88; 7/7; 8/121; 9/37, 79, 93; 10/326; 11/92, 196; 14/15: **mid þǣm þæt** conj *because* 11/308: **III.** (local) *in* 1/h, 100; 2/57; 16/416: **IV. mid ealle** adv completely 4/131, 282; 11/95; 14/126, 144: see also **riht, wiht**

mid adv *therewith, along with* (him, them etc) 1/h; 4/144; 17/106: *with* (them) 8/38: see also **forð**

middan–eard = **middan–geard**

middan–geard m (§13.2) *earth, world* 2/35, 60, 100; 9/h, 12, 47, 110; 11/77, 203f, 311; 16/395; 17/104; 18/4 etc; 19/62 etc; 20/67n, 90

middan–winter m n (§15.2) *midwinter, Christmas, the Christmas season* 6/2

midde adj *the middle of, mid–* 1/44; 4/90, 284f; 10/146, 169, 263; 17/2; 23/68

middel m (§13.3) *middle* 18/65

Middel–tūn m (§13.2) *Milton next Sittingbourne* (Kent) 4/139 etc

midde–neaht f (§15.7) *midnight* 2/83

midde–weard adj *in the middle* 8/53

middun–geard = **middan–geard**

mid–winter m n (§15.2) *midwinter, Christmas* 6/87

Miercan, Mierce m pl (§14.7, 5) *Mercians*, also the region they inhabited: *Mercia* (see 4/2n, 12/128a n) 1/93, 182n; 4/14, 15 etc; 5/24; 12/151 etc; 24/217

miht I. sb f (§14.6) *might, power* 1/59, 127; 2/30; 11/80, 230 etc; 16/336; 17/102; 18/6 etc; 20/108: **II.** 2 sg pres indic of **magan**

mihte pret 1 and 3 sg of **magan**

mihton pret pl of **magan**

mihtig adj *mighty* 16/253 etc; 17/151; 19/h; 20/116; 23/h, 92 etc: *able* 10/119

mīl f (§14.2) *mile* 4/133 etc; 8/53 etc

milde adj *merciful* 24/175: with dat 9/6; 13/101

mild–heortnes(s) f (§14.2) *compassion, mercy* 10/69f, 104; 11/193

milts f (§14.2) *mercy* 9/27, 128; 19/2; 23/85 etc

*(ge)***miltsian** II with dat obj *have mercy on* 10/290; 11/194, 195; 12/161

miltsung f (§14.1) *mercy* 11/183 etc

miltsiend m (§15.5) *one who takes pity* 10/318

mīn possessive adj (§10.8) *my* 2/90; 9/98; 10/184; 11/99; etc

minster = **mynster**

mis–bēodan 2 *injure, harm, wrong, offend* 14/27

mis–dǣd f (§14.6) *misdeed, sin* 13/62; 14/107, 120 etc

mislic adj *various* 7/55; 9/18; 12/193; 13/75; 14/57 etc; 20/99

mislīce adv *variously, diversely, in different ways* 6/57; 21/28/12 (*erratically*?)

mis–limpan 3 impers with dat *go wrong* 14/104

missenlic adj *various, diverse* 1/17

missenlīce adv *in various places* 19/75

mist m (§13.2) *mist* 16/391

mistlic = **mislic**

mis–wendan I *go astray* 11/170

mið = **mid**

mīðan I *conceal, hide* 22/20: with dat *avoid, refrain from* 21/8/4

mōd n (§13.4) *mind, spirit* 1/7, 27, 43 etc; 2/6, 82 etc; 7/32; 10/9, 13 etc; 11/45 etc; 12/59 etc; 16/302 etc; 17/122 etc; 19/15, 41, 51 etc; 20/12, 36 etc; 22/20;

23/57 etc; 24/313

mōd–cearig adj *"heart–anxious," troubled in heart* 19/2

mōd–cearo f (§14.1) *heart–ache, anxiety* 22/40 etc

mōde–lic adj *magnificent* 9/69, 84

mōde–līce adv *bravely* 24/200

mōder = mōdor

mōd–geþōht m (§13.2) *mind, understanding* 16/253

mōd–geþanc m (§13.2) *wisdom, purpose* 2/30

mōd–gidanc = mōd–geþanc

mōdi(g) adj *great spirited* 18/10: *proud* 9/40; 12/21 etc; 23/26 etc: *bold, courageous* 17/41; 19/62; 23/334; 24/80 etc

mōdor f (§15.4) *mother* 11/18, 152 etc; 14/75; 17/92

mōdrie f (§14.7) *mother's sister, maternal aunt* 11/3

mōd–sefa m (§14.7) *heart, soul, mind* 17/124; 19/10, 19; 20/59

mōd–wlonc adj *proud in spirit, haughty* 20/39

Moises = Moyses

molde f (§14.7) *earth* 9/95; 17/12 etc; 20/103; 23/343: *ground* 9/44: *soil* 12/236: *land* 18/10

mold–ern n (§13.2) *"earth–house," sepulcher* 17/65

*ge***molsnian** II *moulder, decay* 9/44, 101

*ge***mon** = *ge***man** (pres 1 and 3 sg of *ge***munan)**

mōna m (§14.7) *moon* 11/130

Mōnan–dæg m (§13.2) *Monday* 6/48

mōnað m (dental stem, see Campbell §637) *month* 4/42, 51 etc; 8/67 etc; 18/66; 23/324

mon–dryhten m (§13.3) *liege lord* 19/41

moneg = manig

*ge***mong** = *ge***mang**

mongum = manigum (dat pl of **manig**)

(*ge*)**monian** = (*ge*)**manian**

monig = manig

*ge***monig–fealdian** II *multiply, increase* 9/13

mon(n) = man(n)

monna = manna

mon(n)–cyn(n) = man(n)–cyn(n)

mōnð = mōnað

monung f (§14.1) *admonition, advice* 1/5, 65

mōr m (§13.2) *mountain* 8/50 etc: *mountain range* 8/55, 58 etc

mōr–fæsten(n) n (§13.6) *"moor–fastness"* (a place secure from attack due to the swampy character of the terrain) 4/93

morgen m (§13.3) *morning* 1/41; 3/19; 10/51, 102 etc; 12/25 etc

morgen–colla m (§14.7) *morning–slaughter* 23/245

morgen–tīd f (§14.6) *morningtide* 5/14; 23/236

Morkere personal name *Morkere* 6/19, 39 etc

morð–dǣd f (§14.6) *murder, deadly deed* 14/107

morðer, morðor n (§13.4) *crime, murder, injury* 22/20; 23/90, 181: *punishment, torment* 16/297 etc

morðor–wyrhta m (§14.7) *murderer* 14/131

mōst pres 3 sg of **mōtan**

mōste pret 1 and 3 sg of **mōtan**

mōston pret pl of **mōtan**

*ge***mōt** n (§13.4) *meeting* 24/199: *encounter* 5/50; 24/301

mōtan pret–pres vb (§23.3) *may, be allowed, be permitted* 1/92 etc; 8/118; 9/43; 11/299; 13/8; 16/359 etc; 23/89 etc; 24/30 etc: *must* 14/14, 17

moððe f (§14.7) *moth* 21/47/1

Moyses personal name *Moses* 2/61; 13/10 etc

*ge***munan** pret–pres vb (§23.3) *remember* 1/70, 107; 7/23 etc; 9/60, 98; 10/127; 17/28; 19/34, 90; 22/51; 24/196 etc: with gen 24/212

mund f (§14.1) **I.** *hand* 23/229: **II.** *security, protection* 14/26

mund–byrd f (§14.6) *protection* 23/3: *hope of protection* 17/130

munec = munuc

munt m (§13.2) *mountain* 18/21

munuc m *monk* 9/38; 13/1

munuc–hād m (§15.2, 13.2) *monastic life*

2/53
munuclic adj *monastic* 12/54
munuclīce adv *as a monk* 12/81
murnan 3 *mourn* 23/154: *care about, trouble about* 24/96 etc
mūð m (§13.2) *mouth* 1/h; 2/59; 10/219, 267 etc; 11/260 etc; 21/8/1; 25/37
mūða m (§14.7) *estuary* 4/132, 135, 264 etc
myc(c)el = mic(c)el
mylen–scearp adj *"grindstone–sharp," sharp from grinding* 5/24
myltestre f (§14.7) *harlot* 14/131
*ge***mynd** n f (§14.5, 6) *memory* 2/38; 7/2; 19/51: *reminder, warning* 9/108
*ge***myndgian** II *remember* 2/57
*ge***myndig** adj *concerned, attentive* 23/74: with gen *mindful of, remembering* 19/6
*ge***myne** imper sg of *ge***munan**
myngian II *exhort* 9/1, 28
mynster n (§13.5) *monastery, church, cathedral* 2/1, 54; 7/64; 12/109 etc
mynster–hata m (§14.7) *persecutor of monasteries* 14/130
mynsterlic adj *monastic* 12/86
mynster–man(n) m (§15.7) *monk* 12/179 etc
myntan I *intend* 12/213: *suppose* 23/253
Myrcan, Myrce = Miercan, Mierce
myrcels m (§13.3) *trophy* 12/163
mȳre f (§14.7) *mare* 1/162; 8/99
myrhð f (§14.1) *joy* 11/2; 14/161

N

nā adv *not, not at all, by no means* 4/55 etc; 6/27 etc; 11/4; 13/3 etc; 14/65 etc; 16/412; 18/72 etc; 19/66, 96; 20/66; 21/26/10; 22/4 etc; 23/117; 24/21 etc: see also **næs I.**
nabban = ne + habban (§7.4)
naca m (§14.7) *boat, ship* 20/7
naced, nacod adj *naked* 11/128, 129 etc: *bare, plain* 13/38
næbbe = ne + hæbbe
næfde = ne + hæfde
nǣfre adv *never* 1/33; 2/11; 3/26; 9/71, 90; 10/253; 11/109; 18/38; 19/69 etc; 23/91
næfð = ne + hæfð
nægl m (§13.2) *nail* 17/46
nægled–cnear(r) m (§13.2) *nailed ship* 5/53
nǣnig I. pron *none, no one, not any* 1/83, 124; 2/9; 3/16; 10/175; 21/29/13; 23/51; 25/63: **II.** adj *no* 2/15, 88; 3/25; 8/101; 9/h, 40; 10/134, 161
nǣnig–wuht adv *by no means, not at all* 10/117
nǣnne m acc sg of **nān**
nǣre = ne + wǣre
nǣren = ne + wǣren
nǣron = ne + wǣron
næs I. sb m (§13.2) *cliff* 23/113: **II.** adv (**= nales**) *not at all*: **næs nā** *by no means at all* 9/36: **III. = ne + wæs**
nafað = ne + hafað
nāh = ne + āh
nāht I. indef pron (with partitive gen) *nothing* 1/36, 54, 123 etc; 2/11, 23, 24: **II.** adv *not, not at all* 1/169; 6/25; 7/14: see also **lǣs**
nāhte = ne + āhte
nā–hwæðer conj *neither:* **nāhwæðer ne . . . ne** *neither . . . nor* 4/260; 7/20; 14/52
nā–hwār adv *never* 11/302
nalæs, nales = nealles
nalles = nealles
(*ge*)**nam** pret 1 and 3 sg of (*ge*)**niman**
nama m (§14.7) *name* 1/h; 2/22; 7/21 etc; 8/95; 10/131, 182 etc; 11/41 etc; 12/126; 13/103; 14/140; 15/Æ; 16/343; etc
(*ge*)**nāmon** pret pl of (*ge*)**niman**
nān (m acc sg generally **nǣnne**) **I.** pron (with partitive gen) *no one, none* 4/271; 5/25; 9/72; 19/9; 23/68, 233 etc: **II.** adj *no* 4/18, 78; 6/4 etc; 7/35 etc; 8/19 etc; 9/43, 53, 75; 11/76 etc; 12/29 etc; 13/95, 96, 99; 14/104; 18/51
nān–wuht pron (with partitive gen) *nothing* 7/26
(*ge*)**nāp** pret 1 and 3 sg of (*ge*)**nīpan**
nāt = ne + wāt
nāðer, nāðor = nā–hwæðer
nā–wiht = nāht
nāwðer = nā–hwæðer
ne I. adv *not* 1/12; 2/23; etc: **II.** conj *nor*

1/34, 162; etc: **ne . . . ne** *neither . . . nor* 14/51; 20/95

*ge*n**ēadian** I *force, compel* 11/228

nēah I. adj *near* 2/81; 9/12; 24/103: see also **æt: II.** adv *near* 19/26; 22/25: *nearly* 8/27; 23/287: **III.** prep with dat *near* 2/85, 93; 6/36; 4/223

*ge*n**eahhe** adv *frequently, often* 19/56; 21/8/2; 21/26/8; 23/26; 24/269

neahnes(s) f (§14.2) *nearness, proximity* 1/52

neaht = niht

(*ge*)**nēa–lǣcan, –lēcan** I often impers with dat or acc obj *draw near, approach, get close* 1/165; 2/17, 73; 9/27; 10/229; 12/157 etc; 14/5; 23/34, 261

(*ge*)**nēa–lǣhte, –lēhte** pret 1 and 3 sg of (*ge*)**nēa–lǣcan, –lēcan**

(*ge*)**nēa–lǣhton** pret pl of (*ge*)**nēa–lǣcan**

nealles (= **ne** + **ealles**) adv *not, not at all, by no means* 2/9; 15/2864; 16/346; 19/32, 33; 21/26/17: **nales þæt ān** adv *not only* 1/58, 87, 96: *not only that* 10/26

nēar comp adv *nearer* 23/53

nearo adj *anxious, oppressive* 20/7

nearolīce adv *closely, concisely, condensedly* 13/81

nearon = ne + earon

nearones(s), –nis(s) f (§14.2) *anxiety, trouble, vexation* 1/43, 53

nēat n (§13.4) *animal, beast*: pl *cattle* 2/19

*ge*n**ēat** m (§13.2) *companion, retainer* 16/284; 24/310: *attendant, follower* 4/275

nēawest, –wist f (§14.6) *neighborhood, vicinity* 2/76; 4/232: *presence* 9/74

nēd = nīed

nēd–mycel adj *important, urgent* 10/62

nēd–þearf I. sb f (§14.1) *need* 9/49, 60: **II.** adj *necessary* 9/39

need = nēd = nīed

nefne conj *unless* 19/113; 23/52: *except, but* 20/46; 22/22

nēh = nēah

*ge*n**ehe** = *ge*n**eahhe**

nēh–mǣg m (§13.2 footnote 1) *close relative* 9/71, 87

nēh–māgas nom and acc pl of **nēh–mǣg**

nēhst = nīehst

nellað = ne + willað

nel(l)e = ne + wil(l)e

nemnan I *name, call* 1/93, 170; 2/22; 4/123, 254; 7/56; 23/81: *name* 21/57/6

nemne = nefne

nemðe = nefne

nēod = nīed

nēodlīce adv *zealously, assiduously* 1/124

nēosan I with gen obj *go to, visit* 23/68

nēosung f (§14.1) *visitation* 11/2, 132

nēotan 2 with gen obj *make use of, enjoy* 16/401; 24/308

neoðan, neoðone adv *below* 16/375: **under . . . neoðan** *down underneath* 16/311

neowel adj *steep, deep, abysmal* 23/113

Nerfa personal name *Nerva* 11/36

nergan = nerian

Nergend m (§15.5) *the Savior* 15/2864; 23/45 etc

(*ge*)**nerian** I *save, rescue* 1/68, 109, 111; 3/32; 4/204; 5/36; 9/106; 25/63

Nerō personal name *Nero* 11/22

*ge*n**esan** 5 *escape* 10/274

nest n (§13.4) *provisions, food* 23/128

nēten = nīeten

nēðan I *venture* 23/277

nīed f (§14.6) *need, necessity, distress* 1/84; 6/83; 14/140; 23/277: *force, violence* 5/33

nīed–be–þearf adj *necessary, essential* 7/45

nīede adv of *necessity, necessarily* 14/7, 18; 23/287

nīehst I. sup adj *last* 23/73: see also **æt: II.** sup adv *nearest, closest by* 4/99, 145: **III.** prep with dat *nearest* 8/112, 117

nīeten n (§13.5) *beast, animal* 2/57; 10/271; 12/32; 13/79

nigon numeral *nine* 4/264, 284; 10/164; 11/283; etc

nigoða adj *ninth* 12/148

niht f (§15.7) *night* 1/31; 2/20; 4/26, 28 etc; 8/67 etc; 10/258; 12/39 etc; 15/Æ; 16/307; 17/2; 21/29/13; 23/34 etc: *day* 6/63; 11/279: **nihtes** adv (Campbell §627(3) and n 1) (*by*) *night* 4/79, 208; 6/37; 11/144, 178; 23/45 (*at night*)

niht–helm m (§13.2) "*night–helmet,*" *cover of night* 19/96

niht–rest f (§14.2) "*night–rest,*" *couch* (on which one rests at night) 15/2864

niht–scūa m (§14.7) *shadow of night* 19/104; 20/31

*ge***nihtsum** adj *abounding* 11/118

*ge***nihtsumian** II *suffice, be enough for* 1/h: with dat obj 10/241; 11/134

*ge***nihtsumlīce** adv *abundantly, adequately* 11/225

*ge***nihtsumnes(s), –nys(s)** f (§14.2) *abundance* 9/116; 11/135

niht–waco f (§14.1) *night–watch* 20/7

(*ge*)**niman** 4 *take* 4/121; 6/17, 92; 8/117 etc; 10/98, 221; 11/2, 112 etc; 12/98 etc; 15/Æ; 17/60; 23/313: *take up* 4/2, 14, 21 etc: *seize* 1/163; 4/174, 211, 218, 224; 10/7, 10, 159 etc; 15/2930; 22/15; 23/77 etc: *lay hold of* 10/260; 17/30: *carry off, kill* 24/252: *receive* 24/39; 24/71: with dat obj *take on, be adorned with* 20/48 (see n): **niman frið** *make peace* 4/3, 11 etc: **niman sige** *gain the victory, be victorious* 4/22, 28 etc: **niman tō** with dat *make with* 1/36: **niman (tō fulwihte)** *stand sponsor to* (at baptism) 12/133: **niman tō wīfe** *marry* 13/15f

nīo–bed(d) n (§13.6) "*corpse–bed,*" *bed of death* 16/343

nīotan = **nēotan**

(*ge*)**nīpan** 1 *grow dark, darken* 19/96, 104; 20/31

nis = **ne** + **is**

nīð m (§13.2) *wickedness, evil, hatred, malice* 20/75; 23/34 etc: *malicious action* 9/41: *affliction, trouble* 23/287

nīð–heard adj *brave in battle* 23/277

nīð–hycgend m (§13.5) *evil schemer* 23/233

nið(ð)as m pl (§13.6) *men* 21/26/28; 21/57/6; 23/287n

niðer adv *down* 16/343

niðera comp adj (§12.9) *lower* 10/156

nīwan adv *newly, recently* 1/129

nīwe I. adj *new* 1/119, 140; 4/264; 13/8 etc: gen sg used as adv *recently* 22/4: **II.** adv *newly, recently* 10/310

*ge***nīwian** II *renew* 17/148; 19/50, 55; 23/98

nō = **nā**

*ge***nōg, –nōh I.** adj *enough, sufficient, aplenty* 8/101; 17/33: **II.** adv *sufficiently* 14/93

nōht = **nāht**

nō–hwæðer = **nā–hwæðer**

nolde(st) = **ne** + **wolde(st)**

noldon = **ne** + **woldon**

nōm pret 1 and 3 sg of **niman**

noma = **nama**

Noren adj *Norse, Norwegian*: m gen sg **Norna** 6/59

Nor–mand–īg f (§14.2) *Normandy* 6/14, 64 etc

Nor–men = **Norð–men(n)**

norð adv *north, northward* 4/165; 6/18; 8/9, 95: *to the north* 8/3: *in the north* 5/38; 6/30; 16/275

norðan adv *from the north* 8/13; 19/104; 20/31: **be norðan** prep with dat *north of* 4/194; 8/7, 65

Norðan–hymbre m pl (§14.5) *Northumbrians*, also the region they inhabited: *Northumbria* (see 4/2n, 12/128a n) 1/h; 4/4f, 10 etc; 12/3, 8 etc; 24/266

norðerne adj *northern* 5/18

norðe–weard I. adj *the northern part of* 8/58, 59: **II.** adv *in the north* 8/54

Norð–hymbre I. sb = **Norðan–hymbre**: **II.** adj *Northumbrian* 12/12

Norð–hymbrisc adj *Northumbrian* 12/69

Norð–man(n) m (§15.7) *Scandinavian* 5/33, 53: *Norwegian* 6/41, 55: *Norseman* 8/1 etc

norðmest adv *farthest north* 8/2

norðor comp adv *farther north* 8/52

norð–ryhte adv *due north* 8/6 etc

Norð–sǣ m f (§14.5, 6) *the Bristol Channel* 4/165

Norð–wēalas m pl (§13.2) *the Welsh* 4/215 etc

Norð–wēal–cyn(n) n (§13.6) *the people of Wales* 4/195

norð–weard I. adj *northward, north* 8/2: **II.** adv *northward* 6/37

norð–weardes adv *northwards* 5/154

Norð–weg m (§13.2) *Norway* 8/70f

Nor–wege m pl *Norway* 6/30 etc

nos–þyrl n (§13.4, 6) *nostril* 13/93

notian II *use up* 4/159
notu f (§14.1) *employment* 7/50
nō–wiht = **nāht**
nū I. adv *now* 1/38 etc; 2/29 etc; etc: *just now* 1/71: *presently* 11/288: see also **hwīl: II.** conj *now that* 2/85; 9/27, 119; 12/249, 274; 16/404; 24/57, 222, 232, 250: *since* 15/Æ
*ge*numen past pple of (*ge*)**niman**
nȳd = **nīed**
nȳde = **nīede**
nȳd–gyld n (§13.4) *exaction, forced payment* 14/85
nȳd–māge f (§14.7) *near kinswoman* 14/92
nȳd–þearf f (§14.1) *need, necessity* 14/20
nȳhst = **nīehst**
nyllan = **ne** + **willan**
nyman = **niman**
nymðe = **nefne**
nyrwan I *narrow, restrict* 14/38
nys = **nis**
nysse = **ne** + **wisse**
nyste = **ne** + **wiste**
nyten adj *ignorant* 11/80
nȳten = **nīeten**
nytennys(s) f (§14.2) *ignorance* 11/66
nytlic adj *profitable* 9/39
nyt(t) I. sb f (§14.2) *benefit, advantage* 21/26/7: **II.** adj *useful* 1/63
nyt(t)nes(s), –nis(s) f (§14.2) *use, utility* 1/123, 150
nyt–wyrðe adj *useful* 4/261
nyðerian II *abase, bring low, oppress* 23/113: *condemn* 11/64

O

ō = **ā**
od = **oð**
Ōda personal name *Oda* 6/94
of prep with dat **I.** (source, substance) *from, from among, away from, out of, of* 1/33, 138; 2/23, 103; 4/4, 79, 98; etc: **II.** (partitive) *of* 6/17; 10/306; 12/57, 258: *(some) of* 10/157; 12/223, 260, 263: **III.** (temporal) *from* 1/183; 12/116: **IV.** (causal) *on account of, by* 10/76; 22/53: **V.** (reference) *concerning* 8/25
of adv *off, away* 4/266: *therefrom* 4/127; 12/264: *away* 9/75
of–ā–slagen past pple of **of–ā–slēan**
of–ā–slēan 6 *strike off* 12/162 etc
of–dūne adv *down* 23/290; 25/30
ofer prep with acc **I.** (local) *over, across* 4/4, 21 etc; 5/26; 6/80, 91; 8/60, 61; 10/124, 210; 19/24 etc; 22/60; 21/26/9; 21/29/7; 22/7; 23/161; etc: *above* 4/h; 5/15, 19; 10/91, 314; 12/181 etc; 15/Æ; 16/377; 17/91; 21/7/3, 6; 21/44/5; 21/57/2: *upon* 9/115; 10/96, 153, 170, 228 etc; 12/118a n; 13/51; 14/102; 20/39: *throughout* 1/39; 17/12, 82; 18/4: *through* 15/2887: *beyond* 20/58: see also **bæc: II.** (temporal) *after, past* 2/83; 4/48, 90 etc: *throughout* 12/185; 23/28: **III.** (adversative) *in spite of, contrary to, against* 4/142; 17/35; 21/29/10
ofer adv *across* 4/131; 8/72
ōfer m (§13.3) *bank, shore* 24/28
ofer–cōm pret 1 and 3 sg of **ofer–cuman**
ofer–cōman = **ofer–cōmon**
ofer–cōmon pret pl of **ofer–cuman**
ofer–cuman 4 *overcome* 5/72; 23/h, 235
ofer–drencan I *overdrench, oversoak, flood* 23/31
ofer–ēode pret 1 and 3 sg of **ofer–gān**
ofer–faran 6 *pass through, meet with* 6/86
ofer–fēran I *traverse* 6/81; 8/57
ofer–fōron pret pl of **ofer–faran**
ofer–frēosan 2 *freeze over* 8/128
ofer–froren past pple of **ofer–frēosan**
ofer–fyll(u) f (§15.3) *gluttony* 14/149
ofer–gān anom vb (§7.7) *overrun* 24/h
ofer–gietan 5 *forget* 10/86
ofer–hoga m (§14.7) *despiser* 14/115
ofer–hygd n f *pride* 16/328
oferlīce adv *excessively* 14/143
ofer–mēde n *pride* 16/293
ofer–mētto f (§14.1) *pride* 16/332 etc
ofer–mōd I. sb n (§13.4) *great pride, overconfidence* 16/272; 24/89: **II.** adj *proud, insolent* 16/262 etc
ofer–stāh = **ofer–stāg** (pret 1 and 3 sg of **ofer–stīgan**)
ofer–stīgan 1 *surpass* 1/59: *mount above, transcend* 11/214
ofer–swīðan I *overcome* 11/248

ofer–wan(n) pret 1 and 3 sg of **ofer–winnan**

ofer–winnan 3 *overcome, defeat* 12/42; 23/319

ofer–wunnen past pple of **ofer–winnan**

ofet(t) n (§13.5) *fruit* 18/77

ofestlīce = **ofostlīce**

of–faran 6 *overtake* 4/196, 209

of–for–cearf pret 1 and 3 sg of **of–for–ceorfan**

of–for–ceorfan 3 *cut off* 23/h

of–fōron pret pl of **of–faran**

(*ge*)**of(f)rian** II *offer up, sacrifice* 11/188; 13/73 etc; 15/Æ

offrung f (§15.3) *offering, sacrifice* 13/79; 15/Æ

of–geaf pret 1 and 3 sg of **of–giefan**

of–gēafon pret pl of **of–giefan**

of–giefan 5 *leave* 15/2864: *give up, relinquish, abandon* 19/61

of–hrēow pret 1 and 3 sg of **of–hrēowan**

of–hrēowan 2 with gen obj *take pity on* 11/156; 12/262

of–lan(n) pret 1 and 3 sg of **of–linnan**

of–linnan 3 *stop* 10/286

of–longian II *oppress with intense longing* 22/29

ofor = **ofer**

ofost f (§14.1) *haste* 14/5: dat pl used as adv **ofstum** *with haste, speedily* 15/2912; 23/35: **of(e)stum miclum** *with great haste* 15/2931; 23/10, 70

ofostlīce adv *with haste, speedily* 15/2850; 23/150 etc; 24/143

of–rīdan 1 *overtake* 4/86

of–scēat pret 1 and 3 sg of **of–scēotan**

of–scēotan 2 *strike down, pierce to death* 24/77

of–sēon 5 *see, observe* 11/51

of–settan I *oppress, afflict* 11/126

of–slægen past pple of **of–slēan**

of–slagen = **of–slægen**

of–slēan 6 *slay, kill* 1/23, 29, 182 (and n); 3/2 etc; 4/h, 11, 23 etc; 6/19, 41 etc; 8/33; 12/7 etc; 15/Æ; 24/h

of–slegen = **of–slægen** (past pple of **of–slēan**)

of–slōg, of–slōh pret 1 and 3 sg of **of–slēan**

of–slōgon pret pl of **of–slēan**

of–snāð pret 1 and 3 sg of **of–snīðan**

of–snīðan 1 *kill* 15/Æ

of–springc m (§13.2) *offspring, descendants, posterity* 15/Æ

of–stang pret 1 and 3 sg of **of–stingan**

ofste = **ofoste**

of–stingan 3 *stab to death* 3/4

ofstlīce = **ofostlīce**

oft (comp **oftor**, sup **oftost**) adv *often, frequently* 1/h; 2/6; 3/6, 32; 4/55 etc; 5/8; 6/2; 7/18; 9/93; 13/56; 14/42 etc; 17/128; 18/11; etc

Ōht–here personal name *Ohthere* 8/1 etc

Ō–lāf personal name *Olaf* 6/59

ō–leccan I with dat obj *fawn upon, flatter* 16/290

oll n (§13.4) *contempt, scorn* 14/121

ombiht m (§13.3) *servant, attendant* 15/2880

on prep with acc, dat and inst **I.** (local) *on, onto* 1/47, 70, 102, 133, 138 etc; 4/157; 5/35; 8/61; etc: *in, into* 1/53, 148, 163; 2/20, 82; 3/3, 9, 22; 4/2[1], 9, 18; etc: *within* 8/112 etc: *at* 4/27, 116[1] etc; 6/87[2]; 11/286; 17/29; 23/50, 51: *to* 3/11[1]; 16/246n: *among* 4/2[2], 124; 12/17; 14/21; 24/264; 25/23: *upon* 3/11[2]: *from* 11/256; 17/138; 23/314: *at the expense of* 24/129: *for* 9/91; 14/65: *under* 13/10: **II.** (temporal) *on, in, during* 1/44, 134; 2/41, 50; 3/19; 4/7; etc: *at* 4/149; 6/67; 11/56; 16/315: **III.** (comitative) *with* 4/69: **IV.** (adversative) *on, upon, against* 3/12, 13; 4/72, 183, 223; 8/59, 62, 127; 9/86; 10/123; 12/150; 14/117; 16/399; 24/163, 322: **V.** (causal) *by, by means of, with* 1/24; 3/14; 4/204; 9/114; 10/245; 11/18; 12/199, 214: **on þon** adv *thereby* 1/24: **VI.** (manner) *according to, in conformance with, by virtue of* 13/98; 24/38: *in, consisting in* 4/174, 175; 8/4, 36 etc; 7/12; 9/3, 16; 13/80, 98: see also **innan, inne**

on adv *on* 14/92: *inside* 4/137: *upon* 1/160; 9/97

on–ǣlan I *light, kindle* 1/135; 15/2923

on–bærnan I *kindle, fire, inflame* 2/7, 72

on–bēodan 2 *announce, proclaim* 1/26

on–bīdan 1 *wait* 10/27, 148: *await*

10/171: with gen *wait for* 10/77, 80

on–blēot pret 1 and 3 sg of **on–blōtan**

on–blōtan 7 *sacrifice, offer* 15/2934

on–bryrdan I *inspire* 11/13; 23/95

on–bryrdnes(s) f (§14.2) *inspiration* 1/171: *fervor, ardor* 12/116: *feeling, inspiration* 2/5

on–byrigan I with gen obj *taste* 17/114

on–cerran = **on–cierran**

on–cierran I *change, alter* 1/79: *turn* 9/35: *turn aside, be changed* 20/103 (with refl acc)

on–cnāwan 7 *know, recognize* 1/103; 9/11, 99; 11/80, 272; 24/9: *understand* 9/112: *observe, perceive* 15/Æ

on–cnēaw = **on–cnēow** (pret 1 and 3 sg of **on–cnāwan**)

on–cnēow pret 1 and 3 sg of **on–cnāwan**

on–cwæð pret 1 and 3 sg of **on–cweðan**

on–cweðan 5 *reply to, answer* 15/2911; 20/23; 24/245

ond = **and**

ondetta m (§14.7) *one who confesses* or *acknowledges* 1/151

ondettan = **andettan**

ond–git = **and–giet**

ond–long adj *entire* 5/21

on–drǣdan 7 with acc obj and (optional) refl dat *fear* 10/264; 13/7; 15/Æ; 20/105: *dread* 1/106; 9/8f: *be afraid* 10/25, 91, 93f, 94 etc: *be in fear of* 11/127

on–drǣtst pres 2 sg of **on–drǣdan**

on–drēdon pret pl of **on–drǣdan**

on–drysne adj *terrible, awesome* 15/2862n

ond–swarian = **and–swarian**

ond–swaru = **and–swaru**

ond–sworian = **and–swarian**

ond–weard = **and–weard**

ond–wleota, –wlita = **and–wlita**

on–emn prep with dat *close by, beside* 24/184

ōnettan I *hurry* 15/2874; 21/29/11; 23/139 etc: *hurry onward* 20/49 (and n)

on–fangen past pple of **on–fōn**

on–fēng pret 1 and 3 sg of **on–fōn**

on–fēngon pret pl of **on–fōn**

on–findan 3 *discover* 3/10 etc: *perceive* 24/5

on–fōh imper sg of **on–fōn**

on–fōn 7 with gen, dat or acc obj *receive* 1/5, 7, 20 etc; 2/11, 27 etc; 4/106; 10/58, 154, 244; 11/254; 15/2919; 24/110: *accept, adopt* 1/108, 114, 130 etc; 2/53: *gather* 11/307: **onfōn** (**æt fulwihte**) with gen *stand sponsor to (at baptism)* 4/109, 179

on–fongen = **on–fangen** (past pple of **on–fōn**)

on–foran prep with acc *before* 4/206 etc

on–funde pret 1 and 3 sg of **on–findan** (see Campbell §741)

on–fundon pret pl of **on–findan**

on–gan(n) pret 1 and 3 sg of **on–ginnan**

on–gēan I. adv *back again* 11/38; 24/137: *opposite* 8/73: *towards, to meet* 4/100; 6/81; 11/40; 23/165: *in opposition* 16/264: see also **eft**: **II.** prep with dat and acc *to* 6/51: *towards* 11/309: *to meet* 4/155: *against* 4/257, 265; 24/100: *upon* 6/52, 67

on–geat pret 1 and 3 sg of **on–gietan**

on–gēaton pret pl of **on–gietan**

Ongel–cyn(n) = **Angel–cyn(n)**

Ongel–þēod = **Angel–þēod**

on–gemang prep with dat *among* 7/54f

on–gēn = **on–gēan**

on–geotan = **on–gietan**

on–get = **on–geat** (pret 1 and 3 sg of **on–gietan**)

on–gēton = **on–gēaton** (pret pl of **on–gietan**)

on–gieldan 3 *pay a penalty for, be punished for* 16/295: used absolutely *pay for it, atone for it* 25/56

on–gietan 5 *understand, know* 1/5, 30, 73; 7/27; 9/3, 11, 98; 10/104, 198 etc: *perceive* 1/145; 3/10; 9/15, 27; 10/276 etc; 16/334; 17/18; 23/168; 24/84: *recognize* 1/103; 10/106, 116: *realize* 4/236; 6/79; 19/73; 23/238

on–ginnan 3 *begin, proceed* 1/41 etc; 2/27 etc; 4/236; 7/54; 9/91; 10/168; 11/215; 12/45; 13/42; 14/135; 15/2846 etc; 16/275 etc; 17/19 etc; 21/28/11; 22/11; 23/42 etc; 24/12 etc: with refl dat 16/259; 17/65, 67: *attempt, try* 2/8; 10/18

on–gi(o)tan = **on–gietan**

Ongol–þēod = **Angel–þēod**
on–gon(n) = **on–gan(n)** (pret 1 and 3 sg of **on–ginnan**)
on–gunnen past pple of **on–ginnan**
on–gunnon pret pl of **on–ginnan**
on–gyldan = **on–gieldan**
on–gynneð = **on–ginneð**
on–gyrwan I *strip, disrobe* 17/39 (with refl acc)
on–gytan = **on–gietan**
on–gytenis(s) f (§14.2) *understanding, knowledge* 1/167
on–hǣtan I *heat, inflame* 23/87
on–hlīdan 1 *open* 18/12, 49
on–hliden past pple of **on–hlīdan**
on–hrēad pret 1 and 3 sg of **on–hrēodan**
on–hrēodan 2 *adorn* 15/2932
on–hrēran I *stir, move* 20/96
on–hweorfan 3 *change, reverse, transform* 22/23
on–hworfen past pple of **on–hweorfan**
on–hyldan I *incline, lower* 2/97
on–hyrgan I *imitate* 21/8/10
on–innan prep with acc and dat *inside* 16/353: *in among* 23/312
on–lāg = **on–lēah**
on–lēah pret 1 and 3 sg of **on–lēon**
on–lēohtan = **on–līhtan**
on–lēon 1, 2 with gen obj *loan, grant* 16/358; 23/124
on–līcnes(s) f (§14.2) *image, statue* 10/170, 264 etc; 11/243: *likeness, image* 13/57 etc; 16/396: *form* 10/181
on–līhtan I *light up, illuminate* 10/22: *illumine, enlighten* 11/302
on–lūtan 2 *bend down* 7/32
on–lȳsan I *deliver, redeem* 17/147
on–mang prep with dat *among, during*: **onmang þisan** adv *meanwhile, in the meantime* 6/86
on–mēdla = **an–mēdla**
on–munan pret pres vb (§23.3) with gen obj and refl pron (acc) *care for, wish* 3/28
ono = **heonu**
on–rēad pret 1 and 3 sg of **on–rēodan**
on–rēodan 2 *redden* 15/2932n
on–sǣge adj *attacking, assailing* 14/43
on–scungend m (§15.5) *one who shuns, a shunner* 9/73
on–scunigendlic adj *detestable* 9/72ff n
on–scyte m (§14.5) *attack, calumny* 14/56, 126
on–secgan III *offer, sacrifice* 15/2853
on–sendan I *send* 7/62; 10/43, 165; 19/104: *send forth, yield up* 17/49
on–sīen = **an–sīen**
on–slǣpnes(s) f (§14.2) *sleeplessness*
on–slēpan I *fall asleep, sleep* 2/21, 97
on–springan 3 *spring up* 18/63
on–stal(l) m (§13.2) *supply, store* 7/16
on–stealde pret 1 and 3 sg of **on–stellan**
on–stellan I *establish, create* 2/32
on–sund = **an–sund**
on–sȳn I. sb f (§14.6) *lack, want* 18/55: **II.** = **an–sīen**
on–tȳnan I *open* 10/137, 293
on–ufan prep with dat *upon, on top of* 23/252
on–wǣcan I *soften, mollify* 16/403
on–wæcnan 6 *wake up* 19/45; 23/77
on–w(e)ald n (§13.4) *dominion, rule, command* 4/287; 7/4 etc
on–weg adv *away* 1/40; 10/229, 238; 12/231; 19/53; 20/74: see also **cuman**
on–wendan I *turn* 9/34, 101, 104: *divert* 1/82: *take away* 16/431: *derange, distort* 10/9, 13: *change* (for the worse) 16/400; 18/82; 19/107: *transgress* 16/405
on–winnan 3 *attack, invade* 23/h
on–wōcon pret pl of **on–wæcnan**
on–wrāh pret 1 and 3 sg of **on–wrēon**
on–wrēah pret 1 and 3 sg of **on–wrēon**
on–wrēon 1, 2 (§19.3) *reveal, disclose* 1/4, 11, 82; 17/97
on–wrigen past pple of **on–wrēon**
on–wrig(e)nes(s), –nis(s), –nys(s) f (§14.2) *revelation* 1/3, 12, 14 etc; 11/32
on–wrīðan 1 *unwrap* 23/173
on–ȳwan I *show, manifest* 10/111
oo = **ā**
open adj *open* 10/173, 175; 17/47; 18/11
(*ge*)**openian** II *open* 10/34; 11/308f
openlīce adv *openly, plainly* 1/147, 151: *publicly* 11/13, 86
ōr n (§13.4) *beginning, origin* 2/32
orc m (§13.2) *pitcher, cup* 23/18
Orcan–ēg f (§14.2) *Orkney* 6/60

ord m n (§13.2, 4) *point* 16/328n; 24/47 etc: *beginning* 15/2877: *battle–line* 24/69: *front line, van* 24/273
Ord–hēh personal name *Ordheh* 4/202
ōret–mæcg m (§13.2) *warrior* 23/232
orf n (§13.4) *livestock* 13/77
orf–cwealm m (§13.2) *cattle–plague, murrain* 14/45
or–feorme adj with dat *destitute of* 23/271
or–mēte adj *immense, huge* 4/h
or–sāwle adj *lifeless* 23/108
or–sorh adj *without anxiety* 11/135
or–þanc adj *cunning, skilful* 25/2
Ōs–bearn personal name *Osbearn* 4/37
Ōs–bryht personal name *Osbryht* 4/6
Ōs–cytel personal name *Oscytel* 4/72
Ōs–rīc personal name *Osric* 3/20
Ōs–wald, –wold personal name *Oswold* 1/182; 12/2 etc
Ōs–wīg personal name *Oswig* 12/164
oð prep with acc **I.** (local) *up to, as far as* 4/17, 85 etc; 8/58, 89; 10/277; 13/5, 80: **II.** (temporal) *until, to* 1/183; 2/14; 4/39; 7/50; 8/107; 11/292, 325: **oð þis** adv *hitherto* 1/123: **oð þæt, oþ þe** conj *until* 3/3f, 13 etc; 4/168, 191, 219; 6/11 etc; 8/111; 10/77, 157 etc; 12/13 etc; 13/28; 15/2875; 17/26 etc; 19/71 etc; 23/30 etc; 24/278, 324
oð conj *until* 3/2, 11 etc; 5/16; 8/70 etc; 16/340 etc; 18/47; 23/140, 292
oð–bær pret 1 and 3 sg of **oð–beran**
oð–beran 4 *carry off, bear away* 19/81
ōðer I. pron *other* 2/8; 4/200 etc; 9/88; 11/138 etc; 12/74; 14/63, 102; 16/322 etc; 24/64: *another* 7/67; 11/194, 251; 14/12, 50, 53, 55 etc; 24/70, 143, 282; 25/52: *the other* 8/116; 9/106; 14/54, 70, 91: *remainder, rest* 4/76, 92: *one* (of two) 8/128; 24/207: **ōðer . . . ōðer** *one . . . the other* 4/33f, 178; 8/46f: **II.** adj *other* 1/47; 2/62; 4/139 etc; 6/94; 7/21 etc; 8/31 etc; 10/221 etc; 11/205 etc; 13/4: *another* 1/h, 131; 4/183; 7/67; 16/332; 20/h; 23/109: *the other* 8/19, 58 etc; 24/234: *second* 4/288; 8/111: *next* 8/11; 9/14; 10/213; 11/50; 12/25: **ōðer . . . ōðer** *one . . . the other* 1/136; 4/152f
oð–fæstan I *set* 7/49
oð–feallan 7 *fall off, decline* 7/11, 37
oð–rēowon pret pl of **oð–rōwan**
oð–rōwan 7 *row away* 4/278
oððe conj *or, or else* 1/23, 140; etc: **oððe . . . oððe** either . . . or 1/128n; 4/143, 176
oð–þon conj *or* 14/60, 156
oð–þringan 3 *force* (something, acc) *out of* (someone, dat) 20/71; 23/185
oð–wand pret 1 and 3 sg of **oð–windan**
oð–wendan I *alienate* (something, acc) *from* (someone, dat) 16/403
oð–windan 3 *get away, escape* 4/268
ō–wiht I. pron *anything* 1/23, 79, 140; 20/46; 22/23: **II.** adv *at all* 1/66

P

pællen adj *rich, costly; silken* 11/114
Pante f (§14.7) *the R. Pant* (Essex), "now called Blackwater in its lower reaches" (Sweet[15]) 24/68 etc
pāpa m (§14.7) *pope* 1/1; 12/124
papol–stān m (§13.2) *pebble* 11/104
paralisyn Lat acc sg *paralysis, palsy* 12/214
Paulīnus personal name *Paulinus* 1/6 etc
Paulus personal name *Paul*
Paðmas *Patmos* 11/29
Pedrede f (§14.7) *the R. Parret* (Dorset, Somerset) 4/194
Pefnes–ēa f (§14.1) *Pevensey* (Sussex) 6/64
Penda personal name *Penda* 1/182n; 12/150 etc
Peohtas m pl (§13.2) *the Picts* 4/72; 12/106
Pergamum *Pergamon* 11/91
Pētrus personal name *Peter* 12/173; 13/26 etc
plega m (§14.7) *revelry* 8/107, 109: *amusement* 11/47
plegian II *play* 5/52
Pleg–mund personal name *Plegmund* 7/h, 58
pleoh n (§13.5) *danger, peril, responsibility* 13/105
plēolic adj *dangerous, hazardous* 13/6
port m (§13.2) *trading center* 8/65 etc
post m (§13.2) *post* 12/226 etc
prass m (§13.2) *battle array, pomp* 24/68

prēost m (§13.2) *priest* 12/242 etc; 13/21 etc
Pryfet m *Privett* (see 2/4n)
prȳte f (§14.7) *pride* 14/128

R

racente f (§14.7) *chain* 16/372, 434
racu f (§14.1) *account, narrative* 11/7
rād I. sb f (§14.1) *mounted expedition, raid* 4/55: *ride, journey* 12/215: **II.** pret 1 and 3 sg of **rīdan**
*ge***rād** pret 1 and 3 sg of *ge***rīdan**
radost = hraðost
*ge***rǣcan** I *reach, get at* 4/219; 24/142: *obtain, attain* 14/17: *pierce* 24/158, 226
rǣd m (§13.2) *advice* 12/124: *good counsel* 9/102: *plan* 16/286: *good fortune* 16/424: *sense, reason* 23/68, 97
(*ge*)**rǣdan** I *read* 9/61; 11/7; 13/7 etc: *give instruction* 24/18: *decide* 11/35; 24/36: *rule, govern* 16/289
rǣd–bora m (§14.7) *adviser, counsellor* 13/95
rǣding f (§14.1) *reading* 12/75: *passage of scripture* 12/78
*ge***rǣdu** n pl (§13.6) *trappings* 24/190
Rǣd–wald, –wold personal name *Rædwald* 1/4 etc
ræfen = hræfn
ræfnan I *perform* 23/11
rǣran I *raise, lift up, exalt* 2/94; 14/12
rǣsan I *rush, make an attack* 1/h: *rush* 3/12
rǣswa m (§14.7) *leader, chief* 23/12 etc
rǣt = rǣdeð
ram(m) m (§13.2) *ram* 15/2927 etc; 15/Æ
ranc adj *proud, important* 14/93
rand m (§13.2) *shield* 24/20: *shield–boss* 25/37
rand–wiggend m (§15.5) *shield–warrior* 23/188
rāp m (§13.2) *rope* 10/204, 207
rārigan II *wail, lament* 11/153
raðe = hraðe
rēad adj *red* 11/102; 21/26/15; 23/338
Rēadingas m pl (§13.3) *Reading* (Berkshire), lit "the people of *Rēad*(*a*)" (see 4/2n, 12/128a n) 4/26 etc

rēaf n (§13.4) *armor* 24/161
rēafere m (§13.6) *robber, reaver* 14/133
rēafian II *rob, plunder* 14/101
rēaf–lāc n (§13.4) *robbery, rapine, depredation, spoliation* 4/h; 14/46, 145
rēc m *smoke, fume* 16/325
reccan I (pret 3 sg **rōhte**) *care, be concerned* 4/120; 14/105: with gen *be interested in, care about* 24/260
(*ge*)**reccan** I (pret 3 sg (*ge*)**rehte**) *explain, relate, tell* 2/47; 12/33 etc: *explain* 12/65: *interpret* 9/61: *guide, direct* 15/2933n
rēccan = rēocan
recceléas adj *careless, negligent* 7/37
reced n (§13.5) *building, hall* 25/37
*ge***recednis**(**s**) f (§14.2) *narrative* 13/38 etc
recene adv *quickly* 19/112; 23/188; 24/93
*ge***rēfa** m (§14.7) *reeve* 4/h, 274
Regen–here personal name *Regenhere* 1/95
regollec, –lic adj *in accordance with a monastic rule, regular, canonical* 2/70
regollīce adv *according to religious rule, regularly, canonically* 14/51
(*ge*)**rehte** pret 1 and 3 sg of (*ge*)**reccan**
(*ge*)**rehton** pret pl of (*ge*)**reccan**
reliquias m pl *relics* 12/258
rēn m (§13.2) *rain* 18/14
*ge***rēne** n *ornament* 21/26/15
(*ge*)**rēnian** II *set, lay* 9/42: *adorn, ornament* 23/338; 24/161
rēn–scūr m (§13.2) "*rain–shower*," *rainstorm* 11/131
rēocan 2 *reek, smoke, steam* 15/2933; 23/313
(*ge*)**reord** f (§14.1) *voice* 20/53; 21/8/1: *language* 12/65 etc
reord–berend m (§15.5) "*speech–bearer*," *human being, man* 17/3 etc
*ge***reordung** f (§14.1) *meal* 11/48
rest f (§14.2) *rest; bed, couch* 2/20, 82; 17/3; 23/54 etc
(*ge*)**restan** I *rest, repose* 1/31, 47, 78; 2/79: with refl acc 1/31n; 15/2881; 16/434; 17/64; 23/44: *remain* 17/69; 23/321: with gen *find rest from* 22/40
rēðe adj *dire, terrible* 4/h: *cruel, savage*

12/23: *raging* 23/348

*ge***rēðru** n pl *oars* (including the rudder) 4/118

rīce I. sb n (§13.6) *kingdom* 1/h, 88 etc; 2/66; 3/1, 24; 4/1, 50 etc; 7/15 etc; 9/57; 11/319; 12/47 etc; etc: *empire* 11/22: *reign* 1/174, 183: *sovereignty* 1/59: **II.** adj *powerful, mighty* 8/99; 14/93; 15/2846; 17/44, 131; 23/11 etc; 24/36: used as sb 14/145: *rich* 11/118, 131; 12/58

ricene = recene

rīcsian II *reign, rule* 3/33; 4/48; 9/129; 11/21, 222: *hold sway, prevail* 14/10

rīdan 1 *ride* 1/162; 3/20; 4/h, 21, 26 etc; 6/28; 8/118; 12/80 etc; 15/Æ; 24/18 etc: *oppress, chafe* 16/372

*ge***rīdan** 1 *ride* 4/99: *obtain by riding, overrun, conquer* 4/91, 92

ridda m (§14.7) *rider, horseman* 12/212 etc

ridon pret pl of **rīdan**

*ge***ridon** pret pl of *ge***rīdan**

*(ge)***riht I.** sb n (§13.4) *law* 11/292 and n: *what is due* 9/81: *what is right, justice* 14/122, 153; 16/360: *right, privilege* 14/33: **Godes gerihta** *God's dues* 14/21, 23, 30: **mid rihte** adv *rightly* 14/118; 16/424: *fairly, honestly* 14/21: **on gerihte** adv *straight on, directly* 23/202: **II.** adj *right, proper* 9/32, 33, 50 etc; 16/289; 17/89; 23/97; 24/190

*ge***rihtan** I *direct* 17/131: *correct* 13/103, 106

rihte adv *properly, correctly* 24/20: *justly* 14/54

riht–gelēfed adj (past pple) *orthodox, Catholic* 9/55

*ge***riht–lǣcan** I *direct* 12/137

riht–lagu f (§14.1) *right, proper* or *just law* 14/116

rihtlic adj *right, appropriate* 11/234

rihtlīce adv *virtuously* 9/29; 14/157: *justly* 12/22

rīman I *count* 4/55

rīnan I *rain* 1/135

rinc m (§13.2) *warrior, man* 15/2846 etc; 16/286; 23/54 etc; 24/18

rīp n (§13.4) *harvest* 4/233

*ge***rīpan** 1 *reap* 4/232

*ge***risene** n *what is decent or fitting, dignity, honor* 14/33

*ge***risenlece** adv *suitably, appropriately* 1/157

*ge***risenlic** adj *suitable, appropriate* 1/141; 2/2

rīxian = rīcsian

rōd f (§14.1) *cross* 1/8; 10/242; 11/78; 12/17 etc; 17/44 etc

rōde–hengen(n) f (§14.2) *crucifixion* 11/18

roder m (§13.3) *heaven, sky* 15/2912; 18/14; 23/5, 348

rōde–tācn, –tānc n (§13.4) *cross* (as Christian symbol) 10/137, 229, 232, 265: *sign of the cross* 2/96; 11/260

rōf I. sb = **hrōf: II.** adj *strong, brave* 16/286; 23/20 etc

rōhtan = rōhton

rōhton pret pl of **reccan**

Rōm *Rome* 4/64; 12/123 etc

Rōmāne m pl (§14.5) *Romans* 11/22

Rōmānisc adj *Roman*: **þā Rōmāniscan** *the Romans* 12/41

Rōme–burg f (§15.7) *Rome* 12/120

Rōme–byrig dat sg of **Rōme–burg**

rōmigan II with gen obj *strive after, try to obtain* 16/360

rom(m) = ram(m)

rond–wiggend m (§15.5) *shield–warrior* 23/11 etc

rōp adj *liberal, generous* 21/57/3

rōse f (§14.7) *rose* 11/115

rōtlīce adv *cheerfully, merrily* 2/85

rūm I. sb m (§13.2) *opportunity* 23/313: **II.** adj *spacious, extensive, wide* 18/14; 23/348; 25/37

rūme adv *spaciously, roomily* 23/97

rūm–mōd adj *generous* 9/30

rūn f (§14.1) *consultation, council, meditation* 19/111; 23/54

rycene = recene

ryht = riht

ryht–fæderen–cyn(n) n (§13.6) *direct paternal ancestry* 3/34

ryht–norðan–wind m (§13.2) *a wind from due north* 8/14

rȳman I *extend, enlarge, expand* 7/7; 12/104: *open, open up, clear* 17/89;

24/93
rȳmet(t) n (§13.6) *space, room* 4/145
*ge***rȳne** n (§13.6) *mystery* 1/8
rȳpan I *plunder, rob* 14/101
rȳpere m (§13.6) *robber, plunderer* 14/46, 133
*ge***rypon** = *ge***ripon** (pret pl of *ge***rīpan**)

S

sacan 6 *fight, contend* 25/53
sācerd m (§13.3) *priest* 10/177
sacu f (§14.1) *strife* 18/54
sǣ m f (§14.5, 6) *sea* 4/63, 75 etc; 6/8 etc; 8/5 etc; 10/48; 11/59, 104; 12/5 etc; 14/97; 15/Æ; 19/4; 20/14 etc: gen sg **sǣwe** 10/76, 86
sæcc f (§14.1) *battle, strife* 5/4, 42; 23/288
sæd adj with gen *sated with* 5/20
sǣd n (§13.4) *seed* 15/Æ
*ge***sǣd** = *ge***sægd** (past pple of (*ge*)**secgan**)
(*ge*)**sǣde** = (*ge*)**sægde** (pret 1 and 3 sg of (*ge*)**secgan**)
Sæfern f (§14.1) *the R. Severn* 4/191 etc
sǣ–fōr f (§14.1) *sea voyage* 20/42
sǣgan I *lay low, fell* 23/293
sægde pret 1 and 3 sg of **secgan**
sægdon pret pl of **secgan**
sǣl m (§14.5) *time, occasion* 11/90, 226; 12/87; 17/80
sǣlan I *bind, fasten* 19/21; 23/114
sǣ–lida m (§14.7) *seafarer, Viking* 24/45 etc
*ge***sǣlig** adj *blessed* 12/52 etc: *happy* 16/411
*ge***sǣliglic** adj *happy* 7/3f; 16/252
sǣ–mæn = **sǣ–men(n)**
sǣ–man(n) m (§15.7) *seaman, Viking* 14/96; 24/29 etc
sǣ–men(n) dat sg and nom and acc pl of **sǣ–man(n)**
sændan = **sendan**
*ge***sǣne** = *ge***sīene**
sǣ–rima m (§14.7) *"sea–rim," coast* 4/263; 6/10
sǣ–rinc m (§13.2) *sea–warrior, Viking* 24/134
sǣ–strand n (§13.2) *seashore* 11/198
sæt pret 1 and 3 sg of **sittan**
*ge***sæt** pret 1 and 3 sg of *ge***sittan**
sǣtan = **sǣton**
sǣting, sǣtung f (§14.1) *machination, plot* 1/19, 96
sǣton pret pl of **sittan**
*ge***sǣton** pret pl of *ge***sittan**
(*ge*)**saga** imper sg of (*ge*)**secgan**
sāh pret 1 and 3 sg of **sīgan**
sāl m (§13.2) *rope; collar, halter* 16/372 etc
salde = **sealde** (pret 1 and 3 sg of **sellan**)
saldon = **sealdon** (pret pl of **sellan**)
salo–pād adj *dark–coated* 21/57/3
salowig–pāda, saluwig–pāda m (§14.7) *dark–coated one* 5/61; 23/211
sam conj: **sam . . . sam** *whether . . . or* 8/128
same adv: **swā same** adv *in the same fashion, likewise* 7/42; 16/399
(*ge*)**samnian II** *assemble, gather* 1/90, 92; 2/43; 4/153; 8/113
samod adv *at the same time, simultaneously* 1/h, 8; 23/269, 282: *together* 8/93; 11/83, 152 etc; 23/163, 288: *as well* 12/6, 227; 15/Æ: **samod ætgædere** adv *acting in unison* 19/39
sām–worht adj *half–built, half–completed* 4/137
sanct m (§13.2) *saint* 12/173, 180 etc
sand f (§14.1) *course of food, victuals* 12/95
sand–ceosel m *sand* 15/Æ
Sand–wīc n (§13.4) *Sandwich* (Kent) 6/11 etc; 24/h
sang m (§13.2) *song, poem* 2/39, 58; 20/19; 21/57/3
(*ge*)**sang** pret 1 and 3 sg of (*ge*)**singan**
sār I. sb n (§13.4) *pain* 20/95: **II.** adj *sore, grievous, painful* 16/425; 17/80; 19/50; 23/182
sāre adv *sorely, grievously* 17/59; 14/35, 129
sārgian II *wound* 4/278
sārlic adj *sorrowful, doleful* 12/248
sārnys(s) f (§14.2) *pain, agony* 11/319
sār–wracu f (§14.1) *sore suffering* 18/54
Sātan personal name *Satan* 16/345 etc
sāul = **sāwol**
*ge***sawen** past pple of (*ge*)**sēon**
sāwl = **sāwol**
sāwol, sāwul f (§14.1) *soul* 9/22, 76, 106; 10/325; 11/66, 120 etc; 12/160; etc
*ge***sāwon** pret pl of *ge***sēon**

*ge***scæpen** past pple of **scieppan**
scǣron pret pl of **scieran**
scafan 6 *scrape* 12/263
scalde = **sceolden** (see 2/16n)
scamian II impers vb with acc of person *be ashamed, feel shame* 14/119, 125, 126, 135[2]: with gen *be ashamed of* 14/135[1]
scamu f (§14.1) *shame, dishonor* 2/17; 14/80: **tō sceame** adv *shamefully* 12/11
scān pret 1 and 3 sg of **scīnan**
scandlic = **sceandlic**
sceacan 6 *hasten, hurry* 23/291
sceadu f (§14.3) *shadow, darkness* 17/54; 19/h
*ge***scēad–wīsnys(s)** f (§14.2) *discretion* 12/82
scēaf pret 1 and 3 sg of **scūfan**
sceaft m (§13.2) *shaft* 24/136
*ge***sceaft** f (§14.6) *created thing, creature* 5/16; 11/214; 13/45; 14/72 etc: *creation* 17/12 etc: *ordained course* 19/107: *establishment* 25/65
scealc m (§13.2) *man, warrior* 23/230; 24/181
sceal(l) pres 1 and 3 sg of **sculan**
sceamu = **scamu**
sceān = **scān** (pret 1 and 3 sg of **scīnan**)
sceandlic adj *shameful* 14/55 etc
scēap n (§13.4) *sheep* 8/40; 10/145
*ge***sceap** n (§13.4) *creation* 2/60
*ge***sceapen** past pple of **scieppan**
*ge***sceapenis(s)** f (§14.2) *creation* 13/42
sceard adj *gashed, hacked, mutilated* 5/40
scearp adj *sharp* 21/28/2; 23/78
scearpnys(s) f (§14.2) *sharpness, keenness* 11/29f
scēat I. sb m (§13.2) *region, part* 18/3: *garment, cloak* 1/h; 21/44/2: pl with sg meaning *surface* 17/8, 37, 43: *expanse* 20/61, 105: **II.** pret 1 and 3 sg of **scēotan**
sceat(t) m (§13.2) *coin, tribute money* 23/40 etc
scēað f (§14.1) *sheath* 23/79 etc; 24/162
sceaða m (§14.7) *criminal* 11/267: *enemy* 23/193
scēawend–wīse f (§14.7) *the manner of an actor* or *singer* 21/8/9
scēawian II *behold, examine, look at* 9/3, 92, 96; 11/317; 17/137
scēawung f (§14.1) *reconnoitering, examination* 8/28
scencan I *give drink* 15/2907
(*ge*)**scendan** I *confound* 10/227: *insult, shame* 14/91, 100
scēne = **scīne**
Scēo–burg f (§15.7) *Shoebury* (Essex) 4/189
Scēo–byrig dat sg of **Scēo–burg**
sceocca m (§14.7) *demon* 11/172
sceolde pret 1 and 3 sg of **sculan**
sceoldon pret pl of **sculan**
sceolon = **sculon**
(*ge*)**sceōp** pret 1 and 3 sg of (*ge*)**scieppan**
scēot m (§13.2) 25/40 (see n)
scēotan 2 *strike, pierce* 5/19; 24/143: *thrust* 1/166: *shoot* 24/270: *put in, go in* 14/69
scēotend m (§15.5) *shooter, warrior* 23/304
Sceottas = **Scottas**
Scepen = **Scieppend**
*ge***scerian** I *bestow upon, ordain for* 16/258 etc
scēð = **scēað**
sceððan 6 with dat obj *injure* 17/47; 18/39
scield m (§13.2) *shield* 1/h; 5/19; 23/204; 24/98 etc; 25/37
(*ge*)**scieppan** 6 *create, form* 2/33; 9/113; 11/20; 13/43 etc; 16/251 etc; 18/84; 23/347: *design* 4/260
Scieppend m (§15.5) *Creator* 2/27, 34 etc; 9/9; 11/163; 12/244; 19/85; 23/78
scieran 4 *shear, cleave* 23/304
scild = **scield**
scild–burh f (§15.7) *shield–wall* 23/304
scīma m (§14.7) *radiance* 17/54
scīnan 1 *shine* 1/48; 6/7; 11/173, 316; 17/15; 25/49: *be resplendent* 11/93, 96, 115
scinddan = **scyndan**
scīne adj *beautiful, radiant* 11/119; 16/265 etc; 23/316
scip n (§13.4) *ship* 4/84, 95 etc; 6/28 etc; 8/61 etc; 10/49; 14/101; 24/h, 40 etc
scipen f (§14.2) *shed* 2/19
scip–flota m (§14.7) *sailor* 5/11
scip–fyrd f (§14.6) *naval force, fleet* 6/13
scip–here m (§13.6) *naval force, fleet*

4/75, 83 etc; 6/31

scip–hlæst m (§13.2) *"ship–load," ship's crew* 2/76

scipian II *provide with ships* 4/130

scip–rāp m (§13.2) *"ship–rope," cable* 8/30 etc

scīr I. sb f (§14.1) *shire, district, region* 6/51; 8/64; 12/186: *division* (of an army) 4/160: **II.** adj *bright, shining, clear* 17/54; 23/193; 24/98

Scīre–burne f (§14.7) *Sherborne* (Dorset) 4/13

scīren–īge adj *bright–eyed* 21/8/9

Scīrin(c)ges–heal see 8/66n

scīr–mǣled adj (past pple) *brightly adorned* 23/230

Scittisc = **Scyttysc**

scōf pret 1 and 3 sg of **scafan**

scōl f (§14.1) *quarter* 4/65

scoldan = **scoldon**

scolde pret 1 and 3 sg of **sculan**

scoldon pret pl of **sculan**

scomu = **scamu**

Scōn–ēg f (§14.2) *Skåne* 8/85

(*ge*)**scōp** pret 1 and 3 sg of (*ge*)**scieppan**

scop–gereord n (§13.4) *language of poets, poetic language* 2/4

scorian I *refuse* 11/245

scoten past pple of **scēotan**

Scot–land n (§13.4) *Scotland* 6/20; 12/5 etc

Scottas m pl (§13.2) *the Scots* 4/118, 124; 5/11 etc; 6/20; 12/106

scrīfan 1 *have regard to, be concerned about* 14/71

scrīn n (§13.4) *shrine, reliquary* 12/172 etc

scrīðan 1 *glide* 25/13, 40

scrūd n (§13.4, and see Campbell §622, note 2) *garment* 11/136

scūfan 2 *shove, thrust* 24/136

sculan pret–pres vb (§23.3) *shall, be going to, be about to, be assumed to, have to, ought to, be supposed to, must* 1/86 etc; 2/16 etc; etc

scūr m (§13.2) *shower* 20/17; 23/79 etc; 25/40

scylan = **sculan**

scyld = **scield**

(*ge*)**scyldan** I *shield, protect* 1/h, 19

scyld–burh f (§15.7) *shield–wall* 24/242

*ge***scyldnys(s)** f (§14.2) *protection* 11/25f

scyle pres subjunc sg of **sculan**

scylun = **scylen**

scylen pres subjunc pl of **sculan**

scyndan I *hasten to an end* 9/120, 124

scȳne = **scīne**

scyp = **scip**

Scyppend = **Scieppend**

*ge***scyrian** = *ge***scerian**

*ge***scyrpan** I *equip, outfit, accouter* 1/164

*ge***scyrpla** m (§14.7) *clothing, garments* 9/78

Scyttysc adj *Scottish* 5/19: *the Scottish language* 12/67

sĕ̄ m, **þæt** n, **sēo** f, dem pron and def art (§9.1, 2) *that, the*: personal pron *he, she, it, that*: rel pron (§9.4) *who, which*: see also **æfter, mid, tō**

*ge***seah** pret 1 and 3 sg of *ge***sēon**

(*ge*)**seald** past pple of (*ge*)**sellan**

(*ge*)**sealde** pret 1 and 3 sg of (*ge*)**sellan**

(*ge*)**sealdon** pret pl of (*ge*)**sellan**

sealm m (§13.2) *psalm* 12/78

sealt I. sb n (§13.4) *salt* 25/45: **II.** adj *salt, salty, corrosive* 10/270

sealt–ȳð f (§14.2) *salt sea–wave* 20/35

Sēal–wudu, –wydu m (§15.2) *Selwood* (Somerset) 4/100 etc

seara–cræft m (§13.3) *fraud, treachery* 14/109

sēarian II *grow sear, wither, fade* 20/89

searo n (§13.6) *skill, art, contrivance*: *snare* 9/42: dat pl used as adv *cunningly, skilfully* 21/29/6

searo–þoncel, –þoncol adj *wise, cunning* 23/145 etc

searwum dat pl of **searo**

sēað m (§15.2) *pit* 17/75: *cistern* 10/124–5n

Seaxan, Seaxe m pl (§14.7, 5) *the Saxons* 5/70; 8/75

seaxs n (§13.4) *knife* (a single–edged knife varying in length from 3″ to 2′ 6″) 21/26/6

(*ge*)**sēc(e)an** I *seek, set out for, look for* 1/147, 153; 4/146 etc; 7/10; 10/182, 195 etc; 17/133; 19/25, 114; 20/h; 22/9; 23/96; 24/193: *seek out* 1/18; 11/278: *attack* 1/26; 4/8: *visit, go to,* *come to* 4/h; 5/27, 55 etc; 8/36; 12/237; 16/302, 332, 406; 17/104, 119, 127; 20/38; 23/14; 24/222; 25/44: *look for, commit* 16/263: *invade* 5/71: *sink to, fall to* 24/287

secg m (§13.6) *man, retainer* 5/13 etc; 17/59; 19/53; 20/56; 23/201; 24/159 etc

(*ge*)**secgan** III *say, tell* 1/h, 31, 52, 81 etc; 2/41, 44; 4/186; 5/68; 6/14; 8/1 etc; etc: *relate* 20/2: *speak* 9/23: *recite* 9/61: **segð** *it says, it tells* 10/1, 3, 6: **(ge)secgan þanc(as)** with dat and gen *give thanks* to (someone) for (something) 9/127; 12/118a n; 15/2934f; 24/120, 147f: similarly **secgan wuldor** 23/341f: see also *ge***hīeran**

secggan = **secgan**

sefa m (§14.7) *mind, spirit, heart* 19/57; 20/51

sēfte comp adv *more comfortably* 16/433 (see n)

sēft–ēadig adj *blessed with comfort* 20/56n

sege imper sg of **secgan**

segel–gyrd f (§14.2) *sailyard* 25/25

*ge***segen** past pple of (*ge*)**sēon**

segeð pres 3 sg of **secgan**

segl m n (§13.2, 4) *sail* 8/83

seglan = **siglan**

*ge***seglian** = *ge***siglan**

*ge***segnian** II *sign, cross* 2/96, 102

segð pres 3 sg of **secgan**

*ge***seh** = *ge***seah** (pret 1 and 3 sg of *ge***sēon**)

*ge***selda** m (§14.7) *one who lives in the same hall, a comrade, companion* 19/53

seldon adv *seldom, rarely* 12/80

sele imper sg of **sellan**

sele–drēam m (§13.2) *"hall–joy," festivity in the hall* 19/93

sele–drēorig adj *sad for want of a hall, homesick* 19/25

sele–secg m (§13.6) *"hall–warrior," retainer* 19/34

sēlest sup adj (§12.10) *best* 1/h, 42, 100; 4/249; 17/27 etc

self I. pron *self, himself, herself, itself, myself, yourself, ourselves, themselves; own* 1/h, 100, 158 etc; 2/46, 102 etc; 4/5, 68 etc; 7/20 etc; 8/26 etc; 12/22 etc; 13/32 etc; 15/2853; 15/Æ; 16/341; etc: **II.** adj *same, very* 1/33, 147, 148; 2/59; 10/91, 288

(*ge*)**sellan** I *give* 1/52, 56 etc; 4/66, 67 etc; 7/19; 10/7, 64 etc; 11/138 etc; 12/96 etc; 13/55; 24/38 etc: *give up* 1/88; 24/184: *deliver* 1/37; 10/19: *sell* 11/87; 13/65, 66; 14/36, 66 etc: *devote* 14/36, 66 etc: see also **hand**

sēlra comp adj (§12.10) *better* 9/5: *happier* 9/63

*ge***sēman** I *decide the terms between, reconcile* 24/60

semninga adv *suddenly* 1/h, 44, 72

(*ge*)**sendan** I *send* 1/h, 1, 22; 10/28, 145 etc; 11/312; 12/48 etc; 19/56; 20/h; 23/190; 24/29 etc; 25/9: *put* 10/204, 207 etc: *cast* 10/2, 11; 23/224; 24/134: imper sg **sænd** 10/266

*ge***sēne** = *ge***sīene**

sēo see **sē** (§9.2)

seofan–wintre adj *seven years old*

seofen = **seofon**

seofian II *lament, moan, sigh* 20/10

seofon numeral *seven* 1/182n; 5/30; 8/31 etc; 10/135; 173 etc; 11/279

seofon–niht f (§15.7) *"sennight," week* 6/7

seofon–nihte adj *lasting seven days, a week's* 4/121; 11/279n

seofon–tēone numeral *seventeen* 1/182n

seofoða adj *seventh* 4/99

*ge***seoh** imper sg of *ge***sēon**

sēoles gen sg of **seolh**

seolf = **self**

seolfor n (§13.4) *silver* 12/173; 13/71 etc; 17/77

seolh m (§13.2) *seal* 8/43, 47

seomian II *abide, remain* 18/19: *hang* 25/25

sēon 5 *see* 2/103; 4/h; 6/4; 8/72: *look* 9/97: past pple **gesawen, gesegen, gesewen** (used impersonally with dat in passive constructions) *seems, appears* 1/119, 132; 2/46 1/119, 132; 2/46

*ge***sēon** 5 *see, observe, perceive* 1/h, 6; 2/17 etc; 6/5; 7/23 etc; 8/26; 9/11, 68 etc; 10/34, 169 etc; 11/92, 98 etc; 12/158; etc: with refl dat 15/2927:

consider 1/129: *behold* 10/113, 150: *catch sight of* 10/193

sēoðan 2 *seethe, boil; afflict, torment* 1/44

seoððan = **siððan**

*ge***seowen** past pple of **sēon**

set n (§13.4) *encampment* 4/152 etc

*ge***set** n (§13.4) *seat, habitation* 25/66: **symbla gesetu** *banqueting–halls* 19/93

(*ge*)**seten** past pple of (*ge*)**sittan**

setl n (§13.4) *sitting place, seat* 1/50; 5/17: *abode, residence* 16/411: *see* 1/1

*ge***setnys(s)** f (§14.2) *decree* 11/36; 13/97, 98: *account, narrative* 11/215, 220: *foundation* 12/86

(*ge*)**set(t)** past pple of (*ge*)**settan**

settan I *set, place, put* 1/h, 69, 102; 6/89; 10/96, 153 etc; 11/302; 16/312; 21/26/4: *set up* 12/163: *situate* 1/85; 2/14: *ordain* 13/33: *set down* 11/47: *compose, write* 11/225; 13/81: *establish, decree* 11/119; 13/10, 94

*ge***settan** I *set, place* 17/67: *settle* 2/21: *seat* 17/141: *ordain* 9/h; 10/307; *establish* 15/252; 18/10: *compose* 2/101; 11/210: *people* 16/364, 396

*ge***setton** pret pl of *ge***settan**

seðel = **setl**

*ge***sewen** past pple of **sēon**

sex = **siex**

sī = **sīe**

sib(b) f (§14.2) *peace* 7/6; 9/31, 116, 121; 10/30: *friendship, love* 15/2922: *relationship* 11/4

*ge***sib(b)** adj *near, close, familiar* 21/26/22: used as sb *kinsman, relative* 14/49

siblec adj *peaceful* 9/50

sib–leger n (§13.4) *incest* 14/111

sibling m (§13.3) *relative* 13/18

*ge***sīcclian** II *be taken ill* 12/205

sīd adj *ample, wide, spacious* 23/337

sīde I. sb f (§14.7) *side* 17/49: **II.** adv *widely* 17/81: see also **wīde**

Sidroc personal name *Sidroc* 4/37

sīe pres subjunc sg of **wesan** (§7.2)

*ge***sīe** pres 1 sg of *ge***sēon**

sīen pres subjunc pl of **wesan** (§7.2)

siendon = **sindon**

*ge***sīene** adj *visible* 17/46; 25/1: *evident* 14/42 etc

siex numeral *six* 1/182n, 183; 4/262 etc; 8/33 etc; 11/10

sīgan I *sink* 5/17

sige m (§14.5) *victory* 4/22, 28 etc; 12/26: *success* 4/44: see also **niman**

sige–bēam m (§13.2) *"victory–tree," cross* 17/13 etc

Sige–bryht personal name *Sigebryht* 3/1 etc

sige–fæst adj *victorious, triumphant* 21/26/19

sige–folc n (§13.4) *victorious people* 23/152; 25/66

sigelan = **siglan**

sige–lēas adj *without victory, defeated* 14/88; 16/312

Sigen f (§14.1) *the R. Seine* 4/246

sige–rōf adj *victorious* 23/177

sige–þūf m (§13.2) *"victory–standard," triumphant banner* 23/201

sige–wong m (§13.2) *field of victory* 18/33; 23/294

siglan I *sail* 4/83; 8/13 etc

*ge***siglan** I *get by sailing* 8/11 etc

sigor m (§13.3) *victory* 17/67; 23/89 etc

sigor–fæst adj *victorious* 17/150

sigor–lēan n (§13.4) *reward of victory* 15/2919; 23/244

*ge***sihst** pres 2 sg of *ge***sēon**

*ge***sihð I.** sb f *sight* 2/100; 9/29; 10/154, 199 etc; 11/55, 123 etc; 17/41 etc: *vision* 17/21, 96: **II.** pres 3 sg of *ge***sēon**

silf = **self**

Sillende see 8/73n

sim(b)le adv *always, constantly, continuously, at every opportunity* 3/17; 4/150; 8/52; 10/13, 26, 187; 11/193 etc; 12/73; 13/79f; 16/316; 20/68: *ever* 11/15; 18/76

sīn possessive adj (§10.8) *his, her, their* 15/2863 etc; 16/295 etc; 23/29 etc

sinc n (§13.4) *treasure* 17/23; 19/25; 23/30 etc; 24/59; 25/10

sin–caldu f (§14.1) *perpetual cold* 18/17

sinc–gyfa m (§14.7) *treasure–giver* 24/278

sinc–þegu f (§14.1) *treasure–receiving* 19/34

sind pres pl of **wesan** (§7.2)

sinder n *impurity* (in a metal), *dross* 21/26/6
sindon pres pl of **wesan** (§7.2)
sin–gāl adj *continuous, perpetual* 12/111
sin–gālīce adv *continually, incessantly, perpetually* 14/100
(*ge*)**singan** 3 *sing* 2/13, 59 etc; 10/31, 139; 11/293; 20/22, 54; 21/7/8; 21/8/2; 23/211; 24/284
sin–sorg f (§14.1) *perpetual sorrow* 22/45
sint = **sind** (pres pl of **wesan** (§7.2))
sīo = **sēo**
siodo m (§15.2) *morality* 7/6
siolh = **seolh**
*ge***sīon** = *ge***sēon**
sittan 5 *sit* 1/h, 40, 47 etc; 4/136 etc; 10/52, 139 etc; 12/87 etc; 14/79; 16/260 etc; 21/8/8; 22/37 etc; 23/15 etc: *stay, remain encamped* 4/20, 74 etc: **sittan on** *oppress, weigh on* 14/16, 79
*ge***sittan** 5 *sit* 19/111: *sit down* 10/73, 170: *settle, remain* 4/64: *occupy* 4/91, 115: *sit out, finish* 4/159: *encamp* 4/113
sīð I. sb m (§13.2) *time* 1/24, 61; 4/153 etc; 16/319; 18/69; 23/73 etc: *journey* 4/131; 10/48; 15/2860; 20/51; 21/29/14; 23/145: *movement* 16/378: *experience, trial* 20/2: *lot, plight* 22/2: **II.** adv *late, tardily* 23/275: **III.** comp adv (§24.5) later: **sīð ond ǣr** *always* 15/2935
*ge***sīð** m (§13.2) *comrade, companion* 23/201; 25/14
sīð–fæt, –fat n (§13.4) *journey* 10/45: *expedition* 17/150; 23/335
sīðian II *travel, journey* 12/6 etc; 15/2869; 17/68; 21/26/11; 24/177 etc
siðða = **siððan**
siððan I. adv *afterwards* 4/147; 6/15, 95; 8/55 etc; 9/73; 11/15 etc; 12/25 etc; 13/54; 14/61 etc; 15/Æ; 20/78; 21/26/2 etc; 21/29/13; 23/114; 25/58: *subsequently* 6/80; 7/51: see also **eft**: **II.** conj *after* 1/177; 9/75; 7/42, 59; 15/2854 etc; 15/Æ; 17/3, 49, 71; 23/160, 168 etc: *from the time when* 5/13: *once* 9/73: *since* 5/69; 7/19; 10/243, 248; 14/32n; 19/22; 20/h; 22/3: see also **sōna**
six = **siex**
sixtig numeral *sixty*
*ge***slægen** past pple of (*ge*)**slēan**
slǣp m (§13.2) *sleep* 2/38; 11/49; 12/38 etc; 18/56; 19/39; 23/247: **weorðan on slǣpe** *fall asleep* 12/217
slǣpan 7 *sleep* 1/47, 48; 2/38; 10/90, 97, 98 etc
slāt pret 1 and 3 sg of **slītan**
slēan 6 *strike* 23/103 etc; 24/117, 163, 285: *slay, kill* 1/94, 182n; 6/56; 12/11; 15/2914; 23/31: *pitch* 12/180: *forge* 16/383
*ge***slēan** 6 *obtain by striking, strike out, win, achieve* 5/4: **geslēan wæl** *make a slaughter* 4/10, 30; 6/40, 69
slege m (§14.5) *slaying, death* 1/97; 9/122; 12/16
slege–fǣge adj *death–doomed* 23/247
*ge***slegen** past pple of (*ge*)**slēan**
slēp pret 1 and 3 sg of **slǣpan**
slēpon pret pl of **slǣpan**
slītan 1 *slit, tear, rend* 20/11
slīðen adj *cruel, fierce, harsh* 19/30
slīð–heard adj *cruelly hard* 16/378
slōgon pret pl of **slēan**
*ge***slōgon** pret pl of *ge***slēan**
slōg pret 1 and 3 sg of **slēan**
slōh pret 1 and 3 sg of **slēan**
smæl adj *narrow* 8/48, 52
smalost sup adj *narrowest* 8/54
smēade pret 1 and 3 sg of **smēagan**
smēagan II *think* 12/45; 14/11: *examine* 14/138: *meditate on* 1/h: *ponder* 1/100; 9/28
smēagung f (§14.1) *thought, contemplation* 11/60
smið m (§13.2) *smith, craftsman* 21/26/14
smiððe f (§14.7) *"smithy," a goldsmith's or jeweller's workshop* 11/107
smolt adj *mild, gentle* 2/87
smylte adj *tranquil, calm, serene* 2/99; 18/33
smyltnes(s) f (§14.2) *tranquillity, serenity* 9/115; 10/93
snac(c) m *small vessel* 6/16–21n
snāð pret 1 and 3 sg of **snīðan**
snāw m (§13.6) *snow* 18/14; 19/48
snel(l) adj *bold, keen* 23/199; 24/29
snīðan 1 *cut* 21/26/6

snīwan I *snow* 1/135; 20/31
Snotenga–hām m (§13.2) *Nottingham* (Nottinghamshire) 4/14 etc
snot(t)er, snot(t)or adj *wise, discerning* 9/2; 19/111; 23/55 etc; 25/11 etc
snūde adv *quickly, at once* 23/55 etc
snytru f (§14.1) *wisdom* 1/158
soden past pple of **sēoðan**
sōfte adv *easily* 24/59
sōhtan = **sōhton**
(*ge*)**sōhte** pret 1 and 3 sg of (*ge*)**sēcan**
(*ge*)**sōhton** pret pl of (*ge*)**sēcan**
*ge***sōhtun** = *ge***sōhton**
somed = **samod**
*ge***somnian** = *ge***samnian**
*ge***somnung** f (§14.1) *company, assembly* 2/55
somnunga adv *immediately* 10/179
somod = **samod**
sōna adv *immediately, at once, straightway* 1/h, 13, 103, 138 etc; 2/27; 4/h, 122 etc; 6/8; 7/35; 9/72; 12/17 etc; etc: **sōna siððan** conj *immediately after* 1/88f: **sōna** (. . .) **swā** conj *as soon as* 4/181; 12/46, 210: **sōna swā . . . swā** *as soon as . . . then* 4/181f: **sōna þæs** (**þe**) conj *as soon as* 1/165, 178; 6/65
song = **sang**
song–cræft m (§13.2) *art of song* 2/11
sorg f (§14.1) *sorrow, care, anxiety* 1/79; 16/364; 17/20 etc; 18/56; 19/30, 39, 50; 20/42, 54; 23/88 etc
sorgian II *sorrow, grieve* 1/75; 16/347
sorh–lēoð n (§13.4) *"sorrow song," dirge* 17/67
sōð I. sb n (§13.4) *truth* 1/57, 147 etc; 8/26; 14/147; 25/10: **ful sōð** adv *very truly* 13/13: **for sōð, tō sōðe** adv *in truth, for a fact* 19/11; 25/64: **II.** adj *true* 1/158, 167, 171: 9/5, 31; 11/73 etc; 12/82 etc; 13/59; 14/5, 30 etc; 15/2919; 21/26/22; 23/89 etc: **tō sōðan** adv *truly, truthfully, as a fact* 6/14
sōð–cyning m (§13.3) *king of truth, God* 15/2895
sōð–fæstnys(s) f (§14.2) *truth* 11/303
sōð–gied(d) n (§13.6) *a true song* or *tale* 20/1
sōðlīce adv *truly, really, certainly, indeed* 1/62; 9/33; 10/84, 296, 333; 11/66 etc; 15/Æ: *frankly* 1/122: *literally* 13/44, 92
*ge***spæc** = *ge***spræc** (pret 1 and 3 sg of *ge***sprecan**)
spǣcan = **sprǣcon** (pret pl of **sprecan**)
spǣtan I *spit* 10/128
spanan 6 *urge, persuade, entice* 16/274
sparian II *spare* 23/233
spearca m (§14.7) *spark* 12/229
spearwa m (§14.7) *sparrow* 1/136
specan = **sprecan**
spēd f (§14.6) *wealth, means* 7/49; 8/104: *riches* 8/35, 121; 11/62, 99 etc
spēdan I *be prosperous, be wealthy* 24/34
spēd–dropa m (§14.7) *useful drop* 21/26/8
spēdig adj *prosperous* 8/35: *abounding in* 18/10: *successful* 17/151
spel(l) n (§13.4) *story, narrative, history* 2/47, 56 etc; 8/24: *homily* 9/1n: *message* 24/50
spēonon pret pl of **spanan**
(*ge*)**spēow** pret 1 and 3 sg of (*ge*)**spōwan**
spere n (§14.5) *spear* 1/163, 166; 24/109: *spearhead* 24/137
spillan I *destroy* 24/34
*ge***spong** n (§13.4) *joining, fastening, clasp, buckle* 16/377
spor n (§13.4) *track, trail* 7/31
(*ge*)**spōwan** 7 impers vb with dat *prosper, succeed* 7/7; 23/175 etc
spræc pret 1 and 3 sg of **sprecan**
sprǣc f (§14.1) *speech, utterance* 1/132; 12/68; 13/74, 85; 15/2911
sprǣcan = **sprǣcon**
sprǣcon pret pl of **sprecan**
*ge***sprǣcon** pret pl of *ge***sprecan**
sprang pret 1 and 3 sg of **springan**
*ge***sprec** n (§13.4) *speech, words* 1/56: *discussion, conversation* 1/71, 115 etc
sprecan 5 *speak* 1/h, 62, 69, 72 etc; 2/25, 75 etc; 4/129 etc; etc: *utter* 19/70
*ge***sprecan** 5 *speak* 16/271: *agree* 6/33, 46
*ge***sprecen** past pple of (*ge*)**sprecan**
sprengan I *cause to spring* or *quiver* 24/137
spric(e)ð = **sprec(e)ð**
springan 3 *spring* 24/137
spyri(ge)an I *follow the track* 7/30: *make a track, travel* 21/26/8

staca m (§14.7) *stake* 12/166
Stacteus personal name *Stacteus* 11/169 etc
stæde–fæst = **stede–fæst**
stæf m (§13.2) *letter, writing* 2/4
stǣlan I *institute* 25/54
*ge***stǣlan** I *accuse* (someone, dat) *of* (something, acc) 16/391
stæl–giest m (§14.5) *thieving stranger* 21/47/5
stæl–here m (§13.6) *marauding band* 4/256
stæl–hrān m (§13.2) *decoy reindeer* 8/37
stæl–wyrðe adj *serviceable* 4/240
stǣnen(n) adj *stone, made of stone* 1/179; 10/264 etc; 11/10
stǣr n (§13.6) *history* 2/56, 60
stæð n (§13.4) *bank, shore* 4/197; 24/25: dat sg **staðe** 8/93
stafas nom and acc pl of **stæf**
*ge***stāh** pret 1 and 3 sg of *ge***stīgan**
stalu f (§14.1) *stealing, theft* 14/45, 108
stān m (§13.2) *stone, rock* 1/41, 47; 17/66: *gem* 11/79, 198
Stān m (§13.2) *Folkestone* (Kent) 24/h
stān–clif n (§13.4) *rocky cliff, crag* 18/22; 20/23
standan 6 *stand* 2/21; 4/265; 7/24; 8/75 etc; 9/36; 10/170 etc; 12/31 etc; 15/2923 etc; 17/7 etc; 18/22 etc; 19/74; etc: *last, endure* 20/67 and n: *shine* 4/127; 12/184: with dat *come to* 11/125
*ge***standan** 6 *stand, take up one's stand* 10/222; 15/2899; 17/63 (with refl dat); 24/171
Stān–ford–brycg f (§14.2) *Stamfordbridge* (Yorkshire) 6/50
stang pret 1 and 3 sg of **stingan**
stan–hleoð, –hlið n (§13.4) *rocky slope* 19/101; 22/48
starian II *stare, gaze* 23/179
stað = **stæð**
staðel = **staðol**
(*ge*)**staðelian** II *establish, fix* 9/51, 109; 10/48; 20/104: *confirm, make steadfast* 20/108
staðol m (§13.3) *(fixed) position, foundation* 17/71; 20/109; 21/47/5
*ge***steal(l)** m (§13.2) *foundation, frame, framework* 19/110
stēam m (§13.2) *moisture, blood* 17/62
stēap adj *steep* 15/2854 etc; 17/22: *tall* 23/17: *protruding* 25/23
stearn m (§13.2) *tern* 20/23
stēda m (§14.7) *stallion* 1/163
stede m (§14.5) *place* 12/237; 16/356: *position* 24/19: *situation, site* 21/44/3
stede–fæst adj *steadfast, firm* 24/127
stede–heard adj *"socket–hard," with a socket of hard iron* 23/223 (see n)
stefn I. sb f (§14.1) *voice* 10/22, 24, 189 etc; 11/239, 277; 12/248; 15/2849 etc; 17/71; 21/8/7: **II.** sb m (§13.2) *term of service* 4/159: **III.** sb m (§13.2) *root* 17/30
stefna m (§14.7) *prow* 5/34; 20/7
stemn = **stefn I.** and **II.**
stemnettan I *stand firm* 24/122
stem(n)ing f (§14.1) *term of service* 4/159n
stenc m (§14.5) *fragrance, scent* 18/8, 81: *smell, stench* 11/177
stent pres 3 sg of **standan**
stēor–bord n (§13.4) *starboard* 8/8 etc
steorfa m (§14.7) *pestilence* 14/45
steorra m (§14.7) *star* 4/125, 126; 6/5 etc; 15/Æ; 16/256
stēor–rēðra m (§14.7) *helmsman, captain* 10/55, 73, 106
steppan 6 *step, go, advance, march* 11/42; 21/26/10; 23/39 etc; 24/8 etc
sterced–ferhð adj *stout–hearted, determined, resolute* 23/55 etc
stician II *stick* 1/166
(*ge*)**stīeran** I *steer, control* 20/109: *restrain* (someone, dat) *from* (something, gen) 23/60
*ge***stīgan** 1 *climb, mount, ascend* 15/2854 etc; 17/34 etc
Stīgand personal name *Stigand* 6/92
stihtan I *incite, exhort* 24/126
*ge***stillan** I *grow still* 10/93
stille I. adj *still, motionless, silent* 15/2910: **II.** adv *silently* 15/2910: *motionlessly* 21/8/7
stilnes(s) f (§14.2) *peace* 7/48: *tranquillity* 2/97
stincan 3 *rise up* 21/29/12
stingan 3 *stab, pierce* 24/138

stīð adj *hard, harsh, cruel* 6/91; 24/301: *firm, strong* 20/104; 21/44/3: *stern* 15/2849: *severe* 13/76
stīð–hycgende adj (pres pple) *firm of purpose, resolute* 24/122
stīð–hȳdig adj *firm–minded, resolute* 15/2897
stīðlīce adv *sternly, harshly* 24/25
stīð–mōd adj *resolute, unflinching* 17/40: *stern* 23/25
stoc(c) m (§13.2) *stake* 12/260
stōd pret 1 and 3 sg of **standan**
*ge***stōd** pret 1 and 3 sg of *ge***standan**
stōd–hors n (§13.4) *"stud–horse," stallion* 1/160
stōdon pret pl of **standan**
*ge***stōdon** pret pl of *ge***standan**
stōl m (§13.2) *throne* 16/260 etc
stonc pret 1 and 3 sg of **stincan**
stondan = **standan**
stōp pret 1 and 3 sg of **steppan**
stōpon pret pl of **steppan**
storm m (§13.2) *storm* 1/137; 19/101; 20/23; 22/48
stōw f (§14.3) *place* 1/17, 169; 2/79; 7/28 etc; 8/4 etc; 10/111, 169 etc; 12/40 etc; 13/81; 15/2900; 15/Æ: *religious foundation* 7/39; 14/64
Stræcled–wālas m pl (§ 13.2) *the Britons of Strathclyde* 4/72
strǣl m (§13.2) *arrow* 17/62; 23/223: *goad, provocation* (?) 10/186
strǣt f (§14.1 or uninflected) 11/51; 12/92
strand m (§13.2) *shore* 11/104; 12/174
strang adj *strong, powerful, vigorous* 1/129; 11/125; 17/30 etc: *mighty* 14/89; 15/2900; 16/284; 21/47/5: *violent* 9/41: *headstrong* 20/109
(*ge*)**strangian** II *strengthen, comfort* 10/24f, 245, 250: *confirm* 10/320, 328
strēam m (§13.2) *stream* 24/68; 25/23: *water, sea* 20/34; 23/348: *liquid* 21/26/10
strēgan I *strew, spread* 20/97
strenglic adj *strong, firm* 16/273
strengu f (§14.1) *strength, power, force* 21/7/5
*ge***strēon** n (§13.4) *treasure* 9/69, 84; 21/28/3: *wealth* 11/53: *riches* 8/119
strīc n *plague* (?), *strife* (?) 14/45
strīð m (§13.2) *fight, battle* 16/284
strong = **strang**
stronglic adj *strong, firm* 16/366
strūdung f (§14.1) *robbery, spoliation* 14/108
*ge***strȳnan** I *acquire, get* 11/300, 307
stund f (§14.1) *a time, while, moment* 24/271
Stūr–mere m (§14.5) *Sturmer* (Essex) 24/249
stycce–mǣlum adv *here and there* 8/4
styde = **stede**
styng m (§14.5) *thrust* 1/h
stynt pres 3 sg of **standan**
*ge***stȳran** = *ge***stīeran**
styrman I *storm, rage* 1/135; 23/25: *cry out* 21/8/7; 23/223
styrn–mōd adj *stern–hearted* 23/227
sub–dīacon m (§13.3) *subdeacon* 9/38
suē = **swā**
sum I. pron *one* 4/107, 250; 8/33; 9/87; 15/2909; 19/81 etc; 20/56, 68; 23/148, 275; 15/2909; 19/81 etc; 24/149, 164: *a certain one* 21/26/1; 21/47/3; 24/285: *some* 4/9, 10, 244; 6/17 etc; 13/72, 90; 19/80: **II.** adj *some* 1/44 etc; 2/21 etc; 4/89, 126 etc; 6/5 etc; 7/44 etc; 8/50, 55 etc; 12/37, 50 etc; 13/4 etc; 14/65 etc; 16/317 etc; 24/271: *a certain* 1/h, 3; 2/1; 8/6; 9/83; 10/88, 169 etc; 11/21 etc; 12/2 etc; etc: *some of, part of* 4/70: *one* 4/233: *a* 11/59
sumer = **sumor**
sumor m (§15.2) *summer* 4/75 etc; 6/21 etc; 8/5 etc; 20/54; 25/7: **sumores** adv *summer* 18/37
sumor–lang adj *"summer–long," as long as in summer* 22/37
sumor–lida m (§14.7) *"summer army"* (an army which does not spend the winter in the country) 4/47
Sumor–sǣtan, –sǣte m pl (§14.7, 5) *the men of Somerset* 4/98 etc
Sumur–sǣtan = **Sumor–sǣtan**
sun–bearo m (§13.6) *sun(ny) grove* 18/33
*ge***sund** adj *sound* 9/7: *unharmed* 3/27; 10/261: *well* 11/295: *prosperous, happy* 21/26/19
*ge***sundful** adj *sound, uncorrupted* 12/103

sundor adv *apart, by oneself* 19/111

sundor–yrfe m (§13.6) *private inheritance* 23/339

sundur–lond n (§13.4) *private land, property*

Sunnan–dæg m (§13.2) *Sunday* 6/47f; 11/288

sunnan–ūhta m (§14.7) *dawn on Sunday* 11/291

sunn–bēam m (§13.2) *sunbeam* 12/184

sunne f (§14.7) *sun* 4/114; 5/13; 11/129; 12/116; 18/17; 21/26/4

sunu m (§15.2) *son* 1/95; 4/177, 288; 5/42; 6/59; 9/53; 11/3 etc; 13/4 etc; 15/2853 etc; 15/Æ; 17/150; 24/76 etc

sun–wliteg adj *beautiful with sunshine* 25/7

sūpan II *sip, drink* 12/264

sūsl n (§13.4) *torment, torture* 23/114

sūð adj *south, southward* 4/164 etc; 6/46; 12/240: **be sūðan** adv *in the south* 6/35

sūðan adv *from the south* 8/94: **be sūðan** prep with dat *south of* 4/54; 7/15: **wið sūðan** prep with acc *south of* 8/71

sūðerne adj *southern* 24/134

sūðe–weard adj *the southern part of* 8/57, 65

sūð–rima m (§14.7) *south coast* 4/282

sūð–ryhte adv *due south* 8/15 etc

Sūð–seaxe m pl (§14.5) *South Saxons*, also the region they inhabited: *Sussex* (see 4/2n, 12/128a n) 4/223 etc

sūð–stæð n (§13.4) *south coast* 4/256

swā I. adv *so, thus, in this fashion* 1/19, 36, 47, 60, 62 etc; 2/58, 80 etc; 4/106, 235; 6/7, 45 etc; 7/11 etc; 8/116, 126; 9/7, 18, 24 etc; 10/118, 119, 203 etc; 11/65, 82 etc; 12/64, 69 etc; 13/44, 96; 14/6[3], 41, 89 etc; 15/Æ; 16/297, 307, 322; 18/47; 19/6, 85, 111; 20/51; 21/8/9; 21/29/6; 23/28, 32 etc; 24/h, 59, 122 etc: *consequently, thus, therefore* 16/289, 381, 385: (emphatic) *exceedingly, very* 9/103; 10/270; 16/252 etc, 373, 425; 23/126: **swā þæt, swā þætte** conj (introducing a result clause) *so that, with the result that* 1/57; 2/3; 4/130, 146, 150; 20/91, 124, 209 etc; 11/200; 12/77 etc; 13/87; 14/125: **swā þēah** adv *however, nevertheless* 6/90; 13/23, 45: see also **ēac, same, swilce: II.** conj *as, just as* 1/87; 2/31; 4/185 etc; 5/7; 7/17, 60[3]; 9/48, 120; 10/55, 100, 106, 107, 110 etc; 12/169 etc; 14/48, 65, 106 etc; 15/2873, 2874 etc; 16/279, 283; 17/108, 114; 18/23, 29 etc; 19/14, 19, 62, 75; 20/h[4], 90; 23/38 etc; 24/290; 25/49: *as when, just as when* 18/41; 19/43: *as if, just as if* 1/133; 10/89; 19/96; 22/24; 23/68: (concessive) *although* 16/391: (purpose) *so that, in order that* 23/102: see also **eal(l), sōna: III.** adv + conj **A.** (together) **swā swā** *as, just as* 1/99, 117; 2/46, 57, 81 etc; 7/57, 60[1,2], 65, 8/109 (*according to what*); 10/120, 145, 290, 329; 11/115, 139, 155 etc; 12/26 etc; 13/9 etc; 14/27, 51 etc; 15/Æ: *as if, just as if* 1/h: (purpose) *so that, in order that* 4/219: **B.** (separated) **swā . . . swā, swā . . . swā swā** *as, just as* 1/20f; 12/74, 102: *so . . . as* 6/12f; 11/4: *as . . . as* 1/185; 4/87, 142, 258; 6/8f, 37, 39, 44, 89f; 8/9, 10, 13 (with ellipsis), 16 (with ellipsis), 55 etc; 11/319f; 12/175; 14/11, 54: *in such a fashion . . . as* 13/18, 82: *either . . . or* 20/h[2,3]: with comp *in proportion as . . . so, the . . . the* 6/75f; 8/52; 14/6[1,2]: similarly **swā micle swā . . . swā** 1/146: **swā hwā (hwǣr, hwæt, hwæðr, hwider, hwilc) swā** see **hwā, hwæt** etc

swǣ = swā

(*ge*)**swǣs** adj *dear, beloved* 19/50; 21/26/22: *gentle* 11/237

swǣsendo, swǣsendu n pl (§13.6) *food, dinner, banquet, feast* 1/134; 23/9

swǣtan I *bleed* 17/20

swæð n (§13.4) *track, trail* 7/29

swālic pron and adj *such, such a thing* 1/133

swālice adj *thus* 10/280

swān m (§13.2) *swineherd, peasant* 3/4

Swāna–wīc n (§13.4) *Swanage* (Dorset) 4/84f

swanc pret 1 and 3 sg of **swincan**

swār adj *heavy, oppressive, grievous* 18/56

swāt m (§13.2) *blood* 5/13; 17/23

swātig adj *bloody* 23/337
swaðu f (§14.1) *track*: **on swaðe** adv *behind* 23/321
swealg pret 1 and 3 sg of **swelgan**
sweart adj *black, dark, dusky* 5/61; 15/2858; 16/312 etc; 21/57/3
sweart–lāst adj *leaving a black track* 21/26/11
swef(en) n (§13.4) *dream* 2/21, 44; 17/1; 19/h
swēg m (§14.5) *sound, noise, music* 20/21
sweg(e)l n (§13.4) *heaven, sky* 15/2879; 23/80 etc: *sun* 25/7
swelce = swilce
swelgan 3 with dat obj *swallow* 21/26/9; 21/47/6
sweltan 3 *die* 10/205, 257; 12/159; 24/293
swenc(e)an I *oppress, harass* 6/95 and n: *afflict, distress* 1/42; 10/75f, 162
sweng m (§14.5) *blow, stroke* 24/118
Swēo–land n (§13.4) *the land of the Swedes* 8/58
sweolt = swealt (pret 1 and 3 sg of **sweltan**)
Swēon m pl (§14.7) *the Swedes* 8/88
swēora m (§14.7) *neck* 10/204, 208, 277; 15/Æ; 23/106
*ge***sweorcan** 3 *darken, become gloomy* or *despairing* 19/59
sweorcend–ferhð adj *with darkening thought, gloomy in mind* 23/269
sweord n (§13.4) *sword* 1/162; 5/4 etc; 15/2858 etc; 15/Æ; 23/89 etc; 24/15 etc; 25/25
sweorfan 3 *rub, polish* 21/28/4
sweoster = sweostor
sweostor f (§15.4) *sister* 11/20; 13/15; 24/115
swēot n (§13.4) *troop, army* 23/298
sweotol adj *clear, plain, manifest, evident* 14/42, 103; 25/10
sweotole, sweotule adv *clearly* 1/103; 23/177: *openly, plainly* 19/11
sweotollīce adv *clearly, plainly* 23/136
swer m *column, pillar* 10/170, 263 etc
swerian 6 *swear* 4/67, 78 etc; 6/61 etc; 15/Æ
swēte adj *sweet, pleasant* 2/57: used as sb *sweetness* 20/95
swētnes(s), –nis(s) f (§14.2) *sweetness* 2/5, 66
*ge***swīcan** 1 *fail, betray* 16/284: with gen *cease from, give up* 11/234f
swic–dōm m (§13.3) *treason, betrayal* 14/109
swicol adj *treacherous, deceitful* 25/10n
swician II with dat obj *deceive* 14/54
Swifneh personal name *Swifneh* 4/124
swift adj *swift, fast* 4/259; 8/113 etc; 25/3
swigian II *be silent, be still* 21/7/1: pres pple **swīgende** (see Campbell §764) *unspeaking, silent* 1/h, 43
swilc I. pron *such* 14/150; 16/286: relative *such as* 20/83; 23/65: **II.** adj *such, such a* 6/4; 16/283 etc
swilce I. adv *likewise, and also* 5/19, 57; 10/213; 17/8; 20/53; 22/43: **swilce ēac, swilce . . . ēac** *moreover, also, furthermore* 1/3, 94, 177; 2/67, 101; 5/30, 37; 16/325; 23/18 etc: **swylce swā** conj *just as* 17/92: **II.** conj *as* 6/4: *just as* 12/184; 19/h: *as if* 7/27; 11/49, 55; 23/31
swīma m (§14.7) *stupor, swoon* 23/30, 106
swimman 3 *swim, float, drift* 19/53
swincan 3 *toil, labor* 12/111
*ge***swinc–dæg** m (§13.2) *"affliction–day," day of toil* or *hardship* 20/2
*ge***swinc–dagas** nom and acc pl of *ge*-**swinc–dæg**
swingan 3 *scourge* 10/128: *strike* 10/218
swinsian II *sound melodiously* 21/7/7
swinsung f (§14.1) *melody, harmony* 2/48
*ge***swippor** adj *cunning, sly* 1/h
switol = sweotol
swīð adj *strong, powerful* 16/252; 20/115; 25/5: comp **swīðra** *right* (hand, side etc) 1/69, 102; 12/99, 101 etc; 17/20; 23/80
swīðe adv *very* 1/40 etc; 2/70 etc; 4/167, 269 etc; 6/31 etc; 7/2 etc; 8/3 etc; 9/84; 10/90; 11/36; 12/43 etc; 13/6, 37 etc; 14/7 etc; 16/356; 19/55; 21/57/2; 24/282: *greatly* 1/5, 74 etc; 6/96; 9/13, 91; 10/91; 12/104 etc; 14/46 etc; 15/Æ: *fiercely* 10/277; 12/229; 23/88; 24/115, 118: *much* 9/21, 72; 14/9, 32 etc: *completely* 14/36: *strongly* 12/3:

readily 9/65, 66: *swiftly* 15/2873; 21/26/4: *seriously* 3/18; 4/256: **swīðe swīðe** *very greatly* 7/33: comp **swīðor** *more* 4/248; 9/87; 11/195; 12/112; 14/119; 23/182: sup **swīðost** *most* 4/249 etc; 16/337 etc: *for the most part* 8/28, 121; 11/205; 14/117 etc

swīðlic adj *great* 12/116

swīðrian II *diminish, destroy* 23/266

swīð–mōd adj *"vehement–souled," arrogant, insolent* 23/30 etc

Swīð–ulf personal name *Swīðulf* 4/170; 7/h

swōgan 7 *resound, make music* 21/7/7

swōr pret 1 and 3 sg of **swerian**

sworfen past pple of **sweorfan**

swōron pret pl of **swerian**

*ge*swugian II with gen obj *keep silent about* 14/147

swungon pret pl of **swingan**

swura = **swēora**

swurd = **sweord**

swuster = **sweostor**

*ge*swustra f pl (§15.4) *sisters* 13/13

*ge*swutelian II *reveal, show* 11/31; 12/182 etc; 15/Æ: *portend, signify, symbolize* 13/56, 59; 23/285

swutol = **sweotol**

swyft = **swift**

swylc = **swilc**

swylce = **swilce**

swȳn n (§13.4) *pig* 8/40

swyra = **swēora**

swyrd = **sweord**

swyrd–geswing n (§13.4) *sword–brandishing* 23/240

swȳð = **swīð**

swȳðe = **swīðe**

swȳðlic = **swīðlic**

sȳ = **sīe**

syfan = **seofon**

*ge*syhð = *ge*sihð **II.** (pres 3 sg of *ge*sēon)

sylen f (§14.2) *generosity* 1/106

sylf = **self**

sylfren adj *silver* 12/190 etc

sylf–wylles adv *voluntarily* 12/269

syllan = **sellan**

syllic (= **seldlic**) *rare, wondrous* 17/4 etc

sylð pres 3 sg of **sellan**

symbel I. sb n (§13.4) *banquet, feast* 2/18; 17/141; 19/93; 23/15: **II.** adj *continuous*: neut used as sb **on symbel** adv *always* 23/44

symble = **simble**

symle I. dat sg of **symbel I.**: **II.** = **simble**

syn = **sind**

sȳn = **sīen**

syn–byrðen(n) f (§14.2) *burden of sin* 9/43

syndan = **syndon**

synd = **sind** (pres pl of **wesan** (§7.2))

synde = **sende**

synderlīce = **syndriglīce**

syndon = **sindon** (pres pl of **wesan** (§7.2))

syndrig adj *private* 12/115

syndriglīce adv *separately, one by one* 1/118: *specially, particularly* 2/1; 11/3

*ge*sȳne = *ge*sīene

syngian II *sin, transgress* 14/125

syn–lēaw f *stain of sin* 14/129

synlic adj *sinful* 9/20

syn(n) f (§14.2) *sin* 2/68; 6/72 etc; 9/55; 11/132, 148; 13/53 etc; 14/7 etc; 16/391; 17/13 etc; 18/54; 20/100; 25/54

synt = **synd**

*ge*syntu f pl (§14.2) *prosperity, success* 1/127; 23/90

syrwan I *arm* 24/159

syððan = **siððan**

syx = **siex**

syxtig numeral *sixty* 8/33 etc

T

tāc(e)n n (§13.4) *portent* 4/h; 6/4: *sign* 1/70, 103; 9/22; 11/78, 82: *miracle* 11/12, 14, 78, 201 etc

*ge*tācnian II *betoken, symbolize, prefigure* 13/25, 72 etc; 23/h: *show, portend* 23/197, 286

*ge*tācnung f (§14.1) *signification, type* 13/23: *betokening, prefiguration* 13/66 etc

Tāda *Tadcaster* (Yorkshire) see 6/48n

(*ge*)**tǣcan** I *teach* 11/193; 13/34 etc; 14/127 etc: *show* 9/32; 15/2855 etc; 24/18: *direct* 15/2901: *interpret* 13/86

tægl m (§13.2) *tail* 13/78 etc

tǣhte pret 1 and 3 sg of **tǣcan**

tǣhtest pret 2 sg of **tǣcan**

tǣhton pret pl of **tǣcan**

*ge***tæl** n (§13.4) *sequence* 2/55
tǣlan I *reproach* 14/121
tǣsan I *wound, lacerate, tear* 24/270
tæt = **þæt**
talian II *impute to* 1/49
tam adj *tame* 8/36
tēah pret 1 and 3 sg of **tēon**
teala interj *well! good!* 2/95
*ge***teald** past pple of (*ge*)**tellan**
tealt adj *unstable* 14/48
tēar m (§13.2) *tear* 11/165
*ge***teld** n (§13.4) *tent* 12/180 etc: *tabernacle* 13/67 etc
telg m (§13.2) *dye, ink* 21/26/15
telga m (§14.7) *bough, branch* 18/76
(*ge*)**tellan I** *consider, reckon* 11/203
Temes f (§14.1) *the R. Thames* 4/54, 113 etc; 7/15
Temese–mūða m (§14.7) *the estuary of the R. Thames* 4/138
temp(e)l n (§13.4) *temple* 1/149; 11/233, 238 etc
tēn = **tīen**
*ge***tengan** I *hasten, hurry* 11/255
*ge***tenge** adj with dat *resting on, in contact with* 21/7/8
teola adv *rightly, properly* 1/165
teolian = **tilian**
teolung f (§14.1) *income, revenue* 11/145
(*ge*)**tēon I.** st vb 2 *draw* 1/h; 9/46, 117: *row* 4/135, 225: *drag* 10/204, 208 etc; 23/99: *instruct, educate* 12/76: **II.** wk vb II *make, create, adorn* 2/36
tēona m (§14.7) *injury, wrong* 1/68
(*ge*)**tēorian II** *subside* 9/91: *grow exhausted* 10/241
tēoðe adj *tenth* 16/246n
teran 4 *tear* 23/281
Ter–finnas m pl (§13.2) see 8/23n
tēð dat sg and nom and acc pl of **tōð**
thā = **þā**
tīan = **tēon**
tīber n *sacrifice, victim* 15/2853 etc
tīd f (§14.6) *time* 1/1; 2/14, 75; 7/4; 13/9; 14/142; 16/369 etc; 18/77; 20/124; 23/286 etc; 24/104: *hour* 1/33, 46; 2/73, 93, 96; 4/114; 10/242; 11/263, 316
tīen numeral *ten* 8/45; 12/90 etc; 16/248
tihtan I *urge, persuade* 11/237

tiid = **tīd**
til I. adj *good, praiseworthy* 19/112; 21/26/23; 25/20: **II.** prep with dat *for, for a*
tilgan = **tilian**
tilian II *strive, endeavor* 9/63; 20/119: with gen obj *provide for, support* 4/82: *provide* 23/208
tīma m (§14.7) *time* 11/56, 286; 12/119; 13/11 etc
*ge***timbre** n (§13.6) *building* 1/168; 16/276
timbran I *build* 1/179; 4/257 etc
*ge***timbrian** II *build, construct* 1/177; 10/304
*ge***tīmian** II impers with dat *befall* 12/215
Tīne f (§14.7) *the R. Tyne* 4/71; 6/30
tintreg n (§13.5) *torment* 1/111; 9/106; 10/18, 123 etc
tintreglic adj *infernal* 2/65
tīr m (§13.2) *glory* 5/3; 21/26/23; 23/93 etc; 24/104
tīr–fæst adj *glorious* 18/69; 25/32
tīð f (§14.1) *grant, concession* 23/6
(*ge*)**tīðian II** with dat of person and gen or dat of thing *grant* 11/328; 12/49 etc; 13/3
tō prep with gen, dat and inst **I.** (local) *to, into* 1/7, 13, 15, 18 etc; 2/6, 7, 18; etc: *towards, against* 2/88, 89, 91; 3/22; 12/14: *in* 11/184; 13/57; 20/45; 23/7, 345; 24/12: *at* 17/141; 23/15: *next to* 4/78n; 16/254: *from* 14/15; 17/86; 19/115: (object of thought) *on, about, of* 20/44; 24/4, 127: **tō þæs, tō þǣm, tō þon** adv *so* 2/75; 4/278; 9/h, 68, 69, 71, 72, 116f; 20/40[2], 41; 23/275: see also **weard**: **II.** (temporal) *at, during* 6/1[2], 26; 17/2: *for* 1/139; 11/114; 12/138[2]: *until* 2/95: **tō dæge** adv *today* 1/170: **III.** (purpose) *for, for purposes of* 4/25[2], 69, 121; 6/45[2]; 8/30; 11/55[2]; 12/201; 13/17; 14/18, 22; 15/2861; 15/Æ; 17/129; 23/54, 189: *as, as a(n)* 1/157; 2/34; 4/25[1]; 6/74, 83, 87; 9/82, 108; 10/306; 11/37, 55[1], 203; 12/18[1], 44, 61 etc; 13/15, 33 etc; 14/24, 52; 15/2853, 2892; 16/285, 318, 407; 17/31, 102, 153; 19/30; 20/20, 69, 101; 21/26/27; 23/96, 174 etc; 24/46

etc: **tō hwǣm** *why* 10/60: see also **āwiht, sōð**: **IV.** with the inflected infinitive (§7.2 footnote 1) *to* (do something), *for* (doing something) 1/2, 5, 42 etc; 2/58; 4/67; etc

tō adv **I.** *to, thither* 4/173, 264; 6/10; 20/119: **II.** *too* 1/h; 9/20, 40; 14/9 etc; 16/340; 19/66 etc; 22/51; 24/55, 66 etc: see also **forð**

tō–æt–ȳcan I *add, expatiate* 1/143

tō–bærst pret 1 and 3 sg of **tō–berstan**

tō–berstan 3 *break* 12/34; 24/136: *split* 24/144

tō–brǣcon pret pl of **tō–brecan**

tō–brecan 4 *break* 14/78; 24/242: *break up* 4/176, 240: *shatter* 11/58f, 77

tō–brēdan 3 with dat obj *shake off, start awake from* 23/247

tō–brocen past pple of **tō–brecan**

tō–ceorfan 3 *cut in pieces* 12/96

tō–clēofan 2 *cleave asunder* 9/47

tō–cnāwan 7 *know, acknowledge, recognize* 11/241

tō–cwȳsan I *crush to pieces, smash* 11/54, 72 etc

tō–cwȳsednys(s) f (§14.2) *shattered condition, fragmentation* 11/82f

tō–cyme m (§14.5) *advent* 13/18: *coming, arrival* 14/7

tō–dǣlan I *divide* 8/108: *part, separate, estrange* 22/12

tō–dāl n (§13.4) *difference, distinction* 13/14

tō–ēacan prep with dat *in addition to* 8/28; 14/63

tō–emnes prep with dat *alongside* 8/57 etc

tō–faran 6 *disperse, split up* 4/244

tō–fōr pret 1 and 3 sg of **tō–faran**

tō–gædere adv *together* 12/156; 14/69, 98; 24/67: see also **fōn**

tō–gēanes prep with dat *against* 1/91; 6/66; 20/76; 24/h: *towards* 11/42; 18/11; 23/149

tō–gegnes = **tō–gēanes**

(*ge*)**togen** past pple of **tēon**

tō–gēnes = **tō–gēanes**

tō–geþēodan I *add* 2/40: with dat *join* 11/90

*ge***toht** n (§13.4) *battle* 24/104

tohte f (§14.7) *battle* 23/197

tō–lēsan I *undo, dissolve* 10/9, 13

tō–lēsnes(s) f (§14.2) *dissolution* 9/121

tō–licgan 5 *divide* 8/90

tō–līð pres 3 sg of **tō–licgan**

tō–middes prep with dat *in the midst of* 12/228; 16/324

tō–niman 4 *divide* 4/150

tō–numen past pple of **tō–niman**

torht adj *bright, radiant, glorious* 18/28; 23/43: *splendid* 15/2891

torhte adv *clearly* 21/7/8

torhtlic adj *splendid* 23/157

torht–mōd adj *glorious* 23/6 etc

torn n (§13.4) *violent emotion* (of anger or grief), *passion* 19/112; 23/272: dat (inst) sg used as adv *grievously* 23/93

tō–somne adv *together* 1/92: see also *ge***faran**

tō–stencan I *drag* 10/124

Tostig personal name *Tostig* 6/8 etc

tō–twǣman I *divide, split in two* 24/241

tōð m (§15.7) *tooth* 23/271: *tusk* 8/29

tōð–mægen n (§13.5) *strength of tusk* 25/20

tō–ward = **tō–weard**

tō–weard I. adj *coming, impending, imminent, future* 1/51, 57; 2/65; 8/115; 11/32; 13/24, 25; 23/286: with dat *in store for* 1/62; 23/157: **II.** prep with dat *toward* 8/116: *on the way to, approaching* 6/16

tō–wearp pret 1 and 3 sg of **tō–weorpan**

tō–weorpan 3 *throw down, overthrow, destroy* 1/156, 157 etc; 11/232 etc

tō–wurpan = **tō–weorpan**

tō–wurpon pret pl of **tō–weorpan**

træf n (§13.4) *tent, pavilion* 23/43 etc

tredan 5 *tread, walk upon* 21/7/1; 21/57/5

trēo(w) n (§13.6) *wood* 1/177; 12/263: *tree* 10/255; 17/4 etc; 18/76

trēow f (§14.3) *faith, good faith* 1/80, 85; 19/112; 25/32: *pledge, promise* 4/142

*ge***trēowe** adj *faithful, loyal* 1/30; 21/26/23

*ge***trēowð** f (§15.3) *loyalty, faith* 14/9, 48 etc

*ge***trimman** = *ge***trymman**

trum adj *strong, firm* 23/6; 25/20

*ge***trum** n (§13.4) *troop, company* 25/32

*ge***truma** m (§14.7) *troop* 4/35, 36
Trūsō see 8/82n
*ge***truwian II** with dat obj *trust* 16/248
trym n (§13.6) *step, pace* 24/247
trymenes(s) f (§14.2) *exhortation* 1/9
trymian = **trymman**
(*ge*)**trymman I** *strengthen, fortify* 2/92; 12/15: *marshal, array, put in order* 24/17, 22: *arrange* 10/48: *establish* 16/248: *construct* 16/276: *urge, exhort* 1/2; 24/305
*ge***trȳwlīce** adv *truly, loyally* 14/53
*ge***trȳwð** = *ge***trēowð**
tū I. numeral (n nom and acc dual of **twēgen**) *two* 4/150, 235 etc: **II.** adv *twice* 4/258
tuǣm = **twǣm**
tūcian II *ill–treat* 12/11
tūddor n (§13.4) *offspring, progeny* 9/116
tuelfta adj *twelfth* 4/90
tugon pret pl of **tēon I.**
tūn m (§13.2) *residence, manor* 4/h: *village* 8/111, 112: *cemetery* 4/13
tunece f (§14.7) *tunic* 11/270 etc
tunge f (§14.7) *tongue* 2/13, 100
tūn–gerēfa m (§14.7) *reeve, steward, bailiff* 2/41
tungol n (§13.4) *star* 5/14; 11/130; 25/48
Tureces–īeg f (§14.2) *Torksey* (Lincolnshire) 4/60f
turf f (§15.7) *turf, soil* 18/66
tuwwa adv *twice* 4/152
twā numeral (n f nom and acc dual of **twēgen**) *two* 4/198 etc; 6/63; 10/163; 12/13 etc
twǣm dat of **twēgen** numeral *two* 4/145; 6/34; 11/167, 186 etc; 12/10; 15/Æ
twām = **twǣm**
twēga gen of **twēgen** numeral *two* 15/2883; 24/207
twēgen numeral (m nom and acc dual) *two* 4/177, 210; 8/45 etc; 10/55; 11/52, 86 etc; 12/10; 13/93; 14/96; 15/2868; 24/80
twelf numeral *twelve* 4/140, 213; 11/244; 13/31; 14/91; 18/28 etc
twentig numeral *twenty* 8/39 etc
twēo m (§14.7) *doubt, uncertainty* 16/276: *matter of doubt* 20/69
twēon II with gen obj *doubt* 23/1, 345
twī–ecge adj *double–edged* 1/h
twī–feald adj *two–fold, double*: **twīfeald hrægl** *a change of clothing* 10/69
twȳnian II impers vb with dat or acc of person *have doubts, be uncertain* 11/267
twȳnung f (§14.1) *doubt* 11/269
tȳddernys(s) f (§14.2) *frailty* 10/244
tȳdran I *propagate, bring forth* 25/48
*ge***tȳhð** pres 3 sg of *ge***tēon**
tȳman I *beget offspring* 13/16; 25/48
tȳn = **tīen**
tȳr = **tīr**
tyrf dat sg and nom and acc pl of **turf**

Þ

þā I. see **sē** (§9.2): **II.** adv *then, at that time* 1/6 etc; 2/18 etc; 3/8 etc; etc: see also **gēn, gīet: III.** conj *when* 1/4 etc; 2/18 etc; etc: **IV.** adv + conj **þā þā** *when* 4/184; 7/15, 20; 11/26, 149, 160 etc; 12/149, 275, 279; 13/45
þǣm see **sē** (§9.2): see also **æfter, ǣr, būtan, for, mid, under**
þæne = **þone**
þænne = **þonne**
þǣr I. adv (§24.1) *there, in that place* 1/21 etc; 2/15 etc; 3/3; etc: **II.** conj *where* 1/h, 30, 101, 171; 3/22; 4/87; 6/10; 8/23, 54; 9/95; 10/304; 11/91; 12/48 etc; 14/28, 92, 148; 16/305, 295; 17/123; 18/81; 19/115; 20/121; 21/26/4; 23/40; etc: *to where, to the place where* 12/208; 16/418; 17/139 etc: *whereas, while* 20/10: *if* 16/388: III. adv + conj **þǣr þǣr** *where* 4/145; 7/19; 12/42; 15/Æ
þǣra = **þāra**
þǣr–binnan adv *therein* 12/136
þǣre see **sē** (§9.2)
þǣr–inne adv *therein, inside* 3/30
þǣr–on adv *therein* 17/67: *into it* 8/23; 11/25
þǣr–rihte adv *immediately, instantly* 11/14, 252 etc; 13/30
þǣr–tō adv *thither, thereto* 3/23; 4/h, 171, 186: *for that purpose* 4/236: *pertaining thereto* 13/23
þǣr–tō–ēacan adv *in addition* 11/70, 142

þæs I. see **sē** (§9.2): **II.** = **þes**: **III.** = **þās** (10/233): **IV.** adv *with respect to that, as regards that, about that* 1/86; 13/100: *after that, afterwards, later* 4/26, 28 etc: *to that extent, so* 20/39, 40[1]: *therefore* 14/39: **þæs (þe)** conj *because* 5/51; 16/303; 23/6f, 344: *after, from the time that* 3/7; 4/63, 140, 213, 226, 243; 23/13: *according to what, as* 5/68; 14/145: see also **sōna, tō**

þæt I. dem and rel pron, see §9.2, 4: see also **oð, þurh**: **II.** = **þæt þæt** dem + rel pron *that which, what* 1/122; 2/51; 4/121; 10/214, 223, 266; 11/137, 196; 12/269; 14/5, 30, 68, 124[1], 151, 154; 24/289: **III.** conj *that* (introducing object clauses) 1/6 etc; 2/68 etc; 3/24; etc: (introducing purpose clauses) *so that, in order that* 1/h, 7, 91, 116; 2/44[3], 79; 4/16[2], 232, 234; 7/50; 9/28, 35; 10/129, 196, 219, 273, 274, 301, 302, 310; 11/19, 24, 73, 80, 114, 115, 116, 120, 230, 252, 271, 300, 309; 12/62 etc; 13/35; 15/Æ; 20/34, 37; 23/48, 89, 184; 24/177; 25/45: (introducing result clauses) *so that, with the result that* 1/28, 88, 166; 4/144, 163, 208, 230, 238, 271[1]; 11/143; 12/34; 15/2899; 16/341, 352; 23/105, 106, 110, 136; 24/63, 119, 135, 136, 142, 144, 150, 157, 226, 227, 286: (introducing causal clauses) *inasmuch as, because* 11/95; 12/236[1]; 17/19, 34, 107; 24/221, 243, 251: (introducing explanatory clauses) *in that* 16/361: *when* 17/81; 24/105: **IV.** = **þæt þæt** conj + dem pron 8/3

þæt–te I. rel pron *who* 1/53: *when* 2/93: **II.** conj *that* 1/73, 83; 2/58, 98; 7/14 etc; 18/1, 69

*ge***þafa** m (§14.7) *one who assents* 16/414

(*ge*)**þafian II** *assent to, agree to* 1/28, 116 etc; 2/54: *allow* 7/20f n: *tolerate* 23/60

(*ge*)**þafung** f (§14.1) *assent* 1/131: *permission* 11/37; 14/89

þām = **þǣm**

þan = **þon**

þān = **þām** = **þǣm**

þanc m (§13.2) *thanks* 7/16, 65: with gen *thanks for* 20/122: *grace* 4/247: gen sg used as adv *willingly* 6/17: **on þance** *pleasant, gratifying* 1/34: see also **dōn,** (*ge*)**secgan**

*ge***þanc** m (§13.2) *thought, mind* 14/125; 23/13; 24/13

(*ge*)**þanci(g)an** II *thank* (someone, dat) *for* (something, gen) 11/312f; 16/257f; 24/173f: with dat + clause 11/297

þancol–mōd adj *thoughtful, attentive* 23/172

þane = **þone**

þānian II *become wet* 5/12b n

þanon(ne) adv *thence, from there* 6/10, 45; 8/3 etc; 10/39, 164, 221 etc; 15/2928; 19/23; 21/29/10; 23/118, 132; 24/h: *whence* 4/119: *after that* 10/146: *out* 21/26/3

þār = **þǣr**

þāra see **sē** (§9.2)

þār–æfter adv *thereafter* 6/8

þās see **þēs** (§9.3)

þat = **þæt**

þe I. indecl rel particle (§9.4) *who, which, that* 1/3 etc; 2/14 etc; 3/10; etc: *in which, when* 1/46; 2/78; 12/148; 23/287; 24/212: *on which, when* 8/108: *during which, when* 6/2: see also **oð**: **II.** conj (= **oððe**) *or:* **þe . . . þe** *either . . . or* 1/48: **III.** conj (= **þonne**) *than* 3/29; 4/288; 14/49

þē I. see **þū** (§6.2) *you, yourself, to you, to yourself, for you* etc: **II.** = **þȳ**

þēah I. adv *nevertheless, however, yet* 3/32; 4/8, 142 etc; 6/68 etc; 7/54; 8/3 etc; 13/82 etc; 16/360, 392; 23/257; 24/289: see also **swā**: **II.** conj *though, although, even though* 4/254; 6/25; 8/127; 10/236; 11/249; 14/10, 41 etc; 16/359; 20/97, 113; 23/20: *if* 14/104: **þēah þe** *although* 13/64; 19/2: *even if* 13/104

*ge***þeaht** f (§14.6) *thought, counsel* 1/115, 118: *advice, plan* 1/63

þeahte pret 1 and 3 sg of **þeccan**

*ge***þeahtere** m (§13.6) *counsellor* 1/142

þēara = **þāra**

þearf I. sb f (§14.1) *need, necessity* 2/85; 10/63; 12/244; 14/30 etc; 16/278; 23/3 etc; 24/175 etc: *what is necessary* 24/232: *service* 4/69: *benefit, advan-*

tage 12/61: **II.** pres 1 and 3 sg of **þurfan**

þearfa adj *poor, needy:* used as sb *poor man, the poor* 9/3; 11/4, 69, 74 etc; 12/59 etc

þearfan I *need* 9/42: pres pple **þearfende** *needy, in need* 9/30; 23/85

þearle adv *very, extremely* 23/74, 268: *fiercely* 5/23; 23/262: *sorely, grievously* 14/46; 17/52; 23/86; 24/158

þearl–mōd adj *stern–minded, mighty* 23/66 etc

þēaw m (§13.6) *custom* 2/76; 8/102 etc; 13/70: *habit* 12/252: *trait* 19/12: *virtue* 7/22; 12/84; 14/116; 23/129

þec see **þū** (§6.2) *you*

þeccan I *cover* 18/42

þeg(e)n m (§13.2) *"thane," servant, retainer, attendant, follower, courtier* 1/h, 29, 124, 134; 2/78, 80; 3/14, 19 etc; 4/55, 66 etc; 12/91; 14/27, 83 etc; 15/2908; 16/409 etc; 17/75; 23/306; 24/151 etc

þegen–gyld n (§13.4) *wergild for a thane, compensation for a thane killed* 14/85

þegenlīce adv *as befits a thane, loyally* 24/294

þegnian II with dat obj *serve, minister to* 2/78

þegnscipe m (§14.5) *service* 16/326

þegnung = **þēnung**

þēgon pret pl of **þicgan**

þēh = **þēah**

þēn = **þegn**

(*ge*)**þenc(e)an** I *think, consider* 1/75, 100; 9/112; 10/202; 16/272 etc; 19/58; 20/96: *think about, consider* 7/19; 9/60; 19/88; 20/118: *take thought* 9/65, 112: *call to mind* 7/15: *intend, purpose, plan* 14/54; 15/2892; 16/401; 20/51; 23/58 etc; 24/258, 316 etc: *conceive, devise* 16/286: *imagine* 17/115; *desire* 17/121: with gen *think about* 9/125

þenden conj *while* 16/410; 20/102; 23/66

þenian I *stretch out, rack* 17/52

þēninc–man(n) m (§15.7) *serving man, attendant* 11/10

þēning, þēnung f (§14.1) *service, obeisance* 10/288: *divine service, office* 7/12: *service of food, banquet* 12/89: *mission* 10/77: pl *retinue, household* 11/20

þēo dat sg of **þēoh**

þēod f (§14.1) *people, nation* 1/9, 93, 173; 4/5, 78; 5/22; 6/95; 7/44; 9/15; 12/105; 14/9 etc

(*ge*)**þēodan** I join 1/182n; 2/55: with dat obj *attach oneself to, be a follower of* 1/128; 9/126

þēode pret 1 and 3 sg of **þēowian**

*ge***þēode** n (§13.6) *language* 7/27 etc; 8/27: *race* 8/123

þēoden m (§13.3) *lord, prince, king* 16/268; 17/69; 18/68; 19/95; 23/3 etc; 24/120 etc

þēoden–māðm m (§13.2) *"lord–treasure," treasure given by a lord* 16/409

Þēod–ford m (§15.2) *Thetford* (Norfolk) 4/21

þēod–guma m (§14.7) *warrior* 23/208 etc

þēod–land n (§13.4) *world* 9/14

*ge***þēodnis(s)** f (§14.2) *association* 2/7

þēodscipe, –scype m (§14.5) **I.** *nation, people* 6/89; 14/106: **II.** *discipline* 2/70; 9/32

þēod–wita m (§14.7) *learned man* 14/142

þēof m (§13.2) *thief* 11/256; 21/47/4; 25/42

þēoh n (§13.4) *thigh* 21/44/1

*ge***þēon** 1, 2 *succeed, be successful, thrive* 25/44

þēos see **þēs** (§9.3)

þeosse = **þisse**

þeossum = **þissum**

þēosterful(l) adj *dark* 11/175

þēostru n f (§13.6, 15.3) often pl (like Lat *tenebrae*) *darkness* 11/309; 16/326 etc; 17/52; 21/47/4; 23/118; 25/51

þēoðen = **þēoden**

þēow m (§13.6) *servant* 2/55; 7/25; 10/17, 109 etc; 14/26 etc

þēowa m (§14.7) *servant* 10/296; 11/92 etc: *slave* 8/99, 11/142

þēowen f (§14.1) *handmaiden* 23/74

þēowi(g)an I, II with dat obj *serve, be subject to* 2/99; 11/142, 273; 16/264 etc; 23/h: *enslave* 14/37

þēre = **þǣre**

þēs m, **þis** n, **þēos** f, dem pron and adj (§9.3) *this*
þet=**þæt**
þī=**þȳ**
(*ge*)**þicg(e)an** 5 *accept* 3/15: *partake of, take, drink* 12/202; 23/19
þider adv *thither, there, to that place* 3/15, 20; 6/20 etc; 8/28 etc; 10/45, 61 etc; 20/118; 23/129: *to where* 12/213
þider–weard adv *thither* 8/76
þider–weardes adv *thither* 4/159: *on the way there* 4/161
þīn I. see **þū** (§6.2) *you:* **II.** possessive adj (§10.8) *your* 1/50; 2/85; 10/44
þincan=**þyncan**
þinceð=**þynceð**
þincg=**þing**
þincð=**þyncð**
*ge***þincðu** f (§14.1) *dignity* 12/113
þīnen f (§14.2) *handmaiden* 13/13; 23/172
þing n (§13.4) *thing* 1/30, 66, 71 etc; 2/82; 9/20, 24; 11/76, 219 etc; 12/56 etc; 13/24 etc; 14/24 etc; 18/h; 19/h; 23/153: *deed* 23/60: *condition* 16/259: *case, situation, circumstance* 20/68
(*ge*)**þingian II** *intercede* 14/153: with dat obj *intercede for* 11/186; 12/255: *orate, harangue* 21/8/8
þingð=**þyncð**
þingung f (§14.1) *intercession* 11/328
*ge***þīode**=*ge***þēode**
þiossum=**þissum**
þīow=**þēow**
þīowot–dōm m (§13.2) *service* 7/9
þis see **þēs** (§9.3) *this*: see also **oð**
þīs=**þȳs**
þisan=**þissum**
þisere=**þisse**
þislic=**þyslic**
þisne see **þēs** (§9.3)
þisre see **þēs** (§9.3)
þissa see **þēs** (§9.3)
þissan=**þissum**
þisse see **þēs** (§9.3)
þissera=**þissa**
þisses see **þēs** (§9.3)
þissum see **þēs** (§9.3): see also **āmang, onmang**
þisum=**þissum**
*ge***þōht** m (§13.2) *thought* 1/41; 9/40; 20/34; 22/12 etc: *purpose, design* 1/81: *mind* 19/88n
(*ge*)**þōhte** pret 1 and 3 sg of (*ge*)**þencan**
(*ge*)**þōhton** pret pl of (*ge*)**þencan**
þolian II *suffer, endure* 14/99; 16/323 etc; 17/149; 23/215 etc: *hold out* 24/201 etc
*ge***þolian** II *tolerate, put up with* 24/6
þon I. see **sē** (§9.2): with comparatives *the* 23/92: see also **æfter, ǣr, for, in, lǣs, mā, nōht, tō, wið**: **II.**=**þonne**
þonan=**þanon**
þonc=**þanc**
*ge***þonc**=*ge***þanc**
þoncunc f (§14.1) *thanks, gratitude* 1/61: see also **dōn**
þonc–wyrðe adj *gratifying, pleasing* 23/153
þone see **sē** (§9.2)
þonne I. adv *then, at that time* 2/17[2]; 3/15; 4/143; 11/231 etc; 14/8; 16/370: *consequently* 13/38: **II.** conj *when* 1/70; 2/15; 6/96; 8/102, 119; 9/10; 10/68; etc: *although* 11/134[2]: *since* 11/141, 142: **III.** conj *than* 1/25; 125 etc; 3/25; 4/152 etc; 8/31 etc; 9/87; 11/134; 12/112; 13/84; 14/15 etc; 15/2922; 15/Æ; 16/270; 17/128; 18/31; etc
þonon=**þanon**
þorfte pret 1 and 3 sg of **þurfan**
þorftun=**þorfton** (pret pl of **þurfan**)
þoterung f (§14.1) *howling* 11/178
þrǣl m (§13.2) *"thrall," slave* 14/81,83 etc
þrǣl–riht n pl (§13.4) *rights of slaves* 14/38
þrāg f (§14.1) *time* 19/95; 23/237: dat pl used as adv *at times* 18/68; 25/4
*ge***þrang** n (§13.4) *throng, press* 24/299
þrēa f (§14.3) *affliction, oppression* 16/389
þrēade pret 1 and 3 sg of **þrēagan**
þrēagan II *afflict* 9/91: *rebuke, reprove* 11/170
þrēat m (§13.2) *troop, throng* 23/62 etc
þrēo=**þrie**
þrēora gen pl of **þrīe**

þridda adj *third* 1/23, 61 etc; 4/120; 8/111; 15/2869 etc; 15/Æ

þrīe numeral *three* 4/118, 243 etc; 8/9 etc; 10/43; 11/205, 211 etc; 13/61 etc; 14/96; 16/307; 20/68; 24/h, 299

Ðrihten = Dryhten

þrim dat pl of **þrīe**

*ge***þring** n *commotion*

þringan 3 *throng, press forward* 23/164 etc: *oppress, constrict, pinch* 20/8

þrītig numeral *thirty* 4/107, 134; 8/53; 11/152, 187 etc; 12/149

þrittig = þrītig

þriwa adv *three times* 11/160

þrosm m *smoke, vapor* 16/326

þrōwian II *suffer* 1/37; 10/127, 242; 11/149; 17/84 etc; 20/3

þrōwung f (§14.1) *suffering, passion* 2/63

*ge***þrungen** past pple of **þringan**

þrungon pret pl of **þringan**

þrȳ = þrīe

þryccan I *oppress* 2/74

þrym = þrim (dat pl of **þrīe**)

þrymfæst adj *glorious* 17/84; 21/47/4

þrymful(l) adj *glorious* 23/74

þrymlic adj *magnificent, glorious* 23/8

þrymlīce adv *mightily, majestically* 18/68

þrym(m) m (§13.6) *glory, majesty* 19/95; 23/60, 86; 25/4: *torrent* 18/41: *host, multitude* 23/164: *force, might* 23/331

Þrȳn(n)es(s), –nys(s) f (§14.2) *Trinity* 10/133; 13/56, 58 etc; 23/86

þrȳðe f pl (§14.6) *multitudes, hosts* 19/99

þū personal pron (§7.2) *you*

*ge***þūht** past pple of *(ge)***þyncan**

(*ge*)**þūhte** pret 1 and 3 sg of (*ge*)**þyncan**

þunar m (§13.2) *thunder* 25/4

*ge***þungen** adj (past pple) *distinguished, excellent* 1/84; 4/254; 23/129: sup acc pl m wk **geðungnestan** 4/339

þurfan pret–pres vb (§23.3) *need, have reason to* 5/39 etc; 13/3 etc; 16/290; 17/117; 23/117 etc; 24/34 etc

þurh I. prep with acc and dat: (place) *through* 14/97; 17/18; 23/303; 24/141 etc; 10/169, 204 etc: *throughout* 1/17 etc: (time) *for, during* 1/99; 10/333: (means or agency) *through, by means of, by virtue of, by* 1/105; 2/9; 7/28 etc; 9/105, 117; 10/285; 11/78, 161, 219 etc; 12/33 etc; 13/47, 48 etc; 14/37 etc; 15/2918; 15/Æ; 16/247 etc; 17/119; 18/6; etc: **þurh þæt** adv *thereby* 9/35: *therefore* 14/123: **þurh þæt þe** conj *because* 14/64f, 122f: **II.** adv *through* 23/49

þurh–drifan = þurh–drifon

þurh–drīfan 1 *pierce* 17/46

þurh–drifon pret pl of **þurh–drīfan**

þurh–flēon 2 *fly through* 1/136

þurh–longe adv *for a very long time* 16/307

þurh–scēotan 2 *shoot through, pierce* 9/46; 11/94

þurh–scoten past pple of **þurh–scēotan**

þurh–slēan 6 *smite through* 9/46

þurh–slyhð pres 3 sg of **þurh–slēan**

þurh–stingan 3 *stab through, run through* 1/h

þurh–stong pret 1 and 3 sg of **þurh–stingan**

þurh–tēon 2 *bring it about* 11/117

þurh–ūt prep with acc *right through* 6/48

þurh–wadan 6 *pierce, go through* 24/296

þurh–wōd pret 1 and 3 sg of **þurh–wadan**

þurh–wunian II *persevere, continue, remain* 10/31; 11/7

þus adv *thus, in this fashion* 1/70; 2/85; 4/123; 8/119; 9/94, 118; 10/96, 201 etc; 11/108, 160 etc; 12/100 etc; 13/42; 15/Æ; 23/93; 24/57

þūsend n (§13.5) *thousand* 4/39; 11/137 etc

þūsend–mǣlum adv *in thousands* 23/165

*ge***þwǣr–lǣcan** I with dat obj *agree to, assent to* 11/236f

*ge***þwǣrnes(s)** f (§14.2) *concord* 9/31

þwēan 6 *wash* 12/190

*ge***þwing** n *torment* 16/317

þwōh pret 1 and 3 sg of **þwēan**

þwȳrnys(s) f (§14.2) *obstinacy, perversity* 11/246

þȳ I. see **sē** (§9.2): with comparatives *the* 7/38[1]; 9/63; 16/429; 19/49; 21/26/19, 20 etc; 21/47/6; 23/53; 24/146, 312, 313[1]: see also **ēac, for, lǣs, mā, māra, mid**: **II.** adv *for that reason, therefore* 8/126; 14/6, 43, 118, 152: **III.** conj *because* 4/h; 21/47/6: *(in proportion) as* 7/38[2]; 24/313[2]

þȳdan = **þēodan**
þyder = **þider**
þȳfð f (§14.1) *theft* 14/37
*ge***þyldig** adj *patient* 19/65
(*ge*)**þyncan I** impers vb with dat *seem, appear* 1/119, 129; 2/80; 4/260; 7/44 etc; 8/27; 9/17, 74; 13/2, 22 etc; 14/48 etc; 15/2896; 16/267 etc; 17/4; 19/41; 21/47/1; 24/55: *seem fitting* 10/280: **bēon geþūht** *seem* 11/234: impers with dat *seem good to, suit* 6/44
þȳrel adj *pierced, perforated* 21/44/2
þyrfen pres subjunc 1–3 pl of **þurfan**
þyrran I *dry* 21/28/4
þyrs m (§14.5) *giant, troll* 25/42
þys = **þis**
þȳs see **þēs** (§9.3)
þysan = **þyssum**
þyses = **þisses**
þyslic pron and adj *such a* 1/55, 62: *such a thing* 1/132: *of this nature* 9/23: *in this fashion* 2/70
þysne = **þisne**
þyssa = **þissa**
þysse see **þēs** (§9.3)
þyssere = **þisse**
þysson = **þissum**
þyssum = **þissum**
þȳstre adj *dark, gloomy* 23/34; 25/42
þȳstro = **þēostru**
þysum = **þissum**

U

uard = **weard**
uerc = **weorc**
ufan adv *from above* 15/2909 etc: *above* 16/375: *down* 16/306
ufe–weard adj *the inner part of* 4/266
ufon = **ufan**
ufor comp adv *farther away* 11/238
ūhta m (§14.7) *dawn, daybreak* 16/315; 19/8; 22/35
ūht–cearu f (§14.1) *grief at dawn* 22/7
ūht–sang, –song m (§13.2) *matins* 2/94; 12/114
uii–niht = **seofon–niht**
un–æðele adj *ignoble, mean* 1/38
un–ā–secgendlic adj *unspeakable* 11/176; 16/333n
un–be–boht adj (past pple) *unsold* 8/36f
un–be–fohten adj (past pple) *unfought, unopposed* 24/57
unc see **ic** (§6.2) *us (two)*
uncer I. see **ic** (§6.2) *of us (two)*: **II.** possessive adj (§10.8) *our* (i.e. *your and my*) 1/71; 22/25
un–coðu f (§14.1) *disease* 11/123; 14/45
un–cræft m (§13.2) *deceit* 14/158
un–cūð adj *unknown* 1/133; 7/64: *unfamiliar, strange* 1/45
un–cyst f (§14.6) *niggardliness, parsimony* 11/138
un–dǣd f (§14.6) *evil deed, crime* 14/125
under prep with dat or acc **I.** (local) *under, beneath* 1/h; 4/287; 8/83; 10/157; 13/10 etc; 17/55; 18/14; etc: see also **bæc, neoðan**: **II.** (temporal) *during*: **under þām** adv *in the meantime, meanwhile* 4/79
under–be–ginnan 3 *undertake, embark upon* 13/7
under–fēng pret 1 and 3 sg of **under–fōn**
under–fēngan = **under–fēngon**
under–fēngon pret pl of **under–fōn**
under–fōn 7 *take, accept* 4/6: *receive* 9/199; 12/61 etc; 14/156
under–geat pret 1 and 3 sg of **under–gietan**
under–gēaton pret pl of **under–gietan**
under–gietan 5 *understand* 6/19: *perceive* 11/97
undern m *the third hour* (i.e. 9:00 A.M.) 11/292
under–standan 6 *understand* 7/12; 12/12, 21 etc; 14/8 etc: *consider* 14/159
under–stondan = **under–standan**
under–þēodan I *subject* 2/70; 9/36: *devote* 1/125
un–earg adj *intrepid, undaunted* 24/206
un–ēaðelīce adv *not easily, with difficulty* 1/6; 4/93: *awkwardly, inconveniently* 4/269
un–ēðelīce = **un–ēaðelīce**
un–fæger adj *unpleasant* 9/74
un–feor adv *not far* 15/2928
un–for–bærned adj (past pple) *unburned, uncremated* 8/103 etc
un–for–cūð adj *undisgraced, not infamous, reputable* 24/51
un–forht adj *unafraid* 17/110: *undaunted*

24/79

un–forht–mōd adj *unafraid* 11/254

un–for–worht adj (past pple) *innocent, uncondemned* 14/36

un–frið m (§13.2) *hostility* 8/18

un–gecynde adj *not of the royal race, having no hereditary right* 4/6

un–gecyndelic adj *unnatural* 9/14

un–geendod adj (past pple) *unending, endless* 11/313

un–gefōge adv *immensely* 8/119

un–gefullod adj (past pple) *unbaptized* 12/154

un–gehȳrsum adj *disobedient* 13/101

un–gelǣred adj (past pple) *unlearned, ignorant* 13/21, 39 etc

un–gelēafful(l) adj *unbelieving* 11/226

un–gelēafulnes(s) f (§14.2) *unbelief* 10/126f, 216

un–gelīc adj with dat *unlike, unequal* 1/91; 16/356

un–gelimp m n (§13.3, 4) *misfortune, disaster* 14/86

un–gelimplic adj *disastrous* 9/15

un–gemet adv *immensely, immeasurably* 16/313

un–gemetlic adj *immense, immeasurable* 4/9f

un–gerec(c) n (§13.4) *tumult, fracas, mêlée* 1/h

un–gerīm n (§13.4) *countless number* 6/54; 14/134

un–gesǣlig adj *unhappy* 11/133

un–getrȳwð f (§14.1) *treachery, disloyalty, unfaithfulness* 14/56

un–geþuærnes(s) f (§14.2) *discord, disagreement, dissension* 4/5

un–gewemmed adj (past pple) *undefiled, immaculate* 11/6: *unharmed* 11/26

un–gyld n (§13.6) *excessive tax* 14/46

un–hēanlīce adv *not meanly,* by litotes: *valiantly* 3/11

un–hold adj *unfriendly, hostile* 1/96

un–īeðēlice = un–ēaðelīce

un–lǣd adj *miserable, wicked* 23/103

Un–lāf personal name *Óláfr* (Tryggvason), K. of Norway (995–1000) 24/h

un–lagu f (§14.1) *injustice, legal abuse* 14/12, 37 etc

un–lifigende adj (pres pple) *lifeless, dead* 23/180, 315

un–lybba m (§14.7) *poisonous drug* 11/257 etc

un–lyfigende = un–lifigende

un–lȳtel adj *"unlittle," much* 14/19

un–meodomlīce adv *carelessly* 9/39n

un–miltsiendlic adj *unforgivable, unpardonable* 13/55

(*ge*)**unnan** pret–pres vb (§23.3) with dat (of person) and gen (of thing) *grant, allow* 3/24; 6/72; 12/26; 15/2916; 23/90, 123 etc; 24/176

un–nyt adj *useless* 19/h

un–orne adj *humble, simple* 24/256

un–rǣd m (§13.2) *folly, bad policy* 6/84

un–riht I. sb n (§13.4) *sin* 9/34, 48: *wrong, injustice* 14/10, 12, 48, 154: **on unriht** adv *wrongfully* 14/34: **II.** adj *wicked, evil* 10/32, 172

un–rihtlīce adv *wrongfully* 14/55

un–rihtnes(s) f (§14.2) *wickedness* 10/187

un–rīm n (§13.4) *countless number* 5/31; 16/335

un–rōt adj *cheerless, sad, dejected* 1/41, 47; 23/284

un–rōt–mōd adj *dejected in spirit, sad at heart* 9/89

un–rōtnis(s) f (§14.2) *sadness, dejection* 1/50

un–ryht adj *wrong, wicked, unlawful* 3/1

un–scyldig adj *innocent* 14/63

un–sidu m (§15.2) *vice, abuse* 14/109

un–smēðe adj *with a surface of uneven height, unsmooth* 18/26

un–sōfte adv *ungently, not gently* 23/228

un–spēdig adj *poor* 8/99

un–stilnes(s) f (§14.2) *disturbance, uproar* 3/14

un–strang adj *weak* 23/h

un–swǣslic adj *unpleasant, cruel* 23/65

un–sȳfre adj *unclean, impure* 23/76

un–trum adj *sick, infirm* 2/76, 77; 11/64, 122 etc; 12/32

un–trumian II *become sick* 12/246

un–trumnes(s), –nys(s) f (§14.2) *weakness, infirmity, sickness* 2/74; 12/274

un–trymnes(s) = un–trumnes(s)

un–twēolīce adv *indubitably, clearly* 23/h

un–þanc m (§13.2) *disinclination:* gen sg used as adv *unwillingly* 6/17

un–þēaw m (§13.6) *bad habit, vice* 11/66
un–þinged adj (past pple) *unprepared for, unexpected, sudden* 20/106
un–wāclīce adv *without weakening* 24/308
un–wær adj *unaware, unprepared:* **on unwær, on unwaran** adv *unexpectedly, by surprise* 6/31, 52, 67
un–wærscipe m (§14.5) *imprudence, folly* 11/174
un–wæstm m (§13.2) *crop failure* 14/47
un–waran see **un–wær**
un–wealt adj *not given to rolling, stable, steady* 4/259
un–wearn f (§14.7) *refusal, hindrance:* dat pl used as adv *irresistibly* 20/63
un–weaxen adj (past pple) *not fully grown, youthful* 15/2872; 24/152
un–weder n (§13.4) *bad weather, storm* 14/47
un–wemme adj *uninjured, inviolate* 18/46
un–windan 3 *unwrap, uncover* 11/160
un–wīs adj *foolish* 4/66; 9/2
un–wið–metenlīce adv *incomparably* 11/118f
un–wrītere n (§13.6) *bad scribe* 13/106
un–wurðlīce adv *unworthily* 16/440
ūp adv *up* 1/104; 4/131, 157, 190 etc; 5/13; 8/17 etc; 12/184 etc; 15/2856 etc; 16/415; 17/71; 22/3; 24/130: *to land, ashore* 5/70; 6/36 etc: *inland, up country* 4/27, 135, 223; 6/28, 34, 79: see also **cuman**
ūp–ā–hafen adj (past pple) *upraised, uplifted* 11/159
ūp–ā–stīgnes(s) f (§14.2) *ascension* 2/64
ūp–ā–wendan I *turn upwards* 12/118
ūp–gang m (§13.2) *rising* 12/116
ūp–ganga m (§14.7) *passage, access up onto land* (from water) 24/87
ūp–hēa adj *tall, steep* 22/30
ūp–hebban 6 *raise, lift up* 16/259
ūp–lǣdan I *extend upwards* 17/5n
upp = **ūp**
uppan prep with dat *on, upon* 11/274; 15/Æ: **wið uppon** adv *toward the interior* 8/50
uppe adv *up* 4/266; 17/9: *above, aloft* 25/38
uppon = **uppan**
ūp–rodor m (§13.3) *the heavens above* 20/105
ūp–stige m (§14.5) *ascension* 11/21
ūp–weard adv *turned upwards* 12/118a n
ūre I. see **ic** (§6.2) *of us:* **II.** possessive adj (§10.8) *our* 1/125; 9/109; 10/147; 12/23; etc
ūrig–feð(e)ra m (§14.7) *dewy–feathered one* 20/25; 23/210
urnon pret pl of **iernan**
ūs see **ic** (§6.2) *us, to us, for us, for ourselves* etc
Ūse f (§14.7) *the R. Ouse* (Yorkshire) 6/34
ūsic see **ic** (§6.2) *us*
ūt adv *out* 1/31; 2/19; 3/12; 4/75, 134 etc; 8/81 etc; 10/7, 28, 32 etc; 11/295; 23/70 etc; 24/72: *abroad* 7/6
utan = **wuton**
ūtan adv *on the outside, from without* 1/180; 3/10; 4/158, 197 etc; 8/25; 16/354: **on ȳtan** adv *outside, along the coast* 24/h
ūtan–bordes adv *outside the country, abroad* 7/9
ūte adv *out* 4/152, 220: *outside* 1/40, 48, 135; 14/24 etc; 16/369 etc; 23/284: *abroad* 7/10; 14/44: *in the field* 4/151
ūter–mere m (§14.5) *open sea* 4/265
ūte–weard adj *outward, the outermost limit of*, i.e. *the mouth of* 4/136, 267
ūt–gong m (§13.2) *departure, exodus* 2/61
uton = **wuton**
ūt–setl n (§13.4) *sitting outside* 1/50n
ūðe pret 1 and 3 sg of **unnan**
ūðon pret pl of **unnan**
ūð–wita m (§14.7) *wise man* 5/69: *philosopher* 11/52, 61 etc
uuið = **wið**
uundor = **wundor**
Uuldur–fadur = **Wuldor–fæder**
uuoldon = **woldon**
vton = **wuton**

W

wā interj (with dat) *woe! alas!* 10/278, 294; 22/52
wāc adj *timid, unreliable* 19/66: *pliant, slender* 24/43: comp *inferior, degenerate* 20/87

wacian II *wake, be awake* 1/48
wācian II *weaken, lack courage* 24/10
wāclic adj *poor* 11/95
wācnys(s) f (§14.2) *meanness, worthlessness* 11/190
(*ge*)**wadan** 6 *go, advance, travel* 15/2887; 24/96 etc: *journey* 19/24: *traverse, tread* 19/4
wado nom and acc pl of **wæd**
wǣcan I *soften* 21/28/5
wæccan I *watch, wake, stay awake, be sleepless* 1/47; 23/142
wæcen f (§14.2) *wakefulness* 1/50
wæd n (§13.4) *water* 21/7/2
wǣd f (§14.1) *garment, covering* 17/15 etc
wǣdl f *poverty, want* 18/55
wǣdla m (§14.7) *beggar, poor man* 11/88; 12/59
wǣdlian II *beg* 11/95: *go begging* 11/116
wǣfels m n (§13.3, 5) *garment* 11/95
wǣfer–sȳn f (§14.6) *something to be gazed at, a spectacle, exhibition, show* 11/55; 17/31
wæg pret 1 and 3 sg of **wegan**
wǣg m (§14.5) *wave, billow* 18/45; 19/46; 20/19
wǣgan I *distress, oppress* 4/199
wǣgon pret pl of **wegan**
wæl n (§13.4) *slaughter; the slain* (collectively) 4/10, 30; 5/65; 6/40 etc; 24/126 etc: see also *ge***slēan**
wǣl n *deep pool* (in a river) 25/39
wæl–cyrie f (§14.7) *sorceress* 14/133
wæl–feld m (§15.2) *field of slaughter, battlefield* 5/51
wæl–gīfre adj *greedy for slaughter* 19/100; 23/207 etc
wæl–(h)rēow adj *cruel, savage, bloodthirsty* 11/22, 27 etc; 12/42; 14/37
wæl–ræst f (§14.1) "*slaughter–bed,*" *resting place among the slain* 24/113
wæl–scel n (?) *carnage* 23/312
wæl–sleaht, –sliht m (§14.5) *slaughter* 4/44; 19/7, 91
wæl–spere n (§14.5) *deadly spear* 24/322
wæl–stōw f (§14.3) *place of slaughter, battlefield* 4/31, 45 etc; 5/43; 6/41 etc; 24/h, 95 etc
Wæl–þēof personal name *Wælþeof* 6/93
wæl–weg m (§13.2) "*whale–way,*" *sea* 20/63
wæl–wulf m (§13.2) *slaughter–wolf* 24/96
wǣpen n (§13.4) *weapon* 1/h, 160, 162; 8/120; 19/100; 23/h, 290; 24/10 etc
wǣpen–gewrixl n (§13.4) "*weapon–exchange,*" *trading of blows, conflict* 5/51; 14/82
*ge***wǣpnian** II *arm* 11/261
wǣr f (§14.1) *compact, agreement* 1/35: *covenant* 9/50
wǣran = **wǣron** (pret pl of **wesan**)
wærd = **wearð**
wǣr–fæst adj "*covenant–firm,*" *faithful, trusty* 15/2901
Wǣr–ferð personal name *Wærferð* 7/h, 1
wærlīce adv *carefully, warily* 14/158
wǣr–loga m (§14.7) *troth–breaker, traitor* 23/71
wǣron pret pl of **wesan** (§7.2)
wǣrun = **wǣron**
wæs pret 1 and 3 sg of **wesan** (§7.2)
wæst = **west**
wæstm m n (§13.2, 4) *fruit* 1/150; 10/157, 255, 317; 18/34 etc; 25/9: pl *form, stature* 9/93; 16/255
wæstmian II *flourish* 9/20
wǣt n (§13.4) *drink, liquid* 11/144
wǣta m (§14.7) *moisture, liquid* 17/22
wǣtan I *wet, soak* 21/26/2
wæter n (§13.4) *water* 4/271; 5/55; 8/127; 10/5, 124 etc; 11/306; 12/194 etc; 13/51 etc; 14/21; 15/2876; 18/41 etc; 21/26/3; 22/49; 24/64 etc; 25/27
wæter–fæsten(n) n (§13.6) *stronghold by the water; the natural protection* (or *barrier*) *offered by water* 4/146
wā–lā interj *ah! alas!* 16/368: with dat *alas for* 14/95
wald = **weald**
*ge***wald** = *ge***weald**
waldan = **wealdan**
walde = **wolde**
*ge***walden** adj (past pple) *small, tiny* 4/167f
waldend = **wealdend**
Walh–færeld n (§13.5) see 4/383n
wamb f (§14.1) *stomach* 11/136
wand pret 1 and 3 sg of **windan**

wandian II *hesitate, waver, flinch* 24/258 etc

wan–hȳdig adj *reckless, foolhardy* 19/67

*(ge)***wanian** II *fade, decline* 9/120; 14/30, 38; 18/72: *diminish, lessen* 14/23, 38: *dwindle* 14/30

wan(n) I. adj *dark, black* 17/55; 19/103; 23/206: **II.** pret 1 and 3 sg of **winnan**

wan(n)–hāl adj *ill* 12/202, 276

wan–spēdig adj *poor, impoverished* 11/146

ward = weard III.

*(ge)***war(e)nian II** *guard* (something, dat) *against* (something, acc) 1/39, 96: with dat obj only *take warning* 14/150

warian II *preoccupy, claim the attention of* 19/32

waroð n (§13.5) *shore* 10/48, 49 etc

waru f (§14.1) *defence* 12/147

was = wæs

wāst pres 2 sg of **witan**

wāt pres 1 and 3 sg of **witan**

*ge***wāt** pret 1 and 3 sg of *ge***wītan**

waðem m (§13.2) *wave* 19/24, 57

wē see **ic** (§6.2) *we*

wēa m (§14.7) *woe, misfortune, grief, trouble* 25/13

wēa–gesīð m (§13.2) *companion in crime* or *misery* 23/16

*ge***wealc** n (§13.4) *rolling, tossing* 20/6, 46

weald m (§15.2) *forest, wood, woodland* 4/135, 147; 5/65; 15/2887; 18/13; 23/206

*ge***weald** n (§13.4) *control* 4/31, 45 etc; 6/42 etc; 13/104; 16/368 etc; 24/h: *power* 10/224, 332; 14/36, 72 etc; 16/280; 17/107; 24/178

*(ge)***wealdan** 7 with gen obj *wield* 24/83 etc: *control, govern, rule* 12/46 etc; 15/2862 (see n); 16/253 etc; 24/95: *manage* 23/103: *bring about, cause* 14/47

wealdend m (§15.5) *ruler, lord* 11/117; 12/26; 15/2862 (see n); 16/260 etc; 17/17 etc; 19/h, 78 (*owner?*); 23/5 etc; 24/173: *leader* 10/159: *master* 10/233

wealdendras late nom and acc pl of **wealdend**

weal–gate dat sg of **weal–geat**

weal–geat n (§13.4) *wall–gate, city gate* 23/141

Wealh m (§13.2) *Welshman*: acc pl **Wēales** 5/72b

Wealh–gefēra m (§14.7) see 4/383n

Wealh–gerēfa m (§14.7) see 4/383n

wealh–stod m (§13.2) *interpreter* 12/67: *translator* 7/43

weal(l) m (§13.2) *wall* 1/181; 12/41; 19/76 etc; 21/29/7; 23/137 etc

weallan 7 (implying abundance and/or agitation) *boil, surge* 11/24; 14/160; 16/353: *well, flow* 25/45

weall–stān m (§13.2) *wall–stone*: pl *masonry* 25/3

weal–steal(l) m (§13.2) *"wall–foundation," site* 19/88

wealweode pret 1 and 3 sg of **wealwigan**

wealwigan II *roll* 12/206 etc

weard I. sb m (§13.2) *guardian, keeper* 2/29, 35; 15/2866 etc; 17/91; 20/54; 23/80: **II.** sb f (§14.1) *watch* 23/142: **III.** adv *toward*: **tō. . .weard** prep with dat *toward* 6/33f: **wið. . .weard** prep with gen *toward* 12/118; 23/99: **IV.** = **wearð** (pret 1 and 3 sg of **weorðan**)

weardian II *occupy, lie in* 22/34

wearg, wearh m (§13.2) *criminal, felon* 17/31; 25/55

wearm adj *warm, hot* 18/18

*ge***wearonian** = *ge***warenian**

wearp pret 1 and 3 sg of **weorpan**

wearð pret 1 and 3 sg of **weorðan**

*ge***wearð** pret 1 and 3 sg of *ge***weorðan**

wearðan = **weorðan**

wēa–tācen n (§13.4) *"woe–token," sign of grief* 18/51

wēa–þearf f (§14.1) *woe(ful) need* 22/10

weaxan 7 *grow* 22/3: *increase* 9/19; 11/143, 325: *rise* 10/277

webgian II *weave, contrive* 9/42

weccan I *kindle* 15/2902

wecg m (§13.6) *lump, ingot* 11/59

wēdan I *be mad, rage* 1/165

wed–bryce m (§14.5) *pledge–breaking, violation of a pledge* 14/112

wed(d) n (§13.6) *pledge* 14/78, 158

weder n (§13.4) *weather, wind* 18/18, 57; 25/42

weg m (§13.2) *way, path* 8/122; 9/33;

10/46, 316; 12/212; 15/2875, 2933n; 16/381; 17/88: **his weges** adv *on his way* 8/118: **ealne weg, ealneg** *adv always* 7/65; 8/8 etc; 20/67n

wēg I. sb m (§13.2) *altar* 15/2933 (but see n): **II.** = **wæg**

wegan 5 *carry* 1/h, 162; 23/325

weg–farende adj (pres pple) *wayfaring* 12/204

weg–nest n (§13.4) *provisions for a journey, viaticum* 2/92

wēgon = **wǣgon (pret pl of wegan)**

wela m (§14.7) often pl *wealth, riches* 7/29 etc; 9/68, 77, 84 etc; 11/118, 120; 18/55; 19/74: *goods* 11/68: *prosperity* 16/420 etc

*ge***welede** past pple of **welwan**

weleg = **welig**

weler m f *lip* 13/93

(*ge*)**wel–hwǣr** adv *nearly everywhere* 4/263; 7/65; 14/26

*ge***wel–hwilc** adj *almost every* 14/44, 88

welig adj *rich, wealthy, prosperous* 9/2, 83; 11/116; 19/h

wel(l) adv *well* 2/5; 6/89; 8/22; 12/67 etc; 13/80; 14/10; 16/248: *eagerly* 2/54, 95; 17/129: *indeed* 6/74: *abundantly, fully* 12/73; 17/143: *generously* 4/180: *properly* 9/39, 53; 13/35, 36; 23/103: *appropriately* 23/27: *carefully* 13/104

welwan I *huddle* 14/97

wel–willende adj (pres pple) *benevolent* 12/59

welm = **wielm**

(*ge*)**wēman** I *attract, win over* 12/51: *entertain* 19/29

wemman I *corrupt* 1/28: *destroy* 10/267

*ge***wemmednys(s)** f (§14.2) *defilement* 11/321

wēn f (§14.6) *probability, likelihood* 10/43, 115, 159 etc

wēnan I *suppose, think, hold* 1/165; 7/14 etc; 12/29; 13/8; 14/41; 24/239 (with gen obj): *look forward to* 17/135 (with refl dat): with gen obj *imagine, expect* 9/43; 23/20

(*ge*)**wendan** I often with acc refl pron *turn* 4/167, 185, 218 etc; 12/63, 266: *go, head* 4/218, 244; 6/18; 11/50, 289; 12/123; 24/205, 252 etc: *change, alter* 16/259; 17/22; 24/193: *translate* 7/35 etc: *bring it about* 16/428

wenian I *accustom, habituate* 19/36

wēofod n (§13.6) *altar* 1/149, 154 etc; 11/294f; 15/Æ

(*ge*)**wēold** pret 1 and 3 sg of (*ge*)**wealdan**

wēoldan = **wēoldon** (pret pl of **wealdan**)

wēol(l) pret 1 and 3 sg of **weallan**

Weonod–land n (§13.4) *the land of the Wends* 8/83f etc

Weonoð–land = **Weonod–land**

wēop pret 1 and 3 sg of **wēpan**

weorc n (§13.4) *work, deed* 2/31; 9/22, 26, 59; 10/94, 227; 12/73, 245, 267; 13/36, 74, 92 etc; 14/156; 15/Æ; 23/h: *construction* 13/70: *ornament* 21/26/14: *trouble, grief, pain* 16/296

*ge***weorc** n (§13.4) *work* 1/177, 182; 19/87; 25/2, 3: *fortified encampment, fortress, stronghold* 4/18, 97 etc

weorld = **woruld**

weorod = **werod**

weorpan 3 *throw, cast, hurl* 4/279; 16/300 etc; 23/290

weorst = **wierrest**

weorð n (§13.4) *price* 14/71 etc: *proceeds* 11/69: *value* 11/74

weorðan 3 *become, come to be* 1/46, 59, 104; 3/15; etc: *get* 4/9; 16/369: *change, turn* 14/82; 16/305: *occur* 4/18: *happen* 2/98; 14/61, 68: *come about* 6/96: past pple **geworden** (= Lat *factus*) *come, come about* 10/90, 93, 102 etc: **wæs geworden** *happened* 14/145: see also **flēam**

*ge***weorðan** 3 *happen* 12/150; 14/74, 93; 18/41: *come to pass* 9/24; 14/82: impersonal with acc *agree* 16/387; 23/260: *please* 13/95

weorðe adj *worthy, noble, of high rank* 4/78n, 108: *worthy, deserving* 13/20: with gen or dat *worthy of, deserving of* 1/141; 2/39 (and see n); 12/254: comp with dat *dearer to* 16/421

(*ge*)**weorðian** II *honor* 2/2; 4/11; 16/310 etc; 17/90 etc; 20/123: *revere* 12/143; 17/81: *worship* 11/266; 12/108, 117; 17/129: *adorn* 17/15; 23/298

weorðlīce adv *worthily, honorably, splendidly* 17/17; 24/279

weorð–mynd f (§14.1) *honor* 23/342
weorðscipe m (§14.5) *honor* 14/99
weorðung f (§14.1) *worship, honor* 14/22
weoruld = **woruld**
weoruld–hād = **woruld–hād**
wēox pret 1 and 3 sg of **weaxan**
wēpan 7 *weep* 10/213, 313 etc; 11/171, 196; 17/55; 22/38
wer m (§13.2) *man* 1/101; 9/2; 10/52, 153 etc; 11/40; 12/203 etc; 15/2865 etc; 19/64; 20/21, 110; 21/26/18; 21/29/14; 21/44/1; 21/47/3; 23/71 etc; 25/33
wēr f (§14.1) *pledge, agreement* 20/110
*ge*werc = *ge*weorc
wered = **werod**
Wēr–ferð = **Wǣr–ferð**
werg = **wearg**
Wer–hām m (§13.2) *Wareham* (Dorset) 4/77 etc
werian II *defend* 3/11: with refl acc 24/82, 283
wērig adj *weary, exhausted, tired out, discouraged* 5/20; 24/303; 19/15, 57; 20/29
wērig–ferhð adj *weary–hearted* 23/249 etc
wērig–mōd adj *weary–spirited, disconsolate* 22/49
werod, werud n (§13.5) *force, troop, band, company, army* 1/90f etc; 3/9; 4/51, 93 etc; 5/34; 6/39; 12/15 etc; 17/69 etc; 24/51 etc: *host* 16/255, 352, 370 etc; 17/51, 152; 23/199 etc
wesan anom vb (§7.2) *be, occur*
Wes–seaxan, –seaxe = **West–seaxan, –seaxe**
west adv *west, westward* 4/83, 167 etc; 8/95; 21/29/10; 24/97: *in the west* 4/188, 198; 16/275
westan adv *from the west* 4/169: **be westan** prep with dat *west of* 4/194 etc
westan–wind m (§13.2) *a wind from the west* 8/12
wēste adj *deserted, waste* 4/208; 8/3 etc: *desolate* 19/74
wēsten(n) n (§13.6) *waste, uninhabited land* 8/7: *wilderness* 11/324; 13/68; 15/2875
west–lang adv *to the west* 4/133
West–mynster n (§13.5) *Westminster* (Middlesex) 6/1 etc
West–sǣ f (§14.6) *West Sea* 8/3
West–seaxan, –seaxe m pl (§14.7, 5) *West Saxons*, also the region they inhabited: *Wessex* (see 4/2n, 12/128a n) 1/h; 3/1; 4/1, 15 etc; 5/20 etc; 12/121 etc
West–sexan, –sexe = **West–seaxan, –seaxe**
west–weard adv *westward* 4/130
Wēð–mōr m (§13.2) *Wedmore* (Somerset) 4/109
wexan = **weaxan**
wīc n (§13.4) pl often with sg meaning *place* 15/2882: *encampment, camp* 4/102: *dwelling, abode, village* 21/7/2; 21/8/7; 22/32 etc
wicce f (§14.7) *witch* 14/133
wīceng = **wīcing**
wicg n (§13.6) *horse, steed* 24/240
wīc–gerēfa m (§14.7) *town–reeve* 4/253
(*ge*)**wīcian** II *camp* 8/4, 23f, 67 etc: *encamp* 4/144, 201, 231, 236
wīcing m (§13.3) *Viking, pirate* 4/113; 14/82; 24/26 etc
wīd adj *wide:* see **ealdor**
wīde adv *far and wide, widely* 6/95; 12/239; 14/8, 13, 28, 32, 36; 20/60; 21/7/5; 21/26/16; 22/46; 23/156: **wīde ond sīde** adv *far and wide* 14/118; 17/81: sup *farthest, most widely* 20/57
*ge*wīde adv *far apart*: sup *as far apart as possible* 22/13
wīd–gil(l) adj *extensive* 12/207
wīdl m n (§13.2, 4) *defilement* 23/59
wīd–sǣ f (§14.6) *open sea* 8/9 etc
wiece = **wuce**
wielm m (§14.5) *surge* 2/71
wierrest sub adj (§12.10) *worst* 10/18, 159 etc; 11/165
wiersa comp adj (§12.10) *worse* 10/235; 14/6, 151; 16/259 etc: nom sg n **wyrre** 6/76
wīf n (§13.4) *woman* 3/14; 4/175, 207 etc; 9/2; 10/164; 11/40; 20/45; 23/148 etc: *wife* 4/177, 181; 13/13, 16 etc: see also **cyn(n)**
wīf–cȳððu f (§14.1) *company of a woman* 3/9
Wī–ferð personal name *Wiferð* 3/21
wīfian II *take a wife* 11/8, 151; 13/17

wīg n (§13.4) *war* 7/7; 19/67, 80: *battle* 5/20 etc; 24/10 etc

wiga m (§14.7) *warrior* 19/67; 23/49; 24/75 etc

wīg–bed(d) = **wēofod**

wīgend m (§15.5) *warrior* 23/69 etc; 24/302

wigge = **wīge** (dat sg of **wīg**)

wiggend = **wīgend**

wīg–heard adj *fierce in battle* 24/75

wīg–plega m (§14.7) *war–play, fighting* 24/268 etc

wīg–smið m (§13.2) "*war–smith,*" *warrior* 5/72

wī–haga m (§14.7) "*battle–hedge,*" *shield–wall* 24/102

wiht n f (§14.5, 6) *creature, being, thing* 10/161; 21/28/8, 13; 21/29/1 etc; 21/57/1: with gen *anything, aught* 16/394; 18/26: dat or acc sg used as adv **wiht(e)** *at all* 16/278; 21/47/6; 23/274: *by any means* 16/400: *in any way* 18/19: **mid wihte** adv *by any means* 16/381, 428

Wiht *the Isle of Wight* 4/262; 6/8 etc

wihtæ = **wihte** (dat sg of **wiht**)

wiite = **wīte**

wīl = **hwīl**

wil–cuma m (§14.7) *welcome thing* 21/8/11

wilde adj *wild* 8/38 etc; 25/18

wildor n (§15.6) *wild animal* 8/36

willa I. sb m (§14.7) *will* 1/110; 10/237; 12/45 etc; 13/97; 14/161; 16/250; 21/29/10: *pleasure* 9/80; 21/28/10: *joy* 16/400; 23/295: *desire* 17/129: **II.** sb m (§14.7) *spring, fount, fountain* 1/116; 18/63

willan anom vb (§7.5) *will, be willing, wish, want, desire, intend, mean, be in the habit of, be about to* 1/7 etc; 2/71 etc; 3/7; etc

Will–elm personal name *William* 6/14, 64

(*ge*)**wilnian** II with gen, dat or acc obj *long for, desire* 1/107; 11/67, 298; 12/56

wilnung f (§14.1) *desire* 7/37

Wīl–sǣtan m pl (§14.7) *the men of Wiltshire* 4/101

wilsumnes(s) f (§14.2) *devotion* 2/99

Wīl–tūn m (§13.2) *Wilton* (Wiltshire) 4/51

Wīl–tūn–scīr f (§14.1) *Wiltshire* 4/24, 284

wīl–wendlec, –lic adj *temporal* 1/108, 109

wīn n (§13.4) *wine* 11/9; 23/29 etc

Wīn–burne f (§14.7) *the R. Allen* (Dorset); still called the Wimborne as late as the sixteenth century 4/49

wind m (§13.2) *wind* 8/67; 10/90, 93; 16/315; 19/76; 23/347; 25/3 etc

windan 3 *twist* 19/32; 21/28/5: *fly* 12/229; 16/418; 24/322: *roll* 23/110: *wave, brandish* 24/43: *circle* 24/106

windig adj *wind–driven* 18/61

wine m (§14.5) *friend* 20/115; 22/49 etc; 24/228: *lord* 24/250

Winedas m pl (§13.2) *the Wends* 8/75

wine–drihten, –dryhten m (§13.3) *lord* 23/274; 24/248 etc

wine–lēas adj *friendless, lordless* 19/45; 22/10

wine–dryhten m (§13.3) *friend(ly) lord* 19/37

wine–mǣg m (§13.2) *friend and kinsman* 19/7; 20/16; 24/306

wine–māgas nom and acc pl of **wine–mǣg**

wīn–gāl adj "*wine–wanton,*" *flushed with wine* 20/29

wīn–gedrinc n (§13.4) *wine–drinking* 23/16

wīn–hāte f (§14.7) *invitation to wine* 23/8

(*ge*)**win(n)** n (§14.5) *battle* 12/18; 24/248, 302: *struggle, strife, conflict, warfare* 8/100; 16/259 etc; 17/65; 24/214; 25/55: *labor* 10/317: *affliction* 18/55

winnan 3 *fight* 4/7, 98; 12/22: *make war* 1/182n; 12/150: *strive, struggle* 1/10; 16/298 etc: *toil* 16/278: *gain, get, win* 14/144; 16/301; 22/5

*ge***winnan** 3 *make war, fight* 1/90: *win* 12/26; 24/125: *conquer* 14/144: *bring about* 16/402: *achieve* 16/437

Winod–land = **Weonod–land**

wīn–sade nom pl m st of **wīn–sæd**
wīn–sæd adj *wine–sated* 23/71
wīn–sæl n (§13.4) *wine–hall* 19/78
wīn–salo nom and acc pl of **wīn–sæl**
Wintan–ceaster f (§14.1) *Winchester* (Hampshire) 3/33; 4/253 etc; 12/142
Winte–ceaster = **Wintan–ceaster**
winter mn (§15.2) *winter* 1/137, 138; 4/22, 90, 94, 207 etc; 8/4 etc; 19/103; 20/15; 25/5: *year* 1/182n; 3/7, 33; 4/13, 63, 288; 9/h, 90; 15/2889; 19/65; 24/210: gen sg used as adv *winter* 18/37
winter–cearig adj *"winter–sorrowful," desolate as winter* 19/24
winter–geweorp n *winter storm*, or perhaps *snowdrift* (= that which has been piled up by winter) 18/57
winter–scūr m (§13.2) *winter shower* 18/18
winter–setl n (§13.4) *winter quarters* 4/2, 14 etc
winter–stund f (§14.1) *winter hour* 16/370
winter–tīd f (§14.6) *wintertime* 1/134
Wiogora–ceaster f (§14.1) *Worcester* (Worcestershire) 7/title
wiota = **wita**
wiotan = **witan**
wīr m (§13.2) *(decorative) wire* 21/26/14
Wīra–mūða m (§14.7) *Wearmouth* (Durham)
Wīr–hēalh m (§13.2) *the Wirral* (Cheshire): dat sg **Wīrhēale** 4/215: dat pl **Wīrhēalum** 4/209
*ge***wis** = *ge***wis(s)**
wīs adj *wise* 13/49; 19/64, 88n; 24/219: *learned* 7/43
wīs–dōm m (§13.2) *wisdom, knowledge, learning* 7/7 etc; 13/48; 18/30; 25/33
wīse I. sb f (§14.7) *way, fashion, manner* 2/71; 13/85; 14/27, 57; 15/Æ; 20/110; 21/8/4: *matter, thing, business* 2/49: *idiom* 13/87, 88: **II.** adv *wisely* 19/88
wīsfæst adj *wise, sagacious* 21/28/13
wīsian II *guide, direct* 24/141
Wīsle f (§14.7) *the R. Vistula* 8/89 etc
Wīsle–mūða m (§14.7) *the estuary of the R. Vistula* 8/89 etc
wīslic adj *wise, prudent* 1/129
*ge***wislīce** adv *verily, truly* 19/h
wisnian II *wither* 9/119
*ge***wis(s)** adj *trustworthy, reliable* 20/110: with gen *aware of, prescient of* 2/104: **tō gewissan** adv *for certain, with certainty* 6/50f
wisse = **wiste** (pret 1 and 3 sg of **witan**)
wissian II with dat obj *guide, direct* 13/35
wist f (§14.6) *feast, feasting* 9/77; 11/173, 297; 19/36
(*ge*)**wiste** pret 1 and 3 sg of (*ge*)**witan**
wist–fulligan II *feast* 11/286
wiston pret pl of **witan**
wit see **ic** (§6.2) *we two*
*ge***wit** n (§13.4) *intelligence, understanding* 16/250
wita m (§14.7) *wise man, councillor, advisor* 1/115, 118 etc; 3/1; 4/15; 7/2 etc; 12/65; 19/65: *senator* 11/35: gen pl **wiotona** 7/46
(*ge*)**witan** pret–pres vb (§23.2) *know* 1/42, 51, 72 etc; 7/26 etc; 8/12 etc; 10/44, 97, 105n, 109 etc; 12/22 etc; 13/10; 14/18 etc; 16/385; etc: *know about, be familiar with* 19/27; 21/29/14: *know of* 2/89; 14/151: *be in one's senses* 1/165: *perceive* 10/105: *recognize* 13/28: *realize* 13/89: *show* 14/66
*ge***witan** = *ge***witon** (pret pl of *ge***wītan**)
wītan 1 *guard, keep, look after* 21/26/17
*ge***wītan** 1 often with refl dat *go, depart* 1/137; 5/35, 53; 9/89, 100 etc; 10/81; 11/147 etc; 15/2850 etc; 17/71, 133; 20/52, 80; 21/29/10, 13; 22/6, 9; 23/61 etc; 24/72 etc: *come* 2/24: *die* 11/129: *pass away* 10/252, 253; 19/h, 95; 20/86
wīte n (§13.6) *punishment, torment, pain* 2/66; 7/19; 9/14, 106; 11/149, 168 etc; 16/296 etc; 17/61 etc; 20/h; 22/5; 23/115
wīt(e)ga m (§14.7) *wise man, sage* 18/30: *prophet* 11/139
*ge***witen** past pple of *ge***wītan**
*ge***witenes(s)** f (§14.2) *departure, death* 2/73
*ge***witenlic** adj *as if passed away* 9/111n

Wīt–land n (§13.4) *the region east of the Vistula estuary* 8/90 etc
*ge***wit–loca** m (§14.7) *mind* 23/69
witodlīce adv *indeed, in fact* 11/17, 137, 140; 12/123
*ge***witon** pret pl of *ge***wītan**
wið prep with gen, acc, dat and inst **I.** (comitative) *with, in the company of, among* 1/62, 80 etc; 4/3; etc: **II.** (adversative) *against, in opposition to, with, upon* 1/19, 90 etc; 2/71 etc; 3/6 etc; 4/7, 16 etc; 5/9; 6/40 etc; 9/15; 11/301; 12/23; 14/126; 18/44; 20/75; 24/82, 290; 25/16: *from* 12/21; 13/65: **III.** (local) *toward* 1/44; 4/167; 11/287; 12/229; 23/162; 24/131: *along* 8/2, 49: *by, near* 4/108; 12/41, 204: *next to* 11/294; 16/438: see also **ēastan, sūðan, uppon, weard**: **IV.** (reciprocal) *in exchange for, for* 1/25; 14/71, 74; 24/31 etc: **wið þon þe** conj *on condition that* 1/23
wiðer–lēan n (§13.4) *requital* 24/116
wiðer–sac(c) n (§13.4) *apostasy* 12/63
wiðer–trod n (§13.4) *way back, return journey* 23/312
wið–feohtan 3 with dat obj *fight against* 12/14
wið–hogian with dat obj *disregard, intend to resist* 15/2865
wið–metenes(s) f (§14.2) *comparison*: **tō wiðmetenesse** with gen *in comparison with* 1/133
wið–sacan 6 with dat obj *renounce, abandon, forsake* 1/152
wið–standan 6 with dat obj *resist, be a match for, withstand* 12/29; 19/15
wlanc adj *proud, bold, valiant* 5/72; 19/80; 20/19; 24/139 etc: *exultant, high–spirited* 20/29; 23/16, 325: with dat *proud of, exulting in* 25/27
wlāt pret 1 and 3 sg of **wlītan**
wlencu f (§15.3) *pomp* 9/77
wlītan 1 *look* 23/49; 24/172
wlite m (§14.5) *beauty* 9/117; 20/49: *countenance* 9/93: *glory, ornament* 18/75
wliteg, wlitig adj *beautiful, fair* 9/17; 18/7 etc; 23/137 etc
wlitigian II *beautify* 20/49
wlonc = **wlanc**
wōd adj *mad, crazy* 12/206
(*ge*)**wōd** pret 1 and 3 sg of (*ge*)**wadan**
Wōdnes–dæg m (§13.2) *Wednesday* 6/42
wōdnys(s) f (§14.2) *madness* 12/199
(*ge*)**wōdon** pret pl of (*ge*)**wadan**
wōg n (§13.4, 6) *error* 13/104
wōh–dǣd f (§14.6) *evil deed* 9/13
wōh–dōm m (§13.2) *unjust judgment* 14/146
wōh–gestrēon (§13.4) *ill–gotten gains* 14/146
wolc = **wolcen**
wolcen n (§13.4) *cloud, sky* 10/273 etc; 16/418; 17/53 etc; 18/27 etc; 21/7/5; 23/67; 25/13
woldan = **woldon** (pret pl of **willan**)
wolde pret 1 and 3 sg of **willan**
woldon pret pl of **willan**
wō–lic adj *unjust, evil* 9/16
wō–līce adv *wickedly* 9/33
wōma m (§14.7) *tumult* 19/103
wom–ful(l) adj *foul, evil* 23/77
wom(m) m (§13.2) *sin, iniquity, stain* 9/82; 17/14; 23/59
wō–nes(s) f (§14.2) *wrongdoing* 9/13, 34
wong m (§13.2) *plain, field, meadow, land* 18/7 etc; 20/49
won(n) **I.** sb n (§13.4) *want, lack, dearth* 19/103n: **II.** = **wan(n)** adj: **III.** = **wan(n)** (pret 1 and 3 sg of **winnan**)
wōp m (§13.2) *weeping, lamentation* 9/121; 10/14, 240 etc; 11/46, 192; 18/51
worc = **weorc**
*ge***worct** = *ge***worht**
word n (§13.4) *word, speech, statement* 1/9 etc; 2/28 etc; 7/1 etc; 11/289; 13/56 etc; 14/54 etc; 15/2849; etc
*ge***worden** past pple of **weorðan**
word–on–drysne adj *"word–reverend," awesome of word* 15/2862
woreldlic = **woruldlic**
*ge***worht** past pple of **wyrcan**
worhtan = **worhton** (pret pl of **wyrcan**)
(*ge*)**worhte** pret 1 and 3 sg of (*ge*)**wyrcan**
worhton pret pl of **wyrcan**
worhtun = **worhton**
wōrian II *moulder, crumble* 19/78

world = **woruld**
world–frēond m (§15.5) *friend in this world* 9/72, 87
worldlic = **woruldlic**
world–rīce I. sb = **woruld–rīce**: **II.** adj *"worldly–powerful,"* 9/16, 83
worn m (§13.2) *a great number, many* 19/91: *swarm* 23/163
worold = **woruld**
worold–scamu f (§14.1) *shame in the eyes of the world, public disgrace* 14/95 etc
worol–strūdere m (§13.6) *despoiler, robber* 14/133
woruld f (§14.6) *world* 2/6, 78; 7/20; 11/118, 148; 12/112 etc; 13/15 etc; 14/5 etc; 17/133; 18/41; 19/h, 58 etc; 20/h, 45, 49 (and n), 87; 22/46; 23/66 etc; 24/174; 25/41 etc: *way of life* 16/318: *eternity* 11/314: **ā tō worulde** adv *forever and ever* 12/287: **on worulda woruld** (= *in saecula saeculorum*) *forever and ever* 9/129; similarly 10/333
woruld–būend m (§15.5) *world–dweller, man* 23/82
woruld–caru f (§14.1) *worldly concern* 12/55
woruld–cund adj *worldly, secular* 7/3
woruld–gesǣlig adj *blessed with this world's goods, prosperous* 24/219
woruld–hād m (§15.2, 13.2) *secular life* 2/14, 53
woruldlic adj *worldly* 9/20; 11/55f, 62 etc
woruld–rīce n (§13.6) *kingdom of the world* (as opposed to **heofonrīce**), *this world* 9/40; 19/65; 22/13
woruld–strengu f (§14.1) *"world–strength," vital power* 21/26/2
woruld–þing n (§13.4) *worldly affair* 7/18
woruld–wīs–dōm m (§13.2) *secular wisdom, philosophy* 11/57
wōð f (§14.1) *eloquent speech* or *song* 21/8/11
wracu f (§14.1) *revenge, vengeance* 16/393: *suffering, pain* 18/51
wræc pret 1 and 3 sg of **wrecan**
wræcca m (§14.7) *exile* 1/4, 12, 87; 20/15; 21/29/10; 22/10
wræc–lāst m (§13.2) *"exile–track," path of exile* 19/5, 32: **wræclāstas . . . lecgan** *"lay tracks of exile," direct their exiled steps, travel* 20/57
wrǣcon pret pl of **wrecan**
wræc–sīð m (§13.2) *"exile–journey," exile* 11/28, 32 etc; 20/h; 22/5, 38: *misery* 22/5n
wrǣtlic adj *beautiful, splendid, wondrous* 18/63; 21/23/14; 25/3: *amazing, curious, odd* 21/44/1; 21/47/2
wrǣtlīce adv *wondrously, splendidly* 18/75
wrāh pret 1 and 3 sg of **wrēon**
wrāð adj *cruel, fierce* 17/51; 19/7: with dat *angry at* 16/405
wrāðe adv *cruelly, fiercely* 22/32
wrāðlic adj *cruel, bitter* 16/355
wreahte pret 1 and 3 sg of **wreccan**
wrec = **wræc** (pret 1 and 3 sg of **wrecan**)
(*ge*)**wrecan** 5 *avenge, "wreak"* 3/4; 23/92; 24/208 etc: *utter, recite* 20/1; 22/1
wrecca = **wræcca**
wreccan I *deliver* 1/h: *awake, arouse* 23/228 etc
wrēgan I *accuse, denounce* 13/62
wrehton pret pl of **wreccan**
wrenc m (§14.5) *modulation* (of the voice) 21/8/2
wrēon 1, 2 *cover* 21/26/11
wrīdian II *flourish, thrive* 18/27
wringan 3 *wring, twist* 16/317n
wreoton = **writon** (pret pl of **wrītan**)
*ge*__writ__ n (§13.4) *letter* 1/2: *writing* 7/51 etc; 13/106; 18/30: *writ* 2/63: **hālige gewritu** *the Holy Scriptures*
wrītan 1 write 2/59; 7/67; 13/38
wrītere m (§13.6) *writer* 13/83: *scribe* 13/105
writon past pple of **wrītan**
wrixendlīce adv *in turn* 2/84
wrixlan I with dat obj *change, shift, vary* 21/8/2
*ge*__wrixlan__ I *get in requital* 16/335
wrōht m (§13.2) *false accusation, slander* 9/42
wuce f (§14.7) *week* 4/99, 107 etc
wudewe = **wuduwe**
wudu m (§15.2) *wood, forest* 4/93, 132

etc; 11/100, 198; 18/37 etc; 22/27; 24/193; 25/33: *wood* 15/2887; 15/Æ: *tree* 17/27

wudu–bēam m (§13.2) *forest tree* 18/75

wudu–fæsten(n) n (§13.6) *stronghold in the woods; the natural protection* (or *barrier*) *offered by a forest* 4/145

wudu–holt n (§13.4) *wood, forest* 18/34

wuduwe f (§14.7) *widow* 11/43, 150 etc; 14/33

wuldor n (§13.4) *glory* 1/97; 10/332; 11/93, 96 etc; 12/282 etc; 15/2916; 17/14 etc; 20/h, 123; 23/59 etc

wuldor–blǣd m (§13.2) *glorious success* 23/156

Wuldor–fæder m (§15.4) *glorious Father* 2/31

wuldor–gāst m (§13.2) *glorious spirit* 15/2913

wuldor–gesteald n (§13.4) *glorious treasure* 21/26/16

wuldorlīce adv *gloriously* 1/182n

wuldor–torht adj *gloriously bright* 15/2875

wuldor–þrym(m) m (§14.5) *heavenly glory* 9/62

wulf m (§13.2) *wolf* 5/65; 10/146; 19/82; 23/206 etc; 25/18

Wulf–heard personal name *Wulfheard* 4/274

Wulf–red personal name *Wulfred* 4/252

Wulf–rīc personal name *Wulfric* 4/283

Wulf–stān personal name *Wulfstan* 8/82

*ge***wuna** m (§14.7) *habit, practice* 12/118a n; 14/119

wund I. sb f (§14.1) *wound* 1/h; 5/43; 24/139 etc: dat pl **wundun** 5/43b: **II.** adj *wounded* 24/113 etc

wunden past pple of **windan**

wunden–loc(c) adj *with braided locks* 23/77 etc

(*ge*)**wundian** II *wound* 1/h; 3/12, 18, 32; 4/162; 24/135

wundon pret pl of **windan**

wundor n (§13.4) *wonder, marvel* 2/31; 9/75; 12/273; 14/104; 16/280; 21/47/2; 23/8: *miracle* 11/277, 304; 12/268, 286: *wondrous thing, monster* 10/178: dat pl used as adv *wonderfully, extraordinarily* 18/63; 19/98; 25/13

wundorlic adj *wonderful, strange, marvellous* 13/68; 21/29/7

wundorlīce adv *wondrously, in a marvelous fashion* 21/29/1

wundrian II *wonder, marvel* 2/80; 12/186: with gen *wonder at, marvel at* 7/33; 12/235

*ge***wunelic** adj *usual, customary* 11/56

wunian II *dwell, remain, stay* 3/3; 6/21; 9/51, 90; 10/167, 309, 327; 11/20; 12/136 etc; 15/2867; 17/121 etc; 18/32; 20/87 (*remain*); 22/27; 23/67 etc; 25/66: *be, occupy* 17/3: *live, endure* 12/44: *inhabit, live on* 20/15

*ge***wunian** II *dwell, remain, stay* 1/40; 25/18, 42: *continue living* 9/89: *be accustomed, make it one's habit* 2/2

wunung f (§14.1) *dwelling, habitation* 11/175

wurdon pret pl of **weorðan**

wurdun = **wurdon**

wurpon pret pl of **weorpan**

wurð = **weorð**

wurðan = **weorðan**

*ge***wurðan** = *ge***weorðan**

wurðe = **weorðe**

wurðian = **weorðian**

wurðlīce = **weorðlīce**

wurð–mynt f (§14.6) *honor* 11/38, 283 etc; 12/18, 31 etc

wutan = **wuton**

wuton 1st person pl subjunc of **wītan**, used to introduce imperative or hortatory clauses *let us. . .* 2/95; 9/26, 63, 112 etc; 10/204 etc; 12/19; 13/57 etc; 14/140 etc; 16/403; 20/117

wydewe = **wuduwe**

wylc = **hwilc**

wylla = **willa**

wyllan = **willan**

Wyllelm = **Willelm**

wynlic adj *pleasant, beautiful* 16/255; 18/34; 22/52

wyn–lond n (§13.4) *joy(ous) land* 18/82

wyn(n) f (§14.6) *joy, pleasure, delight* 16/367; 18/12, 70; 19/29, 36; 20/27, 45; 21/26/7; 22/32 etc; 24/174: dat pl

used as adv *beautifully* 17/15: *delightfully* 18/7, 27
wynsum adj *delightful, pleasant* 2/58; 9/119; 18/13 etc
wynsumlic adj *pleasant, agreeable* 9/18, 70, 117
wynsumnes(s) f (§14.2) *delight* 9/85, 114, 118
(*ge*)**wyrc(e)an I** *make* 4/120; 8/43 etc; 10/47, 137; 11/219; 12/228; 13/44, 47 etc; 14/52, 94; 16/252 etc; 17/31; 20/115: *construct, build* 1/180; 4/97, 138 etc; 6/65 etc; 12/41; 13/68; 16/275 etc; 17/65; 24/102: *effect* 8/126; 16/256: *produce* 8/125: *accomplish* 14/105: *do* 9/59; 14/162; 16/250: *commit, perpetrate* 14/114: *bring about* 9/45; 24/264: *bring it about* 20/74: *perform* 11/13, 305; 16/280: *compose* 2/2, 6, 8 etc; 18/h: *work, toil, strive* 23/65: *send out* 23/8: with gen *acquire, achieve* 25/21: see also **flēam**
wyrd f (§14.6) *what happens, the course of events* 19/5, 15, 107: *experience, event, phenomenon* 17/51 etc; 19/107; 21/47/2: *fateful event* 9/44: *fate, destiny* 19/100; 20/115; 25/5
*ge***wyrdan I** *cause damage* 18/19
*ge***wyrdelic** adj *historical* 11/7
*ge***wyrht** f (§14.6) *deed, desert* 14/81
wyrhta m (§14.7) *worker* 9/57, 58: *maker, creator* 18/9
wyrm m (§14.5) *worm* 9/76, 95; 21/47/3: *snake, serpent* 23/115
wyrman I *warm* 1/135
wyrm–līc n (§13.4) "*worm–body,*" *serpent(ine) form* 19/98
wyrm–sele m (§14.5) *hall of serpents* 23/119
wyrnan I *withhold* (something, gen) 24/118: *refuse* (something, gen) *to* (someone, dat) 5/24
*ge***wyrpan I** *recover* 12/265
wyrre = **wierse**
wyrsa = **wiersa**
wyrsian II *worsen, grow worse* 14/31
wyrst = **wierrest**
wyrð pres 1 and 3 sg of **weorðan**
*ge***wyrð** pres 1 and 3 sg of *ge***weorðan**
wyrðe = **weorðe**
wyrðelic adj *suitable, appropriate* 1/61
wyta = **wita**

Y

ȳcan I *add to, augment* 21/26/24; 23/183
ȳdel = **īdel**
yfel I. sb n (§13.5) *evil, wickedness* 9/19, 122; 14/12; 16/246n; 25/50: *trouble* 1/51: *injury, harm* 1/36; 4/263; 13/105; 16/394; 24/133: *suffering* 1/111: **II.** adj *evil, wicked* 1/82; 14/119 etc
yfele adv *miserably, wretchedly* 10/281: *badly* 16/387
yf(e)lian II *get bad, grow worse* 6/96; 14/7
yfelnys(s) f (§14.2) *wickedness, villainy* 12/13
ylca = **ilca**
yldan = **ieldan**
yldest = **ieldest**
yldo = **ieldu**
yldran = **ieldran**
yldu = **ieldu**
ylfetu f (§14.1) *wild swan* 20/19
ymb–clyppan I *embrace* 17/42
ymb(e) prep with acc or dat **I.** (local) *around, about* 1/180; 3/30; 5/5; 8/25; 16/354, 371 etc; 20/11; 23/48, 268; 24/249; 25/46: **II.** (temporal) *about, after, at, during* 3/6; 4/26 etc; 12/208; 24/271: see also **ǣfre, lang**: **III.** (reference) *about, concerning, in regard to* 1/32; 4/129, 134; 7/8 etc; 12/45 etc; 14/11; 16/388 etc; 20/46; 24/214; 25/53 etc: *with* 11/205
ymb–hēpan I *crowd around, assail* 1/h
ymb–hwyrft m (§14.5) *circle, circuit* 18/43
ymb–sealde pret 1 and 3 sg of **ymb–sellan**
ymb–sellan I *surround* 10/275
ymb–settan I *set round, surround* 1/155
ymb–sittan 5 *besiege* 4/165 etc
ymb–sǣton pret pl of **ymb–sittan**
ymb–ūtan adv *around, around the coast, along the coast* 4/84, 164 etc
*ge***yrgan I** *dishearten, demoralize* 14/89

yrhðo, yrhðu f (§14.1) *slackness, cowardice* 14/147; 24/6
yrmð(u) = **iermðu**
yrnan = **iernan**
yrre I. sb n (§13.6) *anger, wrath* 14/40, 79 etc: **II.** adj *angry* 24/44, 253: with dat *angry at, enraged with* 16/342; 23/225
ys = **is**
ȳst f (§14.6) *storm, tempest* 4/84
ȳtan = **ūtan**
yteren adj *otter–skin* 8/45
ȳt–mǣst sup adj (§12.9) *last* 2/101
ȳð f (§14.2) *wave* 10/91; 20/6, 46; 22/7; 25/23
ȳðan I *lay waste, ravage, depopulate* 19/85
ȳð–faru f (§14.1) *deluge, flood* 18/44

SCANDINAVIA
(Nordkinn)
(Cape Svyatoy Nos)
(Murmansk)
FINNAS
(POLUOSTROV KOL' SKIY)
TERFINNAS
Varzuga
BEORMAS
(Tromsö)
(Kandalakshskaya Guba)
(WHITE SEA)
HALGOLAND
WESTSÆ
NORÐMEN
CWENAS
SWEON
Sciringesheal
EOWLAND
GOTLAND
DENE
Truso
ESTE
WINEDAS
æt Hæðum